sixth edition
INTERNATIONAL ORGANIZATIONS
Principles and Issues

A. LeRoy Bennett
University of Delaware

PRENTICE HALL, *Englewood Cliffs, New Jersey 07632*

Library of Congress Cataloging-in-Publication Data

Bennett, A. LeRoy (Alvin LeRoy),
    International organizations: principles and issues / A. LeRoy
    Bennett. — 6th ed.
        p.   cm.
    Includes bibliographical references and index.
    ISBN 0-13-227018-8
    1. International agencies.   2. International organizations.
    3. Regionalism (International organization)   I. Title.
    JX1995.B43   1995
    341.2—dc20   94-35664
                                                                      CIP

Acquisitions Editor: Charlyce Jones Owen
Production Editor: Alison Gnerre
Copy Editor: Lynn Buckingham
Cover design: Jerry Votta
Buyer: Robert Anderson
Editorial Assistant: Nicole Signoretti

Printed in the United States of America
10   9   8   7

ISBN   0-13-227018-8

Prentice-Hall International (UK) Limited, *London*
Prentice-Hall of Australia Pty. Limited, *Sydney*
Prentice-Hall Canada Inc., *Toronto*
Prentice-Hall Hispanoamericana, S.A., *Mexico*
Prentice-Hall of India Private Limited, *New Delhi*
Prentice-Hall of Japan, Inc., *Tokyo*
Simon & Schuster Asia Pte. Ltd., *Singapore*
Editora Prentice-Hall do Brasil, Ltda., *Rio de Janeiro*

CONTENTS

chapter 3

THE GENESIS OF THE UNITED NATIONS

chapter 4

BASIC PRINCIPLES AND ORGANIZATION OF THE UNITED STATES

chapter 5

SOME BASIC ISSUES OF THE UNITED NATIONS

chapter 6

PEACEFUL SETTLEMENT OF DISPUTES

chapter 7

COLLECTIVE SECURITY AND ITS ALTERNATIVES
Theory and Practice

chapter 8

THE SEARCH FOR JUSTICE UNDER LAW   *178*

chapter 9

CONTROLLING THE INSTRUMENTS OF WAR   *211*

chapter 10

VARIETIES OF REGIONALISM   *229*

chapter 11

TRANSNATIONAL RELATIONS AND INTERNATIONAL ORGANIZATION   *265*

chapter 12

PROMOTING ECONOMIC WELFARE

chapter 13

MANAGING GLOBAL RESOURCES

chapter 14

PROMOTING SOCIAL PROGRESS

chapter 15

HUMAN RIGHTS AND THE STRUGGLE
FOR SELF-GOVERNMENT

chapter 16

INTERNATIONAL ADMINISTRATION AND THE SEARCH FOR LEADERSHIP   *405*

chapter 17

INTERNATIONAL ORGANIZATION IN RETROSPECT AND PROSPECT   *432*

BIBLIOGRAPHY   *444*

appendix I

COVENANT OF THE LEAGUE OF NATIONS   *454*

appendix II

CHARTER OF THE UNITED NATIONS   *466*

appendix III

PREFACE

This book is the culmination of nearly fifty years as an observer, student, and teacher of international organizations. During that period of time the United Nations, as the primary general-purpose intergovernmental organization, has fluctuated between success and failure and has met with both public support and skepticism. The author is normatively committed to the indispensability of global and regional international and transnational organizations in an age when people and nation-states must adapt to a shrinking and increasingly interdependent globe.

In this study the author follows no single model and is eclectic in his interests. The focus is on the philosophy and principles of international organizations and on a broad range of issues with which these organizations try to deal. A balance is struck between comprehensive coverage of the problems, inquiries, and decisions that face these organizations daily and the limitations that must be observed in tailoring a textbook for a one-semester course. The use of several tables, charts, and case studies provides devices for summarizing and illustrating detailed activities. Yet comprehensiveness has not been sacrificed by omitting discussion on any major activity of international organizations. Neither has it been assumed that the student possesses prior detailed knowledge of the subject.

In the sixth edition the main outlines of the previous editions have been maintained. However, adjusting to changing world conditions has prompted major modifications in the text. The breakup of the Soviet Union and the resultant East-West accommodation have provided a newly emerging world order which places altered demands on global, regional, and private international and transnational organizations. Demands on these institutions have actually broadened as regional, civil, and ethnic conflicts have multiplied. United Nations peacekeeping operations have increased at an unprecedented rate and have, in several cases, become peacemaking and peace-enforcing operations. The new emphasis in North-South relations has become "sustainable development." All of these aspects of global change have, of necessity, been reflected in the present edition. In Chapter 7 a more recent and significant peacekeeping case study, that of the United Nations Transition Assistance Group (UNTAG) in Namibia has replaced the case of the West Irian operations. As in previous editions, all topics have been updated to reflect recent developments.

The author would like to thank the reviewers: Don B. Rhoades, Southern Oregon State College, and Frederick H. Gareau, Florida State University, for their valuable and constructive suggestions. He also acknowledges the excellent support of the Prentice Hall staff in every phase of publication.

A. LeRoy Bennett

1

INTRODUCTION

The foundation of international organizations was built in ancient times, but the organizations themselves did not appear until the nineteenth century, when they were formed among political structures known as nation-states. Before being linked by these organizations, the nation-states already had diplomatic, economic, legal, and war relationships.

The international system as a whole consists of these nation-states, their interactions, international organizations, and the interactions of private actors. As only one part of the whole, international organizations are necessarily affected by the other parts. Because these international organizations are new, they have a minor rather than a major influence on world relationships and, again, are shaped by these relationships more than shaping them.

Nevertheless, the idea of international organization is gradually becoming more complex and influential, as shown by both the words and actions of government spokespeople. Although they may not go so far as to surrender sovereign powers to international organizations, they do find them indispensable for other purposes. New nations demonstrate this in their eagerness to be admitted to the United Nations. Despite great differences, the big powers in the UN do not seem anxious to withdraw, and all countries find the organization useful for sounding out ideas and for contact with other nations.

The United Nations has a more elaborate structure than the League of Nations did, which in turn was more complex than pre-World War I organizations. At the same time, regional and private international organizations since

1945 also have increased in both numbers and influence. We may assume then that this process will continue, and that international organizations will become an increasingly important part of international relationships.

THE ROLE OF INTERNATIONAL ORGANIZATIONS IN TODAY'S WORLD

International organizations have been viewed, at one extreme, as the vanguard of an emerging world government and, at the other, as an exercise in futility in fostering cooperation among sovereign states. Neither of these extreme views does justice to the role of international organizations in the present age. Today the state, possessing ultimate power and authority, remains the primary political unit. Yet change, accommodation, and a proliferation of interstate and transnational contacts are the hallmarks of an increasingly interdependent world.

The state system shows no sign of rapid deterioration or transformation into new forms. States are reluctant to sacrifice any sovereignty to supranational entities. Yet humans are rational and capable of effecting adjustment or modification of the system. Change is not only a major phenomenon of the modern world but is occurring at an accelerating rate. Many changes have already taken place that must be considered in analyzing the relations of nations. The post-World War II world is vastly different from the world of the 1930s. The range of changing conditions is indicated by the rise of superpowers armed with superweapons; the collapse of the old colonial empires; and the focus of attention upon new problems of economic development, overpopulation, the environment, the use of outer space, and control of ocean resources. The end of the Cold War shifted the international political focus to severe outbreaks of violence in such places as Somalia, Kuwait, and Yugoslavia, and to the need to supervise transitions to new political regimes in such countries as Namibia, Nicaragua, and Cambodia. Another change is the rapid development within the present century of an elaborate structure of international organizations, private and public, universal and regional, multipurpose and specialized.

Modern international organizations may be classified as intergovernmental organizations (IGOs) and nongovernmental organizations (NGOs, or INGOs, to distinguish international private agencies from those limited to a single country). The major emphasis in this study is on IGOs because of the impact on world affairs of governmental actors. However, the increasing influence of nongovernmental actors, of both profit-seeking and non-profit-seeking varieties, is noted at several points throughout the text. The common characteristics of both IGOs and non-profit-seeking INGOs include: (1) a permanent organization to carry on a continuing set of functions; (2) voluntary membership of eligible parties; (3) a basic instrument stating goals, structure, and methods of operation; (4) a broadly representative consultative conference organ; and (5) a permanent secretariat to carry on continuous administrative, research, and information functions. IGOs are, additionally, established by treaty and usually, in order to safeguard state sovereignty, operate at the level of consent, recommendation, and cooperation rather than through compulsion or enforcement.

States continue as the dominant political units, but international organizations can perform useful functions within the state system. For the present these organizations are more the adjuncts (and perhaps only minor ones) of the state system, rather than the incipient units of a new political system.

As adjuncts of the state system, international organizations can and do play a number of significant roles. Their chief function is to provide the means of cooperation among states in areas in which cooperation provides advantages for all or a large number of nations. In many cases they furnish not only a place where decisions to cooperate can be reached but also the administrative machinery for translating the decisions into action. Another function is to provide multiple channels of communication among governments so that areas of accommodation may be explored and easy access will be available when problems arise. In conflict situations not only may grievances by the parties directly involved be aired but also the influence of other nations may be exerted to prevent precipitous action that may threaten the interests of many states.

States will continue to exercise power, and many conflicts will result. In a nuclear age, states are not free to exercise ultimate force in most conflict situations. They must exercise self-restraint and accept stalemate, a change in conditions, or compromise. If states are willing to explore the possibilities of accommodation and compromise, modern international organizations have made available a new dimension beyond the previously existing channels of diplomacy and peaceful settlement. The United Nations, the Specialized Agencies, and regional organizations provide multiple and continuous contact points through which accommodation can be exercised.

States are still the parties in conflict. They are free to bring their disputes to an international agency or refuse to participate. They are free to bargain or to make no concessions. They may accept decisions and comply with the spirit of resolutions agreed to by a majority of the members of the agency or refuse to cooperate in carrying out these recommendations. If a state must be coerced, it will be by action of other states. International organizations generally have no independent means of carrying out coercion. Even if world public opinion is a sometimes mildly effective pressure influencing the behavior of states, the expression of that opinion is as likely to be through government spokespersons in international agencies as through other channels.

But states, needing to minimize the effects of conflict, find the many and diverse agencies of international organization useful for that end. The United

Nations, for example, provides several major organs whose functions include the resolution of conflict. In addition, the principles of the Charter provide a yardstick for guiding deliberations toward peaceful solutions. The influence of other members can be readily brought to bear in meetings and in private consultations.

In other situations not involving sharp clashes of interests, as in some of the technical work of international organizations, cooperation is facilitated by the existence of these organizations for reaching agreements that have mutual advantages for all states concerned. An agreement to control the spread of disease across international boundaries or to facilitate the interchange of mail can have few possible disadvantages to any nation involved.

Since the states of the modern world must, in so many areas, cooperate, adjust, accommodate, and compromise to promote their common welfare, to solve problems not limited to national boundaries, and to lessen conflict, it is entirely logical for them to create elaborate agencies of international organization for these ends. These agencies are more diverse and numerous than at any previous time in the rather short history of international organization. It is also logical to assume that they will continue to be used by states as indispensable though limited tools for a wide variety of purposes. The range of their purposes is a reflection of the complex set of relationships among nations at this stage in history. Since the trend of world events is toward increased contacts and a growing diversity of problems, we may reasonably expect international organizations to also become increasingly diverse in number and purposes rather than to diminish in significance.

INTERNATIONAL ORGANIZATION IN A WORLD OF PARADOXES

The major political forces and the economic and social factors influencing those political forces produce a most confused and bewildering pattern of international relationships today. The confusion of the pattern is the result of countervailing forces working at cross-purposes. The result is a series of dilemmas and paradoxes that confound those who would seek easy or quick solutions to international problems.

One of the most basic of these paradoxes is the insistence upon state sovereignty, supremacy, and independence in a shrinking, interdependent world. Each state declares its right to determine its own course of action regardless of the effects upon other states and, at the same time, is increasingly dependent upon the actions of other states in vital areas of mutual concern such as trade, communications, economic development, and world peace. Rigid adherence to the absolute right of each state to be bound in international affairs only by its own positive assent to the specific course to be followed places formidable obstacles in the path of resolving conflicts of interest. Only when a high coincidence of interests occurs can agreements be reached, since majority rule is incompatible with the necessity of unanimity based on the sovereignty of each and every state. Many world problems cannot be dealt with effectively as long as no other agency than the sovereign state has the power or means to make or enforce decisions affecting large numbers of states.

Closely related to the paradox of the sovereign power of states in an interdependent world is the conflict between convergent and divergent national interests. Each state may try to enhance its own power, prestige, and economic prosperity partially by seeking advantages at the expense of other states, or it may find mutual advantages with other states through agreements to cooperate for the supposed or real benefit of all parties. An ideology may act as a unifying force within a group of states yet act as a divisive factor in relation to states with competing ideologies. A defense pact may represent a mutuality of interests among the members of the pact but serve as a threat to nonmembers. Weak nations may feel threatened by powerful nations yet, on occasion, find protection in their power. Poor nations may envy rich nations, but both may find advantages in measures that enlist the resources of the rich in an effort to develop the economic prosperity of the poor. Even the chief adversaries of the Cold War found an increasing number of areas of mutual advantage, including the avoidance of nuclear holocaust.

Interdependence and convergent national interests lead to cooperative actions. These cooperative actions may take place inside or outside of international organizations such as the United Nations, but the existence of such organizations facilitates cooperation and thus serves the interests of the member states.

On the other hand, divergent national interests and the emphasis upon state supremacy and sovereignty lead to conflict among states. Since the means of waging economic and political conflict reside in the individual states, and since engaging in conflict may seem to be advantageous to the parties to a dispute or situation, international peace and tranquility are frequently threatened by clashes of interests. In these situations, agencies such as the United Nations are limited in their utility because their power and means are limited. They have never been endowed with the powers of a government or of a superstate. They may serve as a place where disputes may be discussed and pressures may be exerted by other states wishing to avoid extreme forms of conflict between the disputants, but they lack effective or independent means for intervention to preserve peace or dictate a solution. The custodians of the means for protecting the interests of the world as a whole are still more than 180 sovereign states, especially the rich and powerful states, which can wield the strongest pressures. The need for more effective international controls to resolve conflicts may seem apparent to many people, but the world continues to rely upon and perhaps even strengthen the role of the individual state. International organizations may serve as occasionally useful tools of the state, but they constitute no threat to the state's sovereignty.

Another paradox of the modern world lies in separation of international and domestic concerns. As the world shrinks through the effects of technology and communications, the line between domestic and international problems becomes increasingly blurred. Internal events have their international implications. Both the theory and practice of the United Nations recognize this dilemma. The United Nations Charter in Article 2 declares that the United Nations may not "intervene in matters which are essentially within the domestic jurisdiction of any state," but in the same sentence says, "but this principle shall not prejudice the application of enforcement measures under Chapter VII." Chapter VII deals not only with breaches of the peace and acts of aggression but also with threats to the peace. The authors of the Charter foresaw the difficulty of delineating domestic and international issues. It is sufficient to note at this point that their foresight has been borne out in practice and that the impossibility of drawing a satisfactory division between domestic and international matters is one of the recurrent dilemmas of the United Nations and of the world.

The lag in the rate of development of political and social institutions in a rapidly changing world is a frequently noted theme among social scientists. This lag is apparent in the development of international organizations. We are willing to create such organizations as long as they are based primarily on the principle of voluntary cooperation, preserving all the major prerogatives of the state that have been developed over a period of 500 years. The result is the creation of a great deal of machinery with very little power or ability to resolve the rising tide of issues resulting from the international contacts, which seem to increase by geometric proportions. A rising tide of revolutionary international problems is met with the slow, evolutionary development of international institutions. This increasing imbalance between the scope of our problems and our means to solve them can lead to disillusionment, frustration, disaster, a breakdown of the international system, or controlled or uncontrolled revolutionary political changes. Tradition and an excessively conservative set of attitudes toward international political change could easily be humankind's own worst enemy.

Another anomaly becomes apparent by comparing the elements that produce order within national societies with the inadequacy of these elements at the international level. A relative degree of order is a value clearly sought in most national states. The means to achieve such order include government machinery backed up by a monopoly of force, and attempts to build support and unity through education, language, religion and/or ideology, economic ties, tradition, symbolism, culture, and appeals to loyalty. Of course, national states vary widely in the degrees to which they have achieved internal order and unity.

In general, however, the international system is marked by less development of integrative factors than is found at the national level. In most cases, member states are unwilling to accord to international organizations independent decision-making powers of a legislative, executive, judicial, or enforcement nature. Exceptions in the European Community or in the supposedly binding effect of certain United Nations Security Council decisions only prove the general rule. The means available for building a sense of world community are weak in contrast to those available within national states for strengthening the elements of national unity.

However, these contrasts between national and international factors may be overdrawn by ascribing to states an anthropomorphic quality that ignores the fact that individuals and groups, not abstractions called states, are the actors in both national and international affairs. Also, recognition must be given to Dag Hammarskjöld's two concepts of the United Nations: (1) as static conference machinery for resolving conflicts of national interests, or, more realistically, (2) as a dynamic instrument of governments for developing cooperative executive- and legislative-type actions. These more complex approaches to analysis of national and international political processes, when considered along with a variety of stages of political development within states, will prevent the oversimplification of too sharply contrasting national with international conditions.

Behind many of the paradoxes discussed above is the paradox of human rationality and humanitarianism versus the individual's egoistic, selfish, and emotional qualities. If enough attention and intellectual talent are directed to the problem, rational persons may decide that present international relationships are unsatisfactory and that humankind has common values, including survival, that should take precedence over lesser values. Some few intellectuals have come to these conclusions, but thus far these ideas have not permeated the power centers of national governments to any great degree. Not only would such ideas have to become more widely held and greater amounts of research be directed to the problems of international order, peace, and conflict management, but also means would have to be devised for bringing about the revolutionary changes required in the international system. Such developments would encounter tremendous counterpressures from vested interests whose immediate economic interest, political power, or emotional attachments to existing political and social institutions would be seemingly or really threatened. The greatest obstacle of all, however, would be, in a compartmentalized world, to bring about a focusing of major intellectual talents upon the common interests of humankind. The allocation of national resources and talents will more probably continue to be directed toward the enhancement of national power, political advantage, and economic prosperity in short-run perspective, without sufficient regard for their effects on other major segments of the globe. Rational, intelligent individuals may also differ in their assessment of the necessity for greater emphasis upon the common interests of humankind.

A restatement of some of the dilemmas and their attendant conditions discussed above would bring into focus the paradox of maximum international problems and limited means of resolving these problems. World problems become more severe both as a result of increasing contacts of states and people and as a consequence of more sophisticated means of influence and destruction. Science and technology applied to many areas, including the military, create multiple tensions and conflict. We are frequently reminded that these same developments may be used for the benefit of humanity to help eliminate the greatest threats to human security and well-being. The truth seems to be, however, that the means are largely lacking for mustering the benefits of science for the solution of people's major problems. We are constantly reminded that the gap between rich and poor nations continues to widen. Trade and balance-of-payment problems sometimes have overtones of a relationship between an exploited area and its exploiter, and even among relative equals, trade barriers continue to exist. Foreign capital needs of underdeveloped countries are frequently unmet because potential investors feel the risks involved are too great, or because of a lack of guarantees against expropriation, or because the indigenous economy and government are unable to use effectively the resources that might otherwise be furnished for economic development.

Minor wars continue to break out and threaten to spread to greater proportions. Confrontations between nuclear powers are rare but dangerous. The means of dealing with economic, military, and political problems remain inadequate. The methods of dealing with twentieth-century problems are essentially outmoded. New initiatives and a spirit of cooperation are sorely needed, but a shift of focus to regional and global levels will be difficult to achieve.

IDEOLOGICAL ROOTS OF INTERNATIONAL ORGANIZATION

One feature of today's world scene is the existence of approximately 300 public and 5,000 private international organizations. Nearly all these have been established within the past century, with the greatest development since World War II. Although this movement to establish international organizations is mostly confined to the past 100 years, the ideas and practices upon which modern international organization is built can be traced through many centuries. This heritage of ideas and practices is related to the purposes and procedures of today's international organizations, whose goals, generally speaking, stress accommodation and cooperation across national boundaries.

The basic concepts and practices underlying modern intergovernmental organizations involve diplomacy, treaties, conferences, rules of warfare, the regulation of the use of force, peaceful settlement of disputes, the development of international law, international trade, international economic cooperation, international social cooperation, cultural relationships, world travel, world communications, cosmopolitanism, universalism, peace movements, the formation of leagues and federations, international administration, collective security, and movements for world government. All these ideas and practices originated prior to the last 100 years, but they constitute the basic building blocks for existing international organizations and for any emerging organizations of the future.

Many political philosophers, in every period of recorded history and in eastern as well as western civilizations, have advocated theories and practices compatible with and supportive of international accommodation and the easing of intergovernmental tensions. At the opposite extreme were such writers as Hegel, Hobbes, and Machiavelli, who upheld the power and aggrandizement of individual states or rulers. It is to the group of philosophers who formulated ideas for resolving state differences and for promoting intergovernmental cooperation that today's organizations owe their major ideological debt.

War prevention and regulation have been a primary purpose of both the League of Nations and the United Nations. A broad legacy of ideas for controlling warfare can be found in the literature of political philosophy. Attitudes toward war, from ancient to modern times, ranged from those who advocated war as state policy to those who considered it a paramount evil to be eliminated. Between these extremes fell a substantial number of scholars who deplored war but accepted it as inevitable or necessary under some circumstances. In this last category were such ancient Greek philosophers as Plato (427–347 B.C.) and Aristotle (384–322 B.C.). In his *Laws*, Plato esteemed wisdom and justice above courage. He believed that a state should not neglect its military defense, but the ideal state would be an isolated, self-sufficient unit with as little dependence on the rest of the world as possible. Aristotle was also ambivalent in his attitude toward war. He generally opposed war except in self-defense, but in his *Politics* he justified the conquest of inferior people because he believed that some people were suited only to serve as slaves.

In this same pattern, major spokesmen for the Church during the Middle Ages generally accepted war under certain conditions, although deploring it in general. Wars should be just. Wars against the infidel (for example the Crusades) were approved, but wars among Christians were undesirable. St. Augustine (354–430) set the pattern for much of the later Church doctrine. He disapproved of wars of conquest but accepted wars of defense and wars that were intrinsically justified as means of redressing grievances. Thomas Aquinas (1225–74) deplored war as inhuman and wasteful but accepted St. Augustine's doctrine of just wars and approved the Crusades.

Many philosophers have taken an unequivocal position against war and have viewed it as an evil to be eliminated. Ancient Chinese philosophers such as Confucius (551–479 B.C.) deplored the use of coercion and advocated good faith and moderation as the key doctrines of interstate relations. Another Chinese, Mo Ti (fifth century B.C.), showed an even greater aversion to war. Based on his view that killing and conquest in war are crimes similar in kind to murder and theft, though greater in degree, Mo Ti totally rejected war, not only as a criminal act but also as an economic waste.

The Dutch scholar Desiderius Erasmus (1466–1536), as a humanist, pacifist, and internationalist, expressed clearly his rejection of war. His aversion to military action was based on his respect for human life. Erasmus deplored war as brutal, wicked, wasteful, and stupid. Furthermore, he believed that wars result from the ambitions of princes and are generally unprofitable to both victors and vanquished.

Among other philosophers totally opposed to war was William Ellery Channing (1780–1842), who was one of the pioneers of the American peace movement. Channing attacked war as the greatest of all moral evils because it dehumanizes man and makes him a destroyer of his fellow men. It was his contention that war always brings more evils than it removes. The resultant human suffering and destruction are inexcusable. Channing was not sanguine about the rapid elimination of military conflict, for he believed that education was the only effective means to eliminate war.

Just prior to World War I, Norman Angell (1874–1967), an English publicist, drafted an indictment of war that attracted wide attention and was translated into several languages. His book *The Great Illusion* had as its main theme the idea that modern wars were unprofitable for both the victors and the vanquished. Furthermore, military preparedness was socially and economically wasteful and futile. Like Channing, he believed that people's ideas would have to change before effective peace machinery could be erected.

Condemning war does not provide an alternative for settling disputes or for channeling peaceful change. Substitutes that have been proposed have taken a variety of forms, which may now be examined.

One alternative to state conflict is world unity in the form of universal empire. Historically, the most extensive and durable approximation of world empire was the consolidation of territory under the Roman emperors for a period of several hundred years. Dante Alighieri (1265–1321) looked back to this "golden age" with admiration and nostalgia, for to him the restoration of the conditions of the Roman Empire represented the most hopeful approach to universal peace. His ultimate goal was an opportunity for people to develop their intellect, but this could only be accomplished under conditions of universal peace, and peace was most easily attained through universal empire. Dante believed that the success of Roman rule served as proof that it represented a natural order.

A world unity based on political authority may be compared with and contrasted to the world view of cosmopolitanism based on such concepts as the brotherhood of man. The schools of philosophy represented by the Cynics and the Stoics were basically cosmopolitan in their outlook. These philosophies were influential in the late centuries of the pre-Christian era and the early centuries of the Christian era in both Greece and Rome. Because they involved a world outlook, these patterns of thought could serve as a bridge from the era of Greek city-states to the era of the Macedonian and Roman empires. Both the Cynics and the Stoics believed that one person or one place was as good as any other. The Cynics' view was essentially negative and rejected patriotism and the need for separate states. The Stoics held a positive philosophy based on the idea of humans joined by universal reason in a universal society. Reason was the essential ingredient in human universal equality. Both Cicero and Seneca were influential Roman Stoics. Cicero believed in a universal and superior law of justice derived through reason, whereas Seneca emphasized virtue through service to a world society. Erasmus, whose views on war were previously noted, was also cosmopolitan in his beliefs and experience. He was an international scholar who traveled widely throughout Europe, exchanging ideas with leading scholars from England to Italy and maintaining an extensive correspondence with them.

During the past four centuries, philosophers have advocated such diverse approaches to world order as the development of international law, decolonization, disarmament, and free trade. As will be noted in the later discussion of more elaborate plans for peace, some of these approaches appear in combination with other suggested methods for attaining international order, but a few scholars have stressed a single-factor approach as the key to peace. One of the latter was Hugo Grotius (1583–1645), often referred to as the father of modern international law. Grotius believed that law is necessary in the relations among nations and that it serves as a limitation upon sovereignty. In his 1625 *De Jure Belli et Pacis* ("On the Law of War and Peace"), he expanded the principles developed by earlier scholars for a comprehensive system of international law. Jeremy Bentham in his *Principles of International Law* (1786–89) focused on the emancipation of all colonies and general disarmament as twin fundamental principles for attaining an orderly world. One of the ablest critics of colonialism was J. A. Hobson, a British economist. In *Imperialism* (1902) he attacked colonialism on both economic and political grounds. Hobson anticipated the mandate and trusteeship systems of the League of Nations and the United Nations by advocating international responsibility for colonial states to ensure against exploitation of non-self-governing peoples. A principal advocate of free trade as the main key to world peace was Richard Cobden (1804–65), an influential member of the British

Parliament in the mid-nineteenth century. Cobden linked colonialism to war and believed that free trade would eliminate both.

Several elaborate plans for international peace machinery are worthy of special attention. Each of these proposals involves the setting up of confederacies or loose political unions of one type or another, but none goes so far as to advocate the creation of a superstate or world federation with direct representation of citizens.

The earliest of the more intricate proposals for lessening conflict was that of Pierre Dubois (1250–1322). He suggested an alliance of Christian rulers under French leadership. Wars against the infidel would be encouraged, but peace among Christian nations would be enforced by cooperative action against violators. Penalties would be severe, including confiscation of goods, cutting off food supplies, and military sanctions. Dubois proposed that all disputes be settled by arbitration, with final appeals to the Pope. As a counselor to Philip the Fair of France, Dubois also called his plan to the attention of Edward II of England and of the Pope, but his suggestions received no official support.

In 1623, another Frenchman, Émeric Crucé, addressed a detailed proposal for peace to monarchs and princes in Europe. Basing his ideas on the principle of the interdependence of states, he proposed a universal organization, not limited to Christian rulers, primarily for the promotion of trade. Crucé emphasized, as adjuncts to increased trade, the practical arts, travel, and agreements for the stabilization and exchange of currencies and for the standardization of weights and measures. Disputes would be heard by an assembly of permanently accredited ambassadors, with decisions by majority vote. Enforcement, if necessary, would be by mutual military sanctions.

In 1694, William Penn published his *Essay toward the Present and Future Peace of Europe*, and early in the following century the Abbé de Saint-Pierre circulated his *Plan of Perpetual Peace* among rulers and philosophers in Europe. Both of these plans proposed the establishment of a general parliament or assembly to settle all disputes by a three-fourths vote, with collective sanctions including armed force. The Abbé thought that peace would promote the greater prosperity of all, and he proposed a series of bureaus to develop cooperation in commercial law, weights and measures, and monetary systems.

In his thinking about plans for peace, Immanuel Kant begins with an analysis of the nature of humanity. People have two sides: on the one hand, they are selfish, egoistic, and acquisitive; on the other hand, they are reasonable. Reason provides the discipline to balance the selfish side of their nature. People escape from political anarchy to the acceptance of law and government through the discipline provided by reason. Nations, too, will gradually move from international anarchy to order when reason dictates that wars are too costly and unprofitable. Since despotic rulers are not likely to promote peace, Kant foresaw in *Perpetual Peace* (1795) a world society made up of republican states as the ideal basis for peace. The main elements in Kant's plan included a federation open to voluntary membership of any state; a congress to settle disputes; no standing armies; no territorial changes by conquest, inheritance, or purchase; no loans for external purposes; no interference by one state in the internal affairs of another; the right of self-determination; and world citizenship and freedom of movement between countries based on a universal law of hospitality.

Prior to the League of Nations, the most elaborate and revolutionary set of proposals for international peace machinery was detailed by William Ladd, an American Quaker, in his *Essay on a Congress of Nations* (1840). He used the institutions of both the Swiss and American governments as his models. He advocated the establishment of a Congress of Nations and a Court of Nations with legislative and judicial powers to develop and apply international law. The congress, composed of ambassadors, would develop law by unanimous decision in the form of treaties. The court would hear cases submitted with the mutual consent of contending states and would apply principles of international law, if established, or, in their absence, principles of equity and justice. Ladd provided no executive authority, for he thought that public opinion would serve as an adequate means of enforcement. Believing that an enlightened public opinion is more effective than physical power, Ladd advocated the abolition of standing armies, and he stated that people generally obey law more because of opinion than because of compulsion.

In spite of the access of many of the philosophers discussed above to rulers or to government circles, the impact of their ideas upon governmental practices seems to have been minimal. The growth of international institutions has come only in the nineteenth and twentieth centuries. The development of internationalism was retarded for a number of reasons. In the first place, the ideas presented in the preceding pages, while often familiar to rulers, were not necessarily dominant or exclusive in their impact upon the rulers' thoughts and behavior. Second, no age until the present one was marked by a set of conditions conducive to an increased emphasis on international cooperation. Some of these conditions are of very recent origin. Among them are new weapons of war and the potential for wars to become global and the emergence of dozens of newly independent states whose aspirations for development cannot be achieved without external policies of support. Other more gradually developing factors are encompassed within the term *interdependence*, with all its complex components.

Throughout most of human history, the forces of political fragmentation have been dominant. In the modern era, national states had to emerge and engage in competition before the climate for increased cooperation could develop. The seventeenth and eighteenth centuries were marked by a consolidation of state power, rivalries in war and for colonial empires, and the intensification of nationalism. These tendencies were bolstered by philosophies that stressed individualism. As applied to states, an emphasis on individualism tends more toward rivalry than cooperation.

Even today the forces of nationalism outweigh those of internationalism. In newly emergent states, nation building is a primary concern. Older states emphasize national security, economic interests, and prestige. Cleavages between nations are more potent factors than the forces of unity. The world is segmented by elements of language, customs, religion, ideology, political structure, economic rivalry, human acquisitiveness, fear, and suspicion. The impact of the implications of interdependence has not yet penetrated human consciousness to a significant level of influence. Entrenched interests, backed by powerful instruments of influence and enforcement, will resist changes in the international system that are perceived as a potential threat to those interests. The forces of social and political conservatism will, in all probability, prevent radical change in the direction of world unity. Furthermore, parochialism may better represent the capacity and inclination of human thought than the complexities of a global philosophy. If some exponents of theories of human aggression and territorial drives are correct, this tendency toward philosophical parochialism is powerfully reinforced by basic human emotions and drives.[1] Altogether, the movement toward political internationalism has but limited momentum, and the forces of fragmentation remain dominant.

IN SEARCH OF THEORY

As stated previously, international organizations are only one segment of the larger picture of global politics. Therefore, international organization theory will fit logically within the broader framework of theories applying to international politics. Yet some of the more recent developments in such areas of theory building as transnationalism, complex interdependence, regime theory, and epistemic communities have emerged from the efforts of scholars identified with the study of international organizations. One of the principal vehicles for the publication of the seminal work on these theories has been the quarterly *International Organization.*[2]

But what are the meaning and utility of theory? Simply put, theory is a systematic body of generalizations of descriptive, explanatory, and predictive value. Every field of study requires the development and use of theory for analysis and comprehension of the phenomena in that field. The human mind is incapable of encompassing the objective reality of all the data involved and the meaning of that data in such a complex field as international politics. Human perceptions of reality are both incomplete and approximate. Theories of international politics, by concentrating on certain phenomena,

---

[1] See, for example, the writings of Robert Ardrey, Konrad Lorenz, Sir Arthur Keith, and Raymond A. Dart.

[2] Cf. issues of Summer 1971, Autumn 1981, Spring 1982, and Winter 1992.

perceptions, and judgments, provide a simplified and more comprehensible approximation of reality or a significant segment of the larger reality. These theories should aid the scholar, student, and informed member of the public in the selection and utilization of data, in providing meaning, in explaining the data and phenomena involved, in providing hypotheses, and in suggesting methods for testing the validity of these hypotheses. The "best" or most powerful theories are those perceived to possess the greatest descriptive, explanatory, and predictive value.

Theorizing about international politics has been marked by controversy throughout the twentieth century. In a field of study so vast, complex, and changing, a lack of agreement on approaches and theories should not be surprising. Before World War II, many studies of international politics were descriptive, historical, legalistic, institutional, or a combination of these approaches. In the early decades of the twentieth century, theories based on geographic determinism were widely circulated. United States Navy Captain Alfred Mahan declared that sea power was the most important element of national power. Sir Halford Mackinder, while agreeing with the Mahan doctrine of the significance of sea power, predicted the eventual emergence of a world empire based on control of the "heartland" of Eurasia. This geopolitical theory apparently influenced Hitler's plans for global dominance. The emergence of the League of Nations was accompanied by a philosophy of idealism concerning the possibility of world order through national restraint and cooperation utilizing the principles of collective security. By the early 1950s, theoretical battles were being fought over "idealism versus realism," with the keystones of the gospel of realism centering on national power, national interests, and the balance of power.[3] Shortly thereafter the struggle over theory shifted to that of traditionalism versus behavioralism, with the behavioralists stressing empiricism, quantification, and scientific rigor. Behavioralism took many forms and often concentrated on pretheory by stressing the development of data bases and appropriate methodologies for analyzing fragments of the larger reality. Some behavioralists defended this fragmented approach on the grounds that no previous scientific theory existed and that a body of theory would have to be developed piece by piece until the parts began to form a coherent whole.

Hans Morgenthau, the most influential spokesperson for the realist school in the 1950s, stressed that the essence of politics was a struggle for power and that power could not be measured since it was more qualitative than quantitative. Critics of the Morgenthau thesis not only disagreed with this argument but also raised objections to realist theory on two major counts: (1) that concentration on power relationships among states left out of the calculus other important *motivations* for state behavior, and (2) that the realist

---

[3]Cf. Hans Morgenthau, *Politics among Nations* (New York: Knopf, 1948) and *In Defense of the National Interest* (New York: Knopf, 1951).

approach was state-centric and omitted from consideration other *actors* whose impact on the authoritative allocation of values should not be ignored.

The criticisms of the realist approach to international political theory illustrate one of the dilemmas facing all scholars in the field. Since each person's perception of reality is limited, what elements from the vast array of possibilities warrant analysis in order to produce theories of significant descriptive, explanatory, and predictive utility? Do we concentrate our studies on the behavior of individuals, groups, nations, regions, or something so all-encompassing as an international system? J. David Singer caught the attention of most of the profession by raising this issue in 1961.[4] Past and present international political theorists have focused on each of these levels of analysis, each convinced of the relevance and power of the theories applied or developed. The result has been a plethora of contending subtheories and pretheories that individually or collectively shed some light on segments of the field but fail in the quest for an accepted general theory of international politics.

The purpose of this summarization is not to explore in detail every nuance and variation of diverse approaches to international political theory. Numerous methods of analysis, such as decision making, game theory, content analysis, the study of elites, communication theory, conflict resolution, group behavior, development theory, deterrence theory, and integration theory, will be omitted here, although some of these will resurface in various contexts in subsequent chapters. Although each of these approaches may contribute to certain understandings in a complex field, brevity dictates concentration on a few broad trends of theory that are of special significance for international organization.

Among the theorists who seek a more peaceful and orderly world, one group sees functionalism as the most satisfactory and realistic approach to that end. The functionalist believes in the efficacy of a gradualist approach to world order with the attainment of political federation by installments. Since the political rivalry of states is so intense and since state sovereignty is so firmly entrenched, these areas must be bypassed and habits of cooperation must be established and expanded in "nonpolitical" matters in the economic and social spheres. In these spheres, problems exist that are relatively free from the conflict of national interests, that appeal to the human sense of social justice, that require international cooperation for solution, and the resolution of which works to the mutual advantage of all. As the world shrinks through science and technology, the amount of economic and social cooperation multiplies, while political rivalry and national loyalties seem as intense as ever. The functionalist believes, however, that an ever-increasing amount of economic and social cooperation will eventually build habits of interaction and a

---

[4]J. David Singer, "The Level-of-Analysis Problem in International Relations," in *The International System*, eds. Klaus Knorr and Sidney Verba (Princeton, NJ: Princeton University Press, 1961), pp. 77–92.

broader base of common values that will "spill over" into the political arena. Thus, according to the theory, the obstacles to political integration will gradually be eroded and world unity will be achieved. Functionalism can also be interpreted as applicable at the regional level and thus could be a factor in integration theory pertaining to regional organizations.

Functionalist theory in its basic elements is not new. Émeric Crucé, with his emphasis upon travel, trade, the practical arts, and the interdependence of states, was in the seventeenth century essentially a functionalist. Modern exponents of functionalist theory include David Mitrany and Ernst Haas.[5]

Several possible flaws in functionalist theory need to be considered. The first is the assumption that a clear distinction can be drawn between the political and nonpolitical areas. Examples of politicization in organizations established to promote economic and social cooperation are numerous. The possibility of transferring habits of cooperation from the economic and social to the political areas may also be questioned. Economic cooperation in the European Community, which is often cited as the shining example of the movement toward functional integration, has yet to prove that it will lead to political integration. Global integration will be much more difficult to achieve. Functionalists also tend to underestimate the strength of state sovereignty as a barrier to the transfer of loyalties to the international level. Finally, functionalists often claim that ignorance, poverty, hunger, and disease are the "root causes of war." Historical and empirical evidence furnishes meager substantiation for this claim. Examples are World Wars I and II, instigated in Europe, not in economically and socially less developed areas of the globe.

One of the most influential developments in the search for postwar political theory has been the widespread interest in systems theory. The idea of what constitutes a system can be applied in many academic areas and was borrowed by political scientists largely from the natural sciences. The human body can be studied as a system, as can its brain, muscular, skeletal, and circulatory systems. In political science the concept of system can be applied to a national government, a bureaucracy, a city government, or a political party. It may also be used as a tool for analysis of the interactions of states or other influential actors in something that may be labeled the global political system.

A simple definition of a system "is a set of interrelated entities and their interrelationships."[6] A fuller exposition of the elements and characteristics of a system include the following:

Every system has boundaries which distinguish it from its operating environment. Every system is, in some sense, a communications net which permits the flow of information leading to a self-adjusting process. Every system has inputs

---

[5]David Mitrany, *A Working Peace System* (Chicago: Quadrangle Books, 1966); and Ernst Haas, *Beyond the Nation-State* (Stanford, CA: Stanford University Press, 1964).

[6]Patrick M. Morgan, *Theories and Approaches to International Politics: What Are We To Think?*, 3rd ed. (New Brunswick, NJ: Transaction Books, 1981), p. 222.

and outputs; an output of a system may reenter that system as an input, or what is termed feedback.[7]

Among the leading scholars utilizing various forms of systems theory are Charles McClelland, David Easton, Richard Snyder, Karl Deutsch, Morton Kaplan, J. David Singer, and Richard Rosecrance, to name but a few. Variations in the application of systems theory at the global level may include emphases on foreign policy decision making, communications theory, integration theory, interdependence theory, and a diversity of others.

In developing theoretical models of global systems, Morton Kaplan originally suggested six alternative systems, only two of which may have existed at certain historical periods, the others being hypothetical.[8] These he designated as (1) a balance-of-power system, (2) a loose bipolar system, (3) a tight bipolar system, (4) a universal international system, (5) a hierarchical international system, and (6) a unit-veto system. Kaplan and others interpreted the Cold War period of the 1950s as approximating a loose bipolar system. Many scholars in the 1970s and 1980s perceived that none of these systems suggested by Kaplan fit the emerging pattern of global relations in which various aspects of multipolarity are apparent, economic forces share center stage with political and military considerations, and nonstate actors are involved in the authoritative allocation of values. However, systems theory was widely viewed as a useful approach to global political analysis.

While systems theory offers the attraction of focusing attention upon a comprehensible pattern of relationships that simplifies the task of the student of politics, its critics point to its deficiencies in either describing the real world or providing a productive method of analysis. Bits and pieces of the processes involved have been studied, but little progress toward broad workable theory has been produced. Voluminous data have been gathered, but gaps in necessary data still exist. Accuracy in determining the boundaries of a system as distinguished from its environment is often a problem. Charges are made that systems analysis is status quo-oriented and deterministically rigid and that the variables involved in global models are too complex. Difficulties are also encountered in quantifying and operationalizing concepts.

A further development in the 1970s stemming from systems theory was an interest in the idea of interdependence. One definition of interdependence "is that interdependence exists when changes in one nation produce significant changes in one or more others, or where the effects of one government's actions are partially determined by what other governments do."[9]

[7]James E. Daugherty and Robert L. Pfaltzgraff Jr., *Contending Theories of International Relations: A Comprehensive Survey*, 2nd ed. (New York: Harper & Row, 1981), p. 135.

[8]Morton Kaplan, *System and Process in International Politics* (New York: John Wiley, 1957), pp. 21–53.

[9]Morgan, *Theories and Approaches to International Politics*, p. 238.

Interdependence may have either positive or negative effects leading to either cooperation or conflict. Because of the assumption of many scholars that since 1945 transactions across national boundaries have increased greatly, that economic forces have surpassed military options in importance as instruments of foreign policy, and that private actors are assuming an increased role in global relationships, the result is a condition of complex interdependence among nations. Visualizing global relations as a complex web of interdependencies, if accurate, may complicate the construction of workable models for theory building by proliferating the range of significant variables that might influence outcomes.

Not all scholars agree that global interdependence is significantly increasing either as compared with current national internal patterns or as compared with global interdependence in earlier historical periods. Among the dissenters on these points are Karl Deutsch and Kenneth Waltz.

Does the concept of interdependence further our search for workable theory in world politics? On the positive side we may applaud the efforts of large numbers of scholars to clarify our understanding of global relations by seeking to develop theories that they perceive as more congruent with real world conditions than competing theories. Yet difficulties must still be recognized. Patrick Morgan summarizes these difficulties as follows:

> Analysts do not agree on how to define interdependence. They do not agree on how to detect and measure it. Therefore they do not agree as to whether it is increasing or, if it is, just what that means. Aside from that the subject is perfectly clear.[10]

Closely intertwined with interdependence theory is the question of the relevance of nongovernmental actors in global relationships. This phenomenon is usually identified as transnationalism (although some classes of governmental actors are also included within certain definition of the term). Since an entire chapter (Chapter 11) of this text is devoted to the subject of transnationalism and transnational actors and their influence, no further attention will be given to the topic at this point.

Another recent development in the search for useful theories in world politics is the examination of regimes. Many of the same scholars involved in the elaboration of interdependence theory in the 1970s contributed to the emphasis upon regime theory in the 1980s.[11] Three dozen scholars meeting in Los Angeles and Palm Springs in 1980 and 1981 agreed to accept the following definition of regimes: "International regimes are defined as principles, norms, rules, and decision-making procedures around which actor expecta-

---

[10]Ibid., p. 237.

[11]Cf. the entire issue of *International Organization*, 36, no. 2 (Spring 1982) and articles in *International Organization* 34, no. 2 (Spring 1980) and 35, no. 4 (Autumn 1981).

tions converge in a given issue-area."[12] Furthermore, these principles, norms, rules, and procedures are perceived as intervening variables between basic causal factors (power, interests, and values) and related outcomes and behavior. Thus the concept of regimes, for purposes of research analysis, has been somewhat narrowed from previous general understandings of regimes as government and authority within societies.

The relationship of regimes to the basic causal variables and to related outcomes and behavior may be depicted schematically.

Basic Causal Variables→Regimes→Related Behavior and Outcomes[13]

Scholars who most actively endorse regime research view principles and norms as more fundamental than rules and decision-making procedures in regime identification and analysis. In many areas they perceive norms as well-established and persistent variables affecting decision-making outcomes. They reject the view of international relations as anarchical and the role of power as predominant. Donald Puchala and Raymond Hopkins describe the importance of regimes as follows:

> Regimes constrain and regularize the behavior of participants, affect which issues among protagonists move on and off agendas, determine which activities are legitimized or condemned, and influence whether, when, and how conflicts are resolved.[14]

Regime analysis not only seeks to identify the principles and norms that operate in particular regimes, but also searches for the reasons why regimes are created, how they persist, and why they change or disappear.

Doubts concerning the value of regime research are abundant. By its very definition the concept of regimes focuses on only that portion of the processes of global interaction that lies between power, interests and values on the one hand and behavior and outcomes on the other. Yet, as Arthur Stein indicates, scholars have been imprecise in applying the suggested definition.

> [S]cholars have fallen into using the term "regime" so disparately and with such little precision that it ranges from an umbrella for all international relations to little more than a synonym for international organizations.[15]

---

[12]Stephen D. Krasner, "Structural Causes and Regime Consequences: Regimes as Intervening Variables," *International Organization*, 36, no. 2 (Spring 1982), 185.

[13]Krasner, "Structural Causes and Regime Consequences," 189.

[14]Donald J. Puchala and Raymond F. Hopkins, "International Regimes: Lessons from Inductive Analysis," *International Organization*, 36, no. 2 (Spring 1982), 246.

[15]Arthur Stein, "Coordination and Collaboration: Regimes in an Anarchic World," *International Organization* 36, no. 2 (Spring 1982), 299.

If the term "regime" can encompass such a range of meanings, its theoretical utility may reasonably be questioned. Most regime studies are of a particular perceived regime in such areas as GATT (trade), the oceans, food, security, or the monetary system. Will case studies of particular regimes contribute in a major way to the search for a more comprehensive theory for understanding global politics? The most severe critics, such as Susan Strange, label regime research as a fad, diverting attention from more basic elements of global relationships. She also elaborates on her judgments that regime analysis is imprecise, value biased, and static, emphasizing the status quo and neglecting dynamic elements of change.[16]

In spite of doubts and criticisms, regime analysis retains a high degree of academic influence. In the search for workable theory to illuminate global politics, it takes its place as one part of the spectrum of contending theories outlined in this section.

In 1992 a group of nine scholars collaborated in producing a special issue of *International Organization* devoted to epistemic communities.[17] The editor, Peter M. Haas, defines an epistemic community as "a network of professionals with recognized expertise and competence in a particular domain and an authoritative claim to policy-relevant knowledge within that domain or issue area."[18] These scholars feel that the role of knowledge and information in the shaping of policy is a neglected but promising area of international relations research. They therefore examine the influence of networks of knowledge-based experts "in articulating the cause-and-effect relationships of complex problems, helping states identify their interests, framing the issues for collective debate, proposing specific policies, and identifying salient points for negotiation."[19] They reject the arguments of some critics that they are contributing to elitist theory. For those who hope for the emergence of a comprehensive theory of international relations, the study of epistemic communities makes no claim to generality. Instead, as in regime theory, it examines the influence of networks of knowledge-based experts on the policy process in such specific areas as trade in services, food aid, management of whaling, and ozone depletion.

Finally, what is the current status of theory in making world politics more explicable? Middle-range theories or subtheories have proliferated since 1945. No widely accepted general theory has emerged. Christer Jönsson raises the question of why "the relation between general organization theory and the study of international organization has largely been one of mutual neglect," and develops a framework for applying interorganization theory to a

---

[16]Susan Strange, "*Cave! hic dragones:* A Critique of Regime Analysis," *International Organization*, 36, no. 2 (Spring 1982), 479–96.

[17]*International Organization*, 46, no. 1 (Winter 1992).

[18]Ibid., p. 3.

[19]Ibid., p. 2.

case study of fare setting in international commercial aviation.[20] At the same time, he points out that several other scholars have explored the appropriateness of using organizational theory for international organization analysis with negative conclusions.

The field of theory building remains fragmented. The explanation of this condition is manifold. The amount of reliable data that must be gathered, the multiplicity of variables that may be significant, the profusion of hypotheses that may seem plausible, the range and degree of change in global conditions, and the multitude of case studies to which all the foregoing factors may be applied complicate the search for understanding, explanation, and prediction that theory should supply. In a field so vast and complicated as world politics, it is probably necessary to build theory in small segments and at the same time try to sense the elements that may be most important in describing and explaining behavior within something perceived as the overall global system.

Without theory the study of world politics and international organizations has no meaning nor sense of direction. Theory provides the simplified and comprehensible approximation of reality necessary for explaining complex global phenomena. However, since there is so much disagreement about the "best" or most valid approach to theory, and since so many partial theories exist that provide a degree of understanding of certain areas of world politics, no single theoretical approach will be applied in subsequent chapters of this book. Rather, a diversity of theories will be either obvious or implicit throughout the ensuing examination of the various aspects of international organizations.

CONCLUSION

Although nation-states or their spokespersons are the primary actors and nationalism is the chief motive force in world politics, a few developments have occurred in recent decades to enhance the possibilities of international cooperation and unity. The industrial revolution and scientific development have shrunk global distances and resulted in increased international and transnational contacts. Within the past century there has been an accelerating trend in the formation of international private and public organizations. New problems have arisen that are of global proportions and that may respond only to global treatment. Among these are population, food supply, energy supplies, mass poverty, environmental controls, outer space, the oceans and seabed, and insurance against human annihilation. To a degree never existing before, all humans are interdependent for their lives and welfare. Yet the

---

[20]Christer Jönsson, "Interorganization Theory and International Organization," *International Studies Quarterly*, 30, no. 1 (March 1986), 39–57.

number of states and the intensity of nationalistic feelings are at an all-time high. This persistent paradox requires either resolution or the application of intelligence to controls, restraint, and cooperation among independent political units. The very impact of the burgeoning contacts and transactions across national borders may gradually force the lowering of barriers that interfere with human freedom of interaction. Any shift toward internationalism must be accompanied by confidence that the new arrangements offer as much individual security as is now afforded by sovereign states. World community will not evolve quickly or without the serious growing pains that accompany philosophical, emotional, social, and political change. But even before fundamental changes occur, international organizations may serve a useful function in channeling a portion of state interactions and in providing vehicles for increased cooperation. In spite of their limited role, international organizations have become indispensable instruments within the international system.

2

A GREAT EXPERIMENT— THE LEAGUE OF NATIONS

World Wars I and II engendered two rather contradictory forces. One was a unity and a determination in each country to make every effort and sacrifice necessary to win the war. Thus, nationalism and patriotism were intensified. But, at the same time, the hatred of all wars and the resolution to prevent them also were increased. Although not everyone thought that international cooperation was the best way to avoid future conflict (for example, those Americans opposed to the League of Nations), most citizens and world leaders became convinced during these wars that international organizations could help to prevent future military conflict.

But the problem of reconciling these contradictory forces—heightened feelings of nationalism and a greater hatred of war—was carried over into the newly created organizations for peace. Because existing nationalism had been reinforced by the wars, no leaders would surrender any important area of national sovereignty. The result was a really toothless international organization, dependent on the collective power of individual member states and on their desire to cooperate to avoid crises.

Another problem preventing these organizations from having any potency was the establishment of a peace policy enforced by the victorious powers. The enemy states at first were refused membership in these postwar international organizations and then were admitted only by permission of the major Allied powers. Too, the dominance of these powers was secured by assigning them permanent positions on the main enforcing organ of the international agency and by protecting them against enforcement penalties by the privilege of a veto. Thus the great powers had a double guarantee that no effective action could be directed against them, and yet they were the ones directing enforcement action. The major Allies dictated territorial settlements and executed them through self-help assisted by the new international machinery of a League of Nations or a United Nations. Potentially explosive tensions were almost assured, because there still were no satisfactory means of peaceful change, and because the ultimate sanction continued to be military interference, despite the hope that the new organizations would assist in preventing armed conflict.

FOUNDING OF THE LEAGUE OF NATIONS

The war in Europe had scarcely begun when groups were organized in several European countries and in the United States for the specific purpose of planning how to maintain peace in the postwar period and prevent future wars. The first efforts were private, although leading political figures in some instances expressed an interest in the same kind of ideas at an early stage. Organized official support came somewhat later than the initial private activities, and in several cases the official documents borrowed heavily from the ideas of the private groups. Opinion leaders in the citizenry thus influenced and shaped governmental policy with regard to the postwar peace-maintenance system.

In the United States the most important private group in postwar planning was the League to Enforce Peace, founded in Philadelphia in June 1915. Former President William Howard Taft was a major leader of this movement.

At first President Woodrow Wilson was reluctant to identify himself with the ideas of the League to Enforce Peace, but in May 1916, he addressed a meeting of the organization, and gradually he came to endorse many of its principles. By January 1917, Wilson, in an address to the United States Senate, advocated a "League for Peace" backed by superior collective force. One year later, in an address to Congress, he presented his famous Fourteen Points as the war aims of the United States government. The last of the points called for a League of Nations in the following terms: "A general association of nations must be formed under specific covenants for the purpose of affording mutual guarantees of political independence and territorial integrity to great and small States alike." The Fourteen Points were subsequently adopted, with minor exceptions, as the war aims of all the Allied powers. Thus the Allied heads of governments were committed to the establishment of a security organization as a part of their plans for peace.

In Great Britain the first government-sponsored plans for a League of Nations were initiated by a committee of historians, diplomats, and lawyers under the chairmanship of Lord Phillimore, a judge and professor of international law. The official French version, produced by a ministerial commission under the chairmanship of Léon Bourgeois, laid considerable stress on an elaborate system of sanctions.

The Phillimore plan had the greatest influence on the first American draft prepared by Colonel E. M. House, a close personal adviser of the president. Having prepared his own first draft for a League of Nations, Wilson left for Paris in December 1918, a month after the armistice and a month before the peace conference was to open and, on a tour of European capitals, was received with great enthusiasm by huge crowds.

After President Wilson's arrival in Paris, a plan for the proposed League authored by General Jan Christiaan Smuts of South Africa attracted wide attention because it was released to the general public and because it was clearly and persuasively presented with each proposal accompanied by supporting explanation. This *Practical Suggestion*, as it was entitled, among its innovations suggested a mandate system for the colonies of the defeated powers, a council of permanent and rotating members, and a series of technical committees to carry on the economic and social work of the organization.

This brief outline of some of the main threads of planning during 1914–18 for a League of Nations demonstrates the variety of contributions and sources that preceded the work of writing the Covenant. Although President Wilson was credited with being the main champion of this development private and public groups and individuals in many countries deserve recognition for playing highly significant roles.

On January 18, 1919, the peace conference convened in Paris. Just one week later, at the instigation of the United States and British delegations, a resolution was adopted which provided that the plans for a League of Nations would become an integral part of the peace treaties, and that a commission should be created to work out the details of the League's constitution. President Wilson was then designated as chairman of a nineteen-member commission composed of two members from each of the great powers and one each from nine smaller states. The membership was notable for its inclusion of all the major contributors to preliminary planning for a league who were present in the Paris delegations. These were Wilson and House from the United States, Robert Cecil and Smuts representing the British Empire, and Bourgeois of France. The commission was aided by David Hunter Miller of the United States and Cecil Hurst of Great Britain, who produced a combined draft proposal of the Covenant, which became the working document for all further commission deliberations.

The commission met in the evenings beginning February 3 and eleven days later had hammered out a draft Covenant, which it presented to the plenary conference and to neutral and other smaller states for their comment and suggestions. Wilson immediately sailed back to the United States to assess the reaction at home, which might necessitate further modifications in the proposals.

The most significant changes that resulted from this period of general discussion and criticism were in response to American reactions, especially those originating among United States senators, including the opponents of the League idea. Several revisions to meet the objections were made when Wilson returned to Paris. The most important were (1) specific mention of the Monroe Doctrine's consistency with Covenant obligations, (2) recognition of the right of withdrawal from League membership, (3) a statement that unanimity in voting was required except in cases exempted by the terms of the Covenant or peace treaty, and (4) a safeguard against interference in domestic questions.

The commission held only five more meetings after Wilson's return to Paris on March 14 and was able to agree on the incorporation of the major additions outlined above and other minor modifications from a variety of sources. Decisions also had to be made concerning the location of the seat of the League at Geneva, the appointment of Sir Eric Drummond as the first Secretary-General, the provision for an organizing committee to plan for the permanent establishment of the League, the selection of the four states that would serve as initial nonpermanent members of the Council, and the agreement upon a list of neutral states that would be invited to become original members of the organization by acceding to the Covenant.

The final draft of the Covenant was laid before a plenary session of the peace conference on April 28, 1919, and the Covenant and all the supporting agreements were approved unanimously. A week later Acting Secretary-General Drummond received authority from the organizing committee to begin the recruitment of the Secretariat staff and the preparatory work for the first sessions of the League organs. He established temporary headquarters in London. Since the League Covenant was a part of the Treaty of Versailles, the official birthday of the organization was delayed for eight additional months until the treaty was ratified and took effect on January 10, 1920.

ESSENTIAL FEATURES OF THE LEAGUE

All except three of the forty-five states named in the annex to the Covenant deposited the necessary notices of ratification by early 1920 and became original members of the League of Nations. Some question had been raised at the peace conference concerning the eligibility of the British Dominions, especially India, for inclusion in the list. The most severe critics claimed that Great Britain was given six votes in the Assembly.[1] In addition to the original members, other "fully self-governing States, Dominions, or Colonies" could be admitted to membership by a two-thirds vote of the Assembly, provided that they gave "effective guarantees" of their willingness to accept the necessary

[1]This argument is an interesting prelude to the dispute in 1945 over separate memberships for the Union Republics of the Soviet Union in the United Nations.

international obligations.[2] The right of withdrawal with two years' notice was specifically provided, and a member could be expelled by unanimous vote of all other members of the Council for violation of Covenant obligations.

The United States was the only major state that never joined the League. With this exception, the League approximated universal membership with sixty-three states as sometime members, although, with withdrawals in the 1930s, the maximum at any given date was sixty.

Because of President Wilson's preeminent role in promoting the League idea, it is ironic that the United States defected from League membership. Although a majority of the members of the United States Senate favored membership, the opponents, led by Senator Lodge, used the device of burdening the treaty with reservations to prevent the required two-thirds approval. Throughout the history of the League, the official attitude of the United States toward the League gradually changed from one of hostility and aloofness to increasing cooperation in a variety of League activities, primarily through the agency of a most able consul in Geneva, Prentiss Gilbert, and his staff.

Germany was admitted to the League in 1926, and the Soviet Union was admitted in 1934. Both, immediately on admission, were given permanent seats on the Council in recognition of their importance. The first withdrawals became effective in 1927 and 1928 when Costa Rica withdrew because of the financial burden of membership, followed by Brazil, whose national pride suffered from a refusal to grant it permanent membership on the Council. Germany and Japan announced their intention to withdraw in 1933, and in the late 1930s there was a rash of defections.

The only case of expulsion was against the Soviet Union in late 1939 for its invasion of Finland. This was ironic since in most respects the Soviet Union, during its five-year membership, insisted more strongly than any other state on scrupulous observance by all members of Covenant obligations, and since there were several acts of aggression by other League members against whom there was no demand for expulsion.

The most important set of goals of the League of Nations related to promoting peace and preventing wars. Ten of the twenty-six articles of the Covenant dealt with the means for achieving this set of goals. Although war was not totally outlawed by the Covenant, the intention was clear that through peaceful settlement of disputes wars should be prevented, and that any aggressor who resorted to war in violation of the Covenant should be dealt with promptly and effectively by the collective action of all other members.

Two basic principles underlay the League system for peace maintenance: (1) members agreed to respect and preserve the territorial integrity and political independence of other states, and (2) any war or threat of war was a matter of concern to the whole League. If states were unable to settle

---

[2]Covenant of the League of Nations, Art. 1, sec. 2.

their disputes by negotiation, they agreed to submit them to arbitration, judicial settlement, or consideration by the League Council. The disputants agreed not to go to war in any circumstances until at least three months following a decision of the body hearing the dispute. To facilitate judicial settlement, Article 14 of the Covenant charged the League Council with responsibility for establishing a court, and this duty was promptly carried out. If in hearing a dispute the Council made a unanimous set of recommendations, excepting any disputing parties, all League members agreed not to go to war with any state that complied with the recommendations. If unanimity could not be achieved, the members were free to take individual action.

Article 16 of the Covenant provided the teeth for enforcement action against a state that broke its agreements to keep the peace. The sanctions provided under collective action were potentially severe and effective, if the obligations had been vigorously and scrupulously fulfilled. A violation of Covenant obligations was to be interpreted as an act of war against all other members. The offending state was to be subjected to immediate total economic and political isolation with the direct and indirect costs shared equitably by all members. Supposedly, such measures were automatic and obligatory. The Council was empowered to recommend military sanctions, including the allocation of national contributions to a joint military force composed of land, sea, or air contingents. No offending state could withstand such pressures if all other members cooperated in applying maximum available measures against it.

The League's program of war prevention also included provisions for disarmament "to the lowest point consistent with national safety." The success of these provisions depended upon Council initiative and member acceptance of general disarmament plans. The Covenant also criticized the manufacture of arms by private industry and sought its elimination. Finally, the members agreed to publicize information on armaments and industries readily convertible to arms production, and this agreement resulted in the publication by the League of an annual *Armaments Yearbook.*

Although the major emphasis in the Covenant was upon peace maintenance, some recognition was given to the desirability of international economic and social cooperation. The Covenant provided no special machinery for carrying on, supervising, or coordinating these efforts, although a commitment was included for the establishment of one or more organizations to secure "fair and humane conditions of labour for men, women and children,"[3] and an autonomous International Labor Organization was established as a part of the Treaty of Versailles. The Secretariat was designated as a clearinghouse for relevant information not collected by any other international bureau or commission. The Covenant also indicated the desirability of bringing all existing and future public international bureaus under the direction of

[3]Covenant of the League of Nations, Art. 23.

the League. This goal was never achieved, although in very limited areas the League became the central coordinating agency.

In addition to a concern for labor conditions the Covenant included references to several specific economic and social problems. These were (1) just treatment of non-self-governing peoples, (2) supervision of traffic in women and children, (3) supervision of traffic in dangerous drugs, (4) supervision of the arms trade, (5) freedom of communications and transit, (6) equitable treatment of international trade for all states, and (7) the prevention and control of disease. Whether appropriate or not for special emphasis in such a document, another provision of the Covenant singled out voluntary national Red Cross organizations as suitable for encouragement and promotion.

As a substitute for outright annexation of the colonies taken from the Central Powers at the end of the war, a mandate system was instituted declaring that the well-being of the peoples of these territories formed "a sacred trust of civilisation" and that the "tutelage of such peoples should be entrusted to advanced nations." The "advanced nations" who took over this supervision were Britain, France, Japan, Belgium, South Africa, Australia, and New Zealand, with Britain and France assuming a lion's share of responsibility for multiple territories. The Mandatories were declared to be acting on behalf of the League and were to submit an annual report on each territory to the Council through the Mandates Commission. The Mandates Commission, as created, was composed of experts serving in their individual capacities rather than as government representatives.

Three categories of mandates were described in the Covenant, distinguished from one another by their political development or proximity to self government and independence. These became known as A, B, and C mandates, with the A category recognized as nearing statehood and the C category as least able to achieve statehood within the foreseeable future. The Mandatories of the C group were authorized to administer them as integral parts of their own territory.

Another objective of the League of Nations was the abolition of secret treaties. The Covenant provided that all treaties should be submitted to the Secretariat for publication and that no treaty should be valid unless so registered. The *Treaty Series* of the League was the resulting record of compliance. The Assembly was also charged with a general responsibility for the review and revision of outmoded treaties, but this function remained virtually dormant.

The League machinery was centered around three major organs: the Assembly, the Council, and the Secretariat. The first two were delegate bodies in which each member state had one vote; the Secretariat was composed of international civil servants whose role included impartial service to the organization as a whole.

All members of the League were automatically members of the Assembly. Although casting a single vote, each member state's delegation to the Assembly could consist of three representatives and three alternates with sup porting advisory and secretarial staff. No schedule of meetings was provided by the Covenant, but the practice of annual meetings of approximately one month's duration became the established pattern.

The Assembly accomplished most of its work through six main committees. These dealt with (1) legal questions, (2) technical organizations, (3) reduction of armaments, (4) budget and finance, (5) social and humanitarian questions, and (6) political questions. Each member was entitled to be represented on all committees. Although this arrangement was unwieldy, it had the advantage of providing the spectrum of national viewpoints in the committee stage of consideration of each issue. Small delegations from less affluent countries were hard pressed to participate fully and effectively in every phase of Assembly action.

Committee decisions could be taken by majority vote, but final approval on most issues had to face the requirement of unanimity in a plenary session of the Assembly. This presumably difficult barrier was bypassed by a number of special provisions, practices, and devices. Matters of procedure required only a majority vote. Other important matters, such as admission of members and election of members of the Council, were specifically exempted from the unanimity rule. Members exercised restraint in the use of their liberum veto and, unless a matter was of vital concern to one or more states, they generally abstained rather than choosing to block a resolution supported by a substantial majority of states. Abstentions rather than vetoes could sometimes be assured through bargaining and cooperation concerning the wording of resolutions for the purpose of removing or softening elements irritable to particular national sensibilities. If unanimous agreement was impossible, the resolution could be changed to one expressing a wish or the sense of the Assembly, and it then could be treated as a procedural matter. Since most League sanctions relied more on moral than on physical or tangible force, the differences among the effects of various types of decisions were largely matters of degree.

Although the original size of the League Council was intended to be five permanent and four elected members, the defection of the United States produced an equal balance between the two categories. This was the minimum size of the Council throughout its history. The Covenant permitted the Council and Assembly to prescribe changes in both categories of membership. The total membership varied from eight to fifteen, with permanent membership of three to six members and a variation in elected membership between four and eleven. The permanent members were originally designated as the United States, Great Britain, France, Italy, and Japan. Germany was given permanent Council status upon its admission to the League in 1926, and the Soviet Union was identically treated in 1934. The withdrawals of Germany, Japan, and Italy from League membership in the 1930s decreased the proportion of permanent to nonpermanent Council members. Nonmembers of the Council were invited to sit as temporary Council members whenever a dispute or other matter of special concern to that state was considered by the Council.

The Covenant's allocation of powers and duties between the Assembly and the Council indicates the greater importance attached to the Council by the framers of the document. Another evidence of the lesser role predicted for the Assembly was the intent of some of the participants in the Paris conference that the Assembly meet only at three- or four-year intervals but that Council sessions be much more frequent. The list of powers and duties assigned to the Assembly was brief, although some of the Assembly's roles were basic and significant. They included (1) the admission of members to the League, (2) the control of the budget, (3) the selection of nonpermanent members of the Council, (4) the formulation of rules concerning the selection and terms of Council members, (5) the consideration of matters referred to it by the Council, and (6) the instigation of plans for the revision of treaties.

The list of Council responsibilities was more formidable than that of the Assembly. The Council was assigned (1) the conciliation of disputes, (2) the expulsion of members of the League that violated the Covenant, (3) the supervision of the mandates, (4) the approval of staff appointments to the Secretariat, (5) the authority to move the League headquarters, (6) the formulation of plans for disarmament, (7) the recommendation of methods for carrying out the provisions of the Covenant for the peaceful settlement of disputes and the application of sanctions, and (8) the obligation to meet at the request of any League member to consider any threat to international peace.

A few powers were shared by the Council and Assembly. Instead of sharply delineating the spheres of responsibility for the most basic functions of the League, a broad mandate in identical terms was given to each. Both the Council and Assembly were authorized to "deal at [their] meetings with any matter within the sphere of action of the League or affecting the peace of the world."[4] Both were also authorized to seek advisory opinions from the Permanent Court of International Justice. Three other responsibilities required joint action of the Council and Assembly. These were (1) the appointment of the Secretary-General, (2) the election of members of the Permanent Court of International Justice, and (3) the approval of changes in the allocation of permanent and nonpermanent seats on the Council.

A reading of the Covenant makes it evident that the framers of that document laid greater stress on the Council than on the Assembly. It was natural that the great powers should expect to continue their dominance of the processes for maintaining peace as they dominated the decisions at the peace conference. In practice, however, the Assembly became the main focus of attention within the League. The Assembly, at its first session in 1920, seized the initiative and established precedents that enhanced its prestige vis-à-vis the Council. The practice of general debate involving speeches by the heads of delegations of small as well as large states provided the closest approxima

<hr>

[4]Covenant of the League of Nations, Art. 3, sec. 3; and Art. 4, sec. 4.

tion that had yet been achieved to the establishment of a world forum. The report of the Council was treated as a basis for broad debate, analysis, and criticism so that the Council was assumed to be responsible to the Assembly through an annual review of its activities. The Assembly also called for an annual report by the Secretary-General, the review of which brought the entire range of League activities within its purview. The Assembly was not hesitant to invade spheres of influence assigned in the Covenant to the Council and regularly and extensively dealt with such areas as disarmament and mandates. The Assembly set up committees to consider important matters in the interim between its own annual sessions and expected these committees to report back to the parent body. The members of the League regularly sent their most able and responsible spokespeople to represent them in Assembly as well as in Council sessions. Finally, the first Assembly adopted the policy of annual rather than less-frequent meetings as its permanent pattern. "Thus in a single session the Assembly had definitely constituted itself as the central organ of the League."[5]

Like the Assembly, the Secretariat had to establish most of its own precedents. There was an almost total absence of guidelines in the Covenant. Most of the responsibility and credit for the success of the work of the Secretariat was due to the initiative of the first Secretary-General, Sir Eric Drummond, who served in that capacity from 1919 to 1933. He was succeeded by his deputy, Joseph Avenol, who resigned in 1940. From 1940 until 1946, Sean Lester presided over a skeleton staff in what was essentially a caretaker operation.

From the beginning, the Secretary-General assembled a widely representative staff of able assistants. An important precedent was set in establishing the principle that members of the Secretariat were responsible to the Secretary-General and to the organization as a whole and were not answerable to their own governments. This is the basic requirement for a truly international civil service.

Sir Eric Drummond interpreted his role as being mainly limited to efficient administration, rather than assuming a position of political leadership in the policies of the League of Nations. His function was that of impartial civil servant, and, as such, he gained the confidence of the representatives of all members of the organization. The Covenant granted him no broad discretionary powers except in the selection of staff and the direction of the work, and he chose to interpret his mandate modestly. As head of the continuous branch of the League, he efficiently coordinated all of the League's diverse activities, organized and directed the Secretariat, furnished supporting services to the Council and Assembly, and impartially and proficiently carried out their directives. He was available to the delegates for consultation but was

[5]F. P. Walters, *History of the League of Nations* (New York: Oxford University Press, 1952), I, 127.

never accused of a breach of confidence. By playing a limited role, he avoided the political pressures to which the Secretaries-General of the United Nations have been subjected.

Around the main organs of the League, a satellite group of more than twenty auxiliary organizations developed, which varied in the intensity of their affinity to the central organs. These included three major technical organizations: (1) the Economic and Financial Organization, (2) the Organization for Communications and Transit, and (3) the Health Organization. In addition, there were several permanent advisory commissions, such as the Mandates Commission and the Advisory Commission on Opium and Other Dangerous Drugs; a number of temporary commissions, such as the Preparatory Commission for the Disarmament Conference and the Special Committee on Contributions in Arrears; a few administrative bodies, such as the office of the High Commissioner for the Free City of Danzig and the Advisory Commission for Refugees; two autonomous organizations, the Permanent Court of International Justice and the International Labor Organization; and several special institutions, such as the International Institute of Intellectual Cooperation in Paris and the Institute for the Unification of Private Law in Rome. While it might reasonably be assumed that such a diverse and decentralized set of organizations would result in a chaotic and unmanageable pattern of activities, the Assembly acted as a general reviewing body, and the Secretariat provided continuous and fairly effective coordination of the wide range of agency programs.

Although the Permanent Court of International Justice was theoretically a separate organization from the League of Nations, it was in several respects closely affiliated with the League. A previous reference was made to the Covenant's provision that the Council was responsible for formulating plans to establish the Court. The Court was an integral part of the League's formulas for peaceful settlement of disputes, and both the Council and Assembly could seek advisory opinions from the Court. Although membership in the two organizations was separate and independent, the relationship was in most respects as close as is the present one in which the International Court of Justice is designated as a major organ of the United Nations.

The total budget for the League during the years of principal activity varied between 2.5 and 7 million U.S. dollars annually. This included the budgets for the Court and the International Labor Organization as well as the expenses of most of the auxiliary commissions. The attitude of the members always seemed to be one of extreme economy, and the budget was scrutinized thoroughly with an eye to cutting expenses.

The amendment process explained in Article 26 of the Covenant was ambiguous in that it provided a requirement for ratification of amendments but was silent on the process and standards for their proposal. Amendments would take effect when ratified by a majority of League members, including all members of the Council.

In spite of the difficulty of the amending process (a difficulty that increased with the expansion in the size of the Council), three necessary sets of amendments were adopted in the first few years of League history. These provided the Assembly with the authority to allocate expenses of the League and to set up rules for elections to the Council, and clarified the role of judicial settlement through the Permanent Court of International Justice in the League processes for peaceful settlement of disputes.

SUCCESSES AND FAILURES OF THE LEAGUE OF NATIONS

In spite of any accomplishments in other areas of cooperation, the success of modern international organizations such as the League of Nations or United Nations is most often judged on the basis of their handling of disputes and their utility in avoiding war. This is the case because of the destructiveness of modern warfare and because of the central role assigned to peace maintenance in establishing these organizations. The negotiators who frame the treaties that serve as constitutional documents for a League or United Nations may be unable or unwilling to create the conditions that can realistically control aggression and the resort to war, but the organization's success or failure is ultimately assessed primarily in terms of its utility in the control of political and military conflict.

During the early years of League experience, there were high hopes that the organization could ameliorate tense situations that exhibited the potentiality for erupting into major conflict. The League machinery was utilized for the hearing of at least thirty disputes during the first decade of its existence, and a majority of these were resolved satisfactorily. This successful record was in part due to the involvement of small or middle powers in most of the situations and to the resulting ability and willingness of the large powers to bring sufficient pressure to assure a settlement without recourse to war.

One of the potentially most serious incidents of the early years was expeditiously handled and successfully resolved in 1925. This was a Greek-Bulgarian border dispute in which an invasion of Bulgarian territory by Greek troops was brought to the Council's attention by the Bulgarian government. The Council President, Briand of France, requested a cease-fire and a withdrawal of troops, and the Council met within three days. The Council dispatched military observers to the scene to determine whether normal conditions had been restored, and a commission of inquiry was set up to recommend terms of settlement and indemnity. The prompt and positive action of Briand and the Council restored peace with a minimum of hostilities and damage.

The great tests of the League's ability to settle disputes involving the major powers began in 1931. In September of that year the Japanese launched a series of attacks in Manchuria on the initial pretext that they were protecting their rights involved in their lease of railway property. With the capture of Mukden, their purpose to take over Manchuria became apparent. The League Council hesitated to take effective action since Great Britain and France were unwilling to apply economic or military sanctions and the United States indicated that it would not support any drastic measures. An attempt, under Article 11 of the Covenant, to send a commission of inquiry was vetoed by Japan, but China later appealed to Article 15 under which the votes of the disputing parties could not block a decision. China also asked for a transfer of the question to the Assembly to indicate its disappointment with the Council's performance. The United States somewhat stiffened its attitude with the publication of the Stimson Doctrine of nonrecognition of territorial changes in violation of the Kellogg-Briand Pact for the renunciation of war, and the Assembly gave approval to this doctrine as the official attitude of the League.

The Lytton Commission, a five-member group from the big powers, was eventually dispatched to Manchuria but arrived there nearly seven months after the original incident. In the meantime the Japanese had completed their conquest of Manchuria and had established a puppet government with the name of the new state changed to Manchukuo. The Lytton Report castigated the Japanese for their military aggression, but no further action was taken by the League or its members to force the government of Japan to comply with its recommendations. The ineffectiveness of the League in the face of aggression by a major power was a blow to the prestige of the organization and served as an indication to other states bent on conquest that the will to apply sanctions was lacking on the part of the most powerful League members.

Perhaps the greatest challenge to the League's political effectiveness was Italy's conquest of Ethiopia. By early 1934, Mussolini was building up military forces and supplies in Eritrea and Italian Somaliland. In December of that year an armed clash of serious proportions occurred at Wal-Wal in what was generally conceded to be Ethiopian territory. Emperor Haile Selassie requested that the matter be submitted to arbitration under the terms of an earlier treaty with Italy, but Italy responded with demands for an apology and reparations. The Ethiopian government then requested that the matter be placed before the League Council, whereupon Italy, in order to postpone Council action, agreed to the proposed arbitral procedure.

The British and the French, fearful of Hitler and courting the support of Mussolini in Europe, gave to the Italian dictator tacit assurances that they would not unduly interfere with his African ambitions and aided in delaying Council consideration of the Ethiopian complaints. In August, representatives of the British and French governments met with Italian representatives to try to negotiate an African territorial settlement, but the suggested concessions to Italy were rejected by Mussolini as unacceptable.

Finally, on October 3, 1935, a full-scale invasion of Ethiopia was launched by the Italian forces in Eritrea. The small, poorly trained, and inadequately equipped Ethiopian army was no match for the modern, mechanized Italian divisions and bomber squadrons, and the final result could never be in doubt unless Italian supply lines were cut. The Italians also resorted to the extensive use of mustard gas, in spite of other advantages that made this violation of treaty obligations seem unnecessary as well as inhumane.

The response of the League to the news of the attack was prompt and unprecedented. Within four days of the initial invasion, the Council voted unanimously, except for Italy, that the Italian government was an aggressor in violation of the Covenant and that Article 16, providing for economic and possibly military sanctions, should be applied against Italy. This was the first time that the collective security provisions of the Covenant had been invoked, and, surprisingly, they were to be employed against a major power.

To bring Article 16 into effect, action by the Assembly was required. Although that article seems to demand the automatic application of economic sanctions, the members, in 1921, had adopted an interpretation that each state reserved the right to determine if it would engage in sanctions. On October 11, fifty of the fifty-four League members endorsed cooperative action against Italian aggression.

To provide for uniformity in the application of sanctions, a coordinating committee of the fifty states endorsing the League action was formed. The members agreed to stop the sale of arms to Italy but not to Ethiopia; to cut off credit to the Italian government and to Italian businesses; to prohibit imports from Italy; and to embargo the sale to Italy of strategic war materials (including rubber, tin, aluminum, and manganese), which were substantially controlled by the boycotting states.

These measures struck a severe blow to the Italian economy but were insufficient to prevent the conquest of Ethiopia. Within a few months the Italian gold reserves were dwindling to a critical point, and the lira had to be devalued. Italy's foreign trade was reduced to a small fraction of its previous level. Additional effective sanctions, which undoubtedly could have stopped the military action, were rejected. Embargoes were excluded on food, coal, steel, and oil. The sanctions committee refused to cut off Italian access to the Suez Canal or to blockade the Italian mainland. Diplomatic relations were continued with Italy. The British and French governments had agreed not to push sanctions to the point of risking war with Italy, and in December 1935, the Hoare-Laval proposal for giving Italy control of most of Ethiopia shocked public opinion in most of the world. The proposal was, however, unacceptable to Mussolini as well as to Haile Selassie.

In July 1936, sanctions against Italy were abandoned, just two months after Mussolini's announcement of victory and his assumption of the title Emperor of Ethiopia. The initiative for the conciliation of Italy came from the British, who feared the resurgence of a German threat and were reacting to Hitler's remilitarization of the Rhineland in March of that year. Although the hope proved vain, Italy's support was courted in the resistance to German belligerence. Other European states, including the Scandinavian countries, opposed the lifting of sanctions but could do little but accede to the British proposal. The effectiveness of continued limited sanctions was never tested, and the first such application had to be branded a failure. The League members, in their anxiety over European threats to the peace, were unwilling even to refuse to recognize the legitimacy of the Italian hegemony over Ethiopia.

The first experiment in applying sanctions against a major power ended in disillusionment concerning their effectiveness, although there had been limitations placed upon their application. The Russian spokesperson in the League pointed out that the failure was due to halfhearted measures rather than to any deficiency in the formula of Article 16. The proof that collective security measures cannot work was not convincing in this situation, since the will to apply sanctions was the real subject under test. The disappointment in the results was best expressed in a warning by the Haitian delegate to the Assembly, who pleaded, "Let us never forget that one day we may be somebody's Ethiopia."

Following the failure to take effective action against Japanese and Italian aggression, the League processes for the collective control of political conflict degenerated. The faltering will for dynamic response to crises was now dead. Each member concentrated on its own desire to avoid involvement in acts of aggression against other states. Following Hitler's abrogation of the Treaty of Versailles and the Locarno Pact through the remilitarization of the Rhineland, Germany met no League opposition in taking over Austria and Czechoslovakia. The League failed to intervene in the Spanish civil war in spite of the internationalization of the war through Italian, German, and Soviet involvement. China was virtually rejected in its pleas for League action against Japan when Japan invaded China in 1937 as the opening stage of World War II in the Far East. In September 1938, the Council approved the application of sanctions against Japan, by individual League members, but this was a hollow gesture, and no appreciable change of policy by any state resulted.

From the earliest days of the League, the members realized that the procedures of the Covenant lacked guarantees that all disputes would be settled peacefully. Several attempts were made, both inside and outside the League, to close the gaps and build an airtight security system. Most of these proposals were linked to plans for general disarmament. After years of preliminary planning, a League-sponsored general disarmament conference convened in 1932 but failed to reach any compromise among competing formulas for disarmament.

As a part of its search for security guarantees, France, in 1925, succeeded in obtaining the agreement of other European states to the Locarno Pact. France feared the resurgence of German power on the continent, and the Locarno Pact guaranteed the boundaries between Germany, France, and Belgium with British and Italian adherence to the agreement. The League Council was to act as the agent for determining boundary violations. Other pacts were concluded between France, Germany, Poland, and Czechoslovakia, which attempted to assure the freezing of the territorial status quo in East Europe.

The Kellogg-Briand Pact, or General Treaty for the Renunciation of War, in 1928, was widely acclaimed as a landmark in the search for peace but proved ineffective as a bulwark against aggression. Because it was promoted by the United States, it was hailed as an important link between the League ideas and United States policy. The two major principles were simple: (1) war was renounced as an instrument of national policy, and (2) the parties agreed to settle all disputes by peaceful means. The treaty was received so enthusiastically that sixty-four states quickly ratified it. In subsequent years its weaknesses became apparent. It provided no means of enforcement and was therefore only a moral declaration. Wars of self-defense were declared by Secretary Kellogg to be outside the treaty's purview, yet every state is the judge of its own reasons for taking up arms, and all conflicts tend to be self-judged as defensive.

In spite of scant attention paid to economic and social matters in the Covenant, a vast amount of valuable work was carried on in these areas, and in the 1930s these activities became the most successful contributions of the League to the attempted solution of world problems. Starved by a lack of adequate funds, the economic and social work of the League nevertheless ran the gamut of activities that were continued on a grander scale by the United Nations and furnished valuable experience on which the United Nations Economic and Social Council and more than a dozen specialized agencies could build. A network of committees, organizations, and conferences was developed to foster this wide range of activities, and a major portion of the Secretariat was devoted to supporting this work. One of the valuable services in the economic and social sphere was the gathering and dissemination of knowledge, and the Secretariat furnished much of the necessary effort in research in acting as a central clearinghouse for information and in publishing reports.

The growing importance of the economic and social work of the League culminated in a demand during the late 1930s for reorganization of that aspect of the basic League structure with a view both to greater recognition of the role of economic and social activities and to a more detached and independent status for the agencies in those fields. Greater independence would relieve the economic and social organs from dominance by the political arms of the League and would encourage greater cooperation by nonmembers such as the United States. In May 1939, a committee under the chairmanship of Stanley Bruce of Australia was formed to study the problem of reorganization. The report, published in August, proposed a new Central Committee for Economic and Social Questions to supervise and coordinate all League social and economic affairs. It would be open to nonmember states who would make financial contributions to its work. It would not be subject to close supervision by the Council or Assembly, and its composition could include experts as well as government delegates.

In addition to its recognition of the expansion of the economic and social work of the League at a time when its political efficacy was suffering eclipse, the Bruce Report represented the experience of the League in providing an adequate structure for a wide range of activities that the architects of the Covenant had not foreseen. The demands for more and more activities in the economic and social spheres culminated in this landmark report, which, though never implemented in the League because of the advent of war, laid all the essential groundwork for the elaborate economic and social structure of the United Nations. The report is a prime example of the ways in which League experience made valuable contributions to the establishment of an improved international organization at the close of World War II.

GENERAL ASSESSMENT OF THE LEAGUE OF NATIONS

The League of Nations represented both a radical and a conservative trend in the development of international relations. It was radical because, for the first time, the ideas and ideals of several philosophers who had advocated a universal organization for promoting peace and cooperation among nations were incorporated into state policy. It was radical because it dared to encompass within a single organization the means for dealing with a wide range of problems on which international action was desirable if not imperative. It was radical because it was innovative in creating the political, judicial, economic, social, and administrative agencies that would serve basically as a model for the United Nations. The lessons of the League's twenty years of experience also served well to modify and strengthen the pattern of the United Nations.

The trend in establishing the League was conservative because it was based on an existing international order, and no attempt was made to redirect the sources of authority and power. The sovereignty of national states remained undisturbed in an organization based primarily on the principle of voluntary cooperation among those states. The innovations of the League did not include any radically new practices. The methods for settling disputes, the use of conferences, the techniques of international administration, and the principles of equality of states and of the right of a state to be bound only by its own consent were long-established features of the international scene. The new element was the superimposition upon the existing order of a comprehensive and permanent system of periodic conferences and continuous administration. The fact that the new direction received substantial approval in spite of the League's inability to prevent World War II is evidenced by the demand for a similar but expanded organization after that war and the survival without significant change of such auxiliary agencies as the World Court and the International Labor Organization.

The early optimism concerning the League may be attributed in part to the general desire for peace and cooperation among nations in the aftermath of World War I. Because of its lack of independent power and authority, the League was destined to reflect the general state of international relations, rather than to represent a positive force for redirecting the course of international affairs. As long as all members realized mutual advantages through cooperation, the League provided them with a useful avenue for achieving their common goals. When Germany, Italy, and Japan began to challenge the status quo and when each nation was prompted by economic distress to resort to measures that increased economic rivalry, the League mirrored the lack of cooperative will among its members.

Many reasons have been advanced for the League's failure to survive. The absence from membership of major states such as the United States and, during shorter periods, the Soviet Union and Germany was a handicap to concerted action. The Covenant suffered from some gaps and technical weaknesses, but in the critical tests it was the lack of will of the members rather than of available devices that accounted for ineffective measures. Even the halfhearted sanctions against Italy came within inches of stopping aggression or reversing its results. The attempts to use the League as an instrument for maintaining an unsatisfactory and unstable status quo established in Europe by the victors in World War I doomed those attempts to failure, since no safety valves were provided to allow adjustment through the channels of peaceful change. The problem of providing means for peaceful adjustment as a substitute for military conflict remains a dilemma of international organizations today.

Basically, the League of Nations failed (and the United Nations may fail) because it was ill equipped to accomplish its goals. It was based on principles that were inadequate to assure peace and cooperation. All national confederations have collapsed or been transformed due to lack of centralized power and due to rivalries among the component units. An international organization with real enforcement powers is incompatible with the principle of absolute national sovereignty. The world was not ready in 1919 or in 1945 to transfer effective control over military forces and compulsory jurisdiction over disputes to the international level.

The fading distinction between domestic and international problems may hasten the creation of more effective international agencies in the future, but the basic cleavages that divide one nation from another are not much different today from those in the period of the League. Economic rivalries; differences in languages, culture, levels of prosperity, and political systems; prejudice; and a lack of trust stand as barriers to the creation of the kind of international system that may be required to make a League of Nations or United Nations a more effective instrument for dealing with world problems.

If the League of Nations is measured against a yardstick of hopes and possibilities for achieving world peace and cooperation, it fell short of its goal. If, on the other hand, it is measured by the standard of previous advances toward world order, it represented a breakthrough in the development of international organization. If the process of development does not reverse itself, the League will continue to stand as a landmark in the evolutionary process of achieving a more orderly world.

3

THE GENESIS
OF THE UNITED NATIONS

Just as World War I led to the formation of the League of Nations, World War II led to the establishment of the United Nations. In each case, both statespeople and scholars tried to develop ways of maintaining peace and stability when the war ended.

Despite the desire for peace, after each war there were many conservative elements working to prevent the creation of an international organization radically different from that existing before the war. Included in these conservative elements were nationalism; existing international relationships; the desire to continue and to promote national and individual economic, social, political, and ideological interests; and also suspicion and fear of alien political and cultural systems in a hostile world climate.

The United Nations, established in 1945, is a balance of conservatism and change. Because the League of Nations had failed to prevent war, the United Nations Charter sought to correct the League Covenant's deficiencies. The architects of the UN also attempted to divorce the new organization from any lingering stigma of the League and to convince others that the UN was a completely new creation, not just a revised League. But at the same time, the negotiators were unwilling, and perhaps unable, to think in terms other than those of nationalism, national sovereignty, national interests, and established patterns of international relationships. The result was no more radical than a new automobile model might be, in which the lines and trim are different, but basic engineering is the same.

PRELIMINARY STAGES OF POSTWAR PLANNING

With much of Europe overrun by Axis military forces or under threat of anni-hilation by bombing, a greater proportion of postwar planning during World War II than during World War I was concentrated in the United States. Dozens of private organizations in the United States generated ideas and plans for a peace-maintaining organization and reacted to proposals from other sources. The Department of State created some modest planning machinery by January 1940 and gradually intensified postwar planning efforts as the deadline approached for translating ideas into a finished Charter.

The Department of State was able to draw ideas for a postwar organiza-tion from a wide range of private organizations. One of the most active and influential was the Commission to Study the Organization of Peace, estab-lished in 1939 under the chairmanship of James T. Shotwell and composed of leading scholars concerned with international organization. This commission has continued in existence to the present time, but its first four reports, issued during the period 1941–44, outlined a basic philosophy and detailed propos-als for a world organization. Another active agency was the Commission for a Just and Durable Peace, established by the Federal Council of Churches of Christ in America. John Foster Dulles, subsequently Secretary of State, served as the commission's chairman. Another group of Catholic, Jewish, and Protes-tant religious leaders in October 1943 published the *Declaration on World Peace.* A Universities Committee on Postwar International Problems with headquar-ters at the World Peace Foundation in Boston coordinated the deliberations and ideas of approximately 100 local cooperating faculty groups. Both labor and management demonstrated their interest in postwar peace plans through committees of the American Federation of Labor and the United States Chamber of Commerce. A select committee of fifteen United States citizens experienced in the work of international organizations, under the chairman-ship of Judge Manley O. Hudson, published in 1944 a comprehensive *Design for a Charter of the General International Organization.* Other active groups included the Council on Foreign Relations, the League of Nations Associa-tion, the Americans United for World Organization, and the Foreign Policy Association.

All the above efforts, and others among private groups in the United States, antedated the first official plans made public in the form of the Dum-barton Oaks Proposals in the fall of 1944. The State Department recognized the widespread public interest in the Dumbarton Oaks proposals and responded to a request from the Americans United for World Organization and the Commission to Study the Organization of Peace for a briefing session for representatives of interested national organizations. Arrangements were made for delegates from nearly 100 organizations to participate in a briefing and discussion of the proposals on October 16, 1944. This high degree of interest of concerned citizens, acting through private organizations, was sustained throughout the period of the drafting of the United Nations Charter at San Francisco and continued into the initial years of the new organization.

The impetus for a postwar international organization was not confined to the United States. In Great Britain the League of Nations Union, under the leadership of Lord Robert Cecil, published proposals for an international authority closely paralleling the League of Nations provisions. Some efforts in private planning were international in scope. In 1940 the International Chamber of Commerce and the Carnegie Endowment for International Peace jointly initiated a planning project through the cooperation of national committees. The major concentration of these committees was upon postwar economic reconstruction and trade relations. Two cooperative enterprises between citizens of the United States and Canada concentrated on the field of international law. One involved a series of discussions in 1942–43, participated in by 200 judges, lawyers, professors, government officials, and others with special competence and interest in international law. The final report of this group was entitled *The International Law of the Future: Postulates, Principles, Proposals*.[1] The second United States–Canadian cooperative effort was sponsored by the Canadian and American bar associations. As a result of a series of regional conferences attended by more than 600 lawyers, judges, teachers, and legal practitioners, a joint statement was issued entitled *The International Court of the United Nations Organization*.[2]

From this review of private planning activities, it is evident that government agencies could draw upon a wide cross section of concerned and informed opinion in formulating postwar organization plans. The United States Department of State gathered, organized, and analyzed the proposals from dozens of sources and incorporated some of the ideas into the official planning process.

The willingness of American leaders to help create and to play a leading role in a general international organization represented a significant departure from the refusal of the United States to join the League of Nations. President Roosevelt and Secretary of State Cordell Hull were committed to the establishment of a general international organization and were determined to avoid the disillusioning experience of President Wilson with the League of Nations. Congressional leaders of both major political parties declared their support for cooperation in a postwar organization. Senator Arthur Vandenberg of Michigan was instrumental in securing the endorsement of a conference of Republican leaders at Mackinac Island in September 1943 for United States participation in an international organization. Later that month the House of Representatives passed the Fulbright Resolution, favoring the creation of postwar international peace-maintaining machinery and participa-

---

[1] *International Conciliation*, no. 399 (April 1944), 251–374.

[2] *International Conciliation*, no. 411 (May 1945), 343–62.

tion therein by the United States. A corresponding resolution sponsored by Senator Connally was adopted by the Senate in early November.

Although the Department of State initiated postwar planning activities in January 1940, the most intensive and important work in this area was begun after United States involvement in the war against the Axis. Early in 1942 a new Advisory Committee on Postwar Foreign Policy with an elaborate system of subcommittees was established within the department. Most of the personnel for these committees were co-opted from outside the State Department from both public and private sectors. Supporting all the planning activities of the State Department from 1940 through the completion of the United Nations Charter was the Division of Special Research of the department. Under the capable direction of Leo Pasvolsky, the research division acted as secretariat for the series of planning committees and subcommittees throughout the war years. In addition to serving as head of the research division, Pasvolsky also held the portfolio of Special Assistant to the Secretary of State for International Organization and Security Affairs and the title of Executive Director of the Advisory Committee and of its successor agencies that drafted the Charter. During 1942, as the tempo of postwar planning activities within the department rapidly increased, the personnel of the research division was expanded from ten to more than seventy.

During the period 1940–43 the pressures for a postwar organization of a regional or a decentralized nature seemed dominant. President Roosevelt during these years favored a decentralized system of agencies for nonsecurity matters and advocated "great power" responsibility for curbing aggression. Winston Churchill leaned toward a regional approach to peace maintenance, and early British plans reflected this bias. Functional decentralization was bolstered by the United Nations Conference on Food and Agriculture at Hot Springs, Virginia, in May 1943, which agreed upon the establishment of the Food and Agriculture Organization, and by the Bretton Woods Conference of July 1944, which established the International Bank for Reconstruction and Development and the International Monetary Fund. The State Department Advisory Committee in 1942–43 tended to move so much in the direction of a regional emphasis under the chairmanship of Under Secretary Welles that in June 1943 Secretary Hull took over the active role of chairman and redirected the plans along the lines of his own global preferences. By late 1943 a global approach seemed assured, with accommodation within the comprehensive organization for separate and cooperating regional and functional organizations.

World attention was focused upon postwar planning through a series of meetings of heads of the major Allied states or of their foreign ministers. Each of these meetings resulted in the signing and proclamation of a document declarative of postwar goals. The first in this chain of pronouncements was the Inter-Allied Declaration signed in London in June 1941 by representatives of British Commonwealth governments and European governments-in-exile.

Without referring specifically to the establishment of an international organization, the signatories pledged their cooperation in working for the elimination of the threat of aggression and in striving for economic and social security for all free people.

Two months later President Roosevelt and Prime Minister Churchill met aboard ship off Argentia, Newfoundland, and agreed upon the terms of a document referred to as the Atlantic Charter. In arriving at a compromise concerning some of the points to be included and the phraseology, Churchill was persistent in pushing for a reference to the establishment of an "effective international organization." Roosevelt considered the phrase too strong but finally accepted the principle that aggressor nations should be disarmed "pending the establishment of a wider and permanent system of general security." The Atlantic Charter was promulgated before the United States entered the war, but in January 1942 the representatives of twenty-six nations allied against the Axis powers signed the Declaration by United Nations in Washington, D.C. This document included the first use of the term *United Nations*, and in it the signatories subscribed to the principles of the Atlantic Charter as their war-and-peace aims, in addition to a pledge of full cooperation and effort in defeating the Axis states. As they later became involved in the war, a score of additional states adhered to the declaration.

On October 30, 1943, the foreign ministers of the USSR and the United Kingdom, Secretary of State Hull, and the Chinese ambassador to the Soviet Union issued a declaration in Moscow that, for the first time, clearly pledged their efforts for the establishment of a general international organization. The paragraph which contained this pledge stated that the four governments

> recognize the necessity of establishing at the earliest practicable date a general international organization, based on the principle of the sovereign equality of all peace-loving states, and open to membership by all such states, large and small, for the maintenance of international peace and security.

One month after the Moscow Declaration, President Roosevelt, Premier Stalin, and Prime Minister Churchill, meeting in Teheran, announced in their final communique:

> We recognize fully the supreme responsibility resting upon us and all the United Nations to make a peace which will command the goodwill of the overwhelming masses of the peoples of the world and banish the scourge and terror of war for many generations. . . . We shall seek the cooperation and active participation of all nations large and small . . . [for] the elimination of tyranny and slavery, oppression and intolerance. We will welcome them, as they may choose to come, into a world family of Democratic Nations.

From this series of declarations it is apparent that by the end of 1943 the leaders of the major powers were committed to the establishment of a postwar general international organization. The task that remained was the formulation of detailed plans to which a large number of governments could subscribe. This process involved not only compromise among the divergent views and interests of the big powers but also the eventual resolution of some of the differences between the goals of the small and the large states.

THE DUMBARTON OAKS CONVERSATIONS

By mid-1944 the pace of detailed planning within individual major Allied governments had acquired sufficient momentum to provide working plans for a conference of those big powers. The purpose of this conference was to produce a tentative or preliminary draft of a constitution for a postwar international organization, subject to further elaboration and modification by an expanded conference of Allied and neutral states. This two-step conference process allowed the big powers first to agree among themselves on the essential elements of the organization and then to present a united front in resisting fundamental changes proposed by the smaller states, while accepting their suggestions for filling in details and modifying provisions which the major powers considered nonvital.

The United States government suggested an exchange of preliminary plans and invited the other major Allies to meet in Washington, D.C., in August 1944. Because the Soviet Union was not at this time involved as an ally of China in the Pacific war, the parties agreed that the conversations would take place in two phases. During the first phase the representatives of the United States and the United Kingdom would confer with the Soviet representatives, and immediately afterward the Chinese delegates would replace the Soviet delegates for a second round of consultations. The meetings were held at Dumbarton Oaks, an extensive estate in the Georgetown section of Washington, D.C. The informal conversations at Dumbarton Oaks may be characterized as a working conference of a technical nature at a fairly high diplomatic level.

The Dumbarton Oaks conversations brought about substantial agreement on the major elements of a plan for an international organization. The final document, published on October 9, 1944, was neither complete nor in satisfactory form for a finished Charter, but it served, together with subsequent additions by the Big Four, as the fundamental framework of the emerging United Nations. While it was presented to the world merely as a working document to be used as a basis for further discussion, comment, and amendment, it represented much more in reality. It embodied the areas of agreement on essential principles among the major powers, and from these principles those powers could not readily be detached. Throughout the subsequent San Francisco Conference, the Dumbarton Oaks participants demonstrated their tenacity in adhering to their previous mutual agreements and commitments, in spite of attacks, suggestions, and criticisms from other states.

The participants at Dumbarton Oaks concentrated their efforts on the security provisions of the emerging Charter. The dominance of the great powers in the war effort was to be carried over into the peace-maintenance measures for the postwar period. The central organ for this purpose was to be a Security Council in which the Big Five would have permanent membership. The agreements provided for three other major organs: a General Assembly, a Secretariat, and a Court. Except for the incorporation of the Court into the general organization, the basic structure was similar to that of the League of Nations. At Dumbarton Oaks no provision was made for a trusteeship system, and the Economic and Social Council was to be subsidiary to the General Assembly rather than being declared a major organ.

The Dumbarton Oaks Proposals left a number of gaps to be subsequently filled. The most important was the voting formula in the Security Council. At Dumbarton Oaks an impasse had been reached on this issue. The Soviet Union insisted on an unlimited veto privilege for the permanent members of the Council, whereas the other parties thought that such a provision would result in excessive rigidity and stalemate. The Soviet Union also requested individual membership in the organization for all sixteen of her Union Republics on the basis of their constitutional autonomy, a claim somewhat analogous to, but more exaggerated than, membership by India and the Philippines prior to their complete independence. Other unsettled questions included the nature of the Court (whether it should be new or a continuation of the Permanent Court of International Justice) and arrangements for transition from the League of Nations to the new organization. Some sections of the proposals needed elaboration also. Notable among these were the provisions for the Secretariat and for the economic and social activities of the organization.

FROM YALTA TO SAN FRANCISCO

In early February 1945, Roosevelt, Churchill, and Stalin, accompanied by their foreign ministers, met at Yalta in the Crimea to discuss a wide range of subjects relating to the war and postwar plans. Many of the discussions were unrelated to proposals for a United Nations organization; among these subjects were the Polish and Balkan questions, the establishment of occupation zones in Germany, and the entry of the Soviet Union into the Pacific war.

The most important decision reached at Yalta concerning the unfinished business of Dumbarton Oaks was the acceptance of the United States proposals for the voting formula in the Security Council. Under this formula, unanimity of the big powers would be required on substantive matters, including any enforcement action in response to a breach or threat to the peace or act of aggression, but none of the permanent members could use the power of veto to block a procedural vote, and a party to a dispute was required to abstain on a decision by the Security Council to discuss the dispute. Since the proposal provided the means for the big powers to prevent enforcement action against themselves, Stalin finally became convinced that their position was adequately safeguarded by this arrangement.

Stalin accepted the Western position on the voting formula partially in exchange for a concession on multiple membership for the Soviet Union. The original demand for membership for sixteen Union Republics was first reduced to three and then to only two—the Ukraine and Byelorussia. Roosevelt reluctantly accepted this offer, although he anticipated some difficulty concerning Congressional and public acceptance at home, and he stated that he would have to keep open the possibility of asking for a similar multiple vote for the United States. The question of whether the Ukraine and Byelorussia would be invited as full and equal participants in the forthcoming conference to write the Charter was not fully settled at Yalta.

The conferees further agreed that the general conference on international organization would be held at San Francisco beginning on April 25 and that the United States would issue the invitations. China and France would be asked to cosponsor the conference if they so desired. France subsequently attended but did not act as sponsor. It was agreed that the invitations would declare that the Dumbarton Oaks proposals and the Yalta voting formula would serve as a basis for conference discussion.

The Big Three at Yalta also reached an understanding concerning the essential principles of trusteeship in the Charter. No territories were to be specifically designated as trust territories until after the San Francisco conference, but the three categories to which trusteeship could be applied were: (1) existing mandates under the League of Nations, (2) territories detached from the enemy as a result of the present war, and (3) any other territory voluntarily placed under trusteeship. Further details concerning the trusteeship system were to be elaborated on the basis of additional consultation among the sponsoring states prior to the San Francisco conference.

Rumblings of discontent with the Dumbarton Oaks Proposals became apparent at a special Inter-American Conference on Problems of Peace and War held in Mexico City from February 21 to March 8, 1945. Secretary of State Stettinius traveled directly from Yalta to Mexico City to chair the United States delegation. In spite of attempts by that delegation to head off attacks on the big-power agreements, the Latin American representatives expressed their dissatisfaction with the Dumbarton Oaks Proposals. In a broad resolution on the subject of the establishment of a general international organization, the conference listed several suggestions for change, including (1) stress on universality of membership, (2) amplification of the powers and role of the General Assembly, (3) expansion of the jurisdiction and competence of the International Court, (4) an expanded role for regional organizations within the general framework, and (5) adequate representation of Latin America on the Security Council. The voting formula agreed upon at Yalta was published too late to be a target for attack at Mexico City. The attitudes expressed, however, gave due notice of the battles to come at San Francisco between the large and the small states.

THE SAN FRANCISCO CONFERENCE

The United Nations Conference on International Organization (UNCIO), which opened in San Francisco on April 25, 1945, faced not only the problems of reconciling conflicting positions among states but also problems of size, effective organization, communications, and national pride and prestige. All forty-six states that had adhered to the United Nations Declaration and that had declared war on one or more Axis powers accepted invitations to participate and, by agreement of the participants, Argentina, Byelorussia, the Ukraine, and Denmark were added to the roster. The Soviet Union urged the inclusion of the provisional government of Poland, but that recommendation was rejected, although Poland was subsequently allowed to sign the Charter as an original member. The fifty participating states were represented by 282 official delegates and by more than 1,400 delegation advisers and staff members. A Secretariat of more than 1,000, furnished by the United States as host country, served the conference in official roles, and more than 4,000 auxiliary personnel provided less professional services. News coverage was provided by more than 2,600 accredited press and radio personnel.[3] After some debate over the languages to be used, English and French were adopted as the working languages of the conference, and these two plus Russian, Chinese, and Spanish were accepted as official languages. The resulting requirement of reproducing debates in two languages and many documents in five languages placed a heavy burden on the Secretariat.

In San Francisco the smaller states made their most concerted attack on the voting formula in the Security Council. The attack was led by H. V. Evatt, Australian Minister for External Affairs, and was joined by spokespersons from most of the other medium and small states. The objections were both to the principle of a privileged position for the five permanent members of the Security Council and to the lack of clarity concerning the application of the veto in specific situations. All attempts at modification of the formula or the removal of its applicability from such areas as pacific settlement of disputes were rebuffed by the major powers. On one occasion Senator Connally of the United States dramatized the intransigence of the Big Five by tearing to pieces

---

[3]These conference statistics are adapted from Clyde Eagleton, "The Charter Adopted at San Francisco," *American Political Science Review*, 39 (October 1945), 935.

a copy of the proposed Charter and announcing that without the veto there would be no Charter. In the end the smaller states had to accept the formula without change. The applicability of the veto even outside the strict areas of peace and security, such as Charter amendment, admission of members, and selection of a Secretary-General, withstood all attacks and remained a bastion of great-power privilege.

The small powers achieved slight gains in San Francisco in the matter of clarification of the voting formula. They collectively submitted to the sponsoring powers a twenty-three–part questionnaire requesting answers to questions concerning the applicability of the veto in specific situations. After some disagreement among the Big Four over the issue of the right to use the veto to block preliminary discussion of a dispute (settled only through an appeal to Stalin in Moscow to relax the Soviet hard line), the sponsoring powers issued a general reply to the questionnaire. The reply carried the label "Statement by the Delegations of the Four Sponsoring Governments on Voting Procedures in the Security Council." The statement clarified the interpretation of the Big Four without answering the questionnaire item by item. The smaller states were dissatisfied with the general rigidity of the applications of the veto but had to accept the interpretations as representing the limits of big-power concessions. On one point the small states were particularly disappointed. If an issue arose over whether a question was substantive or procedural, the sponsoring powers stated that that preliminary question would be settled by a substantive vote. Thus the way was opened for the so-called double veto. The statement did include a list of matters that could be decided by a procedural vote of any seven of the eleven Security Council members. This list became a future guarantee against further invasions of the procedural areas through interpretation by the permanent members of the Security Council, and also limited the range of future possibilities for using the double veto. In general the big powers have treated their published statement in San Francisco to be as binding as the Charter.

Although the smaller states were unsuccessful in removing the veto power from the process for amending the Charter, they received some concessions toward calling a review conference to revise the Charter. Provision was made that such a conference could be called at any time by a two-thirds vote in the General Assembly and by a vote of any seven members of the Security Council. Furthermore, the proposal to call such a conference would be placed on the agenda of the tenth annual session of the General Assembly, at which time the required vote in the General Assembly would be reduced to a majority, together with any seven affirmative votes in the Security Council. However, any amendments proposed by a conference would still require ratification by all the permanent members of the Security Council as well as by two-thirds of all members of the United Nations.

Many other states shared the concern expressed by the Latin American states at the Mexico City conference with regard to the continued importance of regional arrangements and the relationship of regional organizations to the United Nations. The chapter on regional arrangements was redrafted at San Francisco to strengthen the emphasis on the importance of regional organizations in the peaceful settlement of disputes and in enforcement actions. The most significant change resulting from small-state pressure was the recognition in Article 51 of the Charter of the right of collective self-defense in cases in which the Security Council was immobilized. This provision left a wide latitude for action by such a group as the Organization of American States.

Since the Dumbarton Oaks Proposals contained no provisions on trusteeship or colonial matters, nearly all details of this section of the Charter had to be developed at San Francisco. The sponsoring powers intended to confer prior to the San Francisco conference on the details of a trusteeship plan, but other pressures prevented this consultation, and the door was thus open to diversified influences in developing these chapters of the Charter. The final result was two lengthy chapters on the trusteeship system, including the creation of the Trusteeship Council, which was accorded major-organ status. The creation of the Trusteeship Council as a major organ and the raising of the status of the Economic and Social Council to similar rank increased the number of major organs from four, as suggested at Dumbarton Oaks, to six.

One of the greatest accomplishments of the small states in San Francisco was the drafting of Chapter XI of the Charter, entitled "Declaration Regarding Non-Self-Governing Territories." This unprecedented statement has been hailed as a bill of rights for all politically dependent peoples. It contained the key principle that in the administration of such territories the interests of the inhabitants are paramount, and it obligated the colonial powers to advance the inhabitants' political, economic, social, and educational welfare. It further obligated the administering states to transmit regular reports to the Secretary-General on the economic, social, and educational conditions in these territories. This concern for politically subjugated peoples carried over into the experience and practice of the United Nations and culminated in the adoption by the General Assembly in 1960 of a declaration stating that all peoples have a right to independence and self-determination.

In enlarging the emphasis upon economic and social activities of the United Nations, the smaller states received support from the United States delegation. In San Francisco the Economic and Social Council was declared to be a major organ, although constitutionally, as well as in practice, its activities have been reviewed and closely scrutinized by the General Assembly. A comparison of the Dumbarton Oaks Proposals with the adopted Charter demonstrates the expansion of the role of the Economic and Social Council. Areas of competence were spelled out in greater detail. Specific references were added for promoting respect for and observance of human rights and fundamental freedoms. The powers and functions of the Economic and Social Council were expanded to include the drafting of conventions and the

calling of international conferences on subjects within its areas of competence. The greater detail of this section of the Charter provided a firm base
for the widely diversified program of economic and social work that has been
developed by the United Nations since 1945.

In trying to diminish the influence of the big powers through the Security Council, the small powers in San Francisco sought to increase the importance of the General Assembly, the Secretariat, and the International Court of
Justice. The most significant addition to the powers of the General Assembly
was incorporated into Article 10 of the Charter, which gave to the General
Assembly the broad authority to "discuss any questions or any matters within
the scope of the present Charter or relating to the powers and functions of
any organs provided for in the present Charter." This sweeping grant of power
has served to justify a broad range of General Assembly activities both of a
supervisory and of an initiatory nature. The meager provisions of the Dumbarton Oaks Proposals concerning the Secretariat and the Secretary-General
were enlarged, and the staff received additional guarantees in the Charter of
their independence from undue interference by the member states. A decision to establish a new Court was made before the Conference convened, and
prior to the San Francisco sessions, a committee of jurists had been assembled
in Washington, D.C., to draft a statute for the Court. This statute was adopted
in San Francisco as a part of the Charter. The new statute was nearly identical
to that of the Permanent Court of International Justice. Nevertheless, the
International Court of Justice was incorporated into the United Nations as a
major organ rather than having an independent status as in League days.
Attempts by several states to confer compulsory jurisdiction on the Court were
unsuccessful. Such a step would have constituted a major surrender of sovereignty, a step that a majority of nations were not ready to take.

LAUNCHING THE NEW ORGANIZATION

The Charter provided that it would become effective upon ratification by the
five permanent members of the Security Council and by a majority of the
other signatories. The Charter was signed by representatives of all the participating states on June 26, 1945. The first state to deposit its instrument of ratification was the United States. In late July the Senate approved the Charter by
a vote of 89–2, a far cry from the debates on and defeat of the Covenant in
1919–20. By October 24, 1945, the required number of ratifications had been
deposited with the United States government, and the Charter came into
force.

A preparatory commission had been working in London prior to the
effective date of the Charter to make the necessary arrangements for launching the new organization. This work was continued through the ensuing

weeks until a permanent organization could be created. With the first meeting of the General Assembly in London on January 10, 1946, the United Nations as a functioning entity was under way.

During late 1945 the decision had been made to locate the headquarters of the United Nations in the United States. Temporary quarters were used at Hunter College in the Bronx and at Lake Success on Long Island, with additional facilities in the New York City building on the grounds of the New York World's Fair. After months of search for a suitable site for a permanent headquarters, an offer was made by John D. Rockefeller, Jr., to give for this purpose a tract of land between Forty-second and Forty-eighth streets and adjacent to the East River in Manhattan. Although this site was much more restricted in size than the space previously sought, the offer was accepted. With an interest-free loan of $65 million from the United States government, the principal buildings were planned, built, and occupied by the early 1950s.

The period from conception to launching for the United Nations, like that for the League of Nations, was of several years' duration. Both organizations were the products of major wars. Both were based on ideas and experience from a variety of sources, but both were promoted primarily by the United States presidents and their advisers. Both primarily represented the principles and ideas acceptable to the major powers, but the United Nations Charter was debated by a broad cross section of states, and the small powers managed to make some significant changes and additions to the proposals of the powerful states. With rapid acceptance by all the signatory states, the United Nations held out somewhat greater promise at its inauguration than had the League with its truncated membership. However, the proof of its efficacy remained to be tested through experience and trial.

4

BASIC PRINCIPLES AND ORGANIZATION OF THE UNITED NATIONS

The United Nations Charter outlines all the United Nations' subsequent relationships and programs. The Charter also is a multilateral treaty establishing the pattern of agreements among and obligations of its members and, as such, is an important addition to international law. As a written constitution, the Charter provides the UN's organizational structure, principles, powers, and functions.

Because the United Nations is, at most, a weak confederation, its members' obligations are limited and only their cooperation can bring about the implementation of UN functions. The organization has no means of enforcing its measures, unlike individual governments, and even the final interpretation of Charter obligations is made by its members.

As with most constitutions, not all principles and practices can be determined by merely reading the Charter. Interpretation and actual usage of the document have been far more important than the few amendments added to it. Only by examining United Nations practices can its Charter's functions, nonfunctions, and malfunctions really be understood. Sometimes its constitutional principles have acted either as catalysts or as barriers to action; at other times, the attitude and will of the members have been more influential.

OBJECTIVES OF THE UNITED NATIONS

Obviously, a statement of objectives or goals for an organization guarantees nothing toward their fulfillment, and, if the goals have real importance or significance for the welfare of humankind, the process of fulfillment is of greater value than the verbalization of aims. However, the coming together of fifty nations to form an international organization indicates a desire to accomplish certain common purposes, and the agreement on a statement of these purposes, usually incorporated into the opening passages of the basic final document of such a conference, specifies the range and limits of the areas of mutual concern. Whether achievable or not, this statement of objectives points the direction for action and gives shape to the program for the organization.

The statement of purposes in the United Nations Charter is both general and redundant. The aims are broad enough to express the desire of war-weary nations for an organization and program capable of helping them to avoid future military contests and to improve economic and social relationships among states. At the same time, general and vague goals provide a basis for ready agreement because they can suggest to the representatives of nations with divergent interests a variety of subgoals, interpretations, and means of implementation. The redundancy results from the repetitious character of the Preamble and Article 1 of the Charter.

The primary goal of both the League of Nations and the United Nations is to maintain international peace and security. The means for goal achievement include peaceful settlement of disputes and collective measures for the prevention and removal of threats to the peace or acts of aggression. Major sections of the Charter detail the instruments and methods for implementing this objective. The Security Council is assigned primary responsibility for peace maintenance but shares this function with the General Assembly and the International Court of Justice. Chapter VI of the Charter is devoted to methods of peaceful settlement of disputes, and Chapter VII outlines measures to be taken in the more serious situations involving threats to the peace, breaches of the peace, and acts of aggression. In an additional chapter, the role to be played by regional organizations in maintaining peace is suggested.

Second only to peace maintenance, the Charter emphasizes the aim of promoting international economic and social cooperation. The Economic and Social Council is to serve as the major organ for implementing this goal with substantial support from the General Assembly and from such autonomous international specialized agencies in the economic and social sphere as governments may create and bring into formal relationship with the United Nations. Additional support in promoting economic and social cooperation may come from subsidiary bodies of the Economic and Social Council and through consultations with nongovernmental organizations. Some of the obligations under the trusteeship provisions of the Charter and some of the guarantees made to all non-self-governing peoples also fit into the economic and social category.

A third professed purpose of the United Nations is to promote respect for human rights for all peoples. The reference in Article 1 to human rights and fundamental freedoms lacks any specific or detailed meaning and provides no guidelines for implementation. No further definition appears elsewhere in the Charter. Major responsibilities for promoting human rights are assigned to the General Assembly and to the Economic and Social Council. The Economic and Social Council is directed to set up one or more commissions in the area of human rights and is empowered to make recommendations and prepare draft conventions on human rights. The encouragement of respect for human rights and fundamental freedoms is declared to be a basic objective of the trusteeship system. The safeguarding of human rights may be inferred from the obligation of colonial powers to recognize "that the interests of the inhabitants of [non-self-governing] territories are paramount . . . to promote to the utmost . . . the well-being of the inhabitants of these territories, and . . . to ensure . . . their political, economic, social, and educational advancement."[1]

All other statements of purposes in either the Preamble or Article 1 of the Charter are more notable for their vagueness than for their specific meaning and for their lack of citing means of implementation than for their specifying means for effecting change. These vague goals include (1) developing friendly relations among nations, (2) acting as a center for harmonizing the actions of nations in the attainment of the more specific goals, (3) taking appropriate measures to strengthen universal peace, (4) practicing tolerance and living together in peace as good neighbors, and (5) establishing justice and respect for international law.

BASIC PRINCIPLES OF THE CHARTER

Immediately following the primary statement of purposes, the Charter, in Article 2, establishes the basic rules of conduct or principles upon which the United Nations is founded and, it is hoped, upon which it will operate. In addition to the list in Article 2, several other general rules are scattered throughout the Charter. Although all provisions of the Charter are, in theory, legally binding, these principles are statements of basic standards or norms undergirding the structure and operation of the United Nations system

---

[1]Charter of the United Nations, Art. 73.

These principles, therefore, represent the most fundamental obligations of members of the United Nations and are the basic legal standards to which they promise adherence.

The first, and probably the most fundamental, principle is the sovereign equality of the members. Of course, equality refers to legal status rather than to size, power, or wealth. Some inequality is recognized in according permanent Security Council membership to the great powers and in the unequal assignment of responsibilities and financial assessments. Nevertheless, the Charter substantially perpetuates and reinforces the well-established principle of international law of the legal equality of states and generally accords voting rights on the basis of one state–one vote.

The fact that the United Nations is an organization of sovereign states places drastic restrictions on the independent power of the organization. Sovereignty indicates that the members reserve the power of ultimate decision making for themselves and confer no real authority upon the international agency. This reservation of authority requires the United Nations to depend for its effective performance on the willingness of the members to cooperate in collective action and to accept stalemate or frustration when cooperation is withheld in favor of national interests. A few restrictions upon sovereignty are incorporated into the Charter, as, for example, in the mandatory obligation to carry out certain decisions of the Security Council; but, in practice, this obligation has proved to be nearly meaningless. The admission to membership of non-self-governing political units such as the Ukraine serves as an exception to the strict application of the principles of sovereignty. However, the principle of sovereignty is one of the cornerstones upon which the United Nations is constructed.

Closely related to the primary goal of the United Nations to maintain international peace and security are the twin principles that all member states (1) shall refrain from the threat or use of force in any manner inconsistent with United Nations purposes, and (2) shall settle their international disputes by peaceful means. The substitution of peaceful settlement for the reliance on force has been disappointing in the United Nations record. Portions of the Charter that envision the establishment of international military forces have not been implemented. The United Nations has lacked the means to ensure either, in the first instance, that disputes will be submitted to international agencies for settlement, or, in the second place, that settlement procedures or enforcement will be effective. Although international peace will always be a relative rather than an absolute condition, the number of unsettled disputes, the numerous instances of recourse to force, and the frequent refusals to submit disputes to United Nations agencies attest to the lack of success since 1945 in substituting peaceful settlement for reliance upon force.

Two other Charter principles closely related to those of peaceful settlement and international enforcement are (1) the obligations of members to support enforcement actions of the United Nations and to refrain from giving assistance to states that are the objects of United Nations preventive or enforcement action, and (2) collective responsibility to require nonmember states to conform sufficiently to Charter principles to ensure the maintenance of international peace and security. The obligation to support United Nations enforcement actions is essential to the integrity and reasonable degree of effectiveness of the organization. Without the cooperation of nonmember states, any assurance of efficacious action by the United Nations is diminished. The experiences of the League of Nations with the lack of will by members to apply and enforce League principles and the uncertainties concerning support for League measures by a nonmember, such as the United States, serve as cogent reminders of the importance of both principles.

An essential but self-evident principle of the Charter is the obligation of all members to fulfill in good faith all the obligations assumed by them in the Charter. This promise is nothing more or less than a statement of the basic norm underlying all international treaties and international law. Without this obligation the United Nations Charter has no real meaning beyond its literary value, since enforcement is dependent upon the actions of the individual members. Because the right to interpret such obligations also rests ultimately with individual states, the possibilities for state commitment to Charter obligations vary from vigorous action to a nullity.

The list of principles in Article 2 of the Charter concludes with a severe limitation upon United Nations authority. This limitation is the "domestic jurisdiction" clause, which forbids the United Nations "to intervene in matters which are essentially within the domestic jurisdiction of any state." The impossibility of always drawing a clear distinction between domestic and international affairs makes reconciliation of this clause with the positive obligations of the Charter difficult. Practice demonstrates that varying interpretations of specific dispute or conflict situations often produce disagreement over the domestic or international nature of these situations. Such disagreements are inevitable, but the United Nations is so generally ineffective that individual nations have little to fear concerning interference from the United Nations in their internal affairs. An exception to the application of the domestic jurisdiction principle is granted in the last clause of Article 2, in which the Security Council is authorized to take enforcement action under Chapter VII of the Charter without restriction by the domestic jurisdiction rule. Chapter VII deals with the most drastic measures that the Security Council may apply with respect to threats to peace, breaches of peace, or acts of aggression.

Although the whole of Article 2 of the Charter is devoted to basic principles, at least a half dozen other Charter provisions can reasonably be put in the same category of fundamental standards. The Preamble and Article 1 contain references to human rights not only as goals but also as recognized principles. The phrase in the Preamble "to reaffirm faith in fundamental human rights, in the dignity and worth of the human person, [and] in the equal rights of men and women" should be interpreted more as a matter of principle than as guidelines for a program. Article 1, which deals primarily with the purposes of the United Nations, also includes an obligation for "respect for the principle of equal rights and self-determination of peoples."

Another principle of the Charter is the statement found in Article 51 of the "right of individual or collective self-defence" against armed attack. The primary responsibility for dealing with acts of aggression resides in the Security Council, and member states are obligated to report their responses to attack to the Security Council but are not required to wait for effective United Nations action before taking self-defense measures. The possibilities for using regional self-defense arrangements in lieu of United Nations channels have in practice proved to be another major obstacle to the maximum utilization of the Security Council or the General Assembly for restoring peace in situations in which armed force is involved. By ignoring the obligation to report individual or collective self-defense measures to the Security Council or by the use of the veto in the Security Council, a major power may nullify the role of the United Nations and proceed to handle the situation either independently or through regional channels. Whether Article 51 provides mainly a supplement to or a substitution for the effective role of the Security Council in disputes involving armed force depends upon the cooperative attitude of the member states, but the implications for the United Nations as a dynamic instrument for peace are far-reaching.

Greater detail concerning regional arrangements and their relationships to the United Nations is provided in Articles 52–54 of the Charter. The major principle stated in this portion of the text is that regional arrangements shall not, in general, be considered as precluded by the Charter as long as their provisions and activities "are consistent with the Purposes and Principles of the United Nations."

Several additional principles are incorporated into the chapter of the Charter on miscellaneous provisions, which includes Articles 102–5. The first of these provides that every treaty and international agreement shall be registered by the members with the Secretariat and that no treaty not so registered shall be invoked before any United Nations organ. A second principle in this chapter declares that, in case of conflict, obligations under the Charter shall take precedence over obligations in other international agreements. Both of these principles are duplicates in all but the precise phraseology of provisions of the League of Nations Covenant.

Articles 104 and 105 provide the standards for establishing the juridical capacity of the United Nations and its privileges and immunities and those of its agents and representatives. The details of these provisions remained to be supplied in subsequent conventions. The two principal instruments for supplying these details are the Convention on the Privileges and Immunities of the United Nations, to which most members subscribe, and the Headquarters Agreement between the United States and the United Nations.

The principles discussed in this section constitute a substantial body of basic norms on which the United Nations structure and functions are superimposed. Although this group of norms is not always clear as to meaning and is not internally consistent, it represents, in combination with the purposes of the organization, the essential statement of the philosophy of the United Nations. Since a philosophy is not very useful without implementation, the international behavior of states will determine whether these norms or others are predominant in world politics.

PRINCIPAL ORGANS OF THE UNITED NATIONS

The Charter designates six agencies as principal organs of the United Nations (see Figure 4–1). These are (1) the General Assembly, (2) the Security Council, (3) the Economic and Social Council, (4) the Trusteeship Council, (5) the Secretariat, and (6) the International Court of Justice.

The General Assembly

If any of the six principal organs of the United Nations is paramount and central to the organization, it is the General Assembly. This centrality was not necessarily established by design in the Charter but was soon achieved through vigorous exercise by the General Assembly of its clearly designated functions and through its assertion of additional authority in areas, such as the maintenance of peace and security, in which its Charter mandate is ambiguous. The growth in the relative importance of the United Nations General Assembly is comparable to the transition by which the League of Nations Assembly asserted its precedence over the other League organs. The details that illustrate the enhancement of the General Assembly's relative importance will emerge in the further study of the functions and proceedings of the United Nations.

The General Assembly serves as an arena for general debate for the United Nations and as the only existing approximation of a world forum. Of the six principal organs, the General Assembly is the only one in which all member states are represented. Each year the delegates from almost all the recognized states in the world meet and discuss an agenda encompassing an extremely broad range of general and specific international issues. The General Assembly exercises coordinating and supervisory functions for all other agencies within the United Nations orbit and thus brings to a focus in its debates the most complete scope of United Nations activities. With so many viewpoints to be ex-

THE UNITED NATIONS SYSTEM

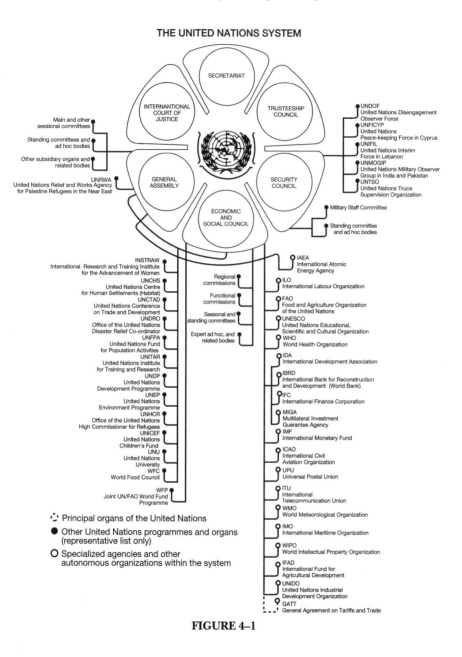

FIGURE 4–1

pressed and with so many functions and issues centered in one body, it should not be surprising that the General Assembly has difficulty working its way through its complicated agenda within a three-month period each year.

The Charter provides for regular annual sessions of the General Assembly and such special sessions as may be required. Regular sessions begin on the third Tuesday in September, and delegates usually anticipate adjournment before Christmas, but the pressure of normal business or a crisis situation, such as the Congo crisis, will prompt a reconvened session after a Christmas holiday.

The Charter provides for the calling of special sessions of the General Assembly, and through 1993 eighteen such sessions have met. The subjects and years are Palestine (1947), Palestine (1948), Tunisia (1961), Financial and Budgetary Problems (1963), Review of Peacekeeping Operations and Southwest Africa (1967), Raw Materials and Development (1974), Development and International Economic Cooperation (1975), Financing of United Nations Interim Force in Lebanon (1978), Namibia (1978), Disarmament (1978), International Economic Cooperation (1980), Disarmament (1982), Critical Economic Situation in Africa (1986), Namibia (1986), Disarmament (1988), Apartheid (1989), Drug Problems (1990), and International Economic Cooperation (1990).

In the summer of 1950 the Security Council was able to avoid a stalemate over the Korean situation because the Soviet Union boycotted the Council meetings during the first seven months of that year. Several resolutions on Korea were adopted by the Council during the Soviet absence. When the General Assembly met in the fall of 1950, the United States and six other states introduced a Uniting for Peace Resolution providing, among other related matters, for the convening, on as little as twenty-four–hour notice, of emergency special sessions of the General Assembly. Under the threat of future Security Council impotence in the face of Korea-type situations, the Assembly members overwhelmingly adopted the resolution in spite of Soviet-bloc opposition and claims of illegality. However, in June 1967, the Soviet delegation called for an emergency special session of the General Assembly under the provisions of the Uniting for Peace Resolution. This emergency session dealt with the crisis in the Middle East. Four previous emergency sessions had been held on the Suez crisis (1956), the Hungarian crisis (1956), Lebanon and Jordan (1958), and the Congo crisis (1960). After a lapse of more than twelve years, a series of further Security Council stalemates led to the convening of four additional emergency special sessions of the General Assembly. These dealt with Afghanistan (1980), Palestine (1980 and resumed in 1982), Namibia (1981), and the Occupied Arab Territories (1982).

The bulk of the work of the General Assembly is carried on in the seven main committees to which the agenda items are allocated according to subject matter. These committees are the First or Political and Security Committee; Special Political Committee, created to relieve the overworked First Committee; Second or Economic and Financial Committee; Third or Social, Humanitarian, and Cultural Committee; Fourth or Trusteeship Committee, to which questions relating to non-self-governing territories are also assigned; Fifth or Administrative and Budgetary Committee; and Sixth or Legal Committee. Each member of the United Nations is entitled to be represented on each of the main committees, a formidable assignment for small under-staffed delegations who find full participation impossible and who must allo-cate their limited resources according to their best assessment of national pri-orities. Subcommittees are also appointed to expedite the work of the main committees.

The General Assembly has used generously its authority under Article 22 of the Charter to "establish such subsidiary organs as it deems necessary for the performance of its functions." In addition to its main committees, there are in existence, at any given time, approximately fifty other subsidiary bodies created by the General Assembly.

The most comprehensive and important function of the General Assem-bly is its power to discuss and recommend. Article 10 of the Charter grants an almost unlimited mandate to the General Assembly in regard to the range of subjects that the body may consider. The mandate extends to "any questions or any matters within the scope of the present Charter or relating to the pow-ers and functions of any organs provided for in the present Charter." Two sig-nificant limitations restrict an otherwise indeterminate list of matters that may be of concern to the General Assembly. The first limitation is the provision in Article 12 of the Charter that specifies that the General Assembly may discuss but may make no recommendation on "any dispute or situation" that is con-currently under consideration by the Security Council. This limitation may be avoided by action in the Security Council to remove the item from its agenda, an action that requires a procedural vote not subject to veto. The second lim-itation involves the fundamental nature of international organization at this stage of development. Since states are reluctant to surrender sovereign pow-ers to international agencies, the General Assembly's authority is limited to recommendations that are not binding on member states. Whether recom-mendations will be enforced or even observed as guidelines depends upon the cooperation and action of individual states.

The General Assembly's powers of discussion and recommendation are supplemented by powers of inquiry, study, and investigation. If the grants of power to study and investigate were not specifically included in the phraseol-ogy of Articles 10–14 of the Charter, they could be implied as a necessary adjunct to the powers of discussion and recommendation. In practice, the General Assembly has liberally interpreted its scope of functions and powers.

A second function assigned to the General Assembly is the supervision and review of all activities of the United Nations. The General Assembly acts as a central coordinating body for the other United Nations organs and agen-cies. In this capacity it receives and reviews annual reports from the Secretary-General, the Security Council, the Economic and Social Council, and the Trusteeship Council. The General Assembly also considers periodic reports from the subsidiary agencies that it has created under its broad grant of authority in Article 22 of the Charter.

Although the Charter designates the Economic and Social Council and the Trusteeship Council as principal organs of the United Nations, Articles 60 and 85 seem to place them in a subordinate role to the General Assembly. This dichotomy results both in an unclear relationship between the General Assembly and the respective councils and in some duplication of effort when the work of the councils is annually reviewed in the Second, Third, and Fourth main committees of the General Assembly.

Deciding financial matters constitutes a third major function of the General Assembly. The General Assembly has the authority to consider and approve the budget, to apportion expenses among the members, and to examine and make recommendations on the budgets of the separate specialized agencies. Budgetary powers may be used as instruments of control in substantive areas, and, in fact, clashes over policy control through financial means caused a major crisis in the 1960s.

The General Assembly exercises the most important elective functions within the United Nations, and these responsibilities constitute a fourth major area of powers and functions of the Assembly. Within the General Assembly resides the exclusive power to elect the nonpermanent members of the Security Council, all members of the Economic and Social Council, and the non-administering members of the Trusteeship Council that are not permanent members of the Security Council. The selection of judges of the International Court of Justice is the joint responsibility of the General Assembly and the Security Council. The General Assembly also appoints the Secretary-General upon the recommendation of the Security Council. Thus, the Assembly has a voice in the composition of all the other major organs of the United Nations, with the single exception that, since 1969, due to the reduction in the number of trust territories, all elective posts on the Trusteeship Council have been eliminated.

Another power that may be interpreted as a part of the elective function is the General Assembly's control over admission of states to membership in the United Nations. Except for the original members, the General Assembly shares with the Security Council control over admission of states. A two-thirds vote is required in the General Assembly to admit an applicant. By a similar vote the Assembly may suspend the rights and privileges or may expel a member state, but all these actions are dependent upon a prior recommendation of the Security Council. In summary of its elective functions, the General Assembly's influence extends not only to the composition of all other organs of the United Nations but to its own composition as well.

The final area of major responsibility of the General Assembly is its role in Charter amendment and revision. This constituent function includes the General Assembly's power to propose amendments by a two-thirds vote. However, any such proposal must be ratified by two-thirds of the member governments, including all the permanent members of the Security Council. The constituent function also extends to the General Assembly's authority to call a general conference for Charter revision. Although two-thirds of the General Assembly and any nine members of the Security Council may, at any time, call a revision conference, such a move would be futile unless all the permanent members of the Security Council were favorable toward ratification of any resulting proposed amendments.

Because the General Assembly has such a broad variety of functions and responsibilities, and because its large membership, which has more than tripled since 1946, makes it an unwieldy body, there have been several proposals for increasing the efficiency of the Assembly. Studies and suggestions have been produced at frequent intervals, but few changes have been effected. Criticisms have been aimed at the number and length of speeches in general debate, at the lack of promptness in convening meetings, at the delays in starting and completing committee work, at the ineffective use of subcommittees, and at the time consumed in roll-call votes. An electric voting device has been installed, but other reforms to limit debate or speed up committee work depend more on human factors of speakers and chairpersons than on devices or rules. The right of all members to be heard in a world forum probably dooms any hopes for radical streamlining of Assembly procedures and shortening of sessions.

The Security Council

The big powers, which dominated both the war effort against the Axis and postwar planning for an international organization, visualized the Security Council as the paramount organ of the United Nations. Providing a mechanism to aid in maintaining international peace and security was to be the primary purpose of the new organization, and enforcement would depend upon the power of the large states. With a continuation of the cooperation that had existed in wartime among the Allies, threats to international peace and security could be effectively met and solutions to disputes could be found. Without cooperation among the most powerful states, solutions were virtually impossible. Therefore, the big powers, it was felt, should have positions of authority on the Security Council commensurate with their responsibilities for maintaining world peace and security.

The four powers that participated in the Dumbarton Oaks conversations—the United States, the Soviet Union, the United Kingdom, and the Republic of China—invited France to join them as permanent members of the Security Council. At first, six other nonpermanent members of the Security Council were to be elected for two-year terms but, according to an amendment adopted in 1965, the number of nonpermanent members was expanded to ten. Primary responsibility for maintaining peace and security was concentrated in the Security Council, and unanimity among the permanent members was required on all votes on substantive matters.

During the early months of United Nations history, the preeminence of the Security Council seemed likely to develop. During the first three years the Security Council held an average of more than 130 meetings per year and debated a substantial number of critical political issues. The development of the Cold War, however, doomed the continued collaboration among the great powers that was necessary for effective Security Council action. Growing disagreement manifested itself in the increasing use of the veto by the Soviet Union, in stalemate in trying to agree on effective measures for Security Council action, and in the use of special sessions and other devices by which peace and security questions could be transferred to the General Assembly. The nadir of Security Council activity was reached in 1959 when that body met only five times. In recent years the Security Council's role and activity have considerably revived due in part to the common interests of the United States and the Soviet Union in resisting mounting pressures of small, underdeveloped nations that can, and often do, dominate voting in the General Assembly. The end of the Cold War and the outbreak of numerous peace and security crises also contributed to a revival of Security Council activity since 1988.

The nonpermanent seats on the Security Council are distributed according to both Charter principles and non-Charter agreements and rules. The term is for two years, with half of the number elected by the General Assembly each year. The Charter specifies that a member may not be immediately reelected. In 1946 a "gentlemen's agreement" was made to allot two seats to Latin America, and one each to Western Europe, Eastern Europe, the British Commonwealth, and the Middle East. The Soviet Union assumed that the East European choice would be subject to Soviet control. These expectations were dashed when, beginning in 1950, that seat was filled, in succession, by Yugoslavia, Greece, and Turkey, and later, under growing pressure for Asian and African representation, by the Philippines, Japan, and Liberia, among others. The growing demands for Asian and African representation finally resulted, in 1965, in the adoption of the first amendments to the Charter, providing for an enlargement of the Security Council from eleven to fifteen members. The General Assembly adopted a resolution allotting the ten elective seats as follows: five for Africa and Asia, two for Latin America, one for Eastern Europe, and two for Western Europe and other states.

Because the Security Council is compact in size and because its types of responsibilities are not diverse, its organizational structure has remained relatively simple. The most important subsidiary agencies have been ad hoc bodies established to deal with aspects of disputes and situations on the Security Council agenda. The length of service of such bodies is dependent upon the nature of the assignment and the duration of the dispute. Fact-finding commissions can finish their assignments within a few weeks, but agencies such as the United Nations Representative for India and Pakistan or the United Nations Force in Cyprus assume a tenure of several years' duration.

To deal with crisis situations, the Security Council is a continuous organization capable of meeting on any given day. Each member state must keep a representative available in the headquarters area at all times. The rules of the Security Council require meetings of the Council at intervals of no more than fourteen days, but this rule is frequently breached by common consent. The frequency of meetings is pragmatically determined by such considerations as the existence of disputes or threatening situations, the willingness of states to bring these situations before the Security Council, and the nature of the dispute and parties involved in relation to any prospects for the Security Council to contribute to the resolution of the controversy or to provide a propaganda advantage for any state or group of states.

In contrast to the full-year term of the General Assembly's president, the presidency of the Security Council rotates monthly by English alphabetical order of states. The president has some control over the agenda, the calling of meetings, and Council debate, but his rulings are subject to challenge by the Security Council.

The primary function of the Security Council is to maintain international peace and security. In carrying out this function the Security Council may place on its agenda for consideration any dispute, threat to the peace, breach of the peace, or act of aggression, with due consideration to the principle of domestic jurisdiction. In accepting the Charter, all members agree that the Security Council acts on their behalf and that they will carry out any Council decisions. This means, in theory, that Security Council decisions are binding, but compliance is difficult to enforce. A preliminary difficulty is the problem of reaching agreement among Security Council members on a firm and effective course of action in any given dispute or situation. Details and examples of Security Council action with regard to peaceful settlement of disputes will be dealt with in Chapter 6.

As a subsidiary aspect of its responsibility for maintaining international peace and security, the Security Council is also charged with the obligation to formulate plans for the international regulation of armaments. The term *regulation* seems to have been deliberately adopted rather than *reduction* or *disarmament*. Until recently relatively little progress has been made in carrying out this Charter provision.

A secondary but important function of the Security Council is its participation in the elective process that it shares with the General Assembly. Before the General Assembly can admit a state as a new member of the United Nations, the Security Council must recommend admission. Since admission of states is a substantive matter, any permanent member of the Council may block admission by a negative vote. The process of selecting a Secretary-General is identical to the requirements for admission of members and is, therefore, also subject to the veto. The only instance in which a majority vote of the Security Council is sufficient for a decision is in the selection of judges of the International Court of Justice. The judges are elected by an absolute majority vote of the General Assembly and of the Security Council, proceeding independently of each other.

The Security Council has the responsibility to supervise, through the agency of the Trusteeship Council, any strategic trust territories. All others are subject to General Assembly supervision. Only one trust territory, the Territory of the Pacific Islands, with the United States as trustee, was ever designated in this category.

Throughout the history of the United Nations the prestige of the Security Council has fluctuated greatly. From an optimistic beginning, through a period of growing frustration manifested by frequent exercise of the veto and the use of the Council as an East-West propaganda arena, the Security Council sank in world esteem to a low point in the 1950s. As disillusionment with the effectiveness of the Security Council grew, attempts were made to strengthen the General Assembly or to utilize the initiative of the Secretary-General to fill the gap. In the 1960s some signs of revitalization of the role of the Security Council began to appear. Meetings were more frequent, and stalemate was avoided by the increased use of abstentions, the adoption of resolutions by consensus, restraint in the exercise of the veto, and efforts to accommodate conflicting views in the formulation of resolutions before they were brought to a vote. In the period since 1988 the Security Council has enjoyed a further upsurge in the spirit of accommodation among its members. The effectiveness of the Security Council is inextricably tied to the utility of the whole United Nations, and that utility ultimately depends on the attitudes and cooperation of the member governments.

The Economic and Social Council (ECOSOC)

At the insistence of the smaller powers and based on the League of Nations experience, appropriate emphasis and structure in the economic and social areas were incorporated into the Charter in San Francisco. The Economic and Social Council of eighteen members (enlarged by amendment in 1965 to twenty-seven and in 1973 to fifty-four members) was created as one of the six principal organs of the United Nations. All members are elected by the General Assembly for three-year terms, with one-third of the terms expiring each year. No state is entitled to continuous membership, but as a practical matter, to assure adequate support of programs, all the permanent members of the Security Council except the Republic of China have been regularly reelected. Other seats are rotated on a regional basis. Small and underdeveloped states are in the majority in ECOSOC and can pass resolutions favorable to their own interests, since all measures are adopted by simple majority vote. Implementation is another matter, because financial support from prosperous states is necessary to give effect to most economic and social programs.

In broad terms, the mission of the Economic and Social Council is to promote the welfare of all peoples everywhere. To consider the diversified agenda necessary for such a sweeping mandate, ECOSOC met twice annually, with a spring session in New York and a summer session in Geneva, until 1992 when a shift was made to a single annual lengthened session.

Because the economic and social activities of the United Nations are less spectacular and less controversial than the area of political disputes and confrontation, the work of ECOSOC and its associated agencies is little heralded in world headlines. Yet, more than three-fourths of the United Nations budget is spent in support of economic and social programs.

The functions of the Economic and Social Council may be divided into three general categories: (1) deliberation and recommendations, (2) research and reports, and (3) coordination. Since each category is significant in the work of ECOSOC, the order of listing is not indicative of any rank order of importance.

The field of Economic and Social Council deliberation includes matters related to human rights, refugees, economic and social development, culture, education, health, food supply, trade and transportation, population, narcotic drugs, housing, labor conditions, and communications. All these topics appear on the Council agenda from time to time, but some topics receive major emphasis. Various aspects of human rights have been of persistent concern since the 1940s. Since 1960, with the adoption of General Assembly declarations proclaiming the 1960s as the First Development Decade and the 1970s, 1980s, and 1990s as the Second, Third, and Fourth Development Decades, ECOSOC has been heavily engrossed in the problems and aspirations of the developing nations.

The Economic and Social Council performs an indispensable function in calling for a wide variety of research studies and reports on subjects within the range of its competence. Adequate statistical data as a basis for rational programming are often nonexistent. Methods of statistical measurement lack standardization, and the results, therefore, lack reliability. ECOSOC has attempted to fill the gaps, standardize procedures, and act as a clearinghouse for information. United Nations studies and reports constitute a primary source of data for governments and private researchers. A portion of the research function is carried out through the subsidiary regional and functional commissions of ECOSOC. Substantial numbers of the United Nations Secretariat personnel are engaged in research and in the preparation of studies and reports in support of ECOSOC activities. Some of the major results of the economic and social research activities of the United Nations include the *World Economic Survey,* the *Report on the World Social Situation,* the *United Nations Statistical Yearbook,* the *United Nations Demographic Yearbook,* and the *United Nations Yearbook on Human Rights.* The specialized agencies affiliated with the United Nations carry on extensive research projects, with ECOSOC acting as a coordinating agency.

Because of the diversity of programs and the numerous agencies involved in international economic and social work, the task of coordination is of signal importance and difficulty among the functions of the Economic and Social Council. Ideally, ECOSOC should operate as a focal point for all efforts in this area, should set up priorities, should allocate projects, and should eliminate duplication of effort and conflict of interest among agencies. Such perfection in coordination is never attained in complex organizations, and the types of relationships among the agencies involved contribute to the difficulties of the Economic and Social Council in achieving an orderly and efficient program. So many activities lie outside the effective jurisdiction of ECOSOC that, even with ideal conditions of budget, will, personnel, unity of purpose, and organizational efficiency, a well-coordinated program would nevertheless be difficult to establish. Furthermore, a fifty-four-member body with limited powers is not an ideal agency of coordination.

In recognition of these problems, the General Assembly in 1974 called for the appointment of a committee of experts to propose structural changes for enhancing the effectiveness of the economic and social programs of the United Nations. One of the results of the committee's recommendations was the creation in 1978 of a Secretariat post of Director-General for Development and International Economic Cooperation, second only in rank to the Secretary-General of the United Nations. This and other measures for streamlining the diverse machinery and programs under the aegis of ECOSOC may help to lessen the most severe problems of coordination.

Further information concerning the range of types of economic and social agencies in the United Nations system and their relationships to ECOSOC are detailed in Chapter 12.

The Trusteeship Council

The Trusteeship Council, like the Economic and Social Council, is in the anomalous position of being designated as a principal organ of the United Nations and yet being subject to General Assembly authority and review of its activities. In supervising the administration of strategic territories, the Security Council theoretically replaces the General Assembly as the final review agency, but this function is never exercised. At the San Francisco meeting the purpose of conferring principal-organ status on the Trusteeship Council was to emphasize the importance attached by some representatives to the task of safeguarding the rights of non-self-governing peoples.

The role of the Trusteeship Council is to provide, on behalf of the international community, supervision of those non-self-governing territories that are designated as trust territories. The administration of each territory is carried out by a specified state, but certain supervisory responsibilities are performed by the General Assembly through the agency of the Trusteeship Council. Articles 87 and 88 of the Charter indicate the main methods for exercising this supervisory role. These methods are (1) the preparation of a detailed questionnaire on the political, economic, social, and educational advancement of the inhabitants of the territory, to be used as a basis for an annual report by the administering authority; (2) a comprehensive oral examination of the spokesperson for the administering authority based on the reply to the questionnaire, and a written report from the Trusteeship Council to the General Assembly; (3) the receipt and examination of petitions from individuals or groups within the trust territory; and (4) periodic visits to each trust territory by delegates of the Trusteeship Council. More effective supervision of conditions within trust territories is provided by these devices than existed under the mandates system of the League, although publicity and persuasion are today, as they were in the League period, the only sanctions available to pressure an administering authority into compliance with recommendations. However, the use of inspection by visiting missions is a new device that was not available to the League agencies, and petitions no longer need be submitted through the administering government, as was the case under the mandates system.

By 1950, eleven territories had been put under trusteeship, with seven states acting as trustees. All except Somalia under Italian trusteeship had been former mandates within the League system. South Africa refused to place its former mandate, South-West Africa, under a trust agreement, insisting instead on the unilateral right to annexation. Only one territory, the Trust Territory of the Pacific Island under United States trusteeship, was declared a strategic area, making it theoretically subject to Security Council rather than General Assembly supervision.

The Trusteeship Council's composition is determined by a complex formula. All members of the United Nations that administer trust territories are ex officio members of the Trusteeship Council. Any permanent members of the Security Council that are not administering powers also have automatic membership. To attain parity in numbers between administering and nonadministering states, the General Assembly elects sufficient additional members to achieve this equality. At the maximum, during the 1950s the Trusteeship Council had fourteen members, with the United States, the United Kingdom, and France among the seven administering states, the Soviet Union and China as nonadministering permanent members of the Security Council, and five other members elected by the General Assembly. As trust territories gained their independence, the number of elective members diminished to one and then to none, leaving only the five permanent members of the Security Council on the Trusteeship Council in the unequal ratio of four nonadministering to one administering member. After 1975 the only remaining area under Trusteeship Council supervision was the Trust Territory of the Pacific Islands with the United States as trustee. Although negotiations for terminating this trusteeship were initiated in the late 1960s, conflicting interests of the inhabitants of the various parts of Micronesia and those of the United States delayed the transition into the 1990s. A solution of this many-faceted problem will leave the Trusteeship Council with no business to perform, and it will cease to exist. Details concerning several aspects of the goals and work of the Trusteeship Council during its active years will be elaborated in Chapter 15.

The Secretariat

The United Nations Secretariat is a body of international civil servants headed by the Secretary-General. Unlike the General Assembly and the three councils, the Secretariat is not composed of delegate spokespersons for their respective governments. Rather, it is constituted of full-time employees of the organization, who must preserve their neutrality in the interests of serving the entire membership and of promoting the international goals of the United Nations. This neutrality is safeguarded by the provisions of Article 100 of the Charter, which provides for the following:

1. In the performance of their duties the Secretary-General and the staff shall not seek or receive instructions from any government or from any other authority external to the Organization. They shall refrain from any action which might reflect on their position as international officials responsible only to the Organization.
2. Each Member of the United Nations undertakes to respect the exclusively international character of the responsibilities of the Secretary-General and the staff and not to seek to influence them in the discharge of their responsibilities.

These paragraphs indicate clearly the double responsibility incumbent upon both staff and governments to preserve the international character of the Secretariat. The independence of the Secretariat members from national pressures was a principle not clearly stated in the Covenant but established at the inception of the League of Nations by its first Secretary-General.

The Secretary-General is appointed by the General Assembly, acting by a two-thirds vote, upon recommendation of the Security Council. In the absence of any Charter specification, the first General Assembly established the length of term for the Secretary-General as five years. The greatest hurdle to selection is agreement on a candidate by the major powers, since any permanent member of the Security Council may exercise a veto. Stalemates are a general threat in the selection process, and the term of the first Secretary-General had to be extended by the General Assembly without concurrence by the Security Council.

Six Secretaries-General have served the organization. Trygve Lie of Norway held the office from 1946 to 1953. He was succeeded by Dag Hammarskjöld of Sweden, who served until his death in an airplane crash in central Africa on September 17, 1961. After an interval of nearly seven weeks,

U Thant of Burma was appointed first as Acting Secretary-General and later for two successive terms as Secretary-General. Kurt Waldheim of Austria served for two full terms and was succeeded on January 1, 1982, by Javier Pérez de Cuéllar of Peru. In January 1992 Boutros Boutros-Ghali of Egypt became the sixth incumbent of the office.

The major functions of the Secretary-General are outlined clearly in the Charter and include the following: (1) to be the chief administrative officer of the organization; (2) to act as secretary to all the major delegate bodies of the United Nations; (3) to perform functions assigned by the General Assembly and the three Councils; (4) to make an annual report to the General Assembly on the work of the organization; and (5) to appoint the Secretariat staff under regulations established by the General Assembly. The Secretary-General also has the authority to act on his own initiative to bring to the attention of the Security Council any matter that in his opinion threatens international peace and security.

In practice, the role of the Secretary-General has expanded far beyond the anticipations of the architects of the Charter. This expansion has resulted both from circumstances and from the initiative of each of the incumbents in the office. The role of the Secretary-General and other facets of the theory and practice of an international civil service will be detailed in Chapter 16.

The International Court of Justice (ICJ)

The sixth principal organ of the United Nations is the International Court of Justice, with headquarters in The Hague. The Statute of the ICJ is an integral part of the Charter and is almost identical to the Statute of the previous Permanent Court of International Justice (PCIJ). However, unlike the League arrangement in which the PCIJ and its membership were independent of the League, all members of the United Nations are automatically members of the ICJ. Additional states may become parties to the Court Statute under arrangements approved by the General Assembly and the Security Council. Switzerland has adhered to the Statute under these conditions.

The Court is composed of fifteen judges elected by concurrent vote of the General Assembly and the Security Council. No two judges may be of the same nationality, and the Court as a whole should represent the principal legal systems of the world. Judges serve nine-year terms, with the terms of five judges expiring every third year. No limit is set on the number of terms for which a judge may be reelected.

In hearing a specific case, if there is no judge on the Court of the nationality of one or more of the states that are parties to the case, such state or states may appoint a national judge to sit for that case. These additional judges participate with full voting rights.

Cases are decided by majority vote of the participating judges. Nine judges constitute a quorum. In case of a tie, the President of the Court has a casting vote.

The Court hears those cases that are referred to it by the contending parties. The Court may, however, determine that the case, because of its nature, is not subject to judicial determination or that the parties have no legal right to submit the case to the Court. Only states may bring cases before the Court, but no state is required to submit any case for hearing and decision. This lack of compulsory jurisdiction is a major deficiency of international as contrasted with national legal systems.

In addition to hearing cases, the ICJ is authorized to give advisory opinions on legal questions. The Charter provides that the General Assembly and the Security Council may request such opinions and that the General Assembly may authorize other organs and the specialized agencies to request opinions on legal questions within the scope of their activities. The Economic and Social Council, the Trusteeship Council, and all the specialized agencies except the Universal Postal Union have been granted general authority of this kind, but three-fifths of all requests to the Court for advisory opinions have been made by the General Assembly.

Although suffering from numerous deficiencies, the Court plays an important role in the development of an international legal system. This role will be explored further in Chapter 8.

5

SOME BASIC ISSUES
OF THE UNITED NATIONS

Besides the principles and the major organs discussed in the previous chapter, certain issues should be understood as a background for a later examination of the programs and activities of the United Nations and its agencies. These issues are questions of membership, representation, voting, amendment, and finance. Among these are constitutional issues as fundamental as the matters of principle and structure covered in Chapter 4. Other parts of these questions reach beyond legal relationships into United Nations practices.

THE MEMBERSHIP ISSUE

Membership in an international public (intergovernmental) organization may be either exclusive or inclusive, limited or universal. Regional organizations or certain special-purpose organizations may naturally be limited in membership, since the vital interests of all states will not be sufficiently affected by the activities of the organization to warrant universality. However, a strong argument can be made for universality in organizations that are concerned with worldwide problems, whether the programs of those organizations are general and complex, as in the case of the League of Nations or United Nations, or whether they are more limited in scope, as exemplified by the specialized agencies of the United Nations. Inherently weak organizations, dependent on the cooperation of members for effective action, are further handicapped if one or more major power centers lie outside the organization's consultation agencies. The absence of the United States from League membership and the limited duration of Soviet and German participation are generally cited as major deficiencies of League efficacy. The absence until 1973 of representatives of East and West Germany and the refusal from 1950 to 1971 to seat delegates from the People's Republic of China in United Nations bodies similarly weakened the implementation of adopted resolutions and introduced an element of uncertainty into the negotiating process itself. For example, arms-control measures or territorial and political settlements, when arranged through United Nations channels, will be more secure if backed by Chinese and German guarantees in addition to the support of the other major powers.

Universal membership was a vague goal but was rejected as a basic principle in both the League of Nations and United Nations. Enemy states in the preceding world war were excluded as original members. A list of original members was drawn up, and these were able to activate their membership by ratifying the Covenant or the Charter. All other states had to submit to an admission process involving a set of imprecise admission criteria. At the San Francisco conference, several states, primarily from Latin America, advocated automatic and universal membership in the United Nations for all independent states. Lip service was given to the desirability of universality, but the hurdles of an admission procedure were retained. In spite of the rejection of the principle of automatic membership by both the League and United Nations, the goal of universality may be achieved if three conditions are present: (1) if the terms and procedures for admission are not too difficult or rigid, (2) if the existing members are cooperative and committed to achieving universality, and (3) if nonmembers are willing to seek membership. Prevalent theories of sovereignty preclude the possibility of compulsory membership.

In general practice, autonomous states are considered the units eligible for membership in international organizations. The League of Nations expanded the list of eligibles by stating that "any fully self-governing state, dominion or colony" might be admitted by a two-thirds vote of the Assembly. India was included as an original League member, although its full sovereignty was not established until 1947. The United Nations also granted exceptions to the requirement of statehood in its list of original members. The Soviet Union claimed a right of separate membership for each of its sixteen union republics; the concession to include the Ukraine and Byelorussia as original members did not meet generally accepted standards of statehood. India and the Philippines were also accorded the status of original members prior to the transfer of sovereignty.

The membership provisions of the League Covenant proved no obstacle in moving toward near-universal membership. The mini-states of Liechtenstein, San Marino, and Monaco were rejected on grounds that their small size precluded their ability to effectively carry out the obligations of membership. The United States was the only major state that never joined the organization.

The provisions of the Covenant that permitted termination of membership thwarted any hopes for sustaining the near universality of the League. The methods for terminating membership included (1) withdrawal with two years' notice of intent, (2) expulsion by the affirmative vote of all other members of the Council, and (3) refusal to accept the terms of an amendment to the Covenant. The third method (a manifestation of one of the principles of sovereignty) was never invoked. The Soviet Union was expelled in 1939 after its military attack on Finland and was the only case of expulsion. Withdrawals, on the other hand, were frequent, beginning with notification of intent by Costa Rica in 1924 and Brazil in 1926, continuing with similar action by Japan and Germany in 1933, and concluding with a flurry of twelve such announcements in 1936–40.

The United Nations closely followed the League pattern in setting up categories of original membership and admitted membership. The original members included the states that participated in the San Francisco conference or previously signed the Declaration of the United Nations issued in January 1942. All fifty-one states that were eligible for original membership ratified the Charter before the end of 1945. The process of admission involves a recommendation by the Security Council (a substantive matter subject to veto by any permanent member) followed by a two-thirds vote of the General Assembly. Membership is open to all "peace-loving states which accept the obligations contained in the present Charter and, in the judgment of the Organization, are able and willing to carry out these obligations."[1]

From 1945 to 1955 the admission of members to the United Nations became a Cold War issue between the Soviet Union and the West. The battleground was the Security Council. Between 1946 and 1950 nine states that were not clearly candidates of one or the other bloc were admitted to the United Nations. From 1950 to 1955 the membership remained frozen at sixty, although by 1952 twenty-one additional states had applied for admission, with a majority of these applications dating from the first two years of United Nations existence. A stalemate developed in which the Soviet Union was unwilling to vote for prowestern candidates and vice versa. The western strategy, led by the United States, was to force as many Soviet vetoes as possible in order to dramatize the "obstructionist" stance of that power. The Soviet Union was compelled to veto Italy's admission on five different occasions, and more than half of all Soviet vetoes in these early years were on membership applications. Since Soviet-sponsored candidates were unable to obtain the required seven affirmative votes in the Security Council, the United States was saved from the use of the veto. The Soviet Union on occasion accused the West of a "collective veto."

[1]Charter of the United Nations, Art. 4.

States on both sides of the Iron Curtain that, by any objective standards, met all the Charter criteria for membership were hapless victims of Cold War politics. Justifications were given by both sides for their opposition to candidate states. The West opposed Bulgaria, Hungary, and Romania for alleged violations of human rights; Bulgaria and Albania for their role in the Greek border incidents; and Albania for its lack of cooperation with the United Nations in the Corfu Channel dispute. The Soviet Union objected to candidates because they had no diplomatic relations with the Soviet Union (Portugal, Jordan, Ireland); because peace treaties with them had not been concluded (Italy, Austria); because of Axis sympathies (Ireland, Portugal); because of membership in the "aggressive Atlantic bloc" (Italy); because of doubts concerning their status of full sovereignty and independence (Jordan, Ceylon, Japan); and because of serving as a base for United States aggression (Japan). These excuses for prolonged exclusion of states from United Nations membership provided a thinly veiled legality that was intended to disguise the unexpressed motives of the Cold War adversaries. However, the underlying motives become clear when it is noted that all pro-Communist candidates were opposed by the West and all non-Communist applications were vetoed by the Soviet Union. Charter criteria for admission were robbed of significant meaning in a contest for political power in the United Nations.

During the ten-year impasse over the admission of more than a score of potential members, several attempts were made through the General Assembly to break the deadlock. In 1946, Australia proposed changes in the admissions procedure to grant the General Assembly sole power over admissions. Similar plans had been previously rejected at the San Francisco conference. In 1947, Argentina proposed that the General Assembly interpret the Charter as permitting General Assembly action on either *positive* or *negative* membership recommendations of the Security Council. Peru in 1952 suggested that the General Assembly proceed on the assumption that all votes on candidates in the Security Council were procedural and not subject to veto. The Argentine and Peruvian suggestions were clearly in conflict with an advisory opinion issued in 1950 by the International Court of Justice at the request of the General Assembly in which the Court declared that the Charter required a Security Council recommendation for admission prior to General Assembly action and that no recommendation could be made in the event of a negative vote by any permanent Council member. The General Assembly also passed a series of resolutions and set up special committees to study the question and consult with Council members; these measures were intended to pressure the Security Council into finding a solution to the impasse.

Since the admissions problem was basically political rather than procedural, compromise of competing interests had to be the final solution in the form of a "package deal" or admissions en bloc. The United States had proposed such a trade-off in 1946, and the Soviet Union had objected, but during most of the ten-year stalemate, the positions of the two major powers were reversed. In December 1955, the deadlock was finally broken under increased pressure from many sources, and a package deal was agreed upon to admit sixteen states simultaneously. In the period since 1955, admissions procedures have proved no impediment to a burgeoning membership approaching universality.

During the period since 1955, the membership more than doubled, and new anxieties arose concerning the impact of a large membership on the organization. As soon as a territory achieved statehood, it generally sought and was accorded United Nations membership. Most of the newly admitted members were located in Africa or Asia. Some new members were so small in population, area, and resources that increasingly they were referred to as mini-states. Small states with voting power equal to that of large states could carry resolutions in the General Assembly by the sheer volume of votes, although they might represent a small proportion of the world's population, resources, or other indices of power. Emphasis shifted in the General Assembly to the issues of development and anticolonialism. Neither the United States nor the Soviet Union seemed to be any longer capable of delivering automatic majorities for their own measures, and the initiative in many areas passed to the underdeveloped nations. The new vocabulary of international affairs deemphasized the East-West split and accorded new emphasis to North-South rivalry and the demands of the Third World. The wisdom of according equal status to political units as small as St. Kitts and Nevis, the Seychelles, Dominica, Antigua and Barbuda, Liechtenstein, and San Marino, with populations of less than 100,000 each, and to more than twenty-five other members with populations under a million each, may reasonably be questioned. The resources of some of these mini-states are so limited that payment of the minimum scale of the United Nations budget and the expense of maintaining representation at United Nations meetings are a serious financial burden. The size of the General Assembly and its main committees has become more and more unwieldy. The pressure for increased representation of the Afro-Asian bloc resulted in Charter amendments to expand the membership of the Security Council and the Economic and Social Council. Suggestions for limited membership or weighted voting have had no impact on the United Nations practice of admitting mini-states to membership.[2]

Few states remain outside the United Nations. Switzerland, although it provided the headquarters and was an active member of the League of Nations, has interpreted some of the obligations of the Charter as inconsistent with its traditional policy of neutrality. It has, however, joined most of the specialized agencies and is a party to the International Court of Justice. Geneva also serves as the European headquarters of the United Nations as well as headquarters for the United Nations Conference on Trade and Devel-

---

[2]Michael M. Gunter, "What Happened to the United Nations Ministate Problem?" *American Journal of International Law*, 71 (January 1977), 110–24.

opment (UNCTAD) and for five of the United Nations specialized agencies. From its inception in 1949 until November 1971, the People's Republic of China was unrepresented at the United Nations, but this problem was primarily one of credentials, recognition, and representation rather than of membership.

No provision is made in the Charter for withdrawal from membership, and this omission seems to have had a salutary influence on the trend toward universality. Only one state, Indonesia, has ever announced its withdrawal, but after an absence of twenty months, it returned to full participation. Indonesia's complaint was the election of Malaysia to a Security Council seat. No readmission process was deemed necessary, since only a notice of Indonesia's statement of intent but no official acceptance of its withdrawal had been issued by the United Nations. Other representatives have absented themselves from meetings of United Nations organs for periods of days or months, but these boycotts were not intended as more than gestures toward the potential threat of withdrawal.

Articles 5 and 6 of the Charter provide for suspension and expulsion of members from the United Nations. The procedural requirements are the same in both cases. The General Assembly may suspend or expel a member by a two-thirds vote upon the recommendation of the Security Council. The suspension or expulsion of a permanent member of the Security Council or one of its client states is impossible since that member can, through its veto power, block action against itself or its client. No action has ever been taken under Article 5 or 6, although African states have exerted pressures to try to bring about the expulsion of South Africa and Arab states have urged Israel's expulsion.

Membership in the specialized agencies affiliated with the United Nations is independent of United Nations membership. Most states belong both to the United Nations and to most of the specialized agencies. Several of the specialized agencies have a membership larger than that of the United Nations. Several specialized agencies admit non-self-governing territories as full or associate members. The Soviet Union initially was reluctant to join any of the agencies except the Universal Postal Union, the International Telecommunication Union, and the World Meteorological Organization, but gradually extended its interests to include membership in most agencies.

PROBLEMS OF REPRESENTATION

The practices regarding representation of members in the United Nations are based to a greater degree upon custom and necessity than upon specific Charter provisions. However, Charter specifications do provide, both concretely and by implication, a skeletal framework for the representation pattern. Member states may have not more than five representatives in the General Assembly and one each in the Security Council, Economic and Social Council, and Trusteeship Council, if a member of those bodies. Nothing in the Charter itself anticipates the practice of appointment of alternates or the extensive use of advisers attached to the larger delegations. The elaborate committee structure developed by the General Assembly and the numerous commissions established by the Economic and Social Council contribute to the practicability of involving a wide range of experts as representatives of governments in these subsidiary bodies.

Consistent with the basic principle of the sovereignty of members, the Charter does not specify any qualifications for representatives. Representatives are the spokespersons for their governments and, as such, are subject to those governments with regard to qualifications, appointment, tenure, and compensation. With modern communications, representatives can receive detailed instructions from the home government concerning the content of speeches, bargaining positions, and voting patterns.

Nearly all member states maintain a permanent mission to the United Nations. The mission is similar to an embassy, except that its personnel are accredited to the United Nations rather than to a host government. The head of the mission normally carries ambassadorial rank as well as the title "permanent representative to the United Nations." The total working force in a mission varies from less than a half-dozen to approximately 200, depending on the resources of the country and the depth of its involvement in United Nations affairs.

Can the host government restrict the size of missions? In 1986 the United States notified the missions of the USSR, Byelorussian SSR, and Ukrainian SSR that over a two-year period their mission staffs must be reduced from 275 to 170. This demand was justified on security grounds, claims of inappropriate activities of mission personnel, and charges that the size of missions exceeded staffing needs for conducting United Nations business. No clear legal basis for this demand can be found either in the Charter of the United Nations or in the 1947 Headquarters Agreement between the United States and the United Nations. Under interpretations of international law by the International Law Commission and the United Nations Legal Counsel, although the United States cannot solely determine the size of a mission, the proper procedures involve consultation among the host state, the affected member state, and the Secretary-General with final resort to dispute settlement procedures.

Another set of related issues involves the right of the United States, as the host state, to deny to persons or groups access to United Nations headquarters in New York. In addition to member states, nonmembers and other entities, including the Palestine Liberation Organization (PLO), have been accorded observer status at the United Nations and maintain missions in New York. In 1987 the United States Congress adopted legislation requiring the closing of the PLO mission. The General Assembly by a vote of 143 to 1 condemned the proposed action and asked for a legal opinion by the International Court of Justice. The Court unanimously ruled that the legislation was in violation of the 1947 Headquarters Agreement, and this position was sustained in a United States district court case. In December 1988, the United States refused to grant a visa to Yasir Arafat, leader of the PLO, to address the United Nations General Assembly in New York. The General Assembly, in turn, reconvened its session in Geneva (at an estimated cost of $600,000,000) to hear Arafat's address. Ironically, a few days later, United States representatives opened negotiations with the PLO on the basis that Arafat had modified and clarified his positions on terrorism and Israel's right to exist, the grounds for denial of the visa.

The Charter does not clearly indicate the necessity for each member to maintain a permanent mission in New York. Only the members of the Security Council are required "to be represented at all times at the seat of the Organization" so that the Council may function continuously. However, all United Nations members are involved in the annual General Assembly sessions, which last at least three months and which occasionally may be prolonged for most of the year. Most members also serve on one or more councils or commissions, which meet at intervals throughout the year. Additionally, New York provides a center for continuous negotiation and consultation among the governments of the world on a one-to-one basis or in larger groups. Finally, the adoption of the Uniting for Peace Resolution in 1950 obligated all members to keep representatives available for emergency sessions of the General Assembly, which can be called on twenty-four-hour notice. The representatives on the permanent staff of their missions find their assignments in New York as demanding of time and energy as an assignment to most other diplomatic posts.

During General Assembly sessions, the mission staff in New York may be augmented at all levels of responsibility, often to the point of doubling the number of personnel. The minister for foreign affairs frequently heads the delegation, although he may remain in New York for only a few days at the opening of the session. Other delegates and alternates from the home government may be designated to serve with the permanent representative to the United Nations and other diplomats on his regular staff. Advisers and supporting personnel from the foreign office or other areas of needed expertise may be assigned to temporary duty at mission headquarters for the duration of the Assembly session. In the larger missions, specialists are useful in such fields as political affairs, finance, economic development, social problems, human rights, arms control, legal questions, military affairs, administration, press relations, public relations, protocol, liaison activities, and various geographical areas of the world. Secretaries, clerks, guards, maintenance personnel, chauffeurs, and other supporting personnel perform necessary auxiliary services for the professional staff of the mission.

In a number of ways the national missions to the United Nations are more important than embassies to individual countries. The United Nations headquarters is the closest approximation to a world capital and serves as a neutral territory where negotiations can take place without loss of prestige by any party to the negotiations. Informal discussions can be arranged outside the meetings of official bodies. Constant contact among representatives facilitates negotiation and communication. No ambassador has greater prestige than that of the head of a mission. The mission staff not only carry out policy determined in their national capital but, to a greater degree than in most embassies, they help formulate foreign policy as well. They serve as a sounding board, a channel for multiple contacts, and a source of information and advice on the widest possible range of matters that come before the United Nations. In the foreign policy process, they not only communicate the outputs of the system but they also furnish valuable inputs for the formulation of the policy.

Governments generally appoint experts in the appropriate areas to represent them in the delegate bodies of the various specialized agencies. A health expert serving in a delegation to the World Health Organization (WHO), an educator as a representative to UNESCO, or a nutritionist appointed to attend the conference of the Food and Agriculture Organization (FAO) will each be convinced that his or her special field is so important that it deserves increased emphasis and greater financial support. The problem for governments is to balance all competing interests, instruct delegates concerning overall policy and limitations on commitments, and coordinate the dozens of strands of policy carried out through the diverse agencies related to the United Nations. Each ministry of foreign affairs (or its counterpart by any other title) must be so organized and staffed as to provide reasonable coordination and control.

For more than twenty years the most persistent and dramatic problem concerning United Nations representation was the China issue. Beginning in 1950, the issue appeared annually, in one form or another, among the General Assembly's items of business. From 1951 through 1960, a debate was avoided by the adoption of a proposal to postpone action, thus eliminating the item from the formal agenda. From 1961 through 1970, the question appeared as a proposal to accept the credentials of the representatives of the Peking rather than of the Taiwan regime. At the same time a resolution, sponsored by the United States, was adopted to treat the problem as an "important question" requiring a two-thirds vote. However, such items may be removed at any time from the "important question" category by a majority decision in the General Assembly. The same thorny problem of Chinese representation was raised from time to time in the Security Council, and the Soviet representatives absented themselves from the Council for nearly seven months in early 1950 in protest against the continued seating of the Taiwan representatives.

Since the question was presented in the General Assembly as a matter of credentials, the issue, in a strict legal sense, was one of representation rather than one of membership. China was an original member of the United Nations and had a permanent seat on the Security Council (Article 23 of the Charter, in naming the permanent members of the Council, uses the title of the Republic of China, the official title retained by the Nationalist Government). Furthermore, agreements made at the close of World War II recognized Taiwan as a part of China, and both rival governments claimed sovereignty and legitimacy over all the area of China. Therefore, the acceptance of the representatives of the Nationalist regime was a recognition of the right of those representatives to speak for all of China—the mainland and Taiwan.

It is clear that the China issue was as much a political contest as it was a legal question. Prior to 1971 the world was more or less evenly divided in the number of states that recognized each rival claimant to legitimacy. Neither Chinese government would exchange diplomats with another country unless that country broke diplomatic relations with its rival. The United States maintained its commitment to the perpetuation of the Taiwan regime and to the defense of the island against attack from the mainland. During the 1960s, many of the United States' closest allies grew restless with the anti-Peking pressure from Washington and refused to follow United States policies of nonrecognition and economic boycott of the People's Republic of China. To those states, recognizing a regime that controlled more than 98 percent of the total population and more than 99.5 percent of the land area of China seemed more logical than maintaining the fiction that a government on Taiwan, after twenty years of exile from the mainland, could speak for 850 million Chinese.

Because of the concern of some United Nations members for the fate of the Nationalists on Taiwan, and because of the desire to encourage self-determination for the island population who have never lived under Communist control, several proposals were made either for a "two Chinas" or a "one China, one Taiwan" solution to the problem. These proposals generally took one of two stances: either that Peking was entitled to the China seat and Taiwan should be admitted as a new member, or that two regimes had succeeded to the original entity of China and that both should be accommodated within the United Nations framework.

For twenty years the United States government led the fight to deny representation in the United Nations to the Peking regime. The principal devices used were the procedural tactics of annually rejecting the question as an agenda item (1951–60) or of requiring a two-thirds vote to seat the Peking representatives (1961–70), plus behind-the-scenes pressures on other delegations and their governments. Figure 5–1 demonstrates the gradual loss of efficacy of these tactics, culminating in the acceptance of the Communist representatives in 1971, when the United States switched its position to one of favoring a Security Council seat for the Peking regime while maintaining

FIGURE 5–1 VOTING IN THE GENERAL ASSEMBLY ON THE
REPRESENTATION OF CHINA (NO VOTE IN 1964)

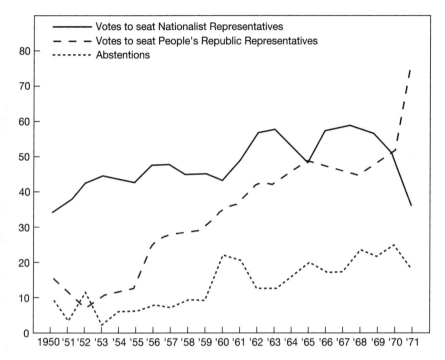

places for both delegations in the General Assembly. By this time the pro-Peking tide was running so strongly that the United States proposal was defeated, and the representatives of the People's Republic were accorded sole representation for China, accompanied by the expulsion of the Nationalist representatives.

The decisions made in the twenty-sixth session of the General Assembly leave the future of Taiwan unsettled. Just prior to the vote to expel them, the Nationalist representatives announced their withdrawal from participation in the United Nations. The People's Republic claims to represent the people on Taiwan but for the near future is unwilling to force the issue. As a separate entity, Taiwan, with a population of 20 million, is larger than three-quarters of the members of the United Nations. For more than forty years the mainlander minority has exercised government domination over 85 percent who are native Taiwanese. No hard evidence exists to prove whether in a free exercise of self-determination the Taiwanese would opt for permanent separation from the mainland. If a new state of Taiwan were created and if it applied for United Nations membership, it would face the grim reality of a Chinese veto on its application. Thus one impasse would be replaced by another.

The General Assembly may deny to a state the right to participate in its deliberations by refusing to accept the credentials of that state's representatives. As explained in the previous discussion of membership issues, expulsion or suspension from the United Nations is highly unlikely because such action is subject to veto in the Security Council. However, in 1974 the General Assembly excluded South Africa from participating in that session by rejecting the credentials of the South African delegation. An Arab threat in 1982 to apply similar measures against Israel was met by a United States counterthreat to withdraw its financial support from the United Nations. The Arab states backed down and settled for a resolution of censure of Israel for its invasion of Lebanon. In September 1992 the General Assembly, in response to a Security Council recommendation, barred the delegation of the Federal Republic of Yugoslavia (Serbia and Montenegro) from participating in the Assembly's session, but also declared that the Federal Republic could not automatically continue the membership of the former Yugoslavia and, therefore, should apply for UN membership.

VOTING RULES AND PRACTICES

Modern international organization, as it has developed over the past century, has been faced with the enigma of reconciling democratic decision-making processes with the theory of the absolute sovereignty of states. The tradition of sovereignty as practiced prior to the twentieth century in international conferences and treaty making required unanimity among all parties according to the principle that no state could be bound without its own consent. States, regardless of population or resources, were also considered equal, and each state was entitled to exercise the right of one vote for each state. Some exceptions to both the principle of unanimity and the principle of state equality developed in the nineteenth century in such agencies as the river commissions of Europe, but the tenacity of these ideas is demonstrated by the first-stated principle of the United Nations Charter that "the Organization is based on the principle of the sovereign equality of all its Members." Although the Charter requires unanimity only among the permanent members of the Security Council on nonprocedural matters (which, it should be noted, constitutes a breach of the equality principle), the formation of the United Nations was intended to fit into long-established patterns of international conduct rather than to revolutionize them.

The League of Nations preserved the principles of unanimity and state equality, although significant exceptions were made to each. Each member of the Council or Assembly could defeat a general recommendation in either body by a negative vote, but abstentions were common and were used as a means of avoiding obstruction of the will of a substantial majority of states when vital national interests were not at issue. The committees of the Assembly operated by majority vote, and procedural matters in either the Council or Assembly required only majority support. When the Council was considering a case under Article 15 of the Covenant, the vote of any party to the dispute was not counted, and under Article 16, a state could not veto its own expulsion from the League. The Covenant specified that the very basic decision of admitting new members to the League could be made by a two-thirds majority. However, the traditional right not to be bound without the state's own consent was preserved in the prerogative of every member to dissent from any amendment to the Covenant, with such dissent constituting termination of membership in the League. Although each state had one vote in the Council or Assembly, the inequality of states was recognized by assigning permanent membership on the Council to the most powerful nations. Membership on the Council carried more than honorific significance because of the powers and functions assigned to that organ.

The gradual abandonment of the unanimity rule in international organizations has been facilitated by the nature of those organizations. As long as international agencies are more administrative than prescriptive, more cooperative than coercive, as long as they are lacking in true legislative and enforcement powers and are limited to discussion and to recommendations that are unenforceable on individual states, the members of such organizations see no great threat to their sovereignty if they agree to modify the requirement of unanimity. Majority or qualified majority votes allow the passage of recommendations that authorize administrative action in the less controversial areas of international relationships; at the same time, each state's retention of ultimate enforcement powers guarantees that its vital interests are not surrendered.

The United Nations preserves this balance of sovereign rights and the necessity to abandon unanimity in order to facilitate the adoption of administrative directives and expressions of the will of a majority of members. The League of Nations rule of unanimity is abandoned in the General Assembly in favor of either majority or two-thirds votes for decisions. Security Council decisions can be taken by a qualified majority, but the permanent members are protected by the rule that any one of them can block action by a negative vote on nonprocedural matters. Since the Security Council was originally intended to deal with the most vital issues of national interest and since the big powers possess the preponderance of means for enforcement, such an arrangement may be considered a necessary departure from the complete abandonment of unanimity. Further flexibility is provided by the interpretation that an abstention does not constitute a veto. Thus, the representative of any one of the permanent members of the Security Council is free to express three choices, ranging from approval, through mild disapproval but unwillingness to be obstructionist, to effective blocking of a decision by negative vote. The net result of the voting arrangements in the General Assembly and the Security

Council is to facilitate activities in the common interest without threatening the sovereign prerogatives of the big powers.

Voting in the lesser agencies of the United Nations is by simple majority. This rule applies to the Economic and Social Council, the Trusteeship Council, and the committees and commissions subordinate to the major organs. Since all actions of these bodies are subject to review by the General Assembly and are not self-executing or automatically enforceable, the less strict criterion for agreement among members may be tolerated without serious challenge to traditional theories of national sovereignty.

In the World Bank group of specialized agencies, the traditional rule of an equal vote for each state has given way to weighted voting roughly proportionate to the financial contributions of the members. In these agencies—the International Bank for Reconstruction and Development, the International Monetary Fund, the International Finance Corporation, and the International Development Association—the United States casts approximately 19 percent of the vote. Except in these financial agencies, proposals to modify the one state–one vote principle in favor of weighted voting based on one or more factors, such as contributions, population, or measures of financial or other resources, have never been seriously debated by United Nations agencies. The influx of numerous mini-states into the organization may raise questions concerning the imbalance between the voting power of states and their ability to contribute to the resolution of world problems or their inequality in the numbers of persons affected by decisions. But although these theoretical considerations may develop, the smaller states will not be inclined to surrender lightly an advantage based on the centuries-old principle of state equality.

The voting formula in the Security Council was discussed in Dumbarton Oaks, hammered out in Yalta, and retained intact in spite of the onslaught of the small and medium states in San Francisco. All votes in the Security Council require the approval of nine of the fifteen members (seven of the eleven members before the amendments of 1965). On substantive (nonprocedural) matters, the nine votes must include the affirmative votes of the five permanent members of the Council. Thus a single negative vote by a permanent member on a substantive question constitutes a veto, although the word veto does not appear in the Charter. According to the explanatory Statement of the Sponsoring Powers issued in San Francisco, certain matters were to be considered clearly procedural, but if a question rose as to whether a matter was procedural or substantive, the preliminary question was subject to the substantive voting requirement. This interpretation opens the door to a double-veto procedure. According to established practice, an abstention or an absence is not equivalent to a veto in spite of the language of Article 27, which specifies "an affirmative vote of nine members including the concurring votes of the permanent members."

The hopes of the smaller states that the permanent members of the Security Council would use their power of veto sparingly have not been borne out in practice. In reluctantly accepting the voting formula established in San Francisco, the spokespersons for the smaller states appealed for restraint in the exercise of the veto. By 1987, each of the big five had used the veto sixteen or more times.

An examination of the pattern of vetoes reveals, however, something less than the flagrant abuse of power. During the first ten years of the United Nations, the Soviet Union cast more than 90 percent of all vetoes in the Security Council, and two-thirds of these were used to block admission of states to United Nations membership. The excessive number of Soviet vetoes on the question of admission is accounted for by the strategy of the western states under United States leadership in forcing separate votes on each candidate and repeatedly asking for admission of the same candidates. The western states, in turn, could block the admission of any pro-Soviet state by any combination of five abstentions or negative votes.

The veto was intended to protect the vital interests of the big powers, and it has operated to accomplish that purpose. During the earlier years of the United Nations, the Soviet Union's vital interests were frequently threatened because of western control of the issues before the Security Council and because of the minority position of the Soviet Union. Since 1970 the United States increasingly resorted to the veto, while the Soviet Union seldom needed recourse to this device. However, the veto is a weapon always available to any of the big five.

During the early years of the United Nations, the General Assembly made a number of efforts to influence the Security Council to eliminate certain categories of questions from the exercise of the veto power. The suggested categories included the admission of members and actions for the pacific settlement of disputes. These efforts were fruitless in instigating any change of rules or attitudes.

In recent years a spirit of restraint has manifested itself in the use of the veto and in the increased use of abstentions. There is evidence also of more frequent consultations to phrase resolutions in terms not seriously objectionable to any major power. This spirit of accommodation is probably due to a realization of a common interest among the big powers in restoring the Security Council, in which they can exercise maximum influence, to a position of greater importance vis-à-vis the General Assembly. With the influx of large numbers of members since 1955, manipulating the General Assembly has become increasingly more difficult for any of the great powers. Under these conditions the arena of the Security Council looks relatively more attractive to the permanent members for the debates over major issues. Restraint in the use of the veto, as well as other forms of accommodation, will avoid transfer of these issues to the General Assembly.

Voting in the General Assembly has presented fewer problems than in the Security Council. Each member, regardless of population or resources, casts one vote. It is theoretically possible for states representing less than 15 percent of the world's population to muster a two-thirds vote in the General Assembly. But since the General Assembly, in most actions, is limited to recommendations that depend for implementation on moral suasion and national cooperation, action by small states is generally not considered a major threat to the larger states. Nevertheless, the passage of resolutions that are meaningless in terms of effecting change may destroy confidence in the United Nations and undermine its future efficacy. In 1974, Ambassador Scali of the United States blasted the Third World members for using "the tyranny of the majority" not only for passing resolutions that are unenforceable but also for making procedural decisions in handling Middle Eastern and South African issues.

In the General Assembly, important matters require a two-thirds majority of the members present and voting. Other decisions can be taken by a simple majority of those present and voting. Article 18 of the Charter lists certain categories of "important questions" requiring the two-thirds rule. These are (1) recommendations with respect to the maintenance of peace and security, (2) the election of nonpermanent members of the Security Council, (3) the election of members of the Economic and Social Council and of the Trusteeship Council, (4) the admission of new members to the United Nations, (5) the suspension of the rights and privileges of membership, (6) the suspension or the expulsion of members, (7) questions pertaining to the operation of the trusteeship system, and (8) budgetary questions. Additional categories of questions requiring a two-thirds vote may be added (and likewise removed) by simple majority. Abstentions are not counted in determining the "present and voting" requirement. With large numbers of abstentions on some questions, a two-thirds affirmative vote on an important matter may represent only a minority of the total membership.

Under some sections of the Charter, either an absolute or a two-thirds majority of all members—not just those "present and voting"—in the General Assembly is required for decisions. Elections to the International Court of Justice require a majority of all states. Amendments to the Charter may be proposed by a vote of two-thirds of the members of the General Assembly. The votes required for calling a general review conference under the provisions of Article 109 of the Charter are based on the full membership. In all these cases abstentions or absences would have the same effect as negative votes in determining the results of the ballots, since the affirmative votes must constitute more than half (or two-thirds when specified) of the membership.

According to Article 19 of the Charter, a member state may have its voting rights in the General Assembly suspended if it is more than two years in arrears in its budget contributions. The crisis of 1964 over the possible application of this provision is detailed below in the section of this chapter dealing with financial problems of the United Nations.

Both the General Assembly and the Security Council in recent years have frequently used the technique of announcing the adoption of resolu tions by consensus without a formal vote. In fact, in several recent sessions of the General Assembly, three-fourths of all decisions were made in this manner. The consensus procedure is a method of adopting measures without formal objection and one that avoids confrontation through voting. Decision making by consensus allows for behind-the-scenes compromise and avoids embarrassment to some states. However, it is no panacea. Consensus resolutions may be watered down to a low level of relevance. Also, nations frequently nullify the appearance of harmony and prolong debate by adding a series of stated reservations to the resolutions after passage by consensus.

Bloc voting and caucusing by groups of states with allied interests have been notable aspects of General Assembly practice. The early dominance of United States influence gradually eroded, to be replaced finally by the unity of the have-not states on issues of economic development and anti-colonialism, which now constitute the bulk of the agenda. Caucusing and informal consultation serve several useful purposes, including the tempering and reconciliation of extreme positions, a saving of time in the sessions of an otherwise unwieldly Assembly, and the planning of advance strategy for the promotion of common interests. However, one should note that votes in the United Nations are an imperfect measure of influence in world affairs, since votes cannot alter world-power relationships to any significant degree.

FORMAL AND INFORMAL CHARTER AMENDMENT

Writing and adopting a constitution is regarded as the most fundamental act of government. Although existing intergovernmental organizations lack many of the attributes of national governments, each has a constitution in the form of a multilateral treaty that prescribes the purposes, structure, and modes of procedure of the organization. Since amendments may generally amplify, modify, or delete any of the provisions of a constitution, the amending process is as basic as the original constituent act. The requirements for adopting amendments to a constitution or charter almost invariably demand a higher order of agreement than is required for ordinary legislation or resolutions. The amending process should be neither so difficult as to make basic change impossible nor so easy as to contribute to frequent tampering with fundamental structures and powers. In an international organization of sovereign states, ease of amendment would run counter to the reluctantly surrendered tradition that no state may be bound without its own consent. Therefore, the difficulty of the amending process of the United Nations Charter should surprise no one.

The Charter provides two methods of proposing amendments but a single formula for ratification. Amendments may be proposed by a vote of two-thirds of the total membership of the General Assembly and will then come into force if ratified by the governments of two-thirds of the members, including all the permanent members of the Security Council. Amendments may also be proposed by a two-thirds vote of a general-review conference. Such a review conference can be convened at any time by the General Assembly and the Security Council. Until 1968 the requirement for calling a conference was a two-thirds vote of all members of the General Assembly and a vote of any seven members of the Security Council. In that year an amendment became effective to raise the Security Council requirement to nine votes as a supplement to the earlier enlargement of Security Council membership. Amendments proposed by a review conference do not become effective until ratified according to the same formula as required for amendments initiated by the General Assembly. Nevertheless, the states most dissatisfied with various provisions of the Charter as adopted in San Francisco insisted on the possibility of calling a review conference in the hope of reexamining a broader range of fundamental changes than might result from piecemeal proposals from the General Assembly.

Article 109 also provides that if a review conference has not been held before the tenth annual session of the General Assembly, the proposal to call such a conference shall be placed on the agenda of that session, and the required vote is reduced to a majority of all members of the General Assembly and any seven members of the Security Council. In 1955 it was clear to most members that a review conference would be an exercise in futility, since there was no basis for agreement upon previously suggested reforms. Instead of calling a conference, the General Assembly created a committee of the whole to study the situation and to revive the question at an "appropriate time" under "auspicious circumstances." This combination of time and circumstances did not occur, and after 1967 the committee became inactive. In 1974 the General Assembly created a new Special Committee on the Charter that has encountered stiff opposition by the major powers to proposals by the nonaligned states for substantial reforms affecting the relative roles of the General Assembly and Security Council.

During the first fifteen years under the Charter, Cold War issues in combination with the difficulty of the amending process blunted all attempts at change through formal amendment. With the influx of large numbers of new members from Africa and Asia, the pressures upon the great powers for structural adjustments in the size of the Councils mounted. In 1963 the General Assembly adopted proposed amendments to increase the size of ECOSOC from eighteen to twenty-seven members and to increase the membership of the Security Council from eleven to fifteen. These amendments entered into force August 31, 1965, upon the deposit of sufficient government ratifications and the enlarged Councils sat for the first time in 1966. In 1973, ECOSOC was enlarged to fifty-four members.

The dynamics of fundamental change in the United Nations have been exercised more through informal than through formal amendment. Most constitutions grow by means of custom, interpretation, and elaboration, and the United Nations Charter is no exception. Examples of such developments are numerous. Although contrary to the terms of the Charter, the custom of disregarding abstentions and absences in Security Council voting is firmly established. The adoption in 1950 of the Uniting for Peace Resolution substantially altered the relative roles of the General Assembly and Security Council without a formal amendment. The phenomenon of bloc voting on certain issues in the General Assembly is a development as fundamental in nature as any provision of the Charter. The General Assembly's liberal interpretation of its authority to demand information from colonial powers, to exercise pressure toward ending colonial rule, and to declare the independence of Namibia from South Africa are examples of expansions of authority in the colonial sphere unforeseen in a strict interpretation of Charter provisions.

Charter provisions may be expanded by custom and usage or may be allowed to atrophy by disuse. One of the most evident examples of the lack of implementation applies to Article 43, according to which armed forces were to be made available to the Security Council by all members of the United Nations for the purpose of maintaining international peace and security. The agreements anticipated by this article were never drawn up because of fundamental disagreements among the major powers over the terms of the agreements and underlying security questions.

The United Nations experience with formal and informal amendment of the Charter suggests several basic questions. Is the formal amendment procedure too rigid to allow necessary adjustment to changing world conditions? Will the members discover enough flexibility through custom, interpretation, and elaboration to overcome the obstacles of a difficult amendment process? Is the disuse and misuse of the United Nations due more to inherent defects in its Charter or to attitudes, practices, and prerogatives of sovereign states in a loosely structured international system? If the members become convinced that a more integrated international system is necessary, is the United Nations Charter a viable instrument on which to build, or must it be replaced with a radically different instrument? If states view the United Nations as tangential to the mainstream of international affairs, those questions remain highly academic and inconsequential. If a more orderly world is ever to be achieved, the answers to such questions become vital.

FINANCIAL PROBLEMS

Since the total annual costs of all United Nations–related activities amount to less than 1 percent of the members' military budgets, one might reasonably assume that budgetary questions should not represent a major difficulty for the organization. Yet, in the early 1960s a financial crisis threatened the continued existence of the United Nations, the organization has been in a precarious financial situation ever since, and in 1986 an even greater menace to solvency emerged as a result of unilateral actions in the United States Congress proposing drastic reductions in United States budget contributions.

Control of the budget is one of the powers lodged in the General Assembly. The Secretary-General annually presents budget estimates to the Assembly, and these estimates are reviewed by the Committee for Program and Coordination and the Advisory Committee on Administrative and Budgetary Questions. The recommendations are examined by member governments both individually and in the Fifth Committee of the General Assembly before adoption in a General Assembly plenary session. In determining the assessment of costs to individual states, the Assembly is assisted by the Committee on Contributions.

In reality, several budgets exist in the United Nations. The basic budget for running the administrative machinery and meeting the costs of the major organs and their auxiliary agencies is the regular budget. This budget has grown from an initial figure in 1946 of less than $20 million to $1.2 billion by 1993. The basic causes of increasing costs are (1) inflationary trends, (2) increased membership, (3) expanding programs and agencies, and (4) currency exchange rate fluctuations. In recent years the big powers have complained of the rates of annual increase, but the more numerous developing nations have defended the expanding costs because the increased activities have been considered vital to their interests.

Contributions to the regular budget are assessed among the members according to a formula that is based ostensibly on ability to pay. In 1946 in the initial determination of the percentage of the total budget to be allotted to each member, the Committee on Contributions was instructed to consider (1) national income, (2) per capita income, (3) economic dislocations resulting from the war, and (4) the ability of members to obtain foreign currencies. On the basis of these factors, the United States should have been asked to pay nearly 50 percent of the original budget, but this figure was arbitrarily reduced by 10 percent to 39.89 percent in order to lessen the financial dependence of the United Nations on a single member. A further agreement was reached to gradually reduce the maximum assessment to one-third and subsequently to a target of 25 percent. A minimum assessment of 0.04 percent was also set for the states with the lowest assets. In 1973 this minimum was reduced to 0.02 percent and in 1978 to 0.01 percent. Since eighty-two members pay the minimum of 0.01 percent each and another eight pay 0.02 percent each, it is theoretically possible for a majority of the General Assembly to represent a total contribution of about 1 percent of the budget. At the other extreme, the ten largest contributors pay three-fourths of the budget but cast fewer than 6 percent of the votes.

Not all costs of maintaining the regular operations of the United Nations must be assessed against the members, but neither does the budget represent the full costs of United Nations membership. The United Nations raises approximately $35 million annually from miscellaneous income from sales and services, and about five times that amount is derived from staff assessments made against Secretariat salaries to offset income-tax payments of employees who are United States nationals. To the assessments levied against each member state must be added the expense of maintaining a mission headquarters and staff in New York and, for most members, maintaining smaller staffs in Geneva and at the headquarters of the specialized agencies. For the least affluent states, these costs generally exceed the amount of the regular budget assessment.

Ever since the establishment of the United Nations Children's Fund (UNICEF) in 1946, the United Nations has supplemented its regular budget with special budgets for economic and social programs. These budgets are supported by voluntary contributions rather than by assessment. Some of the major funds in this category in addition to UNICEF are the United Nations Development Program (UNDP), with an annual budget of more than $1 billion; the United Nations Relief and Works Agency for Palestine Refugees; the World Food Program; and voluntary funds administered by the United Nations High Commissioner for Refugees. Since all members are free to determine whether and how much they will contribute to these funds, the patterns of contribution vary widely from the assessment figures of the regular budget. For many years the United States pledged 30 to 80 percent of these special funds with a fixed dollar limit, but this previous generosity has given way to an attitude in the United States Congress of cutting most voluntary contributions to 25 percent or less.

A third category of budgets is that of the specialized agencies affiliated with the United Nations through the Economic and Social Council. As a part of the autonomous character of these agencies, each enjoys a high degree of independence in determining its budget, with probably the most effective coordinating control operating through member governments. The United Nations General Assembly is limited to reviewing and making recommendations on these budgets. Since the United Nations and the specialized agencies share a great deal of responsibility for economic development and technical assistance programs, including a division of the funds pledged to the United Nations Development Program, controls also operate through administrative coordinating agencies within this sphere of activities.

Within each of the specialized agencies, budgetary assessments are allocated on a scale roughly equivalent to that for the regular United Nations budget. Modifications must be introduced to account for variations in membership. The total of all the budgets of the specialized agencies generally exceeds that of the regular United Nations budget. For the three types of budgets discussed thus far, the total amount in 1992 was more than $5 billion per year. These figures do not include new funds furnished to such financial agencies as the International Development Association and the International Monetary Fund or contributions to special temporary projects, such as the Afghanistan aid program or drought emergency funds for southern Africa.

The fourth category of budgets, peacekeeping expenses, has been the most controversial and has caused the financial crisis that became acute in the 1960s and that has continued as one of the threats to the stability and viability of the organization. The principal problem has resulted from attempts to assess peacekeeping costs on the same basis as regular budget assessments, although separate accounts were set up for each major peacekeeping operation. The high costs of such operations as the Congo, Cambodia, and Somalia also have exacerbated the problem.

The earliest manifestations of the crisis surfaced with the refusal of the Soviet bloc and several Arab states to contribute to the support of the United Nations Emergency Force (UNEF) established in 1956. In spite of opposition and bitter debate, the proposal of the Secretary-General to assess the costs on the same basis as the regular assessments received the necessary support for adoption by the General Assembly. When the United Nations Forces in the Congo (ONUC) was created in 1960, the application of the same formula created greater problems because the annual costs of the Congo operation were greater than the entire regular United Nations budget and because additional members, including France, refused to pay the peacekeeping assessments. The total United Nations cost of the UNEF from 1956 to 1967 was approximately $200 million, and the cost of the ONUC from 1960 until its withdrawal in 1964 was in excess of $400 million. These costs are exclusive of the ordinary costs of salaries and equipment of the forces, which are borne by the states that furnish the forces.

As Ruth Russell suggested in 1970, the United Nations financial crisis is not primarily a result of *incapacity* of the members to pay but a result of their *unwillingness* to do so.[3] The issue is more political and legal than financial. In addition to the legal question of what constitutes "expenses of the Organization" under Article 17 of the Charter, the political disputes involve the legitimate roles of the General Assembly and the Security Council, and the issue of who should pay for peacekeeping operations.

The Secretary-General, backed by the United States and sufficient votes to pass the supporting resolutions, maintained that the expenses of peacekeeping operations initiated by either the Security Council or the General Assembly are expenses that the General Assembly has a right to assess under the authority of Article 17 and that all members are obligated to pay. The Soviet Union, France, and other states that refused to pay the costs of either the UNEF or the ONUC or both declared that only the Security Council can

[3]Ruth B. Russell, *The General Assembly: Patterns/Problems/Prospects* (New York: Carnegie Endowment for International Peace, 1970), p. 35.

authorize a peacekeeping action and that the General Assembly has usurped powers not granted in the Charter. The Soviet Union would assess all peacekeeping costs against the aggressors—France, the United Kingdom, and Israel in the Middle East crisis of 1956, and Belgium in the Congo. Egypt, claiming to be the victim of aggression, also objected to paying the subsequent peacekeeping costs. A third position on the issue of peacekeeping costs is that taken by several Latin American states, who contend that the General Assembly is authorized to assess these expenses but should assess them according to a special formula that would place the primary burden on the permanent members of the Security Council, with token assessments for states with less ability to pay. They would ask the major powers to pay the bulk of such expenses as the price of their special power, privilege, and responsibility in the United Nations.

To clarify the legal aspects of the financial dispute, the General Assembly in 1961 sought an advisory opinion from the International Court of Justice. In July 1962, the Court delivered its opinion sustained by a 9–5 vote. The majority of the Court rejected the contention that the question was purely political and not subject to juridical opinion. On the substantive question, the Court declared that the peacekeeping expenses constitute "expenses of the Organization" within the meaning of Article 17 of the Charter. The position of the Secretary-General supported by General Assembly resolutions was thus vindicated by the Court's opinion.

General Assembly resolutions and Court opinions were insufficient, however, to raise the necessary funds for the peacekeeping operations. The Secretary-General drew on the Working Capital Fund, and some member states made voluntary contributions, but the expense of simultaneously maintaining two peacekeeping forces exceeded the available financial resources of the United Nations. As an emergency measure the 1961 General Assembly authorized the issuance of $200 million worth of United Nations bonds to be repaid in installments over a twenty-five-year period. Approximately 85 percent of the authorized limit was subscribed to, with the United States purchasing 50 percent of the total. This temporary stopgap failed to solve the permanent problem.

The financial crisis came to a head in the 1964 General Assembly session. A provision of Article 19 of the Charter states that a member that is at least two years in arrears in its budget contributions shall be deprived of its vote in the General Assembly. The Soviet Union, because of its refusal to pay peacekeeping costs, was more than two years delinquent, and France would reach that point before the General Assembly was scheduled to adjourn. The United States threatened to apply Article 19, and the Soviet Union indicated that if the sanction were applied it would leave the organization. The contest of wills resulted in a stalemate, and a strange phenomenon ensued. A voteless session of the General Assembly was conducted during which all necessary decisions were taken by consensus through informal consultation of the President of the Assembly with the delegates. Votes were actually registered in the anterooms instead of on the Assembly floor. Thus, a gentlemen's agreement to postpone the showdown permitted the organization to survive what threatened to be its deathblow, at least as a nearly universal organization.

By the opening of the twentieth session of the General Assembly in 1965, the United States abandoned its attempt to enforce Article 19 since it lacked support from most members for such extreme sanctions. In 1965 a Committee of Thirty-three was established to review the financial dilemma resulting from the peacekeeping issue. Since that time a series of committees has not been able to resolve the problems in a manner acceptable to all parties. A suggestion was adopted in 1965 to call for voluntary contributions to alleviate the bankrupt position of the United Nations, and the understanding seemed to be that the Soviet Union and France would contribute if they were free to choose their own terms of contribution. Although more than a score of members made pledges, the Soviet Union and France refused voluntary contributions unless their action was matched simultaneously by the United States. In the game of power politics, the United Nations was the destitute stepchild. The Soviet Union not only refused to pay for peacekeeping operations but withheld from its regular assessments amounts equal to its share of the service debt for United Nations bonds. In the 1980s the United States also withheld funds from UN programs of which it disapproved.

As a practical matter the United Nations has sought alternative means of financing other peacekeeping operations. The Security Council established the United Nations Peacekeeping Force in Cyprus (UNFICYP) in March 1964 and provided that its financing should come from three sources: (1) the governments providing the contingents, (2) the government of Cyprus, and (3) voluntary contributions. The mandate for the force has been continued from year to year, and financial support has been precarious, but the solution has proved less troublesome than the financing of the UNEF or the ONUC. In 1993, however, the Security Council returned to assessments for part of the UNFICYP budget. The costs of a United Nations Observation Mission in Yemen and of an executive authority and a supporting security force in West Irian were split equally by the contending governments.

Somewhat surprisingly, in the light of previous financial difficulties, the Security Council, in authorizing in October 1973 a new 7,000-member peacekeeping force in the Middle East, provided for its costs to be assessed on a modified scale based on the regular budget. The major powers could support this decision since it was made in the Security Council, which is considered by the Soviet Union and France the proper arena for such action. The 1978 peacekeeping force in Lebanon was similarly authorized by the Security Council, but both the Soviet Union and China announced their refusal to contribute to its financial support. However, China later reversed its decision and assumed its share effective January 1, 1982.

The United Nations never recovered from the financial crisis of the 1960s, but a more serious blow to UN solvency and program maintenance threatened after 1985. The United States Congress adopted the Kassebaum Amendment, specifying that the United States pay no more than 80 percent of its assessed dues unless the United Nations adopted weighted voting on budgetary matters and carried out administrative reforms to achieve a more streamlined and cost-effective structure and program. In reality, because of primary concern with reducing the U.S. government's budget deficit, Congress provided less than 50 percent of the U.S. assessment in fiscal 1986.

By 1987 a revised United Nations budgetary procedure was in operation by which the twenty-one-member Committee for Program and Coordination, in which the United States and other major donors are represented, was given the authority to agree by consensus on a budget ceiling and spending priorities. Drastic cuts in top administrative posts were also instituted. Senator Kassebaum and the United States Senate Foreign Relations Committee expressed satisfaction with the reforms and recommended restoration of full funding. However, Congress year after year continued to appropriate considerably less money than its assessed 25 percent of the regular United Nations budget. Arrears also accumulated in the amounts due the specialized agencies and the U.S. share of UN peacekeeping costs. By June 30, 1992, the member states owed the United Nations $1.85 billion. Of this amount the arrears for the regular budget were $911 million, of which the United States owed $555 million. The United States was also the largest debtor for UN peacekeeping operations, the deficit for which totalled $941 million.

Several factors in the recent financial crisis deserve emphasis. First is the illegality of U.S. congressional action. The American Bar Association's House of Delegates adopted a resolution declaring that under the United Nations Charter, which is a binding treaty, withholding of assessed funds is a violation of international law. The resolution also urged cooperation between the executive and legislative branches of government to restore payment fully and promptly. Second, the UN Secretary-General has repeatedly appealed to members to pay past dues to prevent United Nations insolvency. In September 1992, in response to the perennial financial crisis, the Ford Foundation, in cooperation with the UN, announced the creation of an international advisory group of eminent persons on UN financing. A third new factor was a policy change by the Soviet government promising to pay in full its share of all peacekeeping costs over the period since 1956. Suggestions to lower the rate of assessment for the United States would result in a reduction of United States influence in the United Nations. Withholding funds, even though illegal, did result in prompt United Nations budgetary and administrative reform but made it difficult for the organization to maintain its full program and potential and to pay its obligations. As soon as the demanded reforms were instituted, the United Nations threat of bankruptcy should have been removed and simultaneously the United States could have regained its generally established reputation for upholding the rule of law.

From time to time suggestions have been made for future United Nations financing that would give the organization independence from reliance on government assessments. About 3 percent of current revenue comes from such sources as charges for services and sales of publications and stamps, but most proposals for independent financing seek much more substantial sums. Some of the suggestions for future sources of revenue for the United Nations include:

1. A surcharge on international mail or on international communications to be earmarked for the United Nations
2. A fee for the use of international waterways
3. Substantial fees for services performed by the United Nations or the specialized agencies
4. A "finder's fee" for aid in discovering and developing new resources
5. Exploitation of the resources of the oceans and seabeds through a United Nations operating agency or, more likely, through leasing rights to private or national agencies
6. Exploitation of the resources of Antarctica
7. Licensing fees or other charges for the use of outer space
8. Taxes earmarked for United Nations use but collected by member states
9. Taxes on international travel or international passport fees
10. Private or foundation contributions with suitable exemptions from national taxation

Several of these sources seem logical since, for example, no nation can claim jurisdiction under existing international law to the oceans beyond their exclusive economic zones or to unlimited rights in outer space.

Unfortunately, any of these proposals that would raise considerable amounts of independent revenue for the United Nations would face strong opposition from the members. To make the United Nations less dependent on the financial support of its member governments, especially of the larger states, would be a major blow to national sovereignty and control and would radically alter the nature of the organization. The smaller and developing states might welcome the additional leverage and resources available for promoting their economic and social interests. The big powers would view the financial independence of the United Nations as a threat to their influence in the organization. The same attitudes that have produced the financial crises since the 1960s will probably not permit radical innovations in patterns of financing in the foreseeable future.

6

PEACEFUL SETTLEMENT OF DISPUTES

In earlier chapters we discussed the history of the ideology and practice of international organization, the precedents set by the League of Nations, and the legal and organizational framework and the underlying issues of the United Nations. With this background, we will now examine the more specific efforts of the UN to transform theories, goals, and principles into programs for solving world problems.

IMPORTANCE OF PEACEFUL SETTLEMENT

Although the United Nations is a multifunctional organization, foremost among its functions is the maintenance of world peace. Both the League of Nations and the United Nations were created near the end of the greatest wars of the century primarily to act as instrumentalities for eliminating armed conflict and for strengthening means for conflict control and resolution. In the long run, arms reduction and control and the development of world law might serve as means for promoting peace, and on occasion, collective action against threats to or breaches of the peace might be required, but the keystone of the formula for avoiding international violence is to strengthen the commitment to and the machinery for peaceful settlement of disputes.

The primacy of peaceful settlement processes in both the League of Nations and the United Nations is evidenced by the emphasis upon these processes in the Covenant and in the Charter—an emphasis based on both placement and detail within the documents. The goals of promoting peace and security are mentioned first in these texts, and peaceful settlement of disputes is also first and fundamental among the means for goal attainment. Other goals, such as (1) developing friendly relations among nations, (2) harmonizing the actions of nations, (3) taking appropriate measures to strengthen universal peace, and (4) practicing tolerance and living together in peace (included in the United Nations Charter), reinforce the desire for avoiding war. The principles of the organizations emphasize the obligations of member states to refrain from the threat or use of force and to settle international disputes by peaceful means. The means available for the processes of peaceful settlement both outside and inside the new organizations are elaborated in these constitutional documents. In the Covenant the material on pacific settlement of disputes is more detailed than on any other subject. In the Charter the chapter on pacific settlement immediately follows the general provisions on purposes, membership, and organization. These data attest to the concern of the authors of the League Covenant and the United Nations Charter for the processes of peaceful settlement of disputes.

Although the level of anxiety concerning nuclear holocaust has lowered in recent years, other threats to peace have not diminished and the possibilities of the use of weapons of mass destruction still exist. The threat of proliferation of nuclear, biological, and chemical weapons, the size of remaining stockpiles of such weapons, and the increased frequency of civil and regional conflicts, often with heavy casualties and human suffering, emphasize the unmitigated need for conflict resolution. If survival is a foremost human value, then peaceful settlement of disputes is salient to protecting that value. Avoiding the tragedy of war should provide sufficient incentive to use all means available to seek new and imaginative methods for reducing tensions.

CHARTER PROCEDURES AND METHODS

In the area of pacific settlement of disputes the architects of the Charter were not notably innovative. The world's political leaders were not ready to commit their governments to any radical departure from established practices. The sovereignty of states and the protection of the prerogatives of the major powers were the basic conditions around which all other features of the Charter had to fit. Therefore, the familiar methods of pacific settlement, firmly established in international law and practice, were the ones mentioned in the Charter as the devices to be used by states or by United Nations organs in handling disputes; also, the processes to be followed for the consideration of disputes brought before United Nations bodies were singularly similar to the formulas established twenty-six years earlier in the League of Nations Covenant. Except for greater detail and a supposedly clearer delineation of functions between the Security Council and the General Assembly (a distinction that in practice became blurred), the processes for pacific settlement provided for in the two constitutional documents were fundamentally identical.

The Charter provides a logical progression of steps to be followed by states involved in disputes. Each member promises in adhering to the Charter to settle all disputes by peaceful means and to refrain from the threat or use of force. If a dispute does arise, the parties should, before submission to a United Nations organ, "seek a solution by negotiation, enquiry, mediation, conciliation, arbitration, judicial settlement, resort to regional agencies or arrangements, or other peaceful means of their own choice."[1] If the dispute is not so resolved, then a party to the dispute or any member of the United Nations or the Secretary-General may bring the matter to the attention of the Security Council or of the General Assembly. The assumption was originally made that the Security Council would, in most cases, be the referee since primary responsibility for the maintenance of international peace and security was lodged in the Council. When a dispute does come before the Security Council, that body's first and simplest option is to suggest to the disputants that they settle their dispute by one of the means of peaceful settlement listed above.

Since the traditional means of peaceful settlement of disputes listed in Article 33 of the Charter are the basic methods applied to the resolution process both inside and outside the United Nations, a clear understanding of each method is in order. Some variations and refinements of traditional methods have been developed by United Nations organs, but the essential means correspond to procedures and practices developed over hundreds of years.

Negotiation is the most common method for settling international differences. It involves direct discussion between or among the parties to the dispute with the objective of reaching an agreement. No outside party is involved in the process. Negotiation is the essence of the practice of diplomacy.

Good offices is the only traditional method of dispute settlement not listed in Article 33 of the Charter but one frequently used by United Nations organs. Good offices involves the assistance of a third party or state not a party to the dispute. The third party, in adhering strictly to the limits of good offices, may offer only a channel of communications or facilities for the use of the parties but may not offer any suggestions for terms of settlement. By providing a neutral ground for negotiation or by offering to carry messages between the disputants, the third party displays a friendly desire to promote a settlement without getting involved in the issues at stake.

---

[1]Charter of the United Nations, Art. 33.

Inquiry is a process of fact-finding by a neutral team of investigators. Often the facts underlying a controversy are in dispute, and clarification by an impartial commission may facilitate settlement. The report of the investigating commission does not suggest terms of settlement but may help to establish conditions conducive to settlement.

Mediation is a procedure involving the suggestion of terms of settlement by a third party. The mediator enters into the negotiations between the disputing parties seeking terms of compromise acceptable to the disputants. An effective mediator may not impose his will upon the parties without losing the confidence of one or more of them in his neutrality.

Conciliation is similar to mediation except for the legal distinction that the third party is a commission or international body whose aid has been sought in finding a solution satisfactory to the disputants. Special commissions have often been created by the United Nations to attempt conciliation. As in mediation, the object is peace through compromise on terms acceptable to the parties, not the imposition of terms by the commission of conciliation or the application of abstract principles of law or justice. In practice the United Nations organs have tended to use the terms *conciliation, mediation,* and *good offices* without adherence to their strict legal distinctions.

Arbitration is a means of applying legal principles to a controversy within limits previously agreed upon by the disputing parties. A panel of judges or arbitrators is created either by special agreement of the parties or by an existing arbitral treaty. In agreeing to submit the dispute to arbitration, the disputants also agree in advance to be bound by the decision. An arbitral agreement known as a *compromis* specifies the method of selecting the arbitral panel, the time and place of the hearing, and any limitations upon the facts to be considered or the principles of law or equity to be applied in arriving at a decision. Historically, arbitration has enjoyed several periods of popularity, beginning with its use by the ancient Greeks and gaining in use during the nineteenth and early twentieth centuries, but it has almost disappeared from general use in the period since 1945, except for the specific areas of trade disputes and investments.

Adjudication or *judicial settlement* is a process of submitting a dispute to an international court for decision. Unlike arbitration, the court is subject to no preliminary limitations upon its procedures, evidence to be considered, or legal principles to be applied, except those stated in the statute by which it was created. However, nations, jealous of their sovereignty, have been reluctant to grant to international courts any form of compulsory jurisdiction or to submit appropriate cases to existing courts. As a result, the International Court of Justice has languished for lack of business to an even greater extent than its predecessor, the Permanent Court of International Justice. As with arbitration, once the parties have agreed to submit a case to adjudication, the decision rendered is considered binding, although adequate means of enforcement in instances of noncompliance are lacking.

When a dispute is called to the attention of the Security Council, the first step is to adopt the question as an agenda item. Prolonged disputes previously adopted as agenda items and never officially removed from the list of items of which the Council is "seized" (the official United Nations terminology referring to the current agenda) may be taken up again at any future time without this preliminary step. Because the General Assembly may not make recommendations on a dispute or situation under Security Council consideration, the Secretary-General is required to maintain and publish a "list of matters of which the Security Council is seized." If the dispute is new, the preliminary debate on the adoption of the agenda may require from a few minutes to several days. Questions of domestic jurisdiction or other sources of doubt concerning the legality, wisdom, or practicality of Security Council involvement may delay approval of the agenda. By discussing for many hours the pros and cons of the appropriateness of Security Council consideration, some of the substantive issues of the dispute may be thoroughly aired and may serve to focus public attention upon these issues even if the agenda item is subsequently rejected. One example of such prolonged preliminary debate occurred in April 1952, when the Security Council was requested to consider the situation in Tunisia over French objections that the matter was one of domestic jurisdiction. After several days of debate, the item failed to gain the seven votes required to adopt it as an agenda item.

After the Security Council agrees to consider a dispute or situation, the case for each disputant may be presented by sympathetic members of the Council or by the representatives of the disputing states. Any party to a dispute has a right to participate, without vote, in the discussion of that dispute. Other nonmembers of the Council may also be invited, at the discretion of the Council, if their interests are affected. On some occasions these provisions have led to a crowded Council chamber and to lengthy debate because of requests to participate by large numbers of "interested" parties. Of course, every complex question for discussion is also supported by elaborate documentation, including communications from the contending governments. This allows each member of the Security Council to consider evidence other than that presented orally.

If, during the course of debate, some of the Security Council members become convinced that a decision or suggestion by the Council is possible or desirable, one or more resolutions will be introduced with the hope of adoption by Council vote. Resolutions may be sponsored by one or by several members of the Council. In most cases, extensive consultation will occur outside the Council chamber both before and after resolutions are introduced. Amendments to resolutions may be submitted, and not all proposals will necessarily be voted on. In spite of consultation among the members, all proposed resolutions on a given issue may fail for lack of nine supporting votes or because of an occasional veto by a permanent member, although abstentions have been more frequent than vetoes in recent years. Another common phenomenon is that resolutions, in order to receive adequate support from the members, may be so watered down that they fail to be effective in alleviating the conditions of which the aggrieved party or parties have complained. Resolutions of this least-common-denominator variety may contribute to deterioration of public respect for the efficacy of the Security Council.

In dealing with a dispute, the Security Council may decide to refer the matter to another body or may itself suggest terms of settlement. If Security Council action is blocked by a veto, any nine members may remove the item from the agenda and request an emergency session of the General Assembly under the Uniting for Peace Resolution discussed in Chapter 7. By Council resolution the dispute may be referred to a regional organization or to a specially created commission of inquiry or conciliation. The Council may also appoint a mediator or recommend that the Secretary-General arrange for a mediator or for one or more agents to offer good offices. The Council also has the option of suggesting to the parties that they continue or resume negotiations or that they arrange to submit the dispute to arbitration or judicial settlement, although the latter two means have largely fallen into disuse.

One device not mentioned in the Charter, which has been used to good effect while other means for final settlement are being sought, is calling on parties already engaged in armed hostilities to abide by a cease-fire. The drawing of a cease-fire line and the temporary cessation of hostilities may make possible the working out of a permanent settlement, as in the Indonesian-Dutch dispute, or it may contribute only to the checking of large-scale fighting and loss of lives for prolonged periods, as in the Kashmir and Palestine disputes. In either case, whether "settlement" is achieved or not, Security Council members generally prefer an armistice in which the adversaries face each other from their respective sides of a cease-fire line to warfare with its human and economic costs.

Until a dispute is finally resolved, the Security Council may retain the item on its agenda for a period of months or years. This allows for reconsideration on short notice (1) to follow up the results of previous Council recommendations; (2) to seek new, more effective means for settlement; or (3) to consider new developments in the situation. As long as means for international decision making and enforcement are unsatisfactory, the persistence of unresolved issues over long time spans will remain a feature of international relations.

Although it is less well equipped to deal with disputes than the Security Council, the General Assembly may be called upon to consider controversies referred to it by a party to the dispute, by members of the Security Council, or by any other member or group of members of the United Nations. Unwieldy size and lack of binding power for its recommendations are just two of the Assembly's obvious disadvantages as an agent for handling acute international differences. But in spite of these handicaps the Assembly has played a much larger role in dealing with disputes than foreseen by the planners in San Francisco. This enhanced role is discussed at many other points in this book.

If the parties to a dispute can agree that a satisfactory result may be obtained by judicial settlement, they may submit their case, by mutual agreement, to the International Court of Justice. More details of the role of the Court will be developed in Chapter 8, but it may now be noted that the number and the importance of cases submitted to the Court have not been impressive. States are reluctant to use the Court for judicial settlement, and the recent trend has been toward less rather than greater use of this agency for conflict resolution.

The Secretary-General and his staff play a wide variety of roles in dealing with disputes. These range from merely receiving and transmitting information between governments and United Nations organs to calling the attention of those organs to threatening situations or to acting as the principal agent of the Security Council or the General Assembly in mediating a dispute or carrying out the steps called for in United Nations resolutions. The influence and activities of the Secretary-General have been, in practice, much more pervasive than would have been generally predicted in 1945.

The keynote of United Nations responses to disputes and threats to peace has been flexibility. From the variety of procedures outlined above, the organs of the United Nations have been able to select appropriate responses for widely varying circumstances depending upon the limitations imposed by both the situation and the willingness of member governments to support one or another course of action. To the extent that disputes have on occasion been dealt with effectively, the factor of flexibility has made a major contribution.

UNITED NATIONS EXPERIENCE—
SURVEY AND CASE STUDIES

A complete account of United Nations activities in the area of pacific settlement of disputes could not be given in a single chapter or even in a single volume. Although member states do not choose to submit all appropriate controversies or situations "which might lead to international friction or give rise to a dispute" to consideration by United Nations organs, the documentation of the more than 200 disputes debated by the Security Council and General Assembly during a period of forty-seven years is voluminous (see Table 6–1). Even a summary of each dispute would require much space and would be tedious to follow. The data in this section are, therefore, condensed by the use of a table supplemented by sufficient detail concerning selected controversies to sample and illustrate a variety of approaches used by United Nations agencies in dealing with disputes.

TABLE 6–1   DISPUTES CONSIDERED BY THE SECURITY COUNCIL AND THE
GENERAL ASSEMBLY, JANUARY 1946–DECEMBER 1992

	Considered by		Year First Intro- duced	Duration of Consideration		
Dispute	*Security Council*	*General Assembly*		*1 Year or Less*	*1–5 Years*	*More Than 5 Years*
Middle East						
Iranian Question	X		1946	X		
Syrian-Lebanese Complaint	X		1946	X		
Palestine Question	X	X	1947			X
Egyptian Question	X		1947	X		
Status of Jerusalem	X	X	1947		X	
Palestine Refugee Question		X	1948			X
Anglo-Iranian Oil Dispute	X		1951	X		
Israeli Complaint against Egypt on Suez Canal	X		1954	X		
Gaza Area Incidents	X		1955	X		
Suez Canal Question	X	X	1956			X
Syrian Complaint against Turkey		X	1957	X		
Lebanese Complaint against UAR	X	X	1958	X		
Jordanian Complaint against UAR	X	X	1958	X		
Case of Adolf Eichmann	X		1960	X		
Question of Oman		X	1960			X
Question of Kuwait	X		1961	X		
Question of Yemen	X		1963		X	
Complaint by UK against Yemen	X		1966	X		
Situation in the Middle East	X	X	1967			X
Situation in and around Jerusalem	X	X	1968			X

(continued)

TABLE 6–1   (*continued*)

	Considered by		Year First Intro- duced	Duration of Consideration		
Dispute	*Security Council*	*General Assembly*		*1 Year or Less*	*1–5 Years*	*More Than 5 Years*
Israeli Practices Affecting Human Rights in Occupied Territories		X	1968			X
Question of Bahrain	X		1970	X		
Dispute over Certain Islands in Persian Gulf	X		1971	X		
Iraqi Complaint against Iran	X		1974	X		
Middle East Problem Including Palestinian Question	X	X	1976			X
Situation in Occupied Arab Territories	X	X	1976			X
Exercise by Palestinian People of Inalienable Rights	X	X	1976			X
Situation in Lebanon	X	X	1978			X
Situation between United States and Iran	X		1979		X	
Situation between Iran and Iraq	X	X	1980			X
Israeli Attack on Iraqi Nuclear Reactor	X		1981		X	
Israeli Annexation of the Golan Heights	X	X	1981			X
Complaint of Gulf States against Iran	X		1984	X		
Israeli Air Attack against Tunisia	X		1985	X		
Israeli Interception of Libyan Aircraft	X		1986	X		

(*continued*)

TABLE 6–1   (*continued*)

| | Considered by | | Year First Intro- duced | Duration of Consideration | | |
Dispute	Security Council	General Assembly		*1 Year or Less*	*1–5 Years*	*More Than 5 Years*
Downing of Iranian Plane by United States	X		1988	X		
Situation between Iraq and Kuwait	X		1990		X	
Asia and Far East						
Indonesian Question	X	X	1946		X	
Korean Question	X	X	1947			X
Indian-Pakistani Question	X		1948			X
Hyderabad Question	X		1948	X		
Soviet Threats to Political Independence of China		X	1949		X	
Armed Invasion of Taiwan	X	X	1950	X		
Alleged Bombing by United States of Chinese Territory	X	X	1950	X		
Intervention of China in Korea	X	X	1950	X		
Relief and Rehabilitation of Korea	X	X	1950			X
Alleged Bacterial Warfare in Korea	X	X	1952		X	
Complaint of Mass Murder of Korean and Chinese POWs by United States		X	1952	X		
Burmese Complaint against Rep. of China		X	1952		X	

(*continued*)

TABLE 6–1 (*continued*)

	Considered by		Year First Intro- duced	Duration of Consideration		
Dispute	*Security Council*	*General Assembly*		*1 Year or Less*	*1–5 Years*	*More Than 5 Years*
North Korean and Chinese Atrocities		X	1953	X		
Thai Request for Aid of Peace Observation Commission	X		1954	X		
Detention of UN Military Personnel in Violation of Korean Armistice Agreement		X	1954		X	
Acts of Aggression by United States Navy against People's Rep. of China		X	1954	X		
Violations of Freedom of Seas in China Area		X	1954	X		
West Irian Question		X	1954			X
Question of Chinese Coastal Islands	X		1955	X		
Laotian Situation	X		1959	X		
Question of Tibet		X	1959			X
Question of Goa	X		1961	X		
Human Rights in South Vietnam		X	1963	X		
Cambodian Complaints of Aggression by United States and South Vietnam	X		1964	X		
Question of Malaysia	X		1964	X		
Gulf of Tonkin Incidents	X		1964	X		
Situation in Vietnam	X		1966	X		
Complaint by United States against North Korea	X		1968	X		

(*continued*)

TABLE 6–1   (*continued*)

| | | | | Duration of Consideration | | |
	Considered by		Year First Intro- duced	1 Year or Less	1–5 Years	More Than 5 Years
Dispute	*Security Council*	*General Assembly*				
Dispute Concerning Legal Regime in Khmer Republic		X	1973	X		
Situation in East Timor	X	X	1975			X
Question of Kampuchea	X	X	1979			X
Situation in Southeast Asia	X	X	1979			X
Situation in Afghanistan	X	X	1980			X
Downing of Korean Air Liner	X		1983	X		
Bombing of South Korean Air Liner	X		1988	X		
Complaint by Malaysia against Indonesia	X		1989	X		
Situation in Cambodia	X	X	1990		X	
Situation in Tajikistan	X		1992	X		
Africa						
Treatment of Indians in South Africa		X	1946			X
Question of South-West Africa	X	X	1946			X
Former Italian Colonies		X	1948		X	
Apartheid in South Africa	X	X	1952			X
Tunisian Question		X	1952		X	
Moroccan Question		X	1952		X	
Algerian Question	X	X	1955			X
Sudanese Complaint against Egypt	X		1958	X		
French-Tunisian Dispute	X		1958	X		
Congolese Question	X	X	1960		X	
Angolan Situation	X	X	1960		X	

(*continued*)

TABLE 6–1   (*continued*)

Dispute	Considered by		Year First Intro- duced	Duration of Consideration		
	Security Council	General Assembly		1 Year or Less	1–5 Years	More Than 5 Years
Mauritanian Situation		X	1960	X		
Dispute over Bizerte	X	X	1961	X		
Algerians Imprisoned in France		X	1961	X		
Southern Rhodesian Question	X	X	1962			X
Complaints by Senegal against Portugal	X		1963		X	
Situation in Territories under Portuguese Adm.	X	X	1963			X
Intervention in Democratic Republic of the Congo	X		1964	X		
Question of Spanish Sahara		X	1964			X
Complaints of Dem. Republic of Congo against Portugal	X		1966		X	
Complaint of Dem. Republic of Congo Concerning Act of Aggression	X		1967	X		
Situation in Namibia	X	X	1968			X
Complaints by Zambia against Portugal	X		1969	X		
Complaints by Senegal against Portugal	X		1969	X		
Complaints by Guinea against Portugal	X		1969	X		
Complaint by Guinea against Portugal	X		1970	X		
Complaint by Guinea against Portugal	X		1971	X		

(*continued*)

TABLE 6–1   (*continued*)

	Considered by		Year First Intro-duced	Duration of Consideration		
Dispute	*Security Council*	*General Assembly*		*1 Year or Less*	*1–5 Years*	*More Than 5 Years*
Complaint by Senegal against Portugal	X		1971	X		
Complaint by Zambia against South Africa	X		1971	X		
Complaint by Senegal against Portugal	X		1972	X		
Complaint by Zambia against South Africa	X		1973	X		
Occupation by Portuguese Forces of Sectors of Guinea-Bissau		X	1973	X		
Situation Concerning Western Sahara	X	X	1974			X
Situation in the Comoros	X		1976	X		
French-Somalia Incident in Afars and Issas	X		1976	X		
Complaint of South African Aggression against Angola	X		1976	X		
Complaint by Zambia against South Africa	X		1976	X		
Complaint by Mauritius of Act of Aggression by Israel against Uganda	X		1976	X		
Complaint by Lesotho against South Africa	X		1976	X		
Complaint by Botswana against Rhodesia	X		1977	X		
Complaint of Aggression against Benin	X		1977	X		

(*continued*)

TABLE 6–1   (*continued*)

Dispute	Considered by		Year First Intro- duced	Duration of Consideration		
	Security Council	General Assembly		*1 Year or Less*	*1–5 Years*	*More Than 5 Years*
Question of South Africa	X	X	1977			X
Complaint by Mozambique against Rhodesia	X		1977	X		
Complaint by Zambia against Rhodesia	X		1978		X	
Complaint by Chad	X		1978	X		
Status of Mayotte		X	1979			X
Status of Certain Malagasy Islands		X	1979			X
Complaint by Zambia against South Africa	X		1980	X		
Complaint by Chad against Egypt and Sudan	X		1981	X		
Mercenary Aggression against the Republic of Seychelles	X		1982	X		
Fund for OAU Peacekeeping in Chad	X		1982	X		
Complaint by Lesotho against South Africa	X		1982		X	
Complaint by Chad against Libya	X		1983	X		
Complaint by Libya against United States	X		1983	X		
Complaint by Angola against South Africa	X		1983		X	
Air Attack by Libya against Sudan	X		1984	X		
Complaint by Botswana against South Africa	X		1985	X		

(*continued*)

TABLE 6–1   (*continued*)

Dispute	Considered by		Year First Intro- duced	Duration of Consideration		
	Security Council	*General Assembly*		*1 Year or Less*	*1–5 Years*	*More Than 5 Years*
United States Attack on Libya	X	X	1986	X		
Complaint by Chad against Libya	X		1986	X		
Situation in Angola	X		1987			X
Israeli Aggression against Tunisia	X		1988	X		
Complaint by Botswana against South Africa	X		1988	X		
Complaint by Libya against United States Concerning Downing of Planes	X		1989	X		
Situation in Liberia	X		1991		X	
Situation in Somalia	X		1992		X	
Complaint Concerning Libya's Harboring of Airline Terrorists	X		1992		X	
Situation in Mozambique	X		1992		X	
Europe						
Greek Question	X	X	1946			X
Spanish Question	X	X	1946		X	
Free Territory of Trieste	X		1947		X	
Corfu Channel Question	X		1947	X		
Czechoslovakian Situation	X		1948	X		
Berlin Situation	X		1948	X		
Human Rights in Balkans		X	1948		X	
Soviet Wives of Foreign Nationals		X	1948	X		

(*continued*)

TABLE 6–1   (*continued*)

Dispute	Considered by Security Council	Considered by General Assembly	Year First Intro- duced	Duration of Consideration 1 Year or Less	Duration of Consideration 1–5 Years	Duration of Consideration More Than 5 Years
Conditions for Free Elections in Germany		X	1951	X		
Complaint by Yugoslavia of Hostile Activities of Neighbors		X	1951	X		
Complaints of United States Intervention in Domestic Affairs of Other Countries (three separate complaints)		X	1951	X		
		X	1952	X		
		X	1956	X		
Austrian Peace Treaty		X	1952	X		
U.S. Complaint of Attack on Its Aircraft	X		1954	X		
Cyprian Question	X	X	1954			X
Hungarian Question	X	X	1956			X
Flights of United States Armed Aircraft toward Soviet Frontiers	X		1958	X		
Complaints of United States Violations of Soviet Airspace	X		1960	X		
Status of Bozen Residents		X	1960		X	
Relations between Greece and Turkey	X		1964	X		
Situation in Czechoslovakia	X		1968	X		
Complaint by Iceland against United Kingdom	X		1975	X		
Complaint by Greece against Turkey	X		1976	X		

(*continued*)

TABLE 6–1 (*continued*)

	Considered by		Year First Intro-duced	Duration of Consideration		
Dispute	*Security Council*	*General Assembly*		*1 Year or Less*	*1–5 Years*	*More Than 5 Years*
Complaint by Malta against Libya	X		1980		X	
Hijacking of Achille Lauro	X		1985	X		
Attacks on Rome and Vienna Airports	X		1985	X		
Situation in Yugoslavia	X		1991		X	
Situation relating to Nagorno-Karabakh	X		1992	X		
Situation in Georgia	X		1992		X	
Situation in Bosnia and Herzegovina	X		1992		X	
Western Hemisphere						
Aggression against Guatemala	X		1954	X		
Cuban Complaints against United States	X	X	1960		X	
Venezuelan Complaint against Dominican Republic	X		1960	X		
Boundary Dispute between Venezuela and British Guiana		X	1962	X		
Haitian Complaint against Dominican Republic	X		1963	X		

(*continued*)

TABLE 6–1   (*continued*)

Dispute	Considered by		Year First Intro- duced	Duration of Consideration		
	Security Council	*General Assembly*		*1 Year or Less*	*1–5 Years*	*More Than 5 Years*
Panamanian Complaint against United States	X		1964	X		
Situation in Dominican Republic	X		1965		X	
Complaint by Haiti of Act of Aggression	X		1968	X		
Question of Panama Canal	X		1973	X		
Complaint by Cuba against Chile	X		1973	X		
Question of Belize		X	1977		X	
Complaint by Costa Rica against Nicaragua		X	1978	X		
Situation in Nicaragua		X	1978	X		
Situation between Ecuador and Peru	X		1981	X		
Situation in Central America	X	X	1982		X	
Falklands/Malvinas Dispute	X	X	1982			X
Situation in Grenada	X	X	1983		X	
Complaint by Nicaragua against United States	X		1983		X	
Nicaraguan Complaint of Situation in Central America	X		1986	X		
Nicaraguan Complaint of United States Aggression	X		1986	X		

(*continued*)

TABLE 6–1   (*continued*)

| Dispute | Considered by | | Year First Intro- duced | Duration of Consideration | | |
	Security Council	General Assembly		*1 Year or Less*	*1–5 Years*	*More Than 5 Years*
Nicaraguan Complaint against United States	X		1988	X		
Central America: Efforts toward Peace	X	X	1989		X	
Situation in Panama	X		1989	X		
Complaint by El Salvador against Nicaragua	X		1989	X		
Complaint by Nicaragua against United States	X		1990	X		
Complaint by Cuba against United States	X		1990	X		
Situation in Haiti	X		1991		X	
General						
Question of Hostage Taking and Abduction	X		1989	X		
Marking of Explosives for Purpose of Detection	X		1989	X		

No sharp distinctions can be drawn, in United Nations practice, among pacific settlement, collective security, and the newly developed techniques of peacekeeping or preventive diplomacy. All situations that involve the use of collective security or peacekeeping techniques also contain elements of pacific settlement. The accompanying table includes all disputes submitted to the United Nations without classifying certain of them as having been partially dealt with by methods that may be labeled collective security or peacekeeping. However, the theory and practice of collective security and peacekeeping will be treated more fully in the following chapter and will include case studies of several additional disputes to which the techniques of collective security or peacekeeping have been applied.

Through the selection of a few case studies, a wide range of conditions may be illustrated concerning the ability of United Nations organs to contribute to the peaceful settlement of disputes. The case studies that follow have been selected because they demonstrate a variety of circumstances in which the United Nations has been involved in attempts at conflict resolution. The selection is based on these specific criteria: (1) to show examples of a wide variety of techniques utilized, ranging from simple to complex, in attempting to resolve the several disputes; (2) to illustrate varying degrees of great-power involvement or direct interest in the dispute; (3) to include disputes of varying duration; (4) to give examples of consideration by the Security Council only, by the General Assembly only, and by both; and (5) to demonstrate degrees of success or failure in resolving the issues involved or in terminating the dispute.

The Iranian Question

The earliest dispute to come before the Security Council was a complaint by Iran in January 1946 that Soviet troops, still occupying the Azerbaijan region, were interfering with the internal affairs of Iran by encouraging a separatist movement there. The Soviet representative denied the charges and the Council, after brief discussion, requested that the adversary governments resume negotiations and that the Security Council be kept informed of results. In March the matter was discussed again. The issue was dropped in May when Iran reported the withdrawal of Soviet troops.

The Iranian case illustrates several points regarding the handling of disputes by the Security Council. The Council is unable to use strong measures or coercion against a major power. The only weapon available is an appeal to Charter principles and to the good faith of the disputants, supported by publicity and world opinion. There is no way to measure the degree to which international exposure of the situation served as an impetus for the Soviet response. In any event, the matter was shortly settled. There have been several other situations in which no more drastic action by the Security Council or the General Assembly than general debate and an appeal to the parties to negotiate has brought about settlement of disputes. In the absence of contrary evidence, it may be reasonably assumed that in such cases settlement through negotiations was hastened by United Nations exposure and pressure.

Former Italian Colonies

According to the peace treaty with Italy at the end of World War II, the disposition of Libya, Italian Somaliland, and Eritrea was to be determined by France, the United Kingdom, the Soviet Union, and the United States. If within one year they could not agree (and this proved to be the case), they were to turn the matter over to the General Assembly for solution. After much study and debate the Assembly, in November 1949, adopted a resolution that provided for additional investigation with regard to Eritrea and for a decision on the final status of the other two territories.

Libya was to become an independent state not later than January 1, 1952. A United Nations commissioner was appointed and was to be assisted by a ten-member council in drawing up a constitution and preparing for self-government. Since Libya was a poor country with a population of approximately 1 million, all appropriate agencies of the United Nations, including the specialized agencies, were urged to aid it with technical and financial assistance. A National Assembly was chosen, a federal form of government was adopted, and on December 24, 1951, Libya was proclaimed an independent state. Libya immediately applied for United Nations membership, but its application was vetoed by the Soviet Union, and it was admitted only as a part of the "package deal" in December 1955. Libya continued to receive special attention in the aid programs of the United Nations until the discovery of large petroleum resources moved it from very low to very high per capita income in the space of a decade.

According to the Assembly's 1949 resolution, Somaliland was to be placed under trusteeship for a period of ten years and was then to become independent. Italy was to serve as the administering authority with the aid of an advisory council set up by the United Nations. In 1959 a constituent assembly was elected, and a new constitution was approved in May 1960. Independence was declared on July 1, 1960, and in September Somalia (which also includes the former British Somaliland) became a United Nations member.

A brief delay was necessary before a final decision on the future of Eritrea could be reached. An investigating commission was instructed to determine the wishes of the various groups in Eritrea and to suggest a plan for their political future. On-the-spot surveys were taken as a basis for the commission's report. In December 1950, the General Assembly approved a plan according to which Eritrea would be federated with Ethiopia as an autonomous unit under the Ethiopian Crown. A United Nations commissioner was to assist with the transitional steps. A new constitution came into effect in September 1952.

The disposition of the former Italian colonies was handled entirely by the General Assembly as prearranged by the major powers. Although the major powers were unable to agree, the General Assembly rather promptly settled upon distinct plans for each of the three territories. Some criticisms of the proposals were voiced, but the results seemed as satisfactory as could have been expected from any alternative courses of action. The political and economic viability of Libya was questioned, and some special aid was required for several years, but the discovery of oil alleviated major economic problems. Doubts could be raised concerning Italy's role as trustee for Somaliland both because Italy was the former imperial state and because Italy was not yet a United Nations member. However, the administration of Somaliland for a ten-year period under close United Nations scrutiny was conducted as well as the administration of most trust territories, and the transition to full independence was prompt and efficient. Many elements of the Eritrean population were dissatisfied with their status within Ethiopia and, over the years, civil warfare intensified. Finally, in April 1993 Eritrea became an independent state. In general, at the time of the decisions, the Assembly performed a difficult and complicated assignment quite effectively.

Indian-Pakistani Question

One of the most prolonged, and still unsettled, disputes before the United Nations is the Indian-Pakistani question, alternatively referred to as the Kashmir dispute. Military confrontations between the parties have twice flared into major wars that involved fighting outside as well as inside Kashmir. In fact, the 1971 war was fought over the separate issue of the struggle for Bangladesh independence, to which fighting on the Kashmiri front was but incidental.

In 1947, when India and Pakistan were partitioned and became independent, one of the princely states free to accede to either India or Pakistan or to remain independent was the state known by the collective title of Jammu and Kashmir. The majority of the population was Muslim, but the maharajah was Hindu. The maharajah opted for accession to India, and India accepted, subject to later verification by plebiscite.

In January 1948, both India and Pakistan called to the attention of the Security Council the potentially serious situation in Kashmir. The Indians claimed that tribesmen aided by Pakistan had invaded Jammu and Kashmir. Pakistan charged that the accession to India was illegal and that India was violating other agreements with Pakistan.

On January 20 the Security Council established the United Nations Commission for India and Pakistan (UNCIP), to which it assigned responsibilities of investigation, good offices, and mediation. The UNCIP members, representing five states, arrived in the area in July 1948, and the next month proposed a cease-fire and detailed arrangements for a truce and the holding of a plebiscite. Because of disagreements between India and Pakistan over details, the cease-fire did not come into effect until January 1, 1949, and the final delineation of the cease-fire line was not established until nearly seven months later. During this interval a United Nations Military Observer Group in India and Pakistan (UNMOGIP) was set up to observe and report on the cease-fire, and U.S. Admiral Chester Nimitz was nominated as plebiscite administrator.

In December 1949, the UNCIP submitted its final report to the Security Council, voicing its frustration in trying to reach agreement on military withdrawals and the conditions for a plebiscite. The Council then requested the President of the Security Council, General McNaughton of Canada, to negotiate with India and Pakistan, but in February he reported no significant progress. In April 1950, the responsibilities of the UNCIP were turned over to Sir Owen Dixon of Australia, who was given the title United Nations Representative for India and Pakistan. In September he reported failure to reach agreement on outstanding issues and asked to be relieved of his responsibilities. In April 1951, Dr. Frank Graham of the United States was appointed to succeed Sir Owen. The Council vainly suggested that, after three months, any remaining points of difference that could not be resolved with the aid of the United Nations representative should be submitted to arbitration. Graham made limited progress on some points of negotiation, but the unresolved issues after several additional years of effort were crucial to a final settlement, and the general stalement continued.

In January 1957, the Security Council took up the Pakistani complaint that India had held a constituent assembly in Kashmir and drawn up a constitution that provided for the integration of Kashmir into India in violation of earlier agreements for a plebiscite. The Council President, Gunnar Jarring of Sweden, was requested to visit India and Pakistan to explore the possibilities of reaching a settlement on the Kashmir issue. On April 29 he reported no progress. Jarring's suggestion to submit certain basic issues to arbitration had been accepted by Pakistan but rejected by India on the grounds that no other measures were appropriate until Pakistan took steps toward military withdrawal, since it was still engaging in aggression.

In 1962 and again in 1964, Pakistan requested that the Security Council take up the question of Kashmir. In spite of days of debate, no constructive course of action could be agreed upon by the Council.

On September 3, 1965, the Secretary-General reported to the Security Council that between January and mid-June the UNMOGIP had verified 218 cease-fire-line violations by Pakistan and 159 by India. Since August 5, illegal activities on both sides had further increased. These activities included artillery fire, crossing the line by armed Pakistanis not in uniform, and occupation by Indian troops of positions on the Pakistani side of the cease-fire line. The Security Council by unanimous resolution called upon both sides to stop aggression immediately and to return to their respective positions behind the cease-fire line. Instead, military activity intensified, and India invaded Pakistan in areas around Lahore and Sialkot. On September 6, the Security Council called on the parties to stop all hostilities and return their forces to positions held before August 5. The Council requested the Secretary-General to assist in implementing this resolution; U Thant spent the next week in India and Pakistan arranging for a cease-fire, which became effective on September 22. The number of military observers in UNMOGIP was more than doubled, and a new temporary United Nations India-Pakistan Observation Mission (UNIPOM) was dispatched to the areas along the India-Pakistan border where Indian forces had crossed into Pakistan.

Frequent cease-fire violations occurred during the remainder of 1965, and the Security Council pressed India and Pakistan to implement the withdrawal of forces to the positions held before August 5. The Prime Minister of India and the President of Pakistan met in Tashkent under Soviet auspices and on January 10, 1966, issued a joint declaration stating that all troop withdrawals would be accomplished by February 25. The Secretary-General verified that the schedule had been met, the UNIPOM group was disbanded, and the UNMOGIP force was gradually reduced to its normal contingent.

The 1971 civil war in East Pakistan culminated in Indian military invasion of that area in December and resulted in the declaration of Bangladesh as an independent state. Fighting occurred in Kashmir as well, but the war did not bring about any change in the situation in that region. The cease-fire line continues to divide Jammu and Kashmir, the UNMOGIP patrols the line and reports violations, India claims the legitimacy of the incorporation of Kashmir territory into India, and Pakistan insists that its claim to the entire territory is equally valid. The basic issues have been unresolved for more than forty years.

United Nations efforts to resolve the Kashmir issue represent an exercise in repeated frustration, since the parties are unwilling to reach a compromise solution. The prospects for a plebiscite have now receded, and India considers the accession of Kashmir to India a fait accompli. A cease-fire line has divided the area since 1949 with a group of about forty military observers responsible for reporting violations along a line nearly 500 miles long. With the exception of the General Assembly's consideration of the Bangladesh phase in 1971, the Security Council has maintained jurisdiction over the dispute in spite of occasional stalemates due to the use of the veto. On other occasions, when crises occurred, resolutions were passed by unanimous vote or with one or more abstentions. Except for a big-power stalemate over Bangladesh, the ability of the Security Council to take positive action has forestalled demands for General Assembly involvement.

The Security Council has used a very wide range of devices in seeking a solution to the Kashmir issue. It has called repeatedly for cease-fires, and a cease-fire line was established in 1949. Fact-finding or inquiry functions were assigned to the original five-member commission sent to the area and to the two observer groups created subsequently. The instructions to the United Nations Commission for India and Pakistan also included charges to use good offices and mediation. The two United Nations representatives for India and Pakistan acted primarily as mediators. The Security Council twice dispatched its current president to the subcontinent as mediator and authorized the Secretary-General to use his personal influence in bringing the 1965 war to a halt. The Council, on one occasion, and its President, on another, suggested the submission of certain issues to arbitration, but the parties to the dispute would not agree to the use of this procedure. The Soviet Union also exercised good offices and mediation in bringing about the 1966 Tashkent agreement. In spite of flexibility and persistence, the Kashmir issue has remained impervious to resolution. However, for long periods since 1949 fighting has been limited to minor incidents along the cease-fire line rather than breaking out into major military actions.

Race Conflict in South Africa

One of the bitterest, most persistent, and least soluble problems confronting the United Nations has been the question of the racial policies of the South African government. In one form or another the problem has been debated since 1946. The first complaint was made by India concerning South African policies toward the Indian minority in South Africa. In 1952 a second issue—that of apartheid, or separation of the races—was added to the agenda of the General Assembly. After 1962 these separate items were combined into a single question of apartheid in all its aspects. All complaints during the 1940s and 1950s were made to the General Assembly, but beginning in 1960, with prodding from new members (especially those in the African group), the Security Council periodically joined the General Assembly in debating the issue and passing resolutions. If strong measures were required against South Africa, Council action is preferable to Assembly decision because the Charter is more explicit in granting the power to impose sanctions to the Council than to the Assembly. Furthermore, sanctions imposed by the Council are theoretically binding on all members, and the cooperation of the permanent members is necessary to make sanctions effective.

The race issue in South Africa raises some fundamental questions. Are its racial policies, as South Africa claims, purely a domestic question and, therefore, immune under Article 2 of the Charter from United Nations jurisdiction? Or can the United Nations bring action either on the grounds that South Africa has flagrantly violated its human-rights obligations under the Charter, or on the grounds that South African race policies so affect and offend other states as to constitute a threat to international peace and security? In an interdependent world, where can the line be drawn between sovereign rights and collective prerogative; between domestic matters and international concerns? The position of the parties is irreconcilable, yet each is based on fundamental Charter principles.

Political power in South Africa has been concentrated in the less than one-sixth of the population who are white. Those who are black, Asian, or of mixed blood have been denied access to the economic and social resources by which they could escape from poverty and lack of opportunity. The policies of apartheid required the complete separation of nonwhites from whites in the society except for strictly regulated conditions under which nonwhite labor could be used in the nation's economic enterprises. In the 1960s and 1970s, 13 percent of the land was set aside as African Reserves, or Bantustans, where the blacks could live, but economic necessity and the dearth of resources in the reserves resulted in more than half the blacks living outside the reserves. The whites enjoyed a high standard of living, but the apartheid policies perpetuated the poverty of the nonwhites. Since 1976 South Africa has granted independence to Transkei, Bophuthatswana, Venda, and Ciskei, all of them former reserves; but most nations, at the urging of the Organization of African Unity and both the General Assembly and the Security Council of the United Nations, have refused to recognize the transfer of sovereignty, labeling it a device for denying South African citizenship to millions of blacks.

The Asians in South Africa, as well as the blacks, have been the objects of government discrimination. In a total population of nearly 41 million, Asians number about 1.2 million. India made the first complaint to the General Assembly in 1946 and was joined by Pakistan in 1947 in claiming discrimination against the Asian minority in violation of treaties between the countries and of Charter obligations. A series of General Assembly resolutions requesting South African negotiations with India and with Pakistan were ignored by South Africa, and various individuals and commissions authorized by the Assembly to assist in arranging negotiations were rebuffed by South African refusal to cooperate.

On the broad aspects of apartheid, the General Assembly adopted sweeping resolutions requesting (1) South Africa to modify its policies, (2) member states to take retaliatory action against South Africa, (3) special committees to study the situation and recommend action, (4) the Security Council to use economic sanctions or to consider the expulsion of South Africa from the United Nations, and (5) the specialized agencies to take action by all appropriate means to apply pressure on the South African government to modify its policies. An additional resolution called for the dissemination of information concerning the apartheid policies. In protest over the General Assembly's invasion of what South Africa claimed to be a matter of domestic jurisdiction, that government for three years, beginning in 1955, refused to participate in General Assembly sessions and subsequently refused to attend any committee meetings dealing with the apartheid issue. In a reverse move, the Assembly in 1970, for the first time, questioned the legitimacy of the credentials of the South African delegation to the General Assembly, but on technical grounds the delegates were allowed to participate in spite of this manifestation of disapproval. However, on November 12, 1974, the General Assembly upheld a ruling by its President excluding South Africa from participation in the remainder of its twenty-ninth session.

The Security Council first became involved in the apartheid issue in 1960 after the Sharpeville incident in which nearly 250 black demonstrators against South Africa's "pass laws" were killed or wounded. The passbooks serve as identification and as work and travel permits for blacks. The Security Council, on April 1, 1960, adopted a resolution stating that a continuation of South Africa's racial policies might endanger international peace and security. In 1962 the General Assembly requested member states to (1) break off diplomatic relations with South Africa, (2) close their ports to South African vessels, (3) forbid their ships to enter South African ports, (4) prohibit all imports from or exports to South Africa, especially sales of arms or ammunition to that country, and (5) refuse landing rights to all South African aircraft. Some members of the Security Council were not willing to impose such sweeping sanctions, but in 1963 the Council called on all states to embargo the sale of arms, ammunition, and military vehicles to South Africa, including equipment or materials for arms manufacture in South Africa.

According to a report of the Special Committee on Apartheid submitted to the Security Council in 1970, the arms embargo was not effective. Interpretations, loopholes, and violations resulted in a constant strengthening of South Africa's military capabilities. France was accused of being the main supplier of military goods. France defended its position on the grounds that it sold to South Africa arms only for external defense and not for internal repression. The African nations' response to this argument was that no external threat to South Africa existed. Finally, in 1977 the Security Council secured the cooperation of France, the United Kingdom, and the United States in approving a mandatory arms embargo against South Africa.

Pressure on South Africa has been exerted through several of the United Nations specialized agencies, through the Organization of African Unity (OAU), and through the Conference of Non-Aligned Nations. South Africa has withdrawn from some of the specialized agencies including UNESCO, the Food and Agriculture Organization, and the International Labor Organization. It is no longer a member of the Economic Commission for Africa, a regional commission under the United Nations Economic and Social Council. The OAU has acted as a principal mobilizing force behind United Nations actions against South Africa. However, South African overtures for dialogue with other African leaders have broken the united front of OAU opposition, as several black African heads of state have favored such dialogue.

In 1985 and 1986 the level of violence in South Africa increased. The South African government declared a state of emergency and enacted other restrictive measures and, in August 1986, admitted that it had incarcerated more than 8,000 opponents of government policies.

In February 1986 the United Nations Security Council adopted (with abstentions by the United Kingdom and the United States) a sweeping resolution demanding all of the following: (1) an end to violence against and repression of black people and other opponents of apartheid; (2) release of all imprisoned and detained opponents of apartheid; (3) lifting of the state of emergency; (4) eradication of apartheid and rapid movement toward a democratic regime and society; (5) dismantling of the Bantustan structures and cessation of the relocation of peoples; (6) abrogation of bans and restrictions on political organizations and news media opposed to apartheid; (7) return of all exiles; and (8) cessation of acts of aggression by South Africa against neighboring states. However, just three months earlier a proposed Security Council resolution that would have imposed selective sanctions against South Africa was vetoed by the United States and the United Kingdom with France abstaining.

Beginning in 1989 drastic changes in South Africa presaged the end of apartheid and the sharing of political power. In March the South African Law Commission, a government advisory group including lawyers, judges, scholars, and government officials, urged universal voting rights for all South Africans and the adoption of an extensive bill of civil and political rights for all citizens. At about the same time, the leaders of the white Dutch Reformed Church, the predominant church of those exercising political power, declared that apartheid could not be accepted on Christian ethical grounds. In early 1990 the government lifted its ban on the African National Congress, the leading black group opposing apartheid, and released Nelson Mandela, its recognized leader, who had been imprisoned for more than 27 years. In September 1991 Mandela, South African President F. W. de Klerk, and other political leaders signed a pledge to end civil violence. In December, at a meeting of all major political parties and factions, an agreement was reached to put in motion the process of drawing up a nonracial and democratic new constitution for South Africa. In March 1992 President de Klerk held a referendum in which whites supported ending apartheid by a 2 to 1 margin.

Agreement by all parties on the transitional steps and the constitutional details for a democratic South African government has been a difficult process. One of the obstacles was the antagonism, rivalry, and frequent and severe physical violence between the African National Congress and the Inkatha Freedom Party, a large Zulu-based group, who were accused, on occasion, of collaborating with the white government in opposing radical change. However, by the fall months of 1993 President de Klerk and Nelson Mandela had agreed upon the terms of an interim constitution and a schedule for holding a "one-person-one-vote" election in April 1994. For their devotion to the process of a peaceful transition to majority rule in South Africa they jointly were awarded the 1993 Nobel Peace Prize. The UN General Assembly in October 1993 lifted all previous sanctions against South Africa. At first the Inkatha Freedom Party threatened to boycott the elections, but at a late date reversed that decision. The United Nations sent nearly 2,000 persons composing the UN Observer Mission in South Africa (UNOMSA) to monitor the elections. In the April vote Nelson Mandela received nearly two-thirds of the vote and became President. He formed a coalition cabinet including former President de Klerk and Chief Mangosuthu Buthelezi, head of the Inkatha Freedom Party.

The transition from minority to majority rule in South Africa was surprisingly rapid and relatively peaceful. The constituent assembly elected in April 1994 has the task of writing a permanent constitution for the new government. The larger task of the Mandela-led government is to rapidly improve the living conditions and economic opportunities of the former apartheid victims.

Situation in the Dominican Republic

From 1961 to 1966 the political situation in the Dominican Republic was very unstable. General Trujillo Molina ruled the republic as a dictator from 1930 until his assassination in 1961. After a transition period, Juan Bosch was elected president but served only nine months before being overthrown by a military coup. In April 1965, a rebel group under Colonel Caamano Deno temporarily seized power, only to be ousted four days later by a junta under General Wessin y Wessin, which in turn was replaced after nine days by a regime headed by General Imbert Barreras. The city of Santo Domingo was the main battleground in a civil war between the right-wing forces of General Imbert and the left-wing forces of Colonel Caamano.

On the same day that General Wessin y Wessin attained temporary power, President Johnson ordered United States marines into Santo Domingo. The first reason given for intervention was to protect endangered American lives, but official statements soon added the motive of preventing a Communist government from gaining control in the Dominican Republic. The United States response to the situation was massive; within a few days a force of 24,000 men was sent to the island. The contingent was reduced when, under United States pressure, the Organization of American States (OAS), with several members dissenting, authorized the dispatching to Santo Domingo of an Inter-American Peace Force. However, troops from five other countries made up only approximately one-sixth of this peace force, the balance being United States troops already in the republic.

On April 29, 1965, the United States government informed the United Nations Security Council through the Secretary-General that on the previous day United States forces had been sent to the Dominican Republic to protect American citizens and the OAS had been asked to consider the situation. On May 1 the Soviet Union requested an urgent meeting of the Security Council to consider the question of United States armed interference in the internal affairs of the Dominican Republic. The first series of Security Council meetings was held between May 3 and May 25.

The OAS became involved in the Dominican situation earlier than the United Nations, engaged in a wider range of activities, and provided the main channels by which a political settlement was finally achieved. In addition to the authorization of the Inter-American Peace Force mentioned above, the foreign ministers of the OAS, two days before the first Security Council debates, established and sent to Santo Domingo a commission composed of representatives of Argentina, Brazil, Colombia, Guatemala, and Panama. This commission was charged with responsibilities for facilitating the restoration of peace, seeking a cease-fire, and evacuating endangered persons. Less than three weeks later, after the arrival in Santo Domingo of a United Nations representative and a small United Nations military observer corps, the OAS commission issued a report in which the majority of the commission stated that United Nations intervention in the Dominican situation had obstructed their efforts, and they asked to be relieved of their responsibilities. The OAS foreign ministers on May 20 transferred the responsibilities of the commission to the Secretary-General of the OAS, who was already in the Dominican Republic, and requested that he coordinate his efforts with those of the United Nations representative.

On June 2 the OAS notified the Security Council of the appointment of an ad hoc committee, composed of representatives of Brazil, El Salvador, and the United States, to offer good offices for restoring normal conditions in the Dominican Republic. The Inter-American Commission on Human Rights, at the request of both Dominican contending groups, began activities in the republic in early June and continued its investigations and reports for several months. Its work was supported by the Commission of Criminologists, which investigated atrocity charges. The ad hoc committee was finally successful in bringing about negotiations between the parties, leading to the establishment of a provisional government on September 3 under Hector Garcia-Godoy and to the election on June 1, 1966, of Joaquin Balaguer as President. The last contingents of the Inter-American Peace Force left the Republic on September 20, 1966.

The Dominican question was considered by the Security Council in twenty-eight meetings in May, June, and July 1965. The clash of national interests and opinions was apparent throughout the debates and precluded agreement on strong measures for an effective United Nations role in restoring peace in the Dominican Republic. The representatives of the Soviet Union, France, Jordan, and Uruguay were highly critical of both United States intervention in the republic and the primary role of the OAS as the peace-maintaining agency. Uruguay, which had been one of five OAS members to oppose the creation of the Inter-American Peace Force, accused the United States of violating the principles of the United Nations Charter and Articles 15 and 17 of the Charter of the OAS, which specifically prohibited intervention "directly or indirectly, for any reason whatever, in the internal or external affairs of any other State" or military occupation of the territory of any state. The United States was charged with utilizing the OAS for its own ends and with deploying its military forces in such a way as to bring advantage to the right-wing army under General Imbert.

Although several other members of the Security Council supported the United States contentions that the OAS was the most proficient instrument for restoring peace in the Dominican Republic and that the provisions of the United Nations Charter with regard to the role of regional organization were being adhered to, no agreement was possible for authorizing the OAS to act as the agent of the United Nations in the situation. Because of the split among the members, a series of proposed resolutions failed to gain sufficient support for adoption. The only significant resolution was adopted on May 14 when, by unanimous vote, the Security Council approved a call for a strict cease-fire and authorized the Secretary-General to send a representative to the Dominican Republic to report on the situation. A small group of military observers under General Rikhye was dispatched to the republic on May 15, and two days later Jose Antonio Mayobre, Executive Secretary of the Economic Commission for Latin America, who had been designated as the Secretary-General's representative, arrived in Santo Domingo.

From May 1965 until the installation of the new government in the Dominican Republic in the summer of 1966, the work of Mayobre and his staff represented the main contribution of the United Nations to restoring stable conditions there. He consulted with the leaders of the contending factions and with agents of the OAS and others in the Dominican Republic and, through the Secretary-General, kept the Security Council fully informed of the day-to-day situation and new developments in the republic. After June 18, 1965, in spite of sporadic incidents, the cease-fire remained generally effective. Although Mayobre and the Secretary-General continued to report to the Security Council, the Council held no meetings on the Dominican question after July 26, 1965.

The Dominican situation demonstrates the impotency of the United Nations in coercing a major power. Although, by any reasonable interpretation, the United States was guilty of violating Articles 15 and 17 of the OAS Charter and the principles of territorial integrity and political independence guaranteed in the United Nations Charter, it was able to gain the acquiescence of a majority of OAS members for a set of policies substantially supporting its position and actions. Although the United States scrupulously complied with the provisions of Article 54 of the United Nations Charter to keep the Security Council informed of its own and OAS actions, the equally clear mandate of Article 53 that "no enforcement action shall be taken under regional arrangements or by regional agencies without the authorization of the Security Council" was violated. Proposals by the United States for Security

Council approval of OAS actions were unacceptable to other Council members. The United States overreacted both to the threat to American lives and to the possibility of a Communist takeover in the Dominican Republic and lost credibility and prestige in pressuring OAS members for support.

The United Nations and the OAS found themselves as uncomfortable partners in the Dominican situation. The United Nations representative acted mainly as observer and reporter to furnish objective assessments of the situation and the sources of fault in each major incident. The OAS ad hoc committee was an important force in bringing the opposing factions together to work out a permanent settlement. The United States military forces were not used impartially but, at times, acted as a buffer between opposing factions.

No one can accurately predict what internal political developments would have transpired if the Dominican crisis had been treated strictly as a domestic question. It may, however, be asserted that the United Nations, the OAS, and the United States all lost prestige as a result of the episode.

Situation Concerning Western Sahara

In 1975 Spain relinquished its claim to Spanish Sahara in northwest Africa and in early 1976 the territory, since known as Western Sahara, was divided between Morocco and Mauritania, with Morocco receiving about two-thirds of the area. At the same time the Polisario Front, backed by Algeria and Libya, proclaimed the independence of the territory under principles of self-determination. The chief economic asset of the area is rich phosphate deposits.

For a time the Polisario guerrillas were fighting in a three-way war involving both Morocco and Mauritania, but in 1978 the Mauritanian government agreed to a cease-fire with the Polisario, and the following year withdrew from Western Sahara in favor of Polisario claims to legitimacy there. Since that time the Polisario forces have enjoyed sanctuary in Algeria and Mauritania in addition to their control of desert areas within Western Sahara.

In one form or another the question of the status of this territory has been reviewed by the General Assembly each year since 1964. While it was a colony of Spain, the Assembly pressured Spain to grant early independence to Spanish Sahara. The Assembly's main instrument was its special committee created to monitor progress toward independence in compliance with its sweeping resolution of 1960 entitled Declaration on the Granting of Independence to Colonial Countries and Peoples. After 1974 this same declaration continued as a major basis for pressure on Morocco and other interested parties to implement the holding of a general and free self-determination referendum in Western Sahara. An advisory opinion of the International Court of Justice in 1975 supported the Assembly position by declaring that neither Morocco nor Mauritania had any legitimate prior claims to sovereignty over the territory. Therefore, the principle of self-determination should be applied and implemented.

The Security Council and the Organization of African Unity (OAU) have also been involved in the Western Sahara controversy. Security Council involvement was quite limited prior to 1988, when it authorized the Secretary-General to proceed, in cooperation with the OAU, with a plan envisioned as leading to a final settlement of the problem.

For the OAU the issue, for several years, was so divisive as to threaten the organization's continued viability. After the OAU seated a Polisario delegation in 1982, more than one-third of the member governments threatened to boycott meetings or withdraw from membership. In 1984, when the Polisario representatives resumed a seat at the twentieth OAU summit, Morocco withdrew from membership and Zaire suspended participation in the organization. The following year Morocco declared that it would negotiate only with Algeria, not the Polisario, and that the United Nations, not the OAU, was the appropriate body to act as an agent for a settlement.

During more than ten years of fighting, the superpowers supported opposing parties in the Western Sahara dispute. The Polisario used Soviet weapons, and Morocco received arms or other backing from the United States, France, and Saudi Arabia. Within Africa, Tunisia and Egypt were among the leading proponents of the Moroccan claims in opposition to Algerian and Libyan leadership of the majority of the OAU who favored the Polisario.

By 1988, all the immediate parties to the dispute were weary of war and anxious to relieve the military financial burdens upon their economies. In May, Morocco and Algeria, after thirteen years, resumed diplomatic relations. By August, the Secretary-General and the Chairman of the OAU, acting jointly under the auspices of the General Assembly, had induced the representatives of Morocco and the Polisario to negotiate the details of a peace plan. The plan included a cease-fire, a referendum for self-determination of the Western Saharan inhabitants, and the services of a United Nations representative aided by UN observers in implementing the steps leading to establishment of a governmental structure for the area. In September, the Security Council approved the procedure. In June 1990 the Security Council endorsed a more detailed set of proposals and a timetable for the holding of the referendum. This resolution also provided for the creation of a UN Mission for the Referendum in Western Sahara, identified by the French acronym MINURSO. MINURSO was to be composed of civilian, military, and security units under the direction of the Secretary-General's Special Representative. The referendum would determine either independence for the territory or integration with Morocco. In addition to supervising the cease-fire and the referendum, MINURSO would, after the referendum, monitor either the withdrawal of Moroccan troops or the demobilization of Polisario troops, depending on referendum results. In April 1991 the Security Council authorized an eventual strength for MINURSO of nearly 2,900 personnel, but less than 500 had been dispatched to Western Sahara by mid-1993 and were limited to supervision of the cease-fire. Plans for the referendum date were repeatedly delayed because of disagreements over identifying eligible voters. Other obstacles involved organizational details for the referendum and safeguards for various groups affected by the referendum results.

In the United Nations for nearly 14 years the General Assembly was the major forum for the dispute. In turn, the Assembly urged the OAU to act as the principal intermediary in seeking a solution. When the parties became more amenable to a peaceful settlement, the Secretary-General's role, in cooperation with the OAU, became paramount. He personally engaged in extensive negotiations leading to the acceptance of a peace plan. Since major power support for a settlement is desirable, the late involvement of the Security Council is important in securing a successful outcome. A further UN contribution to the process is the use of a special representative assisted by a team of impartial UN observers. The flexibility of the entire process and cooperation between the UN and the OAU are factors facilitating the eventual settlement of a long and bitter dispute.

CHANGING ROLES OF UNITED NATIONS ORGANS

There is little question that the General Assembly has played a larger role in the processes of peaceful settlement of disputes than would have been predicted in 1945. The big powers, who dominated the determination of the basic formulas for the new organization in Dumbarton Oaks and San Francisco, tried to establish the preeminent position of the Security Council in handling disputes. They looked upon the Security Council as an organ designed to perform this one paramount function. They attempted to secure the superior position of the Council over the Assembly by conferring upon the Council "primary responsibility for the maintenance of international peace and security," by making Council decisions legally binding on all members, and by prohibiting the General Assembly from making recommendations on any dispute or situation while the matter is under Security Council consideration. By a number of devices the General Assembly has extended its involvement into this Security Council domain. These devices include generous interpretations of Assembly powers and functions as stated in the Charter and the adoption of special expedients such as an Interim Committee and the Uniting for Peace Resolution. The Uniting for Peace Resolution has served as a basis for calling nine *emergency* special sessions of the General Assembly, each of which dealt with a dispute that the Security Council was unable to resolve. In addition, five of the eighteen General Assembly special sessions called under the regular Charter provisions for such sessions were also concerned with disputes or situations that could possibly threaten international peace and security.

An examination of the table of disputes and a review of the case studies in the preceding section of this chapter can serve as evidence of the degree of General Assembly involvement in the processes of pacific settlement of disputes. Almost 19 percent of all disputes submitted to the United Nations have been dealt with solely by the General Assembly. Another 23 percent have been considered by both the Security Council and the General Assembly. Thus, the General Assembly has been involved in nearly 42 percent of the disputes investigated by the United Nations. Among the six case studies presented in this chapter, the General Assembly exclusively handled the disposition of the Italian colonies and shared with the Security Council the responsibilities for dealing with two other problems—race conflict in South Africa and the Western Sahara dispute.

At the same time, the General Assembly has not superseded the Security Council as the primary agency for considering disputes. Nearly three-fifths of all disputes on the agendas of the United Nations organs have been handled exclusively by the Security Council. When to this list is added the group of cases in which both the Security Council and General Assembly have been involved, the result is that the Security Council has exercised total or shared responsibility for more than 80 percent of all disputes considered.

Predictions in the 1950s that the General Assembly might become the predominant agency for dispute settlement have been proved wrong. In the period when the Cold War was most intense, when the Security Council was most plagued by vetoes and stalemates, and when the General Assembly had lost any inhibitions about encroaching upon Security Council prerogatives and had equipped itself to hold emergency sessions on twenty-four-hour notice, there was some basis for predicting the atrophy of the Security Council. When, in 1959, the Council held but five meetings in twelve months, the trend seemed clear to some persons. Since 1960 the activity of the Security Council in disputes has again accelerated as states have submitted a majority of their complaints first or exclusively to the Council. Since 1970, more than 90 percent of all disputes have been referred to the Security Council.

The reasons for the revival of Security Council activity are many. The Council has always been better equipped than the Assembly to handle disputes, by virtue of size, organization, availability, locus of world power, and authority granted by the Charter. The big powers have always shared a common interest in focusing activity in an organ that is more subject than the Assembly to their control and in which the veto can serve as the ultimate protection of national interests. After 1960, more restraint in the use of the veto, an increase in the use of abstentions, an increase in consultation among Council members, and the frequent use of consensus voting without roll calls all contributed to the ability of the Security Council to reach decisions and avoid stalemate. The end of the Cold War in the 1980s was marked by an even greater energizing of Security Council effectiveness.

A tacit division of labor exists between the Security Council and the General Assembly with regard to consideration of disputes. New disputes, especially of a crisis nature, are generally referred to the Security Council. If a dispute is unresolved and becomes a perennial problem, the General Assembly frequently becomes involved. Exceptions occur but, since 1960, examples of cases submitted solely to the General Assembly are scarce. Even regarding the persistent questions that claim the prolonged attention of both organs, some specialization occurs. Within the broad dimensions of a complex situation, new outbreaks or crises demanding immediate attention will generally be referred to the Security Council, whereas the General Assembly will consider those aspects that allow prolonged study and deliberation. The General Assembly stands ready to deal both with emergencies and the less-urgent aspects of disputes if the Security Council is deadlocked.

The expanded role of the Secretary-General in dispute settlement has been noted at some points in this chapter and will be reinforced in subsequent chapters, but this growing importance should be emphasized in discussing the changing roles of United Nations organs. The case studies in this chapter demonstrate some of the multiple and invaluable functions performed by the Secretary-General in direct negotiation, appointment of representatives or mediators, and furnishing of full, prompt, and accurate information to the Council and the Assembly. In the following chapter his role in the recruitment, deployment, and direction of peacekeeping forces will be explained and illustrated. The Secretary-General and his staff must be not only efficient but also patient, tactful, and impartial in dealing with disputing parties and with members of the Council or the Assembly. The Council or the Assembly may determine broad policy, but the responsibility for implementation falls on the Secretariat. In many cases the critical details of implementation demand a wide range of additional decisions and leave room for initiative by the Secretary-General and his assistants. The history of dispute settlement in the United Nations amply demonstrates that the Secretariat has played a much more important role in this area than did its predecessor in the League of Nations, as well as a more crucial role than was indicated by the specific provisions of the United Nations Charter.

The Secretary-General has also prevented some disputes from being submitted to the Council or the Assembly by arranging for settlement through his good offices when the disputing parties cooperated in such action. On two occasions in 1958–59 and in 1962–64, the Secretary-General, at the invitation of Cambodia and Thailand, sent his personal representative and a small staff to those countries to assist in settling mutual charges of acts of aggression and border disputes. The second mission was invited to stay for two years, with all costs met equally by the two governments. The Secretary-General reported his actions to the Security Council, but no request was ever made for Security Council consideration of the issue. In 1969 the Secretary-General was requested to send a representative to Equatorial Guinea to assure the orderly withdrawal of Spanish military forces and to prevent hostile acts on both sides. Both parties were cooperative, and the representative reported satisfactory conditions in effecting the withdrawal. However, in this instance and again in regard to the appointment in 1970 of a representative to settle the future status of Bahrain, the Soviet representative protested that the Secretary-General was invading the prerogatives of the Security Council. The Secretary-General pointed out that the parties to the disputes sought his assistance for peaceful settlement prior to the necessity for submitting the dispute to the Security Council and that this procedure is in full compliance with the admonition of Article 33 of the Charter: "The parties to any dispute . . . shall, first of all, seek a solution by . . . peaceful means of their own choice." Since the disputes between Cambodia and Thailand and between Equatorial Guinea and Spain were never submitted to the Security Council or the General Assembly, they are omitted from the table of cases in this chapter.

GENERAL APPRAISAL AND FUTURE REQUIREMENTS

The record of the United Nations in the area of pacific settlement of disputes leaves much to be desired. Many controversies develop that are not submitted to the United Nations but are handled through other means. This reluctance to use United Nations channels may result as much from a desire by the parties to maintain their freedom of action as it does from a lack of confidence in United Nations processes. Patterns of national behavior stemming from deeply ingrained feelings of nationalism and sovereign rights stand as bulwarks against the use of international channels for conflict resolution. The forces of nationalism and sovereignty also prevented the establishment, in the first place, of an organization with independent sources of power sufficient to impose solutions upon reluctant minorities. The ability to resist international coercion is abundantly demonstrated by the substantial number of unresolved issues that remain on the agendas of United Nations organs for prolonged periods of time. Weak proposals for responding to threats to peace are also a negative element in the United Nations record and result from the absence of adequate means of enforcement and the necessity to compromise among competing national interests.

In the light of its inherent weaknesses, the record of the United Nations in conflict resolution is surprisingly encouraging. Of more than 200 disputes considered by the Council and the Assembly, approximately 10 percent remain as persistent long-range problems defying final solution. Some have been resolved by action of the parties after United Nations debate, but in others the Security Council, the General Assembly, and the Secretariat have made positive contributions to the final settlement. This success has been due, in part, to the pragmatism and flexibility of the organs in not being unduly hampered by narrow interpretations of grants of authority and in seeking a variety of means for conflict resolution peculiarly adapted to the circumstances of each dispute. Every established device, plus a few innovations and variations on these devices, has been applied to the controversies considered by United Nations organs. Cease-fires and observer missions have been effective in many circumstances in lessening hostilities. The use of peacekeeping forces will be examined more fully in Chapter 7. In prolonged disputes the influence of the United Nations has generally been exerted to prevent escalation or to stabilize the situation at a minimum level of conflict. The substantial number of disputes submitted to the United Nations reflects a need that is fulfilled by the existence of such an organization and a willingness on the part of some of the parties to rely on United Nations contributions to seeking solutions to the problems. Small states have been especially willing to request United Nations aid in conflict resolution.

As the world entered the 1980s, not only was there a rash of serious conflicts but states turned to the United Nations as one means for seeking to lessen the threats to global peace. In rapid succession the questions relating to (1) United States hostages in Iran, (2) the situation in Kampuchea, (3) the Soviet invasion of Afghanistan, (4) war between Iran and Iraq, (5) the Israeli attack on the Iraqi reactor, (6) Israel's annexation of the Golan Heights, (7) the situation in Central America, (8) the Falklands/Malvinas dispute, (9) the Israeli invasion of Lebanon, (10) the Gulf war, (11) Somalia, and (12) Yugoslavia were all referred to the Security Council or the General Assembly or both for debate with the hope of containing or resolving the conflicts.

Regional organizations have played a relatively modest role in dispute settlement. Since 1945 the OAS has assisted in settling several disputes not submitted to the United Nations, but has not been utilized by the Security Council in the manner envisioned in Chapter VIII of the United Nations Charter. Other regional organizations have not achieved notable success in dispute settlement. In the Dominican affair, cooperation between the United Nations representatives and those of the OAS was sometimes grudging and uncomfortable and at other times nonexistent. The dominant influence of a big power may either neutralize a regional organization's capacity for impartial conciliation in a dispute or serve as a lever for settlement if the major power's chief interest is in peace and stability between disputants.

While the availability and the flexibility of United Nations agencies have made major contributions to the positive accomplishments of the organization in dispute settlement or control, the attitudes and the policies of the members are the most critical factors. In a world of sovereign states, which are the final repositories of power, the behavior of those states will determine the spread or containment of conflict. States may defy international pressures, as in the case of South Africa, or they may be willing to seek accommodation through negotiation or the United Nations, or they may work for the strengthening of international means for assuring world order. As contacts multiply among nations, the number of conflicts may proportionately increase.

The end of bipolar suspicion and hostility has diminished the fear of nuclear holocaust but has shifted the theater of serious conflicts to regional and internal arenas. In the peacemaking area, Mikhail Gorbachev and Boris Yeltsin have suggested an agenda for a comprehensive United Nations global security system, including an enlarged role for UN peacekeeping forces, the rejuvenation of the moribund Military Staff Committee, the strengthening of the utility of the International Court of Justice, and the enhancing of the mediating functions of the Secretary-General. Support for some of these measures has been echoed in official and nongovernmental circles, but conservative forces in many states will retard progress toward a significant overhaul of the UN security system. The costs and dangers of conflict should dictate a high priority for a more effective peace-maintenance and settlement process. The range and intensity of threats to peace have not diminished in the 1990s. The dividends in terms of human welfare of preventing, containing, and reducing the use of violence in civil, regional, and global conflicts are vast. The United Nations is the logical, existing agency to be utilized as the instrument for a strengthened system of conflict resolution.

7

COLLECTIVE SECURITY AND ITS ALTERNATIVES
Theory and Practice

There are at least six methods of attempting to settle international disputes. They are (1) no action taken by the disputing parties, allowing the dispute to remain unsettled over a period of time; (2) settlement through the parties' own initiative, using negotiation or other peaceful means of their choice; (3) intervention by an international agency to facilitate peaceful settlement; (4) collective action by an international agency to restore order after international peace has been breached or threatened; (5) coercive self-help, including recourse to war between the parties; and (6) intervention by other states to promote or secure their own interests. A principal reason for founding the League of Nations and the United Nations was to eliminate, as far as possible, the recourse to war. Members of both these organizations also were encouraged to seek by themselves peaceful settlement of disputes through other channels. Chapter 6 investigated the role of international organizations in peaceful settlement. This chapter will explore their role in more serious situations, in which disputes have progressed to actual or imminent hostilities. Implicit here is the question of what can or should an international organization do when peaceful settlement has failed or is avoided?

THE NATURE OF COLLECTIVE SECURITY

The theory of collective security is not unique to the twentieth century. Some scholars credit certain aspects of the Amphictyonic Council of ancient Greece and the Truce of God of the Middle Ages as limited collective-security systems. Several philosophers discussed in Chapter 1 advocated means of controlling conflict that might reasonably be labeled collective-security measures. Nevertheless, the first attempt to adapt the vague concepts of collective security to a worldwide system for preventing war was the establishment of the League of Nations in 1919.

The proponents of collective security viewed it as a method of controlling war in a world of sovereign states. Experience had brought disillusionment with the capability of a balance-of-power system to maintain peace. The world was not ready to surrender enough national sovereignty to make possible the establishment of a world government, even one with limited powers. The idea of collective security seemed to provide the bridge between the crumbling world of past centuries and the kind of ideal world yet to be created.

The theory of collective security rests on the assumption that all nations share a primary interest in maintaining peace. For collective security to operate, peace must be viewed as indivisible, and threats to peace anywhere must be treated as the concern of all members of the international system. Furthermore, all members must agree in advance to react promptly and effectively against threats to peace and must be organized in such a way as to provide the procedures for collective response to such threats, even if the collective action is directed against members with which they are friendly. The aggressor nation will be faced with such overwhelming opposition from all other members of the system that peace will be promptly restored. In fact, the promise of preponderant opposition will usually dissuade incipient aggressors from their inclinations toward breaches of international peace.

Although collective-security theory, in the abstract, sounds plausible, several basic conditions are required for its effective application. The first is a commitment on the part of all members of the international system to peace as a paramount goal requiring the subordination of other goals of foreign policy. If, in practice, collective security is to succeed, each state must commit itself to act in concert with other states as a party interested more in peace restoration than in other national interests or in relationships with the state accused of threatening international peace. A second condition is the ability of the members of a system not only to reach initial consensus for establishing the system, but also to find a consensus in each situation that a threat to peace or a breach of peace does or does not exist. Furthermore, their consensus must extend to the identification of the aggressor state or states against whom collective action is required. Once an aggressor is identified, a collective determination must be made of an appropriate response to apply prompt and effective sanctions against the aggressor for the purpose of stopping the aggressive acts.

A collective-security system will work best if power is widely dispersed. Since the theory requires the possible application of preponderant force against an aggressor, the presence of a very powerful state capable of defying the collectivity reduces the odds for effective action against any and all aggressors.

The ideal collective-security system requires a membership approaching universality. Several reasons for this requirement are obvious. The consensus on peace as a primary goal is reduced to the degree that states exist outside the system. Challenges to the system are less likely from parties committed to all the conditions underlying the system. Impartial decisions can be better guaranteed if all parties can be heard and all relevant evidence examined. Limited membership also restricts the amount of resources available for sanctions against an aggressor and increases the liability of each member for contributions to an effective response. In addition, in an organization of limited membership, the capability of one state to defy the collectivity is enhanced. A powerful state may be immune from the threat of sanctions in a relatively small organization but may respond to pressure when faced with the possibility of preponderant force against it.

Many scholars accept certain regional organizations as collective-security organizations in some of their functions. To qualify as collective-security organizations, they must incorporate the conditions of consensus and commitment to peace and collective response that are fundamental to collective security theory. They must include in their membership most of the states in their region. The collective-security aspects of their terms of agreement are directed against threats from within the region rather than from outside the region. However, the arguments presented above for universality in a collective-security arrangement indicate the possible advantages of a worldwide system.

The term *collective security* has been so distorted from its classical meaning as to jeopardize its precision as a theory of international relations. On occasion it is loosely applied to any arrangement for collective defense against potential enemies outside as well as inside the membership of the collectivity. Such a perversion of meaning disregards some of the essential conditions of collective-security theory and fails to distinguish collective security from the alliance system, which it was designed to replace.

Collective security should be clearly differentiated from collective defense. Collective-defense arrangements, such as NATO, involve alliances for mutual protection against outside attack. The appropriate response to such an attack is war against an enemy, not the restoration of peace through appropriate measured responses. Several collective-defense arrangements will be examined in Chapter 10.

Collective security may be internally consistent as a theory for world order but impractical and faulty in its acceptance and application by sovereign states bent on protecting national interests and suspicious of the motives of other states. In practice, the consensus on peace as a primary goal, which is the basis for collective security, may conflict with other national interests demanding equal or greater priority. Complex forces influence each state in a given situation to diminish that state's commitment to the impartial application of sanctions against an aggressor nation.

The theory of collective security assumes that a situation can be agreed upon demanding collective action and that an aggressor can be identified. However, evidence is seldom clear either that a threat to peace or a breach of peace has occurred or that a particular state has committed the aggressive act. Aggression is difficult to define. This difficulty leaves the determination of aggression in each situation to the subjective and perhaps biased collective judgment of the members of the organization. The determination that a threat to peace or a breach of peace has occurred and demands international action is equally complex and difficult. At what point does a threat assume proportions or characteristics that justify international intervention? Where can a line be drawn or a set of rules established to distinguish between domestic matters and matters of international concern? In answering such questions the subjective judgment of the members of the collective-security organization must again be substituted for objective standards. Such judgments are influenced not only by national interpretation of conflicting evidence and by economic and political ties to the disputing parties, but also by the reluctance of a state to participate in a collective action if there is little promise of advantage to that state from such participation.

Collective security demands a singleness of purpose and devotion to the principle of peace maintenance that states show little evidence of accepting today. Even if the other difficulties of applying collective-security principles could be overcome, the selfish and competitive aspect of international relations would present a major obstacle to success. States are not equally willing and able to participate in collective action against aggression anywhere in the world. National goals, values, and interests and international commitments compete with the demands of collective security for action against aggression. National security takes precedence over collective security. Cultural and traditional ties, trade and investment, military alliances, and ideology are balanced against a general commitment to world peace. Costs and convenience of collective action also enter the calculus of national decisions.

If a common commitment to maintaining peace by prompt, effective, collective action could be guaranteed, there is little doubt that aggressive action by a single state could be checked and, in most cases, deterred. If power is sufficiently dispersed, the threat of massive sanctions would be effective against both large and small states. No state could hope to defy the united will and effort of all other states acting in concert. Faced with such odds, the would-be aggressor, under rational leadership, would avoid the penalties resulting from being subjected to sanctions.

Although certain parts of the theory of collective security are valid, the faults inherent both in some of its basic assumptions and in the reluctance of states to adopt and apply all its principles impair its effectiveness as a keystone for present-day international organization. As some scholars have pointed out, if the world situation were conducive to the success of a system of collective security, we would also be ready for world government.[1] National leaders are not yet prepared to put a common human interest ahead of a host of national interests.

THE LEAGUE OF NATIONS AND COLLECTIVE SECURITY

Woodrow Wilson was firmly committed to the proposition that collective security would stop or forestall wars, and he guided the efforts to incorporate a collective-security formula into the League of Nations Covenant. Article 10 of the Covenant stated that:

> The Members of the League undertake to respect and preserve as against external aggression the territorial integrity and existing political independence of all Members of the League.

The principle of common concern was added to the formula in Article 11 through the declaration that:

> Any war or threat of war, whether immediately affecting any of the Members of the League or not, is hereby declared a matter of concern to the whole League, and the League shall take any action that may be deemed wise and effectual to safeguard the peace of nations.

To provide "teeth" to enforce the general principles of collective security, Article 16 provided for sanctions.

> Should any Member of the League resort to war in disregard of its covenants under Articles 12, 13, or 15 [which outlined procedures for peaceful settlement of disputes], it shall, *ipso facto*, be deemed to have committed an act of war against all other Members of the League, which hereby undertake immediately to subject it to the severance of all trade or financial relations, the prohibition of all intercourse between their nationals and the nationals of the Covenant-breaking State, and the prevention of all financial, commercial or personal inter-

---

[1]See, for example, Inis L. Claude Jr., *Swords into Plowshares: The Problems and Progress of International Organization*, 4th ed. (New York: Random House, 1971), p. 256.

course between the nationals of the Covenant-breaking State and the nationals of any other State, whether a Member of the League or not.

Note that the economic sanctions of the Covenant were intended to be *total* and *automatic.* If military sanctions were required, a further provision of Article 16 obligated the Council to make recommendations to the members concerning their contributions to such forces. Article 17 provided that collective actions could also be taken against nonmembers of the League.

The experience of the League reveals a reluctance by the members to adhere to the collective-security obligations of the Covenant. Instead of total and automatic application of economic sanctions, the obligations were treated as selective and voluntary for each member in each situation. In 1921 the Assembly adopted resolutions that declared that for each state the application of economic sanctions under Article 16 was optional, not mandatory. Loopholes were discovered in the Covenant formula for collective security and taken advantage of to avoid inconvenient enforcement obligations.

League members failed every test in the 1930s to apply effective sanctions against aggressor nations. In 1931 the Japanese invaded Manchuria, and the League response was a belated investigation after Japanese occupation was completed. The resulting report suggested no more effective measures than nonrecognition of the territorial changes that had occurred.

In 1935–36 economic sanctions were actually imposed against Italy after its attack on Ethiopia. Fifty League members agreed to an embargo on arms and on financial aid to Italy and a ban on imports from Italy. Although these measures seriously affected the Italian economy, they did not encompass the most critical sanctions of an embargo on oil, or a blockade of Italian ports, or a denial of access to the sea routes, especially the Suez Canal, through which Italy was able to move and supply its invasion forces. The United States continued to trade with Italy except for arms. The League discontinued its economic sanctions in the summer of 1936 at a time when Italy's economic health was at a critical stage. The opportunity to prove the effectiveness of economic sanctions was missed because of inadequate measures applied for too short a time span. Behind the failure of methods was a failure of national will on the part of League members and nonmembers.

No sanctions were imposed on Germany in Hitler's series of aggressive acts. In 1936 German forces reoccupied the Rhineland in violation of both the Treaty of Versailles and the Locarno Pact. In 1938 Germany further expanded its territory at the expense of Austria and Czechoslovakia. Germany had withdrawn from League membership, and the League seemed paralyzed in the face of spreading aggression.

In 1937 Japan began its further conquest of Chinese territory. Both the League Council and the Assembly reacted to condemn the Japanese action, and the Council invoked Article 16 of the Covenant, but no widespread sanctions were imposed.

In December 1939, the League Council made one last futile gesture in the direction of sanctions by expelling the Soviet Union from the League. The expulsion was prompted by the Soviet invasion of Finland and was ironic for several reasons. This was the only expulsion of a member in the history of the League, in spite of similar patterns of aggression by other states. The League action to expel the Soviet Union came after the beginning of World War II and after the League had been abandoned by numerous states, leaving only a hollow shell in which all confidence had been lost. The condemnation of the Soviet Union had no effect on the course of events, whereas if strong measures had been adopted and enforced in earlier cases of aggression, the chances for success would have been somewhat greater. All opportunities to test the validity of League sanctions as a means to stop aggression had been lost.

CHARTER PROVISIONS AND REALITIES

The architects of the United Nations Charter attempted to distinguish clearly between the functions of peaceful settlement of disputes and of collective security by placing each in a separate chapter of the Charter. Chapter VI of the Charter is entitled "Pacific Settlement of Disputes"; Chapter VII is labeled "Action with Respect to Threats to the Peace, Breaches of the Peace, and Acts of Aggression." All specific references to sanctions are contained in Chapter VII, but the Security Council has maintained flexibility and has avoided legal restraints by dealing with most situations without reference to any particular Charter provision. In this way the distinction between peaceful settlement and collective action has become blurred, and a new process not specifically described in the Charter has evolved in United Nations practice. This process is referred to as *peacekeeping* and will be further explored in subsequent sections of this chapter.

The Charter provisions for sanctions may be viewed in some respects as improvements over and in other respects as retrogressions from the corresponding Covenant terms. No automatic sanctions are mandated. United Nations members are legally obligated under Article 25 of the Charter to accept and carry out Security Council decisions under any section of the Charter. If the Security Council invokes Article 39, it then shall determine that a threat to the peace, breach of the peace, or act of aggression exists and shall decide on a course of action to maintain or restore peace. Article 40 allows the Security Council to take interim or provisional measures. Article 41 outlines the provisions for applying economic, communicatory, and diplomatic sanctions. Article 42 authorizes the Security Council to call for military sanctions. Other articles in Chapter VII foresee supplementary treaty agreements to provide, for immediate use at the call of the Security Council, national military contingents for United Nations enforcement action; specify the functions of a Military Staff Committee to assist the Security Council; and guarantee the right of individual or collective self-defense until the Security Council has acted. In Chapter VII of the Charter the possible role of the General Assembly is not mentioned, showing the original intention to make the invoking of sanctions the exclusive prerogative of the Security Council.

All the major shortcomings of collective-security theory apply as much to the United Nations provisions for invoking sanctions as they did to the League provisions. Before sanctions can be applied, there must be (1) an agreement that an aggression or threat to peace exists, (2) the identification of the guilty party, and (3) unanimity or acquiescence among all permanent members of the Security Council that action is warranted. States maintain all the means to impose sanctions and are reluctant to take coercive actions against allies, trading partners, or states with whom they share cultural or ideological affinities or friendly relations. Every state is not equally interested in maintaining peace or resisting violent change. Because of cleavages among the permanent members of the Security Council, a coincidence of interests, necessary for prompt and effective application of sanctions, infrequently occurs. National interests of the powerful states take precedence over international obligations to support the principle of the indivisibility of peace.

The "teeth" that were lacking in League enforcement were supposed to be furnished under the terms of Article 43 of the Charter. That article provides for prompt negotiation of agreements by which United Nations members will make available on the call of the Security Council "armed forces, assistance, and facilities" for use in applying military sanctions. Depending upon the terms of the subsequent agreements, either a standing international force or standby contingents of national forces subject to immediate Security Council call will be created. The Military Staff Committee, representing the chiefs of staff of the permanent members of the Security Council, is to advise the Council on the implementation of Article 43 and to direct any armed forces called into United Nations service. However, the members were able to agree on only two major principles: (1) that most forces should be furnished by the big powers, and (2) that any forces should remain under national jurisdiction until summoned for specific duty by the Security Council. On all other principles and details there was total stalemate. No agreements could be reached on the size of standby forces, the allocation of quotas to individual members, or the types of forces to be furnished by each state. Because of the suspicions and intransigence of the major powers, Article 43 has become dormant, and the anticipated international forces available for military action against aggressors have never materialized.

One major problem in applying collective-security theory is the identification of aggressors and acts of aggression. One possible approach is to develop a comprehensive definition of aggression that can act as a standard and be applied to each situation as it arises. The alternative approach is to determine for each situation, by vote of an authorized agency and on the basis of the total body of available evidence, whether a state is guilty of aggression. In the absence of objective standards such an approach is necessary and, according to some authorities, is the preferred method of dealing with the problem of aggression. Those who oppose the adoption of a definition of aggression argue that a formula can never be comprehensive or will be too inflexible, and that the application of a formula cannot give proper weight to provocation and various forms of subversion and propaganda in a variety of complex situations.

United Nations efforts to define aggression were initiated in San Francisco in 1945. Subsequently, the question received study by the International Law Commission and was then assigned by the General Assembly to a series of special committees. Finally, in 1974, the last of these special committees agreed on a rather general definition limited to the use of armed force. This definition was approved by the General Assembly as a guide to the Security Council in determining the existence of acts of aggression. Whether the adoption of such legal criteria will actually influence political decisions of this nature is problematical.

Although the Security Council was intended as the exclusive agent to apply sanctions under Chapter VII of the Charter, the General Assembly has invaded this field and the closely related areas of dispute settlement and peacekeeping. The Security Council is frequently immobilized, by disagreement among its permanent members, in taking action in response to threats to or breaches of international peace. Only the accident of Soviet absence, in pique over the Chinese-representation issue, allowed the Security Council, in 1950, to authorize collective action in Korea. The return of the Soviet representative to the Council table on August 1, 1950, precluded any further agreement on the basic issues in Korea. At the initiative of the United States, the General Assembly proceeded at its next session to add specific means of dealing with breaches of the peace to its general grants of authority in the Charter, such as its power in Article 10 to "discuss any questions or any matters within the scope of the present Charter."

The specific instrument for enlarging the General Assembly's realm of concern and action is the Uniting for Peace Resolution adopted on November 3, 1950. The most important provision of the resolution is the agreement for calling an emergency special session of the General Assembly within twenty-four hours whenever the Security Council is deadlocked and "fails to exercise its primary responsibility for the maintenance of international peace and security in any case where there appears to be a threat to the peace, breach of the peace, or act of aggression." Emergency sessions of the Assembly can be called by any nine (previously seven) members of the Security Council or by a majority of United Nations members. The resolution also requests member states to designate and train armed-forces units for United Nations service on the call of either the Security Council or the General

Assembly. This provision is an attempt to plug the gap left by the nonimplementation of Article 43. To further assist the General Assembly in carrying out its expanded functions, the resolution established a Peace Observation Commission and a Collective Measures Committee, both of which lapsed into inactivity after performing brief useful functions in support of the general purposes of the Uniting for Peace Resolution.

The General Assembly has never called for collective military sanctions of the type envisaged in the Uniting for Peace Resolution, but it has been involved in many other actions in the field of peace and security. It has authorized peacekeeping forces in the Middle East and has branded the people's Republic of China as an aggressor in Korea. Nine emergency special sessions of the Assembly have dealt with important aspects of disputes when the Security Council was deadlocked. The adoption of the Uniting for Peace Resolution clearly expanded the General Assembly's potential role to cover all the areas of competency in the area of collective security established for the Security Council in Article 39. The Assembly can now substantially accomplish by a two-thirds vote what the Council can achieve by unanimity of the permanent members and a total of nine affirmative votes. The one remaining difference is that the Assembly can only recommend action while Council decisions are supposedly binding on all members. However, in a world in which states are jealous of their freedom of action, this difference is more apparent than real.

Prior to 1990 the use of sanctions in the practice of the United Nations was very limited and singularly ineffective. During this period the lack of specific reference, in most cases, to Chapter VII of the Charter permitted each state freedom of action in deciding whether or not to comply. Economic sanctions under Article 41 were invoked only twice. In 1966 the Security Council applied partial economic sanctions against Southern Rhodesia, and in 1968 extended them to comprehensive sanctions. The sanctions had little effect upon the white-dominated Ian Smith regime because of the noncooperation of South Africa and Portugal. In 1977 the Security Council also adopted a mandatory arms embargo against South Africa.

In a few cases the Security Council or the General Assembly has adopted a resolution calling for sanctions without designating the action as falling under Chapter VII of the Charter. Under these conditions, states have treated compliance with the resolution as voluntary. In 1946 the General Assembly requested United Nations members to break diplomatic ties with the Franco government in Spain and recommended that Spain be barred from membership in the specialized agencies affiliated with the United Nations. The charge against the Franco regime was that it was illegally instituted with aid from the Axis powers. In 1950 these recommendations were rescinded by the General Assembly. In May 1948, the Security Council, in a resolution calling for a cease-fire in Palestine, requested all governments "to refrain from importing or exporting war material into Palestine, Egypt, Iraq, Lebanon, Saudi Arabia, Syria, Transjordan, and Yemen during the cease-fire." In 1951 the General

Assembly, after branding the people's Republic of China as an aggressor in Korea, asked for an embargo on strategic goods to China.

Sanctions have been requested by both the General Assembly and the Security Council against South Africa. In 1962 the General Assembly, in a sweeping request, included the breaking of diplomatic relations, a total trade embargo, and the closing of ports and airports to South African ships and aircraft. The following year the Security Council asked all states to embargo arms, ammunition, military vehicles, and materials for arms manufacture. In 1977, as noted above, these measures were made mandatory with specific reference to Article 41 of the Charter. However, as described in the previous chapter, all these measures had little economic or political impact on South Africa.

Beginning in 1990 the Security Council has applied economic sanctions several times, with specific reference to Chapter VII of the Charter. Two sets of sanctions have been imposed on Iraq as a result of its attack on Kuwait. The first set of economic sanctions was incorporated into the series of fifteen Security Council resolutions condemning the attack and authorizing retaliatory collective measures. The second set were the measures imposed on Iraq in Security Council Resolution 687 adopted in April 1991, which included the destruction of all Iraqi chemical, biological, nuclear-capable, and long-range armaments, and which affirmed Iraq's liability for war damages to be repaid out of future oil export revenues. All measures were subject to international inspection and supervision. Other examples of post-1990 Security Council–invoked sanctions include (1) commercial, financial, arms, and air embargoes against Yugoslavia; (2) air and arms embargoes against Libya; (3) an arms embargo against Liberia; and (4) an economic embargo against Haiti.

Military sanctions, specifically invoking Article 42 of the Charter, have never been utilized. While not referring to Article 42, the Security Council, in adopting Resolution 678 in November 1990, authorized the use of "all necessary means . . . to restore international peace and security in the area" if Iraq did not comply with previous applicable Security Council resolutions by January 15, 1991. This language was interpreted as justifying and legitimizing the military attacks on Iraq which began on January 16. But the attacks were carried out by the forces of the United States and a few allies under a coordinated United States command structure independent of United Nations direction or control which had been envisaged in the original elaborate provisions of Articles 42–49 of the Charter. Similarly, the Korean action in 1950 fell short, in significant ways, of fulfilling the requirements of a true application of collective-security principles. These shortcomings are explained in detail in the Korean case study included in a subsequent section of this chapter.

The total experience of the United Nations with regard to handling threats to the peace, breaches of peace, and acts of aggression has been filled with disappointment and frustration. No permanent international military force has been formed, and the Military Staff Committee has become a body without substance. Compulsory economic sanctions have seldom been applied and, with rare exceptions, have proved ineffective. The search for a definition of aggression has been full of pitfalls. Prior to 1990 the permanent members of the Security Council were seldom unanimous in applying strong coercive measures and General Assembly attempts to fill the breach encountered sufficient noncooperation to frequently blunt the impact of the proposed measures.

The failure of collective-security measures calls for substitute innovations that can contribute to international peace and security in situations that do not respond to peaceful settlement procedures. United Nations agencies and personnel have shown some ingenuity in developing peacekeeping techniques not anticipated in the Charter. These innovations are considered in the following sections of this chapter.

PEACEKEEPING INNOVATIONS

If the United Nations' experience in handling disputes were based solely on the peaceful settlement and collective-security procedures of the Charter, the degree of success would be considerably lower than history has proved it to be. The Charter has grown, not only through formal arrangements such as the Uniting for Peace Resolution but also through innovative practices of United Nations agencies. One such development is the technique of peacekeeping, which has been applied to more than thirty critical problems brought before the United Nations.

Peacekeeping is unique in that it fits neither the classical pattern of peaceful settlement nor the model of collective security. Peacekeeping techniques have been applied both to disputes between states and to internal situations threatening civil war. By the time the term *peacekeeping* came into the United Nations lexicon, the techniques involved had already been applied in several cases, which have retroactively been considered a part of the peacekeeping experience of the United Nations. Other terms, including *preventive diplomacy* and *United Nations presence* have become closely identified with the process of peacekeeping. It was during the tenure of Dag Hammarskjöld as Secretary-General that these techniques were clearly recognized as a unique contribution to conflict resolution, and Hammarskjöld's name became associated with the successful development and refinement of peacekeeping practices.

Peacekeeping may be compared with collective security only in the respect that each *may* involve the deployment of military forces. In all other attributes the two processes are different. In peacekeeping operations the objective is not to defeat an aggressor but to prevent fighting, act as a buffer, keep order, or maintain a cease-fire. Peacekeeping forces are generally instructed to use their weapons only in self-defense. Their mission is to keep the peace using measures short of armed force, a role more closely resembling that of police than of military. To be effective, they must maintain an attitude of neutrality and impartiality regarding the adversaries. Furthermore, the peacekeepers must be present with the consent of the disputing parties, or at least the consent of one of them and the toleration of the other. One or all disputants must have invited the peacekeeping force since there is no international territory on which they can be stationed, and sovereignty requires consent for their presence on national soil. This consent indicates a desire by the disputants to avoid conflict. A group carrying UN insignia interposed between contending forces will, in most cases, dampen hostilities because neither side wishes to incur international opprobrium by attacking a symbol of a global desire for peace.

In contrast to the intention to draw collective-security forces mainly from the great powers, the practice in peacekeeping, prior to 1990, was to insulate each situation from major-power involvement, influence, or confrontation. Peacekeeping forces were mainly supplied by medium and sometimes smaller powers whose neutrality was unquestioned by the disputants. The major powers contributed transport and other forms of logistical services and substantial financial support, but, by relying upon direct involvement of military or patrol units from smaller states, they avoided the otherwise inevitable charges of intervention. Special circumstances occasionally permitted an exception to the rule of major-power nonparticipation, as in the case of British contributions of personnel to the United Nations Force in Cyprus where British troops were already stationed. Since 1990, with the advent of expanded and more complex role assignments for large-scale peacekeeping operations in such places as Western Sahara, Yugoslavia, Cambodia, and Somalia, the major powers abandoned their earlier policy of noninvolvement. Participation by military contingents of the permanent members of the Security Council became feasible in the new era of consensus among these states on the dispute-management role of the United Nations in the post–Cold War period.

Peacekeeping operations, because of diverse circumstances leading to their creation, vary widely in function and size. They may perform duties of observing, patrolling, acting as a buffer force, keeping or restoring order, or negotiating. Occasionally, as in the Congo situation in the 1960s, or in the more recent chaotic situation in Somalia, they may be permitted or requested to move beyond the traditional peacekeeping principles into peace-enforcing actions. Peacekeeping contingents may range in size from less than a score of observers to an authorized military and civilian complement of 22,000 in Cambodia, 26,000 in the Congo, and 30,000 in Somalia.

According to a report issued by the President of the General Assembly and the Secretary-General in 1965, United Nations peacekeeping operations may be divided into two categories: observer operations and operations involving the use of armed-forces units. Of the thirty-seven peacekeeping missions, sixteen have been of the armed-forces type: the United Nations Emergency Force (UNEF) in Egypt from 1956 to 1967; the United Nations Congo Operation (ONUC), established in 1960 and terminated in 1964; a United Nations Security Force (UNSF), composed primarily of 1,500 Pakistani troops serving as the military arm of the United Nations Temporary Executive Authority (UNTEA) in West Irian in 1962–63; the United Nations Force in Cyprus (UNFICYP), in existence since 1964; UNEF-II dispatched to the Middle East in 1973 and terminated in 1979; the United Nations Disengagement Observer Force (UNDOF), placed on the Golan Heights since 1974 as buffer between Israel and Syria; the United Nations Interim Force in Lebanon (UNIFIL), created in 1978; the United Nations Transition Assistance Group (UNTAG), sent to Namibia in 1989 to oversee that nation's transition to statehood; the United Nations Mission for the Referendum in Western Sahara (MINURSO), established in 1991; the United Nations Protection Force (UNPROFOR), sent to Yugoslavia in 1992; the United Nations Transitional Authority in Cambodia (UNTAC), authorized in 1992; the United Nations Operation in Somalia (UNOSOM), created in 1992; the United Nations Operation in Mozambique (ONUMOZ), founded in 1992; the expanded version of the United Nations Iraq-Kuwait Observer Mission (UNIKOM), under a new Security Council mandate in 1993; and UNISOM-II in Somalia, authorized in 1993 as the largest of all the peacekeeping forces with the broadest agenda.

The twenty-two observer-type missions are as follows: the United Nations Special Committee on the Balkans (UNSCOB), established in 1947 to investigate the Greek border situation; the United Nations Truce Supervision Organization (UNTSO), operating since 1949 to report on cease-fire and armistice violations by Israel and its neighbors; the United Nations Commission for Indonesia (UNCI), charged with observing cease-fires and with aiding negotiations for Indonesian independence in 1949; the United Nations Military Observer Group in India and Pakistan (UNMOGIP), responsible since 1949 for patrolling the cease-fire line in Kashmir; the United Nations Observer Group in Lebanon (UNOGIL), dispatched to Lebanon briefly in 1958 to check allegations of infiltration across Lebanese borders; the United Nations Yemen Observation Mission (UNYOM), charged with supervising the disengagement of military forces during 1962–64 in the civil war in Yemen; the United Nations India-Pakistan Observation Mission (UNIPOM), established to patrol the border between India and Pakistan during and immediately after the 1965 war between those countries; the UNTSO–Suez Canal observer group under the UNTSO direction but stationed in the Suez Canal area after the June 1967 war; the UN Good Offices Mission in Afghanistan and Pakistan (UNGOMAP), created in 1988 to assist in implementing the Geneva Accords on Afghanistan; the UN Iran-Iraq Military Observer Group (UNIIMOG), dispatched in 1988 to monitor the cease-fire in the Iran-Iraq war; the United Nations Angola Verification Mission (UNAVEM) sent in 1989 to monitor Cuban troop withdrawals from Angola; the United Nations Observer Group in Central America (ONUCA) to aid in the peace process there; the United Nations Iraq-Kuwait Observer Mission (UNIKOM), deployed in the demilitarized zone in 1991 at the end of the Gulf War and upgraded to armed-forces status in 1993; the United Nations Observer Mission in El Salvador (ONUSAL), established in 1991; the United Nations Angola Verification Mission (UNAVEM-II), authorized in 1991 to supervise the peace accords leading to elections in Angola; the United Nations Advance Mission in Cambodia (UNAMIC), dispatched to Cambodia in 1991 to prepare the way for the more elaborate UNTAC the following year; the United Nations Observer Mission in South Africa (UNOMSA), created in 1992 to assist in the peace process in South Africa and to coordinate their efforts with observers from several regional organizations; the United Nations Observer Mission Uganda-Rwanda (UNOMUR), established in 1993 to monitor the Uganda-Rwanda border to prevent military assistance from reaching Rwanda; in addition to the above, two election observer groups were constituted in 1990 to monitor elections in Nicaragua and Haiti, another in 1993 for Eritrean elections, and a fourth in 1994 for South African elections.

Although four of the United Nations peacekeeping missions were established before Dag Hammarskjöld became Secretary-General, he is generally identified with the development of peacekeeping practice and the refinement of its techniques. Two of the larger operations, the UNEF and the ONUC, were initiated during his tenure in office. These large-scale undertakings placed heavy demands upon the Office of Secretary-General for the recruitment, organization, deployment, and administration of multinational forces. Hammarskjöld also developed much of the philosophy, terminology, and rationale in support of peacekeeping as a distinctive feature of United Nations practice, and defended peacekeeping against those who questioned its legitimacy, its sources of authority, its methods of financing, and the role of the Secretary-General in its operation.

Peacekeeping was part of a broader approach of Dag Hammarskjöld to maintaining and promoting peace. The term *quiet diplomacy* has been used to describe his style in skillful negotiations, conducted with tact, persistence, and impartiality, but without fanfare. The term *United Nations presence* refers to all the peacekeeping operations, but, in addition, refers to the use of personal representatives of the Secretary-General in the settling of controversies such as the border disputes between Cambodia and Thailand in 1958–59 and in 1962–64. The term *United Nations presence* has also been applied to United Nations mediators and their staffs, commissions of good offices or conciliation, smaller groups of military observers such as the one sent to the Dominican Republic in 1965, and other similar groups dispatched to the scene of a conflict by the authority of either the Security Council or the General Assembly. *Preventive diplomacy* is a term associated with Hammarskjöld's approach to problems of peace, encompassing all aspects of peacekeeping and the related activities mentioned above. The theory of preventive diplomacy rests on the assumption that it is better to forestall conflict than to allow it to spread. All peacekeeping and related techniques contribute to that end.

Peacekeeping represents, on the one hand, one of the most innovative developments in United Nations practice, but, on the other, a source of major problems to the world organization. The larger operations have been relatively expensive and have put a strain on the United Nations budget from which it has never recovered. The combined costs of the ONUC and the UNEF were approximately $600 million, and the attempt to assess these costs on the members on the same basis as the regular expenses of the organization led to refusals to pay and a mounting indebtedness and series of deficits in United Nations financing. Most peacekeeping projects since 1960 have sought alternative means of financing to avoid exacerbation of an already acute situation. More details of these financial problems were discussed in Chapter 5. In spite of the difficulty of financing the larger operations, three of the largest and most expensive peacekeeping forces in UN history have been created since February 1992 in Yugoslavia, Cambodia, and Somalia.

The United Nations financial crisis is a manifestation of a more deeply seated political and philosophical conflict over peacekeeping. Although all but two peacekeeping operations were initially approved by the Security Council, the Soviet Union saw the exceptions, particularly the first UNEF operation, as part of the attempt to alter the control of the big powers over all aspects of peace and security matters. The Congo undertaking was also transferred in certain stages to the General Assembly, so that two of the most expensive peacekeeping enterprises were removed from the possibility of Soviet veto. Thus, the General Assembly asserted its authority to create, direct, and assess the costs of peacekeeping forces. The Soviet Union not only affirmed the exclusive jurisdiction of the Security Council over peacekeeping activities but also argued that costs should be mainly borne by states engaging in aggressive action. Other states joined the Soviet Union in refusing to pay for undertakings of which they did not approve, and many small states suggested that the big powers should pay the lion's share of peacekeeping expenses. After 1987 the permanent members of the Security Council worked cooperatively in approving nineteen new peacekeeping missions, but the potential for disagreement is always present.

The General Assembly has agreed that special accounts, separate from the regular budget, should be established for each of the peacekeeping operations (with a few exceptions). The assessment schedule for payment into each of these accounts has been modified from those of the regular budget. Four categories of assessment rates are provided. These vary from higher than normal rates for the five permanent Security Council members to only 10 percent of the regular rate for the least-developed countries. This arrangement in no way solves the deficit problem for peacekeeping operations, which in 1993 exceeded $1 billion.

One problem of peacekeeping is the source of personnel for participation in peacekeeping missions. Some middle powers, including the Nordic states, Canada, Ireland, and India, have been enthusiastic supporters of the peacekeeping philosophy, have furnished personnel and material for peacekeeping missions, and have provided leadership in short- and long-range planning for more effective United Nations peacekeeping activities.

Why have the middle-sized powers been such a strong source of support for peacekeeping activities? They are in a unique position to contribute personnel because of their reputation for neutrality. They have not been tainted with imperialism or, with the exception of the North Atlantic Treaty Organization, with association with movements that jeopardize their reputation for impartiality. They have sufficient economic resources to meet the costs involved without undue citizen sacrifice. Their position in world affairs is such that they have a heavy stake in the avoidance of military conflict. Leaders such as Lester Pearson of Canada have emerged as enlightened advocates for the strengthening of techniques, including peacekeeping, that may ensure world peace. The humanitarian concerns of a discerning citizenry furnish a base for generous support for causes that promote world peace as well as for a wide range of United Nations economic and social activities. These countries perceive a close affinity between their national interests and United Nations goals and principles. All the Nordic states and Canada have furnished forces for more than half of all peacekeeping missions undertaken by the United Nations including a majority of the ten largest operations. The Nordic countries have cooperated in limited ways in joint planning and training for future peacekeeping requirements, and Canada invited other states to participate in a conference in Ottawa in 1964 to discuss United Nations peacekeeping.

Although the number of missions in which a state has participated is an indicator both of its willingness to contribute and of its acceptability as an impartial party, other factors are significant in assessing the contribution of any given country to United Nations peacekeeping efforts. India, because of relatively large military contingents in the ONUC and the UNEF, outranked in the 1970s all other states in the size of total forces that had served in peacekeeping missions.[2] However, in relation to the number of men in its armed services, less than 2 percent of India's forces were in United Nations missions at any given time, whereas for Ireland's small army the corresponding figure exceeded 15 percent. Prior to 1971, the Netherlands had been involved in more United Nations missions than India, but only in observer missions or in furnishing small contingents of specialists. Therefore, the total number of

---

[2]Larry L. Fabian, *Soldiers Without Enemies: Preparing the United Nations for Peacekeeping* (Washington, D.C.: The Brookings Institution, 1971), p. 161.

Dutch personnel involved was less than 1 percent of the number from India or Sweden.[3]

Factors to be considered in assessing the contributions of states to United Nations peacekeeping must include the following: (1) number of missions, (2) number of personnel, (3) population, (4) size of armed forces, (5) gross national product and per capita income, (6) size of defense budget, (7) financial and logistical support, and (8) basis for deployment (that is, whether military contingents have volunteered for United Nations duty or whether they are regular units of the armed services). No single index can adequately measure the cooperation and commitment of a nation to United Nations peacekeeping efforts. However, an assessment based on all available factors would indicate that the Nordic states, Canada, Ireland, and India deserve special credit for their leadership and support.

A major problem in United Nations peacekeeping is the availability and training of personnel for emergency situations. The necessity to dispatch quickly a force of several thousand to the Middle East in 1956 resulted in the use of military contingents that had no previous training in the special techniques of peacekeeping. In 1958 and 1959, Secretary-General Hammarskjöld took the initial steps toward correcting this deficiency. He recognized that both nation states and the Secretariat must plan for effective peacekeeping participation. The Secretariat first issued a study based on the UNEF experience, and the Secretary-General then directed a letter to the states that had previously furnished personnel for peacekeeping missions in the Middle East. At approximately the same time the Nordic states began preliminary consultations aimed at providing standby forces specially trained for United Nations peacekeeping duty. Several other states indicated a willingness to earmark forces for possible use in emergencies. During the 1960s a dozen states authorized or promised standby forces. Some planned to earmark units of their regular armed forces, and others visualized the use of volunteers, often from military reserve personnel. The training of medical, communications, and other specialized units was recognized as part of future needs. States have responded generously to emergencies, but the need for planning and special training continues.

CASE STUDIES IN COLLECTIVE SECURITY AND PEACEKEEPING

Examples of United Nations peacekeeping activities are numerous, but collective-security theory has been only imperfectly applied in United Nations practice. One approximation of collective security by military means is the

---

[3]*Ibid.*, p. 144.

case of the Korean conflict. In a situation similar to Korea, the Security Council's legitimation of the use of force in the Gulf War of 1991 fell short of invoking the military provisions of Chapter VII of the Charter. Several attempts to apply economic or diplomatic sanctions were described in a previous section of this chapter. Few of these attempts were notably successful in bringing to terms the state against which sanctions were imposed.

United Nations peacekeeping missions are so integrated with other problems of dispute settlement as to be inseparable for purposes of analysis. The case studies of peaceful settlement presented in the previous chapter incorporated substantial information concerning two of the thirty-seven United Nations peacekeeping missions. These groups—the United Nations Military Observer Group in India and Pakistan (UNMOGIP) and the United Nations India-Pakistan Observation Mission (UNIPOM)—were associated with the prolonged Indian-Pakistani dispute. Additional information concerning the theory, practice. and problems of peacekeeping as applied to peacekeeping missions has been previously presented in this chapter. Some gaps in our data can perhaps be best filled by a further examination of the Korean dispute (as an attempt to apply the principles of collective security) and of several of the peacekeeping missions not previously discussed in detail.

The Korean Question

Korea became divided at the thirty-eighth parallel of latitude as a result of the agreement in 1945 between the Soviet Union and the United States that each power would temporarily occupy one of the two sectors, accept the surrender of the Japanese forces there, and work out provisions for establishing a permanent government for an independent and unified country. When negotiations for a unified Korea reached an impasse, the United States in 1947 first submitted the question to the General Assembly. The Assembly adopted a resolution providing for elections for a National Assembly to be conducted under the surveillance of a United Nations Temporary Commission on Korea and subsequently for the prompt withdrawal of occupying forces. The commission was refused access to the territory north of the thirty-eighth parallel but observed the conduct of elections for a government in the southern half of the territory, which was recognized by the General Assembly as the only legitimate government in Korea. Immediately thereafter, a government was established in the zone of Soviet occupation also claiming legitimacy for all of Korea.

In 1948 the General Assembly created a second commission charged with facilitating the political, economic, and social unification of Korea and observing and verifying the withdrawal of occupying forces. The commission reported in 1949 that United States forces had been withdrawn from South

Korea but could not verify the claims of Soviet withdrawal from the North. No progress was made toward unification.

On June 25, 1950, the United Nations Commission on Korea reported a large-scale invasion across the thirty-eighth parallel by North Korean forces. At the request of the United States government, the Security Council met that Sunday afternoon. The Soviet boycott of the Security Council permitted the adoption of three crucial Council resolutions during the next two weeks. The first declared the armed attack by North Korean forces a breach of the peace (but not necessarily an act of aggression) and called for the cessation of hostilities and the withdrawal of North Korean forces. The second, adopted two days later, recommended that member states assist the Republic of Korea in repelling the attack and in restoring international peace and security in the area. The third resolution authorized a unified command using the United Nations flag and requested the United States to designate a commander and organize the combined forces.

The Security Council resolutions gave legitimacy to United States massive involvement in assisting the South Korean government and furnished the basis for the incorporation of contingents from other members into a United Nations army under United States command. Before the Security Council resolution on June 27, President Truman had already ordered United States forces to give air and sea support to South Korea. General Douglas MacArthur, who was directing United States operations in Japan, was designated on July 8 as the Commanding General of the unified forces in Korea, including the forces of the Republic of Korea.

The unified force that fought in Korea under the United Nations banner was far from a model of an ideal collective-security force. The United States supplied 50 percent of the ground troops, 85 percent of the naval forces, and more than 90 percent of the air units. When the South Korean contingents are added to these figures, more than 90 percent of ground and naval personnel and almost all of the air forces came from these two countries. Fifteen other states furnished military units of at least battalion size, and an additional five states sent medical units to serve under the unified command. Token offers of smaller size were not accepted. Almost forty states and several specialized agencies and nongovernmental organizations contributed to the relief and rehabilitation work in Korea, but in this area also the United States furnished the bulk of the contributions. Security Council and General Assembly resolutions and a multilateral force under a unified command using the United Nations flag were symbols of great moral and psychological significance, but they mainly supplied international legitimacy for United States efforts to aid South Korea in repelling aggression. The United States possessed the combination of resources, national interests, and military forces stationed nearby to play the primary role in resisting the invasion. Other countries had obligations elsewhere that restricted their degree of involvement.

Examples include French military commitments in Indochina and British commitments in Malaya. Soviet absence from Security Council sessions permitted United States policies to receive endorsement as United Nations policies. Further support at the international level came in the form of General Assembly resolutions passed by overwhelming majorities. The reality of "collective defense" by the non-Communist nations against a Communist aggression from North Korea thus underlay the formality of "collective-security" action by the United Nations.

Virtually all of Korea became a battleground in 1950 and 1951. Several weeks elapsed after the attack on June 25 before United States forces could launch a successful counterattack against the North Korean invaders, who had overrun nearly the entire peninsula. As the battlefront moved northward, a major question of purpose had to be faced. If the goal was to repel an invasion, a crossing of the thirty-eighth parallel by United Nations forces was unjustified. If the primary objective was to establish a unified Korea, the pursuit and defeat of the North Korean forces could be warranted. A resolution on October 7, 1950, by the General Assembly recalled the original goal of unification, and General MacArthur's army continued to advance toward the Yalu River, which separates Korea from China.

Early in November contact was first reported with military units of the People's Republic of China, and a few weeks later substantial numbers of Chinese attacked the United Nations forces. The war had suddenly assumed a new dimension. The Chinese forces assisted the North Koreans in driving the United Nations armies southward beyond the thirty-eighth parallel. Seoul, the South Korean capital, was captured by the northern invaders for the second time within six months. In January 1951, the retreat southward was halted, the North Korean and Chinese forces were gradually pushed back across the thirty-eighth parallel, and the front became relatively stabilized near that location.

In January 1951, the General Assembly established a cease-fire commission to recommend the appropriate measures for ending the conflict. The commission's proposals were rejected by the government of the People's Republic of China. On February 1 the General Assembly adopted a resolution branding the People's Republic as an aggressor in Korea and on May 18 recommended that all states embargo the shipment of arms, ammunition, implements of war, items useful for producing war material, petroleum, and transportation items to the People's Republic and to North Korea.

Armistice negotiations began in July 1951. For two years these negotiations were stalled over questions relating to the exchange and repatriation of prisoners of war. An armistice agreement was signed in July 1953, and a demilitarized zone was established. Negotiations for a final settlement were carried on in Panmunjom in the demilitarized zone, but no agreement could be reached, and in December these sessions were terminated.

In February 1954, the foreign ministers of France, the Soviet Union, the United Kingdom, and the United States announced that a conference would be called in Geneva in April to discuss a settlement of both the Korean and the Indochinese questions. Participants for the Korean issue would be the four convening powers, the People's Republic of China, North Korea, South Korea, and other countries that had contributed armed forces for the United Nations action in Korea.

The Geneva Conference debated the Korean question for several weeks, but the participants were unable to agree on a settlement. Both sides favored unification, but on irreconcilable terms. From time to time the rival governments have raised the issue of economic cooperation, as well as unification, but without real progress toward change. A divided Korea with hostile forces on each side of a demilitarized zone and frequent charges of armistice violations remained as features of the Korean scene into the 1990s.

Although the Korean problem is one of the two nearest approximations by the United Nations to collective security through military sanctions, it falls short of the conditions for applying the classical theory of collective security. Unanimity among the great powers did not exist. One great power carried out a policy that it would have executed with or without United Nations support. That great power and the invaded political unit furnished most of the forces for repelling the invasion. Small contingents from fifteen other states lent credibility to the action as a United Nations mission but served more as a symbolic than as a decisive factor in fighting.

Security Council and General Assembly resolutions were couched in broad general terms rather than advocating specific actions. States were left free to comply voluntarily with these directives to whatever degree suited their purposes. The General Assembly branded the People's Republic of China as an aggressor, but the Security Council declared only that there had been a breach of the peace. The Council invoked Article 39 of the Charter but never utilized the stronger measures of Articles 40–42. The only specific sanctions, which were voluntary, not binding, were those requested by the General Assembly.

The Korean action ended in a stalemate. However, the invasion was repulsed. A United Nations commission was present to observe the invasion and to give impartial reports to United Nations headquarters. The Security Council was able to act in the absence of the Soviet representative. More than fifty states in a total membership of sixty declared their moral support in the General Assembly for the action taken in the name of the United Nations. As a result of the situation in the Security Council, the General Assembly proceeded at its earliest opportunity to strengthen its ability to deal with disputes when the Security Council is deadlocked. In spite of the failure to apply collective-security techniques fully, the Korean episode was a landmark in United Nations history and furnished some limited positive contributions to United Nations practice.

United Nations Emergency Force (UNEF)

Hostility, incidents involving violence, and a series of wars have marked the history of Israel's relations with its Arab neighbors since 1947, the year before Israel was proclaimed as an independent state. The original UNEF force was created in 1956 during the second major war in that area and remained as a buffer between Israel and Egypt until Egypt requested its removal in 1967 at the outbreak of the six-day war.

The first war between Israel and its neighbors had been brought to a close by the signing of armistice agreements in 1949. The United Nations Truce Supervision Organization (UNTSO) was created at that time to supervise the armistice. From 1949 until 1956 an uneasy truce existed, with many complaints to the Security Council concerning incidents and clashes. The refugee situation was also acute and defied solution.

In 1956 the Palestine dispute assumed a new dimension in a war involving invasions of the Suez Canal area by Israel, the United Kingdom, and France. In July, Egypt announced the nationalization of the canal. Some temporary progress was made toward negotiating differences among Egypt, the United Kingdom, and France over issues of canal ownership, management, and use, but these negotiations were abruptly halted by news that Israeli forces had invaded Egyptian territory and were advancing toward the canal. The Security Council met promptly on October 30, but on the same day the United Kingdom and France, fearing the interruption of canal traffic, issued an ultimatum to Egypt and Israel to pull back from the canal or face British and French military intervention. Proposed Council resolutions requesting immediate withdrawal of Israeli forces were vetoed by France and the United Kingdom, whereupon a Yugoslavia-sponsored resolution was adopted to call for an emergency special session of the General Assembly under the 1950 Uniting for Peace Resolution. Next, on October 31, British and French air attacks against Egypt in the canal area were begun, followed two days later by invasion by land forces. The Egyptians sank ships in the canal, blocking navigation for several months.

On November 1, 1956, the General Assembly began its first emergency special session with the subject matter limited to the Suez crisis. On the following day a resolution was adopted calling for a cease-fire, a withdrawal of forces, and prompt action toward reopening the canal. The British and the French indicated that they would comply only if a United Nations force moved into the area to insure the carrying out of details concerning the armistice and the reopening of the canal. On November 4 Lester Pearson of Canada introduced a resolution calling for the creation of the United Nations Emergency Force (UNEF). Plans for the force were formulated by the Secretary-General and approved by the Assembly on November 5 and 7. By November 15 the first contingents arrived in Egypt, which had agreed to accept the force on its soil. Twenty-four states offered to contribute military personnel, but a force of 6,000 from ten countries was assembled in Egyptian territory by February 1957, none of whom were drawn from the permanent members of the Security Council. UNEF personnel continued to patrol the borders between Israel and Egypt in the Gaza and Sinai areas for more than ten years.

The arrival of UNEF units did not immediately assure the withdrawal of all forces to their prewar positions. The last British and French troops left Egypt on December 22, 1956. Israel had occupied most of the Sinai peninsula, including controlling positions over navigation in the Gulf of Aqaba and the Straits of Tiran. Not until arrangements were made for the UNEF to assure freedom of navigation in these waterways was Israel willing to withdraw its forces. The process was completed by March 8, 1957.

Tensions, incidents, and complaints to United Nations organs concerning the Middle East situation did not disappear during the period that the UNEF patrolled the buffer zone. The UNEF's presence kept incidents along the Israeli-Egyptian borders to a minimum, but during these years the Security Council heard frequent charges of armistice violations from Israel and its neighbors.

Ominous signals of impending war became apparent in May 1967. In a report to the Security Council on May 19, the Secretary-General highlighted the deterioration of the situation in the Middle East. The number of incidents between Syria and Israel had been steadily increasing for several months, and a major armed clash had occurred on April 7. The activities of El-Fatah had also become especially inflammatory and unsettling. In mid-May, Egyptian troops advanced to the Gulf of Aqaba and demanded that UNEF units turn over key strategic positions to them. On May 18, the Egyptian representative to the United Nations, Mohamed Awad El-Kony, delivered to U Thant an official request from his government for the withdrawal of UNEF forces from Egyptian territory. U Thant inquired of Israeli authorities whether they would accept the forces on the Israeli side of the border but, consistent with the original refusal by Israel in 1956 to allow UNEF personnel on its territory, the reply was negative. The Secretary-General consulted his advisory committee on UNEF and the states furnishing contingents, and they agreed that the buffer force was in an untenable position and that there was no choice but to remove it. U Thant flew to Cairo to try to get a reversal of the Egyptian decision but was unsuccessful.

The Security Council, which, in spite of the chain of threatening conditions, had not been called into session previously in 1967, held twenty-one meetings between May 24 and June 14. Before June 5 the Council engaged in general debate on the Middle East situation, but no resolutions were adopted. The Council seemed impotent to find a course of action to stem the tide of events leading to another Middle East war.

In the early hours of June 5, the Security Council representatives were summoned to an urgent session by the news of the outbreak of full-scale warfare between Israel and its neighbors. One of the first results of the fighting was the killing of nine UNEF soldiers from India by Israeli gunfire. Although the evacuation of UNEF forces had begun in May, the last units could not be removed from the area until June 17, and these units were unhappily caught between the lines of the belligerent armies. Other reports to the Council on June 5 dramatized the gravity of the general situation.

During the brief period of fighting, the Israeli forces were successful on all fronts. They occupied the Sinai Peninsula and advanced to the Suez Canal. They occupied the west bank of the Jordan River and pushed the Syrians back from the Golan Heights area. These occupied territories then became a major issue in subsequent negotiations for a settlement of the Middle East question.

On June 6, 1967, the Security Council unanimously adopted a simple cease-fire resolution, attaching no blame for the war nor specifying any conditions for a return to relative peace. Within the next three days the cease-fire was accepted by all belligerents. During succeeding months the situation remained impervious to solution, in spite of the convening of another emergency session of the General Assembly, the passage in November of a Security Council resolution establishing principles on which a settlement should be based, and the prolonged efforts of a United Nations special representative, Gunnar Jarring. The UNTSO observers were present in small numbers on the various fronts, but the larger UNEF force was not re-created until after another major war in October 1973.

The creation of the UNEF is especially significant because it furnished a model for the peacekeeping movement. Although previous small observer forces came to be retrospectively labeled as peacekeeping actions, the scale of the UNEF and the principles clearly enunciated for its operation provided a pattern of organization and a philosophy for all subsequent peacekeeping units. The development was innovative since it did not follow Charter prescriptions. The foresight and imagination of men like Lester Pearson and Dag Hammarskjöld generated a new concept, which has proved useful in numerous situations.

The UNEF was an instrument for relative peace in the Middle East for more than ten years. However, its ultimate success or failure was dependent not only on the skills and initiative of the Secretaries-General but also on the cooperation and support of the disputing states and the major powers. In spite of the lack of financial support by the Soviet Union and France and the demand by Egypt in 1967 to withdraw the force, the acceptability and durability of the basic concepts established in 1956 were attested to by the creation in 1973 and 1974 of two new similar forces in the area with the endorsement of all parties that had previously withheld support and cooperation.

The United Nations Congo Operation (ONUC)

Of all United Nations peacekeeping operations, the ONUC (the acronym follows the French word order) was, until the 1990s, the largest, most controversial, and most expensive. Military units were present in the Congo for four years, and for three of those years numbered 15,000 to 20,000 men. Thirty countries participated in the ONUC, and other countries, including the major powers, contributed transport and logistical support. Costs assigned to the United Nations budget amounted to $400 million in addition to expenses borne by states contributing forces. These amounts do not include the costs of extensive civil and technical aid to the Congo through both the regular and special-aid channels of the United Nations.

The Congo operation was controversial because there was no clear mandate for the ONUC and because several sets of internal and external interests sought to exploit the ONUC or the chaotic internal conditions in the Congo for their own ends. Two Secretaries-General attempted to follow a noninterventionist course in restoring order and in assisting a Congo government to acquire the capability for handling its own political, economic, and social problems. But in the process they were attacked by self-seeking internal and external spokespersons and were denied the necessary financial support to keep the United Nations solvent. The Soviet attacks on Dag Hammarskjöld were especially virulent and took the form of demands for his resignation and the replacement of a single Secretary-General with a troika, which would have extended the veto to the top echelon of the Secretariat.

The former Belgian Congo (presently named Zaire) is a large, almost landlocked state in Central Africa, ranking third among African states in area and fifth in population. At the time independence was granted, only thirty Congolese in a population of 14 million were university graduates, and all middle- and upper-echelon government posts and military officer positions were filled by Belgians or other Europeans. The decision to grant independence to the Congo was made suddenly, with no preparation of the Congolese for the responsibilities of self-rule.

On July 5, 1960, five days after independence, Congolese soldiers mutinied against their Belgian officers, and civil disorder occurred in many parts of the Congo. Belgian authorities requested permission to use Belgian troops, stationed at two bases retained by treaty, to restore order in the Congo but were refused by Prime Minister Patrice Lumumba. On July 10 after riots spread and many Belgians fled the Congo, the Belgian troops intervened to restore order in several cities. On the following day President Moise Tshombe of Katanga declared the independence of his province as a separate state.

Unable to cope with the growing chaos, President Joseph Kasavubu and Premier Lumumba first requested aid from the United States and were advised to appeal to the United Nations. On July 14 the Security Council adopted a resolution calling upon Belgium to withdraw its troops from the

Congo and authorizing the Secretary-General to provide military and technical assistance to the Congolese government until the national security forces were capable of maintaining internal order.

In response to the resolution of July 14, the Secretary-General, with the cooperation of member states, created the United Nations Operation in the Congo (ONUC). On July 15 more than 1,350 troops from Ghana and Tunisia arrived in the Congo, and within a month the United Nations force exceeded 14,000. According to the guidelines established by Hammarskjöld, no units were accepted from permanent members of the Security Council or from any state that, in the judgment of the Secretary-General, had a special interest in the situation. Priority was also given to participation by African states, twelve of which contributed units. The guidelines also provided that the troops were responsible only to the Secretary-General, that they must not intervene in the internal affairs of the Congo, and that they should use force only in self-defense. All these conditions were consistent with the general principles that had been gradually evolved for peacekeeping operations.

The goals for the ONUC were established by a series of Security Council resolutions in 1960–61 and by a resolution adopted on September 20, 1960, by the General Assembly's emergency session on the Congo. These goals are summarized by Ernest W. Lefever in his study of the Congo operation as follows:

> Restore and maintain law and order.
> Protect life and property throughout the country.
> Transform the Congolese army into a reliable instrument of internal security.
> Restore and maintain the territorial integrity of the Congo.
> Prevent civil war and pacify tribal conflict.
> Protect the Congo from external interference in its affairs, particularly through the elimination of foreign mercenaries hired by secessionist Katanga.[4]

All these purposes and the guidelines for the conduct of the operations were generally adhered to, although continued crises in the Congo after the withdrawal of the ONUC demonstrated the absence of stability. This lack of stability should surprise no one, since the transformation of the Congo from a chaotic to an orderly society in four years under the most adverse conditions would have been an achievement beyond reasonable expectation.

The chaotic conditions in the Congo are epitomized by the situation there between September 1960 and August 1961, when no single government existed with which the United Nations could deal. On September 5, 1960, President Kasavubu dismissed Prime Minister Lumumba, and Lumumba retaliated by dismissing Kasavubu. On September 12 the army chief of staff,

---

[4]Ernest W. Lefever, *Crisis in the Congo: A United Nations Force in Action* (Washington, D.C.: The Brookings Institution, 1965), p. 177.

Joseph Mobutu, arrested Lumumba and subsequently took over the government in Leopoldville (now Kinshasa) and suspended Parliament. Lumumba later escaped, was rearrested, transferred to Katanga province, and executed by one of Tshombe's mercenaries in January 1961. By early 1961, at least four separate governments claimed legitimacy in the Congo. Kasavubu and Mobutu in Leopoldville were recognized by a majority of United Nations members and claimed national jurisdiction. Gizenga, a Lumumba supporter with headquarters in Stanleyville in Orientale province, also claimed national jurisdiction and was recognized by the Soviet bloc and by several African states, which withdrew their forces from the ONUC in protest over the failure of the United Nations to support the legitimacy of Lumumba and Gizenga. In Katanga, Tshombe claimed the right of that province to separate statehood and continued to engage Belgian mercenaries to enforce his autonomy. Albert Kalonji in Kasai province sought autonomy through agreements at various stages with Tshombe and with Kasavubu. In August 1961, the eleven-month constitutional crisis was ended with the selection of Cyrille Adoula as premier of a government that all factions endorsed as the only legitimate government of the Congo.

Tshombe soon proved that he was unreliable in his support of the Kasavubu-Adoula government. Tshombe was motivated by personal ambition, but other factors encouraged his secessionist plans. Katanga was by far the richest province of the Congo. Belgian interests, including financial ones, favored the secessionist movement. Mercenaries from Belgium, France, South Africa, and the Rhodesias willingly supported the political intrigues. Sympathy for Tshombe's plans could also be found in Rhodesia, Britain, France, and some segments of the United States population. Fighting occurred between Tshombe's forces and the ONUC in August and September 1961. After the second incident, Secretary-General Hammarskjöld arranged a personal conference with Tshombe and was on his way to keep that engagement when he was killed in the crash of his plane. A cease-fire was agreed to on September 21 but was soon violated by Katangese mercenaries and native armed forces. On November 24 the Security Council gave Acting Secretary-General U Thant an unprecedented mandate "to take vigorous action, including the use of a requisite measure of force, if necessary, for the immediate apprehension, detention pending legal action and/or deportation of all foreign military and paramilitary personnel and political advisers not under the United Nations Command, and mercenaries. . . ."[5] To defend themselves and carry out their mandate, ONUC forces were required to engage in limited military activities rather than adhere to the ideal role of police officers. Tshombe made a series of agreements for the unification of the country and promptly broke each one. It was not until January 1963 that all military and political opposition ceased in Katanga.

[5]Security Council Resolution S/5002, November 24, 1961.

Partially because of financial problems and partially because its principal mandate had been achieved, the ONUC was withdrawn from the Congo by June 30, 1964. The country was still deficient in many elements required for unity, order, and political and economic progress, and internal disorders and political upheavals were frequent during the next four years. After the withdrawal of the ONUC, technical assistance and development aid programs of the United Nations and the specialized agencies continued to serve some of the basic economic, social, and political needs of the Congo.

In concluding his study of the Congo operation, Ernest W. Lefever summarizes his overall assessment of its shortcomings and successes as follows:

> The Congo peacekeeping effort was a novel, controversial, and a less-than-efficient enterprise. It sometimes fumbled. It made many small mistakes. It was assailed on all sides. It precipitated a financial crisis for the United Nations. But in the final analysis, the U.N. Force must be judged by its contribution to international stability, regardless of what other interests it might have served. So judged, the mission succeeded. It contributed to peace and security in Central Africa and in the wider world.
>
> As the largest and most complex internationally authorized and administered operation in history, the Congo peacekeeping effort is rich in lessons and warnings for the future.[6]

United Nations Interim Force in Lebanon (UNIFIL)

Lebanon since 1970 has been the battleground for rival internal factions and for intervention by Syria, Israel, and the Palestine Liberation Organization (PLO). Fighting was intermittent for many years, but since the full-scale invasion of Lebanon by Israel in 1982, bloodshed and violence have become almost daily features of Lebanese life. Raids and counterraids have been frequent across the Lebanese-Israeli border.

After a large-scale Israeli military operation into southern Lebanon, the UN Security Council established the United Nations Interim Force in Lebanon (UNIFIL) in March 1978. The general purpose, which followed the pattern for earlier peacekeeping forces, was to act as a buffer between contending parties. It was hoped that the UNIFIL presence would prevent most attacks by the hostile forces.

The Security Council, on the recommendation of the Secretary-General, originally authorized a force of 4,000 personnel but shortly after approved an increase to 6,000. After the major invasion of Lebanon by Israeli forces in 1982, UNIFIL grew to 7,000. After 1985 the number stabilized at approxi-

[6]Lefever, *Crisis in the Congo*, p. 181.

mately 5,800. Fourteen neutral nations have at various times contributed military units to UNIFIL.[7]

The mandate for UNIFIL included the following major purposes:

1. To confirm the withdrawal of Israeli forces from Lebanese territory, restore international peace and security, and assist the government of Lebanon in reestablishing its effective authority in the area
2. To establish and maintain an effective buffer zone in southern Lebanon
3. To use its best efforts to prevent recurrence of fighting and to ensure that its area of operation is not utilized for hostile activities of any kind
4. To take all measures deemed necessary to ensure the effective restoration of Lebanese sovereignty and authority
5. To cooperate with and support personnel of the United Nations Truce Supervision Organization (UNTSO) already on duty in southern Lebanon

According to well-established principles, UNIFIL personnel were to use force only in self-defense.

From its inception, UNIFIL encountered numerous obstacles to fulfilling its mandate. Israel, fearing raids or shelling across its border with Lebanon, opposed effective occupation and control of the area adjacent to its border by UNIFIL forces. Israeli policymakers and military commanders felt secure in withdrawing from Lebanese territory only if surrogate Christian forces, equipped and trained by Israel, remained in control of substantial areas of southern Lebanon. These Christian forces, under the command of Major Haddad until his death in 1984, were later renamed the South Lebanon Army (SLA). The PLO was only slightly less obstructive of UNIFIL's attempts to establish and control a well-defined area of operation. Other Lebanese armed elements, not controlled by the central government, also frequently challenged and impeded UNIFIL's activities. Small military groups, including affiliates of the PLO and Haddad's army, were located inside UNIFIL's zone of operation and resisted UNIFIL's efforts to take control of new positions to facilitate its mission. UNIFIL established checkpoints and patrols along the borders of its area of operation in order to stop infiltration by armed elements. Although several thousand infiltration attempts were stopped, unknown numbers penetrated the zone and the goal of freeing the area from its use for hostile activities could not be achieved.

When Israel launched its full-scale invasion of Lebanon in June 1982, UNIFIL soldiers were under orders to impede the Israeli advance through their positions. Obstacles were placed in the roadways and confrontations occurred, but the UNIFIL positions were quickly bypassed or overrun. In fact, UNIFIL had to operate behind Israeli lines for a period of nearly three years. Even when Israel carried out the final stage of its withdrawal in May and June

---

[7]Canada, Fiji, Finland, France, Ghana, Iran, Ireland, Italy, Nepal, Netherlands, Nigeria, Norway, Senegal, Sweden.

1985, it established a "security zone" in southern Lebanon, varying in depth from two to twenty kilometers in which Israeli forces acted in support of the SLA contingents. This "security zone" overlapped with portions of UNIFIL's area of operation.

In 1982, Israeli forces drove forward to the Beirut area for the purpose of forcing the withdrawal from Lebanon of PLO armed elements in that region. Ideas for a United Nations expanded role in assisting in an orderly withdrawal were rejected by the Lebanese government in favor of inviting a multinational force to perform this function. Troops numbering 4,000 were furnished by the United States, France, and Italy, with a small contingent from the United Kingdom. These forces were deployed near Beirut from August 21 to September 13, 1982, during the PLO evacuation, but returned at the request of the Lebanese government two weeks later and remained until the spring of 1984. President Reagan of the United States called the multinational force a "peacekeeping" force, but at least two principles established by United Nations practice in developing the peacekeeping technique were violated in the use of the multinational force: (1) the forces were drawn from major powers who should be kept insulated from direct involvement, and (2) the forces became embroiled in the fighting and did not maintain a position of neutrality.

Financing of UNIFIL also presented a major problem. Although opposition of the Soviet Union to the establishment of UNIFIL was mitigated by its creation and renewal by authorization of the Security Council, the General Assembly apportioned the costs among the United Nations members and established a special UNIFIL account. Since some members, for political reasons, refused to pay their assessments, supplemental funds were sought through voluntary contributions from governments, international organizations, and private donations. By November 1988 the deficit had reached $330 million. The burden fell on the troop-contributing countries, which were not being reimbursed for their costs.

Another problem for UNIFIL has been the loss of lives among UNIFIL peacekeeping personnel. UNIFIL units have been fired upon by various armed factions involved in the Lebanese imbroglio. By early 1993 more than 180 peacekeeping personnel had been killed and a larger number wounded. Only in the Congo peacekeeping operation, in which the force was three times as large, were the casualties higher.

With all these difficulties and frustrations, can it be said that UNIFIL has made positive contributions toward lowering the level of conflict in Lebanon? Certainly a most important prerequisite for success of any peacekeeping mission is a high degree of cooperation with and respect for the peacekeeping personnel by the contending parties. Such cooperation and respect were lacking throughout much of the UNIFIL experience. On the other hand, UNIFIL stopped thousands of infiltration attempts into and through its zone of operation and disarmed many of the intercepted parties. The beleaguered and often unstable Lebanese central government repeatedly requested the continued presence of UNIFIL in southern Lebanon. Most major fighting since 1978 occurred in the Beirut and other areas of Lebanon, not in the UNIFIL zone of operation. From June 1982 until 1985, while operating behind Israeli lines, UNIFIL's activities were shifted to include humanitarian assistance and activities as a communications channel among contending force commanders. One strong indicator of UNIFIL's perceived value is the renewal of its mandate by the Security Council at two- to six-month intervals year after year. Although all permanent members of the Security Council have not met their financial obligations in support of UNIFIL, they were unwilling to terminate the force and risk contributing even further to the level of chaos and violence in this unfortunate country. Solutions to larger problems of Lebanon lie outside UNIFIL's limited functions, but that is true of all peacekeeping missions. Under extremely malevolent conditions, UNIFIL carried out its mandate as well as could be expected.

United Nations Transition Assistance Group (UNTAG)

South-West Africa (now Namibia), located between South Africa and Angola, was a former German colony until it was assigned to the administration of South Africa as a class C League of Nations mandate in 1919. After World War II South Africa refused to place the territory under United Nations trusteeship and, instead, claimed the right to annex it. This position was challenged over the years by the General Assembly and the Security Council, and was refuted by two advisory opinions of the International Court of Justice. In 1966 the General Assembly declared the mandate to be terminated and subsequently renamed the territory and set up a Council for Namibia and a United Nations commissioner who acted as a government in exile.

After years of intransigence by the South African government, prolonged negotiations were begun in 1978 for a transition of control leading to Namibian independence and self-rule. The process was protracted by the reluctance of both South Africa and the South-West African People's Organization (SWAPO, the leading Namibian resistance group) to agree to the details of the proposals and timetable. The United States acted as principal mediator with support from major western states and the Soviet Union. Finally, in December 1988 a plan was signed at UN headquarters by Angola, Cuba, and South Africa. Angola, assisted by Cuban forces, had served as a staging base and refugee sanctuary for SWAPO. The plan included timetables for the withdrawal of South African troops from Namibia and Cuban troops from Angola, the holding of elections, and the establishment of a new government in Namibia.

In January 1989 the Security Council adopted a resolution setting April 1, 1989, as the starting date for the transition process. To oversee the process, the Council authorized the creation of the United Nations Transition Assistance Group (UNTAG) to assist the Special Representative of the Secretary-General in monitoring the cease-fire, the withdrawal of troops, the holding of elections, the writing of a constitution, and the installation of a new government. UNTAG was composed of 4,500 military personnel, 1,500 police forces, and 2,000 civilians assigned to election supervision. The personnel were dispersed among forty-two offices throughout Namibia. To confirm the stages of Cuban troop withdrawals from Angola the Security Council also authorized a ninety-member United Nations Angola Verification Mission (UNAVEM). All stages of the schedule were carried out as projected with elections in November 1989 for a Constituent Assembly and the swearing in on March 21, 1990, of Sam Nujoma, leader of SWAPO, as the first President of Namibia. One month later Namibia became the 160th member of the United Nations.

UNTAG must be considered one of the most successful UN peacekeeping efforts. It involved approximately 8,000 personnel of diverse categories, it completed all its assignments in slightly less than a year, and it operated on a budget of $373 million (more than 10 percent under the amount the General Assembly had authorized). It performed effectively under adverse physical conditions and contained numerous incidents threatening to disrupt the peaceful fulfillment of the schedule. UNTAG represented the major instrument for completing a process toward self-rule that had frustrated the United Nations for nearly forty-five years.

GENERAL ASSESSMENT OF UNITED NATIONS PRACTICE

Given the world situation from 1945 into the 1990s, the principle of collective security is probably unworkable and unrealistic. The strength of nationalism and the safeguarding of sovereignty preclude automatic collective responses by states whose interests are not directly promoted by stopping aggression wherever it may occur. National rivalries and competing alliance systems prevent universal responses to threats to international peace. Basic disagreement over the terms for implementing Article 43 of the Charter to provide an international police force was the prelude to other clashes that have frequently immobilized the United Nations as an instrument for peace. The general lack of recourse to Chapter VII of the Charter reflects the lack of unanimity of the United Nations members in seeking solutions to the most serious situations threatening world peace and stability. Until international peace becomes the *primary* goal of the foreign policies of the world's nations, collective security or any adequate substitute at the global level will remain an unattainable solution. The Security Council has imposed economic sanctions in several situations but with limited effect.

In the face of collective-security stalemate, the United Nations has devised new methods for dealing with a limited range of threatening situations. Military forces from the lesser powers have been utilized, not to defeat aggressors, but to keep or restore peace, generally without recourse to arms, at the invitation of a host country on whose soil they are stationed. The ingenuity of statesmen such as Lester Pearson has been linked with the resourcefulness and administrative capability of successive Secretaries-General and the cooperation of governments furnishing troops to make possible innovations in peacekeeping procedures. Going beyond peaceful settlement, but stopping short of enforcement by collective might, these procedures have been dubbed "Chapter Six and One-half," since they fill the interstices between peaceful settlement and collective-security actions. In most of these situations the presence of observer or military corps, supplemented by preventive diplomacy efforts of the Secretary-General or his representatives or assistants, have acted to stabilize or defuse crisis conditions. The financial costs have threatened the United Nations with bankruptcy, but the positive benefits may be immeasurable in monetary terms. A symbol of the value and widely acclaimed contributions of United Nations peacekeeping forces was the awarding to them of the 1988 Nobel Peace Prize. With the exception of the Organization of American States, regional organizations have seldom been effective as agents for conflict management.

Since 1988 new applications and modifications of the peacekeeping technique have put strains on the system and raised questions concerning its future viability. More new peacekeeping missions (including some of the largest and most expensive) were initiated in a six-year interval than in the previous forty years. In less than two years in 1992–93 the number of peacekeeping personnel increased by sixfold to approximately 70,000, and the annual costs rose to more than $3 billion, three times the regular UN budget. Arrearages increased, and proposals to establish a substantial peacekeeping revolving fund were not implemented.

During this same period the sources of peacekeeping personnel and the mandates of peacekeeping missions were modified and expanded. Instead of insulating the areas of conflict from major power involvement, forces from the permanent members of the Security Council participated in missions in Yugoslavia, Cambodia, Somalia, and Western Sahara. Contrary to earlier practice, half of the recent peacekeeping operations have been involved in internal conflicts. New roles have included the supervision of elections, the overseeing of transitions to new governments, the monitoring of referenda on national self-determination, the supervision and delivery of humanitarian assistance, the verification of troop withdrawals, surveillance over the demobilization and disarming of irregular forces, the protection of refugees, the establishment and training of police forces, and (most extremely) the use of force against factions that threaten law and order.

The combination of factors described above calls into question the future role of the United Nations in situations involving threats to or breaches of the peace. Will the nations that vote for the creation of numerous peace-keeping forces be willing to solve the problem of adequate financing? Should the United Nations continue to involve itself in states' internal disputes? Have the original principles of peacekeeping been stretched beyond reasonable limits, thus blurring the boundaries that distinguish it from peacemaking and peace-enforcing? Will the United Nations be overwhelmed by involvement in a plethora of regional, national, and ethnic conflicts? Will the members of the United Nations be willing to strengthen the organization along some of the lines suggested by Secretary-General Boutros Boutros-Ghali in his "Agenda for Peace" issued in 1992 to make it a more effective agency for conflict resolution? The future role of the United Nations in the peace and security arena will be largely determined by the answers to these questions, and the answers lie within the collective wisdom and will emanating from the member states.

8

THE SEARCH FOR JUSTICE UNDER LAW

Humans are political beings who develop orderly processes and institutions to establish relationships among themselves. All human societies have rules substituting order for chaos in intersocietal relations. Laws establish norms governing a society. As a society becomes more complex, its laws also become broader and more detailed. Some laws may be written; others are not, but rather are established customs and usages followed by the society, which are as binding as written laws.

Societies exist on many levels. But there is not yet an effective world society, with laws to govern the relationships between persons or political units.

Today's international organization is an underdeveloped, imperfect, yet potentially useful step toward world order. Evolving and implementing more effective international laws are two goals of such organizations as the League of Nations and the United Nations. Other goals necessary for world order are settling disputes peacefully and maintaining peace, which pertain more to the very basis and activities of these organizations, and which were examined in Chapters 6 and 7. Applying international legal principles to such disputes or threats to international peace is one way of resolving conflict. International law also is used in other aspects of international organizations and relationships. In this chapter we will show further how law is established at the international level.

LAW IN NATIONAL AND INTERNATIONAL SYSTEMS

Today's world is characterized by the existence of more than 180 national states that claim attributes of independence and sovereignty and that are organized for governmental purposes on the basis of law. We have previously defined law as a body of established norms for the governance of a society. The essential condition for law is the recognition of rules that are binding as a result of a group conviction to that effect by the members of the community.

States vary widely in the characteristics of their legal systems. Newly established states may possess little written law and in some cases a minimum of customary law. A state may have within it a high degree of consensus on the basic norms for governance, or it may be divided by factions among which struggle and compromise will produce a stormy and uncertain further development of legal rules. Lawmaking powers may be concentrated in few hands, or they may be widely shared. A central body of law may regulate most of the relations of the members, or legal authority may be decentralized through several levels of government. Government regulation may impinge on every aspect of individual existence, or minimal controls or support may exist.

In spite of wide variations, certain common characteristics of national legal systems are notable. Except for occasional rebellions the members of the society agree that state authority should exist and that the laws should be generally respected and obeyed. Some of the rules should be written in the form of political creeds, constitutions, legislation, court decrees, executive orders, and administrative rulings. There should be both duly constituted authority to enact new law and the means to enforce the law on reluctant or dissident members or groups within the society. Courts or similar agencies should interpret and apply the law to controversies. Consensus should generally provide compliance with the law so that violations of law are the exception, not the rule. Legal norms should be sufficiently stable to maintain the understanding necessary as a basis for consensus. Both individuals and groups are the subjects and beneficiaries of the law.

International law is deficient in several of the attributes that contribute to the effectiveness of national legal systems. Traditionally, only states have been considered the subjects of international law although, in recent years, in such areas as human rights and war crimes, a trend toward the applicability of international law to individuals has been emerging. These same states have retained a monopoly of the means of coercion and have only slowly and reluctantly created supranational agencies vested with the authority to enforce the will of the collectivity upon the individual state. War, means of peaceful settlement, collective security, and world public opinion seem inadequate substitutes at the international level for the kind of action that may be taken against recalcitrant individuals or dissident groups to force compliance with established legal norms within national states.

Other deficiencies of international law include the lack of satisfactory means for developing, applying, and enforcing legal norms. Although national as well as international law is developed, in part, through custom, no true legislative bodies with responsibility for developing new law exist at the international level. Legislation is a swifter and more flexible means of adding to or changing a body of law than the slower and uncertain process of development through custom. The counterpart of national legislation at the international level is the multilateral lawmaking treaty, but these treaties are produced by ad hoc conferences or by international agencies performing other major functions, not by permanent bodies established to exercise primarily legislative functions. Although occasional claims are made that international agreements may be enforced against nonsubscribers to the agreements, the general interpretation of international law is that treaties are binding only on states that specifically assent to their terms. Legislation by majority rule, binding on all members of the society, has few counterparts in international practice.

With limited exceptions the few international courts that exist exercise no general compulsory jurisdiction. In broad terms each state decides when to submit disputes to court jurisdiction subject to its own convenience and interests. States may agree in advance to submit certain types of controversies to court decision, but reservations and interpretations applying to such obligations allow international courts to languish from inactivity. However, national courts also apply international law in their decisions.

Perhaps the inadequacy of enforcement machinery is the most unsatisfactory aspect of the international legal system. No international agencies are authorized to enforce international law. The means of enforcement are monopolized by national states, which are reluctant to curtail their own power and to entrust their security to international agencies.

In summary, each state claims sovereign authority to be its own interpreter of its rights, its own source of authority, and its own strength to maintain its rights. In these respects the international legal system is a primitive arrangement under which threats to order and impediments to justice are as much to be anticipated as their antithetical conditions within well-developed national legal systems.

An assessment of the deficiencies of international law may lead erroneously to the conclusion that no legal principles operate across national boundaries, but an inadequate system does not signify the absence of any system. The impression that international law is of little significance may be reinforced by the resort of states to self-help in those dramatic situations that elicit emotional responses and make world headlines. Emphasis upon deficiencies and crises tends to obscure the broad utility of international law in the daily and orderly relations of states.

The two most important sources of international law are the customs of states and lawmaking treaties. The development of customary law is dependent on the length of time required for state practice to become established as law and on the acceptability of majority practice. Nevertheless, custom accounts for a substantial body of international law in the same way that it establishes many norms for accepted behavior in national societies. As international contacts multiplied in recent decades, lawmaking treaties became increasingly common. International treaties or conventions, like national legislation, tend to convert customary law into statutory law and to clarify and extend its principles. That is, the absence of international legislative bodies has not prevented the acceptance by states of hundreds of conventions specifying mutual obligations and prerogatives. When these conventions are negotiated among and ratified by a large proportion of the world's national governments, or when a pattern of bilateral or limited-party treaties forms a network binding most of the world's states to common terms, a body of international legislation is established by treaty.

Article 38 of the Statute of the International Court of Justice specifies three other sources of international law that the Court may apply. These secondary sources are (1) general principles of law recognized by civilized nations, (2) judicial decisions, and (3) the teachings of the most highly qualified publicists of various nations.

One of the imperfections of international law is that it does not cover all subjects and circumstances. However, even with gaps, courts should be able, by applying analogies from the primary and secondary sources cited above, to "find the law" necessary for deciding cases not specifically covered in previously established principles of international law. Although the gaps may be wider in international than in municipal law, national courts also are required, on occasion, to fill the lacunae in the law and, thus, to establish new law.

For all its imperfections, international law plays an important role in the twentieth century. A substantial body of such law has accumulated because nations have been dealing with each other for hundreds of years and the contacts and legal agreements multiply with each decade. The significance of international law is dramatized by Louis Henkin in a negative approach to the subject.

> If one doubts the significance of this law, one need only imagine a world from which it were absent. . . . There would be no security of nations or stability of governments; territory and airspace would not be respected; vessels could navigate only at their constant peril; property—within or without any given territory—would be subject to arbitrary seizure; persons would have no protection of

law or of diplomacy; agreements would not be made or observed; diplomatic relations would end; international trade would cease; international organizations and arrangements would disappear.[1]

If the absence of organized sanctions is the greatest deficiency of international law, this inadequacy may cause one to overlook the most important sanction of both national and international systems. The main reason national systems work is the broad acceptance of legal norms by the bulk of the community—not the provision of punishment for violators. The convenience of the society is buttressed by this broad consensus. The regularity of relations among states is also guaranteed by consensus and reciprocity. The means for handling violations are inadequate, but the mutual interests of the members of the international community require compliance with international law as the normal pattern of behavior.

LEGAL DEVELOPMENTS BEFORE 1945

The modern state system was of European origin, and a body of international law developed as an adjunct of the state system. In the seventeenth century the law established by the practices of states was clarified in the writings of such scholars as Suarez and Grotius. During this early period of development of international legal principles, the emphasis upon the law of war was much greater than upon the peaceful relations of states.

In the nineteenth century, arbitration of disputes came into practice under the leadership of the United States and Great Britain. A settlement of the *Alabama* claims was made in 1872 through arbitral procedure. In the early twentieth century a number of standing arbitration treaties were agreed to, and several disputes were submitted to the jurisdiction of the Permanent Court of Arbitration, created as a result of the Hague Peace Conference of 1899. The Court continues in existence but has been little used since 1914.

The Permanent Court of International Justice (PCIJ) was not a part of the official organization of the League of Nations, and membership in the Court was separate from League membership, but other linkages were very close. Article 14 of the Covenant specified that the League Council was responsible for formulating plans for the PCIJ, which was to be competent to hear and determine international disputes and to give advisory legal opinions at the request of the Council or Assembly. The Statute of the Court, in the form of a treaty, was promptly developed, opened to state ratification, and

---

[1]Louis Henkin, *How Nations Behave: Law and Foreign Policy* (New York: Praeger, 1970), pp. 22–23.

came into force in September 1921. Judges were chosen by concurrent majorities of the Council and the Assembly, and the budget of the PCIJ was provided as a part of the League budget. Although more than fifty states became members, the United States never joined the Court.

The Court was never permitted to decide the most vital issues affecting the interests of the major powers, but its work has generally been assessed as significant and highly professional and impartial. By 1940 the PCIJ had handed down thirty-two decisions and twenty-seven advisory opinions. The Court was authorized to exercise jurisdiction over disputes arising under hundreds of treaties drawn up during this period. The reputation of the Court was such that, when the United Nations was formed, the Statute of the new Court was nearly identical with that of the PCIJ.

Whereas the early emphasis of international law had been upon the law of warfare, the main thrust of efforts after 1918 turned to the promotion of peace. The establishment of the League of Nations and the PCIJ reflects this emphasis. The League was recognized as inadequate for guaranteeing peace, so supplementary actions were taken to reinforce the means for preventing war. The movement for disarmament took shape in the Washington and London naval conferences of 1921 and 1930. A general disarmament conference under League sponsorship, after years of preparatory work, foundered under basic national disagreements over the means and methods to be followed in achieving world disarmament. The Locarno Pact of 1925 set up obligations to enforce the territorial integrity of European states. In 1928 the Kellogg-Briand Pact, or Pact of Paris, attempted to outlaw war by renouncing it as an instrument of national policy. This pact was ratified by most of the world's governments but proved ineffective in the face of the aggressive actions of the expansionist states in the 1930s. The General Act for Pacific Settlement formulated the same year was not widely accepted.

Other noteworthy attempts to expand the influence of international law include the adoption, in 1925, of a protocol against gas warfare and the convening of a Hague conference, in 1930, for the purpose of codifying laws of nationality, the territorial seas, and state obligations toward aliens. Although the specific results of the Hague conference were disappointing, it represented a part of a widespread continuing effort to develop and clarify various aspects of international law. The International Labor Organization was more successful than most agencies in securing wide acceptance of international conventions; in this instance the subject matter pertained to the social welfare of workers.[2]

---

[2]See Chapter 14 for further details on ILO contributions to international social legislation.

THE CHARTER AS AN INSTRUMENT
OF INTERNATIONAL LAW

As a multilateral treaty that prescribes principles and rules for the behavior of states and that is subscribed to by most national governments, the United Nations Charter is a part of the developing body of international law. Such a statement, however, does not do justice to the relative contribution of the Charter to the dynamics of the process of legal development. The significance of the Charter as compared with other treaties lies in its principles, its scope, and its capacity for generating a chain of activities that, in turn, produce further additions to international law.

The Charter lays down principles that are of sweeping significance to the relations of states. The most fundamental is the promise of all members to settle disputes by peaceful means and to refrain from the threat or use of force against other states or in any manner inconsistent with the purposes of the Charter. This obligation is a departure from previous reliance on force, and the Charter seeks to make the obligation universal. The means of enforcement and the degrees of compliance have been imperfect, but the principle has been regularly applied in United Nations consideration of disputes and in the behavior of states, with the result that wars of one state against another have been kept down in spite of increased contacts, sources of tension, and numbers of states. Louis Henkin strongly asserts that

> the law of the Charter, the wide acceptance of that law by governments and peoples, the authority of the United Nations and world opinion behind the law, and other political reactions (stronger because war has been outlawed) can claim substantial credit for the fact that the world has avoided major war since 1945. The sense that war is not acceptable conduct has taken some hold; nations more readily find that their security and other national interests do not require the use of force after all; even where force is used, the fact that it is now illegal must be taken into account and limits the scope, the weapons, the duration, the purposes, the justifications.[3]

The Charter is more significant in expanding international law than most treaties because of the range of activities provided for in its various articles. The Charter establishes a general, multipurpose organization. It goes beyond a statement of agreed principles and obligations by authorizing the creation of an elaborate set of major and subsidiary agencies. It envisions six major organs, numerous committees or commissions, and the establishment of a pattern of relationships between the central organization and a network of specialized agencies, regional organizations, and nongovernmental organizations throughout the world. Tens of thousands of persons are thus involved in a wide range of political, legal, economic, social, and humanitarian activi-

---

[3]Henkin, *How Nations Behave*, p. 137.

ties, with the United Nations as the focal point of the efforts. The Charter is significant because it is the fundamental law or constitution for the only general-purpose, nearly universal organization that exists in today's world. Even if it does not establish a true government, it creates an elaborate structure through which states have obligated themselves to cooperate for many mutually advantageous ends.

The United Nations is a dynamic organization in which many agencies engage in active programs and in which a wide range of decisions are made. One by-product of these activities and decisions is the gradual expansion of international law. Not only do agencies such as the International Court of Justice and the International Law Commission (to be discussed in more detail in the following sections of this chapter) play a major role in developing law, but some of the decisions of other organs gradually acquire the status of law as well. An extensive analysis of this process has been made by Rosalyn Higgins, who states in the introduction to her study:

> Collective acts of states, repeated by and acquiesced in by sufficient numbers with sufficient frequency, eventually attain the status of law. The existence of the United Nations—and especially its accelerated trend toward universality of membership since 1955—now provides a very clear, very concentrated, focal point for state practice. Here, then, is the reason for looking to United Nations practice in a search for the direction of the development of international law.[4]

At exactly what point the collective action of states taken in United Nations organs becomes accepted as customary international law is not easily ascertainable, but that the process occurs is beyond reasonable doubt.

The United Nations Charter is not a static legal instrument but has grown through interpretation and usage. International law has been altered as the Charter has been modified and amplified by such interpretation. The Charter was written in general and often deliberately ambiguous terms. It is subject to interpretation by the member states and by each organ, and, as with any flexible constitution, the Charter expands and takes on new meaning with widely accepted interpretation and the resulting practice. Examples are myriad and include the practice of abstentions in the Security Council, the assumption of unforeseen powers by the General Assembly, the degree of initiative exercised by the Secretary-General, and the substitution of peacekeeping procedures for an unworkable system of collective security.

The United Nations General Assembly, the International Law Commission, the specialized agencies, and United Nations commissions under the aegis of the Economic and Social Council have all taken initiatives and carried on preparatory work resulting in treaties that are significant landmarks in the growing body of international law. A few of the most important examples

---

[4]Rosalyn Higgins, *The Development of International Law through the Political Organs of the United Nations* (New York: Oxford University Press, 1963), p. 2.

include the Treaty Governing the Exploration and Use of Outer Space (1967), four conventions on the law of the seas (1958), the Vienna Conventions on Diplomatic and Consular Relations (1961 and 1963), the Convention on the Settlement of Investment Disputes (1965), the Genocide Convention (1948), the Covenants on Human Rights (1966), the Convention on the Law of Treaties (1969), the Convention on the Succession of States in Respect of Treaties (1978), and the Convention on the Rights of the Child (1989).

Although international law may emerge from many sources within the United Nations, the General Assembly is assigned special responsibility for its development. Article 13 of the Charter specifies that the "General Assembly shall initiate studies and make recommendations for the purpose of . . . encouraging the progressive development of international law and its codification." These responsibilities are exercised in part through (1) the Assembly's Sixth (Legal) Committee, (2) the International Law Commission, (3) the Assembly's own interpretations and practice, and (4) international conferences that are called for formulating treaties on specific subjects.

Another way in which the General Assembly reinforces and verifies international law is by declarations of the existence of legal principles. When such declarations, referring to specific principles, are sustained by the supporting votes of nearly all members, the legal norms involved are given added weight as clearly established elements in international law. Examples of such declarations include the Declaration on the Granting of Independence to Colonial Countries and Peoples (1960), which was adopted by a vote of 89–0 with nine abstentions, and the 1961 General Assembly resolution on apartheid in South Africa as a flagrant violation of the Charter, which was adopted by a vote of 97–2 with one abstention.

THE ROLE OF THE INTERNATIONAL COURT OF JUSTICE

The International Court of Justice (ICJ) is the principal judicial arm of the United Nations. It is designated as one of the six major organs of the United Nations and is the successor to the Permanent Court of International Justice (PCIJ) established by the League of Nations. The Statute of the Court is an integral part of the United Nations Charter, and a government's act of ratification involves acceptance of both documents. Under special provisions, Switzerland, which is not a United Nations member, and Liechtenstein and San Marino prior to becoming members in 1990 and 1992 respectively, adhered to the Court Statute. The general facts concerning the composition, procedures, headquarters, and functions of the Court were outlined in Chapter 4 of this text and will not be repeated here.

One deficiency of the international legal system as compared with national systems is the lack of compulsory jurisdiction of the ICJ. One attribute of sovereignty that states refuse to surrender to international authority is their freedom to choose whether or not they will submit any particular case for judicial determination. Once they have agreed to submit a case to the Court, they are bound by the principles of international law to accept and carry out the decision, although there is no satisfactory means for enforcement of decisions, and refusal to comply has, on more than one occasion, occurred.

An attempt to partially overcome the lack of compulsory jurisdiction was written into the Statute of the ICJ in Article 36. This article provides in section 2 that any party to the Statute may declare that it recognizes as compulsory, in relation to any other state accepting the same obligation, the jurisdiction of the Court in all legal disputes concerning:

a. the interpretation of a treaty;
b. any question of international law;
c. the existence of any fact which, if established, would constitute a breach of an international obligation;
d. the nature or extent of the reparation to be made for the breach of an international obligation.

Article 36, section 2, was an attempt to build a bridge between the principle of sovereignty and that of compulsory jurisdiction. The aim was to open an area in which a degree of international order could be established through the judicial process.

This "optional clause" has not resulted in the submission of a wide range of disputes over legal questions to the Court for settlement. By July 1993, only fifty-six states had filed declarations of acceptance of the "optional clause" that were currently in effect. The acceptances of eleven other states had, through the years, expired or been terminated. Several states have attached reservations to their acceptance of the compulsory jurisdiction of the Court. The most sweeping of these reservations was made by the United States in the Connally Amendment, which specified that the jurisdiction of the Court would not apply to "disputes with regard to matters which are essentially within the domestic jurisdiction of the United States *as determined by the United States of America*" (italics added). Not only did this reservation practically nullify the compulsory jurisdiction clause by allowing the United States to decide unilaterally that any case it wished not to submit was "essentially" one of domestic jurisdiction, but it also allowed, under the legal principle of reciprocity, any other party to a case involving the United States to invoke the same privilege. All attempts at repeal of the self-judging Connally reservation were futile. However, on April 7, 1986, this issue became moot when the United States, with the required six months' notice, withdrew its adherence to the "optional clause." Six weeks later Israel also terminated its adherence to Article 36(2).

The proportion of economically underdeveloped countries that have accepted the compulsory jurisdiction of the Court, with or without reservations, is smaller than that of the developed countries. The high response from Europe and from such countries as Canada, Australia, and New Zealand is often attributed to the reflection of the Court and of the body of international law of European norms and standards of justice, since that area is the source from which modern international law developed.

The Court's jurisdiction in contentious matters is by no means limited to the "optional clause" of its Statute and the voluntary submission of cases by parties to disputes. Hundreds of bilateral and multilateral treaties contain clauses agreeing that the parties will submit disputes arising under the terms of each treaty to the International Court of Justice. In fact, most recent cases submitted to the Court have been based on such treaty agreements.[5]

Court Judgments

With 185 states as parties to the Statute of the ICJ and with 56 of them as adherents to the compulsory jurisdiction provisions (albeit with some significant reservations), it might reasonably be assumed that the Court would have a full docket of cases. Since only one such court exists and since international conflicts of interest are legion, one would expect that the Court would be swamped with pending litigation. These assumptions concerning the amount of business before the Court have not been borne out in practice. The reasons include (1) distrust of the Court, (2) distrust of the judicial process, (3) unwillingness of states to submit their interests to outside determination, or (4) bad faith by states in carrying out their obligations assumed under the United Nations Charter and the Court Statute. The reasons for the neglect of the Court will be further examined in the subsequent sections of this chapter.

Table 8–1 lists all the cases placed before the ICJ from the election of the first panel of judges in 1946 through 1992. The first case, the Corfu Channel Case, was referred to the Court a year after the Court's initial organization. The peak periods for the submission of new cases came in 1949–51, 1953–55, 1957–59, and 1989–92.

The 1960s are in sharp contrast with the 1950s in the amount of business before the Court. In the 1950s, twenty-nine cases were submitted to the ICJ; in the 1960s, the number was only six cases on four subjects, as both the South-West Africa question and the North Sea Continental Shelf controversy involved pairs of related cases on single subjects. In fact, in spite of six years of

---

[5]Thomas M. Franck, *Judging the World Court* (New York: Priority Press Publication, 1986), pp. 27–33.

TABLE 8–1   INTERNATIONAL COURT OF JUSTICE CASES AND ADVISORY
OPINIONS (1947–92)

I. Cases In Which Judgments Were Rendered		
Title	*Parties*	*Dates*
1. Corfu Channel	United Kingdom v. Albania	1947–49
2. Fisheries	United Kingdom v. Norway	1949–51
3. (a) Asylum	Colombia/Peru*	1949–50
(b) Request for Interpretation of Judgment in Asylum Case	Colombia v. Peru	1950
(c) Haya de la Torre	Colombia v. Peru	1950–51
4. Rights of Nationals of the United States in Morocco	France v. United States	1950–52
5. Ambatielos	Greece v. United Kingdom	1951–53
6. Anglo-Iranian Oil Co.	United Kingdom v. Iran	1951–52
7. Minquiers and Ecrehos	France/United Kingdom*	1951–53
8. Nottebohm	Liechtenstein v. Guatemala	1951–55
9. Monetary Gold Removed from Rome in 1943	Italy v. France, United Kingdom, and United States	1953–54
10. Certain Norwegian Loans	France v. Norway	1955–57
11. Right of Passage over Indian Territory	Portugal v. India	1955–60
12. Application of Convention of 1902 Governing the Guardianship of Infants	Netherlands v. Sweden	1957–58
13. Interhandel	Switzerland v. United States	1957–59
14. Aerial Incident of 27 July 1955	Israel v. Bulgaria	1957–59
15. Sovereignty over Certain Frontier Land	Belgium/Netherlands*	1957–59
16. Arbitral Award Made by the King of Spain on 23 December 1906	Honduras v. Nicaragua	1958–60
17. (a) Barcelona Traction, Light and Power Co., Ltd.	Belgium v. Spain	1958–61
(b) Barcelona Traction, Light and Power Co., Ltd. (New Application)	Belgium v. Spain	1962–70
18. Temple of Preah Vihear	Cambodia v. Thailand	1959–62
19. South-West Africa	Ethiopia v. South Africa; Liberia v. South Africa	1960–66
20. North Cameroons	Cameroon v. United Kingdom	1961–63
21. North Sea Continental Shelf	Federal Republic of Germany/Denmark; Federal Republic of Germany/Netherlands*	1967–69

(continued)

TABLE 8–1   (continued)

I. Cases In Which Judgments Were Rendered

Title	Parties	Dates
22. Appeal Relating to the Jurisdiction of the ICAO Council	India v. Pakistan	1971–72
23. Fisheries Jurisdiction	United Kingdom v. Iceland	1972–74
24. Fisheries Jurisdiction	Federal Republic of Germany v. Iceland	1972–74
25. Nuclear Tests	Australia v. France	1973–74
26. Nuclear Tests	New Zealand v. France	1973–74
27. Continental Shelf	Tunisia v. Libyan Arab Jamahiriya	1978–82
28. Continental Shelf	Libyan Arab Jamahiriya/Malta*	1982–85
29. Application for Revision and Interpretation of Judgment of 24 February 1982 Concerning the Continental Shelf	Tunisia/Libyan Arab Jamahiriya	1984–85
30. Arbitral Award of 31 July 1989	Guinea-Bissau v. Senegal	1989–91
31. Territorial Dispute	Libyan Arab Jamahiriya v. Chad	1990–94

II. Cases In Which Special Order Was Rendered

Title	Parties	Dates
1. United States Diplomatic and Consular Staff in Teheran	United States v. Iran	1979–81
2. Libyan Application against the United Kingdom	Libyan Arab Jamahiriya v. United Kingdom	1992
3. Libyan Application against the United States	Libyan Arab Jamahiriya v. United States	1992

III. Cases Pending

Title	Parties	Dates
1. Maritime Delimitation in the Area between Greenland and Jan Mayen	Denmark v. Norway	1988–

(continued)

TABLE 8–1   (continued)

III. Cases Pending

Title	Parties	Dates
2. Aerial Incident of 3 July 1988	Islamic Republic of Iran v. United States	1989–
3. Certain Phosphate Lands in Nauru	Nauru v. Australia	1989–
4. East Timor	Portugal v. Australia	1991–
5. Maritime Delimitation between Guinea-Bissau and Senegal	Guinea-Bissau v. Senegal	1991–
6. Maritime Delimitation and Territorial Questions between Qatar and Bahrain	Qatar v. Bahrain	1991–
7. Projected Diversion of the Danube	Hungary v. Czech and Slovak Federal Republic	1992–
8. Destruction of Offshore Oil Platforms	Iran v. United States	1992–

IV. Contentious Cases before a Chamber

Title	Parties	Dates
1. Delimitation of Maritime Boundary in Gulf of Maine Area	Canada/United States*	1981–84
2. Frontier Dispute	Burkina Faso/Mali*	1983–87
3. Land, Island, and Maritime Frontier Dispute	El Salvador/Honduras	1986–92
4. Elettronica Sieula S.p.A (ELSI)	United States v. Italy	1987–

V. Cases Removed without Judgment

Title	Parties	Dates
1. Protection of French Nationals and Protected Persons in Egypt	France v. Egypt	1949–50
2. Electricite de Beyrouth Co.	France v. Lebanon	1953–54
3. (a) Treatment in Hungary of Aircraft and Crew of United States	United States v. Hungary	1954
(b) Treatment in Hungary of Aircraft and Crew of United States	United States v. USSR	1954

(continued)

TABLE 8–1   (continued)

V. Cases Removed without Judgment

Title	Parties	Dates
4. Aerial Incident of 10 March 1953	United States v. Czechoslovakia	1955–56
5. (a) Antarctica	United Kingdom v. Argentina	1955–56
(b) Antarctica	United Kingdom v. Chile	1955–56
6. Aerial Incident of 7 October 1952	United States v. USSR	1955–56
7. Aerial Incident of 27 July 1955	United States v. Bulgaria	1957–60
8. Aerial Incident of 27 July 1955	United Kingdom v. Bulgaria	1957–59
9. Aerial Incident of 4 September 1954	United States v. USSR	1958
10. Compagnie du Port, des Quais et des Entrepots de Beyrouth and Société Radio-Orient	France v. Lebanon	1959–60
11. Aerial Incident of 7 November 1954	United States v. USSR	1959
12. Trial of Pakistani Prisoners of War	Pakistan v. India	1973
13. Aegean Sea Continental Shelf	Greece v. Turkey	1976–78
14. Military and Paramilitary Activities in and against Nicaragua	Nicaragua v. United States	1984–91
15. Border and Transborder Armed Actions	Nicaragua v. Costa Rica	1986–87
16. Border and Transborder Armed Actions	Nicaragua v. Honduras	1986–92
17. Passage through the Great Belt	Finland v. Denmark	1991–92

VI. Advisory Opinions

Title	Requested by	Dates
1. Conditions of Admission of a State to Membership in the UN	UN General Assembly	1947–48
2. Reparation for Injuries Suffered in the Service of the UN	UN General Assembly	1948–49
3. Interpretation of Peace Treaties with Bulgaria, Hungary, and Rumania	UN General Assembly	1949–50
4. Competence of the General Assembly for the Admission of a State to the UN	UN General Assembly	1949–50

(continued)

TABLE 8–1   (continued)

VI. Advisory Opinions		
Title	*Requested by*	*Dates*
5. International Status of South-West Africa	UN General Assembly	1949–50
6. Reservations to the Convention on the Prevention and Punishment of the Crime of Genocide	UN General Assembly	1950–51
7. Effect of Awards of Compensation Made by the UN Administrative Tribunal	UN General Assembly	1953–54
8. Voting Procedure on Questions Relating to Reports and Petitions Concerning the Territory of South-West Africa	UN General Assembly	1954–55
9. Judgments of the Administrative Tribunal of the ILO upon Complaints Made against UNESCO	UNESCO Executive Board	1955–56
10. Admissibility of Hearings of Petitioners by the Committee on South-West Africa	UN General Assembly	1955–56
11. Constitution of the Maritime Safety Committee of the Inter-Governmental Maritime Consultative Organization	IMCO Assembly	1959–60
12. Certain Expenses of the UN [Art. 17(2) of the Charter]	UN General Assembly	1961–62
13. Legal Consequences for States of the Continued Presence of South Africa in Namibia (South-West Africa) Notwithstanding Security Council Resolution 276 (1970)	UN Security Council	1970–71
14. Application for Review of Judgment No. 158 of the UN Administrative Tribunal	Committee on Applications for Review of Administrative Tribunal Judgments	1972–73
15. Western Sahara	UN General Assembly	1974–75
16. Interpretation of Agreement of 25 March 1951 between the WHO and Egypt	World Health Assembly	1980
17. Application for Review of Judgment No. 273 of the	Committee on Applications for Review of Administrative Tribunal	1981–82

(continued)

TABLE 8–1   (continued)

VI. Advisory Opinions		
Title	*Requested by*	*Dates*
UN Administrative Tribunal	Judgments	
18. Application for Review of Judgment No. 333 of the UN Administrative Tribunal	Committee on Applications for Review of Administrative Tribunal Judgments	1984–87
19. Applicability of the Obligation to Arbitrate under the UN Headquarters Agreement	UN General Assembly	1988
20. Applicability of Article VI, Section 22, of the Convention on the Privileges and Immunities of the UN	Economic and Social Council	1989

*Proceedings instituted by special agreement

litigation in the South-West Africa case and eight years in the Barcelona Traction Light and Power Company case, the ICJ was twice for the brief periods in 1970 and 1971 completely without any pending business of any kind including requests for advisory opinions. In the period since 1971 a moderate increase in the workload of the Court has developed, with more cases since 1989.

The table of ICJ cases also demonstrates that a substantial number of controversies are removed from the Court's jurisdiction in the preliminary stages with the result that the Court never reaches the point of formulating a judgment. These removals before judgment fall into two categories. The larger group are those in which a plaintiff state presents a case to the Court with a request that the defendant state agree to accept the Court's jurisdiction for the settlement of the dispute. When the state against which the charge is made refuses to submit to the Court's jurisdiction, the Court has no choice but to remove the case from its list. Most of the cases involving aerial incidents and the two cases relating to Antarctica claims are in this category. The remaining cases that fail to reach the judgment stage are removed at the request of the plaintiff, usually on the grounds that a satisfactory settlement or method of settlement has been agreed to by the parties. This procedure is similar to a settlement out of court in civil cases in municipal law. Since these cases require relatively little of the judges' time and consideration, the Court's workload has been lighter than the list of cases and opinions might suggest.

One special provision of the Statute of the ICJ had never been used until the 1980s. This provision allows greater flexibility in the handling of disputes by permitting the Court to establish special chambers of three or more judges to hear a specific case or to deal with a particular category of cases. The judgment of a special panel shall be considered as rendered by the full Court. Three boundary disputes have been handled by five-judge chambers at the request of the parties to the disputes. These were a dispute between the United States and Canada over the maritime boundary in the Gulf of Maine, a frontier dispute between Burkina Faso and Mali, and a boundary and maritime frontier dispute between El Salvador and Honduras. A special chamber was also established for a 1987 dispute between the United States and Italy.

Another point, obvious to any well-informed person who examines the list of ICJ cases, is that the major international conflicts since 1945 have been dealt with by bodies other than the Court. Judgments by the ICJ have been requested in none of the more serious clashes that have come before the political organs of the United Nations—clashes such as Korea, the Congo, Palestine, Suez, Cyprus, Rhodesia, or Afghanistan. The level of conflict involved in Court cases is also low as compared with the situations dealt with mainly outside the United Nations, such as Vietnam, Biafra, the Cuban missile crisis, Northern Ireland, or the Chinese border clashes. This is not to say that no questions of legal principles are involved in all these examples or that the issues involved are unsuitable for judicial determination. Rather, it is an indication that the nations of the world, and particularly the most powerful states, do not entrust questions of national interest to impartial determination based on the established rules of international law.

If the cases decided by the Court are not notable for their involvement with world headlines, they may, nevertheless, help to establish an ever-growing set of principles that, by slow accretion, add to the body of international law. Another major significance of Court judgments is the avoidance by the parties of settlement through resort to violence or other means not based on the rule of law. Willingness to submit a case to legal determination not only establishes patterns of compliance with legal norms for the states involved but, it is hoped, serves as an example to other states of the desirability of this method of peaceful settlement of disputes.

A brief summary of a few of the Court's most important cases will illustrate the ICJ's adjudicatory role. The selection is based on the significance of legal principles involved and on the degree of general interest in the cases.

Corfu Channel Case. On October 22, 1946, two British destroyers passing through the Corfu Channel adjacent to Albania struck mines, and forty-four naval personnel lost their lives. The channel had been swept in 1945, so the assumption was made that the mines had been recently laid by Albania or another party. The British on November 12 and 13, without Albania's consent, used minesweepers to clear the channel. In January 1947, the United Kingdom submitted the dispute to the Security Council, which, after some investigation and debate, adopted a resolution recommending that the parties refer the dispute to the ICJ for settlement.

Albania had voluntarily been represented before the Security Council during the Corfu Channel debate and had accepted the resolution to refer the question to the Court but raised preliminary questions challenging technical aspects concerning the Court's jurisdiction. The Court rejected Albania's preliminary objection by a vote of 15–1. The only judge dissenting was the ad hoc judge from Czechoslovakia appointed by Albania under the right of a party to a case not represented on the Court to choose a person to sit for that case.

After disposing of the preliminary objection, the Court turned to the main issues of the case and handed down a judgment on April 9, 1949. The Court ruled that the mine field could not have been laid without the knowledge of Albania, that Albania was responsible for the loss of life and damages, and that compensation should be paid. The Court also decided that the British ships enjoyed the right of innocent passage through an international waterway, although part of the channel lies within the territorial waters of Albania. In sweeping the mines on November 12 and 13, 1946, the British were held by a unanimous Court to have violated Albanian sovereignty. In a third judgment on December 15, 1949, the ICJ fixed the amount of compensation due the United Kingdom from Albania at 843,947 pounds sterling.

The Corfu Channel case is significant because it is the only situation in which the Security Council ever recommended referral of a dispute to the Court. The case is also notable as the only judgment of the ICJ that one of the parties refused to honor; Albania has never paid the assessed compensation to the United Kingdom. Important questions concerning the law of the seas were basic to the judgments, and the Court performed impartially on the basis of legal principles.

Fisheries Case. In 1935 the Norwegian government issued a decree reserving exclusive fishing rights for its nationals within a four-mile zone along its northern coast. In 1949 the United Kingdom instituted proceedings before the ICJ objecting, not to the four-mile zone, but to the manner in which Norway had determined the limits of the zone. Norway's coastline is very irregular and it had used straight baselines drawn between fixed points on the mainland and islands rather than following the configuration of the coast. The Court was asked to determine whether the method used and the specific baselines were contrary to international law.

The Court decided both basic questions in favor of Norway. The majority opinion found that the method used by Norway was well established in international law and that Norway had been using a similar method for several decades without objection by other states. Baselines must follow the general direction of the coast and Norway's specific methods did so.

The case was followed with particular interest by many maritime states since it involved significant questions concerning territorial waters. Other aspects of such questions persist to the present, and the International Law

Commission and a series of conferences have attempted to resolve some of the related issues.

South-West Africa Cases. South-West Africa was assigned as a Class C Mandate under Article 22 of the League of Nations Covenant to the jurisdiction of South Africa. Class C status permitted South Africa, subject to safeguards for the interests of the indigenous population, to administer the area as an integral part of its own territory. When the United Nations was formed, all former Mandates not granted independence, except South-West Africa, were placed under trusteeship. South Africa claimed that, with the demise of the League, it was under no obligation to place South-West Africa under trusteeship, and stated its intention to annex the territory under its sovereign control. In 1949 South Africa discontinued its annual reports on South-West Africa and refused to forward petitions from inhabitants of the territory to the United Nations.

In December 1949, the General Assembly requested an advisory opinion of the ICJ concerning the international status of South-West Africa and the resulting obligations of South Africa. In July 1950, the Court rendered an opinion covering several aspects of the issue. The Court advised that (1) South Africa's obligations under the original Mandate continued and it was required to submit reports to the General Assembly as the successor organ to the League machinery; (2) although Chapter XII of the Charter provides a means by which South-West Africa could be placed under trusteeship, it was not mandatory that South Africa do so; (3) the degree of supervision by the General Assembly was to be, as far as possible, neither greater nor less than that exercised by the League; and (4) South Africa could not unilaterally alter the status of South-West Africa and would have to obtain the consent of the General Assembly for any such modification.

South Africa refused to recognize the validity of the Court's advisory opinion and continued to ignore all United Nations attempts to work out means for compliance with its terms. The General Assembly established a series of committees to seek means for implementing the terms of the opinion and to investigate conditions in South-West Africa. Beginning in 1957 the Assembly pointed out to member states the possibility of taking legal action through the ICJ under the terms of the original Mandate. Such a case would necessarily have to be instituted by a state that was a member of the League of Nations.

In 1960 Ethiopia and Liberia instituted proceedings against South Africa before the ICJ. They charged that South Africa (1) had failed to carry out its duties as a mandatory power, (2) had extended the policy of apartheid to South-West Africa, (3) had violated the human rights of the population of South-West Africa and prevented progress toward self-government, and (4) had failed to render annual reports or to forward petitions to the General Assembly. South Africa responded by raising preliminary objections to the jurisdiction of the Court and to the right of Ethiopia and Liberia to act as plaintiffs. In 1962 the Court replied to the preliminary objections by ruling that, as had been indicated in the 1950 advisory opinion, South Africa's obligations under the Mandate continued, that the ICJ was the appropriate forum in which to air the complaint, and that Ethiopia and Liberia, as former members of the League, were entitled to bring charges of violation of the obligations under the Mandate. The fact that the Court was sharply divided 8–7 on the preliminary questions was an omen of the possibility of a final opinion unfavorable to the Ethiopian and Liberian position. Changes in Court personnel between 1962 and 1966 contributed to converting this possibility into reality.

After four more years of written and oral proceedings and after consideration of two additional procedural motions by South Africa, the ICJ in July 1966 handed down its final judgment in the South-West Africa cases. The judgment did not deal with the substantive issues raised by Ethiopia and Liberia but rested upon the legal status of the plaintiffs and their right to institute proceedings to enforce the Mandate, a question that, according to widely held opinion, had been disposed of in the 1962 Court rulings. The Court found that the plaintiffs had failed to establish their right or interest to enforce the Mandate since the Covenant did not provide for the right of each League member individually to require from the Mandatories the performance of their obligations. Such a right was vested only in the League organs, and since the League was now defunct, no means of legal enforcement was possible. The Court noted that the absence of a means of legal enforcement in the international field occurred frequently.

The ICJ's ruling was greeted with dismay by most African states as well as by a majority of United Nations members, which had been carrying on a campaign against the remnants of colonialism and against all forms of racial or ethnic discrimination. The dismay was compounded by the expectation that the Court would rule on the substantive, not the procedural, aspects of the case since the 1962 preliminary judgment had been based, in part, on Article 7 of the Mandate, which established the right of League members to invoke the compulsory jurisdiction of the Court in any dispute involving the Mandate. The ruling was made more unpalatable by the fact that the vote of the justices was 7–7 with Sir Percy Spender of Australia using his prerogative in such cases, as President of the Court, to cast an additional "casting vote" to break the tie.

The members of the United Nations were frustrated in their hopes for using the ICJ as one more avenue for putting pressure on South Africa to grant early independence to South-West Africa. After the adverse decision, they turned from legal means to an intensification of their efforts through political channels. Disillusionment with the court increased as a result of the 1966 decision, and the movement away from the adjudicatory process was intensified.

Advisory Opinions

The ICJ may be requested to give advisory opinions on any legal questions by the Security Council, the General Assembly, or any other organ or specialized agency of the United Nations that has been authorized by the General Assembly to make such requests. The General Assembly has extended such authorization to the Economic and Social Council, the Trusteeship Council, the Interim Committee of the General Assembly, the Committee on Applications for Review of Administrative Tribunal Judgments, the International Atomic Energy Agency, and all the specialized agencies except the Universal Postal Union. Prior to 1993 the ICJ had rendered twelve advisory opinions at the request of the General Assembly, one at the request of the Security Council, one at the request of the Executive Board of UNESCO, one at the request of the Assembly of the Inter-Governmental Maritime Consultative Organization, three at the request of the Committee on Applications for Review of Administrative Tribunal Judgments, one at the request of the World Health Assembly, and one at the request of the Economic and Social Council.

Advisory opinions are not binding but are authoritative statements of the principles of international law applying to the specific situations on which the advice of the Court is sought. Advisory opinions often delineate the rights and duties of states or international agencies, or provide an interpretation of an international treaty or other instrument. Advisory opinions are useful to establish a basis for further action and could be sought much more frequently by international bodies. The Security Council has been particularly delinquent in seeking the Court's advice on legal issues, a delinquency that reflects the emphasis upon political, not legal, approaches by that body, and an indication of the reluctance of the major powers to subject their policies to international legal norms.

A majority of Court opinions have been accorded due respect through compliance with the terms of the rulings, but the record is far from perfect. In an advisory opinion of March 1950, the Court ruled that Bulgaria, Hungary, and Rumania were obligated to cooperate in setting up commissions to safeguard human rights as provided in the peace treaties with those countries. When all three refused to comply, the Court further advised that a substitute method of appointment of commissioners was not justified, and a stalemate resulted. It has been noted above with regard to the South-West Africa situation that South Africa refused to respect the advisory opinion of the Court concerning its several continuing obligations under the terms of the Mandate. A number of states, led by the Soviet Union and France, refused to honor a 1962 Court opinion on the right of the General Assembly to assess the costs of certain peacekeeping operations of the United Nations on the same basis as the regular budget of the organization. Lack of respect for Court opinions contributes to the weakening of the international legal order and is one more evidence of the need for means of enforcing international legal rules and standards.

Only ten requests for advisory opinions have been registered with the ICJ since 1955 as compared with ten between 1947 and 1955. In part this decline is due to the greater need in early years for legal opinions to clarify points of confusion in a newly created set of international organizations. In substantial measure, however, the trend is one aspect of the direction of international relations in which states use political rather than legal means for conducting their foreign policies.

Some of the ICJ's advisory opinions have dealt with fundamental and significant legal matters. A few examples will illustrate this aspect of the work of this Court.

Conditions of admission of a state to membership in the United Nations (Article 4 of Charter). In 1946 and 1947, fifteen states applied for admission to membership in the United Nations and, during that period, only four were admitted. The unsuccessful candidates were the victims of an East-West political contest in which the United States and the Soviet Union each managed to block the candidates favored by the other through the voting requirements in the Security Council. There was little doubt that most of the applicants could meet the standards for admission, if impartially applied, but the reasons given for the rejections served as legal rationalizations for political expediency in which neither major power was willing to see the influence of the other in the United Nations extended.

To clarify some of the issues behind the deadlock, the General Assembly asked the ICJ for an advisory opinion. The request raised two major questions. One question was in regard to whether a member state is juridically entitled to make its consent to the admission of a new member dependent on conditions not expressly provided by Article 4 of the Charter. The second question concerned whether a member can make its consent subject to the condition that other states be admitted at the same time.

In rendering its advisory opinion in May 1948, the Court disposed of two preliminary questions. It found that the issues involved in the request were properly legal, not political, questions, and it upheld its own competence under the Charter and the Statute of the Court to interpret the Charter.

In dealing with the substantive issues raised by the General Assembly, the Court advised that the conditions for admission of members specified in Article 4 of the Charter were exhaustive and that members were not justified in adding other conditions. From this conclusion it then follows that the admission of one member cannot be made contingent upon the admission of another. Each member's admission should be based solely on its own qualifications.

The handing down of this opinion did not immediately resolve the membership impasse but it clarified some of the issues involved in the admission process. The major powers continued to block membership applications on grounds that, in their self-judgment, would fall within the qualifications for membership specified in Article 4 of the Charter. Another attempt to escape the stalemate was made by the General Assembly in 1949 by requesting the Court to advise on whether the General Assembly could admit a state to membership in the absence of a positive recommendation by the Security Council. The Court replied that such a procedure would violate the clear intent of the Charter. The membership dilemma was finally resolved in 1955 with a "gentleman's agreement" for a "package deal" in spite of the Court's previous advice that one state's admission should not depend upon the simultaneous admission of another state.

Reparation for injuries suffered in the service of the United Nations. By 1948 several agents of the United Nations had been killed or injured while carrying out their official duties. The assassination of the United Nations mediator in Palestine, Count Folke Bernadotte, was the most publicized of these incidents. The United Nations had provided compensation in these cases and wished to establish its legal right to attempt to recover these amounts by claims against the states responsible for the deaths or injuries.

In December 1948, the General Assembly sought an advisory opinion from the ICJ in which the principal issue was whether the United Nations had the capacity to bring an international claim against the responsible government with the purpose of obtaining reparation for damage caused to the United Nations and to the victim. In the event of an affirmative reply to the main issue the General Assembly also wished to know how the action by the United Nations could be reconciled with such rights as might be possessed by the state of which the victim was a national.

The advisory opinion of the Court was a landmark in establishing the international personality of the United Nations with attendant rights in international law. The Court ruled that the member states in setting up the United Nations intended to confer upon it the capacity to operate on the international plane and to exercise rights and duties necessary to carry out its functions. Its privileges are not necessarily identical with those of a state, but the organization must be deemed to have such powers as, even if not expressly stated in the Charter, are essential to the performance of its duties. This is a principle of implied powers that opens the door to a generous interpretation of the prerogatives of international organizations. With regard to the secondary question of reconciling the United Nations' right to claim damages with those of an interested state, the Court advised that neither party has priority and that any conflict of interest might be resolved by accommodation.

Effect of awards of compensation made by the United Nations Administrative Tribunal. In December 1952, Secretary-General Trygve Lie dismissed or suspended a number of Secretariat employees who were United States nationals. The grounds for dismissal were the refusal of the staff members to testify before a United States federal grand jury or before congressional committees on questions of subversion. Twenty-one of these former employees appealed their cases to the Administrative Tribunal established by the General Assembly in 1949 to review charges of violation of staff members' contracts. The Administrative Tribunal awarded compensation to eleven of those dismissed in the amount of $179,420. The United States led the opposition in the General Assembly to appropriating the funds for compensation and, as a compromise measure, the Assembly decided to request an advisory opinion of the ICJ.

The question answered by the Court was whether the General Assembly had the right on any grounds to refuse to give effect to an award of compensation made by the Administrative Tribunal in favor of a United Nations staff member whose contract had been terminated without his assent. In determining the answer the ICJ examined the nature of the Administrative Tribunal and found that, although the Tribunal was created by the General Assembly, it was intended to be a judicial, not an advisory, body with authority to make decisions from which there was no appeal. The judgments were, therefore, binding on the General Assembly, which was obligated to appropriate funds for the awards. Challenges to the power of the Assembly to create the Tribunal or to confer upon it its assigned powers were rejected. Thus a broad interpretation of implied powers not explicitly stated in the Charter was relied upon by the Court to arrive at its ruling, an approach consistent with the earlier Reparation for Injuries opinion.

The Awards of Compensation ruling was made against the dramatic background of hysteria in the United States concerning alleged subversion among government and United Nations employees. Although the United States government lost the battle for refusing to pay compensation to its dismissed nationals, it managed to get major concessions from the Secretariat concerning the future screening of United States personnel employed by the United Nations. The costs of such concessions were high in terms of the independent international position of the Secretariat and in terms of general morale among its personnel. These factors are examined in more detail in Chapter 16.

Several additional advisory opinions are referred to at other points in this and other chapters of the text. The opinion on the International Status of South-West Africa was discussed above as background for the South-West African Cases decision in 1966. Altogether three separate opinions on questions pertaining to South-West Africa were handed down between 1950 and 1956, and these opinions form a part of the picture of the struggle for independence treated in Chapter 15. A fourth opinion on South-West Africa delivered in 1971 is the latest important development in this sequence. The opinion by the Court in 1962 on the right of the General Assembly to assess peacekeeping costs as a part of the regular expenses of the United Nations was discussed in relation to the section on financial problems in Chapter 5 and in regard to peacekeeping practices in Chapter 7. Together with the preceding treatment of selected advisory opinions, these references form a basis for judging the significant role played by the Court in delivering advisory opinions on basic legal problems that have faced the United Nations.

THE ROLE OF THE INTERNATIONAL LAW COMMISSION

The Charter makes the General Assembly responsible for initiating studies and making recommendations "for the purpose of. . . encouraging the progressive development of international law and its codification."[6] To carry out this function, the Assembly established the International Law Commission as its principal instrument for making the necessary studies and recommendations. After some delays in the General Assembly over details for its establishment, the International Law Commission began its work in 1949. Its thirty-four members are chosen as experts in law representing the major legal systems of the world, and no two may be of the same nationality. The pattern of composition was thus copied from that of the ICJ.

The procedures of the International Law Commission have been slow, but this slowness is inherent in the processes of developing international law. The commission has also followed a pragmatic and flexible course in drawing no sharp distinction between its two functions of progressive development and codification of law. In many instances its efforts on a single subject involve clarification and standardization as well as the filling of gaps in existing law. The steps usually followed in developing and codifying law are (1) selection of an appropriate topic by the commission, (2) approval of the topic by the General Assembly, (3) appointment of a member of the commission as rapporteur on the subject, (4) report and preliminary suggested draft by the rapporteur, (5) discussion and revision by the commission, (6) submission to governments for comment, (7) revision by the commission on the basis of governments' suggestions, (8) submission of the revised draft to the General Assembly, (9) consideration in the Assembly's Sixth Committee, (10) decision by the General Assembly to convene an international conference to consider the draft, (11) consideration and revision by the international conference, (12) signature of any adopted convention by state representatives, (13) ratification by governments, and (14) deposit of sufficient ratifications to bring the new convention into force. With so many hurdles to overcome, many efforts at codification become stalled or are aborted.

However, the International Law Commission has been successful in initiating studies that have led to the adoption of important conventions. At its initial session the commission drew up an agenda of fourteen topics for its inves-

---

[6]Charter of the United Nations, Art. 13, sec.1.

tigation. The General Assembly has from time to time requested additional studies. One general area in which a series of multilateral treaties has been adopted as a result of groundwork by the commission is the law of the sea. A conference in Geneva in 1958 adopted four separate conventions on the territorial sea, the high seas, fisheries, and the continental shelf. Further complex, unresolved problems concerning the oceans were considered by a conference in 1960 and by the Third United Nations Law of the Seas Conference, which began in 1973 and was prolonged by the difficulties of achieving compromise among diverse interests. Additional details on these issues are given in Chapter 13. Initial work by the International Law Commission also resulted in the adoption of the Vienna Convention on Diplomatic Relations (1961) and the Vienna Convention on Consular Relations (1963). These conventions modified and clarified diplomatic and consular practices, some of which had been established at Aix-la-Chapelle in 1818. A third area in which the work of the International Law Commission led to the formulation of a multilateral treaty is with regard to the problem of statelessness. International conferences at Geneva (1959) and New York (1961) finally adopted and opened for ratification a Convention on the Reduction of Statelessness.

According to many legal experts, the most fundamental accomplishment of the International Law Commission has been its preparatory work concerning the law of treaties. Treaties are especially important because they constitute a major source of international law. Careful work by the commission resulted in the adoption by a two-year conference of the Vienna Convention on the Law of Treaties (1969). By this convention, many uncertainties in the customary law of treaties are removed.

In addition to its contributions to the formulation of international conventions, the International Law Commission has submitted other significant reports to the General Assembly. The studies include, *inter alia,* (1) model rules of arbitral procedure, (2) the principles of the Nuremberg trials, (3) a declaration of the rights and duties of states, (4) a code of offenses against the peace and security of humankind, (5) the question of defining aggression, and (6) the effect of reservations to multilateral conventions. In the 1980s and 1990s the International Law Commission has given major attention to developing a Draft Code of Crimes against the Peace and Security of Mankind and to the related question of the feasibility of establishing an International Criminal Court.

Evaluations of the contributions of the International Law Commission vary. There is little doubt of the eminence of some of its members. The original membership of the commission included such distinguished legal experts as Sir Benegal Rau of India, James L. Brierly of the United Kingdom, Manley O. Hudson of the United States, V. M. Koretsky of the USSR, and George Scelle of France. Its meticulous preparatory work for the law of treaties might alone justify the existence of the commission for its more than forty-five years.

Edward McWhinney has described the approach of the International Law Commission to the carrying out of its mandate as "sober, cautious, conservative, and technical, and very, very slow-moving."[7] He further states that the Commission has been "overly preoccupied with the petit-point needlework of international law rather than with the imaginative reshaping and rewriting of international law to meet new conditions in international society."[8]

Percy E. Corbett points to another of the difficulties that the International Law Commission has faced from the beginning.

> The division of the world into competing power blocs, aggravated, if not caused, by the conflict of ideologies, made the International Law Commission a forum for political polemics, a distortion undeterred by the fact that its members were supposed to be independent experts rather than representatives of governments.[9]

Yet, in general, Corbett praises the commission, calling its total output "a remarkable achievement"[10] and highlighting

> its merits not only as a standing drafting committee, but as a body where, in spite of the nonofficial character of its members, even the political and cultural differences of their countries undergo a first round of reconciliation. . . . The enlargement of the Commission from the original fifteen experts in 1948 to twenty-five in 1961 gives new assurance that all main currents of legal thought will find representation, and at the same time gives the newly established nations of Asia and Africa a necessary sense of participation in the adaptation to present needs of a legal order which they had little or no part in elaborating.[11]

OTHER AGENCIES PROMOTING WORLD LAW

If the International Law Commission is slow and tedious in its methods of contributing to the progressive development of international law, then other arenas will be utilized to supplement this effort. One of the most comprehensive treaties of recent decades is the United Nations Convention of the Law of the Sea developed by the Third United Nations Conference on the Law of the Sea after nearly a decade of intensive work. This conference and treaty are discussed more fully in Chapter 13. Additional organizations for expanding and modifying international law are outlined below.

The Sixth (Legal) Committee of the General Assembly deals with a wide range of legal problems assigned to it by the Assembly. It regularly reviews the recommendations and reports from the International Law Commission. The Sixth Committee could be used more extensively, but many legal questions are

---

[7]Edward McWhinney, *United Nations Law Making: Cultural and Ideological Relativism and International Law Making for an Era of Transition* (New York: Holmes & Meier, 1984), p. 98.

[8]Ibid., p. 99.

[9]Percy E. Corbett, *The Growth of World Law* (Princeton, NJ: Princeton University Press, 1971), pp. 51–52.

[10]Ibid., p. 60.

[11]Ibid., p. 68. Membership was again increased to thirty-four in 1982.

often assigned to one of the committees handling political issues in situations in which political and legal questions are intertwined. The Sixth Committee was utilized to draft one important treaty, the Convention on Genocide.

One of the earliest acts of the General Assembly was its approval and opening for ratification of the General Convention on Privileges and Immunities of the United Nations. Because of its fundamental importance to the operation of the United Nations, this convention was drafted by a subcommittee of the Legal Committee of the United Nations Preparatory Commission and was ready for consideration at the first session of the General Assembly. After review by its Sixth Committee, the Assembly approved the Convention in February 1946.

The General Assembly occasionally declares and even creates law by resolution. In 1961 and 1963 it adopted unanimous resolutions declaring principles for space that were later incorporated into the 1967 Treaty on Outer Space. On other occasions, actions by the Assembly have led to important subsequent treaties. As a result of the cooperation stemming from the proclamation of an International Geophysical Year in 1957 and 1958, the Antarctic Treaty was made possible among the states having claims in that area. The treaty provides for continued cooperation among the parties and prohibits all military activity in Antarctica.

To support the legal work of the United Nations and to advise on legal matters, the Secretariat incorporates within its structure an Office of Legal Affairs. Because of the initiatives taken by the Secretary-General, the advice of the legal counsel, who heads the office, and of his staff is vital to the Secretary-General. The Secretariat also registers and publishes international treaties and agreements in the United Nations Treaty Series.

From time to time the General Assembly establishes bodies to study or promote a discrete aspect of international law. In 1963 the Assembly created a Special Committee on Principles of International Law Concerning Friendly Relations and Cooperation among States. The committee was asked to assist the Assembly with the study of seven principles for improving state relations and cooperation. In 1965 the Assembly established a ten-member Advisory Committee on a Program of Technical Assistance to promote the Teaching, Study, Dissemination and Wider Appreciation of International Law. The advisory committee was assigned the task of advising the Secretary-General in a program carried out by the Secretariat, UNESCO, the United Nations Development Program, and the United Nations Institute for Training and Research. In 1966 the Assembly created a twenty-nine-member (later expanded to thirty-six members) United Nations Commission on International Trade Law (UNCITRAL) with a broad program to promote the improvement of the law of international trade and with a close relationship to the United Nations Conference on Trade and Development. UNCITRAL has produced several treaties, including the UN Convention on the Carriage of Goods by Sea (1978) and the UN Convention on Contracts for the International Sale of Goods (1980). It has given much attention to rules of arbitration and conciliation and has published a Model Law on International Commercial Arbitration.

Since its inception, the Commission on Human Rights, under the aegis of the Economic and Social Council, has devoted its main energies to the development and encouragement of multilateral treaties within its field of competence. After first producing the Declaration of Human Rights, the commission turned its attention to converting the non-binding declaration into two covenants, one on economic, social, and cultural rights and the other on civil and political rights. States were slow to ratify these covenants, but in 1976 they received sufficient ratifications to come into force. Under United Nations auspices, other treaties have been produced dealing with such subjects as equal rights for women, forced labor and slavery, the elimination of all forms of discrimination, the status of refugees, and the reduction of statelessness.

The International Labor Organization (ILO) has since 1919 opened for ratification more than 170 conventions dealing with every aspect of labor welfare. By setting standards and incorporating these standards through ratification into the domestic law of states, these conventions can serve as a model for similar effort in other fields. Fuller treatment of the contributions of the ILO to labor law is presented in Chapter 14.

In 1966 a Convention on the Settlement of Investment Disputes between States and Nationals of Other States entered into force. The treaty had been worked out through several years of preliminary effort by the International Bank for Reconstruction and Development. The unique feature of this convention is its provision for binding arbitration of disputes in which private investors as well as states are involved.

Regional organizations have made significant contributions to the development of international law and judicial practice. The European Court of Justice, which is the judicial arm of the European Community, has handed down hundreds of decisions and rulings on disputes among the Western European members. Parties to the cases may be member states, community organs, or private individuals or agencies. The European court also rules on preliminary questions referred from municipal courts. Court decisions are binding upon the parties and upon municipal organs of government, but the problem of enforcement is not satisfactorily resolved.

The Council of Europe sponsored a European Convention on Human Rights, which came into force in 1953. The convention provides for a European Commission on Human Rights, which screens most complaints, and a court of last resort, the European Court of Human Rights, which is composed of one judge from each of the twenty-two members of the Council of Europe. Although few cases are brought to the court, the degree of satisfaction with the system seems high. Individuals may bring complaints to the commission, and the emphasis is upon quiet adjustment of differences. Unique breakthroughs in the practice of international law are represented by the compulsory jurisdiction and the access of private parties to the European Court of Justice, the European Commission on Human Rights, and the European Court of Human Rights.

Since the creation of a Commission of Jurists by the Inter-American Conference of 1906, a substantial number of conventions have been produced by that body and its successors in the Organization of American States. The conventions cover a broad range of subjects, but none of them has been ratified by every member of the organization. The work of the commission was divided in 1948 between an Inter-American Council of Jurists and an Inter-American Juridical Committee, and less progress has been made since that date.

Dozens of private agencies focus all or a portion of their energies on the promotion of international law as an instrument of world order. For a fairly complete summary of the work of both private and public agencies in this field, the student should examine the May-June 1967 issue of *Intercom,* published by the Foreign Policy Association in New York. Only a partial listing will be included here.

The International Chamber of Commerce has carried on a variety of activities to promote international law with regard to trade and investments. In 1953 it took the initiative through the Economic and Social Council to call attention to the need for enforcement of commercial arbitral awards. An international conference was called in New York in 1958, and the following year the Convention on the Recognition and Enforcement of Foreign Arbitral Awards came into force. The chamber established a Court of Arbitration in Paris in 1924, which has heard more than 3,000 cases involving individuals, corporations, and governments in disputes providing for arbitration in the enforcement of contracts. The chamber has also established standards for fair treatment of international investment and for the terms of international contracts.

The World Peace through Law Center in Geneva was established in 1963. Among its activities are the sponsorship of biennial world conferences and World Law Day; the establishment of sixty subject-matter committees and national committees; the publication of reports, bulletins, and pamphlets; and the maintenance of a world legal information and reference service.

The World Policy Institute in New York carries on a broad educational program through schools and colleges. It makes available publications and films and conducts seminars for students and teachers. It also has conducted a World Order Models Project to promote alternative futures for the world of the future, with an emphasis upon the elimination of war.

The World Federalist Movement has been very active in the United States and elsewhere since World War II in promoting the concept of peace through law. The Federalists spread their influence through publications and meetings, but they also serve as a well-organized pressure group to influence the United States Congress on issues within their range of interests.

Other organizations are too numerous to describe. A partial list would include the American Society of International Law, the American Bar Association's committees on World Peace through Law and on Peace and Law through the United Nations and its section of International and Comparative Law, the International Commission of Jurists, the Commission to Study the Organization of Peace, the Carnegie Endowment for International Peace, and the Fund for Education in World Order.

ASSESSING OUR PROGRESS

Because of certain defects and gaps in the system, the development of international law appears to many critics to be one of the weakest elements in the evolution of international organization and in the struggle for world order. These defects are not difficult to identify, and a comparison with national legal systems dramatizes the deficiencies of the international system.

A single court lacking compulsory jurisdiction is inadequate to meet the minimal standards of a world system of justice. If most international legal disputes were assured of a hearing in a judicial forum, the International Court of Justice would be unable to conduct all the hearings. Instead the Court languishes from a lack of business. The decision in the South-West Africa cases contributed to a loss of confidence in the Court but is not the principal factor in its being neglected. The political organs of the United Nations have failed to utilize the ICJ for advisory opinions on many subjects. More importantly, national governments have refused to submit their differences to impartial judicial judgment, thus subordinating their national interest in the evolution of world order to the supposed advantages of protecting immediate interests. The lack of adherence to the optional clause of the Court Statute and the attachment of crippling reservations to acceptance of that clause are other factors contributing to the inactivity of the ICJ.

Disrespect for established principles and agencies of international law has made news headlines since the late 1970s. When a large contingent of United States diplomatic personnel was held hostage in the United States embassy in Teheran for 444 days, most nations of the world condemned the Iranian government because this situation threatened to undermine long-established principles of diplomatic immunity. In 1984–86, when Nicaragua brought charges against the United States in the International Court of Justice that intrusions into Nicaraguan waters and territory and United States support for antigovernment rebels violated both general and specific norms of international law, the United States refused to recognize the jurisdiction of the Court and the validity of its decision. The United States government first announced that it would not adhere to its commitment under the optional clause of the Court Statute in spite of a six-month requirement in the Statute for rescinding its adherence. Subsequently, it gave the necessary six months' notice and officially withdrew from its previous obligations under the optional clause. In the meantime the United States refused to appear before the Court in its proceedings in spite of an 11–1 ruling by the Court that it did have jurisdiction based on Article 36 of the Court Statute and other treaties. These minority attitudes and unilateral actions by the Iranian and United States governments are distinct setbacks to the hopes for acceptance of international law norms and procedures as components in advancing toward a more orderly world.

Even if a system of courts with compulsory jurisdiction existed, other defects in the international legal system would be apparent. Individuals as well as states and international organizations should have rights and duties under the law. Custom and multilateral treaties produced by occasional conferences are slow and inefficient methods of developing a comprehensive body of law. Means of enforcement will remain unsatisfactory as long as no independent enforcement agencies exist at the international level.

In spite of deficiencies, a substantial body of international law exists. Except in a few critical areas, international law is observed and respected. New states look to legal norms to protect them against insecurity, and mature states find the conduct of international affairs impossible except within the framework of law. An increasing body of commercial law is evolving, and disputes are being settled by recourse to legal agencies and principles. New treaties have been adopted and widely respected not only in the realm of commerce but also with regard to labor, human rights, Antarctica, space, and the seas. A few bright spots appear in the area of arms limitation and regulation. The desire of every state to belong to the United Nations and to a network of regional and world organizations and to use the processes of these organizations for common ends is a beginning toward further development of world law.

In spite of slowness and politicization, the International Law Commission has been successful in developing standards and the texts for conventions in crucial areas of law. It has been willing to pioneer in the codification and development of law on the most fundamental subjects regarding interstate relations.

Perhaps it is the private agencies that most clearly indicate the future hope for a more orderly world. The acceptance of the peace-through-law concept has permeated a wide range of nongovernmental organizations. This concept is fundamental to the philosophy on which the United Nations is built; the renunciation of the use of force and the settlement of disputes by peaceful means is the keystone principle of the organization. National political leaders cling stubbornly to national sovereignty and independence in a world in which traditional approaches are inadequate to the needs of humankind. The realization of the need for orderly legal processes in critical areas of international relations may eventually reach the level of national political leadership in a majority of the world's states. Pressures from private groups will speed this process.

9

CONTROLLING THE INSTRUMENTS OF WAR

War is as old as the existence of competing political units and as ubiquitous as the common cold. Like the cold, people for some time have tried to eliminate it, with about equal success. Theories about the causes of war range from those of the human's supposedly inherent violence to those of war as exploitation in a class struggle. Reactions to war stretch from its acceptance as a continuation of political intercourse by other means to its deprecation as wasteful, inhumane, and irrational.

Although wars have always been devastating, those of the twentieth century have introduced new methods and levels of destruction. The Thirty Years' War during the seventeenth century was perhaps, for the area involved, as bloody and ravaging as any so far. Yet in the twentieth century, the two world wars involved more countries, more men, more widespread combat arenas, more expense, and more lethal weapons than any before. The new nuclear weapon was the first with the capacity to destroy all human life on this planet.

Arms races affect both rich and poor nations alike. Few have been able to resist maintaining expensive military forces and weapons systems. The most powerful countries were for forty years caught up in both an escalating arms race and in the development of more sophisticated weapons—conventional, nuclear, chemical, radiological, and bacteriological. Poor states accept military aid from the rich and spend great sums of their own on military preparedness. Of the ten countries that in 1990 spent 9 percent or more of their gross national product (GNP) on military preparedness, all were developing countries, half of which had per capita GNPs of less than $1,800.[1] Obviously this is a questionable use of resources for countries whose economic and social needs are so great. In spite of declining military budgets since 1987, the affluent donor nations still spend more than ten times as much for military purposes as they contribute to the developing states in official economic aid. World military expenditures exceed the total annual income of the poorest one-third of the world's population.[2] The cost of armaments continues to constitute a heavy drain on resources for both rich and poor countries.

Proposals for disarmament and arms control have been numerous; steps toward their success have been limited. Fear, envy, suspicion, hatred, and pride have acted to frustrate the hopes for a world in which a general sense of political security allows nations to drastically lower their reliance on military strength. The Cold War has been replaced by local wars which continue to feed the appetite for military equipment. Costs in terms of both human lives and well-being remain high.

A DISCOURAGING HISTORY

Throughout history, philosophers have advocated disarmament as one means of controlling international conflict or of lowering the level of suffering and destruction caused by war, but their ideas have made little appreciable impact upon those who wielded political power. This discrepancy between philosophical thought and state practice was noted in Chapter 1. Jeremy Bentham, Immanuel Kant, William Ladd, and Richard Cobden were strong advocates of disarmament as a means to peace.

Occasional state actions or pressures for disarmament appeared in the nineteenth century. As early as 1816 the Russian tsar suggested general disarmament, but this and similar suggestions by several heads of state during the century evoked no favorable response from other governments. In 1817, under the terms of the Rush-Bagot treaty, Great Britain and the United States agreed to the demilitarization of the Great Lakes, an important step in the attitude of friendly confidence that has pervaded most U.S.-Canadian-British relations for 150 years.

The Hague conferences of 1899 and 1907 were called by the Russian tsar in the hope of reaching agreements on disarmament and means of peaceful settlement of disputes. The 1899 conference succeeded only in adopting an innocuous and meaningless resolution urging states to reduce their military budgets, but no firm agreements could be reached. The 1907 conference noted the ongoing increase in armaments and decided that nothing could be

---

[1]Ruth Leger Sivard, *World Military and Social Expenditures 1993* (Washington, D.C.: World Priorities, Inc., 1993).

[2]Ibid., p. 5.

done at the time to stop the arms race. An agreement to meet again in 1915 was aborted by war.

At the close of the war a series of treaties, including the Treaty of Versailles, provided for disarmament and demilitarization in certain areas. Germany was forced to accept severe limitations on its armaments, and the Rhineland, Danzig, and other areas were demilitarized.

Article 8 of the Covenant of the League of Nations dealt with disarmament and related questions. A firm pledge of "reduction of national armaments to the lowest point consistent with national safety" left open the underlying conditions of security that would make agreement possible on levels and formulas for reduction. The League Council was charged with the responsibility for initiating plans for disarmament, and League members pledged the exchange of "full and frank information" on levels of military preparedness, including information on industries convertible to war-support production. The information contained in these reports was published in the League's *Armaments Yearbook*. Finally, the members agreed "that the manufacture by private enterprise of munitions and instruments of war is open to grave objections," and again the Council was directed to "advise how the evil effects attendant upon such manufacture can be prevented."

During the period 1920–24, two commissions appointed by the League Council were unable to agree on plans for disarmament. However, confidence still existed that a universal disarmament agreement could be formulated and adopted, and in 1925 the Council appointed a Preparatory Commission to do the preliminary work necessary before convening a World Disarmament Conference. Commission membership included three nonmembers of the League—the United States, the USSR, and Germany. At this point the intention was clear to call the conference within three years.

During its five years of intermittent effort, the Preparatory Commission came up against fundamental national cleavages concerning approaches to disarmament and the relation of disarmament to security guarantees and to enforcement measures. France wanted security before disarmament. The United States refused to be linked to any system of international sanctions. Germany chafed under the special restraints imposed by the Treaty of Versailles and demanded equality. The USSR insisted on total disarmament. Basically, the United States and Great Britain maintained that disarmament in itself would lead to security, while France argued that disarmament could come only after security measures were instigated and that international enforcement must be incorporated into disarmament plans. Agreement seemed impossible. The final instrument of the Preparatory Commission was a draft convention, which failed to resolve the fundamental national differences and which left numerous gaps to be filled, contrary to all reasonable expectation, by the World Disarmament Conference.

In spite of dim prospects for success, the World Disarmament Conference was finally convened in February 1932. Additional indicators in the international climate foretold the possibility of failure. The Nazis were rising in power in Germany, and Japan had invaded Manchuria. Economic unrest was fed by the Depression. The spirit of political cooperation was fragile.

Instead of following the normal pattern for international conferences of adjournment after a few weeks of intensive effort, the World Disarmament Conference dragged on intermittently for more than two years. Several new and revised plans were considered, but each was unacceptable to one or more major powers. The United States, Great Britain, Germany, France, and Italy consulted during periods of conference recess. Any hope for agreement was shattered when in 1933 first Japan and then Germany announced their withdrawal from the League and from the conference. Final adjournment came in June 1934, with no tangible achievement to show for nearly a decade of planning and negotiation.

The one area of partial success in disarmament efforts during this period was in naval disarmament. At the Washington Naval Conference in 1921–22 the United States, Great Britain, Japan, France, and Italy agreed to limit the size of battleships and aircraft carriers, scrap certain ships, and build no new capital ships for ten years. In the London Naval Treaty of 1930 the United States, Great Britain, and Japan agreed to extend the building moratorium on capital ships, limited the size of destroyers and submarines, and set ceilings for their total tonnages of cruisers, destroyers, and submarines. The resurgence of Japanese militarism and territorial ambitions in the Pacific marked the abandonment of the naval treaties.

The experiences of the interwar years seemed to indicate the fallacy of the direct approach to disarmament, which held that armaments in themselves were the main source of insecurity among nations and that disarmament would automatically bring an easing of international tensions. Negotiators from many countries were unwilling to enter into disarmament agreements unless linked with security and enforcement measures. Such arrangements as were negotiated were readily evaded or discarded when they were incompatible with the political goals of the state. Simplistic approaches to disarmament failed to come to grips with the basic elements of state relations, which included the prerogative of waging war to gain or protect supposed national interests. Armaments, both then and today, are considered as primary instruments of national security—the most fundamental goal of the foreign policy of most states. Therefore, armaments will not be lightly surrendered without substitute means of assuring that security.

ARMS CONTROL ISSUES

From 1945 until approximately 1987 three major developments affected and complicated the desire for arms control or disarmament as factors in maintaining a peaceful world. The first of these was the development of nuclear and other means of destruction thousands of times more lethal than previous weapons. The second factor was the bipolar rivalry of two superpowers, reinforced by a clash of ideologies. The third development was the emergence of dozens of new states whose demands produced a degree of instability in international relations.

The terms *arms control* and *disarmament* are often linked but are neither synonymous nor mutually exclusive alternative approaches to the problem of dealing with armaments. Disarmament means a reduction in the means to engage in war and may be qualitative, quantitative, or both. Arms control may involve a reduction in armaments levels but need not do so. Arms control involves mutual restraint and a seeking of stability in arms competition through regulation. Until 1987 more emphasis was placed on arms control than on disarmament.

For most of the postwar years, the Soviet Union and the United States were the leaders of competing power blocs, each attempting to attain superiority in individual and collective strength. Military alliances were the order of the day. Competing ideologies served as the philosophical basis for rivalry of political, economic, and social systems. These ideologies depicted the world competition in terms of good versus evil—evoking a messianic zeal on each side of the curtain that separated East from West.

As alliances weakened in the 1960s and 1970s, new forces unconducive to arms agreements developed. The nuclear monopoly of the United States and the Soviet Union was broken, and many states developed the potentiality for a nuclear arsenal. The cleavage within the Communist bloc produced an intense rivalry for bloc leadership, with China as the challenger. China possessed limited nuclear capability but remained outside the channels of negotiation for arms control. The French no longer trusted United States assurances of nuclear protection and developed their own capabilities, also refusing to be bound by international limitations.

The emergence of dozens of new states in the Third World, while only indirectly related to arms control, nevertheless complicated the problem of seeking agreements. New lines of cleavage were drawn between North and South, rich and poor. Military assistance was often thrust upon countries that could ill afford to build a military establishment. However, military regimes are in control of the governments of more than fifty developing nations. Discontent with the status quo and the lack of stability in the developing countries are unsettling factors in seeking international agreements on many subjects, including arms control.

The development of nuclear weapons has had a revolutionary effect upon problems of arms control. For the first time in history, the new weapons posed the threat of annihilation of whole populations or perhaps all of humanity. Their full-scale use became unthinkable or likened to an act of madness. Even with limited use, millions would die and no effective defense against attack could be devised. Self-restraint and international control were the only rational alternatives.

A problem that tends to goad nuclear powers to seek limited arms control is proliferation of nuclear capability. Originally, there was but one nuclear power, then two, then five, then six, and tomorrow perhaps dozens. The problem is frequently referred to as the Nth power problem. The spread of nuclear weapons is made possible by the diffusion of scientific and technical knowledge, by the decreasing cost of producing a basic weapon, and by national pride. Fear of the intentions of neighbors may also lead states to seek nuclear capability for protection. This factor was undoubtedly present in the Chinese development of nuclear weapons and may lead to proliferation in the Middle East or in India and Pakistan.

One concern concomitant to disarmament proposals is whether the economy of individual countries will be adversely affected by reductions in military spending. Most analysts agree that sufficient economic knowledge exists to meet the challenge and, to a greater degree than the lack of knowledge, the problem would involve psychological factors, will, and the adequacy of government processes in applying the necessary measures. The talents now absorbed in military research and development could be redirected toward the enrichment of life in developed economies or toward the solution of the most basic problems of the developing nations.

Several national and international, public and private studies have been made of the economic and social consequences of disarmament. One of the most notable was carried out by a team of ten experts representing a cross section of economic systems at various levels of development. The report of this consultative group, transmitted to the Economic and Social Council by the Secretary-General in March 1962, concluded with the following summary of their findings:

> The Consultative Group is unanimously of the opinion that all the problems and difficulties of transition connected with disarmament could be met by appropriate national and international measures. There should thus be no doubt that the diversion to peaceful purposes of the resources now in military use could be accomplished to the benefit of all countries and lead to the improvement of world economic and social conditions. The achievement of general and complete disarmament would be an unqualified blessing to all mankind.[3]

Another United Nations study, issued in 1971 and updated in 1978 and 1982, affirmed the conclusions of the earlier report.

The testing of nuclear weapons has been a perennial issue of the nuclear age. The period from 1954 to 1963 was one of increasing concern for the harmful effects of atmospheric testing. Skin burns incurred by Japanese fishermen on the fishing boat *Lucky Dragon* nearly 100 miles from ground zero and thyroid abnormalities discovered among inhabitants of the Marshall

---

[3]UN Document E/3593/Rev. 1, p. 52.

Islands following the United States Bikini test, in 1954, dramatized the dangers of continuing to saturate the atmosphere with radioactive substances. Scientific reports on the possible contamination of food supplies and the long-term effects of certain atomic substances such as strontium 90 distributed over remote areas by air currents heightened the demand for cessation of indiscriminate or unnecessary testing.

With the adoption of the partial test-ban treaty in 1963, which eliminated all except underground tests, these fears were diminished but not entirely eliminated. Some radioactivity is a problem in underground tests, and possible damage to plant and animal life and the danger of setting off earthquakes persist.

In October 1992 the U.S. Congress declared a moratorium on testing and this moratorium was later extended by President Clinton. Other states also voluntarily refrained from testing during this period. Pressure has been growing, both within and outside the United Nations, for a Comprehensive Test-Ban Treaty; but whether pariah states, such as North Korea, or Middle East states with nuclear capability or potential would adhere to such a treaty remains problematical.

Two disarmament issues of the 1990s are the destruction of existing stockpiles of nuclear, chemical, and biological weapons, and the problem of constraining the global arms trade. Recent progress on agreements to destroy stockpiles of various weapons of mass destruction are detailed in a subsequent section of this chapter. Until the breakup of the Soviet Union, that country and the United States accounted for two-thirds of the world's arms exports. Since that time, the United States became the dominant arms source, being responsible for about half of the world's total. Although the global total of trade in arms has fallen to about half its level of the 1980s, heavy sales of sophisticated weapons were made in the early 1990s, especially to Middle East countries. The dangers of nations being "armed to the teeth" are self-evident.

The basic objectives of arms reduction are international security and stability. Phased disarmament must meet the demands for a balanced impact upon the principal negotiators. Because of differences in types of weapons and forces maintained by various parties, the formulas for each stage of arms reduction, in order to maintain security for all concerned, are complicated and difficult to negotiate. Reciprocal reductions cannot be based purely on percentage or numerical cuts by all or major states. Security involves psychological factors that must be weighed before a new balance at a lower level of preparedness can be subscribed to and achieved. Since security is not based on military preparedness alone but upon a total world situation involving political, social, and economic relationships among and within national states, the ability to maintain a sense of relative security free of excessive risks for all nations calls for a delicate balance not easily achieved. In fact, these difficulties explain, in major portion, the painstaking and frustrating nature of disarmament and arms control negotiations.

The lack of international agencies with means to police disarmament or arms-control agreements creates roadblocks for arriving at such agreements. States are unwilling to substitute international authority for self-help in enforcing disarmament arrangements. If the international climate were conducive to the creation of an international agency with means to assure compliance with arms control or reduction measures, then other diminutions of national sovereignty might also be possible. Or, to state the case conversely, disarmament and arms control would be more easily attainable in a world ready to accept limited world government. In fact, a world authority could not tolerate means of massive destruction concentrated in the hands of its component members. Until the forces that drive humankind together outweigh the divisive elements of world politics, the difficulties and problems outlined in the preceding pages dealing with arms-control issues will persist. The risks involved in weapons competition are not in themselves a sufficient compulsion to cause the human race to convert the international system of today into a single world authority capable of controlling the instruments for waging war.

CONTINUED FRUSTRATIONS WITHIN AND OUTSIDE THE UNITED NATIONS

The United Nations Charter contains no firm commitment to arms reduction but charges the Security Council with the responsibility for formulating plans for a system for the "regulation of armaments." The General Assembly is also permitted to consider the principles governing disarmament and arms regulation and is empowered to submit recommendations on these principles to the Security Council or to the member governments. In spite of the Charter's lack of emphasis upon disarmament, as contrasted with the details of Article 8 of the League Covenant, proposals and machinery for both disarmament and arms control have been profuse and varied since 1946, although they have yielded small returns. The immediate pressure for control was heightened by the first use of atomic weapons at Hiroshima just six weeks after the signing of the Charter. The lack of progress is due to the same factors of mistrust, search for security, national intransigence, and lack of effective international authority that prevented the adoption of earlier proposals for disarmament or arms regulation. The issues of arms control remain inextricably interwoven with the fabric of an international system in which states are incapable of performing some of their intended functions (such as affording security to citizens) but in which those same states seem unable to change the system into a more viable form.

Under pressure from the major powers, in January 1946, the General Assembly adopted as its first resolution a proposal to establish an Atomic Energy Commission to be composed of all the members of the Security Council plus Canada. The commission was to formulate and submit to the Security Council plans for eliminating atomic weapons, setting up regulations and safeguards, and assuring the use of atomic energy for peaceful purposes only. The next year the Security Council established the Commission for Conventional Armaments, composed of all Council members, to consider general measures for the reduction of armaments.

Basic differences between the positions of the Soviet Union and the United States on the control of atomic weapons manifested themselves immediately, and elements of these differences persisted throughout subsequent negotiations. The United States submitted to the Atomic Energy Commission the Acheson-Lilienthal, or Baruch, Plan, which provided for an international authority to be set up to exercise a monopoly over the ownership, production, and research for peaceful purposes of all atomic material. Atomic weapons would be prohibited, a system of inspection would be instituted, and severe penalties could be imposed by veto-free Security Council actions. When adequate controls were established, the United States would destroy its stockpile of weapons and turn over to the international authority its scientific information on atomic processes. The Soviet representatives insisted on (1) the destruction of existing weapons before discussion of controls, (2) national ownership of atomic facilities, (3) limited and periodic inspection, and (4) the retention of the veto in the Security Council. The Baruch Plan received the endorsement of the majority of the commission, but the East-West impasse was irresoluble.

The post–World War II stalemate over disarmament revives the familiar dichotomy of national positions that persisted throughout the 1920s and 1930s. The Soviet Union frequently states the theme that "the way to disarm is to disarm" or that security results from disarmament and must rest on the good faith of sovereign states expressed through treaty pledges. This theme is similar to the position and approach of the United States and several other states prior to 1940. The current United States insistence on controls and safeguards is reminiscent of the French position during the League of Nations period when France demanded security before disarmament.

In 1952 the consideration of nuclear arms control was merged with that of conventional or nonnuclear arms reduction through the formation of a single Disarmament Commission replacing the two previously separate commissions, but was composed, like the Atomic Energy Commission, of the Security Council members plus Canada. The Disarmament Commission was enlarged from twelve to twenty-six members in 1957 and, at the insistence of the Soviet Union, to the full membership of the United Nations in 1958. However, subcommittees and ad hoc bodies have played a more significant role in disarmament negotiations. A subcommittee of Canada, France, the Soviet Union, the United Kingdom, and the United States was established in 1953 to seek reconciliation of opposing views through private sessions. In 1959 the major powers announced that they had agreed to the formation of the Ten Nation Committee, composed of equal numbers of states from the East and West blocs. In 1961 the General Assembly approved an arrangement between the Soviet Union and the United States for a new Eighteen Nation Disarmament Committee (ENDC) to report to the General Assembly and the Disarmament Commission. In 1969 the membership was enlarged to twenty-six, and the title was changed to the Conference of the Committee on Disarmament (CCD). In 1975 five more members were added to the CCD. At the recommendation of the 1978 General Assembly special session on disarmament, the CCD was renamed the Committee on Disarmament and expanded to forty members. In 1984 the title was again changed to the Conference on Disarmament. This Conference is the most important United Nations negotiating agency in the field of disarmament. Also, since 1978 the UN Center for Disarmament within the Secretariat has been strengthened and a United Nations Institute for Disarmament Research (UNIDIR) has been created.

Some of the most fruitful disarmament negotiations have been carried on outside the United Nations. The path to agreement is often easiest in private consultations among the major powers. Several of the ad hoc bodies referred to in the previous paragraph have had an ambiguous relationship to the United Nations. This relationship has been described as follows:

> But from 1957 on, the major negotiations on general disarmament have taken place not in the organs of the United Nations but in ad hoc bodies established by agreement of the major powers, in particular the Eighteen Nation Disarmament Committee. These bodies have had only a tenuous connection with the United Nations. They have, at the invitation of the Assembly, utilized the facilities of the United Nations and the services of the Secretariat. At the request of the Assembly, they have submitted reports to the United Nations. The annual discussions on disarmament in the Assembly have taken place largely on the basis of these reports.[4]

Some arms control efforts, such as the Strategic Arms Limitation Talks (SALT) and the Strategic Arms Reduction Treaties (START), have been completely divorced from United Nations sponsorship. Although closed meetings of the major powers may be a more appropriate forum than the United Nations organs for certain stages of negotiation on disarmament, the world organization has played an active role in the movement for disarmament since 1946. The General Assembly, in particular, has annually prodded its members toward agreement by the spotlight of debate, through recommendations, and by obligingly constituting new bodies in which negotiations may be resumed when any of the major powers find the climate in the previous agency oppressive or disadvantageous. Largely at Third World instigation, the General Assembly in 1978, 1982, and 1988 met in special sessions, each of four to five weeks' duration, to focus world attention on the need for disarmament.

---

[4]Leland M. Goodrich, Edward Hambro, and Anne Simons, *United Nations Charter: Commentary and Documents*, 3rd ed. (New York: Columbia University Press, 1969), p. 120.

These special sessions were not intended as negotiating sessions for the formulation of new disarmament proposals, but rather as consciousness-raising devices to stimulate progress in other appropriate fora. The sessions were disappointing in the inability of the last two to produce a final document by consensus. Nevertheless, growing public concern was demonstrated through the 140 nongovernmental organizations that applied to make statements at the 1982 session and by perhaps the largest mass rally ever assembled, with participants from all parts of the globe, which was held on June 12, 1982, in New York.

In addition to the special sessions on disarmament, the General Assembly in 1984 decided to convene an International Conference on the Relationship between Disarmament and Development. After some delay and a shift in the meeting site from Paris to New York, the Conference met August 24–September 11, 1987. The United States did not participate because it objected to linking disarmament with development. The 150 states in attendance produced a Final Document by consensus, providing, in part, for the United Nations to analyze the economic and social consequences of the arms race and to publicize the relationships between disarmament and development. The Secretary-General organized a task force within the Secretariat to implement the mandate of the Conference.

Comprehensive plans for general disarmament were repeatedly put forward by the major powers beginning with a Soviet proposal in 1948 to reduce immediately all military forces by one-third and to prohibit atomic weapons. For nearly forty years proposals and counterproposals were so numerous that a detailed examination of them is of small value. Each of the superpowers submitted plans containing elements that they were aware were unacceptable to other parties. Stalling and posturing by the Soviet Union and the United States in the negotiating bodies of the United Nations led to impatience and frustration of many representatives who hoped for real progress. The only areas of agreement between the two superpowers were outlined in a Joint Statement of Principles issued in 1961 which suggested general disarmament in phased steps with verification at each stage. In 1986 Moscow submitted a proposal for the elimination of all nuclear weapons by the year 2000.

Comprehensive or general disarmament seems an unlikely prospect in the 1990s. However, progress has been made on partial measures or a piecemeal approach to lessening the effects of the arms race. The successes of this fractional effort will be examined in the next section of the chapter.

BREAKTHROUGHS IN ARMS CONTROL

Failure to achieve general disarmament has not prevented a series of lesser agreements on specific areas of arms control. Comprehensive and limited approaches to arms control are not incompatible; in fact, some would argue that the piecemeal approach may pave the way and create the climate for the adoption of more comprehensive plans to follow. A series of partial measures may collectively, over time, cover many aspects of a general reduction in preparedness. In the meantime, each step in the series of agreements may remove a specific source of tensions and may, in itself, serve the cause of a more stable and less threatening international situation.

A development only indirectly related to disarmament is the encouragement, under safeguards, of the peaceful uses of atomic energy. In 1953, President Eisenhower suggested to the General Assembly that governments contribute fissionable materials to a new United Nations atomic energy agency. In 1955 the first United Nations Conference on the Peaceful Uses of Atomic Energy met in Geneva and drew up a draft statute for this agency. The revised statute was approved the following year, and in 1957 the International Atomic Energy Agency (IAEA) began operations with headquarters in Vienna. Although the major aim of the IAEA is to assist countries and disseminate information for the use of atomic energy for peaceful purposes, it has developed a system of controls to prevent the diversion of atomic materials to military uses, and this experience may prove valuable in any control system applied to nuclear weapons. Nuclear disarmament could also make available reservoirs of talent and materials for peaceful purposes.

Following extensive joint research efforts in Antarctica during the International Geophysical Year (1957–58), twelve nations with territorial and/or scientific interests in the area concluded an Antarctic Treaty in 1959, which, without settling conflicting territorial claims, opened the continent to all countries for research purposes. Military activities of all types are forbidden, including nuclear weapons or testing and the dumping of radioactive materials. By setting up a demilitarized and denuclearized neutral zone, the Antarctic Treaty set a precedent for claiming other areas as the "common heritage of humankind." Limited applications of these principles to outer space and to the seabed are noted subsequently.

In the mid-1950s, India repeatedly urged the cessation of nuclear testing because it endangered human health, well-being, and survival. From 1959 through 1962 the General Assembly passed numerous resolutions calling upon states to refrain from testing in all environments. In 1958 the United States and the Soviet Union convened a conference of scientific experts to determine the feasibility of setting up an effective control system for the detection of violations of a test-ban agreement. The conclusions of the conference were favorable, and the United States, the Soviet Union, and the United Kingdom began negotiations for the discontinuance of nuclear-weapons testing.

The three-power Conference on the Discontinuance of Nuclear Weapons Tests was unable to reach agreement on a satisfactory control system for detecting and verifying underground tests, and the conference was adjourned in January 1962. However, these same states resumed negotiations in March as a subcommittee of the recently established Eighteen Nation Disarmament Committee (ENDC). After months of prodding by the full committee and by the General Assembly, the three governments announced that they would hold discussions in Moscow in July 1963.

The Moscow negotiations resulted in agreement on a partial test-ban treaty. Attempts to agree on an inspection or verification system for underground tests were abandoned. The treaty prohibited tests in three environments: the atmosphere, outer space, and under water. Existing detection methods required no additional safeguards or machinery for determining violations in these environments. Parties to the treaty also bound themselves to prevent the escape, beyond their national boundaries, of radioactive debris from underground explosions and promised not to encourage or participate in any nuclear explosion anywhere that would violate the restrictions assumed under the treaty. By 1993 120 states had ratified the partial test-ban agreement, but France and the People's Republic of China refuse to do so, although France has voluntarily complied with its provisions since 1974.

Another significant development in 1963 was the opening of a hot line between Washington and Moscow. By establishing a direct communications link between the heads of government of the superpowers, the risk of nuclear war through error or miscalculation may be reduced.

In the year following the orbiting of the first earth satellite, the General Assembly established a Committee on the Peaceful Uses of Outer Space. The Assembly has since that time repeatedly affirmed that outer space and celestial bodies are free to access by all states but are not subject to national appropriation. The United Nations has promoted peaceful cooperation in space, but a major concern has been to prevent the deployment of nuclear destructive devices in this environment. The test-ban treaty prohibits testing in space but not the orbiting or stationing there of nuclear weapons.

In 1963 the ENDC submitted a draft resolution to the General Assembly on the banning of weapons of mass destruction from outer space. In 1966 these ideas were incorporated into a general Treaty on Principles Governing the Activities of States in the Exploration and Use of Outer Space. Certain provisions of the treaty prohibit the orbiting, installing, or stationing of nuclear or other weapons of mass destruction anywhere in space. The treaty also forbids all military activity on the moon and other celestial bodies. These measures remove a potentially serious threat to the security of nations and to humankind. The treaty came into force in October 1967.

One approach to controlling nuclear weapons is the prohibition of their introduction into certain geographic areas. The Antarctic Treaty in 1959 incorporates such a provision and is a first step in establishing nuclear-free zones. The African states through the Organization of African Unity (OAU) have exerted pressure for many years to have their continent declared a nuclear-free zone. Proposals have also been discussed in the General Assembly, beginning in 1974, for establishing nuclear-free zones in South Asia and the Middle East. A greater measure of success has been achieved in Latin America. In 1967, twenty-one Latin American countries signed at Tlatelolco, Mexico, a Treaty for the Prohibition of Nuclear Weapons in Latin America. Recognizing the importance of peaceful uses of nuclear research and energy, the treaty forbids only the testing, use, production, acquisition, receipt, storage, and deployment of all nuclear weapons in the Latin American area. A control system and an agency to ensure compliance are also established by the treaty. An attached protocol provides for nuclear powers to signify their cooperation in respecting the terms of the agreement, and all five major nuclear powers have done so. The treaty came into force in 1969. In 1985 a South Pacific Nuclear Free Zone Treaty was opened for ratification and has been adopted by eleven states.

Another partial step toward arms control is the Treaty on the Non-Proliferation of Nuclear Weapons, which was opened for signature in 1968 and which entered into force in 1970. The treaty resulted from nearly ten years of effort in the General Assembly and the ENDC, from extensive negotiations among the nuclear powers, and from the prodding of the Secretary-General bolstered by expert opinion and public pressures from many sources. The terms of the treaty obligate the nuclear powers not to transfer, and the nonnuclear states not to acquire, nuclear weapons. The acquiring of nuclear capability, under safeguards, solely for peaceful purposes is encouraged. To ease the qualms of states not possessing nuclear capabilities, the nuclear powers also promise to negotiate as soon as possible effective measures for stopping the nuclear arms race, for nuclear disarmament, and for general and complete disarmament. Thus, the partial step toward arms control is tied to the need for more sweeping measures that would erase some of the possible disadvantages of nonnuclear states in their relations with the members of the nuclear club. Disillusionment on the part of nonnuclear states with the effects of the Non-Proliferation Treaty was manifested in four review conferences held in 1975, 1980, 1985, and 1990. Until 1990 the major powers had made few significant moves toward meeting their assumed obligations to reduce nuclear stockpiles and to negotiate general and complete disarmament. Nonnuclear states also believed that the treaty had not succeeded in restraining nuclear proliferation or in encouraging peaceful uses of nuclear energy.

In the same way that the test-ban treaty of 1963 required supplementation to demilitarize outer space and reserve it for peaceful purposes, the need was also recognized to protect the seabed and the ocean floor outside national jurisdiction. In 1968 the ENDC began intensive consideration of seabed demilitarization proposals from the Soviet Union and the United States. In the same year the General Assembly established a permanent Committee on the Peaceful Uses of the Seabed and the Ocean Floor beyond the Limits of National Jurisdiction. After nearly three years of effort to expand the scope of a demilitarization treaty, a very limited text was opened for signature in February 1971. The treaty merely prohibits the placing of weapons of mass destruction, or structures for storing, testing, or launching such weapons, on the seabed and ocean floor or in their subsoil. It does not interfere with nuclear-armed submarines or detection devices beyond territorial limits or with military installations within territorial waters. Thus, the demilitarization measures adopted for the seabed fall far short of those adopted for outer space.

Since World War I, chemical, bacteriological (biological), and radiological (CBR) weapons have been recognized as potential killers on a massive scale. In 1925 a protocol was signed at Geneva under the terms of which the ratifying states agreed not to use asphyxiating, poisonous, or other gases or biological weapons in war. Pressures for the control of these weapons stemmed from (1) the fact that several states, including the United States, had never adhered to the Geneva Protocol; (2) the knowledge that huge stockpiles of varied and sophisticated CBR weapons had been accumulated in a number of countries; (3) the reaction in various parts of the world to the use by the United States in Vietnam of tear gas, herbicides, and defoliants; (4) the publication of studies and reports, including a 1969 United Nations report by fourteen experts, on the effects of the possible use of these weapons; and (5) evidence of extensive use of chemical weapons in the Iran-Iraq War in the 1980s.

Beginning in 1966 the General Assembly, the Eighteen-Nation Committee on Disarmament (ENDC), and its successor negotiating bodies exerted pressure on all states that had not done so to accede to the Geneva Protocol of 1925 and urged the major powers to reach agreement on a treaty banning the production and stockpiling of chemical and bacteriological weapons. The United States and the United Kingdom were willing to agree to a prohibition of bacteriological but not chemical weapons, while the Soviet bloc and nonaligned states pressed for the inclusion of both. The United States also reserved the right to interpret the coverage of the Geneva Protocol as not applying to tear gas, herbicides, and defoliants. However, in 1969 the United States unilaterally renounced the use or production of bacteriological (biological) weapons. President Nixon also announced that the United States would not use lethal and incapacitating chemical weapons except in retaliation for their use by other parties, and he urged the ratification of the Geneva Protocol. In 1971 the major powers agreed to a Convention on the Prohibition of the Development, Production and Stockpiling of Bacteriological (Biological) and Toxin Weapons and on Their Destruction, which was drafted in the CCD, approved by the General Assembly, and opened for signature in London, Moscow, and Washington, D.C., on April 10, 1972. The Convention entered into force in 1975. After continual pressure in the Conference on Disarmament, two new instruments were drawn up to control chemical weapons. In 1990 the United States and Russia, in a Chemical Weapons Reduction Agreement, undertook to reduce their chemical weapons stocks to a maximum of 5,000 tons by the year 2002. In 1993 the

Conference on Disarmament formulated a Chemical Weapons Convention banning all production of chemical weapons and the destruction of all stockpiles within ten to fifteen years of the treaty's entry into force. For both of these agreements the financial burden of the destruction process will present major problems of compliance.

Outside the United Nations, the United States and the Soviet Union conducted negotiations at Helsinki and Vienna after November 1969 on strategic arms limitation. These Strategic Arms Limitations Talks (SALT) have considered possibilities for halting or slowing the race to stockpile and develop both defensive and offensive weapons. By 1971 it was clear that the first agreement to come out of the SALT talks would concentrate on the limitation of the deployment of antiballistic missile systems (ABMs) in both countries. Following President Nixon's visit to Moscow in May 1972, an announcement of accord on ABM limitation was made, limiting each country to two sites. A collateral agreement placed a numerical ceiling on certain categories of armament such as ICBM launchers, but excluded from the limitation multiple warheads, bombers, medium-range missiles, the improvement of existing systems, and new technological developments. The net result was an announcement of proposed increased defense budgets in each country. In fact, since the ABM was yet to be deployed, and the numerical ceilings limited only substantial *increases* of certain systems, no *decreases* in defensive or offensive levels were provided by the Moscow agreements.

Negotiations in preparation for a SALT II agreement began in 1972. In 1974 a Vladivostok understanding between President Ford and General Secretary Brezhnev set numerical ceilings for strategic missiles and the number of missiles that could carry multiple warheads. The treaty was subsequently completed and signed in Vienna in 1979, but was never ratified by the United States Senate. The Reagan administration rejected the terms of SALT II as disadvantageous to the United States, but agreed to open negotiations with the Soviet Union on strategic and intermediate-range arms reduction, as well as on reduction of theater nuclear forces in Europe.

In 1975 the Helsinki Final Act, resulting from the thirty-five-nation conference on Security and Cooperation in Europe, contained provisions for notification of and inviting observers to certain military activities in Europe. At a follow-up conference in Stockholm in 1984–86, an agreement was reached to considerably expand the Helsinki Accords, including verification by on-site inspection on demand.

On December 8, 1987, at a summit meeting in Washington, D.C., President Reagan and General Secretary Gorbachev signed a treaty to eliminate all intermediate-range nuclear missiles (INF) within three years, with elaborate verification provisions to guarantee compliance. This includes all nuclear weapons of 300- to 3,400-mile range. While this agreement removed only 4 percent of all nuclear warheads, it was hailed as a major breakthrough. It was the first pact to agree to eliminate, not just control, existing nuclear weapons.

In the early 1990s several additional agreements were reached promising to substantially reduce both nuclear and conventional arms. In 1991, in the START I agreement, Russia and the United States committed themselves to reduce long-range nuclear warheads by about one-third. In a 1992 protocol, Belarus, Kazakhstan, and the Ukraine promised to remove the nuclear weapons in their areas. Later, the Ukraine refused to willingly live up to its commitment. In 1993 the United States and Russia negotiated the START II agreement pledging to reduce the number of strategic nuclear warheads deployed by each to 3,000–3,500 by the year 2003. Technicalities prevented the beginning of implementation of either START agreement by early 1994.

With regard to conventional arms, the NATO and former Warsaw Treaty members in 1990, in the Conventional Armed Forces in Europe Treaty, agreed to substantially reduce five categories of conventional weapons deployed on the continent. After the breakup of the Soviet Union the successor states assumed the obligations, and progress in treaty implementation was not impeded. In 1993 a UN Register of Conventional Arms was established to receive annual reports from states on arms exports and imports. This registry is a part of the recent General Assembly's annual discussions of the issue of transparency in armaments and is reminiscent of the publication of the League of Nations *Armaments Yearbooks.*

THE NEED FOR CONTROL

The end of the Cold War lessened some of the anxieties concerning the use of weapons of mass destruction, and the period since 1987 has witnessed the adoption of important arms control agreements, but military threats and loss of lives in wars are still prevalent. Although world military expenditures have been reduced by approximately one-third (but only 10 to 15 percent in constant dollars) from the 1987 peak of nearly $1 billion, national military expenditures exceeded public expenditures for education in thirty-seven countries in 1992.[5] This use of scarce resources is questionable, especially in developing countries. In 1992 there were twenty-nine ongoing ethnic and civil wars with an accumulated death toll of 6 million.[6]

The major powers have undertaken reductions in strategic and intermediate-range nuclear weapons, but after all agreements through 1993 are fully

[5]Sivard, *World Military and Social Expenditures 1993*, p. 5.
[6]Ibid., p. 7.

implemented the number of remaining nuclear warheads would exceed 10,000. The explosive power would be more than capable of causing the annihilation of all humankind. Furthermore, as former major adversaries reduce their mutual threats, the same sense of security does not necessarily apply to other states with nuclear capability or potential. The same uncertainties apply to the possible use of other weapons of mass destruction in regional wars.

Another pressing need is to reduce the accumulation of conventional arms, many of which are capable of great damage and loss of life. Many countries, including most Middle East nations, are saturated with sophisticated weapons. Military regimes are often violence-prone whether against neighbors or their own minorities. Although the arms trade has declined since 1987, the level of lethality in dozens of states is very high, large military forces are maintained, and resources for economic and social well-being are diminished.

The search for disarmament contains both a dilemma and a paradox. The paradox is that each state searches for security by acquiring a military arsenal, and yet the possession of arms by all states results in greater international threats and the lessening of the sense of security. The existence of modern weapons of mass destruction exacerbates the threat, raises it to a level of total destructive capability previously unimagined, and heightens the feelings of insecurity.

The dilemma for each state is how to promote its national interests in a disarmed world and how to be sure that at each stage of the process of disarming no nation violates its pledges and uses its advantage for the purpose of dominating other nations. It is frequently pointed out that armaments are means and are generally not ends in themselves. States acquire arms to achieve certain ends. The elimination of arms can probably never be achieved without the substitution of other means for accomplishing the goals of states. This lesson was apparent in the security demands of states in the disarmament negotiations of the League period and is equally apparent today. Disarmament is primarily a political problem linked to the whole range of problems of the relations of nations in a competitive world.

Disarmament cannot occur in a vacuum or in the abstract. Security must be sought through substitute means in order for disarmament to occur. Restraint and rationality must be exercised until the new means can be developed.

10

VARIETIES
OF REGIONALISM

One phenomenon of the period since 1945 is the rapid growth in the number of intergovernmental regional organizations. In fact, regional organizations founded since 1945 outnumber those of a universal nature by approximately a five-to-one ratio. Obviously, not all regional agencies perform highly significant functions, but some have assumed important roles in world affairs. The contributions and deficiencies of the major regional organizations are the subject matter of this chapter.

THE PROS AND CONS OF REGIONALISM

Regional organizations are variously defined, often on the basis of geographical proximity of the members. Such definitions are subject to the difficulty of delimiting geographic regions, for there is no general agreement on any natural divisions into which the world may be clearly and conveniently divided. Therefore, while geography may be one factor that aids in determining the regional character of many organizations, the lack of proximity of the members or the failure of an organization to conform to a neat generally recognizable geographic area will not be decisive in excluding certain agencies from consideration in this chapter. The United States, for example, is a member of several organizations that claim regional status and that reach to almost every point of the compass, thus variously identifying the United States with the North Atlantic, American, and Southeast Asian areas. None of the organizations involved conforms to any natural geographic region. The North Atlantic area opens to question whether an ocean represents a unifying factor or a barrier for determining a region; the inclusion of Greece and Turkey in the membership of the North Atlantic Treaty Organization throws further doubt on conformity to regional limits. The now defunct Southeast Asia Treaty Organization was *for* the protection of Southeast Asian countries, but it was dominated *by* non-Asian states, which formed a majority of its membership. The membership of the Organization of American States includes all states within North, South, and Central America, but geographers have never viewed both continents as a single well-defined region. The Commonwealth is also frequently classified as a regional organization, although its members are dispersed around the globe.

As the term is used in this chapter, a *regional organization* is a segment of the world bound together by a common set of objectives based on geographical, social, cultural, economic, or political ties and possessing a formal structure provided for in formal intergovernmental agreements. Although bilateral arrangements can qualify under such a definition, attention will be focused here only on arrangements involving three or more members. At the other end of the scale, limited actual membership in organizations open to all states does not affect their global character since their objectives point toward universality. A regional organization is intended to appeal only to a specified category of states, less than global in scope.

In the twentieth century a cleavage has developed between certain advocates of universalism and some advocates of regionalism. Both sets of antagonists agree that the international system must eventually be modified from the primacy of the nation-state in the direction of a partial surrender of state sovereignty to larger political units. The adversaries concur on the goal of world order and stability and on the inadequacy of the state-centered system for this purpose. Extreme universalists and regionalists each see their own approach to order and stability as the *only* feasible alternative to the deficiencies of the present system. Thus a dichotomy is set up in which the choice is presented as either universalism or regionalism.

The regionalists often include the following claims for the superiority of regionalism over universalism:

1. There is a natural tendency toward regionalism based on the homogeneity of interests, traditions, and values within small groups of neighboring states.
2. Political, economic, and social integration is more easily attained among a lesser number of states within a limited geographic area than on a global basis.
3. Regional economic cooperation provides more efficient economic units than the smaller states, and these larger units can compete successfully in world markets.

4. Local threats to the peace are more willingly and promptly dealt with by the governments of that area than by disinterested states at greater distances from the scene of conflict.

5. By combining states into regional groupings, a global balance of power will be maintained and world peace and security will be promoted.

6. The world is not ready to establish global authority sufficient to maintain world peace and promote world welfare. Regionalism is the first step in gaining experience and building areas of consensus toward eventual intergovernmental coordination or integration.

7. Universalists fail to take into account the heterogeneity of political, economic, social, and geographical factors throughout the world that militate against global unity. These differences can be more easily accommodated within a regional framework.

On the other hand, the universalists frequently argue that the following reasons substantiate their preference for universalism over regionalism:

1. World interdependence has created an increasing number of problems that require global solutions. Political, economic, and social problems reach across regional boundaries.

2. Regional resources are often inadequate to resolve the problems of states within the region.

3. Since peace is indivisible only a world organization can deal effectively with threats to the peace that may, if unchecked, spread beyond local or regional limits.

4. Only a universal organization can provide an adequate check on the power of a large state that can often dominate the other members of a regional arrangement.

5. Sanctions against an aggressor are usually ineffective if applied on a regional basis because of sources of aid to the aggressor from outside the region.

6. Regions are imprecise and impermanent. No agreement can be reached on a system of regions into which the globe can be conveniently divided.

7. Regional alliances provide the basis for rivalries and competition for military supremacy among regions leading to greater possibilities for major wars.

8. The existence of numerous, moderately successful universal organizations demonstrates the desire of governments and peoples to cooperate on a global basis without the necessity of first using regional organizations as laboratories for gradually developing enlarged areas of consensus or community.

Although the claims of the universalists and regionalists, by creating a dichotomy between the two approaches, might seem to preclude an accommodation between them, such an accommodation may in fact exist. The choice is not necessarily one of either regionalism or universalism but allows for both regionalism and universalism coexisting in a sometimes competing and sometimes mutually supporting relationship. The relationship of regional with universal organizations may be either antagonistic or harmonious.

In her book *The Majority of One*, Minerva Etzioni discusses the concept of compatibility and incompatibility between regional and universal organizations. Compatibility is defined as the relationship between two organizations by which "the activities of one do not undermine those of the other and vice versa."[1] The antagonism between regionalism and universalism occurs only when the jurisdiction and functions of organizations at the two levels are incompatible. If universal obligations, in case of conflict, prevail over regional obligations, and if regional agencies submit to supervision by global agencies or respond positively to their requests for supportive action, then the basis for a compatible relationship exists. These harmonious or conflicting relationships will be examined with regard to the regional organizations described throughout this chapter. A combination of regionalism and universalism serves to promote the national interests of most states in their advance beyond unilateralism and self-help.

The nature of the problem to be solved determines whether it will best respond to regional or to universal treatment. If the consequences of a problem are regional in nature or scope, then a regional solution is appropriate. On the other hand, a military security system or a form of economic regionalism that tends to foster antagonisms or discriminatory policies toward other states or blocs of states may be considered as subversive of and incompatible with world order and justice through universalism. In determining the balance to be sought between the roles of regional and universal organizations, the effect of each action in promoting order, restraint, and international cooperation should serve as normative guides, while actions that increase international tensions and rivalries should be avoided. Both regional and global agencies can contribute to the promotion of the general welfare of humanity, but the myopic view fostered by rival nationalistic movements prevalent in today's world will continue to bolster the misuse or nonuse of both levels of agencies for immediate, narrow, national advantage.

REGIONALISM UNDER THE UNITED NATIONS CHARTER

At the time that the Charter of the United Nations was being formulated, the forces favoring regionalism were sufficiently strong and diverse to require an accommodation for regional organizations within the universal framework. Winston Churchill at first favored the regionalist over the universalist approach to world order, and the Latin American states formed a strong pressure bloc for a recognition of the legitimacy and importance of the role of regional agencies in promoting the aims of international peace, security, and welfare. However, at the San Francisco conference a proposal to provide specific arrangements for regional agencies in the economic and social work of

---

[1]Minerva M. Etzioni, *The Majority of One: Towards a Theory of Regional Compatibility* (Beverly Hills, CA: Sage Publications, 1970), p. 18.

the United Nations was defeated. Consequently, all the Charter provisions for regional arrangements are limited to the role of regional organizations in the maintenance of international peace and security. However, in practice, regional agencies are extensively utilized in the economic and social spheres, since nothing in the Charter precludes their establishment and since their utility is widely recognized. Those regional economic and social agencies that are part of the United Nations official structure are created under the broad authority of the General Assembly and the Economic and Social Council to establish subsidiary bodies to assist in carrying out their functions.

The primary provisions of the Charter concerning regional arrangements are found in Chapter VIII containing only three articles (Articles 52–54). The most important principles of Chapter VIII are the following: (1) regional agencies may exist for dealing with such issues of international peace and security as are appropriate for regional action as long as their activities are consistent with the purposes and principles of the United Nations; (2) states are encouraged to settle local disputes through regional agencies before referring them to the Security Council; (3) the Security Council may, in turn, utilize such agencies for the settlement of local disputes; (4) with the exception of action against enemy states resulting from World War II, no enforcement action shall be taken by regional agencies without the authorization of the Security Council; and (5) the Security Council shall be kept fully informed of activities undertaken or contemplated by regional agencies for the maintenance of peace and security.

These principles clearly were intended to establish that, in case of conflict between the jurisdiction of a regional organization and the United Nations, universalism should take precedence over regionalism. However, through interpretation of such phrases as "local disputes," "enforcement action," and "fully informed," and through intermittent debate concerning the right of the Security Council to assume priority over disputes while they are under consideration by regional organizations, the supremacy of the universalist claim has been substantially undermined.

The most numerous test cases tending to lessen United Nations authority have involved the Organization of American States (OAS). Because of its dominant position within the OAS, the United States has preferred to use regional channels for dealing with conflicts within the Western Hemisphere. In 1954, on the grounds that the situation was under consideration by the OAS, Guatemala was denied access to the Security Council in bringing its charge of aggression against Nicaragua and Honduras. In 1960, Cuba's charges of aggression committed by the United States, and in 1963 the Haitian complaint against the Dominican Republic, were deferred by the Security Council, honoring the priority claimed by the OAS. Although the right of any party to a dispute to appeal to the Security Council at any time is not denied, expediency and political pressures often dictate leaving the dispute to regional consideration.

Article 53 forbids the taking of "enforcement action" by regional agencies without the authorization of the Security Council. Articles 41 and 42 of the Charter specify that the kinds of enforcement available include both military and nonmilitary measures. Yet the meaning of the term *enforcement action* in Article 53 has been, in practice, systematically narrowed to exclude nonmilitary sanctions applied by regional agencies. In 1960 the necessity for the Security Council to approve economic sanctions against the Dominican Republic imposed through OAS action was denied on the grounds that approval only of military action was required by Article 53. The meaning of *enforcement action* was further narrowed during the Dominican crisis of 1965, when the United States was supported in its claim that United States Marines and OAS military contingents in the Dominican Republic were there as "peacekeeping forces," not as agents of enforcement within the meaning of Article 53.

Similarly, the requirement of Article 54 that the Security Council at all times be kept fully informed of activities "undertaken or in contemplation" by regional agencies has been eroded through practice. The kinds and scope of information have been limited and "after the fact" instead of keeping the Council fully informed during the planning stages in order that United Nations supervision can be maintained throughout all phases of a dispute or conflict. The Security Council has acquiesced in accepting perfunctory reports from regional organizations outlining in documentary form the results only of actions.

One of the most significant modifications of the Charter through interpretation and state practice applying to regional associations has developed, not under Chapter VIII, but under Article 51, dealing with the right of states to take measures for collective as well as individual self-defense against armed attack. Such a right is limited by requirements that the Security Council be immediately informed of such measures, that the Council's authority and responsibility for maintaining peace and security not be affected thereby, and that the right of self-defense exists only until the Security Council has taken necessary measures to restore and maintain international peace and security. No specific mention of regional arrangements is made in Article 51, but the reference to collective self-defense opens the door to the creation and use of regional organizations for this purpose.

Few regional arrangements capable of mobilization for collective self-defense existed in 1945. The Union of American Republics, as the forerunner of the OAS, and the League of Arab States (Arab League) were the only regional agencies that included collective self-defense among their objectives. The breakdown of East-West cooperation after World War II and the increasing tensions of the Cold War presaged the deadlock of the Security Council on issues involving the maintenance of peace and security in which the major powers had important interests.

The great powers sought security through a series of regional pacts in which the United States took the earliest initiative. The first postwar development of this type did not receive its main impetus from the Cold War. In 1947 the Inter-American Treaty of Reciprocal Assistance (Rio Treaty) established a regional security system for the Western Hemisphere. Other United States–sponsored alliances for military defense quickly followed and were aimed at bolstering the emerging Communist containment policy of the United States government. These included the North Atlantic Treaty Organization (NATO) formed in 1949, the ANZUS Pacific Security Pact in 1951, and the Southeast Asia Treaty Organization (SEATO) in 1954 (disbanded in 1976). In 1955 the Soviet Union responded to the threat of military encirclement by setting up the Warsaw Treaty Organization (WTO) as capstone to a series of bilateral security treaties among East European states.

Although Article 51 of the Charter emphasizes the supreme authority of the Security Council in matters of self-defense, this article became an escape hatch from the obligations of universalism toward a revival of an alliance system contributing to a compartmentalization and fragmentation of any potential global unity. The major powers interpreted the collective self-defense clause as justifying the creation of military security alliances. These alliances, in turn, exacerbated existing attitudes of divisiveness and hostility. The Security Council's supposedly preeminent role in self-defense situations cannot be exercised when a major power is involved if that power refuses to inform the Council of its defensive measures, as required by Article 51, or when the veto is available to block Council action. The end of the Cold War and the breakup of the Warsaw Treaty Organization marked the decline of superpower confrontation. However, new potential threats to the security concerns of nations slowed the abandonment of other military alliances and prompted a reexamination of their purposes. At the same time, the potential role of the Security Council in conflict management is thereby enhanced.

MULTIPURPOSE REGIONAL ORGANIZATIONS

Regional organizations may be classified in several ways, based on the nature or scope of their functions or memberships, or possibly on the degree of eventual integration that is sought. One useful and instructive method of classification has been developed by Lynn H. Miller, who divides all regional organizations into three general types, which he labels as (1) cooperative, (2) alliance, or (3) functional.[2] Miller's categories are based on "the single variable of the *security orientation* of component states as expressed through the organizational structure."[3]

[2]Lynn H. Miller, "Regional Organizations and Subordinate Systems," in *The International Politics of Regions: A Comparative Approach*, eds. Louis J. Cantori and Steven L. Spiegel (Englewood Cliffs, NJ: Prentice-Hall, 1970), pp. 357–78.

[3]Ibid., p. 361.

For purposes of this chapter, a variation of the above categories will be adopted. Instead of the "cooperative" classification, a more inclusive category of "multipurpose" organizations will be used. The terms *alliance* and *functional* will be retained, and a fourth distinct category of United Nations Regional Commissions will be added.

These latter regional commissions fit neatly into no other group since they form a link between the universal and the regional systems and serve to promote universal goals within specific geographic areas through regional agencies established as a part of the United Nations system. The multipurpose organizations are those whose broad aims and activities reach across the lines that divide political and military matters from those generally classified as economic and social. Alliance-type organizations are those whose military and political orientation is intended to provide security against external actors. Functional organizations are those that promote economic, social, or political collaboration, with little or no regard to security factors. The dividing line between all other categories and the multipurpose category is somewhat arbitrary and subjective and is determined by the range and variety of activities pursued by the regional organization. Table 10–1 includes the most important regional organizations within this fourfold classification system.

As defined above, multipurpose organizations are characterized by the range and scope of their functions, aims, and activities. The examination of several multipurpose organizations will serve to demonstrate these characteristics and to illustrate the significance of these agencies in the conduct of world affairs.

Organization of American States (OAS)

The OAS is in several respects the most significant of the multipurpose regional organizations. This significance is established on the basis of the elaborate structure and functions of the OAS and its long, continuous history.

The First International Conference of American States in 1890 authorized the establishment of a permanent organization under the title of the International Union of American Republics. As the continuous organ of the union, a central bureau was set up in Washington, D.C., for the primary purpose of disseminating commercial information. Successive Inter-American Conferences in the early twentieth century broadened the functions of the bureau to include a wide range of noncommercial activities. In 1910, in a major reorganization, the title of the organization was changed to the Union of American Republics, and the bureau became the Pan-American Union. A further restructuring in 1948 resulted in the adoption of the present name, the Organization of American States, and the Pan-American Union became the General Secretariat. In 1967 the Third Special Inter-American Conference meeting in Buenos Aires approved a series of Charter amendments that again significantly altered the previous organizational structure. These Buenos Aires amendments took effect in 1970.

TABLE 10–1   MAJOR INTERGOVERNMENTAL REGIONAL ORGANIZATIONS

I. MULTIPURPOSE ORGANIZATIONS

Title	*Acronym*	*Established*	*Membership (1992)*
Organization of American States (originally, International Union of American Republics)	OAS	1948 (1890)	35
League of Arab States (Arab League)		1945	21
Organization of African Unity	OAU	1963	51
Commonwealth (formerly, British Commonwealth of Nations)		1926	50
Council of Europe		1949	26
Organization of Central American States	ODECA, or OCAS	1952	5
Andean Group		1969	5
Association of Southeast Asian Nations	ASEAN	1967	6
Nordic Council	NC	1952	8

II. ALLIANCE SYSTEMS

Title	*Acronym*	*Established*	*Membership (1992)*
North Atlantic Treaty Organization	NATO	1949	16
Warsaw Treaty Organization (disbanded 1991)	WTO	1955	7
Australia, New Zealand, United States Security Treaty Organization	ANZUS	1952	3
Western European Union	WEU	1954	7

III. FUNCTIONAL ORGANIZATIONS

Title	*Acronym*	*Established*	*Membership (1992)*
Benelux Economic Union	BENELUX	1948	3
European Coal and Steel Community	ECSC	1952	12
European Community	EC	1958	12
European Free Trade Association	EFTA	1960	7
European Atomic Energy Community	EURATOM	1958	12

(continued)

TABLE 10–1   (Continued)

III. FUNCTIONAL ORGANIZATIONS (continued)

Title	Acronym	Established	Membership (1992)
Organization for Economic Cooperation and Development	OECD	1961	24
Latin American Integration Association	LAIA	1981	11
Central American Common Market	CACM	1961	5
Council for Technical Cooperation in South and Southeast Asia (Colombo Plan)		1950	26
South Pacific Forum	SPF	1971	15
Caribbean Community	CARICOM	1973	13
Central African Customs and Economic Union	CACEU	1964	6
Economic Community of West African States	ECOWAS	1975	16
Inter-American Development Bank	IDB	1959	44
African Development Bank	AFDB	1964	75
Asian Development Bank	ASDB	1966	52
Central American Bank of Economic Integration	CABEI	1961	5
European Investment Bank	EIB	1958	12
Conseil de l'Entente	CE	1959	5
Organization of Petroleum Exporting Countries	OPEC	1960	12
Arab Monetary Fund	AMF	1976	20
Nordic Investment Bank	NIB	1976	5

IV. UNITED NATIONS REGIONAL COMMISSIONS

Title	Acronym	Established	Membership (1992)
Economic Commission for Europe	ECE	1947	43
Economic and Social Commission for Asia and the Pacific	ESCAP	1947	48 + 10 assoc.
Economic Commission for Latin America and the Caribbean	ECLAC	1948	40 + 6 assoc.
Economic Commission for Africa	ECA	1958	51
Economic and Social Commission for Western Asia	ESCWA	1974	13

The OAS operates through a General Assembly, which meets annually and is designated as the supreme organ. A Permanent Council, consisting of one representative of ambassadorial rank per member state, has its seat in Washington, D.C. The Permanent Council performs special pacific-settlement functions in addition to serving as the preparatory committee for the General Assembly and carrying out other directives of the Assembly. Two other councils, the Inter-American Economic and Social Council and the Inter-American Council for Education, Science and Culture, supervise extensive programs, draft treaties, and initiate conferences under Assembly guidance. In crisis situations a Meeting of Consultation of ministers of foreign affairs may be summoned at the request of member states. An Inter-American Juridical Committee acts as an advisory body to the OAS and promotes the development and codification of international law within the hemisphere. Other agencies include specialized conferences; specialized organizations in such fields as agriculture, child welfare, women's affairs, health, and Indian affairs; and an Inter-American Commission on Human Rights. The General Secretariat, headed by a secretary-general and employing more than 700 staff workers, serves as the administering and coordinating arm of the OAS. The headquarters are in Washington, D.C.

The aims of the OAS are as comprehensive and diffuse as its structure. These include (1) strengthening the peace and security of the continent; (2) preventing difficulties and ensuring the pacific settlement of disputes among members; (3) providing common action in the event of aggression; (4) seeking the solution of political, juridical, and economic problems among members; and (5) promoting by cooperative action the economic, social, and cultural development of the member states.

The OAS operates in part as an alliance for collective defense. In 1947 a special conference at Rio de Janeiro drew up the Inter-American Treaty of Reciprocal Assistance (Rio Pact). This pact and the OAS Charter adopted at Bogotá in 1948 (as amended in 1967) serve as the legal basis for the hemispheric security system. The Rio Pact declares "that an armed attack by any State against an American State shall be considered as an attack against all the American States." This principle is common to the military-alliance arrangements discussed in the next section of this chapter. While the OAS serves a wide range of other functions, this feature establishes an identity of purpose with such organizations as the North Atlantic Treaty Organization and the former Warsaw Treaty Organization. The Rio Pact also defined an inter-American security zone extending several hundred miles into the oceans and from pole to pole within which an attack would be treated as if it were made upon the land area of a state. Members of the OAS were obligated to provide individual assistance to the victim of an aggression until a Meeting of Consultation (either of ministers of foreign affairs or of the OAS Council) or the United Nations Security Council recommended a course of collective action.

The collective defense features of the OAS have served more as a warning against potential external aggression that might threaten states within the hemisphere than as a defense against military attack. During the 1950s the organs of OAS, in response to United States initiative, adopted a series of resolutions urging safeguards against Communist subversion of individual states. Indirect aggression was thus viewed as the major concern of the defense system. The emergence of Communism in Cuba served as "proof" of indirect aggression and established a base for the further spread of Communist doctrine. Cuba was suspended from participation in the OAS, and Communism was declared incompatible with the principles of the OAS. The only direct military threat was the placing of Soviet missiles and missile launchers on Cuban soil in 1962. While the United States carried out all measures for getting the weapons removed, the OAS indicated its willingness to cooperate in collective defensive measures. OAS members served as willing partners, and OAS agencies as convenient tools in supporting United States attitudes in the Cold War.

The OAS has played a much larger role in maintaining peace and promoting the pacific settlement of disputes among states within the hemisphere than it has as a collective defense agency against outside aggression. In these inter-American conflicts, the council of the OAS or the ministers of foreign affairs acting as an Organ of Consultation have served as the instruments through which action was taken. In several cases the assistance of the Inter-American Peace Commission as a fact-finding and conciliation agency was vital to a solution. Among the disputes dealt with by the OAS are the following: Costa Rica and Nicaragua (1948–49, 1955–56, 1959); Honduras and Nicaragua (1957); Venezuela and the Dominican Republic (1960–61); Venezuela and Cuba (1963–64, 1967); the Dominican Republic and Haiti (1950, 1963–65); and Panama and the United States (1964). The OAS was particularly effective in bringing about a resolution of the issues in the so-called soccer war between El Salvador and Honduras in 1969–70. The organization also played a supporting role to that of the United States in the interventions into the internal situations in Guatemala in 1954 and in the Dominican Republic in 1965. In the latter case the United States was hard pressed to muster the necessary two-thirds vote for an OAS force to partially replace United States military contingents unilaterally dispatched to Santo Domingo. Many Latin American states resented the pressures from the "colossus of the North" to turn a unilateral violation of domestic jurisdiction into a face-saving collective "peacekeeping" operation under which the United States could claim immunity from United Nations responsibility and jurisdiction. In the 1982 Falkland Islands (Malvinas) war between Argentina and the United Kingdom, the OAS adopted mild resolutions of support for Argentina, but the organization could play no constructive role in settling the dispute. The United States' swing toward the British brought it into opposition with most Latin American countries. In 1983, under the pretext of applying an Eastern Caribbean Defense Treaty, and without consulting the OAS, the United States unilaterally invaded Grenada.

Throughout their history the OAS and its forerunners have served as instruments of economic and social cooperation. The earliest activities of the International Union of American Republics concentrated on commercial concerns. After World War II economic and social development in Latin America was treated by the United States as secondary to the rebuilding of Western Europe. As a result, the Latin American states, prior to 1961, relied more on the United Nations Economic Commission for Latin America (ECLA) than on the OAS for promoting their aspirations for accelerating the development process. In addition to its direct programs, the ECLA encouraged the founding of the Latin American Free Trade Association (LAFTA), the Central American Common Market (CACM), and the Inter-American Development Bank (IDB). After a period of intensified anti–United States feeling, culminating in the physical attacks upon Vice President Nixon in 1958 in Peru and in Venezuela, a special meeting of foreign ministers in Washington endorsed a number of new economic measures to be carried out through the OAS.

The resurgence of OAS economic and social development activities was manifested in the Charter of Punta del Este, which, in 1961, outlined the terms of the Alliance for Progress. The purpose of the alliance was to accelerate the rate of economic and social development by mobilizing the energies and resources of Latin American peoples and governments. Both national and cooperative programs were stressed. A minimum per capita income growth rate of 2.5 percent was set as a target, and additional goals included increased investment and more equitable distribution of income; diversification of national production; more rapid industrialization; increased agricultural productivity and land reform; the elimination of adult illiteracy; the expansion of educational facilities, including vocational and technical training; improved health and medical facilities, with a target of a five-year increase in life expectancy by 1970; construction of low-cost housing; price stabilization; and the promotion of economic integration. The total investment needs for accomplishing these goals was set at $100 billion for a ten-year period, with 80 percent of the total to be generated internally in each developing state and the remaining $20 billion to come from outside sources, not the least of which was to be the United States government.

The results of the Alliance for Progress were disappointing. The ambitious goals of the program fell short of realization. The rate of economic growth measured in terms of per capita income averaged far below the target of 2.5 percent, although a few states exceeded the goal. As a result of their continued frustrations, Latin American governments became staunch advocates of the United Nations Conference on Trade and Development (UNCTAD), a combined effort with other underdeveloped states to establish a claim for special concessions from the developed states for the purpose of closing the economic gap between rich and poor nations. In the early 1990s a limited number of Latin American states, including Argentina, Chile, Mexico, and Venezuela, achieved growth rates above the average of the world's other developing countries.

The OAS Charter is technically compatible with the United Nations Charter and contains more references to the role of OAS as a regional organization under Articles 52–54 of the United Nations Charter than are found in the basic document of any other regional organization. However, as pointed out in the previous section of this chapter, through narrowed interpretation of the obligations of the OAS to submit to United Nations supervision of enforcement actions, the role of the United Nations in the realm of peace and security has been gradually eroded. In practice, according to Minerva Etzioni, the relationship has been transformed from one of compatibility to one of incompatibility.[4] The United States, as the hegemonic power within the OAS, has used the organization for its own purposes and has insulated these actions from effective United Nations control and responsibility. Even the military measures used in the Dominican Republic in 1965 were first converted from unilateral to regional status and then claimed as "peacekeeping" forces immune from the requirement of prior Security Council approval of enforcement measures. Ellen Frey-Wouters sums up the results of the transformation of the security and peaceful settlement provisions of the OAS Charter from compatibility to incompatibility with the United Nations Charter in these terms:

> The primary role of the Latin American members of the OAS in most collective security cases has been to provide a multilateral legitimacy for essentially unilateral U.S. action. The OAS serves to carry out the extracontinental objectives of the U.S., free from any control by the UN. It can be expected that the OAS will continue, at least in the immediate future, to be misused as a means to intervene against regimes of states which do not meet with approval of the U.S.[5]

More recently, however, the ability of the United States to use the OAS as such a willing tool of United States foreign policy shows some signs of weakening as Latin American states assert greater independence from United States dominance. As stated by a former OAS official, the efficacy of the organization was also weakened by United States official attitudes in the 1980s.

> U.S. policies in recent years have done considerable damage to the concept of inter-American cooperation, principally by ignoring it in the multiple crises the hemisphere has faced in the last decade: the Malvinas, Grenada, the debt crisis, trade, and, most importantly, Central America. In so doing, U.S. policies have

---

[4]Etzioni, *Majority of One*, passim.

[5]Ellen Frey-Wouters, "The Prospects for Regionalism in World Affairs," in *The Future of the International Legal Order*, eds. Richard A. Falk and Cyril E. Black (Princeton, NJ: Princeton University Press, 1969), I, 539.

almost irreparably sundered the underpinnings of mutuality implicit in the inter-American bargain.[6]

The OAS has been wounded but is far from death. Its elaborate network of agencies continues to perform useful functions, keeping alive contacts and habits of collaboration. Even in the political arena, the OAS joined the United States in May 1989 in condemning General Noriega's cancellation of the Panamanian elections, and dispatched a delegation of three foreign ministers to Panama to try to effect a transfer of power and to restore the democratic process there. Again, in the early 1990s, the OAS was a major actor, in collaboration with the United Nations, in the political crisis in Haiti.

Organization of African Unity (OAU)

The OAU is one of the newest multipurpose regional organizations and is the largest in membership. The OAU emerged in 1963 as an amalgamation of several former subregional groupings of states in Africa. From its original membership of thirty it has grown to include fifty-one states. All members are from Africa, since the Charter does not permit non-African states to join. Only independent and sovereign states are eligible, and admission is by simple majority of the members after notice is given by the applicant state of its intention to accede to the charter.

The purposes of the OAU are the following: (1) to promote the unity and solidarity of the African states; (2) to cooperate and coordinate efforts to achieve a better life for the peoples of Africa; (3) to defend the sovereignty, territorial integrity, and independence of the African states; (4) to eradicate all forms of colonialism from Africa; and (5) to promote international cooperation with due regard to the Charter of the United Nations and the Universal Declaration of Human Rights. The basic principles of the organization, in addition to those implicit in the purposes stated above, include (1) peaceful settlement of disputes by negotiation, mediation, conciliation, or arbitration; (2) unreserved condemnation of political assassination and subversive activities; and (3) affirmation of a policy of nonalignment with regard to all blocs. The condemnation of political assassination and subversive activities was prompted by a series of charges against the government of Ghana by neighboring states, which culminated in the assassination of President Sylvanus Olympio of Togo on the eve of the conference for the adoption of the OAU charter.

---

[6]L. Ronald Sheman, *The Inter-American Dilemma: The Search for Inter-American Cooperation at the Centennial of the Inter-American System* (New York: Praeger Publishers, 1988), p. 195.

At the inception of the OAU, Ghana also led an effort to establish a central political organization with power to formulate a common foreign policy, common planning for economic development, a common currency, and a common defense system. These suggestions for the surrender of national sovereignty were unacceptable to most of the heads of states and governments that approved the charter. The Ghanaian proposal for organic political union was rejected in favor of a loose organization with a limited functional approach to unity.

The supreme organ of the OAU is the annual Assembly of Heads of State and Government. The agenda for the supreme organ is prepared by the Council of Ministers, which meets twice a year to supervise the general work of the organization and which is also called into emergency session when crises so demand. The Council of Ministers is charged with the responsibility of implementing the decisions of the Assembly of Heads of State and Government. A permanent General Secretariat carries on the continuous activities of the organization and provides necessary support for the periodic meetings of the policy-determining organs. The General Secretariat is headed by an administrative secretary-general, a title highly significant in designating the limited initiative conferred upon this officer. Five functional specialized commissions and a Commission of Mediation, Conciliation and Arbitration complete the organizational structure of the OAU.

In bringing about peaceful settlement of disputes among African states, the OAU has a mixed record. In an Algerian-Moroccan border dispute in which fighting broke out in 1963, the efforts of individual African heads of states, an emergency session of the OAU council, and the appointment of an ad hoc commission contributed to a gradual lessening of tensions and hostilities, although no permanent settlement was ever formalized. From 1964 until 1967 guerrilla fighting occurred along the borders of Somalia with Ethiopia and Kenya over the claims of Somalia to the right of incorporation into Somalia of territories occupied by Somali minorities in adjoining states. In spite of attempts at settlement by the OAU, sporadic fighting continued for four years until a reconciliation at the 1967 OAU Assembly of Heads of State. In 1966 and 1967 the political activities of refugees from Rwanda who had fled to Burundi caused tensions between the two countries. The Assembly of Heads of State in 1966 requested president Mobutu of the Congo to mediate the dispute, and his efforts were successful.

In three other disputes, disagreement among OAU members led to frustration and stalemate. In the Congo in 1964 and 1965 rebel actions against the Tshombe government split the sympathies of African states. An emergency meeting of the Council of Ministers in 1964 agreed upon the appointment of a ten-nation conciliation commission, but neither this commission nor a subsequent meeting of the council could concur on any course of action. The dispute subsided with the defeat of the rebels and with subsequent changes in the leadership of the Congo government. In the Biafran revolt against the Nigerian government in 1967–70 and the resulting civil war, the OAU proved impotent as a force for conciliation. The majority actions of the OAU were partial to Nigerian sovereignty and violated the requirement of neutrality, which is necessary for conciliation. Some African states supported the Biafran cause, and the OAU made no contribution to the final settlement, which came about by military action. A review of the case study of the Western Sahara dispute, which was included in Chapter 6, will serve as a reminder that the OAU was so badly divided over this issue that the viability of the organization was temporarily threatened.

As might be expected, the failures of the OAU in dispute settlement or amelioration occurred in those situations in which the members were split in their support of the contending parties. Relative success resulted from near unanimity on a course of action or from a desire to provide neutral pressures for a cessation of hostilities.

In numerous areas the OAU has worked closely with the United Nations. In attitudes and sanctions against the previous white-dominated regime in Rhodesia, the OAU organs anticipated and pressed for effective United Nations action. Realizing their own lack of military and economic capacity, the African states agitated through the OAU, the General Assembly, and the Security Council for British measures and United Nations sanctions to bring down the Ian Smith government. Reciprocally, the Security Council in 1965, immediately after the unilateral declaration of independence by the Smith regime, specifically called on the OAU to assist in the implementation of its resolution on Rhodesia. Also in 1965, in the area of economic and social cooperation, the OAU and the United Nations Economic Commission for Africa signed an agreement for mutual cooperation on a continuing basis to facilitate economic and social development in Africa.

The OAU in its short life has survived several crises that have threatened its disintegration. Its effectiveness has not lived up to inflated expectations, and its weakness against targets in South Africa, Rhodesia, and Portugal has been painfully apparent. Recently, its budget has been cut to more realistic proportions. Although a judgment about its value may be premature, the OAU's modest accomplishments in political, economic, and social matters seem sufficient to justify its past efforts and to assume its continued utility.

League of Arab States (Arab League)

Established in 1945 with seven original members, the Arab League expanded by 1992 to a membership of twenty-one states. The elements contributing to basic unity among the members include a common religion, language, and culture. Since 1948 a shared hostility toward Israel has provided a powerful motivating force for collective action, but other factors have frustrated this potential for mustering full and united opposition to Israel. The

League has been split into radical and conservative factions, and no member has been able to emerge as a leader of a Pan-Arab movement. Individual member states have gained little support from the League in their wars and guerrilla activities against Israel. After Egypt and Israel signed a peace treaty in 1979, the League suspended Egypt's membership and transferred the League's headquarters from Cairo to Tunis. In 1989, Egypt's membership in the League was restored.

The scope of activities of the Arab League is extensive, and the work is supported by a Secretariat staff of more than 450. One of the principal instruments (in addition to the pact establishing the League) that outlines the mutual obligations of members is the Treaty of Joint Defense and Economic Cooperation, adopted in 1950. This treaty asserts the principle that armed aggression against any party is an act against all members and obligates each state to assist the attacked state by every appropriate means, including armed force. Such sweeping obligations were ignored by the member states in circumstances such as the attacks by Israel, France, and the United Kingdom against the United Arab Republic in 1956. The League has been wholly ineffective against outside threats.

The record of the Arab League in dealing with disputes and military clashes among its own members has been only slightly better. One notable success was a united effort, including a 3,300-member military force, to prevent Iraq from taking over Kuwait at the time of the latter's independence in 1961. The British first sent troops in response to Kuwait's appeal, and these were replaced by the combined force from five Arab states, with the bulk furnished by Saudi Arabia and the United Arab Republic. These military contingents remained in Kuwait until 1963. Again in 1976 four Arab countries sent a combined military force of 30,000 into Lebanon to stop hostilities among disputing factions and to restore a temporarily stable government. The League seemed incapable of resolving other disputes, including charges of UAR successive interventions in Tunisia (1958), Lebanon (1958), Jordan (1958 and 1960), and Syria (1962). In the cases of Lebanon and Jordan in 1958, these countries sought the protection of the United States and the United Kingdom respectively in the face of Arab League ineffectiveness. In 1963 Morocco and Algeria turned to the OAU rather than to the Arab League for the conciliation of their border dispute. The League was also paralyzed in the Yemen civil war of 1962–67, in which Saudi Arabia and the UAR were supporting opposing factions. The Arab states again failed to act concertedly in the Iran-Iraq war.

On certain issues the Arab states have presented a united front. At the United Nations they have spoken with one voice in opposition to Israel and on questions of decolonization. They consistently opposed France on the Algerian, Moroccan, and Tunisian disputes and exerted pressure on Britain to free its territories in the Middle East.

The diversity of interest in the program of the League is demonstrated by the elaborate League machinery. In the political and security realm there is a Council, a Political Committee, a Joint Defense Council, and a Permanent Military Committee. In the area of economic cooperation, the chief organ is an Economic Council, composed of ministers of economic affairs. The Secretariat has departments dealing with political, economic, legal, cultural, press and publicity, administrative and financial, social, and Palestinian matters. There is also an Institute of Arab Studies, an Institute of Arab Manuscripts, a Refugee Boycott Office, and an Anti-Narcotics Office. An Arab Development Bank has been established, and an Arab Economic Union has been formed with the goal of achieving a common market. Other cooperative agencies include a Postal and Telecommunication Union, a Health Organization, and an Arab League Petroleum Bureau. Cooperation among Arab states has been achieved in such areas as educational standardization and teacher exchange. The League maintains an office in New York to facilitate cooperation among Arab states at the United Nations.

From the preceding summary of agencies and activities, it is apparent that Arab League deficiencies are not the result of a narrowness of interests or instrumentalities. Economic, social, and cultural cooperation has succeeded to a greater degree than cooperation in the political and security realm. In spite of a common basis for political cooperation, intrabloc rivalries and suspicions have prevented closer collaboration and unity of action.

ALLIANCE-TYPE REGIONAL ORGANIZATIONS

As previously defined, alliance-type organizations are those whose military and political orientation is intended to provide security against external actors. All organizations in this category were a response to the Cold War, which developed between the Communist states, led by the Soviet Union, and the so-called free world, led by the United States, in the aftermath of World War II. The attitudes that foster such organizations were based on distrust and hostility rather than on friendly and cooperative relations among nations. The need for security arrangements reflected feelings of insecurity concerning perceived threats from other countries or groups of countries and indicated the conviction that these threats required a collective rather than a unilateral response. The resulting treaty arrangements among allies provided for united military responses to an attack on any member of the alliance so that any use of force would be met with massive counterforce. The intent was to deter aggression by the prospect of collective retaliation against the aggressor. Potential aggressors were envisioned as being states outside the membership of the alliance, and it was assumed that members of the alliance would not initiate armed attacks against each other.

The members of military alliances of this type claim that these pacts are compatible with the United Nations Charter. The provisions of the treaties refer specifically to the right of individual or collective self-defense in Article 51 of the Charter, and the agreements are generally defended as regional organizations within the spirit and purpose of the Charter. The signatories proclaim their support of United Nations purposes and principles and recognize their obligations under the Charter, including the pledge to settle all disputes by peaceful means. The parties also recognize the primacy of the Security Council in the maintenance of international peace and security.

In spite of these declarations of support for United Nations principles, the compatibility of these pacts with the spirit of the Charter is questionable. If all members of the United Nations honor their commitments to renounce the use of force and to settle all disputes by peaceful means, no military alliances would be required. If the collective-security system of the United Nations could be implemented, other military arrangements would be inconsistent with the working of the universal system. By dividing the world into hostile camps, the alliance-type organizations undermine the Charter purposes of developing friendly relations among nations and harmonizing their actions within a universal framework. The attainment of a worldwide spirit of peace, harmony, and cooperation for peaceful change is thus retarded by emphasizing the hostility among blocs of nations suspicious of the intentions of other nations to adhere to Charter principles.

On the other hand, military alliances merely reflect the hostility and lack of harmony among states. The spirit of the Charter was never taken seriously by the world's political leaders. Cleavages and power politics became immediately apparent in the postwar period. Clashes of ideology intensified the rivalries of powerful states. National interests predominated in the interactions among sovereign states. The Cold War became the prime factor of world politics. If military alliances were incompatible with the yearnings for a worldwide system that could assure peace and cooperation among nations, they were a manifestation that such an ideal had not been attained through the creation of the United Nations. Given this kind of world in which national rivalry and suspicion were rampant, a system of rival military alliances seemed necessary for protection of national interests, even if subversive of universal hopes for cooperation and harmony. The response to a potential military threat was an arrangement for military counterforce. Such a response, it may be argued, is not a creator of tensions but only a reflection of existing tensions that must be recognized and acted upon.

Alliance-type organizations have built-in elements of instability. The perceived threat against which each arrangement is directed tends to be greater at the time the organization is formed than on a sustained basis. As changes occur in world relations, the reasons for forming and supporting the alliance become less credible, and the unity of the membership is subject to greater stresses and strains. Doubts arise concerning the legitimacy of maintaining a high degree of hostile relations with the outside power or powers against which the pact is directed. Additional skepticism grows regarding the scope and intensity of the commitment of alliance partners to honor fully their mutual obligations when their own national interests are not vitally affected. Disaffections and disillusionments stem from the practice of the dominant power within the alliance to set a unilateral course in its foreign policy without regard to effects upon lesser alliance partners and frequently with little or no consultation prior to foreign-policy actions. France's withdrawal of forces from NATO and the breakup of SEATO are only two of the more dramatic examples of these tendencies toward alliance instability.

For approximately forty years the superpower rivalry of the Soviet Union and the United States dominated the world political and military scene marked by the formation of competing alliance systems. The examination of the main features of the two leading alliance-type organizations (one of which is now defunct) will illuminate the nature, importance, and evolution of this type of regional arrangement.

North Atlantic Treaty Organization (NATO)

The largest, most highly organized, and most stable military security alliance is NATO. As the original postwar organization of its type, it served as a model for the other organizations in this category. NATO was formed in response to the possible threat of Soviet military incursions into Central and Western Europe. NATO was initiated by the United States as a major element in the containment policy directed against Communist states in general and the Soviet Union in particular. Other closely related elements within the United States containment policy were the Truman Doctrine, the Marshall Plan, the Korean War, SEATO, and the Baghdad Pact.

NATO membership extends geographically from the United States and Canada on the west to Greece and Turkey on the east. Original members included Belgium, Canada, Denmark, France, Iceland, Italy, Luxembourg, the Netherlands, Norway, Portugal, the United Kingdom, and the United States. The treaty was signed in Washington, D.C., in April 1949, and came into force in August of that year. In 1952, Greece and Turkey joined the alliance, and in 1955 the Federal Republic of Germany brought the roster to fifteen members. In 1982, Spain was admitted as the sixteenth member. In 1966, President de Gaulle announced France's intention to withdraw from participation in the combined NATO military organization in Western Europe and requested that military forces and NATO headquarters be removed from French territory. In 1967 the Supreme Headquarters Allied Powers Europe (SHAPE) was moved to Mons, Belgium, and a new Secretariat and Council headquarters was opened in Brussels.

The key provision of the North Atlantic Treaty is the agreement "that an armed attack against one or more of them [the parties to the treaty] in Europe or North America shall be considered an attack against them all." When such an attack occurs, each member state is obligated to assist the member attacked in order to restore and maintain security within the region. However, sovereignty is safeguarded by providing that each member is obligated to take only "such action as it deems necessary." This protection of sovereignty carries over into the command of troops assigned to the European sector. Although an elaborate integrated command structure exists, national officers retain full control over their military contingents, and no orders can be carried out except through national channels. The entire basis for NATO operation consists of consultation, cooperation, and discussion so that each member state retains its full freedom of action. Forces are maintained in the field in Europe, with the largest contingents furnished by the United States and Germany. Agreements on levels of forces have been negotiated but not fully implemented. A large and complicated organizational structure has been created. Meetings for consultation are regular and numerous. But in spite of a large structure and budget, backed potentially by the total military might of the individual members, national decision-making powers remain unimpaired. Attempts to form both an integrated military force and a supranational nuclear capability have failed to materialize. For nearly forty years European members were somewhat frustrated by the realization that only the United States policy toward the Soviet Union, including the decision for nuclear retaliation or other flexible response, would really determine their fate in a major confrontation. Freedom of action in reality involved more freedom of decision for some members than for others.

The supreme organ of NATO is the North Atlantic Council, in which all decisions require a unanimous vote. The Council meets at the ministerial level (generally ministers of foreign affairs or defense) at least twice a year and at the level of permanent representatives (ambassadorial rank) on a weekly basis. The secretary-general of NATO is the chairman of the Council. The permanent representatives (with the exception of a representative from France since 1966) also meet as a Defense Planning Committee for determining military policy.

An elaborate administrative, committee, and military-command structure operates under the general aegis of the North Atlantic Council. The Secretariat headed by the secretary-general is organized to reflect and support all the activities and committee structure of NATO. The secretary-general, in addition to presiding over Council sessions, prepares the budget, arranges the agenda of meetings and initiates agenda items, supervises the administrative functions with powers to hire and release personnel, and represents NATO in relations with governments and with other organizations. The North Atlantic Council is assisted in its work by a dozen major committees and as many more specialized committees. Examples of primary committees are those concerned with political affairs, defense review, armaments, economic affairs, science, and information and cultural affairs. Specialized committees deal with such matters as European air space, pipelines, and communications. In 1969 a Committee on the Challenges of Modern Society was established to consider environmental problems. This latter activity serves as an example of the non-military interest incorporated within the NATO program. Since an elaborate structure already exists, and as military threats decrease, there is a tendency for NATO to seek new activities to justify its continuance near the level previously developed.

The military-command structure is headed by the Military Committee composed of chiefs of staff, or their representatives, of all NATO members except France. The defense area was originally divided into three principal commands: Allied Command Europe, Allied Command Atlantic, and Allied Command Channel, plus a Canada-U.S. Regional Planning Group. Each of the three commands was in turn subdivided into a number of subordinate commands. The Allied Command Europe always enjoyed the highest prestige because of its assigned strategic area in relation to the Soviet Union and because of its coordinating functions over the various national military contingents that provide defense for Western Europe. Persons of the eminence of General Dwight Eisenhower have served as Supreme Allied Commander Europe (SACEUR) at the headquarters in France or Belgium.

Support and enthusiasm for NATO have been subjected to stresses and strains from time to time, and priorities for the organization have been modified. France's disillusionment with United States primacy within the organization and with such problems as the role of German forces in European security culminated in 1966–67 in France's withdrawal from the military arrangements in NATO while retaining membership in the organization for other purposes. In 1974, after Turkey's invasion of Cyprus, Greece withdrew its armed forces from NATO, but in 1980 resumed full participation. NATO's original central purpose of deterrence of the Soviet Union has given way to periodic emphasis on détente between East and West. The Harmel Report, adopted by the Council in December 1967, marked the recognition of détente as a primary function of NATO. Since that time emphasis has been placed upon such policies as disarmament, mutual and balanced force reductions, and accommodation and trade with the Soviet bloc. When the United States shifted its strategic doctrine from massive retaliation to flexible response, the NATO Council was reluctantly forced to also adopt flexible response as its official policy, in spite of questions concerning the firmness of United States commitment to European defense in some circumstances.

With the breakup of the Soviet Union and the Soviet bloc, questions have been raised concerning the future missions or continued existence of NATO. Some suggest that NATO has become an expensive anachronism and that most of its missions could be shifted to other agencies. But security questions, including the proliferation of nuclear and other weapons of mass destruction and their acquisition by terrorist groups or renegade states, dominate the defense policies of NATO members. In spite of plans to cut in half the number of United States forces in Europe within a decade, the continued existence of NATO seems probable. At a summit meeting in Rome in 1991 a new strategy was adopted stressing dialogue and cooperation in Europe. A North Atlantic Cooperation Council (NACC) of thirty-eight states has been formed including states formerly part of the Soviet Union and their former eastern European allies. The trend is toward transforming NATO from a military to a political organization for assuring European security and stability. Another aspect of the new strategy is an increased emphasis on support for the crisis management and peacekeeping operations of the United Nations, the Conference on Security and Cooperation in Europe, and the Western European Union. NATO's command structure is also being streamlined and a rapid reaction corps has been developed.

Warsaw Treaty Organization (WTO or Warsaw Pact) (Disbanded 1991)

Instead of the Soviet Union responding to the formation of NATO by immediately instigating an East European general security arrangement, that country first consolidated its security system by a series of bilateral pacts. However, the entry of West Germany into NATO membership in 1955 is often cited as the trigger that set into motion the formation of the Warsaw Treaty Organization. Other factors that prompted this move were the desire to create a bargaining tool with the West and the provision of justification for keeping Soviet military forces in Hungary and Rumania after the signing of the Austrian State Treaty by the Big Four, which removed the previous grounds for maintaining forces there. Among these reasons, subsequent events seem to indicate that the most important was to furnish a bargaining device in dealing with the West.

In its basic elements the Warsaw Pact was almost a carbon copy of the North Atlantic Treaty, although in practice the organizations did not follow identical patterns of organization or behavior. In case of armed attack upon any member, all other members of the WTO were obligated to come to the aid of the victim by all means, including military, that each member deemed necessary. Members pledged themselves to peacefully settle disputes among themselves, to promote disarmament, and to consult on matters of mutual concern. One unique feature of the Warsaw Pact was the provision to dissolve the organization upon the conclusion of an all-European security agreement, a recurrent project in Soviet proposals. However, in spite of the security guarantees contained in the Helsinki Accords, which were agreed upon at the Conference on Security and Cooperation in Europe in 1975 and which were strengthened in a series of review conferences, the Warsaw Pact in 1985 was extended for twenty more years.

The original members of the Warsaw Pact, which was adopted in the Polish capital on May 14, 1955, were Albania, Bulgaria, Czechoslovakia, the German Democratic Republic (GDR), Hungary, Poland, Rumania, and the USSR. Albania ceased its participation in any meetings in 1961, and Rumania on many occasions demonstrated its discontent with the pact.

Two primary structural devices were provided in the treaty. The first was a Political Consultative Committee, supposedly the supreme policy-determining body. Meetings of this committee were infrequent but were attended by high-ranking party and government officials, including first secretaries of the national Communist parties, premiers, and defense and foreign ministers.

The second major body provided for in the treaty was the Unified Command. A Soviet general always served as commander in chief of the joint forces, and ministers of defense from the other pact countries served as his deputies. A Joint Staff with headquarters in Moscow was established to assist the Unified Command in their direction of WTO forces. Beginning in 1961 frequent joint military maneuvers or exercises were conducted in the various countries allied with the Soviet Union. Soviet troops were initially stationed in the German Democratic Republic, Hungary, Poland, and Rumania, but in 1958 they were withdrawn from Rumania.

The Warsaw Pact was used to enforce Soviet dominance over its allies. In 1956, it was invoked as the authority for using Soviet troops to suppress the Hungarian revolt. In 1968, joint WTO forces displayed their effectiveness in quashing the attempted Czechoslovakian defection from Soviet influence. Rumanian moves toward greater independence of action were temporarily reversed because of the demonstration in Czechoslovakia of WTO effectiveness against insurgent members of the organization.

Centrifugal forces were in operation throughout the history of the Warsaw Pact. Albania's defection was accomplished without serious reprisal in 1961. On the other hand, Polish and Hungarian attempts at establishing independent courses of policy in 1956 and Czechoslovakia's changes of basic doctrine in 1968 were dealt with in such a manner as to prevent a break in the alliance relationship. Members were restive because of the domination of the USSR within the organization. Long before the organization's demise Rumania, Czechoslovakia, and Hungary asserted increasingly independent policies. After the breakup of the Soviet Union and the restoration of full sovereignty in the former eastern European Soviet satellites, the dissolution of the WTO was inevitable and became official in 1991.

FUNCTIONAL REGIONAL ORGANIZATIONS

The largest category of regional organizations includes those of the functional type. Functional organizations, as previously noted, are defined as those that promote economic, social, or political collaboration with little or no regard to security factors. A review of the list of functional organizations in Table 10–1 reveals that the majority of these organizations are formed for the attainment of economic goals of the members. The collaboration of the members achieve mutual economic advantages that cannot be attained through unilateral policies.

According to functional theories of emerging world order, such as those held by David Mitrany, the habits of collaboration developed in functional areas should eventually spill over into the political sphere and lead to the breakdown of political barriers among states. If these theories have any validity, the proof is not yet strongly evidenced in the behavior of states, which continue to safeguard vigorously their political unity and independence. In fact, steps toward economic union have been partial, gradual, cautious, and reflective of little national enthusiasm for merging national economic institutions, except to the degree that national political freedom remains intact. On the other hand, Joseph S. Nye states that

> before a conflict has reached a stage of open hostilities, micro-regional economic organizations may indeed act to raise the price of conflict and to foster communications and help restructure values in a way that may have a restraining effect on political leaders. . . . After major fighting has broken out, the role of the regional economic organization will be primarily to symbolize the possibility of upgrading a common interest.[7]

Thus, without achieving a broader political community, regional economic organizations may contribute modestly to the maintenance or restoration of peace and the integration of policy.

Functional regional organizations are so numerous that even a brief description of each would require too much space in this chapter. Only a small sampling is presented below. For information on other organizations, the student may consult the *Yearbook of International Organizations,* which will serve as a starting point by outlining such features as the aims, membership, structure, and primary activities of each agency.

European Community (EC)

The European Community is unique among regional organizations. It represents the greatest advance toward supranationalism of any such organization. Within the economic sphere, broad national decision-making authority has been voluntarily surrendered to collective agencies. Economic integration has been carried further on a wide scope of activities than in any other regional arrangement. Yet, in the basic political functions the integrative process has not followed that of the economic sector, although the two cannot

---

[7]Joseph S. Nye, Jr., *Peace in Parts: Integration and Conflict in Regional Organization* (Boston: Little, Brown, 1971), p. 112.

be totally differentiated since much economic decision making is a part of the political process, and the surrender of sovereign powers has, to a remarkable degree, already occurred.

The EC is also such an unprecedented success story that it has served as a model for other similar experiments and as the most tangible hope of the functionalists to prove that economic integration will lead to eventual political integration. Although this step still seems remote, the EC has achieved several major economic goals, and this achievement resulted in rapidly rising prosperity for its component states.

The EC is an outgrowth of, and is closely associated with, several other organizational developments. The impetus for a European federation predates World War II, and the first step toward an economic union was the formation of a customs union (Benelux), which came into operation January 1, 1948, among Belgium, the Netherlands, and Luxembourg. In 1950, French Foreign Minister Robert Schuman proposed a coal and steel community to include six countries, and in 1952 the European Coal and Steel Community (ECSC), composed of the Benelux countries and France, West Germany, and Italy, became a reality. In 1954 and 1955, proposals were initiated for expanding the areas of integration of economic policies among the six members of the ECSC into a common market, and in 1957 the Rome treaties were signed creating the European Economic Community (EEC or Common Market) and the European Atomic Energy Community (Euratom). Habits of cooperation among European states were also fostered by the establishment in 1948 of the Organization for European Economic Cooperation (OEEC) to implement the Marshall Plan for European recovery; by the creation in 1960–61 of its successor, enlarged in membership, the Organization for Economic Cooperation and Development (OECD); and by the formation in the political arena in 1949 of the Council of Europe.

The creation of the Common Market also gave rise to the establishment of the European Free Trade Association (EFTA) in 1960. EFTA is less integrated and more limited in aims than the EEC but represents a response by European nonmembers of the EEC to the desirability of international cooperation in establishing enlarged trade areas through reducing barriers to trade. The EFTA membership eventually included Austria, Denmark, Finland, Iceland, Norway, Portugal, Sweden, Switzerland, and the United Kingdom. On January 1, 1973, Denmark and the United Kingdom withdrew from the EFTA and became members of the EEC. Ireland also joined the EEC on this date, thus enlarging the EEC membership from six to nine. The remaining EFTA members retained their own organizational relationships, continued their previous trade arrangements with the United Kingdom and Denmark and negotiated individual trade agreements with the EEC. In 1981, Greece became a full member of the EEC. Portugal and Spain were accepted as members effective January 1, 1986.

Today the EEC, the ECSC, and Euratom share the same common organizational institutions. From the inception of the EEC and Euratom, all three organizations had in common a Parliament and Court of Justice. In 1967, other separate organs were merged into a single Commission and Council of Ministers. Since 1984, as the scope of policy determination expanded, the term "European Community" gradually became the common collective title for the organization.

The Commission of seventeen members, not more than two of whom may be of the same nationality, is chosen by the Council of Ministers for four-year renewable terms and may be removed only by a two-thirds censure vote of the European Parliament. The Commission administers and implements the program of the EC and is assisted by an administrative staff of more than 12,800. The Commission submits an annual report to the European Parliament. It administers a European Development Fund, which has made billions of dollars available to associated countries and territories, mainly in Africa. The Commission is also advised by an Economic and Social Committee of experts representing a cross section of employers', workers', and consumers' interests.

The real center of power in the EC is the Council of Ministers. For the most important decisions the foreign ministers participate, but for specialized subjects the appropriate ministers from each of the member states sit on the Council. The preparatory work for the Council is performed by a Committee of Permanent Representatives of ambassadorial rank accredited to the headquarters in Brussels. This group wields great influence in the activities of the council.

Until 1978 the European Parliament represented the legislatures of the constituent countries, but after that year the members were chosen by direct election. It meets at Strasbourg at least six or eight times annually for sessions of approximately a week in duration. The members of the Parliament are apportioned according to the size and resources of the member states. The representatives sit in political, not national, groups. The Parliament may question the members of the Commission and maintains an elaborate committee structure. The Parliament does not have general legislative powers, but possesses one important and powerful prerogative—the authority to approve, reject, or amend the Community's budget.

The Court of Justice sits at Luxembourg and hears cases and appeals concerning obligations and disputes under the basic treaties and agreements within the community framework. Cases may involve governments, community agencies, private organizations or firms, or individuals. Penalties may be fixed by the court and there is no appeal from its decisions. Hundreds of cases have been brought before the court.

In 1979 the European Monetary System (EMS) was established utilizing a European Currency Unit (ECU). The ECU is a "basket" of currencies of the participating states, which is designed to minimize currency fluctuations through central bank intervention when allowable margins for exchange rates of individual currencies are reached. The ECU is becoming one of the world's most widely utilized monetary units, and it serves as the unit of account for the European Community's budget.

The success of the Common Market may be measured by its specific accomplishments. The transition period for the full development of a customs union was originally set at twelve to fifteen years but was accomplished in approximately ten years. This customs union abolishes customs duties and quantitative restrictions among the member states and establishes common external tariffs on imports. The Community has negotiated much-reduced tariff rates with their outside trading partners. The EEC also adopted a Common Agricultural Policy (CAP) financed from a central fund involving certain subsidies and incentives for improving agricultural production. Labor mobility from one country to another is virtually achieved and guaranteed, and a common transport policy has been adopted. The states in the Community have moved toward a common added-value tax on goods and services and are working to remove restrictions on capital movements. General policies and targets for economic growth have been adopted and the achieved rates of growth have exceeded those of the United States or the EFTA countries. The EEC established a European Investment Bank, which has provided loans for such economically disadvantaged areas as southern Italy.

Sixty-six African, Caribbean, and Pacific countries, through the Lomé Convention, have a unique affiliation with the EC granting them general tariff preferences and development assistance. This arrangement, dating from 1975, has been renewed periodically. These developing countries are permitted freedom from almost all customs duties for exports to the Community without reciprocal concessions. They also receive from the Community almost $2 billion annually in technical and financial aid, as well as loans from the European Investment Bank. The Community also guarantees these countries compensation for export earnings losses for numerous basic commodities.

A new landmark in the development of the European Community was achieved by the signing on February 28, 1986, of the Single European Act and its ratification by all member governments by March 21, 1987. The Single Act amended the previous basic treaties to complete a European internal market and to create an area without frontiers by 1992. Other goals included (1) strengthening of research and technological development; (2) progress toward economic and monetary union; (3) preservation, protection, and improvement of the environment and the prudent and rational use of natural resources; (4) strengthening of economic and social cohesion; and (5) institutionalizing foreign policy cooperation through the activities of the European Parliament, the Commission, and more frequent meetings of ministers of foreign policy. A further development was the Maastricht Treaty proposals of 1991 which provide for a common currency for most members by 1999, a movement toward common foreign and defense policies, and some further expansion of the authority of EC institutions.

The changes since 1986 do not create a supranational entity in the EC, though a gradually expanding pooling of sovereignty has occurred. Although the Maastricht proposals revive the hope of some advocates for a political union, and although some qualified majority voting has been substituted for consensus decisions, the member states still dominate the decision-making process in the EC agencies and retain most of their individual sovereign powers. Yet the European Community is the world's largest trading bloc and serves as a model of substantial economic integration. Whether or not it is the forerunner of a United States of Europe cannot be predicted.

Organization for Economic Cooperation and Development (OECD)

The OECD was created in 1961 as the successor to the Organization for European Economic Cooperation (OEEC), whose original purpose was the administration of Marshall Plan aid and European recovery plans. Membership includes the European states having market economies in the 1960s, plus Australia, New Zealand, Japan, the United States, Canada, and Turkey. The aims of the organization include the promotion of optimum economic conditions and financial stability of the members, the development of the world economy, the promotion of economic development of member and non-member countries, and the expansion of world trade on a nondiscriminatory basis. The headquarters are in Paris.

In addition to a Council, Executive Committee, and Secretariat, the OECD carries on its numerous functions through more than two dozen committees and other subsidiary groups. The broad subject areas include economic policies, the environment, aid to developing countries, trade, financial affairs, science, education, manpower, social affairs, industry, energy, agriculture, and fisheries. The Development Assistance Committee (DAC) includes the eighteen most affluent members, which are the world's principal donors of development aid. The OECD Development Centre aids in research and transfer of knowledge on development problems. A Nuclear Energy Agency is a feature of the OECD operations, and in 1974 an International Energy Agency of eighteen members was created to deal with oil supply and price problems through coordinated policies in stockpiling, conservation, and research into new energy sources.

The OECD maintains working relations with numerous other intergovernmental and nongovernmental organizations. Through consultation, research, exchange of information, and publication the OECD provides a center for coordinating the economic policies of the members among themselves and toward the developing states.

Organization of Petroleum Exporting Countries (OPEC)

OPEC was formed in 1960 with five initial members and was expanded to thirteen members by the 1970s. The membership was reduced to twelve in 1993 with the withdrawal of Ecuador. Although several of the world's largest producers, the USSR, the United States, and Mexico, are not members, OPEC states until recently accounted for 85 percent of oil exports. The early years of the organization provided little evidence of its later potential for a dominant role in affecting world economic conditions. Gradually, the OPEC governments took over control of ownership, production, and pricing from the giant oil companies. The 1973 war in the Middle East provided an opportunity for the large Arab producer states to use the oil weapon by instigating a boycott and by quadrupling oil prices within a few months. European states and Japan are especially vulnerable to threats to their oil supply, and non-oil-producing developing states must expend a larger share of their scarce foreign exchange for oil imports. Huge accumulations of surplus capital flowed to such large oil producers as Saudi Arabia, Kuwait, Libya, Iran, and the United Arab Emirates, and these petrodollars were recycled abroad with profound effects upon patterns of balance of payments.

During the period 1974–78, the world price of oil declined in real terms, but in 1979 demand again exceeded supply and OPEC prices nearly tripled in the next two years. This change in supply partially resulted from disruption of production due to the revolution in Iran and the subsequent Iran-Iraq war. Since 1981 there has again been a glut of oil and a reduction of the world price due to the global economic recession, new supplies of non-OPEC oil, and user conservation measures. As the largest OPEC producer for many years, Saudi Arabia provided leadership in regulating supply and price. More recently, the unity, discipline, and cooperation among members necessary to make OPEC an effective organization have shown signs of breakdown. Quotas have not been adhered to, as many OPEC members are reluctant to reduce their income for carrying out development plans. Overproduction resulted in a drop in world prices as individual countries competed for a larger share of the market.

Regional Development Banks

An international phenomenon of the 1960s was the establishment of several regional and subregional development banks. These banks were set up because of discontent with the policies of the World Bank group of institutions, the inadequacies of the development resources available through existing channels, and the special needs of particular areas that were unlikely to be met by bilateral and global financial programs. The countries in the areas involved sought increased resources, greater flexibility in lending policies, and more local control in the determination of policies and the use of resources. One of the purposes was to provide financing for projects essential to development, such as in education and agriculture, for which loans were not readily available from existing sources. Another was to encourage financial support for broad programs rather than for specific projects.

The regional institutions that were created in response to these demands were the Inter-American Development Bank (IDB), the African Development Bank (AFDB), and the Asian Development Bank (ASDB). The IDB became operative in 1960 and the other two in 1966. Subregional financial institutions include the European Investment Bank (EIB), to which reference was previously made in the discussion of the EC; the Central American Bank for Economic Integration (CABEI), dating from 1961; the East African Development Bank, created in 1967 by Kenya, Tanzania, and Uganda; and the Nordic Investment Bank established in 1976. The establishment of so many regional and subregional financial agencies within a decade is part of the movement by the developing countries to join forces to speed the processes of their economic development.

Of the three large regional banks, the Inter-American Development Bank, because of its longer period of operation and its generous support from the United States, was able by 1992 to commit more than $51.8 billion in loans for about 2,000 projects. The Asian Development Bank grew rapidly and by 1993 had obligated $42.4 billion in loans for 1,210 projects, 30 percent of which were in agriculture. The African Development Bank has suffered from inadequate resources because for many years it limited its membership to African states, all of which are relatively poor. In 1982 it opened its membership to non-African states, and by 1991 its loans totalled $11.6 billion. In the Asian Development Bank, Japan, Australia, and the nonregional members control a majority of the voting power. In the IDB, because of special and weighted voting requirements, the United States has a virtual veto over most decisions.

Thus, the developing states are caught in the dilemma of wishing to control their own destinies but of having to surrender decision-making power to those states who command the bulk of the world's resources in exchange for access to a portion of those resources. Although the major purposes of the regional development banks include the provision for greater flexibility in lending policies and more local control over the allocation of resources, the attainment of these goals is dependent upon the sympathy and cooperation with these aims of the affluent contributors of capital. In spite of these difficulties, the regional and subregional banks have provided for needs not otherwise met through alternate channels. The financing of cooperative enterprises and attention to the unique problems of each region or subregion are among the contributions of these agencies during the short span of their existence.

UNITED NATIONS REGIONAL COMMISSIONS

As previously noted, no regional decentralization of the economic and social activities of the United Nations was provided for in the Charter; all Charter references to regionalism applied solely to security matters. However, the task of reconstruction and rehabilitation in the war-damaged areas provided the initial impetus for the establishment in 1947 of the Economic Commission for Europe (ECE) and the Economic Commission for Asia and the Far East (ECAFE). The title of ECAFE was changed in 1974 to the Economic and Social Commission for Asia and the Pacific (ESCAP). Pressures from the Latin American states, with support from other underdeveloped countries in the General Assembly, after a lack of success in the Economic and Social Council, led to the creation in 1948 of the Economic Commission for Latin America (ECLA). Its title was changed in 1984 to the Economic Commission for Latin America and the Caribbean (ECLAC). Ten years later the beginning of the influx of new African states into United Nations membership brought about the approval of an Economic Commission for Africa (ECA). For many years, proposals for a Middle East commission fell prey to the hostility between the Arab states and Israel. As a substitute, a relatively small United Nations Economic and Social Office in Beirut was opened in 1963. Finally, in 1974, it was converted into a full-fledged Economic Commission for Western Asia. In 1985 its title was changed to the Economic and Social Commission for Western Asia (ESCWA).

Each of the regional commissions is a subsidiary body of the Economic and Social Council, to which it reports. Although the regional staffs of the commissions in Asia, Latin America, and Africa number 600 to 800 each, the regional offices must work closely with the Department of Economic and Social Affairs of the United Nations Secretariat; with the United Nations Development Program; with the United Nations Conference on Trade and Development; with such other regional organizations as the OAU, the OAS, or the Colombo Plan; with the specialized agencies of the United Nations; and with the governments of the countries in the area. Their task of trying to provide coordination in economic development is complicated by their lack of authority and by the diversity of channels of operation in each region. The project and individual country orientation of most bilateral and United Nations aid programs makes their work doubly difficult. Rivalries among states or groups of states in the area compound the problem.[8]

The principal structural components of each United Nations regional organization are the secretariat, which is a branch of the United Nations Secretariat; the commission, made up of representatives of governments belong-

---

[8]For example, see James S. Magee, "ECA and the Paradox of African Cooperation," *International Conciliation*, no. 580 (November 1970), passim.

ing to the regional organization; and a series of specialized committees. Each commission meets annually or biennially and determines general policy within the limits of United Nations guidelines, programs, and resources. The secretariat prepares for commission and committee meetings, carries on research, implements the programs approved by the commission, and attempts to provide coordination of activities for the region. The executive secretary, as head of the secretariat, occupies a crucial position in providing leadership within the organization and in his relations with member governments.

The major purpose of the regional commissions is to assist in raising the level of economic well-being in their region and to strengthen the economic relations of the countries of the region with each other and with other countries outside the area. Originally, the principal activity of each commission was to provide research, surveys, and planning as a basis for coordinated economic development. After 1960 the importance of the commissions was intended to be upgraded by an official United Nations policy to strengthen the commissions and decentralize the United Nations economic activities. This purpose has met with varying degrees of success due to some of the obstacles previously mentioned. The ECLAC has enjoyed extensive popularity among Latin American states and has been credited with major contributions in the establishment of the Latin American Free Trade Association, the Central American Common Market, the Inter-American Development Bank, and the United Nations Conference on Trade and Development. The ESCAP has promoted such projects as the Mekong River development, the Asian Highway, the Asian Development Bank, and the Asian Institute for Economic Development and Planning. The ECA has some credits also, such as the African Development Bank, but it has failed to gain acceptance among African states to the same degree as the other regional commissions, and its effectiveness has been hampered by internal dissension and by rivalry with the OAU. Forces that tend to emphasize individual projects, individual countries, and diverse agencies impede any attempts at regional coordination.

One of the most effective areas of service and coordination engaged in by the regional commissions is in the dissemination of information and the development of needed skills. The specific methods include workshops, seminars, training institutes, information centers, advisory services, provision of fellowships, research centers, symposia, and conferences. Thousands of persons in the areas have received the direct benefits of these activities. The regional commissions provide only part of the needed services and resources, but they act to stimulate governments and other agencies and to provide coordination of diverse activities.

The regional economic commissions of the United Nations system represent a middle approach between the global goals for which the organization was created and the manifold projects and agencies that carry decentralization to a point bordering on chaos. However, because of their limited resources and influence, and because of their dependence upon the cooperation of governments and numerous agencies, they have never attained a central role in the processes of economic development. Persuasion is a relatively weak tool for uniting and coordinating the disparate elements that tend to protect the sovereignty of states and the autonomy of myriad programs and projects.

GENERAL ASSESSMENT OF REGIONALISM

The proliferation of regional organizations within a period of forty years could lead to the mistaken conclusion that regionalism is the wave of the future in the redistribution of world political and economic power. The mere establishment of numerous regional agencies as evidence of a new world order would be as misleading as to assume that the establishment of the United Nations and the subsequent increase in the number of universal organizations heralds a new age of world community. Concomitant with these developments has been the emergence of a host of new independent states, seeking separate identities, jealous of their sovereign prerogatives, and determined to seek the promotion of their national interests, not through an onslaught on the state system but within its framework. The older and more powerful states are equally determined to maintain the established system, to emphasize self-help in their foreign policies, and to exercise extreme caution in movements toward cooperation, coordination, or integration across state boundaries.

No incompatibility need exist between regional and universal organizations. The United Nations has established its own economic commissions to facilitate the achievement of regional goals within a universal framework. Most functional regional organizations are striving for the same kinds of economic and social development as the United Nations family of agencies, and the two levels of effort generally serve to reinforce each other. It is possible for regional economic integration to lead to policies adverse to the interests of other countries, but this problem has not attained major proportions in the broad pattern of functional regional development.

On the other hand, alliance-type organizations, by stressing the hostility between groups of states, tend to retard the attainment of some of the cooperative aims of universal organizations. The OAS, as a multipurpose organization, has also been perverted, through military and political intervention, into an instrument of United States foreign policy within the hemisphere. It has provided a cloak of legitimacy for unilateral United States action. In the process, means were found to isolate the United Nations organs from any effective supervision over disputes within the hemisphere and to rewrite Charter provisions on this subject through restrictive interpretation and practice. This perversion and reinterpretation has occurred in spite of the clear provisions of the UN and OAS charters establishing the priority of United Nations jurisdiction over disputes. However, the economic and social activities of the OAS and other multipurpose organizations are generally supportive of, and compatible with, the goals of universal organizations.

No strong or persistent trend toward regionalism can be discerned on the present world scene. Discontent and dissension are threats to several existing organizations, including the OAS, the OAU, the ECA, and NATO; and the WTO and the Council for Mutual Economic Assistance (COMECON) have already been disbanded. Resentment of the domination of organizations by single powerful states, the clash of interests among groups of states, and reassertions of sovereign prerogatives are among the factors that act as centrifugal forces destroying the unity of regional agencies. A sufficient community of interests has not been established to outweigh the forces of nationalism and unilateralism. Cooperation for mutual benefit is possible, under these circumstances, but regional integration can occur only at a superficial level. The one partial exception is the European Community.

Regionalism (as well as universalism) possesses limited dynamics of its own. Regionalism exerts little magnetic force that tends to pull states away from the poles of national power and purposes. Regional organizations are formed not for their own sake but to promote the enhancement of national interests. If functionalism ever results in a surrender of national sovereignty, the current evidence suggests that the period of time in which this will generally occur is not imminent.

11

TRANSNATIONAL RELATIONS AND INTERNATIONAL ORGANIZATION

The constant change in world relations affects individuals, states, businesses, and organizations—domestic or international, public or private. Better transportation and communication link people, ideas, and commodities across national borders to a degree never before possible.

These changes force states and international organizations to adjust their policies and operations in order to maintain their relevance in international relations. Nongovernmental organizations in business, labor, and many other fields encroach upon states' prerogatives and escape government control. Often the network of contacts and transactions among nongovernmental actors threatens to undermine state sovereignty in important areas and questions the adequacy of the state-centric model of international relations.

Although transnational activities have been carried on for centuries, they have only recently become of major significance. And even more recently have scholars focused attention on these activities as important factors in current and future political relationships deserving increased analysis. There still is much to be learned about these activities, but it is known that transnational relations are now important and will be more so in the future. Because there is sure to be more concentration on the study of transnational relations, the fields of international relations and international organization may even need to be redefined so as to accommodate dimensions previously largely ignored.

DEFINITIONS AND PERSPECTIVES

Because the study of transnational relations is relatively new, some of the terminology applied to this area is little understood and sometimes lacks precision. To guide the student in distinguishing between interstate and transnational relations, a few definitions are in order. Not all scholars would subscribe to the same use of terms, but the definitions adopted below are based on those used in the summer 1971 issue of *International Organization*. These are selected because twenty scholars writing on various aspects of the theme "Transnational Relations and World Politics" agreed to accept the general definitions supplied by the editors of the issue.[1]

The basic term used by the editors, Keohane and Nye, is *transnational interaction*. A transnational interaction is "the movement of tangible or intangible items across state boundaries when at least one actor is not an agent of a government or an international organization."[2] This definition focuses on the activities of nongovernmental organizations and individuals involved in the transfer of goods, money, credit information, or persons from one country to another. States or intergovernmental organizations may be involved in transnational interactions, but they need not be, since the interaction may be between nongovernmental organizations or individuals only.

In the lexicon of Keohane and Nye, the term *transnational interaction* is not as broad as *transnational relations*, since the latter also includes interactions involving governmental subunits and subunits of international organizations as well as nongovernmental actors. Complex organizations, whether governmental or nongovernmental, are scarcely monolithic and may be properly treated as multidimensional. The Secretary-General of the United Nations or the Central Intelligence Agency of the United States government may play independent roles, on occasion, from those taken through "normal" or traditional policy channels.

Transnational or nongovernmental international organizations may be divided into two broad categories. One is the nonprofit organizations, of which there are approximately 4,800. The other category is the multinational business enterprise organized for profit, the number of which varies from 400 to 1,500 depending on the definition of how widespread the activities of such an enterprise must be in order to qualify as multinational.

---

[1]Robert O. Keohane and Joseph S. Nye Jr., eds., "Transnational Relations and World Politics," *International Organization*, 25 (Summer 1971). This publication, which makes no claim to comprehensive coverage of the subject, is at this time the best broad-gauged treatment of the many facets of transnational relations and is a basis and guide for further investigation of the area.

[2]Ibid., p. 332.

Definitions of multinational business enterprises are generally imprecise in setting standards for inclusion or exclusion of particular firms. Some definitions are based primarily on the number of countries in which a corporation or conglomerate has assets, earnings, manufacturing facilities, or sales. Other definitions stress such factors as the percentage of overseas assets or sales, centralized control, or tendency toward a global perspective.

Economic and social historians cite evidence of the prior existence of transnational interactions and relations. One example is the influence of various religious movements over several centuries. In the Middle Ages the Roman Catholic Church was a major political force commanding human allegiance outrivaling that of any secular ruler. The Church straddled the line between temporal and secular power through ownership and political rule over vast territories. In the struggle for supremacy between Church and state in the late Middle Ages, the Roman Catholic Church only gradually lost ground in the political realm to kings and emperors.

Another historical example of the significance of transnational activities is the close affinity of private and public agencies that assured the dominance of British world power in the nineteenth century. British manufacturers, traders, and financiers played a key role in the preponderance of British political influence in an empire encompassing one-fourth of the land area of the globe and in the preeminence in commercial and financial as well as political relations with other states. Robert Gilpin emphasizes strongly the importance of this precedent for modern transnationalism.

> One may reasonably argue, I believe, that in certain respects the regime of the Pax Britannica was the Golden Age of transnationalism. The activities of private financiers and capitalists enmeshed the nations in a web of interdependencies which certainly influenced the course of international relations. In contrast to our own era, in which the role of the multinational corporation in international economic relations is unprecedented, the private institutions of the City of London under the gold standard and the regime of free trade had a strategic and central place in world affairs unmatched by any transnational organization today.[3]

In spite of a plethora of historical examples of transnational interactions, the period since 1945 is particularly noteworthy as the era in which transnationalism has come into its own both as a phenomenon and as a subject for increased scholarly investigation and analysis. Multinational corporations are becoming larger, more numerous, and more influential with each passing year. They cannot yet be described as ubiquitous, but their spread will be watched with interest by governments and by students of international rela-

---

[3]Robert Gilpin, "The Politics of Transnational Economic Relations," *International Organization*, 25 (Summer 1971), 406.

tions, business, and economics. International nonprofit organizations are also proliferating at an unprecedented rate since 1945, and the possibilities for political influence multiply as improved transportation and communications increase the facilities for linking members and groups across national boundaries. Complex interactions are encouraged by close working relationships between intergovernmental organizations, such as the United Nations or its specialized agencies, and nongovernmental organizations. Nongovernmental organizations not only enjoy consultative status with intergovernmental organizations but frequently enter into working relationships with them for the attainment of commonly shared goals. The distinction between public and private functions becomes blurred in this as well as in numerous other areas.

The impossibility of separating public from private, domestic from foreign, and political from economic and social matters calls into question previously narrow concepts of the political process. If the political process is defined in terms of the authoritative allocation of values, then private actions in the economic and social realms, which affect the values available to other actors, are political actions. If these actions have an impact across state boundaries, they are transnational.

A broad definition of the political process points to the inadequacy of the state-centric model of world politics. The state-centric model tends to view the actions of nongovernmental actors as outside the political process. It assigns to them the status of environmental factors affecting the political process but not part of it. The justification for this approach rests on the monopolization of certain forms of coercive power by states. By excluding transnational actions from the main elements of the world political system, the model is simplified and becomes more manageable. At the same time, the state-centric model may lose much potential explanatory power by assigning to transnational factors a secondary status only incidental to world politics. Recent analysis of transnational factors reveals their direct relevance for and participation in the political process. A model that includes them as primary, not secondary, inputs into the political system will undoubtedly prove more satisfactory as a basis for research than the state-centric pattern that may be more manageable but lacking in inclusiveness of significant and perhaps powerful actions that are political in nature.

No specific model for study and research will be endorsed here. What is important is a recognition that any matrix of interactions in world politics is lacking in recognition of important transnational factors if only states and international organizations are included as active units. For the reader the salient fact to consider is the necessity to emphasize the role of nongovernmental actors in political affairs. No picture of world politics is complete if the complex pattern of interactions between transnational actors and governmental actors is ignored or treated as peripheral to the interactions of states and international organizations. The significance of transnational interactions will be clarified further in successive sections of this chapter.

NONPROFIT TRANSNATIONAL ACTORS AND ACTIVITIES

One category of transnational interaction results from the movement of persons across national boundaries. The dimensions of this movement have not been computed with great accuracy, but according to the best estimates, the number of persons involved annually is tens of millions and the rate of increase per year is more than 10 percent. The rapid growth of personal movement is due not only to improved transportation facilities but also to the creation of new governmental and private programs supporting the exchange of persons and to complex economic, sociological, and psychological motives related to increased knowledge about other countries and peoples. The interactions that take place involve both the persons who move across national boundaries and the persons residing in the host countries. If we are interested in the impact of these transnational interactions, we must consider the effects on the host population as well as the influence on the person who goes abroad. The question of impact or influence can also involve contacts with persons or policymakers in the home state during or after the foreign experience.

In relation to world politics, some movements of persons are much more significant than others. One scholar who has attempted to analyze those aspects of personal interchange that have a positive influence toward breaking down barriers among states and promoting accommodative policies is Robert C. Angell. He believes that national barriers may be more easily removed by the pressure exerted by "influentials" on their own policymakers than by the strengthening of international organizations or by any other means. An increasing number of this influential elite are engaging in transnational interactions each year. The thesis stated by Angell is that

> policy-makers are being subjected increasingly to a stream of influence from elites toward accommodation among nations, a stream that derives in part from the growing amount of transnational participation with positive effects on these elites. . . . The present hypothesis emphasizes the influence that the transnational experiences of members of national elites has on their home governments and thus ultimately on the relations among nations. Participation in the world social system is seen as affecting the nature of the world political system via national foreign policies.[4]

In sorting out those transnational interactions that have a positive influence toward accommodation among nations, Professor Angell rejects from his analysis all tourist travel and other transient contacts that make little impact upon the attitudes and values of the participants or the population of

---

[4]Robert C. Angell, *Peace on the March: Transnational Participation* (New York: Van Nostrand Reinhold, 1969), p. 26.

the host country. Among the types of contacts which are of sufficient duration and intensity to affect national elites, he includes

Study abroad
Teaching and research abroad
Migration for long-term or permanent settlement abroad
Visiting relatives and friends abroad
Participation in foreign work camps and the Peace Corps
Technical assistance missions
Work in foreign religious missions
Residence abroad for business reasons
Residence abroad in military service
Participation in international nongovernmental organizations
Membership in secretariats of United Nations agencies[5]

The individuals in these categories are often acting on behalf of or are supported by a private organization or governmental agency, but they engage in *personal* interactions that may change their attitudes and cause them to exert accommodative influence upon governmental policymakers. The identity of purposes between these individuals and public policies or the programs of nongovernmental organizations is demonstrated by other studies.[6] The role of individuals may often be difficult to distinguish from the role of organizations or agencies in which those individuals participate, but their personal impact should be noted as a separate aspect of transnational interactions. Changes in personal attitudes are an additional factor in world politics beyond the actions of governments and organizations.

Personal transnational interaction can have both positive and negative effects upon the development of accommodation among nations. Some contacts may reinforce attitudes of national chauvinism, hostility, and the protection of sovereignty. Interactions that may be negative in their effects include (1) interactions between those in military service abroad and segments of the host population, (2) the impact of foreign religious missionaries upon members of the host population who àre not direct beneficiaries of their religious and social activities, and (3) the interaction between businessmen residing abroad and competitors or others who resent the drain of profits to foreign investors.

[5]Ibid.

[6]Examples include Philip H. Coombs, *The Fourth Dimension of Foreign Policy: Educational and Cultural Affairs* (New York: Harper & Row, 1964); Andrew M. Scott, *The Revolution in Statecraft: Informal Penetration* (New York: Random House, 1965); Robert Blum, ed., *Cultural Affairs and Foreign Relations.* For the American Assembly. (Englewood Cliffs, NJ: Prentice-Hall, 1963); Herbert C. Kelman and Raphael S. Ezekiel, *Cross-National Encounters: The Personal Impact of an Exchange Program for Broadcasters* (San Francisco: Jossey-Bass, 1970); James N. Rosenau, *National Leadership and Foreign Policy: A Case Study in the Mobilization of Public Support* (Princeton, NJ: Princeton University Press, 1963).

In balancing the positive and negative effects of personal interaction, Angell calculates an overwhelming influence on the side of accommodation among nations. Not only is this the case, but annually the increment of positive influence is increasing. With present trends he foresees these forces assuming extensive proportions before the close of the century and predicts that national accommodative policies will reflect the multiple influences of personal transnational participation. To predict an end to international conflict is unrealistic and naive, but the atmosphere in which interstate interactions occur may be ameliorated by the impact of the web of personal relationships.[7]

Several United Nations special programs represent joint efforts between the United Nations and private groups and individuals and embody goals fostering international understanding and amity. One of these is the United Nations International School, which was begun by Secretariat personnel in 1947 to provide basic education in an international atmosphere. In the area of development, a United Nations Volunteers program was initiated in the 1970s to appeal mainly to an international corps of young people anxious to participate in development projects. In 1965 the United Nations Institute for Training and Research (UNITAR) began operations. Its regular staff is supplemented by scholars on temporary assignment to UNITAR. The Institute has published dozens of research studies and also conducts training seminars for new members of government delegations and their staffs and for United Nations–related civil-service positions. Another research enterprise linking the private world of scholarship with the United Nations is the United Nations University, which first began operations in 1975 at its headquarters in Tokyo. The purpose is to energize research on global problems through a network of public and private research institutes and universities.

Another dimension of transnational relations is the development of a web of international nongovernmental organizations (NGOs), with the most rapid expansion occurring since 1945. The *Yearbook of International Organizations* for 1993–94 gives data on 5,102 "conventional" international organizations, of which 4,830 are nongovernmental as compared with only 272 intergovernmental units. Additionally, the *Yearbook* includes information on 3,606 national nongovernmental organizations which are internationally oriented. Although the annual rate of increase since 1945 in the number of NGOs is probably less than half the increment rate of growth in interpersonal transnational interactions, it is nevertheless substantial, with an annual increase of 4.7 percent for the period 1954–68.[8] Even with allowance for the increase in world population, the movement is a dynamic one and promises to continue to be an increasing factor in world politics for the next several decades. International nongovernmental organizations

---

[7]For more details concerning these conclusions see Angell, *Peace on the March*, Chapter 11.

[8]Kjell Skjelsbaek, "The Growth of International Nongovernmental Organization in the Twentieth Century," *International Organization*, 25 (Summer 1971), p. 425.

have been created in almost every conceivable field of human concern, from religion to transport and from art to science.

Nongovernmental organizations do not operate in a vacuum hermetically sealed off from each other or from governments and intergovernmental organizations. One of the major purposes of focusing greater attention on the study of nongovernmental actors is to assess the interactions between them and governments so that the political process may be examined in its fullest dimensions. Knowledge of the importance of these interactions is at an elementary stage, but preliminary investigations indicate a complex pattern of relationships warranting further study.

One indication of the interaction between NGOs and intergovernmental organizations is the provision for consultative status of NGOs with United Nations agencies. The most sought-after consultative status is granted by the Economic and Social Council. The breadth of ECOSOC's mandate explains the large number of NGOs that have been granted consultative status, including more than 800 organizations divided into three categories according to the extent of their involvement in ECOSOC's program. All the specialized agencies except the Universal Postal Union and the financial group also enter into consultative agreements with NGOs. The number of NGOs that have such a relationship varies from fifteen organizations for the World Meteorological Organization to more than 580 for UNESCO. The United Nations Children's Fund, the United Nations Conference on Trade and Development, and the International Atomic Energy Agency also grant consultative status to substantial numbers of NGOs.

The relationships between United Nations agencies and hundreds of NGOs demonstrate the impossibility of effectively separating public from private organizations. The working arrangements involve bonds of mutual support and interdependence. Lines of information, research, and administration flow back and forth between United Nations and private agencies. The pattern is one of cooperation and division of labor for common ends rather than a sharp cleavage between public and private sectors. Transnational interactions operate extensively through these channels.

Many cases can be cited of the political impact of transnational actors. A few examples will illustrate the interrelationships of governmental and private groups.

Plane hijackings have been a cause of much concern to governments, airlines, and the public. It has been estimated that nearly two-thirds of all hijackings have been committed for political reasons. Revolutionary organizations such as the Popular Front for the Liberation of Palestine have engaged in spectacular hijackings for the purpose of securing the release of political prisoners. Passengers and crew have been held hostage, and threats have been made to destroy the aircraft. A series of hijackings culminated in 1970 in the diversion of three aircraft belonging to TWA, Swissair, and BOAC to an isolated airstrip in Jordan and a Pan American 747 to Cairo. After lengthy negotiations, the passengers were freed in exchange for the release of Popular Front members from prisons in West Germany, Switzerland, and the United Kingdom. Similar incidents involving other revolutionary organizations have occurred frequently in various parts of the world.[9]

Nongovernmental organizations play a key role in aerial hijacking and in other aspects of transnational air transport. One of these is the International Federation of Airline Pilots' Associations (IFALPA). Pilots assume primary responsibility for the safety of passengers, crew, and aircraft during a hijacking attempt. IFALPA is composed of national associations of pilots in seventy countries and has among its goals assisting and advising in the development of a safe and orderly system of air transportation and the promotion of safe working conditions. IFALPA has agreed to boycott all air traffic to states unwilling to take effective antihijacking measures. In August 1968, it called for a boycott of routes to Algeria in retaliation for the detention in Algeria of plane, crew, and passengers of an El Al aircraft. The boycott was canceled when the Algerian government gave assurances that the release would be made promptly.

Another example of IFALPA's effectiveness was its threat of a strike in protest of a revision in 1966 by the International Civil Aviation Organization (ICAO) of the safety rules in the North Atlantic air corridor. The proposed rule reduced the distance between planes from 120 to 90 miles. The rule was rescinded as a result of IFALPA's protest.

Governments, intergovernmental organizations, and transnational organizations engage in an intricate pattern of interactions in the air-transport arena. Public and private ownership of airlines complicate the pattern. The International Air Transport Association (IATA), whose members are 165 scheduled airlines from 110 countries, sets fares for scheduled airline service. In addition to the organization of pilots, other airline employees are affiliated with the International Transport Workers Federation. Governments and the ICAO adopt regulations affecting interstate carriers, but private groups—including those mentioned above, manufacturers of aircraft and equipment, and labor organizations—engage in interactions that affect the pattern of airline control, service, and operation.[10]

Since 1970, terrorism has moved from the national to the transnational level and from plane hijacking to a wider range of terrorist techniques. The transnational dimensions of terrorism are established when there is collusion among the popular Front for the Liberation of Palestine, the Japanese Red Army, and the German Baader-Meinhof Gang. Transnational dimensions are demonstrated by Lebanon, Iraq, and Yemen serving as training centers for ter-

[9]For a discussion of many facets of the hijacking problem, see articles by Narinder Aggarwala, Michael J. Fenello, and Gerald F. FitzGerald in "Air Hijacking: An International Perspective," *International Conciliation*, no. 585 (November 1971).

[10]For additional details, see Robert L. Thornton, "Governments and Airlines," *International Organization*, 25 (Summer 1971), pp. 541–53.

rorists of various nationalities and by Libya, Yemen, and Lebanon serving as sanctuaries for various terrorist groups. In recent years Iran has become a major supporter of Middle East terrorist activities. Iraq was the source of an aborted plot to assassinate former U.S. President George Bush on a visit to Kuwait in 1993. Access of terrorist groups to weapons from international sources is another transnational aspect of terrorism. Even the media, as transnational agencies, become partners of the terrorists by giving them the publicity they seek. This publicity, along with the reactions of governments and publics, offers to a few hundred terrorists an influence far beyond their numbers.

The number of international terrorist acts involving violence and intimidation increased slightly throughout the 1980s, but were met by more effective counterterrorist policies and techniques. About 40 percent of terrorist acts occurred in or originated from the Middle East, but terrorism was also on the increase in such areas as Latin America, especially in Colombia. Plane hijackings have decreased, but plane sabotage has increased in recent years. The bombing of Pan Am Flight 103 over Lockerbie, Scotland, in December 1988 was indicative of the technological sophistication in the use of plastic explosives in the hands of terrorists and of the inadequacy of detection techniques and airport security measures to prevent sabotage. In addition to national action and international efforts through the ICAO to prevent air sabotage, the International Maritime Organization, after the *Achille Lauro* seajacking in 1985, developed and opened for signature a new treaty to supplement previous provisions against terrorism involving ships. In another major area of combating terrorism, more than seventy states have subscribed to the International Convention against the Taking of Hostages, which provides for international cooperation in extraditing and prosecuting those accused of hostage taking. However, several countries continue to furnish not only training and sanctuary for terrorist groups, but also to provide money, weapons, identification documents, and diplomatic pouch privileges to such groups. Thus, some lessons have been learned in combating terrorism, but its transnational aspects will remain a persistent problem for the foreseeable future.

Science is inherently and traditionally transnational. An example of a transnational scientific organization of transcendent significance is the International Council of Scientific Unions (ICSU). The ICSU is the coordinating agency for twenty constituent international scientific unions in the exact and natural sciences. Membership also includes the principal scientific academies, national research councils, and associations of scientific institutions in sixty-six countries. The ICSU has consultative status with ECOSOC, UNESCO, the Food and Agriculture Organization, the International Atomic Energy Agency, and the Council of Europe, and working relationships with the World Meteorological Organization, the International Telecommunication Union, and the World Health Organization. Inter-Council coordinating committees have been established with the International Council for Philosophy and Humanistic Studies and with the Council for International Organizations of Medical Sciences. The ICSU was primarily responsible for the organization of the International Geophysical Year, the International Year of the Quiet Sun, and the International Biological Programme. Its committees on oceanic research, antarctic research, space research, water research, and science and technology in developing countries all deal with politically significant and sensitive subject areas. The ICSU is obviously involved in a complex pattern of interactions with governments, intergovernmental organizations, and other nongovernmental organizations.

Several activities of the ICSU demonstrate the meshing of public and private interests. The idea for the International Geophysical Year (IGY) originated with individual scientists. The ICSU soon became interested in the project and, in 1952, established the Special Committee for the IGY, which became the planning and coordinating agency for the program. The IGY lasted officially for eighteen months from July 1, 1957, to December 31, 1958, and enlisted the cooperation of scientists from sixty-six nations. Special areas of concern were space, the weather, the oceans, and the frigid zones. All these are of major interest to governments, and such activities as space probes and satellite programs required governmental cooperation. Governmental financial support was obtained for many IGY projects. UNESCO also makes annual grants for scientific research through the ICSU and, in 1957, made a special grant to the Special Committee for the IGY. During and following the period of the IGY, another of the United Nations specialized agencies, the World Meteorological Organization (WMO) acted as the collecting and publishing agency for meteorological data by establishing an IGY Meteorological Data Centre. In this work the WMO maintained close liaison with the Special Committee for the IGY.

The ICSU is also cooperatively involved with intergovernmental organizations in the promotion of space-research programs. The role of two subagencies of the ICSU—the Committee on Space Research (COSPAR) and the Inter-Union Commission on Frequency Allocations for Radio Astronomy and Space Science (IUCAF)—will serve to illustrate the web of interactions among nongovernmental, governmental, and intergovernmental units.[11]

COSPAR was first established by the ICSU in 1957, a few days before *Sputnik I* was launched into orbit. Membership consisted of both national members—representing scientific academies, research councils, or governments in states most active in space research—and representatives of scientific unions that belong to the ICSU. Almost immediately, political pressure was interjected into the formulation of the terms of the COSPAR charter by pro-

[11]For additional details, see Edward Miles, "Transnationalism in Space: Inner and Outer," *International Organization*, 25 (Summer 1971), pp. 602–25; and Hugh Odishaw, "International Cooperation in Space Science," in *Outer Space: Prospects for Man and Society*, ed. Lincoln P. Bloomfield. For the American Assembly. (Englewood Cliffs, NJ: Prentice-Hall, 1962), pp. 105–22.

posals from the Soviet Union to expand the list of national members to include the Ukraine, Byelorussia, and several states of East Europe. A limited veto power was given to the United States and the Soviet Union over financial assessments and certain relationships with the United Nations. National committees have been formed to cooperate with COSPAR, and some of these are controlled by governments. Thus, COSPAR is linked with governments in its composition and control.

COSPAR also interacts with intergovernmental organizations interested in space research. These working relationships are most involved with the World Meteorological Organization (WMO) and the International Telecommunication Union (ITU). Weather data from satellites and space communication are areas of joint interest with COSPAR. Edward Miles also states that

> among NGOs, COSPAR has played the leading role both by providing advice to the UN General Assembly and by acting as an international referee in disputes involving claims of probably harmful effects of experiments.[12]

COSPAR is at the center of international cooperation in space research because it comprises the greatest reservoir of international expertise in the field. Planning in COSPAR represents the frontiers of space knowledge and research. COSPAR can serve other purposes, such as the provision of a center for the collection and dissemination of scientific space data, but its greatest asset is its pooling of the best talent in space research. Because of this central role, the interactions that exist between it and governments, intergovernmental organizations, and other NGOs are a natural development in an interdependent world.

An area of both competition and cooperation between governments and private agencies is in the allocation of radio frequencies for specific uses. The international agency that registers all frequency requests is the International Frequency Registration Board (IFRB), a subdivision of the ITU. The power of the IFRB does not extend to the allocation of frequencies, which must be determined by bargaining in international conferences. Frequency allocations have great economic value, affecting private business interests, but governments are the agents that engage in the process of compromise to determine the allocation of frequencies within the spectrum.

Radio astronomers and space scientists were dissatisfied with the first allocation of frequencies for space purposes in 1959. In 1960 the ICSU set up the Inter-Union Commission on Frequency Allocations for Radio Astronomy and Space Science (IUCAF) to promote the interests of scientists in lobbying with their governments and with the ITU. The IUCAF is composed of representatives of the International Astronomical Union, the International Scientific Radio Union, and COSPAR, all of which are constituent units or commit-

---

[12]Miles, "Transnationalism in Space," p. 614.

tees of the ICSU. Prior to the 1963 Extraordinary Administrative Radio Conference on Space Radiocommunications, the IUCAF communicated its needs to the IFRB. As a result of IUCAF efforts, approximately 15 percent of the radio-frequency spectrum was allocated for space purposes. Multiple pressures of a transnational nature were required to achieve this end.

Not all foundations perform as transnational actors, but a number of United States and European foundations carry on overseas programs that have a substantial impact on world politics. Two United States foundations stand out in international programming. These are the Ford Foundation and the Rockefeller Foundation. Both have assets in the billions of dollars and annually allocate funds for all purposes in the hundreds of millions. The Ford Foundation has assets nearly three times those of the Rockefeller Foundation, but allocates a smaller percentage of funds to international projects. In 1986 the Rockefeller Foundation adopted a policy that would double its amount previously spent on third-world projects.

The Ford Foundation officially states that its fundamental objective is the advancement of human welfare. More specifically, its aims include contributions toward eliminating the causes of war and the strengthening of democratic institutions and processes. Its international program concentrates on the needs of developing countries. Special areas of emphasis include food production, rural development, education, health, nutrition, population, development planning and management, cultural preservation, refugee assistance, human rights, and the status of women. Both the Ford and the Rockefeller foundations maintain large field staffs in the developing countries to stimulate, plan, coordinate, influence, and oversee local projects.

The official seal of the Rockefeller Foundation proclaims a goal as comprehensive and global as that of the Ford Foundation. This goal is declared to be "the well-being of mankind throughout the world." Any realistic approach to achieving this aim would necessarily involve the foundation in transnational activity.

Since its inception in 1913, the Rockefeller Foundation has been notable for its support of health and biomedical programs particularly in Latin America. In recent years this emphasis continues, but other major preoccupations of the field staff are with programs in Latin America, Asia, and Africa for the conquest of hunger and the development of universities. The largest program expenditures are for research on problems of population and agriculture.

Both the Ford and the Rockefeller foundations deserve special credit for the "green revolution," which provides the means to expand cereal production in many agriculturally primitive societies. The green revolution involves the development of high-yielding seeds together with the use of fertilizers, water, and planting and cultivation techniques to produce remarkably increased yields per unit of land. Other experiments have produced grain varieties with substantially increased protein content. Protein-deficient diets are endemic to many societies living at poverty levels. Ford and Rockefeller foundation funds have jointly supported four institutes largely responsible for the green revolution. These are the International Rice Research Institute in the Philippines, the International Maize and Wheat Improvement Center in Mexico, the International Center of Tropical Agriculture in Colombia, and the International Institute of Tropical Agriculture in Nigeria. In 1970, Dr. Norman E. Borlaug, a member of the Rockefeller field staff attached to the International Maize and Wheat Improvement Center, received the Nobel Peace Prize for his contributions to the development of the new varieties of wheat.

The international programs of the Ford and the Rockefeller foundations bring the foundation personnel into constant and intricate interaction with personnel representing governments, universities, intergovernmental organizations, and other private agencies. The annual reports of the foundations are replete with evidence of these interactions. Governments have given land and financial support to institutes created by the foundations, and repeated references are made in the reports to the necessity for governments to take over projects initiated through Ford and Rockefeller grants. Agencies of host governments with which interactions frequently occur are ministries of health, agriculture, education, home affairs, labor, external affairs, and finance; commissions or offices of national planning; presidential commissions; local planning organizations; population commissions; and publicly supported universities. The United States National Institutes of Health has supported programs in which the foundations played a role. In Latin America, cooperation with such regional organizations as the Organization of American States, the Inter-American Development Bank, and the Latin American Demographic Center is cited in the foundations' reports. Among international intergovernmental agencies, the program with which the foundations interact to the greatest extent is the United Nations Development Program; but frequent interactions also occur with the World Health Organization, the Food and Agriculture Organization, the United Nations Educational, Scientific and Cultural Organization, and the International Bank for Reconstruction and Development.

The pattern of cooperative interactions in which the foundations are involved is, indeed, most intricate and extensive. The impact, in some cases, can already be assessed; other evaluations must be based on future developments. The foundations may be able to generate only modest changes in comparison with the vast needs of underdeveloped nations, but their efforts are made at critical points in terms of the generally recognized reforms that are required and desired.

Organized religion has powerful influences over individuals and affect attitudes that sometimes promote human unity and peace and at other time generate hostility and divisiveness. Iran in 1979 established an Islamic republic merging important elements of divine and secular law under religiou leadership and domination. Throughout history, religious wars have been among the bloodiest. On the other hand, the Roman Catholic Church was previously cited as the most important transnational actor of the Middle Ages. Recent popes who have used their influence for peace and world unity are Paul VI and John Paul II. Church leaders of many denominations have joined in ecumenical movements to bring pressures for disarmament, with special attention to the avoidance of nuclear war. The moral effects of foreign policy bring religious pressures into the governmental arena.

Many more examples of nonprofit transnational actors and their activities could be described, but those already presented may serve as a representative cross section of this phenomenon. By realizing that this presentation is only a portion of the whole, the student may appreciate the complexities of the web of interdependencies that characterize world political affairs and may recognize the need to assess the role of individuals and nongovernmental organizations in the political process.

THE MULTINATIONAL CORPORATION

Multinational business enterprises deserve special treatment because they are different from nonprofit organizations in nature, size, and degree of impact on world politics. Furthermore, they have come under increased scrutiny by governments, businesspersons, and scholars because of the realization of their growing importance in economic and political affairs and because of the complex patterns of interactions between them and other actors, especially states and international organizations. Projections of current growth trends indicate an increasing influence of the multinational corporation (or transnational corporation in United Nations parlance) in world politics. Reactions to this future influence vary from welcoming the process as the key to an emerging world community to pointing with alarm to the prospect of irresponsible concentrations of economic power in the hands of an elite. The future role of the multinational business enterprise in perpetuating or closing the prosperity gap between rich and poor nations is also an area of interest and concern.

One simple measure of the impact of multinational corporations is the enormity of the resources controlled by these conglomerates. The annual *Fortune 500* lists of the largest United States and foreign industrial corporations rank corporations according to their annual sales. In 1986 the sales of six United States, one European, and two Japanese conglomerates exceeded $50 billion each. General Motors sales throughout the world amounted to more than $126 billion, which is larger than the entire gross domestic product of Argentina, Austria, Denmark, Norway, or South Africa.

For decades the United States dominated the field of multinational giants, but by the 1990s the top ten included two from Europe and two from

Japan, and the top twenty included six from Europe, four from Japan, and one from South Korea. A majority of the world's ten largest banks are Japanese.

The simultaneous development of (1) a world market, (2) the rapid expansion of multinational corporations, and (3) the necessity for modern governments to exercise controls in order to maintain stability and economic growth presents dilemmas for both business and government. Economic factors occupy a larger share of the political spectrum than ever before. The doctrine of laissez-faire has been long abandoned even in the least-controlled national economic systems. The multinational business enterprise seeks to gain greater freedom by establishing subsidiaries in many countries, but it is subjected to controls by both the home and the host nations. Multinational corporations have great flexibility in moving goods, money, personnel, and technology across national boundaries, and this flexibility increases their bargaining power with governments. In dealing with such giants, governments must be sure that they maintain control over tax revenues, inflation, trade balances, balance of payments, trade restrictions, monetary values, credit policies, employment, and economic planning. The complex interplay of economic and political factors is greatly affected by the activities of multinational business enterprises. The business conglomerates, by controlling such enormous resources and so great a share of the market, play a leading role in the areas of control sought by governments.

Most multinational firms are highly centralized and are dominated by the parent company. The managers are from the home state, research is centralized, autonomy for foreign subsidiaries is limited, technology is exported from the parent company, profits are often repatriated, and the policies of the firm conform closely to the economic and foreign policies of the home government. As multinational corporations grow larger, as they recognize that not all managerial and research talent in monopolized by one country, and as they accommodate more to local conditions, they may move from an ethnocentric to a geocentric orientation.

Howard Perlmutter uses the term *geocentric* to describe a type of business attitude that is world oriented. Some of the characteristics of a geocentric-type organization include complex and interdependent organization, collaboration between headquarters and subsidiaries in decision making, worldwide perspective, worldwide recruiting and interchange of personnel, and multidirectional communication among units of the corporation.[13] If a number of large and powerful business enterprises eventually shift their orientation from a national to a geocentric emphasis, the implications for state policy could be extensive.

The acquisition of subsidiaries by foreign parent corporations is both welcomed and resisted by the governments of the host countries. Jack

[13]Howard V. Perlmutter, "The Tortuous Evolution of the Multinational Corporation," *Columbia Journal of World Business,* 4 (January–February 1969), 9–18.

Behrman has cogently summarized the dilemma of the host government in facing the incursion of foreign-dominated business enterprises.

> The host government is caught in a "love-hate" syndrome. It wants the contributions to wealth and economic growth that the multinational enterprise can provide because they add to its power within the country, as well as internationally. At the same time it dislikes and fears the results: the incursions on national sovereignty and technological independence. The host government finds multinational enterprises difficult to live with, but, so long as it seeks to increase national power, equally unpleasant to live without. . . . It appears to the host government that a trade-off may be required between sovereignty and greater wealth.[14]

The advantages and the disadvantages to the host government may be analyzed in more specific terms. Behrman suggests, "The contributions lie mainly in the areas of capital formation, technology and management skills, regional development, competition, and balance of payments."[15] The concerns of the hosts include the fear of industrial dominance, the fear of technological dependence, and the disturbance to economic plans.[16]

An aspect of the flexibility of the multinational corporation is its freedom to establish subsidiaries in countries that provide the most favorable conditions. Furthermore, when a parent company decides to close a subsidiary, it may evoke strong repercussions from the host government because of the loss of local employment. Compromise and accommodation mark the bargaining positions of host governments and business enterprises in determining the location and the status of subsidiary business units.

The establishment of foreign subsidiaries also entails both benefits and costs for the home government of the parent corporation. Incentives for businesses to become multinational include not only economy of operation and access to markets but also possible tax advantages through flexible accounting procedures. The outflow of investment is a factor in the international balance of payments. The United States, as the base for the largest multinational business enterprises, has imposed governmental controls over foreign investment, the export of goods or technology to designated areas, and antitrust violations by multinational corporations. Under authority derived from the Trading with the Enemy Act and the Export Control Act, the United States has been able to prohibit sales to such areas as Cuba, Iran, or Nicaragua from both United States–based businesses and from their foreign subsidiaries. When such sales are not contrary to the law of the state in which the subsidiary is located, this amounts to an extension of United States law and foreign policy across national boundaries. A similar situation arises from the extension of

---

[14]Jack N. Behrman, *National Interests and the Multinational Enterprise: Tensions among the North Atlantic Countries* (Englewood Cliffs, NJ: Prentice-Hall, 1970), pp. 7–8.

[15]Ibid., p. 13.

[16]Ibid., *passim.*

United States antitrust jurisdiction to cases affecting the international business holdings of American-based corporations.

The existence of multinational corporations results in many conflicts of law. Host states resent and fear the intrusion of the jurisdiction of the home state in regulating business practices as an invasion of their sovereignty. Even without the application of domestic law across national boundaries, the erosion of sovereignty and independence occurs to some degree because of the identity of interests between corporations and their home governments.

Host governments are not helpless in protecting their interests against the invasion of foreign capital and the threat of diminution of national sovereignty. They may refuse to grant corporate charters to subsidiaries of foreign businesses. They may place conditions upon the ownership and behavior of subsidiaries. They may restrict the freedom of businesses whose products are closely related to national security. They may encourage and subsidize local businesses to increase their competitiveness. Governments may seek protection against undesirable practices through regional and international agreements and associations and through diplomatic channels when conflicts occur. Businesses are subject to the threat of nationalization with or without adequate compensation.

The threat of nationalization carries with it complex economic and political ramifications. The foreign business subsidiary is hostage to the host state. The home state also becomes hostage to the attitudes and the practices of the multinational enterprise in its foreign operations. The corporation seeks guarantees from the home government against loss from confiscation of its foreign properties. The negative attitude of the United States government toward public ownership is reflected in its foreign economic and political policies. Public ownership, in turn, may work to the advantage of a state only if it possesses sufficient resources and technology to compete in the international arena. Again, internal psychological factors may dictate policies not economically advantageous.

The complex interplay of political and economic factors is illustrated by the nationalization of the Anglo-Iranian Oil Company in 1951.[17] The British government owned 51 percent of the stock of Anglo-Iranian. The terms of the agreement regarding oil revenues gave three times as much income to the British treasury as to the Iranian treasury. Several oil-producing countries had won more favorable terms from international oil companies. Premier Mohammed Mossadegh announced the nationalization of the Anglo-Iranian Company, which had a monopoly of Iranian oil production. The British took their case to the International Court of Justice and to the Security Council without attaining satisfaction and, with the cooperation of other states, imposed an oil boycott on Iran. The boycott virtually paralyzed Iranian opera-

[17]These details are reviewed in Michael Tanzer, *The Political Economy of International Oil and the Underdeveloped Countries* (Boston: Beacon Press, 1969), pp. 321–26.

tions for three years as the British drew on oil reserves in Kuwait and elsewhere. Tensions grew between Premier Mossadegh and the Shah as the premier sought new revenues from wealthy Iranians, instituted new land policies, tried to gain control of the military, and moved to cut the Shah's personal income and allowances. The United States Central Intelligence Agency (CIA) played a decisive role in engineering a coup that overthrew the Mossadegh regime. In the new oil agreements that followed, 40 percent of the shares were assigned to British Petroleum and 40 percent to United States firms. The CIA agent who directed the coup later became a vice president of Gulf Oil Corporation.

Other examples of interference by multinational corporations in the internal politics of third-world countries have been widely publicized. For decades the United Fruit Company was able to extract from several Central American governments legislation and policies that were extremely favorable to its profitability. In the early 1970s the International Telephone & Telegraph Company (ITT) first tried to prevent the election of Salvador Allendé, a Marxist, as president of Chile, and later was heavily instrumental in his overthrow. Tragedies have also occurred in poor countries from business practices of large companies. For several years the Swiss Nestlé Corporation aggressively marketed its baby feeding formula as a substitute for breastfeeding in many third-world countries. After widespread public pressure resulted from evidence of a substantial increase in infant deaths attributed to the Nestlé campaign, the company agreed to discontinue these practices.

While industrially developed nations generally welcome multinational subsidiaries as more beneficial than harmful, the same case does not clearly apply to developing areas. In the less developed countries, the industries affected have frequently been extractive in nature, with a major drain of resources to the host country. In general, multinational corporations establish most manufacturing subsidiaries in other developed countries or in the newly industrialized countries (NICs), not in underdeveloped ones. Only one-fourth of the business activities of transnational industries are conducted in the developing states, and these are largely concentrated in twenty countries. Two-thirds of the United States' direct investment has gone to Europe and to Canada; another one-sixth is divided among Japan, four of the NICs of East Asia (Hong Kong, Singapore, Taiwan, and the Republic of Korea), and three Latin American countries (Brazil, Mexico, and Panama). This leaves only one-sixth for the rest of the world. Less than five percent of the world's research and development activities occur in developing states. The repatriation of handsome profits from extractive industries, plus the problem of servicing public and private debts, leaves little investment income within developing countries for economic growth. Furthermore, the technology that is cheaply exported from one developed country to another may be inappropriate for transfer to an underdeveloped economy. Employment of local labor may represent a higher good in a labor-rich economy than mechanized efficiency suitable to Europe or North America. United States or European industries geared to mass consumption buttressed by advertising may, if introduced in areas of low industrialization, create demands inappropriate to national needs and divert resources from enterprises more basic to development. Fundamental problems of economic growth are often ignored by local elites who link their interests with foreign business enterprises backed by a powerful government. Local governments are no match for the bargaining power of large developed states whose means for rewards and punishment are formidable. The identity of government and business interests compounds the problem for the weak state.

The growth of multinational corporations presents ethical and philosophical problems. Democratic values are affected by the emergence of powerful transnational businesses capable of affecting the distribution of goods and of influencing or bypassing governmental policy. Trends toward a deterioration of democratic control resulting from the size, complexity, and bureaucratization of government are exacerbated by the development of powerful transnational actors only partially responsible and responsive to public pressures exercised through governmental channels. The possible threat to democratic values represented by the multinational corporation deserves further attention by philosophers, political scientists, and others concerned with maintaining responsibility in political and social affairs.

Inevitably, the United Nations has become involved with the question of the rapid growth and expanding influence of the multinational corporations. In 1972, ECOSOC created a group of twenty eminent persons to study the role and the impact of these corporate giants and to recommend steps or methods leading toward international accountability or regulation. In 1974, as a first step, ECOSOC created two permanent bodies to keep the problems of the multinationals under scrutiny: a forty-eight-member intergovernmental Commission on Transnational Corporations and a United Nations Center on Transnational Corporations. In 1992 the Center's functions were transferred to a newly-created Transnational Corporations and Management Division. The Commission established as its first priority the development of a code of conduct for the activities of transnational corporations and this task, due to its complexities and to the competing interests involved, had not been completed by 1993. In the meantime, the Organization for Economic Cooperation and Development in 1976 adopted a voluntary code of conduct for transnationals, which, because it represented the position only of affluent states, was considered inadequate by Third World standards.

Several other major tasks were undertaken by the Commission and the Center. The Commission, besides working on the code of conduct, gave special attention to means for halting corrupt practices involving transnational corporations. The Center was requested to work in four primary areas in addition to its support activities on a code of conduct. These were (1) the establishment of a comprehensive information system; (2) research into the political, legal, economic, and social effects of the operations of transnationals; (3) technical cooperation programs to strengthen the negotiating capacities of developing countries in their dealings with transnational corporations; and (4) attempts to more precisely define the term *transnational corporations*. In 1977 the Commission adopted, in a vote divided along North-South lines, a resolution requesting transnational corporations to cease further investment in South Africa and to disengage progressively from that country. The Commission also enlisted the services of a panel of experts to advise on the development of uniform national standards of accounting and reporting by transnational corporations.

The role of multinational corporations will continue as a persistent issue in many forums inside and outside the United Nations. One danger to the welfare of developing countries is that a code of conduct and related measures might contain provisions considered so inimical to the interests of transnational enterprises that they would withdraw from those countries. Such a trend would be a major blow to development aspirations and to the realization of a new international economic order.

Some other recent trends in the role of multinational corporations in developing countries include (1) greater acceptance by developing nations of multinational corporations as necessary contributors to the development process, (2) a substantial increase in the number of joint ventures involving greater participation by public and private parties in host states, (3) the enlarged importance of the service sector in world trade, and (4) the rapid expansion of computing and telecommunications technology, which make possible greater control and flexibility by multinational corporations.

POSSIBLE IMPACT OF TRANSNATIONAL ACTORS

There is little doubt that the accelerated rate of growth of transnational actors of diverse types since 1945 has complicated the political picture and brought into serious question the adequacy of the state-centric model of world politics. This growth is a natural outcome of scientific and technological developments that shrink global distances and increase access from one part of the world to another. The process was well underway before social scientists became aware of its far-reaching implications and realized that current trends indicate a rapidly enlarged future role of transnational actors.

Will the effects of the future expansion of transnationalism be benign or malignant, utopian or disastrous? Informed opinions vary so widely as to be inconclusive. The principal point of agreement is that political relationships will become increasingly complex. Whether methods of dealing with information and ideas can be harnessed to control the complex relationships to the benefit of most of humanity is not clear.

Some students of transnational trends forecast the decline or eventual demise of the national state. Charles Kindleberger welcomes the replacement of the nation-state as an economic unit by multinational corporations as a natural and beneficial development.[18] J. J. Servan-Schreiber points to the lack of adequate political response to the American challenge by European governments or by the European community and predicts that, unless new policies are rapidly adopted, the third greatest industrial power will soon be not Europe but American industry in Europe. As multinational corporations move toward a geocentric perspective, they may become independent centers of economic power rivaling the power of large states.

Other forecasters predict the breaking down of national barriers and the adoption of more accommodative policies among states. The state would continue to operate as the primary political unit, but its freedom to use the most hostile means of persuasion would be circumscribed. Robert Angell attributes a movement toward peace to the increased exchange of elites who will bring growing pressure on their home governments for international accommodation and cooperation.

Those who adopt Marxist theory see the multinational corporation as an extension of the imperialism of powerful capitalist states. In their view the partnership between business and the state is a manifestation of the control of the state by capitalists, who use economic and political power to exploit foreign societies. Underdeveloped countries will continue to become poorer unless they revolt against their oppressors.

Regardless of the philosophical or theoretical orientation of the observer, the fact is that the developing states have been bypassed by the mainstream of the transnational movement. Developed countries have been the principal actors in the programs of international nongovernmental organizations and in the exchange of persons. Multinational corporations are based in developed nations and prefer investing most of their resources in other developed areas rather than risk their capital in less stable political and economic units. Unless prosperous states or multinational actors adopt more accommodative policies toward the poor countries, the escape of those countries from poverty may be indefinitely postponed. Hopeful beginnings have been made through the programs of the Ford and the Rockefeller foundations, the United Nations Development Program, national economic aid programs, the Organization of Petroleum Exporting Countries (OPEC), the United Nations Conference on Trade and Development (UNCTAD), and the United Nations Industrial Development Organization (UNIDO), but the impact has been disappointing in relation to relative needs.

Most observers forecast the continued importance of both the nation-state and transnational actors. States still command a monopoly of certain

---

[18]Charles P. Kindleberger, *American Business Abroad: Six Lectures on Direct Investment* (New Haven, CT: Yale University Press, 1969).

forms of coercive force and elicit the loyalty of millions of citizens. The increase in transnational activity will not radically alter the role of states in the near future. The political process will become increasingly complex, and the web of interactions will affect the behavior of governments. The realization of advantages in the utilization of international organizations may well encourage the further development of such organizations as a means of channeling cooperative actions for mutual gain. The study of political phenomena must encompass a wide range of actors and activities and a pattern of interactions of such complexity as to challenge the ingenuity of scholars. States will continue to serve as instruments of control but will undergo change as pressures from other sources exert influence on world political affairs.

12

PROMOTING ECONOMIC WELFARE

Over three-fourths of the United Nations' budget is allotted to economic and social activities, and most of its or its affiliated agencies' permanent and temporary personnel are engaged in economic and social work. Since 1960, economic and social development and all its ramifications have been the main preoccupation of the General Assembly. Activities in these fields are varied and are carried out in almost every country in the world.

It is impossible to separate completely economic from social matters. Problems in these areas usually have both economic and social characteristics and effects. Projects in these areas thus generally serve both sets of needs of individuals.

The United Nations and its agencies also are organized around both economic and social concerns. The Economic and Social Council is a single coordinating and directing agency. The regional economic commissions deal with a combination of economic and social matters. At first the Secretariat was organized into separate economic and social departments, but soon these were combined into a less artificial, single department. Although some agencies, such as the World Bank, may suggest a predominantly economic character, the country surveys made by the bank cover social as well as economic problems, and the bank's loans are for multiple purposes.

For purposes of presenting such an extensive set of activities, a somewhat artificial and arbitrary separation of economic from social issues will follow. This chapter will focus on certain basic concerns that are primarily economic. Chapter 13 will deal with global resource management that has broad economic and social aspects. Chapter 14 will examine a number of other themes that can be classified as principally social.

WORLD ECONOMIC INTERDEPENDENCE

In the following discussion, the term *world interdependence* should be interpreted as referring to conditions involving reciprocal effects among countries or among actors in different countries.

Although world trade is not a new phenomenon, its growth rate since 1945 has exhibited exponential characteristics. The value of world exports expressed in constant 1970 dollars (excluding the Communist countries with the exception of Yugoslavia) soared from $63 billion in 1948 to $107 billion in 1958 and $280 billion in 1970. By 1977 the value had climbed to $428 billion.[1] However, after 1973 the rate of annual growth slowed and the real value of world trade fell nearly 25 percent between 1980 and 1983. Beginning in 1985, both developed and developing countries experienced a return to a substantial annual growth rate. In spite of fluctuations, world trade since 1948 has grown more rapidly than world production, amounted in 1992 to more than $3.7 trillion at current prices, and is one type of gross indicator of the expanding network of exchanges across national boundaries.

The most important mechanism for promoting and regulating world trade is the General Agreement on Tariffs and Trade (GATT), which was established in 1947 after the failure of state representatives to reach agreement on the details for an International Trade Organization. GATT started in treaty form but was transformed into a permanent international organization loosely associated with the United Nations. Basically, GATT is dedicated to substantial reduction of tariffs and other trade barriers and to nondiscrimination based on the most-favored-nation principle in the trading relations of the member states. These states account for more than 80 percent of world trade. In 1993, GATT had 105 full members and special arrangements with twenty-seven additional states classified as de facto members. In 1986 the Soviet Union sought membership but was rebuffed. Eight series of negotiations for mutual tariff reductions have been held. By the end of the "Kennedy round" of negotiations in 1967, tariff reductions among the major trading nations of approximately one-third had been achieved. The "Tokyo round" of 1973–79 resulted in further reductions in tariffs on manufactured goods, additional agreements on nontariff barriers, and some concessions for less developed countries. In 1986, the "Uruguay

---

[1]*United Nations Statistical Yearbook*, 1978, Table 14, p. 55.

round" of negotiations was begun, but major differences among groups of countries delayed completion until December 1993.

Many obstacles to the achievement of the aims and principles of GATT remain. Adverse internal and global economic conditions since 1973 encourage a return to protectionism against the competition for foreign goods. Many policies of the European Community (EC) conflict with GATT aims. These include the protection of farmers through a Common Agricultural Policy (CAP) and an external trading preference system with developing nations. Japan is accused of various forms of trade restrictions, and the United States has legislation permitting escape clauses from general trading agreements under trigger mechanism formulas. Nontariff controls have increased until nearly half of world trade is subject to such controls. GATT's effectiveness has been weakened. Two big areas of contention in the "Uruguay round" of negotiations were agricultural policies and the inclusion, for the first time, of the growing trade in services.

International monetary and financial relationships represent another type of economic interdependence. As a part of postwar planning, representatives of forty-four nations met in July 1944 at Bretton Woods in New Hampshire to create a monetary and financial system. The International Monetary Fund (IMF) and the International Bank for Reconstruction and Development (IBRD or World Bank) became the key agencies of the newly created system and began operations in late 1945. The United States furnished the leadership for the system and, in the postwar years, became the world's central banker. The system was controlled and dominated by those states of Europe and North America with developed market economies. Until the dissolution of the Soviet Union, the USSR and its Communist satellites were not members; but by 1993 most of the component units of the former USSR and the eastern European states had been admitted, swelling the IMF membership to 175 and the World Bank to 172.

Essential elements of the Bretton Woods system included the following: (1) a set of fixed exchange rates was established with parity in terms of gold and with the IMF as regulator; (2) the IMF could furnish credit to countries with temporary balance-of-payments deficits; (3) funds provided to the IMF by member states were in gold and in member states' currencies; and (4) from its capital of $10 billion and its borrowing power, the World Bank could make loans for postwar reconstruction and for economic development.[2]

In the period of 1945–47 the European states ran very large balance-of-payments deficits, which the World Bank and IMF funds proved insufficient to meet. For the next decade the dollar became the standard world currency and the United States followed a set of policies that provided an outflow of dollars to furnish liquidity for international transactions. Through aid programs for

---

[2]A major source of information on monetary and financial relationships is Joan E. Spero, *The Politics of International Economic Relations*, 4th ed. (New York: St. Martin's Press, 1990).

European states and military expenditures, the United States intentionally ran balance-of-payments deficits to provide dollars for the international economy. By the late 1950s, United States gold reserves became depleted and world confidence in the dollar declined. In the next few years the United States modified its policies for the purpose of correcting the huge overseas accumulation of dollars, which then resulted in another shortage of international liquidity.

As the inadequacies of the Bretton Woods system bolstered by United States policies became evident, greater reliance was shifted to other monetary elite groups. International financial management was shared with the Bank of International Settlements (BIS), which met monthly in Basel, Switzerland, and represented the central banks; with the Group of Ten, which was composed of finance ministers of ten leading states; and with the working party of finance ministers of the Organization for Economic Cooperation and Development (OECD), with membership from all the developed market economy states. Beginning in 1986 the Group of Seven (the United States, Japan, the United Kingdom, Germany, France, Canada, and Italy) through a series of economic summits and regular consultation among finance officials became a principal force for fiscal policy. These groups took concerted measures to support currencies in temporary difficulty, to stabilize gold prices, and to lend additional funds to the IMF. International financial management became further dispersed by the rapid growth of multinational banks and international banking consortia, which loaned large sums to developing countries and provided the main channels for recycling the huge surpluses of the major oil-producing states in the 1970s.

The original Bretton Woods system eventually broke down and had to be modified. In the late 1960s the central banks proved incapable of controlling the large and volatile currency flows and resulting speculation. The fixed exchange rate system showed increasing signs of stress. In spite of United States pressure, European states refused to revalue their currencies. The crisis was brought to a head by President Nixon's sudden announcement on August 15, 1971, of a New Economic Policy. Without consulting European nations or Japan, he dropped the gold standard for the United States and announced a 10 percent surcharge on imports.

The Nixon bombshell was followed by a series of attempts at monetary reform. In the Smithsonian Agreement of December 1971 the price of gold was altered, the dollar was devalued by 10 percent, and more flexibility was introduced into exchange rates. From 1972 until 1974 a Committee of 20 on Reform of the International Monetary System was unable to find an acceptable comprehensive plan for reform. By 1973, fixed exchange rates gave way to floating rates. In this period, sharply rising oil prices compounded the problems of international liquidity. Previously, in 1969, the IMF had created Special Drawing Rights (SDRs), which were the world's first artificial international reserve units that exist only in accounting form, hence often referred to as "paper gold," and which were expected to promote trade and development by increasing the supply of international liquidity. In the Jamaica Agreement, which became effective in 1978, these SDRs, whose value is determined by a market basket of currencies, were increased in volume and were made the principal reserve asset of the system. The dollar, however, tends to retain its primary monetary role because of the size of the United States economy and financial markets. The IMF agreed to sell some of its gold reserves to promote economic development. Floating rates continue. The member states of the European Community (EC) have adopted a European Monetary System (EMS) with fixed exchange rates among the members. They have created a European Currency Unit (ECU) whose value is determined by a basket of EC currencies. Through increased credit arrangements to finance balance-of-payments shortages and through a policy of stabilizing EMS rates with the dollar, the European Community hopes to lessen liquidity problems.

National economic policies produce international monetary repercussions and, because of its preeminent position, United States policies produce the most drastic effects. The shift of domestic policies begun in 1981 under the Reagan administration emphasized a tight monetary policy, increased defense spending, supply-side economics, and reductions in taxes. These policies were unilateral without regard for their impact abroad. At succeeding economic summits there were strong protests concerning the effects of United States policies and United States refusal to intervene in foreign exchange markets. The United States economy was also affected by increasing international trade deficits.

A growing third-world (developing countries) debt problem threatened in the 1980s to produce an international crisis which, if ignored, could potentially lead to world financial panic and economic depression. Private banks had been major conduits of petrodollars invested in third-world countries. The threats of insolvency of both national treasuries and major private banks in the United States and elsewhere led to some modifications of United States monetary policy. The United States assumed leadership in seeking increased financial resources for the IMF, which in turn worked out agreements with such countries as Mexico, Brazil, and Argentina for new loans, rescheduling of debt payments, and austerity measures, to try to prevent insolvency and default on debts. IMF short-term loans were supplemented by new funds from private banks, regional banks, the World Bank, central banks, and national governments.

By 1992, third-world debts had grown to $1.7 trillion, and in many developing countries service charges on previously incurred debt exceeded new receipts of financial aid. Rates of economic growth in the 1980s shrank in much of the developing world to negligible proportions, raising demands for an increase in loans and grants and simultaneously making almost impossible the repayment of the principal and interest on past loans. Access to new loans from public and private sources and rescheduling of debt payments were accompanied by stringent conditions of austerity and reform measures imposed by the IMF and others. In some circles the idea that a portion of the debt might have to be canceled gained acceptance, and France announced the forgiveness of one-third of the debt owed it by sub-Saharan states. If the debt crisis cannot be solved by a reversal of declining rates of economic growth and prosperity in developing states, it will persist or worsen throughout the 1990s.

No permanent solution to the monetary and financial dilemma has been found. Crises regularly occur and no one is in charge. Monetary control is widely dispersed in a situation of complex interdependence. Preoccupation with internal economic problems encourages states to seek short-range national advantage, while an adequate global management arrangement eludes the world's monetary architects.

Another facet of economic interdependence involves the transfer of technical knowledge and skills from one country to another. This transfer occurs at all levels of scientific, technological, and managerial development. The creation of the Economic and Social Council and more than a dozen specialized agencies under the aegis of the United Nations serves mainly to provide technical assistance to developing countries for the primary goal of raising their standards of living. Technical assistance can be furnished by developed nations to developing ones, but sharing of skills and knowledge among developing societies is also a feature of a multilateral system of agencies and programs. The transfer of technology also involves private as well as public agencies. Grants from the Ford and the Rockefeller foundations supported the development of new strains of cereal grains capable of creating a "green revolution" in the developing areas. The multinational corporations serve as a vehicle for the transfer of often highly sophisticated technology throughout the world, although this channel has operated more among developed economies than from developed to developing systems.

Interdependence has manifested itself in the creation of regional economic communities (or common markets) and of regional development banks. The most fully developed common market is the European Community (EC), whose membership includes twelve European states, with a total population of 340 million people. (For a more detailed description and assessment of the EC and other regional agencies, consult Chapter 10.) In general, the tendency of regional economic agencies is to break down barriers to the free exchange of goods and persons and to develop common economic policies among the members.

The rapid growth of multinational corporations has contributed to international economic interdependence in respects other than the transfer of technology across national boundaries. A large number of these corporate giants have scattered their production units in a score or more of countries, thus decentralizing this aspect of their operations. Production resulting from foreign investment is nearly double the value of world exports. The flow of investment, goods, technology, profits, and managerial controls are all stimulated by the complex operations of the multinational corporations.

As the world uses its reserves of minerals and fuels, the number of countries that are nearly self-sufficient in resources diminishes and interdependence increases. The use of petroleum as an economic and political weapon in the Middle East crisis of 1973–74 is dramatic proof of the dependence of Europe, Japan, and the United States upon this resource. Lester R. Brown points out that of thirteen basic industrial raw materials, the United States by the end of the century will have to import more than half its supply of twelve of these and will be nearly self-sufficient in phosphate only.[3] Many of the major reserves of minerals and fuels are in developing countries. If these countries tightly control their resources and demand higher prices as the industrialized economies seek increasing supplies from abroad, their financial problems for supporting the process of development could be partially solved. However, resources are so unevenly distributed throughout the world that this brighter outlook for the future would bypass a substantial number of poor but aspiring states.

Thus, in numerous ways, world economic interdependence exists and grows at an accelerating rate. Future effects may be manifested through both conflict and cooperation. If common goals and solutions are sought, greater prosperity may result for an increasing percentage of humanity.

THE UNITED NATIONS NETWORK OF AGENCIES

The United Nations structure for planning, coordinating, administering, and implementing its economic and social program is very complex, diversified, and decentralized. As stated in the introduction to this chapter, the bulk of the United Nations' resources, both physical and human, is devoted to economic and social activities.

At the apex of the structure are the General Assembly and the Economic and Social Council. The General Assembly, among its manifold responsibilities, provides general direction and supervision for economic and social activities. The Economic and Social Council (ECOSOC) concentrates solely on this work but has difficulty in coordinating the diverse strands of the program. These difficulties are related to the nature of the Economic and Social Council, the scope of the economic and social program, the number and diversity of agencies involved, and ECOSOC's lack of authority over the specialized agencies.

---

[3]Lester R. Brown, *The Interdependence of Nations,* Headline Series, no. 212 (New York: Foreign Policy Association, October 1972), pp. 43–44.

The broad features of the General Assembly and the Economic and Social Council were described in Chapter 4. For a review of the structure and functions of these organs, the reader may wish to refer to that portion of the text.

The complexity of the Economic and Social Council's responsibility for coordination can best be realized by examining, in general outline, the range and types of economic and social agencies in the United Nations system and their relationships to ECOSOC. The United Nations organization chart on page 63 is useful in visualizing the range of agencies and this interrelationship. The general categories include functional commissions, regional commissions, specialized agencies, standing committees, ad hoc committees, and a variety of other bodies and agencies. The relationships of nongovernmental organizations with the United Nations are also carried on primarily through ECOSOC.

ECOSOC operates with the assistance of nine functional commissions. Three have existed continuously since 1946. These are the Statistical Commission, the Commission on Human Rights, and the Commission on Narcotic Drugs. The Commission on the Status of Women was originally a subcommission of the Commission on Human Rights but was raised to full commission status in 1947. The Population Commission was created at the third session of ECOSOC. The Commission for Social Development was established at the initial meeting of ECOSOC as the Social Commission, but the title was changed in 1966 to reflect the main focus in its program. In the 1990s three new commissions were established which represent changing emphases in ECOSOC's agenda. These are the Commission on Science and Technology for Development, the Commission on Crime Prevention and Criminal Justice, and the Commission on Sustainable Development. The Commission on Human Rights has a Sub-Commission on Prevention of Discrimination and Protection of Minorities. The Commission on Narcotic Drugs has a Sub-Commission on Illicit Drug Traffic and Related Matters in the Near and Middle East. Several functional commissions and subcommissions have been established, served their purposes, and been discontinued.

The regional commissions represent a moderately effective method of decentralizing some of the planning and programs of ECOSOC. Each regional commission focuses on the problems salient to its geographic area. Five such commissions have been established: the Economic Commission for Europe (ECE), established in 1947; the Economic and Social Commission for Asia and the Pacific (ESCAP), originally established in 1947 as the Economic Commission for Asia and the Far East (ECAFE); the Economic Commission for Latin America and the Caribbean (ECLAC), originally established in 1948 as the Economic Commission for Latin America (ECLA); the Economic Commission for Africa (ECA), established in 1958; and the Economic and Social Commission for Western Asia (ESCWA), originally established in 1974 as the Economic Commission for Western Asia (ECWA). In general, membership in each commission is open to all states in the region, except that Israel has been refused membership in the ESCWA and South Africa has been excluded from participation in the ECA. In the ECA, states such as France, Spain, and the United Kingdom, with special interests in the area, are accorded associate membership, but in the other regional commissions, outside states with special interests enjoy full membership. The United States is a member of the ECE, the ESCAP, and the ECLAC; the United Kingdom, France, and the Netherlands belong to the ECLAC and the ESCAP; Russia has membership in the ESCAP; and Canada is a member of the ECLAC. Since 1960 the emphasis on regional decentralization has been increased. Each commission determines its own pattern of organization, and all have established a number of committees to facilitate their efforts in special areas of concern. The commissions hold annual meetings and submit annual reports to ECOSOC.

To provide further assistance for its varied responsibilities, ECOSOC has maintained a flexible and frequently changing group of standing, sessional, and ad hoc committees. In 1993 there were standing committees or commissions on (1) Program and Coordination, (2) Transnational Corporations, (3) Human Settlements, (4) Nongovernmental Organizations, and (5) Negotiations with Intergovernmental Agencies.

A number of other bodies exist in the economic and social fields that are not as directly subject to ECOSOC direction or control but that are related to ECOSOC interests and for which ECOSOC provides limited coordinating services. These agencies include (1) the United Nations Development Program (UNDP), (2) the United Nations Children's Fund (UNICEF), (3) the United Nations High Commissioner for Refugees (UNHCR), (4) the United Nations Conference on Trade and Development (UNCTAD), (5) the United Nations Fund for Population Activities (UNFPA), (6) the United Nations Institute for Training and Research (UNITAR), (7) the International Narcotics Control Board, (8) the World Food Program, (9) the United Nations Environment Program (UNEP), (10) the United Nations University (UNU), (11) the World Food Council, (12) the Office of the United Nations Disaster Relief Coordinator (UNDRO), and (13) International Research and Training Institute for the Advancement of Women (INSTRAW). Two other coordinating committees, composed of top-level Secretariat personnel from the cooperating agencies, are the Administrative Committee on Coordination and the Inter-Agency Consultative Board of the United Nations Development Program.

One step further removed from ECOSOC control, but subject to limited ECOSOC coordination, are the specialized agencies of the United Nations family of associated organizations. In fact, the specialized agencies are so highly independent of any effective control by United Nations organs that they are generally described as autonomous organizations. Each has its own headquarters, staff, and budget. Each was created in the same manner as the United Nations, by an international conference that produced a constitution or charter for the proposed organization in the form of a multilateral treaty.

Membership is independent of United Nations membership but is predominantly identical since all agencies aim at near universality, and most agencies have substantially more than 150 members. This overlapping membership probably provides as effective coordination as is provided under the limited controls of ECOSOC, since governments that belong to many agencies will be interested in balancing their interests, controlling relative budgets, and preventing duplication of services or conflict of goals.

After each intergovernmental agency is established by international treaty independently of the United Nations, it becomes a specialized agency of the United Nations by an agreement between the agency and the United Nations. This agreement is negotiated between the agency and the Economic and Social Council subject to approval by the General Assembly. The purpose of the agreement is to spell out the relationships and avenues of coordination between the agency and the United Nations. Although the agreements are not uniform, a pattern of standard provisions exists. The agreements normally include provisions for (1) reciprocal representation at meetings, (2) reciprocal proposal of agenda items, (3) exchange of documents and information, (4) submission of reports by the specialized agencies to the United Nations, (5) prompt consideration by the agencies of recommendations by appropriate United Nations organs, (6) consultation to achieve uniform personnel standards and practices, and (7) submission of agency budgets to the United Nations for review and recommendation. Additional consultation occurs at the administrative level. Coordination also is effected by numerous bodies involved in the planning, financing, and administration of the United Nations Development Program since the United Nations and most of the specialized agencies participate in this cooperative program.

Seventeen specialized agencies operate today in affiliation with the United Nations. One temporary agency, the International Refugee Organization (IRO), existed from 1948 to 1952 and was dissolved. The present agencies follow:

International Labor Organization (ILO)
Food and Agriculture Organization (FAO)
United Nations Educational, Scientific and Cultural Organization (UNESCO)
World Health Organization (WHO)
International Bank for Reconstruction and Development (World Bank or IBRD)
International Finance Corporation (IFC)
International Development Association (IDA)
Multilateral Investment Guarantee Agency (MIGA)
International Monetary Fund (Fund or IMF)
International Civil Aviation Organization (ICAO)
Universal Postal Union (UPU)
International Telecommunication Union (ITU)
World Meteorological Organization (WMO)

International Maritime Organization (IMO)
World Intellectual Property Organization (WIPO)
International Fund for Agricultural Development (IFAD)
United Nations Industrial Development Organization (UNIDO)

Two other agencies that resemble specialized agencies in some, but not all, characteristics are the International Atomic Energy Agency (IAEA), discussed in Chapter 9, and the General Agreement on Tariffs and Trade (GATT), a substitute for an aborted attempt to establish an International Trade Organization.

The Economic and Social Council is also authorized to enter into a consultative relationship with private organizations, generally referred to as nongovernmental organizations (NGOs). These arrangements may be made with international organizations or, with the consent of the government involved, with national organizations. The United States delegation had established a precedent of extensive consultation with national interest groups at the San Francisco conference. Since both public and private resources are limited and interests overlap, reciprocal benefits often result from this type of coordination and cooperation. The specialized agencies also carry on extensive consultative and cooperative efforts with nongovernmental organizations.

Three categories of NGOs have been established. Category I consists of 38 organizations having the broadest range of interests in the work of ECOSOC. Category II, with approximately 350 organizations on the approved list, includes agencies interested in a specific aspect of the work. Other NGOs, numbering nearly 500 and having significant contributions to make to the program of ECOSOC or other United Nations agencies, are placed on what is known as the roster. Organizations on the roster may send observers to meetings and may submit recommendations only on invitation. Category I and II organizations have the additional privilege of submitting written statements to ECOSOC and making oral statements to the Council's commissions. Category I representatives may also submit agenda items to ECOSOC and may be heard on such items if they are approved for inclusion on the agenda.

Some appreciation of the importance and complexity of ECOSOC's responsibility for coordination should be apparent from the listing in the preceding paragraphs of the scores of agencies and subagencies with which ECOSOC has relationships. Since many of these bodies are immune from its direct control, ECOSOC must depend primarily on consultation, persuasion, and the perceived advantages of cooperation. A fifty-four-member body with limited powers is not an ideal agency of coordination. If coordination is reasonably achieved, the results are due in part to the other avenues of cooperation and control—budgetary allocations, subsidiary agencies performing coordinating functions, administrative cooperation, and coordination through member governments.

Recent ECOSOC organizational reforms were prompted by studies and resolutions approved by the General Assembly in 1991. Since 1992 ECOSOC has held one substantive session per year instead of two. The previous time-consuming general debate is eliminated, and a high-level ministerial segment is instituted into the procedures. The two new commissions related to development issues also held initial sessions in 1993. Whether these reforms bring desired effectiveness to ECOSOC remains to be proven.

PROBLEMS OF ECONOMIC DEVELOPMENT

Countries are generally classified as either developing or developed, depending primarily upon their degree of industrialization. Sometimes the categories used are preindustrial, industrial, and postindustrial. In another method of classification, the categories may be underdeveloped, semideveloped, and developed. If only two classes are used to separate developing from developed countries, most experts agree that two-thirds to three-fourths of the world's population live in developing nations.

A profile of the developing states reveals certain common characteristics. These nations, with few exceptions, recently emerged from colonial rule into political independence. Generally, a large proportion of the population suffers from severe deprivation in terms of fulfilling human potential and achieving well-being. The broad forms of deprivation are manifested as widespread poverty, illiteracy, hunger, and disease. The more specific characteristics are numerous. Most of the population is engaged in subsistence agriculture using primitive agricultural methods involving hand labor and few tools. Foreign trade is small, and exports are often primarily made up of a single commodity that is either an agricultural product or an unrefined mineral. Dependence on a single source for foreign exchange creates fluctuations in trade revenues as world markets and prices vary from year to year. The absence of manufacturing results in an economy based on primary or unfinished commodities. Manufactured goods are scarce and, for the most part, must be imported.

In the developing countries, individual income levels are extremely low. The average per capita income generally falls into the $100 to $3,500 range. Furthermore, a small, wealthy, and powerful elite usually controls a large share of the economic resources, while the bulk of the population lives at an even lower level of misery than is indicated by the average income level. A low level of per capita energy consumption is a result of the lack of capital and industrialization. The absence of basic skills and technical knowledge, in combination with other factors, leads to low per capita productivity.

In these countries, health and educational facilities are inadequate. Endemic and epidemic diseases are prevalent. Birth and death rates are usually high. Infant mortality often exceeds 10 percent of all live births, and life expectancy averages eleven years less than in the developed countries. In spite of the high death rates, the population growth rate usually varies between 1.5 percent and 4 percent and is almost universally higher than in developed nations. Lack of access to knowledge about and devices for birth control, religious and social barriers to contraception, and economic pressures and desires for large families contribute to population increase at an exponential rate.

In the developing countries, malnutrition and hunger contribute to a lack of human vigor. Not only is the daily calorie intake much below the standard of the developed countries, but protein deficiency also threatens to undermine physical and mental health. Basic health care is inadequate with a lack of access to doctors, hospitals, and public or private health facilities.

In most of these countries, in spite of efforts to educate the people, a lack of funds, facilities, and trained personnel results in slow progress toward the elimination of illiteracy. Training above the level of basic literacy is even more scarce so that the development of skills and the provision of secondary and higher education are available to an extremely limited portion of the population. Without skills and knowledge among the general citizenry and without a broad corps of adequately trained political leaders and administrators and industrial managers, progress in economic development is slow and difficult and is marked by undue reliance upon nonindigenous personnel in managerial positions, especially in the economic structure.

Because both capital and managerial skills are in scarce supply, the developing countries must continue, for a time, to rely on foreign industry to develop their resources. This dependence results in feelings of inferiority, frustration, and resentment. Foreign personnel receive the highest salaries, profits drain out of the country (often to the former colonial power), and the indigenous people exercise little control over the use or exploitation of their own resources.

Low levels of income and the difficulty of saving result in a vicious circle of poverty. In an illiterate, poverty-stricken population, incentives for saving and investment are almost totally absent. The struggle for survival and the crises of today dominate the economic lives of most individuals.

The needs of the developing states seem infinite. As soon as a determination is made to seek the alleviation of some of the basic problems of development, new sources of frustration arise. Attacks are made upon the causes of endemic and epidemic diseases and the death rate falls, while birth rates continue at a high level. The result is a population explosion, which wipes out a substantial portion of the economic gains in other areas. Population control seems to be almost a necessity in order to generate a rapid rate of economic growth.

Health and educational facilities must be provided for people of all ages. Short courses must be instituted to train midwives and persons with minimal qualifications in a variety of health areas until the cost of more adequate facilities and more highly trained medical personnel can be afforded. Schools must be provided for wiping out illiteracy among the young, but adult education and training are equally important if rapid economic development is to take place. Farmers must learn improved methods of production and the use of simple tools. Enough skills must be taught to facilitate diversification in the economy and a gradual shift toward industrialization and commerce.

The accumulation of capital and its investment in growth-generating economic enterprises is imperative for economic development. Forced savings through taxation may be required even though individual resources are barely enough for subsistence. Foreign loans, grants, and investment may also be necessary, but internal capital must be generated if the economy is ever to reach a takeoff point in energizing the development process. A balance must be attained between incentives for foreign capital to invest and maximization of benefits to the host state. Reinvestment within the country rather than a drain of large profits abroad, adequate compensation to indigenous employees and their progressive access to more highly skilled positions, and the host country's control over the use and conservation of native resources, as well as an adequate return through taxes or joint ownership of business enterprises, are all required if national developmental progress is to be maximized. Bilateral or multilateral grants must be utilized so as to assure their application to growth-generating enterprises or to building the infrastructure essential to an industrializing economy. Loans may be useful unless resources for repayment are accumulated too slowly, in which case loans may become a burden when payment of principal and interest comes due. Such a process might lead to a point where more capital resources are being drained from the country than are coming in.

The complexity of the problems faced within a developing economy and the application of efficient methods for maximum progress in escaping from the human deprivations that are involved necessitate a major role for government in the process. Planning and effective administration of programs are essential for rapid growth. National unity and pride must be instilled among the people. Noneconomic incentives and promises of future well-being must be substituted for immediate material benefits in order to foster rapid economic growth. In addition to the functions of planning and whipping up support, government must also provide, either directly or indirectly, for the necessary organizational structure to carry out the economic measures within the plan.

There is no guarantee of rapid progress in economic development. The obstacles are self-evident in the previous analysis of needs and conditions. Governments often lack capable personnel for wise planning and able administration of programs. The needs are so vast that choosing priorities is difficult and marshaling sufficient resources seems impossible. Apathy on the part of the masses and complacency among the elites must be overcome. Drastic social change must occur if development is to succeed. Entrenched interests must be uprooted and prevailing attitudes must undergo radical change. Internal graft, corruption, and inefficiency may frustrate attempts at progress. Those who control private and public foreign resources may balk at involvement except on their own terms. The delicate balancing of forces for development may be beyond the capabilities of the talent available for the task. It is small wonder that much pessimism prevails over the prospects for a substantially more satisfying existence for two-thirds of humanity.

DEVELOPMENT PROGRAMS OF THE UNITED NATIONS

Plans for postwar relief and rehabilitation in Europe and Asia antedate the establishment of the United Nations. In 1943 and 1944, at the height of war activity, the Allied powers established the United Nations Relief and Rehabilitation Administration (UNRRA), held a conference that took the initial steps for the creation of the Food and Agriculture Organization, and, at the Bretton Woods Conference, drew up the plans for the International Bank for Reconstruction and Development and the International Monetary Fund. The UNRRA was to be a temporary organization, whereas the others were to become specialized agencies affiliated with the emergent United Nations.

The UNRRA served a vital purpose in helping the war-devastated countries of Europe and of Asia to meet their immediate relief needs of food, clothing, and medical supplies at the survival level and to rebuild their economic and social fabric. During 1945–46 the UNRRA furnished more than $3.5 billion worth of supplies for relief and rehabilitation. Recipient governments were required to sell most of the supplies and use the funds for UNRRA-approved rehabilitation projects. UNRRA delivered the goods to the countries, but internal distribution was the responsibility of the receiving state, although the UNRRA maintained surveillance over the process. The entire approach was one of self-help and internal responsibility with external assistance. The United States was the chief donor, supplying more than two-thirds of the goods and money. The program was abruptly terminated in Europe at the end of 1946 and in Asia three months later.

As the organs of the newly created United Nations began operation in 1946, great stress was laid on helping disadvantaged nations and groups. UNICEF was set up to care for the special needs of children. Initially, it took over some of the assets of the UNRRA. A temporary specialized agency, the International Refugee Organization (IRO), was created to cope with the residual problems of wartime refugees unresolved by the UNRRA. The Economic and Social Council, from its inception and by intent, focused heavily upon the problems of development and relief. By 1948 it had created regional commissions in Europe, Asia, and Latin America and functional commissions in such fields as population, transport and communications, commodity trade, social questions, and human rights. Also by 1948, in addition to the IRO, nine of the permanent specialized agencies had become affiliated with the United Nations, and administrative coordinating machinery had been established to assure some degree of cooperation with the United Nations. A large share of the activities of these specialized agencies (particularly the Bank, the FAO, UNESCO, and the WHO) was directed toward technical or other aid to developing countries. Altogether, the United Nations and its affiliated agencies were much involved in aid to developing nations prior to the launching of the Expanded Program of Technical Assistance in 1950.

The Expanded Program of Technical Assistance (EPTA) represented a United Nations endeavor to supplement the scattered technical assistance efforts previously carried out by ECOSOC and the specialized agencies as parts of their regular programs. It involved cooperation and coordination among the United Nations bodies and most of the specialized agencies to weigh requests from states for technical aid and to allocate the tasks and resources for implementing approved projects to the most appropriate agencies. To achieve this coordination and distribution of resources and responsibilities, new coordinating machinery had to be created within the United Nations structure both at the intergovernmental and the administrative levels. The Technical Assistance Administration was established within the United Nations Secretariat, the Technical Assistance Board was charged with administrative coordination among all the agencies involved, and the Technical Assistance Committee of governmental representatives was created to assist ECOSOC in the coordination and supervision of the EPTA.

The initial impetus for the EPTA was President Truman's inaugural address of January 1949, in which he proposed a sharing of technical knowledge and capital resources with the developing nations. The United States Congress later made available resources for international development on both a multilateral and a bilateral basis with the lion's share of resources being allocated to the bilateral channels. The General Assembly, in November 1949, approved the plans for the EPTA as the multilateral program to capitalize on the United States initiative. All members of the United Nations were invited to pledge, on a voluntary basis, support to a special and supplementary budget for the support of the EPTA.

The amounts expended for the EPTA projects were always modest. A target of $20 million was set and fully subscribed to for the first eighteen-month period—from July 1, 1950, to December 31, 1951—with the United States pledging 60 percent of the total. In subsequent years the total pledges increased at a more rapid rate than the number of subscribing states. For example, in 1953, 69 states pledged $22.4 million, while by 1963 the number of states involved was 105 and the subscriptions for the first time exceeded $50 million. By 1961 the United States had reduced the proportion of its pledge to 40 percent of the total.

The EPTA concentrated its efforts on the furnishing of individual experts for work in the developing countries and the provision of fellowships for the training abroad of personnel from these nations. By 1965 approximately 9,000 experts had been sent overseas to provide technical advice in developing countries for periods averaging two to three years. More than three times that number of persons had been granted fellowships for relatively short periods of training abroad. At very low cost, thousands of persons were exchanged for the purpose of raising the levels of knowledge and skills in the developing states and territories. But the effect of such diverse and fragmented efforts was similar to hunting big game with a shotgun loaded with birdshot. The impact made some impression but never reached the vital centers of the problems on which a concentrated and massive effort must be directed if the hunt is to really succeed. The lack of effective coordination and the scattering of resources among small-scale projects—problems that have plagued most United Nations economic and social programs—were prime characteristics of the EPTA. Manifold demands from every corner of the globe led to the apportionment of limited resources among as many countries and projects as possible. Something for everyone was the general rule.

To provide a new dimension for development aid, a United Nations Special Fund began operations in 1959. The developing states had been pressing for several years for a Special United Nations Fund for Economic Development (SUNFED), the establishment of which was resisted by the affluent states, and the Special Fund represented a substitute more acceptable to the big donors of funds. The Special Fund concentrated on preinvestment projects, each of which averaged considerably larger than EPTA projects and which involved modest expenditures for equipment as well as for the provision of experts to carry out surveys of resources, research, training, and pilot projects. A small number of fellowships were also provided by the fund. The main purpose of the fund was to provide the groundwork and then to stimulate investment from internal and external private and public sources to carry out development projects and programs in needy countries.

Over the years, the Special Fund was somewhat more generously supported than the EPTA. After a modest start in 1959, the amounts pledged for the Special Fund gradually outstripped those for the EPTA by ever-widening margins until, in 1965, the total subscribed for the fund was $91.6 million compared with the EPTA's $54 million.

In 1965 the General Assembly decided to merge the Special Fund and the EPTA into a single entity, the United Nations Development Program (UNDP). Better coordination and integration of projects within an overall development plan for each country was thus achieved. The merger was resisted by several of the specialized agencies because of their significant roles in the EPTA. Although the merger resulted in a single administrative structure for coordinating requests for aid, in fact the two components of the program remained identifiable. The level of aid continued to increase yearly under the combined program from $145.6 million in 1965 to nearly $673 million by 1981, but thereafter began to decline as several governments reduced their voluntary contributions. By 1989 the UNDP budget reached $1 billion, but this represented a loss over 1981 in terms of inflation. UNDP's 1993 budget grew to $1.5 billion.

One way to achieve a degree of coordination of development plans and programs at the individual country level is to utilize the United Nations resident representative. While the practice of appointing resident representatives developed gradually, the utility of a single United Nations appointee with a broad perspective over all the multilateral projects within each country is obvious.[4] Because of the breadth of planning and the diversity of international agencies operating in each country, a person who can assist the government in formulating and presenting proposals and who can try to bring some degree of order out of the diverse and scattered field activities of technical advisers from several United Nations agencies can provide a most valuable service.

Ideally, the resident representative should be looked upon by the host government and by the operating agencies as the intermediary channel between the government and the representatives of the agencies. He or she should also serve as chief United Nations spokesperson and diplomat within the country. His or her office should advise the host government in formulating proposals and presenting them to the United Nations for approval. The representative should coordinate and evaluate programs to assure the contribution of each project to the broad goals of development. The representative and his or her staff can furnish administrative support that can assist both the host government and the agencies and their technicians.

The resident representative never totally achieves these ideals and usually falls far short of achieving perfection. Among the many factors that operate to frustrate the achievement of the ideal are (1) a lack of any grant of broad authority to the resident representative, (2) interagency jealousy and competition, (3) inadequate staff to provide all the services that an overall coordinator and administrator should furnish, (4) lack of adequate planning or cooperation by the host government, and (5) human inadequacies both of spirit and of ability. Without the instruments of authority the resident representative must depend upon persuasion, service, personality, effectiveness, and the building of confidence to enhance his or her importance in the development process. But for all the representative's skill, he or she is dealing, in most developing countries, with only the United Nations component of development aid, which is far outstripped by more massive bilateral inputs of human and material resources. Until a greater proportion of aid becomes

[4]Gerard J. Mangone, "Field Administration: The United Nations Resident Representative," in *UN Administration of Economic and Social Programs*, ed. Gerard J. Mangone (New York: Columbia University Press, 1966).

multilateral and until the resident representative is granted greater authority, the potential of his or her role in the development process will not be realized. In the meantime, fragmentation leads to inefficiency in planning and in attaining the goals of economic development.

As the number of new, developing nations entering the United Nations multiplied after 1955, demands for increased attention to their economic and social needs were manifested in new United Nations programs. Through their growing majority in the General Assembly, they were able to create new agencies and to focus world attention upon development issues by declaring the 1960s as the United Nations Development Decade and the 1970s, 1980s, and 1990s as the Second, Third, and Fourth Development Decades. Although the developing nations could not force the affluent states to furnish massive resources for development, they could exert constant pressure for increased attention to their problems and squeeze from the rich reluctant and limited concessions for their benefit.

Planning for the First Development Decade was inadequate and poorly executed. Most of the measures recommended were in the form of exhortations in vague terms, lacking any specificity of procedures, priorities, or commitments by which the aims could be achieved.

Planning for the Second and Third Development Decades was done more carefully and the measures for implementation of goals were spelled out more specifically, but the means to secure the cooperation of those states possessing a majority of the world's resources were still lacking.[5] One of the targets set for each of the decades was an annual resource transfer of 1 percent of the GNP of the developed to the developing states, with 0.7 percent to come from the public sector. The actual record shows that the official development assistance from the eighteen affluent donor nations that are members of the Development Assistance Committee (DAC) of the Organization for Economic Cooperation and Development (OECD) fell from a level of 0.51 percent of GNP in 1960 to a low of 0.33 percent in 1976, and it has been below 0.40 percent since that date. Although Sweden, the Netherlands, Norway, and Denmark have, in recent years, exceeded the target of 0.70, the United States, the most affluent member and, therefore, the largest donor, has varied in recent years in its level of assistance, giving between 0.15 percent and 0.24 percent of its GNP. The United States percentage since 1970 is approximately one-third of its rate in the 1960s. Since most aid is bilateral and since donor states select their recipients, the benefits for the developing world are very uneven. Since 1975 the OPEC nations

[5]"Towards Accelerated Development: Proposals for the Second United Nations Development Decade," Report of the Committee for Development Planning (New York: United Nations, 1970); *International Development Strategy: Action Programme of the General Assembly for the Second United Nations Development Decade* (New York: United Nations, 1970); *International Development Strategy for the Third United Nations Development Decade* (New York: United Nations, 1981).

have been more generous in official development assistance as a percentage of their GNP than the DAC donors, but a majority of this aid went to Arab states.

The 1970s was a difficult decade for both developing and developed states. Prices of energy and food increased sharply and global economic conditions were in a state of disequilibrium. Midway through the decade, the developing states increased their pressure for a New International Economic Order and were vigorously opposed in many of their demands by the developed states. Partially because of these problems, the goals of the International Development Strategy for the Second Development Decade fell much shorter of fulfillment than had the goals of the 1960s.

In spite of previous difficulties and North-South tensions, the General Assembly by consensus adopted on December 5, 1980, the International Development Strategy for the Third United Nations Development Decade, setting generally higher targets for development than had been targeted in the previous decade. Among these, in addition to the goal for the transfer of resources discussed above, were (1) an average annual rate of economic growth of the developing countries of 7 percent, (2) an annual rate of increase of exports of goods and services in developing countries of 7.5 percent and a rate of increase for imports of at least 8 percent, (3) an increase of gross domestic savings for investment in domestic production in those countries to 24 percent of GNP by 1990, (4) an average annual increase of at least 4 percent in agricultural production in developing nations, and (5) expansion of manufacturing output in developing countries at an average annual rate of 9 percent in order to meet the goal that by the year 2000 the developing countries will have a 25-percent share of world production.

Planning for the Second and Third Development Decades was spearheaded by an expert Committee for Development Planning under the aegis of the Economic and Social Council. Review and appraisal of progress toward achieving the proposed goals were the responsibility of the Secretary-General, the Committee for Development Planning, the Economic and Social Council, and the General Assembly. In 1982 the General Assembly established a special Committee on the Review and Appraisal of the Implementation of the International Development Strategy for the Third United Nations Development Decade. Membership was open to all member states. This committee was scheduled to make its first report to the General Assembly in 1984 but could not reach a consensus until a year later. In that report it noted that world economic conditions in 1981–84 had contributed to a failure to meet any of the targets set in the Strategy during those years. In most developing countries, per capita gross domestic product had been negative. In its 1984 report the expert Committee for Development Planning called the outlook for the remainder of the 1980s "thoroughly unacceptable" and labeled the decrease in real terms of concessional assistance flows to the poorest countries as "little short of an international scandal."

Preliminary planning for the Fourth Development Decade (1991–2000) was begun in 1988 with major inputs by the Secretary-General, the Economic and Social Council, the Coalition of Developing States (group of 77), and the General Assembly. At the urging of the developing states, the International Development Strategy was launched at a special session of the General Assembly held April 23–May 1, 1990. The strategy calls for (1) an increase role for the United Nations and the specialized agencies in global development; (2) developing countries to control inflation, promote savings and foreign and domestic investment, and modernize their economies; (3) all countries to reduce military expenditures and redirect resources to meeting social needs; (4) developed countries to increase aid flows including furnishing adequate resources to multilateral financial institutions; and (5) greater emphasis upon the needs of the least-developed countries (LDCs).

The impatience of the developing states with the limited support available through international channels for the attainment of their economic goals led to the formation of the United Nations Conference on Trade and Development (UNCTAD), which was approved by ECOSOC and the General Assembly in 1962 and which met in Geneva for a twelve-week period in 1964. Although 120 countries participated in the Conference, it was dominated by a solid coalition of developing states, "the 77," which, through unity of action, pressed their demands into resolutions adopted by the conference. This group of seventy-seven developing states also signed, at the conclusion of the conference, a joint declaration in which they made clear their intention to treat the conference only as a first step in achieving a greater degree of justice for the impoverished nations. Since 1964 the term *group of 77* continues as a label, although its membership has expanded to well over 125 states. The guiding spirit of the conference was Raul Prebisch, an economist and former executive secretary of the Economic Commission for Latin America, who was selected to become the Secretary-General of the newly created quasi-autonomous secretariat of the permanent organization of UNCTAD. By creating their own agency, the developing states hoped to establish an effective channel for promoting their interests and for partially bypassing the labyrinth of United Nations agencies surrounding ECOSOC.

The principal demands of the developing states as reflected in the conference resolutions included the following: (1) the stabilization of prices for primary commodities by international arrangements, (2) the lowering of tariffs and other trade barriers on primary commodities, (3) the safeguarding of the developing countries against adverse effects of the disposal of surplus agricultural products, (4) the provision of long-term loans at low rates of interest repayable in local currencies or in goods, (5) loans and grants free of obligations to buy from the granting state or to utilize their shipping and insurance facilities, (6) a net flow of aid from developed states equal to 1 percent of their national income, (7) the encouragement of regional arrangements and integration among developing states as a means of promoting trade and economic growth, and (8) special attention to the needs of the least developed among the developing states.

Altogether twenty-seven principles were approved by the conference. In voting on these principles, a dichotomy became evident between the positions of the developing and the developed states. The solid bloc of developing states produced affirmative votes varying in number between 78 and 116 on each principle. Only five principles were unanimously approved. In general the developed states either opposed or abstained on a majority of issues, with the United States opposing more principles than any other state. This dichotomy is significant in forecasting the difficulties during the following years in eliciting cooperation from the affluent states to speed the development process.

Another set of decisions of the conference led to the creation of permanent machinery for the UNCTAD. Conferences were to be held presumably at three-year intervals although, in reality, UNCTAD 2 met in New Delhi in 1968, UNCTAD 3 in Santiago in 1972, UNCTAD 4 in Nairobi in 1976, UNCTAD 5 in Manila in 1979, UNCTAD 6 in Belgrade in 1983, UNCTAD 7 in Geneva in 1987, and UNCTAD 8 in Cartagena, Columbia, in 1992. Between sessions of the conference a Trade and Development Board open to participation by all UNCTAD members meets annually. To assist the board, several specialized and expert committees have been set up. Within the United Nations Secretariat a special UNCTAD unit with its own budgetary allocations has been established in Geneva. The UNCTAD is placed directly under the aegis of the General Assembly, thus bypassing much of the jurisdiction of ECOSOC as a coordinating agency. The developing countries sought and obtained their own agency but, in the process, further complicated the already complex United Nations machinery for dealing with development problems in a somewhat orderly and unified manner.

The hopes of the developing states for special concessions through the UNCTAD to meet their perceived needs have been largely frustrated. The fact that the resolutions of each successive conference generally reiterate the same demands as those of UNCTAD 1, and that speeches of third-world representatives often concentrate upon blaming the developed states for the lack of substantial progress toward the goals of the development process, dramatizes the disappointment of the developing nations in obtaining outside aid and support. However, at UNCTAD 8 in 1992 the final document called for reconciliation in a "new partnership for development." This declaration included an emphasis on sustainable development, on the need for sound management of resources, and on more openness in decision-making processes. Thus, the developing countries shifted a larger share of the responsibility for economic progress to their own policies.

A major thrust of the developing countries' efforts to enlarge their share of global income has been their demand for remunerative and stable prices for primary commodities, the source of most of their foreign exchange. This theme of equitable and reliable prices for their exports has run through every UNCTAD session since 1964. In 1975, in preparation for the fourth general conference, the UNCTAD secretariat drew up plans for an integrated program for commodities. In 1977 the Paris Conference on International Economic Cooperation endorsed in principle a Common Fund to finance buffer stocks for stabilizing commodity prices. In 1980 a modest Common Fund was approved of $750 million (one-eighth of the original amount proposed). Due to lack of enthusiasm by donor states, the Integrated Program for Commodities, covering eighteen products, was never implemented, but international commodity agreements were negotiated for a few individual products.

Because the programs of the UNDP and of the specialized agencies for the promotion of the industrialization process in the developing countries were meager and dispersed, these countries pushed through the creation of another organization, similar in structure to the UNCTAD, in the industrialization field. The United Nations Industrial Development Organization (UNIDO) was approved by the General Assembly in 1965 and began operations in 1967. Its purpose is to accelerate the industrialization process in the developing countries, with particular emphasis upon the manufacturing sector. UNIDO's activities include research, training, pilot projects, surveys, technical aid, seminars, data gathering and analysis, and exchange of information. For the first eighteen years its funds came from the United Nations regular budget, from voluntary contributions, and from allocations from the UNDP. UNIDO was originally established with its own "permanent and full time" secretariat in Vienna as a part of the United Nations Secretariat. As with the UNCTAD, a high degree of autonomy, rather than direction from ECOSOC or the UNDP, was assured. The critics of UNIDO charged that the establishment of another "autonomous" agency added to the chaos of decentralized and overlapping jurisdiction within the economic and social areas of the United Nations and that the activities of UNIDO spread too few resources over too many projects with too little impact on the industrialization process. Those that have directly benefitted, especially from the field activities of UNIDO, are likely to challenge such an assessment. In 1975 a proposal was made to convert UNIDO to the status of a specialized agency and, after years of planning and negotiation, the process was completed in 1985.

Small programs, but significant for development, include Operational Executive and Administrative Personnel Services (OPEX) and United Nations Volunteers. OPEX recruits top-level administrators for government posts in developing countries. While performing their duties, these administrators train indigenous counterparts who will replace them. The United Nations Volunteers program, begun in 1972, recruits young people who use their skills in aiding development programs.

The tendency for several years in the United Nations was to answer each new problem related to development by creating a new agency or program and to escape control by the affluent states by giving autonomy to the new agencies and by structuring them so that in their governing bodies the developing states had substantial majorities. Additional funds for development were also sought each year by the United Nations. The result was the constant expenditure of larger sums on a wider variety of projects through dispersed agencies with inadequate means for central planning and coordination.

In the 1970s the UNDP attempted some reform in its procedures to correct these faults. For most of the developing countries, five-year integrated country programs for development have been worked out and priorities have been established within the longer-range plans. This country-oriented approach has been accompanied by administrative restructuring to place more responsibility at the country level. Such attempts to strengthen the leading component of the United Nations development activities are indeed welcome and overdue.

A new dimension was added to the United Nations development efforts in 1974 when the "group of 77" called for a special session of the General Assembly devoted to problems of raw materials and development. From this session came the demand for a New International Economic Order (NIEO) "based on equity, sovereign equality, interdependence, common interest, and cooperation among all states." The less-developed nations dominated this and subsequent regular and special General Assembly sessions and pressed hard for a radical reordering of the global economic system to correct what they saw as inequalities and injustices that constantly worked to the disadvantage of the poor countries. The general goals were to accelerate economic and social development and to eliminate the widening gap between rich and poor states.

The aspirations and demands of the developing states for the NIEO incorporated the previous programs of the UNCTAD conferences and expanded them. A Charter of Economic Rights and Duties of States adopted by the 1974 General Assembly asserted that every state has the right to exercise exclusive sovereignty over its wealth and natural resources; to regulate foreign investments; and to nationalize, expropriate, or transfer the ownership of foreign property with controversies to be settled under domestic law. This provision was vigorously opposed by the representatives of the developed market economies. Other planks in the NIEO platform stressed the formation of producers' associations and other forms of cooperation among developing countries, the establishment of linkage between the prices of exports of developing countries and the prices of their imports from developed countries, the formulation of commodity agreements, international monetary reforms, and the restructuring of the economic and social sectors of the United Nations system.

By the 1990s the demands for a New International Economic Order had become virtually a dead issue. Means were sought to reconcile North-South differences and to assess more realistically policies and measures by which the developing states could achieve economic progress. Mutual interdependence may, in the long run and with a willingness to cooperate, work to the advantage of a number of nations, both North and South, but no early closing of the North-South gap is probable.

FINANCING ECONOMIC DEVELOPMENT

Some of the programs discussed in the previous section entail substantial financial contributions to the purpose of development. For example, an annual budget of approximately $1 billion for UNDP is a considerable sum to be devoted exclusively to aiding the development process. Sums from the regular budgets of the United Nations and many of the specialized agencies are also earmarked for development-supporting activities. Yet these programs provide none of the basic financial resources in the form of loans or grants that the developing countries need in order to stimulate economic growth. The UNDP, the specialized agencies, and similar organizations merely furnish preinvestment needs through information, surveys, demonstrations, expert advice, and training, which are preliminary to investment in agriculture, industry, roads, dams, schools, and the host of other elements for building a more prosperous economy.

Capital is a primary component for development although, obviously, it can be wasted or misdirected. Infusions of capital, without careful planning and the provision for supplementary conditions for growth, will not necessarily lead to development. Graft, mismanagement, maldistribution of resources, poor planning, or the lack of a balanced social and economic structure of society can lead to failure even though investment capital is available.

The major sources of capital are of four types. In the long run, domestic savings for investment are the most important source if an economy is to be healthy and is to attain an internal dynamic that all developed industrial economies possess. Until this "takeoff" point is reached, outside loans or grants are essential. These monies come through bilateral, multilateral, or private channels. Bilateral sources provide the bulk of these funds, but multilateral sources are the main focus of this study of international organization.

The initial financial agencies of the United Nations family of specialized agencies were the International Bank for Reconstruction and Development (IBRD or World Bank or Bank) and the International Monetary Fund (IMF or Fund). These are conservative agencies, run by hardheaded bankers and financial experts and controlled by the affluent states through weighted voting based on quotas of capital. Both organizations came into being in December 1945, when twenty-eight countries ratified the Bretton Woods Agreements of the previous year.

The World Bank is the largest multilateral source of funds for development. By 1992 the aggregate of all loans made by the Bank passed the $200 billion mark for more than 3,000 projects. Since 1946 the volume of lending has increased steadily, and in recent years has exceeded $20 billion annually.

Loans are made by the Bank under rules requiring (1) that all loans must be made to governments or must be guaranteed by governments; (2) that the rate of interest be consistent with the prevalent rate in the world's money markets; (3) that repayment be made within ten to thirty-five years; (4) that loans be made only in circumstances in which other sources are not readily available; (5) that investigations be made of the probability of repayment, considering both the soundness of the project and the financial responsibility of the government; and (6) that sufficient surveillance be maintained by the Bank over the carrying out of the project to assure that it is relatively well executed and managed. The application of some of these rules has carried the Bank into areas not strictly typical of lending institutions. The Bank is heavily involved in technical assistance activities and has made both comprehensive and limited preinvestment surveys, some of which are financed by the Bank and others by the UNDP. The Bank also provides training for about 2,400 high-level administrative personnel each year through its Economic Development Institute.

To meet a wider variety of financial needs, two affiliates of the Bank have been created since 1956. The first was the International Finance Corporation (IFC), which is intended to stimulate private investment in the developing countries. The IFC acts as a catalyst by furnishing limited investment capital for growth enterprises, in partnership with private investors. To increase its impact as a catalyst for private investment, the IFC frequently sells some of its holdings and uses the returns for investment in new enterprises. Although its resources, as compared with the capital and borrowing power of the Bank, are relatively modest, the IFC by 1991 had cumulatively committed more than $13.5 billion in investments. Since it never underwrites more than 25 percent of each enterprise, and since its projects are carefully selected as making a significant contribution to the overall growth of a country's economy, its impact has been of significant proportions.

In 1960 a second affiliate of the Bank, the International Development Association (IDA), was created to provide for the special financial needs of the least-developed countries. Many of the poorest countries cannot bear the debt burden of conventional middle-term loans on the Bank's regular terms. Repayments of principal and interest provide such a drain on their limited resources as to cancel out much of the input of new capital. Countries are eligible for IDA loans if their per capita GNP is less than $940, but most of IDA lending goes to countries with a per capita GNP of less than $765. Between 1960 and 1993 the IDA committed nearly $70 billion for projects in the world's fifty-five least-developed countries. Loans are made for fifty years (reduced in 1987 to forty years) at no interest, with only an administrative service charge of three-fourths of 1 percent. No repayment is required during the first ten years, 10 percent of the loan is due during the second ten years, and the remaining 90 percent is payable during the last thirty years. Unlike the Bank and the IFC, whose funds are regenerated through repayments of principal and interest on loans made out of their original capital and borrowing power, the IDA must ask for new voluntary contributions on a continuing basis until such time as substantial repayments of previous loans are due. The response to the IDA requests for increasing amounts of funds to meet the expanding needs of the least-developed states is dependent upon the generosity and sense of obligation of the donor states. As the United States reduced its contributions from 41.89 percent of the total for the first three-year replenishment of the fund to 27.00 percent for the sixth replenishment for 1980–83, other countries, most notably Japan, Germany, Saudi Arabia, and Kuwait, filled the gap by substantial increases in their percentage and dollar contributions. When the seventh replenishment for 1985–87 was negotiated, the United States refused to contribute more than 25 percent of a $9 billion total, although most donor states, because of deteriorating economic conditions in many of the poorest countries, favored a $12 billion target. However, for the ninth replenishment for 1991–93, the total agreed upon was $15.5 billion.

Although the Bank and the IDA are legally separate entities, the same administrative structure directs both. After 1968, under Robert McNamara's presidency of the Bank group of agencies, the philosophy common to the two organizations focused upon maximum contributions to the development process, particularly of the poorest states. The IDA's emphasis upon long-range needs became the dominant element in the new philosophy. Attention to the effects of projects on the total economy was intensified. Earlier concentration upon dams, industrial facilities, and transportation was shifted to include substantial support for agriculture, education, water supply, and population planning. Another concern in the new philosophy was the impact of projects upon the lowest 40 percent of the people within each national society, those who suffer the most from dire poverty. This policy was known as a "basic needs" approach. The benefits of past programs that often accrued only to privileged segments of the society were not considered satisfactory. A trickle-down philosophy of economic benefits was rejected.[6] Later administrations have abandoned the "basic needs" philosophy while retaining an emphasis on agricultural development and the special needs of the least-developed countries.

Because of the special problems of developing countries that could not qualify for IDA loans, the World Bank in 1975 opened a "Third Window" for loans at intermediate rates of interest of approximately half those of its regular loans. The Third Window loans are subsidized by a special fund raised by

---

[6]For a more complete discussion of this philosophy, see Paul Dickson, "A Fresh Look at the World Bank," *Vista* (now *Inter Dependent*) (June 1973), 25, 27, 30, 48–49.

voluntary governmental contributions. The money available is relatively small in comparison with IDA or standard Bank lending.

The International Monetary Fund (IMF) provides temporary funds to aid governments in correcting balance-of-payments deficits. The IMF has established an Expanded Fund Facility and a Compensatory Finance Facility, both of which aid developing nations by making funds available for longer than normal periods and which compensate for sharp drops in commodity prices. As balance-of-payments difficulties grew after the energy crises and general global economic problems of the 1970s, the IMF's role as crisis manager increased. However, developing states were reluctant to seek aid from the IMF because of the stringency of the austerity measures demanded as a condition of receiving IMF loans. Under continued pressure some relaxation of the rules has resulted. As part of their NIEO demands, the developing states also pressed unsuccessfully (except for some OPEC states) for greater voting power and, thus, policy control in the IMF. The IMF also offers technical assistance in areas such as tax and budgeting policies, statistics, and central banking. In addition, it operates a training institute for the instruction of fiscal and budgetary officers from developing nations.

One slow-starting venture of the United Nations in the financial area was the establishment in 1966, at the insistence of the developing countries, of the United Nations Capital Development Fund to aid community development projects in the least developed countries. Because of their opposition to its creation, most wealthy states have refused to contribute to the fund, and the resources made available were until recently extremely limited and are mainly in nonconvertible currencies. In the first ten years only $18 million had been pledged, but somewhat larger donations were made subsequently. Because of the disappointing response, the modest resources are administered through UNDP rather than by special machinery provided for in the 1966 General Assembly resolution.

Other important sources of multilateral financing for development include the regional and subregional banks, which were discussed more fully in Chapter 10. Both the Inter-American Development Bank and the Asian Development Bank have been major sources of development financing for hundreds of projects within their respective regions.

In recent years the former figure of only approximately 10 percent of all foreign aid being transferred through multilateral channels has increased to about 25 percent, and private banks have become a relatively larger source of capital for development. In spite of the creation of many new agencies for meeting development needs, the demands of the poor countries for capital and other valuable resources seem unlikely to be met through either multilateral or bilateral channels. Continued sacrifice, misery, and reliance on a high degree of self-help seem likely predictions for the poverty-stricken two-thirds of the world in the light of current attitudes in the affluent segments of the globe.

RICH NATIONS AND POOR

Wealth is very unevenly distributed both within national societies and among them. Economic equality may be relatively more closely approximated in a few countries, but inequality is the rule. The Scandinavian countries and China are examples, at different levels of living standards, of countries that may have eliminated the greatest extremes of affluence and deprivation among their citizens.

One general difference, however, between the industrialized and the preindustrial societies is in the size of the segment of the population that lives in conditions of dire poverty. In a preindustrial society a small elite, perhaps 5 to 10 percent, generally lives either comfortably or extravagantly by twentieth-century standards. The remainder of the population lives far below the standard of minimum essentials that befit human dignity. In the industrial societies, on the other hand, the amenities of social and economic well-being are widely distributed among a large segment of the population.

In the world as a whole the discrepancies between rich and poor are similar to the contrasts of wealth and poverty within a preindustrial nation. If all states are divided into two classes, developed and developing, the developed one-fourth of the world population enjoys the benefits of possessing about 80 percent of the gross world product, while in the developing world three times as many people must survive on the remaining 20 percent of the world's wealth.

Relatively, the gap between rich and poor increases even though small absolute gains are registered by the developing states. A far greater rate of population growth in the poor than in the rich countries exacerbates the problem. Even if a developing country attains a 5.0 percent economic growth rate, if it also has a rate of population increase of 1.9 percent, which is the average for the developing world, it will require twenty-two years to double its per capita GNP. In that same period the discrepancy between the rich and poor nations in dollar amounts will have widened even if the rate of economic growth of the rich states is below 3.1 percent per capita.

In relative terms the developing states lose ground in other ways, too. Between 1950 and 1970 their share of the value of world trade fell from 30 percent to less than 18 percent. By 1989 it had risen to slightly over 20 percent. In light of those statistics, their pressures for higher prices and favored treatment for their exports, as expressed through the UNCTAD, seem reasonable. For countries that are already poor, their debt and debt service burdens become increasingly oppressive. The debts of the developing states doubled between 1965 and 1973 and doubled again in the next five years. By 1992 their total indebtedness was more than $1.7 trillion. For several countries, repayments of principal and interest threaten to exceed receipts of new loans and grants. Again, it should cause no surprise if these countries request easier terms on their much needed capital in the form of long-term, low-interest loans or outright grants.

The economic situation in Africa graphically depicts the desperate conditions of human existence in a region that includes some of the world's poorest countries. Stagnant economic conditions and negative or minimal economic growth rates in a large number of African states prompted the convening of a one-week special session of the UN General Assembly in May 1986. A five-year United Nations Programme of Action for African Economic Recovery and Development was unanimously adopted at the session. The Programme called upon African states to launch new, more intensive programs for economic development and committed the affluent states of the world to provide $9 billion annually to supplement the $16.5 billion per year raised domestically by the African beneficiaries. The Programme focused on five main areas: (1) agricultural development, (2) sectors in support of agriculture, (3) drought and desertification, (4) human resources, and (5) socioeconomic reforms. The final assessment of the Programme termed the 1980s as the "lost decade for Africa," with per capita income falling to less than 70 percent of 1980 levels. In 1991 the General Assembly adopted a United Nations New Agenda for the Development of Africa in the 1990s. Secretary-General Boutros-Ghali assigned high priority to the program and chaired a newly formed Panel of High-Level Personalities to advise on African economic policies. In October 1993 an International Conference on African Development was held in Tokyo with representatives of African states, donor nations, and international organizations to review ongoing efforts and to seek better solutions for the problems of a continent in distress.

In the international arena the frustrations of the developing nations have been expressed through the General Assembly, the Economic and Social Council, the UNCTAD, and conferences of nonaligned states. The poor countries have passed resolutions setting goals for development, creating new machinery, and demanding a New International Economic Order; but the problems multiply and intensify, and the impact for dramatic alteration of their plight is slight. Part of the reason for slow progress is that the goals of the developing states are not shared or given high priority by the wealthy nations. Interdependence has not yet produced a common strategy for mutual prosperity. Robert Gregg has referred to a United Nations "performance gap" between less-developed countries' "numerical control of the UN decision-making process and Western state control of the goods and services toward which those UN decisions are directed."[7] This performance gap in the United Nations is indicative of the dissatisfaction of the developing states with their economic status and progress.

---

[7]Robert W. Gregg, "UN Economic, Social, and Technical Activities," in *The United Nations: Past, Present, and Future,* ed. James Barros (New York: Free Press, 1972), p. 235.

A PERSPECTIVE ON THE FUTURE

Several appraisals of development aid were published during 1969–70. One is a report prepared at the instigation of the World Bank by the Commission on International Development under the chairmanship of Lester Pearson. Another is the Capacity Study of the United Nations Development System under the leadership of Sir Robert Jackson. A third is the report of the UN Committee for Development Planning, which helped set the goals for the Second Development Decade. And a fourth is a study made by a Presidential Task Force appointed by President Nixon and chaired by Rudolph Peterson on the subject of international development, with emphasis upon the United States' role.

As the decade of the 1980s opened, three new landmark studies were published. One of these, whose major goals were outlined in a previous section of this chapter, was the International Development Strategy for the Third United Nations Development Decade, prepared with the cooperation of the Committee for Development Planning and adopted by the General Assembly in December 1980. A second widely circulated publication, often referred to as the Brandt Report, appeared under the title *North-South: A Programme for Survival,* prepared by an independent commission of eminent persons under the chairmanship of Willy Brandt. The third was The Global 2000 Report to the President prepared by the United States Council on Environmental Quality and the Department of State in response to a 1977 directive of President Carter.[8]

All these reports stress the importance of development, point to mutual advantages of rich and poor in promoting it, and set higher goals for the future than the accomplishments of the past in order to accelerate the process. All urge that a larger percentage of aid be distributed through multilateral channels. All agree that the official component of development aid is a more reliable and important stimulus to rapid progress than heavy reliance on private investment for the transfer of resources.

The Jackson report, in particular, stresses the weaknesses of the United Nations system for accomplishing orderly development. Projects have been too small, numerous, and dispersed without sufficient relationship to broad plans either on a global or national basis. Agencies have proliferated and become uncoordinated instead of playing a role in an integrated whole. Clear priorities have not been set and adhered to. The whole process is chaotic and lacks direction.

---

[8] *International Development Strategy for the Third United Nations Development Decade* (New York: United Nations, 1981); *North-South: A Programme for Survival* (London: Pan Books, Ltd., 1980); *The Global 2000 Report to the President; Entering the Twenty-First Century,* 3 vols. (Washington, D.C.: U.S. Government Printing Office, 1980).

Some progress is being made in correcting these deficiencies. Evaluation and review were incorporated into the process for the Second, Third, and Fourth Development Decades. Countries have been pressured to cooperate with the United Nations in drawing up integrated development plans and in establishing priorities. A new high-ranking Secretariat post of Director-General for Development and International Economic Cooperation was created in 1978. The World Bank and IDA have stressed education, agriculture, and population planning as basic to healthy development, and the needs of the least-developed states have received special attention.

Past and present trends, nevertheless, suggest a gloomy prognosis for the next decade. The goals of the first three Development Decades fell substantially short of achievement. The transfer of resources to the developing states is far below the targets set by the reports. Cleavages between North and South as expressed through UNCTAD and the General Assembly seem to grow wider. The entrenched privileged segments of the global society seem inadequately concerned with the conditions faced by the disadvantaged two-thirds of humanity.

Immediate and longer-range prospects for the poor nations to improve their lot rapidly seem bleak. World food supply reserves are inadequate for emergencies, and the prospects for mass starvation in many areas are imminent. Population increases are canceling out many of the potential economic gains of the poor countries. The oil shortage of 1973–74 hit the poorest countries particularly hard because of increased prices, which they could not afford, for energy and fertilizer. Projections of the growth of population and GNP for the year 2000 show that more and more people will be living in the underdeveloped world, while the prosperity gap between rich and poor, in relative terms, will widen.

But do both the record and the prospects for economic development warrant the pessimistic outlook suggested above? Many scholars do not accept the idea that development has failed or that further progress is unlikely. For example, John P. Lewis, in collaboration with eight other development theorists and policy advisers, in a book published under the auspices of the Overseas Development Council, comes to quite positive conclusions concerning past and future roles of development programs.[9] In his introductory overview, Lewis reviews the many sources of pessimism including such recent factors as economic crises in sub-Saharan Africa, the debt problems of developing countries, world economic malaise in the early 1980s, and the international impacts of the Reagan administration philosophy and policies. He then points out with regard to the past record of development that

---

[9]John P. Lewis and Valeriana Kallab, eds., *Development Strategies Reconsidered* (New Brunswick, NJ: Transaction Books, 1986).

In the aggregate, Third World growth has been a rousing success, compared with the earlier productive performances of the same areas and with both the earlier and concurrent growth records of the OECD countries.[10]

With regard to the future, Lewis concludes that we have learned much since the late 1940s, that budgetary constraints on aid donors are determined more by priorities than by affordability, and that "[d]evelopment promotion is pulsating with potential right now."[11]

[10]Ibid., pp. 23–24.
[11]Ibid., pp. 31–32.

13

MANAGING GLOBAL RESOURCES

Prior to 1950, most of the current concerns with regard to global resources had barely surfaced in the agendas of either international organizations or national governments. The industrial revolution had fostered attitudes of human domination over most aspects of nature. Problems of food supply, population control, energy shortages, pollution, and jurisdiction over the oceans did not receive wide attention. Today the management of global resources is a primary area of study and debate in academic, governmental, and intergovernmental arenas. In this chapter some of these concerns will be treated from an international perspective.

FOOD AND AGRICULTURE

From 1960 to 1984, there was great optimism concerning the ability to produce enough food to feed the world's growing population. During that period, world grain production was increased to 2.6 times its 1950 rate, representing a per capita increase of 40 percent. At the same time, however, the countries of Asia, Africa, and Latin America moved from general food self-sufficiency to reliance on huge imports of food grain, especially from North America, which became the world's breadbasket.[1]

---

[1]Lester R. Brown and Alan Durning, eds., *State of the World 1989* (New York: W. W. Norton & Company, 1989), passim.

Since 1984 the former optimism has somewhat faded for a number of reasons. In 1987 and 1988, drought conditions in India, the United States, Canada, and China, and again in 1991 in the United States and the former Soviet Union, contributed to an absolute decrease in grain production, which amounted to an even greater decrease in per capita terms and resulted in a drawing down of world grain reserves. In addition to climatic effects, several other adverse factors are at work. These include substantial erosion of topsoil; falling water tables affecting irrigation and other demands on water supply; a worldwide decrease in the amount of cropland; limits on the use of chemical fertilizers, including cost of fertilizers versus grain prices, limits in marginal productivity from the use of fertilizer, and environmental effects of extensive fertilizer application; and the continuation of maldistribution of food supplies resulting from poverty, the burden of debt, population growth, and the loss of food self-sufficiency in developing countries.

Although nutritional deficiencies exist among the poor living in prosperous countries, the severe problems of world hunger and malnutrition affect mainly the underdeveloped states. The problems include low per capita calorie consumption, protein deficiency, vitamin and mineral deficiencies, high cost of scarce commodities, and inequalities in food consumption among various segments of the population. Hunger and malnutrition lead to health problems and lack of energy. With a rapid growth in population, the poor countries must increase food supplies rapidly and distribute them more equitably if they hope to mobilize the necessary human resources for economic development. The number of people suffering from chronic hunger was estimated at nearly 800 million in 1990. This is a modest decrease since 1970, but possibly another 1 billion persons' diets lack some of the nutrients essential to healthy physical and mental development. The quantity and quality of food that reaches the poorest segments of society will not permit children to attain normal body weight and intelligence.

The recent severe economic conditions in Africa (which is predominantly agricultural) and a United Nations Programme of Action for African Economic Recovery and Development (which failed primarily for lack of promised external financial support) were outlined in the previous chapter. Starvation in sub-Saharan Africa has been a recurrent problem and is linked both to low rates of economic growth and to civil strife in several countries. Massive bilateral, multilateral, and private emergency food aid efforts have been mobilized to prevent mass starvation in such countries as Ethiopia, Angola, Mozambique, Lesotho, Somalia, and the Sudan. In 1983 the United Nations General Assembly, in response to the desperate conditions of millions of Africans, authorized the creation of the United Nations Office for Emergency Operations in Africa (OEOA). This Office was administered by Bradford Morse, who also continued as long-time Director of the United Nations Development Program. The OEOA operated from January 1984 through

October 1986. It was terminated in part because of some improvement in the food situation in several African countries and in part because of the general financial crisis in the United Nations, which forced curtailment of services and personnel. Emergency programs, however, do not address the basic problems of food supply and distribution in the continent with the highest rate of population growth.

A current emphasis in the fight against hunger is to help the small farmer in the developing countries to stay on his land and to improve his welfare and buying power. As a part of their "basic needs" philosophy, the World Bank and its affiliates have stressed programs that directly assist poor farmers and their families. Frances Moore Lappé and Joseph Collins in their investigations of the hunger problem have concluded that the answers lie neither in production of more food nor in better distribution, and that such developments as the "green revolution," which involves the use of new high-yielding varieties of wheat, maize, and rice, have contributed simultaneously to more food production and more hunger. They argue that modernization of agriculture in the developing countries has made a business of farming that is profitable only on a larger scale and thus squeezes out the small farmer, who becomes landless and unemployed. The displaced farmers are eliminated from both the production and consumption processes. Increased food supplies are diverted-from basic human consumption to livestock feed, breweries, or sweeteners for soft drinks. To resolve the problem, the small farmers in developing countries need to regain control of the production process in order to feed themselves.[2]

The key international agency concerned with food production and distribution and with nutrition is the Food and Agriculture Organization (FAO) established in 1945 as a specialized agency of the United Nations. The headquarters are in Rome with regional offices throughout the world.

For an organization with an annual regular budget of approximately $215 million to attack the problems of world food supply and nutrition would appear to be an exercise in futility. However, several factors add to the effectiveness of the FAO's efforts. The FAO administers additional funds from several sources, including the United Nations Development program (UNDP), UNICEF, national governments, and nongovernmental organizations. Each regional commission of the Economic and Social Council has an agriculture division jointly staffed by the FAO and the commission. With the International Atomic Energy Agency (IAEA), the FAO has set up a joint Division of Atomic Energy in Agriculture at IAEA headquarters in Vienna. The FAO collaborates with other specialized agencies, notably the ILO, UNESCO, and WHO. The

[2]Frances Moore Lappé and Joseph Collins, "When More Food Means More Hunger," *War on Hunger*, 10, no. 11 (November 1976), publication of U.S. Agency for International Development, 1–3, 14–15.

World Bank has subsidized surveys of national needs, including agricultural requirements, in many underdeveloped countries, and the financial agencies of the United Nations have furnished loans and grants for agricultural projects promoted through FAO efforts.

Like most of the other specialized agencies of the United Nations, the FAO engages in relatively low cost activities. It does not undertake large-scale operations or furnish extensive funds for implementing its recommendations. Its major programs involve research, fact-finding, publication, technical assistance, and the promotion of conferences and seminars. The FAO's main role is to furnish information, stimulation, and technical knowledge. If the implementation of proposed programs is costly, the financial resources must come either from within the state where a given program is conducted or from bilateral or multilateral grants or loans.

A brief review of some of the FAO's principal projects will serve to demonstrate the breadth of its activities. In 1960 the FAO inaugurated a Freedom from Hunger Campaign based on private citizen support and programs with FAO advice and stimulation. Projects inspired by the campaign range from land use and irrigation to cooperatives and nutrition education. A perennial activity of the FAO is a survey of the world food and agriculture situation and the publication of regular reports showing the status and trends of food supply and agricultural production. For several years the FAO worked on an Indicative World Plan for Agricultural Development setting forth detailed objectives for food production and supplies for the years 1975 and 1985. Regular surveys are also published covering the state of the world's forests and fisheries. Studies have been made of fishing boats and fishing equipment and methods, and research and technical assistance have been furnished to promote "fish farming" in ponds and flooded rice paddies as a means of increasing the protein intake in underdeveloped countries. As a joint enterprise with WHO, the FAO has developed under the *Codex Alimentarius* a set of international quality standards for food products. The FAO also works closely with UNICEF and WHO in improving child nutrition, especially in the production of powdered milk and inexpensive high-protein foods.

Within the broad area of agriculture, the FAO is concerned with such diverse matters as soils, irrigation, the development of new varieties of seeds, the use of farm machinery and fertilizers, and the elimination and control of livestock diseases. One important service of the FAO is the furnishing of fellowships for training personnel in new skills in all the areas of the FAO program. Regional seminars and short courses also contribute to the policy of training for greater self-help in the developing countries, a policy that, it is hoped, will make the maximum contribution to the development process.

In 1961 the General Assembly authorized a three-year World Food Program to begin in January 1963, with a proposed budget of $100 million in commodities, cash, and services pledged by governments. In 1965 the program was made permanent, and new pledging targets were set. By 1993 the annual budget reached $1.7 billion. The program is run as a joint project of the United Nations and the FAO with an Inter-Governmental Committee for policy direction and a special secretariat for program administration. The purposes of the World Food Program are to relieve emergency food needs and to implement the food portion of economic and social development projects. A unique feature is the use of food as a partial substitute for cash wages for persons engaged in development work. Although its emergency relief is important, the program makes little impact on the total food needs of the developing countries. At least 80 percent of food aid moves through bilateral channels.

At the suggestion of the Economic and Social Council, the United Nations General Assembly in 1973 authorized the convening of a World Food Conference. Preparatory work was split among ECOSOC, a preparatory committee established by ECOSOC, the Economic Commission of ECOSOC, United Nations Secretariat personnel under the direction of the Secretary-General of the conference, and the Food and Agriculture Organization. The World Food Conference met in Rome, November 5–16, 1974.

The conference produced a Universal Declaration on the Eradication of Hunger and Malnutrition and a set of twenty other recommendations. Among the principles that made up the Universal Declaration were the following: (1) freedom from hunger and malnutrition is a basic human right; (2) it is a fundamental responsibility of governments to cooperate for higher food production and more equitable and efficient distribution; (3) governments should initiate immediately an attack on chronic malnutrition among lower income groups; (4) each state has a responsibility to remove obstacles and to provide incentives for increasing food production through agrarian, tax, credit, and investment policy reform; (5) developed states should provide increased and sustained technical, material, and financial assistance on favorable terms to developing states; and (6) barriers to food trade should be reduced or eliminated, and special nonreciprocal trade concessions should be made to developing states.

The World Food Conference recommended that the FAO set up a Global Information and Early Warning System on Food and Agriculture. Governments were urged to establish national grain reserves as part of a world food security system. The level of continued food aid was set at 10 million tons of grain annually, and states were urged to channel a greater proportion through the World Food Program.

One significant proposal of the conference was a recommendation that the General Assembly establish a World Food Council at the ministerial level to coordinate all United Nations agencies' food policies and programs, periodically to review problems and policies, and to recommend remedial action. The Assembly promptly established a thirty-six nation council and directed other United Nations agencies to cooperate with it and report to it.

Another organization created as a result of the Rome conference is the International Fund for Agricultural Development (IFAD), which began in late 1977 as a new member of the family of United Nations specialized agencies. The provisions for this agency are unique in that OPEC countries agreed to furnish at least 40 percent of the $1 billion of initial funds, and the Governing Board has a balanced representation of donor-developed countries, donor-developing countries (OPEC), and recipient-developing countries. The purpose of the Fund is to provide grants and loans on concessional terms to help increase food production in developing countries. In the first replenishment of the Fund for 1981–83 the OPEC countries again pledged $450 million of the total of $1.1 billion. However, partially because of decreased oil revenues and world economic distress, the level of funding for the IFAD replenishments through 1990 fell to slightly more than half of the first replenishment, with OPEC countries funding only a 22 percent share. By 1993 IFAD was able to channel $12.8 billion to 337 projects in ninety-six countries by procuring supplemental funds amounting to 2½ times its own resources from cofinancing agencies and recipient governments. Most of these projects were concentrated in sixty-eight low-income food-deficit countries. In 1986 an additional Special Programme for Sub-Saharan African Countries with separate funding was approved by IFAD. The International Monetary Fund since 1981 has also made loans to selected countries through its special Food Financing Facility.

Since 1985 the FAO has suffered from a severe cleavage within its membership over the policies and administrative practices of its Director-General, Edouard Saouma. The criticism was spearheaded by the United States, which was joined by the United Kingdom, Australia, Japan, Canada, Denmark, and other major donors. The dissatisfaction focused in part on the means Saouma used to enhance his personal power and in part on the need to study and implement FAO administrative and program reforms. Saouma was accused of using irregular methods of assuring his reelection in 1987 to a third six-year term. After 1986 the United States withheld funds from FAO, forcing substantial reductions in its projects.

Questions about the global food supply persist. Occasional threats of mass starvation have been met by emergency measures by donor nations and international coordinating agencies. In 1992 the necessity to link food production to environmental concerns, and the role of women in agriculture, were stressed in the United Nations Conference on the Environment and Development (UNCED). IFAD has heavily stressed these same principles in its current programs. Sustainable agricultural development and the improvement of rural women's welfare hold some promise for a reversal of earlier negative trends in the agricultural situation in a large number of poverty-stricken countries.

POPULATION

The problems of feeding a growing world population were noted in the previous section of this chapter. World population in 1987 passed the 5 billion figure and in 1993 5.5 billion. In the preindustrial states the rate of population increase is triple the rate in the industrialized countries. By the year 2000 these trends will result in a concentration of 80 percent of the world's population in those countries now classified as developing. This rapid population growth complicates the planning process for economic development and cancels out a substantial portion of the economic growth in developing countries.

Other demographic factors exacerbate the problems of the underdeveloped states. In a pattern of rapid population increase, the high proportion of nonproductive persons is a significant factor. Children and old persons constitute nearly as high a percentage of the population as those of working age. Finding work for a rapidly growing rural population and for those who migrate to the cities is another formidable problem. The increased demand for health, education, and housing facilities represents a basic drain on the limited available resources for capital investment required for development.

Population control is a sensitive area and limits the possibilities for effective international action. In the first place, several declarations have been adopted since 1966 by the General Assembly and by special conferences that state the principle that the determination of the number and spacing of children is a basic human right of parents. Such declarations have both positive and negative connotations with regard to the relations between individuals and governments. On the one hand, the state may not interfere with the parents' desire to have many or few children. On the other hand, the state may make family planning possible through laws and through informational and educational programs of birth control, abortion, and sterilization. Religious principles may affect individual opinions toward family planning. Other factors include attitudes engendered by high infant mortality and information about and access to effective, inexpensive, and convenient birth-control devices and methods. Government and private programs to promote family planning may have contributed to recent substantial reductions in the rate of annual population growth in the Republic of Korea, China, Sri Lanka, and Cuba, but the rate of increase in India has dropped only moderately in spite of government efforts favoring population control.

Prior to the 1960s the United Nations limited its population program mainly to fact-finding and statistical analysis. These activities were stimulated by the Economic and Social Council and by its subsidiary Population Commission, which meets at two-year intervals. The work of research and publication was carried on by the Population Division and the Statistical Office of the

Secretariat. The program emphasized training in census techniques, the gathering of worldwide census data, and the publication of census data and population trends. The *Demographic Yearbook* published by the Statistical Office is one of the major outputs of these efforts.

As governments became more concerned with population problems, as the relationship between population growth and economic development was more widely appreciated, and as the role of government in population control became more acceptable, the emphasis in the United Nations population program broadened to include technical assistance and a concern for human welfare. Since 1962 the General Assembly has shown an interest in and concern for the reciprocal aspects of population change and economic development. Regional conferences, seminars, and committees of experts have met frequently to discuss general and specific aspects of population matters. An Asian Population Conference met in 1963 and an African Population Conference in 1971. Committees of experts were convened in 1964 and 1966 to plan programs of research and action in the population field. In 1969 the United Nations Development Program financed a Seminar on Population Data and Development Planning in Kiev, Ukrainian SSR. In 1967 the Secretary-General established a United Nations Fund for Population Activities (UNFPA) with a budget target of $5.5 million for five years. From this modest proposal a substantial fund has developed with actual annual pledges of more than $89 million in 1976 and $147 million in 1982. However, in 1985 the largest previous donor, the United States, withheld $10 million from its appropriated contribution as a result of pressure from antiabortion and right-to-life groups and the following year refused to contribute any money to UNFPA. The excuse used was Chinese population policies, although no UNFPA funds were allocated for Chinese abortion or sterilization activities. The United States gives $250 million in annual bilateral support for foreign population programs, but little of this goes to Africa, where the problems are most acute. Through increased contributions by Finland, the Netherlands, Norway, Italy, Australia, Switzerland, Denmark, Germany, Canada, and the United Kingdom, and a first-time donation in 1988 by the Soviet Union, UNFPA's resources rose in 1992 to a new high of $225 million, despite the absence of United States support. In 1993 President Clinton announced his intention to restore United States UNFPA financing, but technical problems in Congress delayed immediate action.

In 1969 an inaugural five-week training course for United Nations Population Program officers was financed by the fund to prepare specialists for field assignments. The nine specialists in the initial course were given eighteen-month field assignments to aid forty-two governments in identifying population problems and in preparing action projects to be submitted for financing by the United Nations or other sources. The United Nations has gradually become involved in population activities that, thirty years earlier, would have been considered inappropriate for such an organization.

World Population Conferences have been held approximately every ten years since 1954. The first two in Rome and Belgrade were mainly technical in nature, but the 1974 conference in Bucharest adopted a World Population Plan of Action setting targets for reducing world fertility, with special emphasis upon developing countries. This Plan of Action set a goal for the reduction of the average birth rate in developing countries from thirty-eight per thousand to thirty per thousand by 1985. Another aim was an average global life expectancy of sixty-two years in 1985 and seventy-four years by 2000. Reduction of infant mortality was accorded high priority. Respect for human life, the quality of human existence, the essentiality of the family, the right of couples to decide the numbers and spacing of their children and to have the information and means to do so, and respect for the sovereignty of states in formulating population policies and programs were declared to be basic principles of the World Population Plan.

Governments were urged to enhance the status of women, to assure them equal responsibility for family planning, and to integrate them fully into the educational, social, economic, and political life of their societies, as possible incentives to smaller family size.

The bulk of the responsibilities for implementing the plan were envisaged as resting on national governments. Each government was urged to formulate its own population policy and program consistent with its overall goals and with the principles and aims of the World Plan of Action. Governments were encouraged to utilize the support and facilities of intergovernmental and nongovernmental organizations. United Nations agencies were to undertake the tasks of monitoring, reviewing, and appraising the results of the plan and were to conduct an intensive review and appraisal every five years for possible modification of goals and recommendations.

In 1984 another major World Population Conference was convened in Mexico City to review the World Population Plan of Action adopted at the 1974 Conference and to formulate recommendations for further implementation of population goals. In contrast to the earlier Conference the impetus for the Mexico City Conference came mainly from the developing countries; and the final document, consisting of eighty-eight recommendations, was entitled the Mexico City Declaration on Population and Development. In spite of heated debate on several issues, all but one of the recommendations were adopted by consensus of the 149 governments. However, a policy paper issued by the United States, declaring that free-market forces were the best guarantee of population equilibrium, raised widespread criticism. The Mexico City Declaration stressed both economic development and increased efforts at family planning as dual approaches to population control. The role of women in family planning also received much emphasis at Mexico City. Elaborate plans for the decennial International Conference on Population and Development (ICPD) in Cairo in September 1994 were begun in 1992. The new emphasis is on the relationship between population and sustainable development, reflecting a major theme of the 1990s.

Many experts have concluded that, without drastic reductions in population growth rates, poverty and lack of economic development are inevitable. In 1988 the President of the World Bank declared that limiting population growth was an absolute prerequisite for raising living standards, especially in Africa, South Asia, and parts of Latin America. Exacerbating the situation is the lack of access to family-planning services in many developing countries. Using China and Japan as examples, a Worldwatch Institute report suggests that countries can cut their population growth rates in half within one generation. The report concludes:

> Some countries may find it necessary to press for one child per couple until the momentum of their population growth is checked. But for the world as a whole, two children may now be a more realistic goal. Accumulating evidence suggests that this is the only population policy that is consistent with restoring a worldwide improvement in living conditions. It is time for international leaders, such as the Secretary General of the United Nations and the President of the World Bank, to urge adoption of such a goal by all governments.[3]

ENERGY

The problems relating to the production, transport, and consumption of energy are multifaceted. These problems involve interests that are private, national, transnational, regional, and global. Energy concerns are also linked to issues in the areas of economic development, the global economy, research and development, security, conflict, and the global environment.

The industrial revolution was dependent upon a huge increase in the consumption of energy. Oil gradually replaced coal as the major energy source for industrialization. A seemingly abundant supply, cheapness, the proliferation of internal combustion engines, and the scientific development of a wide range of petroleum-based products entrenched oil as the dominant commodity in the energy field.

Attempts at monopoly control have punctuated the history of the petroleum industry. In the nineteenth century, John D. Rockefeller built a Standard Oil empire and integrated the production, refining, transportation, and marketing of petroleum products. In the twentieth century, agreements among the "seven sisters" (seven giant companies, five United States–based plus British Petroleum and Royal Dutch Shell) allowed their

---

[3]Brown and Durning, *State of the World 1989*, p. 192.

virtual dominance of the industry. In the list of *Fortune 500*'s world's largest transnational corporations discussed in Chapter 11, these same oil companies and their offspring, the motor-car giants, remain today among the largest of the world's business enterprises. The collaboration between the oil companies and the British and United States governments in overthrowing the Mossadegh regime in Iran was also detailed in Chapter 11.

The rise and fluctuations in the effectiveness of the Organization of Petroleum Exporting Countries (OPEC) were discussed in Chapter 10. Without actually diminishing the profitability of the giant oil companies, the thirteen members of OPEC, operating in the 1970s as a temporarily effective cartel, drove world oil prices up more than twelvefold. They accomplished this through production controls and the use of boycotts against vulnerable user countries. Their monopoly control was broken in the 1980s when new sources of supply and falling global demand reduced their share of the world oil market from more than 50 percent to 27 percent. However, their actions during the 1970s contributed heavily to global economic recession, the slowing of economic development processes, and indirectly to the burden of debt in the third world. Because, in the long run, oil is a finite resource and because in general the OPEC countries have the largest reserves, this cartel could again achieve a dominant world influence in the period before relatively cheap and abundant alternative sources of energy are developed.

The search for alternative sources of energy has not yet produced any major breakthroughs. Recent scientific evidence of the adverse environmental effects of the continued use of fossil fuels adds to the urgency of shifting to cleaner energy sources. In the 1950s, many scientists believed that nuclear energy would replace fossil fuels as an inexpensive energy source. Problems of cost, safety, and waste disposal have dashed these expectations. By 1992, nuclear power was producing just 17 percent of the world's electricity, which is only one of the forms of needed energy. The nuclear accident at Chernobyl in 1986, which spread contamination over a large portion of Europe, raised the level of anxiety concerning the further development of nuclear power. With the adoption of the Treaty on the Nonproliferation of Nuclear Weapons, all nonnuclear weapons states adhering to the treaty are committed to accept the safeguards and inspection of the International Atomic Energy Agency (IAEA). For the IAEA, the carrying out of this function has become perhaps its most important activity. After the Chernobyl accident the IAEA developed two new international treaties, a Convention on Early Notification of a Nuclear Accident and a Convention on Assistance in Case of Nuclear Accident or Radiological Emergency.

A United Nations Conference on New and Renewable Sources of Energy took place in Nairobi during the period August 10–21, 1981. Intensive preparations for the conference involved the work of eight panels of international specialists, six expert groups, two consultant studies, and national reports of participating governments. This background work and the attention of the conference were focused on the whole range of alternatives to the world's reliance on hydrocarbons for energy. These alternative sources include hydropower, fuel wood and charcoal, biomass conversion, solar energy, geothermal energy, wind, ocean energy, oil shale and tar sands, draft animal power, and peat for fuel. Other studies dealt with research, development, and transfer of technology, financing, information flows, education and training, industrial issues, and rural energy.

National interests are at variance on the subject of alternative sources of energy. Petroleum-exporting countries have much at stake in maintaining a high level of demand for oil. In many poor countries the biggest immediate problem is the rapid depletion of the supply of fuel wood. Therefore, it is no surprise that the plan of action adopted by the conference included a recommendation to stress acceleration of forestation programs. The conference also recommended the establishment of an intergovernmental body within the United Nations to monitor and guide the implementation of the plan of action and that new and expanded financial resources be mobilized in support of the program. The United States government made clear its lack of enthusiasm for new agencies or expanded funds for this purpose. The General Assembly, in spite of these obstacles and lack of unanimity of purpose among various interests, has moved to set up a United Nations Energy unit within the Secretariat and a Committee on the Development and Utilization of New and Renewable Sources of Energy to monitor progress on the goals of the plan of action adopted by the Conference.

Omitted from the agenda of the Nairobi conference was the subject of nuclear energy. In 1980 the General Assembly decided to convene a United Nations Conference for the Promotion of International Cooperation in the Peaceful Uses of Nuclear Energy. The next year the Assembly determined that the conference would be held in Geneva, August 29–September 9, 1983. A seventy-member preparatory committee was appointed and the International Atomic Energy Agency was designated as a primary agency to assist at all stages of preparation for the conference and during the conference itself. Disagreement over technical difficulties caused delays in the conference plans and the date was repeatedly rescheduled until March 1987. Delegates from 106 countries, after three weeks of debate, were unable to agree on the terms of a final document. The only positive outcome of the Conference was a full and frank airing of views on the peaceful uses of nuclear energy.

In the mid-1990s there seems to be no global sense of urgency concerning energy problems. This complacency will most likely be shaken only if oil becomes a scarcer and costlier commodity or if the dire effects of pollution from the burning of fossil fuels rises in world consciousness and concern. It is appropriate, therefore, to next consider the subject of the global environment.

ENVIRONMENT

Widespread concern that the human race may be potentially as threatened by pollution as it is by nuclear holocaust is a relatively recent phenomenon. The possibility of nuclear contamination of air, water, and soil in a large-scale nuclear war has been realized since Hiroshima and was reemphasized when Japanese fishermen were affected by nuclear fallout in the Bikini test of March 1, 1954. Localized threats to health from air pollution have existed for many years in such places as Los Angeles and London (before the latter city imposed regulations to reduce the threat), and from water pollution in myriad rivers and lakes, and oil pollution on numerous beaches. But gradually the realization has spread that major environmental problems require international attention in order to anticipate and forestall the various forms of eco-catastrophe that could overtake humankind.

Attention has focused on a wide range of pollutants that threaten the natural balance of the biosphere necessary to sustain healthy human life. A study sponsored by the Massachusetts Institute of Technology identified the following pollutants as worthy of special attention: carbon dioxide; particulate matter; sulfur dioxide; oxides of nitrogen, mercury, and other toxic heavy metals; oil; DDT and other hydrocarbons; radionuclides; heat; and nutrients, especially phosphates.[4] Later studies focusing on the major causes of global warming and depletion of the ozone layer additionally call for controls on chlorofluorocarbons (CFCs), methane, halon, chlorine, bromine, and ground-level ozone. Severe problems may exist locally with other pollutants; but this list represents the main contributors to global effects on the climate, oceans, or terrestrial ecology or that create major problems in many countries.

International agencies have given limited attention to problems of the human environment for many years, but the programs have been selective, low-scale, and often incidental to the main thrust of the efforts of these agencies. The pressure for a comprehensive and better-coordinated effort is of recent origin. A perusal of the activities of the specialized agencies affiliated with the United Nations reveals that the agencies giving the greatest attention to environmental problems are the World Meteorological Organization (WMO), which is concerned with air pollution and the climatic effect of pollutants; the World Health Organization (WHO), which is involved in a wide range of projects in environmental health; UNESCO, which has sponsored several studies and conferences of experts; the Food and Agriculture Organization (FAO), whose interests include pesticide accumulation and misuse of the environment; the International Atomic Energy Agency (IAEA), which is

---

[4]*Man's Impact on the Global Environment,* Report of the Study of Critical Environmental Problems (Cambridge, MA: MIT Press, 1970), 227.

concerned with nuclear wastes; the International Maritime Organization (IMO), which has a special interest in oil pollution of the oceans; and the International Labor Organization (ILO), whose concerns include exposure to toxic substances in the working environment.

Obstacles to the solution of environmental problems have also been evident in the United Nations and its affiliated agencies. In the FAO the pressure to continue to use DDT to eliminate pests threatening food production proved greater than the effects of warnings by scientists of the widespread ecological effects of its continued use. Another attitude that is slow to respond to the threats of terracide by pollution is found in the underdeveloped areas, where the problems of pollution are widely conceived as those of the industrialized nations and any attempt to impose ecological restraints on development programs may be viewed as unnecessary obstacles to rapid development. Such negative attitudes toward placing environmental problems high on the list of global priorities may defer effective measures until the disasters of which many scientists warn are imminent.

The growing concern about global pollution problems came to a focus in the World Conference on the Human Environment in Stockholm in June 1972. Swedish leadership in acting as the host country for this two-week conference was prompted, at least in part, by problems of mercury poisoning of birds and fish and other foods consumed by the Swedish people, resulting in both national action to combat the threat and in the summoning of an international conference in Sweden in 1966 on the threat of mercury poisoning. By 1968 enough delegates to ECOSOC and the General Assembly responded to Swedish prodding for a broad-gauge approach to environmental problems to approve the calling of the 1972 World Conference on the Human Environment.

Preparations for the Stockholm Conference were extensive and received special attention by Secretary-General U Thant. Groups outside the United Nations also took supportive action. Under persistent urging by U Thant, Maurice F. Strong, the energetic director of the Canadian International Development Agency, accepted the posts of United Nations undersecretary general in charge of the Secretariat staff in Geneva for conference preparation and of secretary-general of the Stockholm conference. To convince the developing nations of the importance of their full participation in the 1972 conference, regional seminars were organized to bring the impending environmental crisis to their attention. Maurice Strong also initiated a conference of twenty-seven experts who met at Founex, Switzerland, near Geneva, in June 1971, to study the relationships between development and environment. The report of this conference contributed to an awareness in developing countries that environmental problems were not the exclusive domain of industrialized nations.[5]

[5]For the Founex Report and accompanying commentaries by four of the participants, see "Environment and Development," *International Conciliation*, no. 586 (January 1972).

In spite of initial misgivings, most of the developing countries agreed to participate in the Stockholm conference and altogether 113 countries were represented. The USSR and most East European Communist states refused to send delegations as a result of a controversy that led to a decision to exclude the German Democratic Republic. In addition to official delegates from governments, representatives of United Nations specialized agencies and of international nongovernmental organizations were invited as observers, and in some cases they were permitted to submit statements to the conference. To provide an outlet for other private groups, the Swedish government arranged an Environment Forum to run simultaneously with the conference in another part of Stockholm. Representatives of almost 200 nongovernmental organizations participated in this Environment Forum.[6]

The United Nations Conference on the Human Environment (UNCHE) approved as its theme "Only One Earth" to emphasize the essential unity and interdependence of the global life-support system. The conference adopted a 26-point Declaration on the Human Environment and a 109-point Action Plan for the guidance of governments and international organizations in implementing a program of environmental protection. The conference also proposed the setting up of permanent international machinery within a United Nations Environment Program (UNEP), and this arrangement was endorsed and implemented by ECOSOC in October and by the General Assembly in December 1972.

The permanent machinery created by the General Assembly includes a small Environmental Secretariat of which Maurice Strong served as the first executive director; a fifty-eight-member Governing Council to coordinate environmental activities and to promote governmental cooperation; an Environment Fund raised by voluntary contributions with a target of $100 million for the first five years; and an Environment Coordination Board as a subsidiary of the intersecretariat Administrative Committee on Coordination to foster cooperation among the secretariats of the United Nations and its specialized agencies in carrying out environmental projects. It was anticipated that continued activities in support of environmental protection would be carried out by United Nations regional economic commissions, by the specialized agencies, by nongovernmental organizations, and by governments under the leadership of the Environmental Secretariat and the Governing Council. Since no coercive powers exist, the basic principle for successful coordination and effective programs is voluntary cooperation.

---

[6]For a study of the role of nongovernmental organizations in the Stockholm conference, including preparatory and follow-up activities, see Anne Thompson Feraru, "Transnational Political Interests and the Global Environment," *International Organization*, 28 (Winter 1974), 31–60.

The interests of the developing states are protected in two aspects of the UNEP arrangements. Developing countries have a majority of the seats on the Governing Council, and the selection of Nairobi, Kenya, as the site for the Environmental Secretariat is clearly a concession to pressures from the less-developed states. A balance between environmental and development concerns in rich and poor nations is assured.

One major focus of the action program adopted at Stockholm is an "Earthwatch" network to assess current environmental conditions in all parts of the globe and to monitor changes that presage danger. Atmospheric conditions are monitored for pollutants that threaten health or climatic modification. Marine pollution and the release of toxic substances into the life-support system are checked, and any threatening changes are publicized. Earthwatch activities include an International Referral System connecting national information centers to a central data bank in Geneva, an International Register of Potentially Toxic Chemicals, and a Global Environmental Monitoring Service (GEMS) with a projected 110 monitoring stations throughout the world.

The pace of UNEP activities gradually accelerated after a slow start. In 1982 the Environment Fund dispensed approximately $40 million for a variety of projects. In May 1976 an agreement was signed at Barcelona to combat pollution and other environmental problems in the Mediterranean and its coastal states. In April 1978 a similar agreement was drawn up for the Persian Gulf region by eight major oil-producing states. The threat of oil and industrial pollution is especially severe in this area. UNEP has instigated other antipollution plans for the Caribbean Sea, the Gulf of Guinea, the Red Sea, East Asian seas, and specific areas of the Pacific Ocean. In December 1985, in response to deteriorating environmental conditions in many parts of Africa, a meeting of African environment ministers was convened in Cairo to agree on new programs and cooperative actions to reverse these trends. UNEP cooperated with the Organization of African Unity (OAU) and the Economic Commission for Africa (ECA) in sponsoring this meeting.

During the 1970s the United Nations Environment Program generated three additional global conferences within the environmental context. The first of these was a United Nations Conference on Human Settlements (HABITAT) in Vancouver, Canada, from May 31 to June 11, 1976. The central theme of the conference is summed up in one of the general principles adopted by the delegates, stating that "the improvement of the quality of life of human beings is the first and most important objective of every human settlement policy."

After the conference, until new United Nations machinery was created, the global human-settlement activities continued as a part of the United Nations Environment Program. In 1978 the Economic and Social Council's former Committee on Housing, Building and Planning was replaced by a fifty-eight-member Commission on Human Settlements to assume general supervision of appropriate functions, and a special section of the Secretariat was established under the title HABITAT, Centre on Human Settlements. The new Commission urged governments to act quickly to meet the proposed target of $50 million for 1978–81 for human-settlement activities. Much of the emphasis at Vancouver had been on the necessity for national action, but the United Nations regional commissions were also urged to enlarge their role in human-settlement programs. At its 1986 meeting the Commission urged universal participation by states in its 1987 session in Nairobi, at which HABITAT's tenth anniversary and the International Year of Shelter for the Homeless were observed.

The next global conference within the environmental context had as its subject the problems of water supply and utilization. The HABITAT conference included clean water and sanitation facilities on its list of basic human needs. The United Nations Water Conference met in Mar del Plata, Argentina, March 14–25, 1977.

The problems of water supply and utilization are numerous. Water is a scarce resource and much of it is wasted or misused. The best estimates indicate that today nearly 20 percent of the world's population still lack a supply of safe drinking water, in spite of major gains in the 1980s in alleviating this problem. Many areas suffer from floods, drought, soil erosion, and salination. Agriculture today accounts for 75 percent of water use, but the area of irrigated land in proportion to world population has been decreasing since 1980. Waterborne diseases and the pollution of water supplies remain as problems in many countries.

The recommendations of the conference were wide ranging, but the results were not especially dramatic. The recommendations were embodied in a "Plan of Action of Mar del Plata." At least 85 percent of the recommendations were to be carried out by national governments. The Plan of Action also stressed regional cooperation, including an expanded role for the United Nations regional commissions. Global implementation was to be carried out by the Economic and Social Council, its Committee on Natural Resources, and the United Nations Development Program. No new special funding was recommended, but the Secretary-General was requested to study the mechanisms by which an adequate flow of funds through existing channels could be assured for water-related projects.

A special environmental problem of geographically widespread impact is that of halting the spread of deserts. The problem overlaps not only that of water supply and utilization, but also has dimensions relating to health, food, population, development, meteorology, culture, science, and technology. Deserts presently cover about 25 percent of the earth's land surface, affecting more than 850 million people. The 1972–74 Sahel drought in Africa, with its human suffering and long-range implications, dramatized the threat of desertification. To check the further encroachment of deserts on habitable and productive land requires informed planning in water utilization and in grazing and agricultural practices. The United Nations Conference on Desertification, in Nairobi, Kenya, August 29–September 7, 1977, emphasized human activities that can turn productive areas into deserts, and methods for checking and reversing the spread of desert conditions.

In Africa it is clear that in many areas desertification has not been checked. In the Programme of Action for African Economic Recovery, 1986–90, adopted by the General Assembly special session on Africa in May 1986, further massive actions were recommended to combat the spread of deserts. These included measures for afforestation and reforestation, stabilization of sand dunes, the development of alternative sources of energy to replace wood fuel, and measures to stop soil erosion.

In the 1980s, global environmental activities accelerated and intensified both within and outside the United Nations, with UNEP supplying significant impetus in the process. In 1987 the World Commission on Environment and Development, headed by Gro Harlem Bruntland, Norway's Prime Minister, issued a 374-page report calling for "sustainable development" in which environmental concerns are paramount. The Bruntland Report represented three years of intensive study and served as a primary basis, together with simultaneous studies by UNEP, for the adoption by the 1987 United Nations General Assembly of a document entitled "Environmental Perspective to the Year 2000 and Beyond." The introduction to this Environmental Perspective declares that action must be taken to combat environmental degradation, which threatens "human well-being and, in some instances, the very survival of life on our planet."

The Bruntland Report served as background for the United Nations Conference on Environment and Development (UNCED) in Rio de Janeiro in June 1992. This conference, often referred to as the Earth Summit, was held on the twentieth anniversary of the Stockholm environmental conference, and Maurice Strong was again recruited to guide both the preparatory work and the conference proceedings. Elaborate preparatory planning over a two-year period laid out the detailed agreements for the content of the conference's final documents; and input from interested nongovernmental organizations was encouraged, culminating in the attendance in Rio of 1,500 accredited observers and 30,000 participants in parallel forum sessions. Among the representatives of 170 countries at the conference were more than 100 heads of state and government.

The principal documents given final approval at UNCED included the Rio Declaration on Environment and Development, which laid out twenty-seven principles for sustainable development; Agenda 21, a detailed plan for achieving the broad goals of the conference; and a statement of principles for the sustainable development of the world's forests. Also simultaneously two conventions, one on biodiversity and the other on climate change, were signed in Rio by most nations attending the conference. In order to monitor progress toward the implementation of Agenda 21 a new high-level UN Commission on Sustainable Development of fifty-three members was authorized and has begun its work. The UN Secretary-General, as a part of Secretariat reorganization, has also created a Department for Policy Coordination and Sustainable Development. A Global Environment Facility has also been jointly established by the World Bank, the UN Development Program, and the UNEP.

Not all the results of the conference met the hopes of the more ardent advocates of sustainable development. The developing countries stressed aspects promoting development, while many developed countries were more interested in environmental issues. Compromises resulted in some watering down of commitments. The United States acquired the reputation of being the leading noncooperative state at Rio, and the Bush administration refused to sign the Biodiversity Treaty, a policy reversed by the Clinton administration. However, the general spirit of Rio indicated a desire for stimulating development while protecting the global environment and of maintaining the linkage between the two. On the other hand, the commitments made at Rio are so tenuous and so dependent upon implementation by individual nations and their agencies in international organizations that only time can measure the results.

In addition to the emphasis in the Bruntland Report on the interdependence of economic development and the global environment, the issues of global warming and ozone-layer depletion have received major emphasis in recent years in the science community, in national governments, and through intergovernmental channels. The executive director and governing council of UNEP have focused on global warming as a primary concern. The fact that the nine hottest years on record have all occurred in the period 1980–93 and that scientific studies predict further increases of several degrees in global temperatures by the year 2050 has prompted the proposal of measures to slow or arrest these trends. The chief cause of the "greenhouse effect" is the increase in emissions of carbon dioxide (CO_2) into the atmosphere resulting from the burning of fossil fuels and the destruction of forests. Other greenhouse gases include chlorofluorocarbons (CFCs), methane, and nitrous oxide. The release of large quantities of these gases into the atmosphere traps heat and increases surface temperatures. The effects of an increase in global temperatures could include the flooding of coastal areas, huge shifts in agricultural production areas, and severe health problems. To slow or stabilize the rate of temperature increase requires both increases in efficiency in the use of energy and a shift to new and renewable sources of energy. Additional measures require the elimination of CFCs and massive reforestation. In June 1988, at a world conference in Toronto on "The Changing Atmosphere: Implications for Global Security," the recommendation was agreed to that carbon emissions should be reduced by 20 percent by 2005. A Second World Climate Conference was held in Geneva in 1990 at which the United States refused to assume obligations promised by the other leading industrial nations to stabilize carbon emissions at 1990 levels by the year 2000. This obligation became the centerpiece of the treaty on climate change signed at the 1992 Rio conference. However, at United States insistence, the standards were made voluntary and without any timetable. Later President Clinton announced his acceptance of the standards established at Geneva and Rio.

CFCs not only act as greenhouse gases but also are the chief culprits in the destruction of the ozone layer, which serves as a shield against the sun's ultraviolet rays. These rays can cause skin cancer, damage the eyes and the immune system, and threaten certain forms of animal and plant life. UNEP took leadership in the signing in Vienna in 1985 of the Convention for the Protection of the Ozone Layer and a supplemental agreement, the Montreal Protocol in September 1987. CFCs are widely used in refrigeration, air conditioning, foam insulation, aerosol sprays, packaging, and cleaning solvents. The Montreal Protocol provides for a 50 percent cut in the production of CFCs by 1998. However, in March 1988 the United States National Aeronautics and Space Administration (NASA) issued the results of an extensive study which showed that current damage to the ozone layer was triple the amount assumed as a basis for the Montreal Protocol. UNEP's executive director had previously served notice that any such evidence would require further review and more sweeping measures to deal with the problem. At a 1990 conference in London, ninety-two countries agreed to phase out all CFC production by 2000. After additional evidence of the scope of ozone depletion, the United States and the European Community advanced their phase-out schedule to December 1995.

It is generally recognized that most effective measures for preventing deterioration of the human environment will depend primarily upon national and local regulations and enforcement. It is unlikely that sovereign states will subject themselves to supranational authority in ecological matters in sharp contrast to the lack of such authority in other areas. Nevertheless, the problems of global pollution, with the threat of eco-catastrophes from many existing sources and trends, present to humankind one more opportunity for cooperative action for the benefit, and possibly the survival, of the whole human race. National action without global planning will probably prove insufficient. A failure to meet potential ecological threats on a global front with foresight and imagination could prove disastrous. Should the scientific evidence suggest the necessity for drastic global measures to preserve a healthy environment, is a world of competing sovereign states capable of developing flexible responses in time to avert catastrophe?

LAW OF THE SEA

Until fairly recently the problems with regard to the use of the oceans by national states and private actors were relatively simple. The principle of freedom of the seas governed navigation, fish were plentiful, and most states claimed jurisdiction over a three-mile territorial sea adjacent to their shores.

Since 1945 these conditions have changed drastically. Some states now claim jurisdiction over the adjacent waters and seabed to a distance of 200 miles; new methods of fishing threaten the extinction of many species; ocean pollution has become a threat to the marine life system; vast reservoirs of petroleum are being tapped on the continental margins; other valuable minerals may soon be retrieved from the deep ocean floor; submarines and nuclear weapons make possible the use of the oceans as nuclear bases; the widening of territorial claims may close many straits to free navigation; and ocean research has expanded at a rapid pace.

To exacerbate all these problems, two opposed sets of interests have emerged. On the one hand, a movement has developed to declare the oceans and seabed as "the common heritage of humankind" and to restrict national jurisdictional claims to a narrow range of territorial waters and seabed. At the other extreme is the desire of some coastal states and private interests to claim sweeping national jurisdiction over nearly one-fourth of the ocean and seabed area, wherein lie 90 percent of the mineral and fishing resources. Further compounding the problem of finding a solution to these many-faceted issues is the lack of a simple division of coastal versus landlocked or shelf-locked states or of developed versus developing states. Even within states, policy may be dictated by competing orientations among commercial, military, industrial, fishing, research, conservationist, and political interests.

The definition of several terms is necessary to an understanding of the current ocean controversy. The *continental shelf* is the portion of the ocean bottom from low tide to the point at which the slope begins to decline much more sharply. The width of the shelf varies widely but averages just under fifty miles. However, a 1958 international convention, which sets the limits not by the natural contour but at a water depth of 200 meters, extends this average width to somewhat more than fifty miles. The *continental slope* extends from the edge of the continental shelf sharply downward to the *continental rise*, at which point the angle of decline is much less abrupt until it reaches the *abyssal plains* of the *deep ocean floor.* The term *continental margin* includes the shelf, slope, and rise, or the entire submerged extension of the continental landmass. These features are illustrated in Figure 13–1.

The movement toward the extension of national jurisdictional claims over the resources of the continental margins began with a proclamation in 1945 by President Truman that, while not extending the three-mile territorial sea, declared exclusive United States jurisdiction over the resources of the

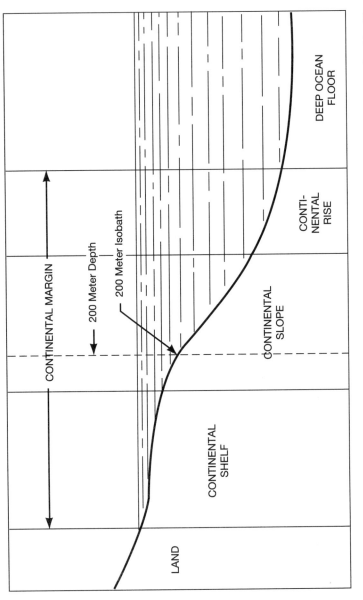

FIGURE 13–1 Adapted from Larry L. Fabian, "The Ocean, the United States, and the Poor Countries," in *The United States and the Developing World: Agenda for Action* (Washington, D.C.: Overseas Development Council, 1973), p. 81, and from John J. Logue, ed., *The Fate of the Oceans* (Villanova, PA: Villanova University Press, 1972), p. 232.

continental shelf, defined as extending to the 200-meter isobath. Other countries, following the lead of the United States, unilaterally enlarged their claims over an extended area, variously covering exclusive jurisdiction over mineral resources, fishing rights, or even full sovereignty over the seas to a distance of as great as 200 miles. By the early 1970s, eight states claimed exclusive jurisdiction over a 200-mile territorial sea and four additional states declared title to fishing rights in a 200-mile zone.

In 1958 the United States' assertion of jurisdiction made by President Truman was institutionalized and universalized by the adoption by the Law of the Sea Conference in Geneva of a Convention of the Continental Shelf. Not only did this convention adopt the 200-meter isobath rule for the boundary of the continental shelf, but, in addition, it included an "exploitability clause," which allows the extension of jurisdictional claims beyond the 200-meter depth wherever exploitation of the natural resources of the seabed and subsoil is technically possible. With today's technology such exploitation for petroleum, for example, is possible well beyond the limits of the continental shelf and may soon encompass virtually all the continental margin.

The 1958 Law of the Sea Conference referred to above was the first in a series of attempts by the international community to reconcile the growing differences among national claims and to create universally recognized standards of international law for the oceans. The United Nations General Assembly instigated this conference, which was preceded by ten years of preparatory work by the International Law Commission. Eighty-six countries (almost every independent state in 1958) were represented in Geneva. The conference approved four conventions and submitted them for ratification by states. In addition to the Convention on the Continental Shelf, these instruments were a Convention on the Territorial Sea and the Contiguous Zone, a Convention on the High Seas, and a Convention on Fishing and the Conservation of the Living Resources of the High Seas. Each of the conventions received sufficient ratifications between 1962 and 1966 to come into force.

The 1958 conference left unanswered certain important questions, including the breadth of the territorial sea and conflicting limits on fishing rights. A second United Nations Conference on the Law of the Sea in 1960 failed to resolve these issues.

During the 1960s the urgency of resolving both previously unsettled issues and newly emerging ones mounted. National claims became more diverse at the same time that conflicts over fishing rights, concern over ocean pollution, and the possibility of placing nuclear weapons on the ocean floor caused increasing anxiety. Partial solutions touching only the periphery of the main body of problems were provided by a 1970 Treaty on the Prohibition of the Emplacement of Nuclear Weapons and Other Weapons of Mass Destruction on the Seabed and the Ocean Floor and in the Subsoil Thereof and by a 1972 Ocean Dumping Convention.

A notable proposal for restoring order out of the mounting chaos was made in the United Nations General Assembly in 1967 by Ambassador Arvid Pardo of Malta. With great imagination, Ambassador Pardo linked the desirability of restoring order and uniformity in the realm of the oceans to the needs of the developing states for substantial and growing financial resources. He warned against further national appropriation of the seabed. He proposed that the resources of the seabed and ocean floor beyond present national jurisdiction be declared "the common heritage of humankind" to be shared by all states both coastal and landlocked. Ambassador Pardo suggested the setting up of an international seabed authority with jurisdiction to regulate, promote, and protect the common heritage for the benefit of all, but with special attention to the needs of developing states. With increasing exploitation of these resources and with curtailment of extravagant national jurisdictional claims, the prospects for a long-term common heritage of billions of dollars could be foreseen.

The General Assembly, in responding to the Pardo initiative, set up an ad hoc committee and, in the following year, a standing committee of forty-two members to study the principles involved in promoting the exploration and exploitation of the resources of the sea and the machinery for an international regime for the seabed. This Seabed Committee, as it is popularly called, was later expanded to eighty-six and then to ninety-one members. In 1970 the committee was converted to a preparatory organ for a third Law of the Sea Conference planned initially for 1973.

As the date for the projected Law of the Sea Conference approached, the difficulties of achieving Ambassador Pardo's goals became increasingly apparent. Some of the most extravagant national jurisdictional claims hardened to the point that the possibility of compromise on universal standards seemed increasingly remote. The diversity of issues to be resolved and of interests to be accommodated added to the difficulty of working out an all-encompassing plan for managing ocean resources. Nations were engaged in enforcement battles over fishing rights in a 12- to 200-mile zone from their shores. States were issuing licenses for oil drilling beyond the limits of the continental shelf. Several companies were preparing to mine manganese nodules (from which could also be obtained valuable resources of nickel, copper, and cobalt) from the deep ocean floor without waiting for the establishment of an international regime. Several states proposed plans that sought to compromise outstanding national differences, but national intransigence was apparent in the vigorous debates over these proposals.

The debate over differences among the members of the Seabed Committee delayed the proposed opening date for the third Law of the Sea Conference. The first session, purely organizational in character, was held in New York for two weeks in December 1973. The second session, lasting the entire summer, met in Caracas in 1974. Slowness in resolving basic disagreements among divergent interests required further extended meetings in Geneva or New York each year from 1975 through 1982.

One reason for the difficulties in formulating a comprehensive treaty was the range of issues with which the conference had to deal. Larry Fabian summed up this problem as follows:

> The conference agenda is awesomely ambitious. Seaward limits of national sovereignty must be drawn. Rights to ocean resources beyond these limits must be spelled out. Ground rules must be set for allocating privileges between coastal states and others wanting access to their adjacent offshore areas beyond national limits—long-distance fishermen, oil drillers, marine scientists, and civilian and military vessels or aircraft seeking rights of transit or overflight. The conference is to settle the status of international straits, to adopt principles for international revenue sharing from ocean exploitation, and to determine methods for providing technical assistance and resolving international disputes. It must take further steps to control ocean pollution, in conjunction with the recent U.N. Conference on the Human Environment and several international agencies with marine environmental responsibilities. For these and many other issues, the conference is charged with creating a comprehensive regime of ocean law and the political machinery to implement it.[7]

Idealists saw in the opportunities facing the Law of the Sea Conference the possibility of the greatest breakthrough ever achieved toward universalism. If an international ocean regime could be established with shared jurisdiction over the rich resources of the continental margins as well as those of the deep ocean floor, and, endowed with real decision-making and enforcement powers, such a step would indeed create a common heritage of great potential. By establishing an international authority with an independent and vast source of revenue, the first substantial penetration would have been made of the wall of national sovereignty. And with these future resources committed to meeting the needs of the development process, the outlook for a stepping up of the rate of development (if combined with other favorable factors of planning, management, and incentives) would be bright.

As the Conference dragged on year after year, compromises were reached on most issues, although individual states were not entirely satisfied with the concessions necessary for consensus on the total complex package. By 1980 the principal issue that required further agreement on details was that of deep-sea mining of manganese nodules under an International Authority. After the United States' change of administration in the 1980 presidential election, the Reagan administration replaced all its chief negotiators and announced that time would be required to thoroughly review all aspects of the treaty. Later it became clear that only the deep-sea mining

---

[7]Larry L. Fabian, "The Ocean, the United States, and the Poor Countries," in *The United States and the Developing World: Agenda for Action* (Washington, D.C.: Overseas Development Council, 1973), p. 80.

provisions were opposed by the new administration, but the objections to those provisions were of such magnitude as to make compromise unfeasible. Most other nations, weary after eight years of negotiation, were determined to conclude their work. The United States delegation requested a recorded vote, and on April 30, 1982, the treaty was approved by a vote of 130 yeas, 4 nays, and 17 abstentions. The United States was joined only by Israel, Turkey, and Venezuela in casting a negative vote. More than half the abstentions came from the solid Soviet bloc but included also the United Kingdom, Germany, and Italy. France, China, Japan, Australia, Canada, and the Scandinavian countries, among others, joined an almost solid third-world bloc in favoring the treaty. Formal signing took place in Jamaica in December 1982.

The treaty covers all aspects of ocean access and usage and is composed of 320 articles. It establishes a 12-mile territorial sea with the right of "transit passage" through and over straits used for international navigation. It provides for a 200-mile exclusive economic zone with respect to natural resources, scientific research, and fishing, in which the coastal state would determine the rules for any sharing of resources. Coastal states would also have sovereign rights over exploitation of resources on the continental shelf to a distance of 350 miles from shore, subject to sharing with the international community part of the revenue from such exploitation beyond 200 miles. Landlocked states would have the right of access to and from the sea and a share in fishing rights in the exclusive economic zone of coastal states when the coastal state cannot harvest all the supply. Measures to prevent and control marine pollution are included in the treaty. Provisions are made for compulsory submission of disputes not settled by negotiation to a variety of arbitral or judicial procedures, including a newly created International Tribunal for the Law of the Sea and a Seabed Disputes Chamber.

The most complicated part of the treaty involves deep-sea mining of manganese nodules. An International Seabed Authority would grant mining concessions and would conduct mining operations through its subagency called the Enterprise. Under a "parallel system," each private agency seeking a mining permit would submit two proposed tracts to the Authority and the Authority could choose one for its own operation. Certain fees and sharing of technology are also involved. Safeguards to prevent undue depression of world mineral prices are included. Revenues accruing to the Authority are earmarked for aid for development.

The treaty technically and legally came into force in November 1994, one year after ratification by the sixtieth state, Guyana. Yet, the lack of adherence to the treaty by the most affluent maritime states limits its effectiveness. Additionally, the operations for deep-sea mining will take time to develop. However, for nations such as the United States, which has withheld ratification, some interesting legal and practical questions are involved. There are many features of the treaty which the United States favors. Can passage of United States vessels through straits be restricted if that country is not a party to the treaty? Do other countries have to honor United States claims over the exclusive economic zone and the continental shelf? If United States companies eventually mine deep-sea nodules without complying with the rules of the Authority, can collective retaliatory action be taken to prevent depression of world prices of those minerals? In other words, in today's world can any state, no matter how powerful, claim the advantages of widely accepted law, but be immune to its consequences? On a shrinking planet, can anarchy over ocean issues be tolerated? Perhaps the task is still far from completion.

14

PROMOTING SOCIAL PROGRESS

As explained in the introduction to Chapter 12, the economic and social activities of international organizations cannot be distinguished completely, either in theory or in practice. However, those programs generally identified as more social than economic are discussed in this chapter. These topics include health, child welfare, aging, labor conditions, education, science, culture, narcotic drugs, and refugee problems.

CHARTER GOALS AND WORLD NEEDS

The social goals of the United Nations are best summarized in the phrase from the preamble of the Charter "to promote social progress and better standards of life in larger freedom." This statement of goals expresses the aspirations of humankind for a fuller, richer, more secure and more satisfying life—a quality of living that promises escape from the meanness of human degradation into the fullness of human dignity. The complete realization of these aspirations would bring about an ideal world from which all pockets of ignorance, poverty, hunger, and disease had been eliminated.

Anyone who views world conditions since 1945 realizes how short of utopia we are and how little positive progress has been made toward a better life for the majority of humankind. As world population rapidly increases, the percentage of that population living at subhuman levels of education, health, nutrition, and economic well-being remains relatively unchanged despite billions of dollar-equivalents devoted annually to programs for raising social and economic standards of living. In comparative economic terms the rich countries continue to get richer and the poor countries get poorer. Pessimistic forecasts for the future of the underdeveloped countries are common. Based on trends of the past forty years, the prospects are not bright for the majority of humankind to escape from misery into a "better way of life" during the remainder of this century.

World social and economic needs are of gargantuan proportions. Massive infusions of capital would be required to bring about rapid improvement in the quality of life of hundreds of millions of people who have not shared in the emancipating aspects of economic affluence. But the problems of social change cannot be solved merely by providing huge amounts of capital, even if sufficient quantities were available. The experiments of the postwar years have demonstrated the fallacies of such an approach. The developing countries may be required to generate most of their own capital rather than to depend primarily on outside sources. But beyond capital needs the requirements of planning, social engineering, and social revolution probably outweigh other factors if the kinds of changes are to occur that will "turn the world around" for the developing societies. Only in those countries where enlightened leadership promotes social revolution can societies hope to achieve their aspirations for an escape from human misery. In countries where that quality of leadership fails to emerge, life for the masses will continue to be, in Hobbesian terms, "solitary, poor, nasty, brutish and short."

Although most of the energy and resources for social and economic development must be generated internally, the attitudes of the decision makers of the affluent states toward the "revolution of rising expectations" in the developing world will affect the course and rate of change in those countries. The examples of Soviet and Chinese development may lead one to conclude that a state can carry on massive reforms with a minimum of outside assistance, or even with outside opposition, but these examples may serve as inadequate models for most of the scores of underdeveloped states today. The Soviet Union and China, with their gigantic political, social, and economic base, are in sharp contrast to most of the political units seeking improved social and economic conditions. Dependence upon outside relations is an inescapable reality for a small state lacking in a myriad of necessary elements for rapid development. Whether the developed states will tolerate or encourage revolutionary change, whether they will cooperate and support internal efforts at reform, or whether they will intervene to maintain the status quo can profoundly affect the course of development of those nations trying to throw off the yoke of past conditions. From the developed states the less prosperous will need capital, technical assistance, goods, markets for their products, and, above all, an understanding of their problems and tangible encouragement and aid in their solutions. Without this aid and encouragement, progress will be either slow or nonexistent.

Social revolution is an essential ingredient for rapid social development, but social change is interrelated with political and economic change. No state can plan for improved social conditions without concomitant expansion of its economic base and adequate attention to improvement of the quality of government personnel, organization, and programs. Any discussion of social factors is, of necessity, certain to impinge upon the economic and political sectors. No attempt will be made to isolate the social issues discussed in this chapter from the political and economic realities to which they are inextricably related.

In a world of more than 180 independent states, of which two-thirds are classified as underdeveloped or preindustrial, the United Nations can play a minor yet essential role in the development process. The resources distributed through United Nations agencies are small when compared to the amounts involved in bilateral aid programs or the expenditures for war preparation or the sums that would be required to relieve human deprivation and suffering. An attitude of skepticism and pessimism concerning the United Nations' impact on world economic and social problems seems justified when one compares a total budget measured in hundreds of millions of dollars against the tens of billions that would be necessary annually to satisfy the needs of all persons who live below a decent standard of human dignity. One might also question the amount of change that can be effected by a few thousand civil servants and experts recruited by United Nations agencies, however skilled and devoted to their tasks they may be, when the total needs for social reform are so vast and progress to date seems infinitesimal. National sovereignty and national sensibilities also preclude any global solution to world social problems. National governments must request aid before it can be granted, existing governmental agencies must act as the channels through which aid is administered, and United Nations personnel can carry on their activities within each state only at the sufferance of the governmental authorities of the host state. Global welfare programs must still conform to the theories and patterns of a compartmentalized world of independent, sovereign states in which no significant authority has yet been transferred to the international level.

In spite of all its obstacles and limitations, the United Nations plays an indispensable role in assisting nations to escape from the intolerable conditions that condemn the majority of the world's population to a brutish existence. Although for each country self-help is the main key to the escalation process toward better social and economic standards, small states are dependent on the rest of the world for supportive conditions for their own efforts. Bilateral arrangements are often unattractive because of the degrading psychological effects of dependence that attend such arrangements. Multilateral channels provide an escape from the stigma of dependence since every state can be both donor and recipient in a cooperative effort. Developing states clamor for the expansion of United Nations development programs as evidenced by the proclamation of the four Development Decades and by the creation of the United Nations Conference on Trade and Development (UNCTAD) and the United Nations Industrial Development Organization (UNIDO). Developed states, among whose primary goals is that of international stability, may gradually see their enlightened self-interest to lie in the direction of channeling increased development effort through multilateral channels. Although United Nations resources may remain small in comparison to both total need and internal national programs, they can provide, if intelligently planned, the necessary catalytic element to turn failure into success in those countries whose own efforts are greatest and best directed.

If any progress is to be made toward a worldwide frontal attack upon ignorance, poverty, hunger, and disease, the United Nations family of agencies is indispensable for coordinating that effort. The United Nations already exists, its goals include the promotion of the better standards of life to which the developing nations aspire, and it has established an elaborate pattern of agencies and programs for working toward the attainment of these goals. No other broad competing or substitute international agencies that can promote world social welfare are in prospect. The present and future role of the United Nations system has been well summarized by David Owen, who was for nearly twenty-five years a key administrator in the development programs of the United Nations:

> The mobilization and application of the resources needed to carry out a combined attack on the problems of global development will be so immense and pervasive a task as to be beyond the resources of any single institution or grouping of institutions now in existence. . . . It is certainly far beyond the capability of the United Nations system as it exists today. It may be suggested, however, that a modest but nonetheless vital role does await the United Nations system as a focal centre for strategic planning, for coordinating programmes of combined action, for harmonizing the actions of governments and international institutions, for directing some key activities, and for assessing the progress made in the implementation of programmes. Financially weak and ill-nourished though it is today, no other systematic grouping of worldwide institutions has the same organizational resources for the purpose.[1]

---

[1]David Owen, "A Combined Strategy," in *International Targets for Development*, ed. Richard Symonds (New York: Harper & Row, 1970), p. 247.

PROMOTING IMPROVED HEALTH STANDARDS

Health problems have been a matter of international concern for centuries. Epidemics of cholera, plague, typhus, and influenza have swept across national borders from ancient times to the present century. Beginning in 1851 a series of international conferences was called to deal with quarantine regulations, and the International Sanitary Convention was adopted in 1903. In 1909 the International Office of Public Hygiene was established in Paris to deal only with quarantine matters. After the establishment of the League of Nations Health Organization, the Paris office continued its functions side by side with the League organization until both were absorbed by the World Health Organization in 1948. In 1902 the Pan American Sanitary Bureau was created and has served, in the scope of its authority, as a model for subsequent organizations. It continues its functions today both independently of and as a regional office of the World Health Organization.

The Health Organization of the League, established in 1923, accomplished much more than its creators or those who limited its financial resources anticipated. It was appraised by most students of League operations as one of the most successful agencies among the League's social and economic divisions. The economic and social work of the League, mainly an afterthought in an organization created primarily to maintain peace, grew throughout the life of the League in importance and prestige, and the Health Organization was a keystone in this development. It carried on activities in epidemic control, research, publication of health information, standardization of vaccines, sponsorship of conferences and lectureships, and direct assistance to governments. It became the principal center for international activities in promoting improved world health standards.

The World Health Organization (WHO) was established as a specialized agency of the United Nations in 1948 and has become the largest of the specialized agencies in terms of budget and one of the largest in membership. Its headquarters are in Geneva, but its operations are decentralized through six regional committees and regional offices.

In trying to carry out its self-imposed mandate of attaining "Health for All by the Year 2000," the World Health Organization has engaged in a formidable array of activities. WHO maintains an Epidemiological Intelligence Network for the rapid dissemination of information by telecommunications concerning the outbreak anywhere in the world of cases of cholera, plague, and yellow fever. It has initiated massive campaigns for the eradication of malaria, tuberculosis, smallpox, and yaws; and, with the cooperation of governments, tens of millions of people have been treated for each of these communicable diseases. In the case of tuberculosis, WHO research helped produce a new, improved vaccine. Costs of effective treatment for mass campaigns against communicable diseases have been reduced through WHO efforts. WHO supports research and control programs against trachoma, bilharziasis, and leprosy.

In the areas of water supply, sewage disposal, air pollution, and the development and use of insecticides, WHO conducts studies, subsidizes research, and furnishes technical assistance. It provides advice to governments on public-health planning. It has assumed leadership in establishing research programs for heart disease, cancer, drug dependence, and mental health. In trying to overcome the severe shortage of personnel in the health professions, WHO aids in establishing schools and training programs and each year makes about 250 training and exchange grants and provides 3,500 fellowships. Each year it organizes approximately forty short courses and eighty technical conferences. In encouraging research it initiates more than 150 research contracts annually. WHO is responsible for administering the Code of International Health Regulations adopted in 1969 by the World Health Assembly. It has established quality control for hundreds of drugs in order to establish standards of content and purity.

In the 1980s, WHO assumed a central role in the global concern with acquired immune deficiency syndrome (AIDS). In November 1986, WHO's Director-General declared AIDS to be a global health priority and early in 1987 he established the WHO Special Programme on AIDS. WHO's role in directing and coordinating global efforts has been affirmed by conferences of national government representatives and by the United Nations General Assembly. In coordinating AIDS programs, WHO maintains close collaboration with national programs; with such other United Nations agencies as UNFPA, UNICEF, UNESCO, UNDP, and the World Bank; and with nongovernmental organizations, including the American Foundation for AIDS Research, the International Council of Nurses, the League of Red Cross and Red Crescent Societies, and the International Union of Immunological Societies. WHO acts as a world center for the collection, analysis, and dissemination of data relevant to the control of AIDS. In spite of the indispensable role of WHO as coordinating agency, most AIDS efforts and expenditures are concentrated at the national level.

By 1991, WHO estimated that there were at least 1.5 million AIDS cases in the world, including 500,000 children under five years of age, with 90 percent of these children in sub-Saharan Africa. At the same time it was estimated that the number of persons infected with the human immunodeficiency virus (HIV), a precursor to AIDS, totaled at least 8 to 10 million, including 3 million women of childbearing age.

In WHO's general program for 1990–95 special emphasis was given to an Expanded Program on Immunization. By 1990, 80 percent of all children had been immunized for measles, whooping cough, tetanus, poliomyelitis, tuberculosis, and diphtheria. WHO's goal is universal child immunization for these diseases.

WHO serves as an information and publication center on health matters by compiling statistics and publishing reports, research studies, monographs, manuals, directories, and several periodicals. It can draw on and disseminate information through several hundred reference centers that have agreed to serve as part of a network that WHO coordinates.

Through collaboration with private and public agencies, WHO expands its influence in every aspect of its program. The reference centers mentioned above are one example of this collaboration; another is the relationship with the Pan American Sanitary Bureau, which serves both as a regional office of WHO and as an arm of the Organization of American States (OAS) with its own program and budget. A substantial portion of the budget of the United Nations Children's Fund (UNICEF) is administered through WHO since the health of children is a prime aspect of their welfare. WHO collaborates with other United Nations specialized agencies in activities that are mutually supportive. The closest relationships are with the Food and Agriculture Organization (FAO); the International Labor Organization (ILO); and the United Nations Educational, Scientific and Cultural Organization (UNESCO). WHO also administers programs and funds as a part of the United Nations Development Program, in addition to the programs financed through WHO's regular budget.

Altogether WHO has working agreements and relationships with more than 150 major public and private organizations in the health field in addition to its hundreds of reference centers. For its expertise it depends not only on its own staff but also on forty-five or more advisory panels and expert committees representing a cross section of health subjects and world talent.

This review of the broad range of WHO activities and collaboration could lead one to assume that great inroads have been made into the problems of world health. When one adds to the picture the fact that, in a country such as the United States, expenditures have been several times as great for bilateral programs as for multilateral activities, and that foundations and private organizations have devoted substantial funds and energy to the alleviation of health problems, the expectations for success might be raised even higher. Signal advances in some areas have, indeed, been made. The world has already eliminated smallpox and is well on the way toward the elimination of malaria, tuberculosis, and yaws. But the attainment of the goal of health for all is nearly as remote as it was in 1948. Hundreds of millions of humans live without access to medical aid, health services, safe drinking water, or sanitary facilities. WHO currently dispenses funds from all sources of more than $800 million annually. The World Bank reports external assistance for all health-related activities, broadly defined, as more than $1 billion annually. Yet the Committee for Development Planning established by the Economic and Social Council suggested in 1970 that, in order to meet the needs and implement the objectives of WHO, an annual expenditure of nearly $10 billion from bilateral and multilateral sources would be necessary. In addition to large sums of money, a substantial increase in personnel and adequate planning would be major requirements. As in most international problems, the reallocation of human and monetary resources is not likely to occur in a highly compartmentalized world. The areas of greatest need are those with scarce resources. Without a restructuring of human values, the attainment of a high level of health for the poverty-stricken populations of the world will be a slow process.

FOCUS ON CHILD WELFARE AND YOUTH

The plight of destitute children has a strong emotional appeal for most persons. Several of the United Nations specialized agencies include in their programs projects that address the needs of the young. WHO is concerned with the health of children, FAO with their nutritional needs, UNESCO with problems of education, and the International Labor Organization (ILO) with child labor. An additional organization, UNICEF, concentrates exclusively on the task of improving the lot of disadvantaged children. Since the 1950s, its main concern has been the condition of children in the developing countries.

At its creation by resolution of the General Assembly in December 1946, UNICEF was intended to be an emergency organization to care for the European children who were victims of World War II. Hence its full original title, United Nations International Children's Emergency Fund, emphasized the crisis nature of what was planned as a temporary agency. In 1953, when it was made a permanent agency and the word *emergency* was dropped from its official title, its familiar acronym, UNICEF, remained unchanged.

When UNICEF was formed, it had available approximately $30 million in unexpended assets from the United Nations Relief and Rehabilitation Administration (UNRRA). During the period 1946–50, when UNICEF's activities were concentrated in Europe, it provided $112 million in direct assistance to needy European children. At the peak of the European operations, 6 million children received a daily supplementary meal, 5 million were given clothing and shoes, and 8 million received a vaccine to inoculate them against tuberculosis.

UNICEF is neither a specialized agency of the United Nations nor an operating agency. Its budget is not raised by assessment but by voluntary contributions from governments and private sources. It was established by resolution of the General Assembly and is not a membership organization, although more than 120 governments make voluntary contributions for its support. It is, as its title suggests, a fund administered under the direction of a thirty-nation executive board with the assistance of a staff incorporated within the United Nations Secretariat and headed by an executive director. UNICEF grants are made to governments for projects benefiting children, and experts are recruited through WHO, the FAO, UNESCO, or other agencies, with UNICEF subsidizing the costs. Governments requesting aid must furnish financial support and personnel so that UNICEF funds have a catalytic or multiplier effect. Government funds for UNICEF-aided projects average 2½ times the UNICEF subsidy. Private sources of income for UNICEF have risen in both absolute and percentage terms. Today they account for more than 25 percent of UNICEF's resources. Personalities from the entertainment and sports worlds, such as Danny Kaye, Audrey Hepburn, and Katarina Witt have acted as special ambassadors for UNICEF, devoting much time to publicizing the needs of children and promoting financial support for UNICEF.

In the mid-1980s, UNICEF focused special attention upon the needs of African children. In a special report entitled *Human Reach: A Future for Africa's Children,* the emphasis was placed on the long-range problems of nutrition and health of the very young in Africa. The report emphasized that, although 5 million children died in Africa in 1985, 4 million die every year when there is no drought, famine, epidemic, or media coverage. Called for was a "Marshall Plan" to assure sufficient financial support on a stable and sustained basis.

After a campaign of many years, the Convention on the Rights of the Child was opened for signature in January 1990, and by December 1993 had been ratified by 154 countries. A World Summit for Children in September 1990 set as its goals by the year 2000: (1) to reduce mortality rates of children under five years of age by one-third from 1990 rates, (2) to reduce maternal mortality rates by one-half, (3) to reduce severe and moderate malnutrition of children under five by one-half, (4) to achieve universal access to safe drinking water and sanitary disposal systems, (5) to achieve universal access to basic education, (6) to reduce the 1990 adult illiteracy rate by one-half, and (7) to provide special protection for children in armed-conflict situations.

In spite of occasional attacks on UNICEF by right-wing groups in the United States, the organization has been widely acclaimed as one of the most significant developments among the social and humanitarian efforts of the United Nations. In recognition of its great contribution, UNICEF was awarded the Nobel Peace Prize in 1965. Hundreds of millions of children in the developing countries require substantial aid if they are to make maximum contributions to the economic, social, and political development of their nations. UNICEF is making more than a token impact upon their prospects for a better life.

The United Nations General Assembly has focused on a number of special problems relating to youth. These problems include unemployment, illiteracy, poverty, juvenile delinquency, and drug abuse. Another emphasis is on young people who are abused, neglected, abandoned, or living in marginal circumstances. The General Assembly designated 1985 as International Youth Year (IYY). United Nations agencies with special programs for youth include UNESCO, WHO, UNICEF, FAO, and ILO. The coordinating agency is the

Centre for Social Development and Humanitarian Affairs (CSDHA) in Vienna. In preparation for the tenth anniversary of IYY the UN Secretariat, the Economic and Social Council, and its Commission for Social Development began work in 1992 on a draft World Program of Action for youth. The Economic and Social Council has also urged that the International Year of the Family in 1994 be utilized as an instrument for promoting youth welfare.[2]

THE QUESTION OF AGING

Global population trends indicate that between 1975 and 2025 the number of persons aged 60 and over will increase by 315 percent to more than 1.1 billion compared to a total world population growth of 102 percent. By 1978 the Economic and Social Council, through its Commission for Social Development, prompted the General Assembly to call for a World Assembly on Aging. After extensive preparatory work at many levels, this World Assembly met in Vienna from July 26 to August 6, 1982. As an important part of the preparatory work, a forum on aging was held in Vienna from March 29 to April 2, 1982, attended by 336 delegates representing 159 nongovernmental organizations (NGOs), which had consultative status with the Economic and Social Council.

The World Assembly issued the Vienna International Plan of Action on Aging, which the United Nations General Assembly endorsed on December 3, 1982. The Plan of Action focused on positive contributions that older persons could make to the society, as well as on such concerns as health and nutrition, housing and environment, the family, social welfare, income security, employment, retirement, and education. In implementing the plan, governments were urged to design national strategies responsive to their own particular needs. At the global level the United Nations Centre for Social Development and Humanitarian Affairs in Vienna was designated as the executing agency to carry out technical assistance projects for the aging. Since most of the implementation was to be accomplished by national governments, the Secretary-General was urged to coordinate these efforts. He was also requested, in formulating overall budgetary plans, to allocate necessary funds for translating the plan into action. Other United Nations agencies with supportive functions were the United Nations Fund for Population Activities, several of the specialized agencies, and the Administrative Committee on Coordination. The Economic and Social Council through the Commission for Social Development was requested to review progress toward implementation every four years and to report to the General Assembly. Nongovernmental organizations were also invited to coordinate their activities with the United Nations.

[2]United Nations Association of the United States of America, *A Global Agenda: Issues before the 47th General Assembly of the United Nations* (Lanham, MD: University Press of America, 1992), pp. 280–82; and *Issues before the 48th General Assembly* (1993), pp. 260–61.

To carry out planning for the World Assembly on Aging, the General Assembly in 1980 had requested governments to contribute to a modest United Nations Trust Fund. In 1991 a Banyan Fund was also established to raise private funds from corporations, foundations, and other private sources. Nevertheless, inadequate funding has been a major factor in limiting desirable measures toward implementing the goals of the International Plan of Action. In 1987 the Economic and Social Council also approved the establishment in Malta of the International Institute on Aging which, in cooperation with the University of Malta, began operations in 1988. It carries on research activities and conducts short-term courses on subjects related to gerontology. In 1989 the 14th International World Congress on Gerontology was held in Mexico City. In 1992 the UN General Assembly devoted four sessions to the subject of the aging. Members adopted a Proclamation on Aging and proclaimed 1999 as the International Year of Older Persons.

In the area of gerontology much collaborative activity is occurring in the private, national, and global sectors. However, the problems of an aging population are expanding so rapidly and the competition for scarce resources is so great that progress toward solutions is slow, and the issues involved will be persistent for decades to come.

IMPROVING CONDITIONS OF LABOR

Although other agencies of the United Nations family of organizations engage in limited activities beneficial to workers, it is in the International Labor Organization (ILO) that the bulk of these efforts is concentrated. Workers are affected by certain aspects of the programs of the Human Rights Commission, UNESCO, and the World Health Organization; the Economic and Social Council discusses and coordinates matters of vital concern to the welfare of the laboring class; the ILO consults with and engages in joint projects with other specialized agencies of the United Nations. But these efforts on behalf of labor are tangential and incidental to the concentration within the ILO of programs for the improvement of conditions for those within each society who are classified as laborers.

The ILO is unique both in its origins and in its system of representation. In response to pressure from several international workers' conferences held during World War I, the Paris peace conference incorporated the Constitution of the ILO into the Treaty of Versailles. Thus, the ILO was established in 1919 in the same manner as the League of Nations as a part of the movement to further world order through international cooperative institutions. In declaring that the ILO should be an autonomous organization associated with the League of Nations, the peace conference established a model that would serve for the relationship of the specialized agencies to the United Nations a quarter of a century later. The ILO's pattern of affiliation with the League based on the twin principles of autonomy and coordination proved more attractive at the San Francisco conference than suggestions for a highly centralized system of agencies. As a continuous organization since 1919, the ILO in 1946 became the first of the specialized agencies to conclude an agreement with the United Nations defining that relationship.

The ILO is typical of most of the other specialized agencies in its tripartite structure. This tripartite organization usually consists of a general conference, or assembly, in which all members are represented, a smaller council, or executive board, which acts as an executive committee between sessions of the larger assembly, and a secretariat, headed by a director-general, which carries out the basic policies established by the conference or assembly. In the ILO these three major organs are given the titles International Labor Conference, Governing Body, and International Labor Office.

Although similar to the other specialized agencies in overall organizational structure, the ILO is unique in its system of representation. The novel feature of ILO representation applies to both the International Labor Conference and the Governing Body, in which there are employers' delegates and workers' delegates as well as government delegates. Each member state is represented in the International Labor Conference by two government delegates, one employers' delegate, and one workers' delegate. In the choice of employers' and workers' delegates, governments are obligated to consult "with the industrial organizations, if such organizations exist, which are most representative of employers or workpeople, as the case may be, in their respective countries."[3] The Governing Body has a similar balance and consists of twenty-eight government representatives, fourteen employers' representatives, and fourteen workers' representatives. Ten of the government representatives are required to be from the states of "chief industrial importance" and the employers' and workers' representatives are "elected respectively by the Employers' delegates and the Workers' delegates to the Conference."[4] In Communist ideology the identity of interests among government, employers, and workers tends to vitiate the purpose of tripartite representation and has led to charges of a lack of divergent interests and viewpoints among Communist delegates. In general, however, the tripartite formula has received praise and support as a device peculiarly suitable to such an organization as the ILO.

The activities of the ILO may be divided into four major categories. These are (1) standard setting, (2) technical cooperation, (3) research and information, and (4) education and training.

The purpose of standard setting is to improve labor conditions and workers' rights. The ILO has pioneered in safeguarding human rights.

[3]ILO Constitution, Art. 3, sec. 5.
[4]Ibid., Art. 7.

Although it works in the limited but significant area of workers' rights, the ILO lost no time after its establishment in 1919 in gradually building a body of law known as the International Labor Code through the development of conventions and recommendations to be adopted by member states. Beginning with the adoption of six conventions and six recommendations by the first International Labor Conference in 1919, the Code today consists of more than 170 conventions and more than 180 recommendations. The number of new ratifications of conventions by governments usually exceeds 150 per year and is now over 5,900. While this number seems substantial, it represents an average of about 34 ratifications for each convention in an organization whose recent membership is approximately 166. States that have most recently joined the ILO tend to be low in number of ratifications, but the United States, whose membership dates from 1934, has ratified only eleven conventions. In contrast, Spain, France, and Italy ratified more than 100 of these international instruments, thus incorporating a substantial portion of the Labor Code into their internal legal systems.

The subjects covered by the Code are diverse, making the Code a comprehensive charter of workers' rights. Most fundamental is the right to organize and bargain collectively, which is recognized in several conventions. Other subjects forbid slavery or forced labor, or regulate hours of work, wages, unemployment, workers' compensation, insurance benefits, and safety. Many parts of the Code give protection to special categories of workers, especially women, young people, miners, and seamen.

Member states of the ILO are required through their governments to call each newly developed instrument to the attention of their respective legislative bodies and, once ratified, to report periodically on compliance. A review procedure for these reports is a part of the monitoring and implementation process of the ILO, which is generally credited with having developed the most effective review methods among the global organizations. Because of this effectiveness and the accumulated experience of the ILO, and since many of the ILO conventions and recommendations are elaborations of the International Covenant on Economic, Social and Cultural Rights (discussed in the next chapter), a method of collaboration has been worked out between the United Nations and the ILO for checking on government compliance with those provisions of the Covenant. The ILO's Committee of Experts on the Application of Conventions and Recommendations acts as a review body and reports to the UN Economic and Social Council.

Another ILO device for encouraging adherence to the standards of the International Labor Code is to seek changes in national legislation to bring it into harmony with the Code. Since 1964 more than 1,850 changes have been made to bring national law into conformity with provisions of conventions in response to observations made by ILO supervisory bodies.

While the standards of the International Labor Code, established by conventions and recommendations, are mainly a reflection of the achievements of the more advanced industrial countries, the ILO's work in technical assistance and economic development is of primary significance to the developing nations, which now make up 70 percent of its membership. Although limited activities involving advisory missions had been sponsored by the ILO since the 1930s, the first expansion of this work into a major program of the ILO was recommended by the director-general, David Morse, in 1949. Supplements to the ILO budget for this purpose became available in 1950 through the United Nations Expanded Program of Technical Assistance. Today more than one-half of all ILO activity is in this area.

Although aid sought from the ILO by governments ranges over a broad spectrum of specific projects, a major portion of the technical-cooperation activities falls within the general field of manpower or human resources, including vocational training. The means include the recruiting and furnishing of experts, providing fellowships and study grants, and conducting seminars and local and regional training courses. In recent years more than 1,000 experts have been assigned, and a similar number of fellowships and study grants have been awarded annually through the ILO.

In the area of research and information the ILO performs a function in labor matters similar to that of most other specialized agencies in their respective fields. The ILO is the only comprehensive organization capable of acting as a research and information agency in the field of labor data. Research and information functions are performed by the Central Library and Documentation Branch, the Central Research and Planning Department, the International Occupational Safety and Health Information Center, the Editorial and Translation Branch, and the Public Information Branch of the Geneva office. Publications include, *inter alia,* the quarterly *Official Bulletin,* the monthly *International Labor Review,* the *Year Book of Labor Statistics,* and a variety of studies, handbooks, and manuals. The Public Information Branch also issues press and media releases, films, photographs, posters, and booklets. As a worldwide organization the ILO must furnish publications in several languages, especially in English, French, and Spanish.

In the field of education and training the ILO has established two institutions of special significance. The first is the International Institute for Labor Studies at Geneva, established in 1961. The institute conducts high-level courses on social and labor policy for government and industrial leaders and researchers, concentrating on labor problems in social and economic development. The institute hopes to act as a catalyst for the establishment of similar programs of leadership education in national education centers of developing countries. The second institution of special note is the International Centre for Advanced Technical and Vocational Training at Turin, Italy, which was opened in 1965. The original mandate of the Turin center was to provide technical and vocational training for persons, primarily from developing countries, at more advanced levels than they could obtain in their own countries or regions and to provide training of instructors in technical cooperation. This mandate has been expanded to include emphasis upon management training for senior and middle-level managers from both industrialized and developing countries. During the first three years of operation, the courses at the center enrolled 500 trainees annually, but a target of 1,500 four-month fellowships was established. In 1992 the center enrolled more than 2,000 trainees in 120 courses.

In recent years the work of the ILO has been somewhat decentralized through the creation of a pattern of area offices, regional offices, regional conferences, regional advisory committees, and industrial committees. This decentralization reflects a means of bringing technical cooperation and informational and research activities closer to local sources.

In its current program the ILO stresses the following themes: (1) standard setting and human rights, (2) employment promotion, (3) training, (4) industrial relations and labor administration, (5) working conditions and environment, (6) industrial sectoral activities, (7) social security, and (8) services to employers' and workers' organizations.

After threatening in 1975 to do so, the United States in November 1977 withdrew from membership in the ILO for a period of more than two years. The reasons given were the erosion of the tripartite principle, the ILO's selective concern for human rights, its growing disregard for due process, and the increasing politicization of the organization. The serious temporary loss of 25 percent of the ILO budget was met mainly by the curtailment of services and functions, although several smaller states offered to make up some of the loss.

The ILO can provide no panaceas for assuring the welfare of workers. As with other international agencies, it lacks teeth for enforcing its standards. It lacks sufficient funds for meeting all the demands for technical cooperation in the areas of its competence. But in many areas the ILO has furnished indispensable services to governments and groups of individuals during its more than seventy-five years of existence. The awarding of the Nobel Peace Prize to the ILO in its fiftieth anniversary year, 1969, was one evidence of esteem and respect. Now that the United States has rejoined the organization and the budget difficulty has been removed, the ILO can continue to play the important role for which it has been noted throughout its history.

COOPERATION IN EDUCATION, SCIENCE, AND CULTURE

One basic factor in the slow advancement of the development process for two-thirds of the world's people is the wasted human potential associated with high illiteracy and a lack of skills. Overcoming these deficiencies could, in combination with other necessary ingredients for growth, go far toward implementing the "revolution of rising hopes and expectations" sought by the more enlightened leaders of the developing nations.

Since its establishment in 1946, the United Nations Educational, Scientific and Cultural Organization (UNESCO) has concentrated much of its major efforts in the educational portion of its program on the elimination of illiteracy and on training in basic skills. Traditionally, literacy has been defined as an ability to read and write. UNESCO has sought a more utilitarian form of literacy through literacy with a social and economic value. The early terminology in UNESCO's program of "fundamental education" has been superseded more recently by a program of "functional literacy," but the goals are essentially identical. The aim of functional literacy is economic and social effectiveness, which includes vocational training and skills linked to social and economic development. UNESCO, in cooperation with nongovernmental organizations and the United Nations Development Program, can furnish encouragement, information, research, technical assistance, and demonstration projects for combating illiteracy; but the major inputs of capital and the planning and execution of programs must come from national and local governments determined to solve their own educational problems.

Progress in eliminating adult illiteracy is not encouraging. The extent of illiteracy in the world is estimated by UNESCO to have decreased from 44 percent in 1957 to 34 percent in 1970. Yet, due to population increase, the number of illiterates actually increased during that period by 48 million to a total of 783 million adults. By 1992 the estimate of adult illiteracy had risen to 945 million. With most of these persons concentrated in the developing countries, the implications for the development process are obvious. Adult illiteracy and the lack of sufficient schools to guarantee even a minimal exposure to formal education of many minors make future prospects for closing the gap between have and have-not nations far from bright.

UNESCO's activities in the field of education, in addition to its literacy program, are far-ranging. The linkage between educational problems and the needs of developing nations is at the forefront of several other types of projects in the UNESCO program. For example, UNESCO has supported pilot projects in education for rural development in both Peru and Uganda. Most of the teacher-education effort of UNESCO has been focused on the problems of the developing countries. Low-cost and practical school buildings have been planned; curriculum development is emphasized; the production of textbooks and educational materials is fostered; conferences are sponsored between ministers of education and ministers responsible for economic planning; dozens of projects have been financed by the United Nations Development Program and administered and staffed by UNESCO. UNESCO has decentralized some of its educational efforts on behalf of disadvantaged areas by establishing regional offices for education for Africa (in Dakar), for Latin America (in Santiago), and for Asia (in Bangkok).

UNESCO also includes in the educational portion of its program a wide range of activities of general and worldwide significance and value. These activities encompass such processes as the holding of conferences, acting as a clearinghouse of information, gathering statistics, conducting research, issuing publications, and cooperating with other organizations interested in educational matters. Important publications that result from UNESCO's role as a clearinghouse of information are the *International Yearbook of Education,* published jointly with the International Bureau of Education; *Study Abroad,* issued biennially in English, French, and Spanish, and listing more than 250,000 scholarships throughout the world; and *Vacation Study Abroad,* listing opportunities for short-term foreign study. UNESCO cooperates with the other United Nations specialized agencies, and several hundred nongovernmental organizations have consultative status with UNESCO, but especially close affinities exist between UNESCO and the International Institute for Educational Planning in Paris.

Two other educational activities implemented by UNESCO resulted from initiatives taken by the United Nations General Assembly. The Assembly declared 1970 as International Education Year, and UNESCO set up special programs to emphasize education during that year. The General Assembly in 1969 agreed to consider a proposal by Secretary-General U Thant for establishing a United Nations or International University and requested that UNESCO prepare a feasibility study. The results of the study were generally favorable to the proposal, and the university began operations in Japan in 1975.

In the total UNESCO program the emphasis upon the natural sciences ranks close behind education in number and variety of projects and budget allocations. The main source of funds for natural science projects is not the regular UNESCO budget but the United Nations Development Program, which supplies more than 70 percent of the resources administered by UNESCO in the natural science area. Projects include the promotion of fundamental research in science; the establishment of a World Scientific and Technical Information System; studies and assistance to member states in science education, engineering education, and agricultural education; the training of technicians; promotion of research on natural resources and ecological research studies of natural disasters and their causes; hydrology projects and research; oceanography projects and research, including the establishment of an Integrated Global Ocean Station System; nuclear research; and research on the earth's arid zones and their possible uses. In 1957–58, UNESCO assisted in sponsoring the International Geophysical Year.

Over a period of several years, UNESCO developed a program called Man and the Biosphere as a contribution to the total United Nations program on human environment and pollution problems. Also, in preparation for the United Nations Conference on the Human Environment (Stockholm, 1972),

UNESCO produced a plan for a World Heritage Foundation to preserve critical environmental areas and endangered animal and plant species.

Since the bulk of UNESCO's funds for the natural sciences are furnished by the United Nations Development Program, most of UNESCO's activities in this area are in the nature of assisting member states to carry out programs in the natural sciences that will contribute to their economic development—for example, projects in science education, engineering education, agricultural education, and the training of technicians referred to in the previous list of UNESCO activities. UNESCO also assists and cooperates with nongovernmental organizations such as the International Council of Scientific Unions. Work is further decentralized through the operation of five field science offices for Africa, Latin America, the Arab states, South Asia, and Southeast Asia.

A third broad area of UNESCO's program encompasses the social sciences, humanities, and culture. Although UNESCO devotes a much smaller portion of its budget to these fields than to education or the natural sciences, the variety of activities in these fields is, nevertheless, quite broad. With assistance from the United Nations Development Program, UNESCO assists member governments primarily in three types of projects. These are (1) social-science teaching and research; (2) preservation, presentation, and development of their cultural heritage; and (3) training of museographers and technicians.

One method by which UNESCO widens its area of influence is through subsidies to numerous nongovernmental organizations with which UNESCO maintains close liaison. A sample list of such organizations includes the International Council for Philosophy and Humanistic Studies, the International Social Science Council, the International Political Science Association, the International Sociological Association, the International Economics Association, the International Committee for Social Science Documentation, the International Theater Institute, the International Music Council, the International Association of Plastic Arts, and the International Council of Museums. UNESCO also cooperates with and gives financial support to international and regional institutions such as the African Training and Research Centre in Administration for Development in Tangiers, the Latin American Social Science Faculty in Santiago, and the Center for Coordination of Research and Documentation in the Social Sciences in Vienna.

For many years UNESCO devoted much attention to questions of race in order to refute myths of racial superiority or inferiority. More recently the emphasis in the social sciences has focused on the contributions of the social sciences to development, the study of population and environment problems, the promotion of human rights, and research and teaching on the problems of peace.

One of UNESCO's primary concerns is the preservation of human culture. Studies of Asian, African, Latin American, and European cultures have been encouraged and supported. A massive *History of the Scientific and Cultural*

Development of Mankind has been published in several languages. Translations of the masterpieces of literature is a part of UNESCO's program linked with the publication of *Index Translationum,* an annual international bibliography of translations appearing throughout the world. Another major project is the mutual appreciation of Eastern and Western cultural values. UNESCO has aided states in the preservation and restoration of cultural monuments, including the Nubian monuments of Egypt. Other projects involve the safeguarding of Venice and the restoration of the art treasures of Florence in cooperation with the Italian government.

In the field of art, UNESCO has produced more than thirty sets of color slides with commentary on painting and sculpture and is continuing to produce three or four new sets each year. UNESCO also publishes a *Catalogue of Colour Reproductions of Paintings,* with one edition for the period before 1860 and another for 1860 to the present. These are updated and revised regularly.

Among the important multilateral treaties developed by UNESCO are a Universal Copyright Convention and a Convention on the Free Flow of Educational, Scientific and Cultural Materials. Each has been ratified by more than eighty states.

Finally, UNESCO publishes or subsidizes the publication of a number of periodicals in addition to those previously mentioned. These include the *UNESCO Courier,* the *International Social Science Journal,* and *Museum.*

One might assume that with such a variety of programs UNESCO's impact in the areas of its competence would be substantial. Yet the resources available are extremely limited in relation to the size of the problems, and the obstacles to be overcome are formidable. The scattering of limited resources over such a broad range of activities may in itself act as a limiting factor in effectively coping with educational, scientific, and cultural problems, and UNESCO has frequently been accused of too much diffusion of effort. This criticism was blunted by the decision of UNESCO's Executive Board in November 1988 to radically reduce the scope of the organization's program. The number of major areas in programming was reduced from fourteen to seven, with specific programs down from fifty-four to only seventeen. Other threats to UNESCO's vitality are the politicizing of the organization and charges of financial and organizational mismanagement. Anti-Israeli actions and resolutions in the 1970s incensed some governments and scholars. Later the focus of complaints centered on Director-General Amadou-Mahtar M'Bow, who was accused of being authoritarian, highhanded, and impervious to complaints. In 1984 the United States withdrew from membership, alleging that demanded reforms had not been made. A year later the United Kingdom and Singapore withdrew. The loss of approximately 30 percent of the organization's budget was a serious blow to UNESCO programs. Other major countries threatened to withdraw from membership if M'Bow were elected to an unprecedented third six-year term as Director-General. In November 1987 the General Conference elected Frederico Mayor Zaragoza of Spain to succeed M'Bow. The new Director-General instituted reforms in both administrative structure and program, thus hoping to woo back into membership the states that had withdrawn. At the same time he was careful not to alienate the third-world members that had constituted the strongest support for his predecessor.

UNESCO has also been embroiled in a North-South issue over the South's demands for a New International Information Order, in which developing states seek greater control over news and information and accuse the affluent states of monopoly control of the information channels. In turn, the North sees these demands as a threat to "freedom of the press." The new Director-General has de-emphasized UNESCO's role in seeking a New International Information Order, but the issue has been kept alive in the UN General Assembly through its Committee on Information.

In spite of all the above criticisms and threats, the fundamental importance of the elements of the UNESCO program for human well-being and enrichment cannot be denied. In UNESCO's revised and streamlined program, literacy receives major emphasis, beginning with the observance of 1990 as International Literacy Year. A return to full membership, together with ongoing reforms, will restore the reputation of UNESCO as an essential element in global cooperation in education, science, and culture.

COMBATING NARCOTIC DRUGS AND CRIME

Narcotic drugs are both a boon to medical science and, at the same time, a threat to individual and societal well-being. The problem is to produce sufficient amounts for medical and scientific needs and to prevent illicit traffic that leads to uncontrolled use or addiction. No one nation can achieve these ends without international cooperation and international instruments of control.

Attempts at narcotics control date back to the period before World War I. In 1912 the first convention on the subject was adopted at The Hague and established essentially the principles and methods of control that have been used in all subsequent agreements. Production, manufacture, and trade in narcotic drugs were to be controlled by law, and permits and records were to be used as regulatory instruments. Opium and its derivatives (morphine and heroin) and cocaine were the chief objects of early regulation. The League of Nations established two new agencies, the Permanent Central Opium Board and the Drug Supervisory Body, with limited regulatory powers, and drew up additional more comprehensive conventions to cover the new developments in narcotic-drug production. The system depended for its effectiveness upon government compliance in submitting annual and quarterly reports on production, consumption, stocks, imports and exports of drugs; upon import and export authorizations; and upon state enforcement of the conventions and national supporting legislation.

The United Nations system of control continues the essential features of the League arrangements. The Economic and Social Council early established as one of its functional commissions the Commission on Narcotic Drugs. The supervisory bodies of the League system continued to operate as United Nations agencies. A proliferation of new treaties resulted in pressure for the adoption in 1961 of a so-called Single Convention on Narcotic Drugs. By consolidating the several previous treaties into one, the problem of uniform regulations for all states adhering to the new convention was resolved since some states had previously been selective in their choice of treaties to ratify. At the same time an International Narcotics Control Board replaced the two previous regulatory agencies inherited from the League of Nations.

Before the single convention was in full operation, it became apparent that its scope was not sufficiently comprehensive to cover new developments and new problems of drug control. The manufacture of synthetic drugs and the widespread use of amphetamines, barbiturates, hallucinogens, and tranquillizers produced increased pressure for bringing their use under control. In 1971 a Convention on Psychotropic Substances was endorsed by an international conference in Vienna, attended by delegates of seventy-one governments. This convention entered into force in August 1976 when ratified by the required forty states. Loopholes in the enforcement provisions of the 1961 Single Convention on Narcotic Drugs also became apparent, and a conference was called in Geneva in March 1972 to strengthen these provisions. The protocol that was adopted, amending the single convention, came into force in 1975. In June 1987 an International Conference on Drug Abuse and Illicit Trafficking produced a comprehensive operational guide concentrating on reducing the demand for illegal drugs, curbing drug trafficking, and treating addicts. In December 1988 a new Convention on Narcotic Drugs was signed in Vienna, further strengthening the earlier treaties and providing for greater international cooperation in law enforcement and seizure of assets derived from illicit trading in drugs. A United Nations Fund for Drug Abuse Control with modest resources was established in 1971 to assist short- and long-term programs directed against drug abuse. Pledges to this fund increased dramatically in the late 1980s as world attention focused on the enormity and complexity of the drug problem.

The United Nations has added to its list of agencies in the drug field a Division of Narcotic Drugs at the UN Office in Vienna to provide professional and technical support for other United Nations bodies. Collaborative efforts are carried out between the United Nations drug agencies and the United Nations Development Program, the World Health Organization, the International Labor Organization, and the Food and Agriculture Organization. In 1991 the International Narcotics Control Board was integrated with the UN

Fund for Drug Abuse Control and the UN Division of Narcotic Drugs into a United Nations International Drug Control Programme.

In the late 1980s the drug problem in many quarters seemed to be intensifying. In the United States, President Bush declared a "war on drugs." In Colombia the drug cartel threatened the very foundations of the government and especially endangered those personnel engaged in law enforcement to control or punish the production and trafficking in cocaine. The heads of state of Colombia, Peru, Bolivia, and the United States held a summit meeting to discuss their common interests in drug control. Major dimensions of the problems are indicated in the 1988 report of the International Narcotics Control Board, which the Economic and Social Council summarized as follows:

> In its report for 1988, the Board notes that the abuse of a variety of drugs remains serious and continues to threaten all countries and all segments of society. . . . Intravenous abusers are at high risk of falling victim to the fatal acquired immuno-deficiency syndrome (AIDS). Illicit production and manufacture of drugs take place in a growing number of countries. These activities continue to be carried out by criminal organizations linked within countries, within regions and interregionally. These organizations, which often join forces with terrorist groups, spread violence and corruption, threaten political institutions, undermine the integrity of national economies and imperil the very security of countries.[5]

As with most social problems, law enforcement alone will not get to the root of the drug-abuse issue. In spite of international conventions and regulatory agencies, national laws and enforcement, and the cooperation of the International Criminal Police Organization (INTERPOL), illicit production, smuggling, drug addiction, and crime committed by sellers and users continue without significant letup. Synthetic drugs are easy to produce and difficult to regulate. The countries of Southeast Asia have been ineffective in controlling the production of opium. Turkey, with United States financial support, cut production by subsidizing poppy farmers to grow substitute crops. Fabulous wealth is accumulated by drug barons as a result of the cocaine trade originating in South American countries. At the users' end of the chain, a larger number of addicts with no source of cheap or legal supply will continue to make illicit sales so profitable as to invite high risks in supplying the demand. Society continues to grope for the "best" answers to this dilemma. To the control of production, manufacture, trade, and distribution of drugs must be added education, research, and treatment and rehabilitation of addicts if any impact is to be made on drug-abuse problems.

In addition to its activities in the criminal aspects of the drug problem, the United Nations has regularly carried on other diverse projects

---

[5]United Nations Document E/1989/38, p. 1.

relating to the transnational and international dimensions of crime. Every five years it sponsors a UN Congress on the Prevention of Crime and the Treatment of Offenders. The Economic and Social Council has established an expert Committee on Crime Prevention and Control, which produces recommendations for the attention of the congresses and other agencies. A Crime Prevention and Criminal Justice Branch of the Centre for Social Development and Humanitarian Affairs at the Vienna headquarters of the UN organizes meetings and develops model legislation and national structures for more effective crime control. Over a period of several years the numerous UN agencies, in suggesting national standards or means of international cooperation in crime control, consider a broad range of subjects. These subjects include the extradition of criminals, curtailing summary executions, the protection of persons under detention, developing a more adequate crime-prevention information system, the treatment and protection of juvenile delinquents, economic offenses, family violence, the dumping of nuclear and toxic waste in developing countries, organized crime, combating terrorist activity, illicit trade in national art treasures, government corruption, and the conduct of law-enforcement officials. In spite of a wide-ranging agenda, UN agencies suffer from a lack of adequate funds to carry on their work.

REFUGEE PROGRAMS AND DISASTER RELIEF

Wars, revolutions, and natural disasters frequently generate large numbers of refugees. Because of fear of persecution for reasons of race, religion, nationality, or political opinion, or in order to escape from unacceptable living conditions, groups of people move across national boundaries and constitute a problem for the host nation. Small numbers might be readily dispersed or assimilated, but mass movements of thousands or even millions of persons confront the host country with a dilemma of such proportions that international assistance is often both welcome and necessary. In addition to the issues involved for the host state, the welfare of the refugees raises questions of individual, local, national, and international concern.

To deal with the post-World War I refugee situation, the League of Nations appointed Fridtjof Nansen of Norway as high commissioner for refugees. Most of the original group of refugees resulted from the Russian Revolution of 1917, but additional numbers at irregular intervals from other sources caused the conversion of a temporary program into a permanent activity. The high commissioner developed the Nansen passport, which was accepted by more than fifty states as a permit for displaced persons to cross national boundaries in search of permanent homes. Without authority or monetary resources, the Nansen office could only solicit cooperation and aid from governments and private agencies and try to guarantee legal rights to displaced persons.

The trauma of World War II created new millions of refugees. The most satisfactory solutions for refugee problems involve (1) repatriation to the state of origin, (2) assimilation into the host state, or (3) resettlement to a new state willing to absorb a given number of displaced persons. The least desirable situation is to maintain refugee camps for sustained periods, since these camps usually result in unsatisfactory levels of nutrition, housing, and health care and in psychological attitudes of dependence and hopelessness.

By 1947 the large majority of World War II refugees were repatriated to their original states through the efforts of the military-occupation authorities with the aid of the United Nations Relief and Rehabilitation Administration (UNRRA). The problem of finding homes for the remaining 1.6 million was transferred in that year to the preparatory commission of a new specialized agency of the United Nations, the International Refugee Organization (IRO). During its short life this organization resettled more than a million persons in countries willing to absorb them and repatriated a few tens of thousands more. By the termination of the IRO's existence in 1951, most of the original group of refugees remaining in the European camps were "hard-core" refugees whom, because of age or other infirmity, no country was willing to accept.

In 1951, on the initiative of the General Assembly, the Office of the United Nations High Commissioner for Refugees (UNHCR) began operations, and through periodic renewals of its authority, continues as the general international agency for refugee protection. The office is nonoperational in its program and is thus dependent on governments and voluntary agencies for staffing the direct-care facilities for refugees. Excluded from the high commissioner's jurisdiction are refugees considered as nationals by the countries granting them asylum and refugees, such as the Palestine group, for whom separate United Nations programs have been established. At first no direct relief assistance was furnished by the UNHCR, but gradually this restriction has been relaxed. However, with an annual budget for both regular and special programs of $500 million raised by voluntary contributions, the office must depend primarily on other agencies for the direct aid that refugees require. The mandate for the UNHCR is thus very similar to that of the League of Nations high commissioner. The main functions are (1) furnishing legal protection to refugees; (2) facilitating repatriation, resettlement, and assimilation of refugees; (3) coordinating the efforts of governments and private agencies; (4) stimulating international action on behalf of refugees; and (5) providing technical assistance on a very modest scale.

As a basis for the legal protection of refugees, a Convention Relating to the Status of Refugees was adopted in 1951 and came into force in 1954, and in 1967 a protocol was added to enlarge its coverage. The convention specifies the minimum rights of refugees, such as the right to work, to education, to social welfare, to religious freedom, and to access to legal processes. It also provides for the issuance of travel documents and guarantees protection against expulsion under conditions threatening the refugee's life or freedom. More than 100 countries have acceded to the convention or protocol or both.

One persistent problem, which has been politically explosive because of emotional overtones, has been that of Palestine refugees displaced as a result of the creation of the Israeli state and the Arab-Israeli conflict. In 1950 the United Nations Relief and Works Agency for Palestine Refugees in the Near East (UNRWA) assumed the responsibilities that had been temporarily carried out since 1948 by other agencies. Although, as in the case of the UNHCR, the UNRWA is supported by voluntary contributions, it is an operating agency with substantial financial requirements. On an annual budget of $200 to $250 million, it has attempted to furnish enough daily food to prevent starvation among more than half of the total of 2.2 million refugees registered with the agency. It has also, because of the large number of children and young people among the refugees, stressed education in its recent programs. UNRWA operates more than 600 schools, most of which are on double shifts, and employs 9,200 teachers, nearly all of whom are refugees, as are the bulk of its other 7,000 employees. Health care is also a necessary element in its services. The snail's pace of the Middle East peace process leaves these unfortunate people in Syria, Lebanon, the Gaza Strip, the West Bank, and Jordan in the position of pawns in a nearly half-century struggle for a political settlement in the area. The Arabs stress the right of the refugees to return to their original homes, while the Israelis point to the lack of Arab effort to resettle or assimilate these people. In the meantime, hundreds of thousands of persons exist at subhuman levels. Ever since the Israeli invasion of Lebanon in 1982, UNRWA has encountered almost insurmountable difficulties in maintaining its operations in that country.

The expectation that refugee problems are transient and will disappear seems ill-founded on the basis of other experience in addition to the Palestine situation. The creation of the IRO for only four years and the original mandate of the high commissioner for only three years demonstrate the illusion that the need for such agencies might be temporary. However, no sooner had the European refugee situation been reduced to manageable proportions (although with fresh inputs, such as Hungarian refugees of 1956) than Africa became the main area of concern. Refugees from Morocco, Tunisia, the Congo, Angola, Rwanda, Mozambique, Portugese Guinea, and the Sudan swelled the numbers to approximately 1 million, with Angola accounting for the largest group. Asian groups included Tibetans and Chinese in Hong Kong. However, all these movements of refugees were dwarfed in 1971 by the sudden influx of at least 7 million persons fleeing to India from the civil war in East Pakistan. Among them disease and starvation became rampant, and the international community was requested to furnish emergency aid at a rate of nearly $1 billion annually. No adequate international machinery exists to channel such massive aid, and the bases of response make the survival (let alone the human dignity) of the refugees highly uncertain.

By 1993 there were 19 million refugees and 25 million internally displaced persons worldwide. The war in the former Yugoslavia had produced 3.5 million refugees and displaced persons, and the conflict in Somalia approximately 1.5 million persons in these categories. In addition to these countries and the Palestinians, the largest numbers of refugees were from Afghanistan, Mozambique, Ethiopia/Eritrea, and Liberia; and the largest numbers of internally displaced persons were from Sudan, South Africa, Afghanistan, Mozambique, the Philippines, and Ethiopia/Eritrea. Thus Africa continued to provide the leading focus for UNHCR attention.

From August 1988 to June 1989, three conferences were called to discuss regional refugee problems. The first met in Oslo with the support of the Organization of African Unity and addressed the Plight of Refugees, Returnees, and Displaced Persons in Southern Africa. An International Conference on Central American Refugees met in May 1989 in Guatemala City. The third regionally focused conference was instigated by the Association of Southeast Asian Nations. This International Conference on Indochinese Refugees met in Geneva in June 1989. In spite of many international efforts and changes of focus, the dimensions of refugee problems remain undiminished and require perennial attention.

Prior to 1970 various United Nations agencies had responded to appeals for aid in areas struck by natural disasters, but two of history's worst catastrophes in that year—an earthquake in Peru and a tidal wave in East Pakistan (now Bangladesh)—prompted the General Assembly to authorize the creation of the Office of United Nations Disaster Relief Coordinator (UNDRO). The Office began operations in Geneva in 1972. The two principal functions of UNDRO are (1) relief coordination (mobilizing, guiding, and coordinating aid to stricken nations), and (2) prevention and preparedness in disaster-prone areas. UNDRO acts as the coordinating agency in emergencies for UNICEF, appropriate United Nations specialized agencies, other private and government donors, and such agencies as the League of Red Cross Societies. Although UNDRO does not operate its own relief programs in the field, it has acted as the channel for more than $150 million to disaster areas. Its predisaster planning program has served more than thirty countries. In its first ten years UNDRO helped coordinate relief projects in more than 215 major disasters.

ASSESSING SOCIAL PROGRESS

There is no doubt that the worldwide promotion of social welfare is a never-ending process. In the competition for limited resources, social programs are often curtailed in favor of military expenditures or private luxuries and pleasures. Huge expenditures and well-administered programs would be necessary for the elimination of hunger, illiteracy, disease, drug addiction, and the plight of refugees. In a world of semisovereign states, most of these efforts must emerge from within each nation. Yet the fact of growing global interdependence plus the emotional human reaction to appeals for raising standards of human dignity and welfare evoke international responses to these appeals.

International agencies are not necessarily the most important channels for the international transfer of resources to aid in carrying out national social programs. Yet the United Nations devotes much of its budget and personnel to those ends. When the efforts of UNICEF, the WHO, the ILO, the FAO, UNESCO, and dozens of other global, regional, and private agencies and programs are added to the equation, the commitments are substantial. Much progress has been made since 1945. Many challenges remain.

15

HUMAN RIGHTS AND THE STRUGGLE FOR SELF-GOVERNMENT

The question of human rights is concerned with interpersonal relationships and with the relationships of the individual to governmental authority at all levels from local to international. Human rights include those areas of individual or group freedom that are immune from governmental interference or that, because of their basic contribution to human dignity or welfare, are subject to governmental guarantee, protection, or promotion. In the past half-century one of the most basic and widely accepted human rights has been the right of political independence and self-government.

Since 1945, the rush to independence has become a stampede, and the old colonialism, based on territorial dominance, has been nearly terminated. The speed of this stampede could not be predicted in 1945. Then, about one-third of the world's population was governed by metropolitan powers in some form of colonialism. Today less than 0.2 percent of the world's population is non-self-governing, and the number of recognized states has considerably more than doubled. India, Pakistan, and Indonesia account for three-fourths of the liberated population. Much of the rest live in numerous small states, many of which have very limited political and economic bases.

From the beginning, the United Nations has declared, in its Charter and in its delegate bodies, its interest in the movement toward self-government. This interest is shown through trusteeship and through decolonialization. The number of trust territories and their populations has represented only a fraction of the colonial domain, with decolonialization making up the bulk of the movement. After India, Pakistan, and Indonesia became independent, and at the peak of the establishment of trusteeship arrangements, only one-tenth as many people lived in trust territories as remained under colonial rule. Today both arrangements have been almost phased out, and only a few remnants of the system are left.

This chapter will trace the struggle for self-government in both its trusteeship and decolonialization dimensions and the problems of the emerging new states. The concluding topic will focus on the other aspects of the human-rights movement in the United Nations and other international arenas.

THE LEAGUE MANDATES SYSTEM

When the League of Nations was founded, the legitimacy of acquiring colonies was already beginning to be questioned, and, therefore, a way was sought by which the victorious powers in World War I could avoid the disapprobation of acquiring the overseas territories of the defeated powers as outright possessions. General Jan Smuts of South Africa included a plan for a League-supervised mandates system in his proposals for an international organization, and this idea was incorporated into the Covenant as Article 22. Territories taken from the defeated powers and not yet ready for self-government were to be placed under the tutelage of "advanced nations" and "this tutelage [was to] be exercised by them as Mandatories on behalf of the League." Each mandatory was to apply "the principle that the well-being and development of such people form a sacred trust of civilization." The League Council was assigned the responsibility of supervising the mandates system. The explicit terms of each mandate were agreed upon between the mandatory and the Council.

To assist the Council in supervising the mandates system, a Permanent Mandates Commission was constituted. The commission was composed of experts nominated by the Council and, to encourage their independence and impartiality, no one in a government role was considered for appointment. Each mandatory was required to submit an annual report on each territory to the Council. The Permanent Mandates Commission, rather than the Council, actually received these reports and supplemented the information through questioning representatives of the administering authority, often the governors of the territories. This useful and enlightening procedure served as a precedent and carried over into the practice of the United Nations Trusteeship Council.

In spite of severe handicaps, the Permanent Mandates Commission was remarkably successful in its efforts. The commission possessed no real authority and had to rely upon its reputation for thoroughness and impartiality to secure cooperation from all parties affected by its work. The annual reports by the mandatory and the interrogation of responsible administrators were the main sources of information on which the Commission could base its reports to the Council. No right of inspection by visiting missions existed. The administering states were the channels through which any petitions were screened and forwarded to the Commission. No right of petition was specified in the Covenant, but the right was sanctioned in Council practice. In the definitive historical work on the League of Nations, F. P. Walters points out that at first the administering states resented the Commission's inquiries and suggestions.

> But as the time went on its reputation for competence and fairness continued to grow. The mandatories themselves gradually discovered that if on the one hand the reprimands of the Commission were painful, on the other hand its suggestions were helpful and its commendations were a valuable encouragement to the administration in the field. In its last years the Commission was consulted and trusted by mandatory and non-mandatory powers alike.[1]

The territories placed under mandate fell into three categories. Territories formerly belonging to the Turkish empire were considered nearly ready for self-government and came to be known as A mandates. These included Lebanon and Syria under French supervision, and Iraq, Palestine, and Trans-Jordan under British supervision. All of the A mandates achieved full sovereignty between 1932 and 1947. The former German colonies in Central Africa were considered to be further from the attainment of self-rule and were classified as B mandates. Cameroons and Togoland were each split into two territories administered by the British and French; Tanganyika was assigned to British administration; Ruanda-Urundi was made a mandate of Belgium. The C mandates were considered to be incapable of self-rule in the foreseeable future, and because of their small size or population, or because of contiguity to the territory of the mandatory, the administering powers were permitted to administer them as integral parts of their territory. The C mandates were the former German colonies of South-West Africa placed under South African supervision; the Marianas, Caroline, and Marshall Islands assigned to Japan; New Guinea and Nauru under the aegis of Australia; and Western Samoa under the control of New Zealand. All of the B and C mandates except South-West Africa became trust territories under the United Nations trusteeship system.

The idea of mandates was frequently criticized as a thinly veiled disguise for expanded colonialism on the part of the victorious powers. Little distinction was drawn between the treatment and administration of mandates and that of other colonies of the metropolitan powers. Progress toward self-rule was slow, and the mandatories were under no pressure to advance self-govern-

---

[1]F. P. Walters, *A History of the League of Nations* (New York: Oxford University Press, 1952), I, 173.

ment in the C group of mandates. However, the constant pressure and publicity furnished by the Mandates Commission probably ensured more protection for the rights and well-being of the indigenous peoples than would have been otherwise guaranteed. The mandates system was a first step among several that foreshadowed the eventual doom of the old colonialism.

RUSH TO SELF-GOVERNMENT

Modern colonialism grew out of the age of exploration and discovery during which European explorers and traders gained access to areas of the globe from which Europe had been previously isolated, and European governments laid political and economic claim to those non-European territories. Territorial empires were accumulated by Spain, Great Britain, France, the Netherlands, Portugal, and Belgium, with Germany and Italy later aspirants to imperial rule. Political ambitions and economic gains provided incentives for empire building. Imperialism was accompanied by the establishment of a superior-inferior relationship, by the exploitation of the resources of the non-European territories by the metropolitan powers through both public and private channels, and by a sense of mission to bring the benefits of European civilization and administration to "less advanced" peoples—an attitude reflected in the phrase "the white man's burden." In the early stages of colonialism the possibilities of self-rule by indigenous populations did not occur to colonial administrators, although paternalistic attitudes concerning the welfare of native inhabitants increasingly developed.

Eventually the European model served as a major force in the dissolution of the overseas empires. Western political and economic revolutions caught the imagination of the dominated groups. Imperial administrators and entrepreneurs, although reserving all top government and management posts for Europeans, found it necessary to train more and more indigenous people for skilled positions and to use education as a means for progressively developing business and government enterprises. Native elites were educated in Western universities and embraced Western values as goals for their own societies. Members of these elites became leaders in the independence movements, were frequently jailed by colonial administrations, but eventually emerged as national heroes. Gandhi and Nehru in India, Nkrumah in Ghana, and Kenyatta in Kenya are familiar examples.

The impact of the European revolutionary model upon the anticolonial movement is cogently summarized by Rupert Emerson.

> . . . imperialism has been drawing to a close precisely because it has been fulfilling the historic but inadvertent function of spreading abroad the dynamism inherent in the great Western revolution of modern times. . . . The peoples who were being driven into the modern world by alien masters had learned enough

of a lesson to insist that, henceforward, they would themselves take control of their further advance into modernity. To sum the matter up in the briefest fashion: through global conquest the dominant Western powers worked to reshape the world in their own image and thus aroused against themselves the forces of nationalism which are both the bitterest enemies of imperialism and, perversely, its finest fruit.[2]

The first independence movements occurred in the Western Hemisphere and involved transplanted Europeans who inherited the values of the Western world. The war for independence in the area that became the United States was followed in the nineteenth century by secession from colonial empires by major segments of Latin America and by Canada. In the early twentieth century, Australia and New Zealand, also predominantly inhabited by British emigrants, attained self-rule.

By 1914 the major areas remaining under colonial jurisdiction were in Asia and Africa. The most prevalent pattern was domination by whites of non-whites. The territories that emerged as independent states between 1910 and World War II were relatively few in number and included South Africa, Saudi Arabia, Yemen, Egypt, and Iraq. Self-rule for hundreds of millions of non-whites remained as an unachieved goal in 1940.

World War II provided the impetus for accelerating the rush to independence. Japan invaded the British, French, Dutch, U.S., and Australian colonies in Southeast Asia and in the Pacific Islands. Only the Philippines, which had been promised early independence, provided formidable resistance to the invaders. Upon the withdrawal of Japanese forces, the Indonesians and Vietnamese seized the opportunity for revolt against the return to Dutch and French rule. India, Pakistan, Burma, Ceylon, and the Philippines rapidly achieved independence after the war. Korea was promised self-rule but became a divided state in the territorial arrangements growing out of the agreements for temporary occupation by Soviet and U.S. armed forces. In the Middle East the long-awaited transfer of sovereignty was promptly made to the remaining mandates, which became the states of Syria, Lebanon, Jordan, and Israel.

The war made an impact on other areas that were not immediately granted independence. Wartime conditions and the invasion of Belgium, the Netherlands, and France by the Nazi war machine disrupted the pattern of control over colonial possessions. Permanent domination of whites over non-whites was challenged. Recruitment of colonial forces for fighting outside their borders and increased contacts with military personnel from other countries both within and outside their home base widened the experiences and aspirations of colonial peoples. Allied slogans and aims in the war provided a philosophical basis for the allure of self-determination. The spread of infor-

---

[2]Rupert Emerson, *From Empire to Nation: The Rise to Self-Assertion of Asian and African Peoples* (Cambridge, MA: Harvard University Press, 1960), pp. 16–17.

mation allowed the attainment of independence by some states to serve as a model and to whet the desire of others for the same goal.

By the early 1950s the major remaining bastion of the old colonialism was in the African continent, and the final assault on this bastion had been clearly heralded. After 1950 the independence movement swept through the continent, adding more than forty-five new states to the four that had previously attained sovereignty. For many years the most stubborn foreign imperial state was Portugal, but after a change of regime, its policy abruptly shifted and it granted independence to Guinea-Bissau in 1974 and to Mozambique and Angola in 1975. Rhodesia, once a British colony, was under what the rest of the world considered to be an illegal white-minority-controlled government after 1965; but it obtained full sovereignty and independence in 1980 as the state of Zimbabwe. After that date the only large non-self-governing area was South-West Africa (Namibia).

THE UNITED NATIONS TRUSTEESHIP SYSTEM

No proposals for a system of trusteeship were included in the conversations of the major powers at Dumbarton Oaks; subsequently, at Yalta an agreement emerged providing only (1) that the Charter should include provisions for trusteeship, (2) that the major powers would consult on the matter before the San Francisco conference, and (3) that three categories of territories should be eligible for inclusion as trust territories. The three categories were those eventually incorporated into Article 77 of the Charter and included (1) former mandates under the League of Nations, (2) territories detached from enemy states as a result of World War II, and (3) any other territories voluntarily placed under the system by administering states. The anticipated consultations among the big powers were not held prior to the San Francisco sessions; instead, these consultations proceeded simultaneously with the drafting of the trusteeship provisions of the Charter, causing inconvenience and delay in committee consideration of the provisions.

At one stage in the postwar planning within the U.S. State Department, a proposal was made to apply the trusteeship principle to all colonies and dependencies, but this plan was resolutely opposed by the military arm of government. The same proposal was suggested in San Francisco by Australia and the Philippines but was not vigorously pushed and was dropped. As a substitute, several states supported the inclusion in the Charter of a declaration on non-self-governing territories, which developed into Chapter XI of the Charter. Details of this declaration, applying to other colonies and possessions not placed under trusteeship, are discussed in a subsequent section of this chapter.

Charter provisions for trusteeship involved several basic changes from those that governed the League mandate system. General supervision of trusteeship matters was shifted from the League Council to the United Nations General Assembly. The Permanent Mandates Commission, composed of experts serving in their private capacity, was replaced by the Trusteeship Council, made up of government representatives. Half of the members of the Trusteeship Council were the states that administered trust territories, thus assuring control over any measures on which the administering states were united. As a gesture toward the desirability of maintaining the services of experts, each member of the Council was requested to "designate one specially qualified person to represent it therein." The goal of self-government was indicated in the League Covenant only for category A mandates; trustees were bound by the Charter to promote the political advancement and the "progressive development towards self-government or independence" of all trust territories in accordance with the "freely expressed wishes of the peoples concerned."

In addition to the obligation to advance trust territories toward self-government or independence, the trustees were committed by Article 76 of the Charter to promote the economic, social, and educational advancement of the inhabitants of the trust territories. Other principles binding the trustees were (1) the promotion of human rights and fundamental freedoms, (2) encouragement of the recognition of the interdependence of peoples, (3) the furthering of international peace and security, and (4) the guarantee of equal treatment in social, economic, and commercial matters for United Nations members and their nationals. On the whole, these obligations served as better protection for the rights and aspirations of the indigenous peoples than had been provided in Article 22 of the League Covenant.

Although three categories of territories were designated as possible subjects of trusteeship agreements, thus opening the door to arrangements that could apply to dozens of non-self-governing territories, only eleven areas administered by seven trustees ever came under the aegis of the Trusteeship Council (as opposed to the fifteen mandated territories under the League). Most of the trust territories were former mandates.

A second category of potential candidates for trusteeship status was territories detached from enemy states as a result of World War II. The Pacific Islands group, over which the United States was granted a strategic trusteeship, can be classified in this category as well as in the group of mandates listed above, since Japan held these islands under mandate from the League of Nations. Of the three African colonies detached from Italy, one, Italian Somaliland (joined since 1960 with former British Somaliland into Somalia), was assigned by the General Assembly to Italy as trustee for a ten-year period beginning in 1950. The territory had been under British control in the interval since World War II. The arrangement was unusual (1) because of the assignment of a former enemy state as trustee, (2) because Italy was not yet a United Nations member in 1950, and (3) because Italy was subjected by the terms of the trusteeship agreement to several restrictions and to a degree of United Nations supervision not applicable to the trustees of other territories.

The third category of territories eligible for trusteeship were "territories voluntarily placed under the system by states responsible for their administration." Since no compulsion existed for colonial powers to submit to the inconveniences of international supervision over territories in this category, it is not surprising that no such offers were made.

Another unused feature of the Charter's trusteeship provisions is the possibility of designating the United Nations itself as the trustee over a specified territory. Suggestions were made from time to time for such an arrangement—for example, with regard to Palestine or Jerusalem—but none ever came to fruition. The United Nations created a Temporary Executive Authority (UNTEA) to administer the area of West Irian for a few months in 1962–63 in the interval between the transfer of jurisdiction from the Netherlands to Indonesia, but this operation most resembled a peacekeeping arrangement, and the Trusteeship Council was not involved. Another provision of the Charter for joint trustees was implemented in the arrangement for Australia, New Zealand, and the United Kingdom to serve as the administering authority over Nauru, but Australia was to act as administrator on behalf of all three.

As plans were being formulated for the trusteeship system, defense spokespersons within the United States government expressed their concern that, on the one hand, outright annexation of territory taken from the Axis powers was contrary to current world opinion, and that, on the other hand, the proposed trusteeship arrangements failed to provide for protection of the security interests of the United States in the Pacific area. To accommodate these military pressures, the State Department proposed a unique variation in the trusteeship arrangements by which all or part of a trust territory could be declared a strategic area. Only one territory, the Trust Territory of the Pacific Islands under United States administration, was offered as a strategic area. The Charter provides that all functions performed by the General Assembly in approving regular trusteeship agreements and in exercising supervisory powers shall be exercised by the Security Council for strategic areas. The purpose of this arrangement was apparently to give the United States a potential veto over any action considered adverse to its security interests. In practice, the Security Council never exercised its supervisory powers, although it annually received reports from the Trusteeship Council, as did the General Assembly for all other territories.

In many respects the obligations assumed by the trustee for a strategic area are identical to those applying to other trust territories. The trustee is obligated to promote the political, economic, social, and educational advancement of the inhabitants and the other rights and protections specified in Article 76 of the Charter as applying generally to the inhabitants of trust territories. Annual reports are submitted to the Trusteeship Council on the basis of a uniform questionnaire, visiting missions are sent to the territory at regular intervals, and petitions from the inhabitants are guaranteed a hearing through established procedures of the Trusteeship Council.

The major departures from the normal operation of the trusteeship system as applied to the Trust Territory of the Pacific Islands are in the closing of certain areas for security purposes and in the lack of a review of the Trusteeship Council's annual consideration of matters concerning the territory resulting from the Security Council's default on its exercise of this function. The United States conducted nuclear tests in the area from 1946 until 1958 and, for a time, declared the Bikini and Eniwetok regions closed to visiting missions. Other members of the Trusteeship Council severely criticized the United States for conducting these tests and charged that the interests and safety of the inhabitants were jeopardized. The fortification of the islands and the establishment of military, naval, and air bases required no special privileges for the United States since this right applied to all trust territories, a right forbidden in class B and C mandates under the League.

To provide for adequate supervision of the administration of the trust territories, the Charter stipulates the establishment of the Trusteeship Council. The composition of the Council was outlined in Chapter 4, and the details need not be repeated here. For the period 1950–55, Italy, as an administering state but a nonmember of the United Nations, sat in the Council without vote but with responsibility for its administration of Italian Somaliland. After the seating of the People's Republic of China delegation to the United Nations in 1971, its representative never participated in Trusteeship Council sessions until 1989.

During the most active years of the trusteeship system, the General Assembly exercised tight control over the Trusteeship Council through its Fourth Committee. Of necessity, however, the Trusteeship Council performed the primary functions needed to check on the administration of the trust territories. The Charter provides a broader range of methods for performing these functions than were available to the Mandates Commission of the League.

The special devices available to the Trusteeship Council are (1) annual reports from the administering authority, (2) petitions, and (3) visiting missions. The annual reports are based on a detailed questionnaire, and a special representative, usually a top administrator from the territory under investigation, is subjected to extensive questioning by members of the Council. At the height of Trusteeship Council activities, the volume of petitions from individuals and groups was of such proportions as to require special procedures for handling them. Both oral and written petitions are acceptable, and visiting missions may receive petitions during their visits to a territory. The use of visiting missions is a wholly unprecedented means of checking on the administration of trust territories. These missions are composed of representatives of two administering and two nonadministering members of the Trusteeship Council, each accompanied by the necessary supporting staff. Each territory was visited at three-year intervals. Each mission attempted to compare by observation the conditions within the territory with the information reported by the trustee and as reflected in previous petitions.

THE RECORD OF TRUSTEESHIP

Because the composition of the Trusteeship Council was dependent upon the prior adoption of trusteeship agreements, fourteen months were required after the initial session of the General Assembly before the Council could be organized. The General Assembly in February 1946 urged the mandatory powers to promptly draw up trusteeship proposals and submit them at an early date for General Assembly approval. Accordingly, eight proposed agreements were submitted to the General Assembly for consideration and approval at its reconvened first session in October–December of the same year. In spite of prolonged and sometimes bitter debate over some of the terms of the proposals, all major suggestions for modification were rejected, partially in recognition of the reality that the administering state had a final veto over changes it found unacceptable, since all trust arrangements were voluntary, not compulsory. On December 13, 1946, the Assembly approved all eight agreements and the following day elected two states to provide the necessary balance in the Trusteeship Council between administering and nonadministering members.

The Trusteeship Council met for the first time in March 1947, with ten members. Within the same year, trusteeship agreements were approved for the strategic Trust Territory of the Pacific Islands and for Nauru, and two more elective members were added to the Council. The only further territory added to the list was Italian Somaliland, but since Italy as trustee was not, in 1950, a United Nations member, it sat as a thirteenth nonvoting member of the Council until 1955. In that year Italy's admission to the United Nations required the election by the General Assembly of one additional nonadministering member of the Trusteeship Council. From 1955 to 1960 the composition of the Council was seven administering members (Australia, Belgium, France, Italy, New Zealand, the United Kingdom, and the United States); two nonadministering permanent members of the Security Council (China and the Soviet Union); and five members elected for three-year terms. The attainment of independence by eight trust territories between 1960 and 1968 left temporary majorities of nonadministering states on the Council until the terms of elected members expired. After 1975 only the five permanent members of the Security Council remained as Trusteeship Council members, with the nonadministering states outnumbering the administering states four to one.

The first trust territory to gain independence was British Togoland in 1957, when it was combined with the Gold Coast, a British colony, to form the new state of Ghana. The future of British Togoland was in doubt for several years preceding 1957 because of conflicting expressions of the wishes of various tribal groups living in the two Togolands and in the Gold Coast. Over a period of ten years the General Assembly and the Trusteeship Council, through the use of visiting missions, the holding of hearings, and a plebiscite, tried to determine the preferences of the various peoples of the area. Although the Ewe tribe, who were scattered across all the involved territories, opposed the union with the Gold Coast, the plebiscite showed a substantial majority in favor of the formation of the new state of Ghana.

Several trustees set up administrative unions by which a trust territory was administered through a single governmental structure common to the trust territory and an adjoining colony. Ardent advocates of the trusteeship system, in the interests of safeguarding the rights of indigenous inhabitants, were suspicious that such an arrangement would subvert those rights by reducing the trust territory to colonial status. In 1950, at the urging of the General Assembly, the Trusteeship Council established a Committee on Administrative Unions to scrutinize such unions to make sure that the fulfillment of all objectives of the trusteeship system, including the attainment of self-government, were not hampered by these arrangements. Most evidence indicates that administrative unions did not jeopardize the rights of the inhabitants of trust territories or slow progress toward self-government. The vigilance and supervision of the General Assembly and the Trusteeship Council may have helped to prevent any tendency to use administrative unions as a device for escaping from Charter obligations.

Progress toward independence has been furthered and expedited by the trusteeship system. Table 15–1 shows that eight of the eleven trust territories had attained self-rule by 1962. Although this process was paralleled by the rapid emergence of colonies as new states, the pressures for independence for the trust territories were increased through the supervision of United Nations agencies. Furthermore, the trust territories were, on the average, better prepared for self-rule than were many colonies. Pressures on the trustees to expand suffrage, to develop institutions of local government, and increasingly to involve the inhabitants as participants in the government and the administration of the territories paved the way for a smooth transition to self-government.

Economic and social gains were also registered in the trust territories during the period before independence. Evidence of these gains could be found in the annual reports on each territory, in the questioning of the spe-

TABLE 15-1 TERRITORIES PLACED UNDER UNITED NATIONS TRUSTEESHIP

TERRITORY	PREVIOUS STATUS	ADMINISTERING AUTHORITY	DURATION OF TRUSTEESHIP	PRESENT STATUS	UN MEMBERSHIP
Cameroons (British)	Class B Mandate (UK)	United Kingdom	1946–61	Portion incorporated into Nigeria; remainder into Cameroon (1961)	
Cameroons (French)	Class B Mandate (France)	France	1946–60	Independent as Cameroon (1960)	1960
Nauru	Class C Mandate (Australia)	Australia (on behalf of Australia, New Zealand, and UK)	1947–68	Independent (1968)	
New Guinea	Class C Mandate (Australia)	Australia	1946–75	Independent (1975)	1975
Ruanda-Urundi	Class B Mandate (Belgium)	Belgium	1946–62	Independent as separate states of Rwanda and Burundi (1962)	1962
Somaliland (Italian)	Italian Protectorate	Italy	1950–60	Independent and joined with British Somaliland as Somalia (1960)	1960

TABLE 15–1 (continued)

Tanganyika	Class B Mandate (UK)	United Kingdom	1946–61	Independent (1961); joined with Zanzibar (1964)	1961
Togoland (British)	Class B Mandate (UK)	United Kingdom	1946–57	Joined with Gold Coast as independent state of Ghana (1957)	1957
Togoland (French)	Class B Mandate (France)	France	1946–60	Independent as Togo (1960)	1960
Trust Territory of the Pacific Islands	Class C Mandate (Japan)	United States	1947–94	Divided into 4 units: 1 U.S. Commonwealth—Northern Marianas; 3 associated with U.S.—Marshall Islands, Micronesia, Palau	1991 1991
Western Samoa	Class C Mandate (New Zealand)	New Zealand	1946–62	Independent (1962)	1976

cial representatives by the members of the Trusteeship Council, and in the reports of the visiting missions to the various territories. The trustees were under constant pressure to advance the fundamental human rights of free speech, assembly, press, and religion, to improve the status of women, and to abolish racial discrimination and corporal punishment. Other pressures were exerted to show continuous improvement in educational and medical and health facilities and to develop transportation, communications, and levels of economic well-being of the local population.

According to most predictions, all trust territories were expected to achieve self-rule and allow the Trusteeship Council to cease functioning before the 1980s. However, the change of status for the Trust Territory of the Pacific Islands (often referred to as Micronesia) became a perennial problem. Inherently, Micronesia represented the ministate problem in its most extreme form. It was composed of three major groups of islands (the Marianas, the Carolinas, and the Marshalls) with a population of only 180,000 scattered over 3 million square miles of ocean. Formation of a single, independent state for the area could not provide a viable political or economic entity. But the problem was further prolonged by conflicts among the State, Interior, and Defense departments of the United States government and the encouragement from the United States for the formation of a separate Commonwealth of the Northern Marianas in political union with the United States upon termination of the Trusteeship Agreement. Plebiscites in other groups of islands approved Compacts of Free Association with the United States, and in 1991 they were admitted to United Nations membership as the Marshall Islands and Micronesia. However, seven plebiscites in Palau failed to achieve a constitutionally required three-fourths approval. Finally, after the Palauans amended their constitution to allow for approval by simple majority vote, the eighth plebiscite in November 1993 approved their Compact of Free Association with the United States. All the territories continued to express their disappointment that the U.S. Congress regularly failed to supply their expected levels of financial and other support. The settlement of the Palau issue finally, after twenty years of a seriously diminished status of the Trusteeship Council, completed the Council's raison d'être, and that UN major organ held its final session in 1994.

The trusteeship system was less than perfect in its operation. Conflicts between General Assembly and Trusteeship Council jurisdiction and functions were apparent, although Assembly supervision tended to prod the Council members and trustees into more diligent efforts to safeguard the interests of indigenous populations. On the whole, the glare of publicity furnished by the varied means of supervision over the administration of the territories produced salutary results in comparison with the League mandates system or with general colonial administration.

THE CHARTER AND NON-SELF-GOVERNING TERRITORIES

In 1945 when the Charter was written, the anticolonialist movement had not yet attained its momentum of later years. The provisions of Chapter XI entitled "Declaration Regarding Non-Self-Governing Territories" represented, therefore, a set of compromises between colonialism and the emerging pressures for terminating the colonial system. States representing the growing anticolonialist sentiment could effectively demand inclusion of guarantees for subjected peoples but could not establish these guarantees on any except a moral basis and without implementing machinery. Yet Chapter XI subsequently became the instrument for a militant campaign for the immediate granting of self-government and independence to all peoples who had not attained self-rule and political independence.

Chapter XI has been characterized as a bill of rights for all non-self-governing peoples. Since it represented a new precedent in asserting certain rights and since all members of the United Nations accepted obligations toward colonial peoples not clearly recognized previously, its revolutionary nature is evident. Colonial powers agreed, in adhering to Article 73 of the Charter, to "accept as a sacred trust the obligation to promote to the utmost, . . . the well-being of the inhabitants of these territories" and to "recognize the principle that the interests of the inhabitants of these territories are paramount." They further promised to ensure non-self-governing peoples political, economic, social, and educational advancement, just treatment, and the development of self-government and of free political institutions (but not necessarily independence). Colonial powers were additionally obligated to transmit to the Secretary-General statistical and technical information "relating to economic, social, and educational conditions in the territories" that they administered. However, such information was designated as "for information purposes," and no provision was made for the further use of this information. At the insistence of the colonial powers, political data were exempted from inclusion in the reports.

From the earliest years of the United Nations, the anticolonialist forces chipped away at the colonial bastions by seeking to put into operation the principles of Article 73 of the Charter, to expand the coverage of the article to establish the principle of international accountability for the administration of non-self-governing territories, and to mobilize world opinion on behalf of the self-determination of dependent peoples. The assault on colonialism was carried on in the General Assembly, in the Assembly's Fourth Committee, and in a series of ad hoc and semipermanent committees created on the authority of the General Assembly. Frequently recurring themes for debates within these bodies included such questions as (1) What is the scope of the obligation to transmit information under Article 73? (2) How shall such information be dealt with and utilized? (3) What are the criteria for determining non-self-governing status? (4) Who has the authority to determine that a territory is non-self-governing? (5) Under what conditions may the submission of reports be terminated? (6) By what authority may reports be discontinued?

From the beginning the General Assembly asserted its authority to examine the information submitted by administering states, to debate the issues relating to conditions in non-self-governing territories, and to recommend steps toward the political, economic, social, and educational advancement of indigenous peoples. In 1946, eight states resolved the problem of deciding which territories were subject to the transmission of information by submitting a list of seventy-four territories on which they intended to forward data to the Secretary-General. This list was accepted by the General Assembly as a basis for compliance with Article 73.

To utilize the information submitted by metropolitan powers more effectively, the General Assembly in 1946 authorized the establishment of a Committee on Information from Non-Self-Governing Territories. This committee was composed of an equal number of administering and nonadministering states, the latter chosen by the Assembly's Fourth Committee. The pattern of representation was copied from that of the Trusteeship Council. Belgium refused to participate in committee deliberations beginning in 1953, although it continued to transmit information on its colonial possessions. The Committee on Information was not a powerful anticolonialist instrument because of its composition, with the colonial states exerting strong influence; because the committee lacked means, such as the receipt of petitions or the sending of visiting missions, for checking on the accuracy of the reports submitted to it; and because the committee was forbidden by its terms of reference from making specific recommendations on individual territories. The Fourth Committee (in relation to which the Committee on Information was essentially a subcommittee) and the General Assembly, each representing the full membership of the United Nations, were more aggressive in their attitudes on anticolonialism.

As a guide to colonial powers in submitting their annual reports to the Secretary-General, the General Assembly approved a type of comprehensive questionnaire entitled "Standard Form for the Guidance of Members in the Preparation of Information to Be Transmitted under Article 73(e) of the Charter." Article 73 deliberately omitted political information from the categories on which data were required, but the standard form included optional sections, and several states voluntarily submitted political information. The standard form served as just one of several means for increasing the pressure on colonial powers to rapidly move toward granting independence to non-self-governing peoples.

The lack of a definition for the term *non-self-governing* was partially remedied by the submission in 1946 of the list of seventy-four territories on which the colonial powers intended to submit information. However, within the first few years, states discontinued the forwarding of information on several of these territories claiming, in most cases, a change of status that warranted the cessation. The United Kingdom, for example, asserted that it would be improper to report on any matters on which local autonomy had been granted. France ceased reports on several overseas departments within the French Union. In 1955, when Portugal and Spain were granted United Nations membership, each asserted that they had no territories on which to report because their overseas territories were integral parts of the homeland. Several colonial powers maintained their exclusive right to determine the status or change of status of territories under their jurisdiction.

The unilateral right of administering states to determine the territories on which they would report and to decide when they would cease to make such reports was disputed by the General Assembly. The Assembly sought to define *non-self-governing territory* through studies conducted with the aid of several special committees, the Secretariat, and the Committee on Information from Non-Self-Governing Territories. The Assembly asserted its role in deciding whether to accept the termination of reports on territories whose status was claimed by the colonial powers to have changed, although, in fact, the Assembly lacked any sanctions except moral suasion over reluctant states.

In general, during the period from 1946 to 1959, the General Assembly and its Fourth Committee exhibited an increasing tendency toward establishing international accountability on the part of colonial powers for their administration of dependent territories. Pressures were exerted to extract more information from metropolitan states and to keep the spotlight of world opinion on their progress in promoting the well-being and political, economic, and social advancement of indigenous populations. The revolution of independence for all non-self-governing peoples was well begun, but its more militant aspects remained to be manifested during the 1960s.

INCREASING PRESSURES FOR EMANCIPATION

The year 1960 marks the turning point from mild pressures on metropolitan powers to encourage independence for their colonies to a frontal assault on the legitimacy of the colonial system, accompanied by demands for the immediate termination of all domination of one people over another. This transformation of attitudes was made possible by the influx of new members into the United Nations. The dozen former colonies that were admitted to the United Nations during the period 1955–58 were augmented in 1960 by seventeen new states, all of which had experienced the sting of colonial domination and had escaped to self-rule and independence. The previous anticolonialist minority now became a majority in the General Assembly.

The forces of anticolonialism lost no time in launching a frontal assault on the remaining bastions of colonialism. On December 14, 1960, they pushed through the General Assembly a Declaration on the Granting of Independence to Colonial Countries and Peoples by a vote of 90–0 with nine abstentions, with the abstentions cast mainly by colonial powers. The sweeping nature of this document is attested to by Rupert Emerson's characterization of it as "almost an amendment of the Charter."[3]

The 1960 declaration moved from previous assertions that political independence should be progressively forwarded by colonial powers to demands for immediate political freedom as a basic right for all peoples regardless of their stage of political, economic, social, or educational development. The seven main provisions of the declaration may be summarized as follows: (1) the subjugation or domination of any people constitutes a denial of fundamental human rights, is contrary to the United Nations Charter, and serves as an impediment to world peace and cooperation; (2) all peoples have the right to self-determination; (3) the inadequacy of political, economic, social, or educational preparedness should never serve as a pretext for delaying independence; (4) all repressive measures directed against dependent peoples shall cease; (5) all powers necessary for complete independence and freedom should immediately be transferred to the peoples of non-self-governing territories; (6) any attempt to disrupt the national unity and territorial integrity of a country is incompatible with United Nations Charter principles; (7) all states shall observe the provisions of the United Nations Charter, the Declaration of Human Rights, and the present declaration in order to secure the sovereign rights and territorial integrity of all peoples.

To convert the declaration into an instrument for action, the General Assembly in 1961 created the Special Committee on the Situation with Regard to the Implementation of the Declaration on the Granting of Independence to Colonial Countries and Peoples. In this special committee, parity of membership between administering and nonadministering states (the pattern followed for the composition of the Trusteeship Council and the Committee on Information from Non-Self-Governing Territories) was abandoned in favor of majority representation of states with a strong anticolonial bias. In 1962 the original committee membership of seventeen was increased to twenty-four, and since that time the Special Committee of Twenty-Four has served as the common title for the body because of the ponderous official appellation. In 1963, in order to concentrate more anticolonial activities in a single body, the

---

[3]Rupert Emerson, "Colonialism, Political Development, and the UN," *International Organization*, 19 (Summer 1965), 493.

Committee on Information from Non-Self-Governing Territories was abolished and its functions transferred to the Special Committee of Twenty-Four.

In spite of its lack of coercive means, the Committee of Twenty-Four has been aggressive in its demands. Early in its existence it decided to ignore the restriction placed on the Committee on Information to make only recommendations of general application and instead to consider territories on an individual basis. It has attempted to use petitions and investigative commissions to supplement its deliberations. It has sought the support of the General Assembly and the Security Council for marshaling world opinion and invoking sanctions against recalcitrant colonial powers. It encouraged the use of the International Court of Justice in the South-West Africa controversy and sought ways to offset an unfavorable decision by the Court.

Empirical proof of the effectiveness of the Special Committee of Twenty-Four in hastening the processes of granting independence to non-self-governing peoples may be difficult to produce, but the pressures on the colonial states have been so sharply focused and world opinion has been so preponderant in favor of self-determination that few countries were defiant of these influences. Anticolonialism as a major issue preoccupying the majority of United Nations members has been rivaled only by concerns for economic, social, and political development. Regardless of the causes of the process, the addition to United Nations membership since 1960 of sixty former colonies is evidence of the continuing process of decolonization.

PROBLEMS OF RESIDUAL COLONIALISM

In spite of the rush to independence, certain remnants of the old colonialism are left. Most of the approximately twenty-five remaining dependent territories are small islands or groups of islands whose viability as independent political units is doubtful. Some form of political relationship with another state under an arrangement for local self-rule may be the most advantageous solution for these microunits. Such an arrangement may be acceptable to the majority of United Nations members, providing that the option is clearly a free choice by the indigenous inhabitants, although this is not a foregone conclusion, since demands for Puerto Rican independence are voiced in the United Nations notwithstanding the islanders clear choice of commonwealth status rather than independence.

A few colonies are larger and more populous than the microunits referred to above and account for the bulk of the approximately 10 million people who are non-self-governing. Hong Kong, a British Crown Colony of about 5.7 million people, will be transferred from British to Chinese control in 1997. The Special Committee of Twenty-Four for more than a decade focused most of its attention upon South-West Africa, Rhodesia, and Portuguese territories in Africa. The problem of the Portuguese territories was resolved with a dramatic shift of policy by the Portuguese government, which resulted in granting independence to Guinea-Bissau, Mozambique, and Angola in 1974–75. Rhodesia, as previously mentioned, became the fully self-governing state of Zimbabwe in 1980 and was promptly admitted to United Nations membership. The permanent status of Western Sahara, a former colony of Spain, has been in dispute since 1974. In 1982 the British and Argentinians fought a war over their conflicting claims to sovereignty over the Falkland Islands (Malvinas). The long-disputed status of South-West Africa (Namibia) was finally settled with the aid of a large UN peacekeeping mission—UNTAG (previously discussed in Chapter 7)—and Namibia's admission to United Nations membership in 1990.

PROBLEMS AFTER POLITICAL INDEPENDENCE

Although self-determination and self-rule are attractive goals for politically dominated peoples, independence is no panacea, and the problems following political liberation may seem greater than those previously surmounted. Most former colonies are economically underdeveloped and must face the dilemmas of gradually overcoming poverty, disease, hunger, and illiteracy. Both outside aid and internal savings are required to build a self-generating economy. Without population controls, gains in total production may be partially or completely wiped out on a per capita basis. Ministates lack the economic base to build a viable economic structure independent of heavy reliance on others. Frustration and impatience with slow progress are almost certain to accompany the struggle for development. The international community may seem deaf to the appeals of the poor nations for special concessions to help them escape from poverty. The self-interests of the rich are not likely to identify strongly with the welfare of impoverished peoples or to be outweighed by humanitarian compassion.

Once the unifying force of the common goal of independence has been removed, the political vitality of the new state must also be strengthened. The development of political consciousness or nation building must be undertaken. Enlistment of all elements of the population is required for rapid development. Heroes of the independence movement may lose their former luster as the hardships and frustrations of economic, social, and political development are faced. Fratricidal factional contests must be avoided in order not to dissipate the energies and resources of the new state. Stability in government is difficult to achieve. The struggles for power in Vietnam, Pakistan, Indonesia, Nigeria, Ghana, and Somalia are but a few reminders of the cleavages that may interfere with the stability required for goal attainment.

The struggle for self-government is a revolution that has nearly run its course. But out of that struggle has emerged the new North-South confrontation of which the world is increasingly conscious. Whether the nations of the globe, with the aid of international machinery and cooperative efforts, can successfully resolve the new challenges remains to be proven. At this stage it seems certain that the new problems are no less formidable than the old.

EMPHASIS ON HUMAN RIGHTS

Two major ideologies encompassing ideas on human rights, which are in substantial degree antithetical, have emerged in recent centuries. One strand of political thought is represented by the humanistic philosophy of the Enlightenment of the eighteenth century; the other is the ideology of Marxism as developed by Lenin, Mao, and others. Advocates of each ideology are certain of the truth and eventual universal acceptance of their doctrines. Their differences in views on property, class struggle, individualism, equality, and the role of the state leave little ground for agreement upon a universal set of values for the international community. Communist doctrine emphasizes economic and social rights, whereas liberal democratic theory concentrates on civil and political rights. Semantic interpretations can occasionally help to bridge the gaps if each side is allowed to read its own set of meanings into terms such as "democratic" and "freedom," which both use but in different contexts. But as long as major groups of individuals differ sharply on their acceptance of basic values and values systems, the adoption of universally accepted standards of human rights will be difficult to achieve and implement.

Although the basic principles of human rights have been accepted in some countries for 200 years, it is only since 1945 that these ideas have been universalized and internationalized. Louis Henkin defines "universalization" of rights as their general acceptance by national governments, and he defines "internationalization" of rights as the recognition that treatment of citizens in one country has become the business of other countries.[4] Impetus for the universalization and internationalization of human rights was provided by the mass murders, concentration camps, and other forms of inhuman treatment of individuals as a part of the official policy of some governments prior to and during World War II.

Since 1945 international organizations have been at the heart of the movement to globalize the basic concepts of human rights. Although the protection of workers' rights by the ILO and the guarantees for certain minorities had been fostered under the aegis of the League of Nations, the Charter of the United Nations is the watershed document that marked the beginning of revolutionary (as compared to previous efforts) expansion of human rights as an appropriate area for international concern. In seven different references

---

[4]Louis Henkin, "The Internationalization of Human Rights," *Human Rights: A Symposium,* Columbia University, Proceedings of the General Education Seminar, 6, no. 1 (1977), 5–16.

to human rights, the Charter declares the promotion of human rights to be one of the basic purposes of the United Nations and specifies the responsibilities of major organs for implementing this goal. The General Assembly and the Trusteeship Council are charged with the promotion of human rights among their obligations, and the Economic and Social Council is given a specific mandate to set up commissions in the area of human rights in addition to such other commissions in economic and social fields as may facilitate its functions.

In 1946 and 1947, the primary commissions, which today are still basic to the human rights program of the United Nations, were created by the Economic and Social Council. These are the Commission on Human Rights, the Commission on the Status of Women (which for one year was a subcommission of the Commission on Human Rights), and the Sub-Commission on Prevention of Discrimination and Protection of Minorities.

The language of the Charter with regard to human rights was so general that it lacked specific definition and content. The first major task of the Commission on Human Rights was to produce a Universal Declaration of Human Rights to provide specific standards for the guidance of the international community. This document represented essential compromises on both substance and semantics among the members of the Commission. In deference to both democratic and Marxist ideals, the Declaration included civil, political, economic, social, and cultural rights. Without negative vote, the General Assembly adopted the Declaration on December 10, 1948. However, the representatives of the Soviet bloc members abstained because of narrowness of coverage of economic and social rights, and the South African delegate abstained on the grounds that this area was reserved for domestic jurisdiction.

Although resolutions of the General Assembly are legally nonbinding, the Declaration of Human Rights had considerable impact. It has been widely publicized and acts as a common standard of conduct for the protection and expansion of individual rights. The Soviet Union and other East European states, in spite of their 1948 stance on the Declaration, agreed in the Helsinki Accords in 1975 that:

> In the field of human rights and fundamental freedoms, the participating States will act in conformity with the purposes and principles of the Charter of the United Nations and with the Universal Declaration of Human Rights. They will also fulfill their obligations as set forth in the international declarations and agreements in this field, including inter alia the International Covenants on Human Rights, by which they may be bound.[5]

The Declaration has also been cited in court opinions, has been partially incorporated into at least forty-five national constitutional documents (including the Soviet and Chinese), has influenced national legislation, has

[5] *Conference on Security and Co-operation in Europe, Final Act*, Helsinki, 1975, Part I (a) VII.

been referred to in international treaties, and is constantly alluded to in United Nations debates and documents. It may be reasonably argued that the Universal Declaration, through this usage and as an explication of Charter purposes and obligations, has progressively attained the status of international law.

The movement to translate the Declaration into one or more treaties or conventions, binding on the states subscribing thereto, was started immediately after 1948 in the Commission on Human Rights. Many differences arose in the course of years of effort and, after an early decision to produce two Covenants instead of one, the texts of the International Covenant on Civil and Political Rights (fifty-three articles) with its Optional Protocol (fourteen articles) and the International Covenant on Economic, Social and Cultural Rights (thirty-one articles) were finally ready for General Assembly unanimous approval in December 1966. Each Covenant required thirty-five ratifications and the Optional Protocol required ten in order to enter into force. Ratifications were, at first, slow in coming and both Covenants were delayed in taking effect until early 1976. More than two-thirds of all United Nations members have subscribed to each of the Covenants, but less than half of these have adopted the Optional Protocol.

The general covenants on human rights have been supplemented by numerous, more specialized treaties on diverse aspects of rights. Some of the subjects include the rights of women, slavery and forced labor, torture, the status of refugees, apartheid, discrimination in employment, and discrimination in education. One of the earliest, best known, and most widely adopted treaties is the Convention on the Prevention and Punishment of the Crime of Genocide (1951). Among the other extensively accepted treaties are the Convention on the Status of Refugees (1954) and the Convention on the Elimination of Discrimination against Women (1979). Most unique is the Convention on the Elimination of All Forms of Racial Discrimination (1969), which has been subscribed to by more than 135 states. This Convention provides for implementation through a special committee of experts to receive reports. An optional clause also provides for the submission of petitions from individuals or groups, but requires that ten states, including the state concerned, must accept this jurisdiction before this provision becomes effective. To date, this requirement has not been met.

An international organization that has played a major pioneering role in the safeguarding of human rights is the International Labor Organization. This role was treated in detail in the previous chapter and need not be repeated here. However, the development since 1919 by the ILO of the International Labor Code and the success of their review procedures constitute major contributions to the movement for expanding and protecting human rights.

Regional organizations have also contributed to the international protection of human rights. The most highly developed regional system is the

European system under the aegis of the Council of Europe. A European Convention for the protection of Human Rights and Fundamental Freedoms was concluded in 1950. A Commission and Court of Human Rights were established to assist the Committee of Foreign Ministers in the protection of human rights within the member states. Nearly all members have accepted the compulsory jurisdiction of the Court.

The Commission of Human Rights receives complaints of violations, decides which ones are admissible, and tries to reach a settlement among the parties involved. Most complaints are disposed of by the Commission, but if no settlement can be negotiated, it issues a report to the Committee of Foreign Ministers and to the states concerned. The Committee of Ministers must decide whether to refer the case to the Court of Human Rights or to make its own decision. In either instance, the decision is considered binding.

Under the Council of Europe's system, economic, social, and cultural rights are promoted through the European Social Charter adopted in 1961. As is true of the rights included in the International Covenant on Economic, Social and Cultural Rights, those in the European Social Charter are not absolute but are goals for progressive implementation. Therefore, the supervisory techniques are modeled on those developed by the ILO, in which reports of compliance are submitted by governments and examined together with comments from private groups by a committee of experts, which reports in turn to the European Consultative Assembly. The discussions may lead to recommendations of the Committee of Ministers directed to member governments.

Another aspect of human rights in Europe has resulted from the Helsinki Accords of 1975, which was the final act of the Conference on Security and Cooperation in Europe. Although this agreement is not a treaty and lacks any adequate enforcing machinery, it includes, among the principles guiding relations among participating states, respect for human rights and fundamental freedoms, including freedom of thought, conscience, religion, or belief. The states affirm their commitment to obligations under the UN Charter, the Declaration of Human Rights, and the International Covenants on Human Rights.

The government of the Soviet Union vigorously advocated the holding of the Conference on Security and Cooperation in Europe. Western countries insisted on the inclusion of human-rights provisions in the final act. All the Eastern bloc countries have also ratified the International Covenants on Human Rights. Therefore, as a part of the Helsinki Accords, these countries have agreed to uphold their obligations under all the international documents mentioned in the last sentence of the preceding paragraph. Yet dissidents in and exiles from the Soviet Union and Czechoslovakia stated that these governments continued to violate the human-rights provisions of the Helsinki Accords. Dissidents were subject to arrest and imprisonment or exile.

A group of 257 Czechoslovakian citizens issued a document called the Charter 77 Manifesto, which detailed human-rights violations and stated that, to a great extent, "basic human rights in our country exist, regrettably, on paper alone."[6] Western attempts to monitor Eastern bloc compliance with the human-rights commitments of the Accords were frustrated because of discord over these issues at the review conferences held in Belgrade in 1977–78, in Madrid in 1980–83, and in Vienna in 1986–89. With the breakup of the Soviet empire these issues were largely mitigated.

Other major regions of the world have made less progress than Europe in creating regional instrumentalities for safeguarding human rights. In 1948 the Organization of American States (OAS) adopted an American Declaration on the Rights and Duties of Man. In 1959 the OAS established an Inter-American Committee on Human Rights and decided to draft an American Convention on Human Rights. The Inter-American Committee has been effective both in investigations of human-rights conditions in several countries and in protecting human rights in such cases as the Dominican crisis of 1965, which was previously examined in Chapter 6. The American Convention came into force among eleven ratifying states in 1978 and additional ratifications rapidly followed. African and Southeast Asian regional human rights systems are in their initial stages.

Private as well as public agencies are active in promoting human rights. Anyone who attends the sessions of the United Nations Commission on Human Rights soon becomes aware of the participation of several international nongovernmental organizations (INGOs) in the proceedings of that body. Not only are representatives of these private organizations in regular attendance as observers at the Commission sessions but also they frequently invoke their privilege of addressing the sessions on such subjects as apartheid in South Africa, violations of human rights in Israeli-occupied territories, the use of torture in several countries, or the problem of missing persons in Latin American states.[7]

One of the most respected INGOs among the promoters of human rights, but one of the most vilified by the regimes accused of gross violations of rights, is Amnesty International. This organization, established in London in 1961, concentrates upon securing the release of political prisoners and upon the eradication of torture. With 500,000 members, the methods used include adoption by the organization of identified prisoners, letter writing to governments to pressure for their release, careful investigations (on the spot

---

[6]For the text of the Charter 77 Manifesto, see James Avery Joyce, *World Labor Rights and Their Protection* (London: Croom Helm Ltd., 1980), pp. 160–64.

[7]For an excellent analysis of the contributions of INGOs, see Laurie S. Wiseberg and Harry M. Scoble, "Monitoring Human Rights Violations: The Role of Nongovernmental Organizations," in *Human Rights and American Foreign Policy*, eds. Donald P. Kommers and Gilbert D. Loescher (Notre Dame, IN: University of Notre Dame Press, 1979), pp. 179–98.

if possible), and publicity and testimony concerning those who are still detained in violation of established human-rights standards. Other prominent INGOs whose representatives often give statements to the Commission on Human Rights are the International Commission of Jurists, the International League for Human Rights, the World Council of Churches, the International Federation for Human Rights, and the International Confederation of Free Trade Unions. Other important INGOs that work for human rights through other methods include the International Institute of Human Rights, Society of Friends (Quakers), and the International Committee of the Red Cross. Individually, collectively, and cooperatively, the private agencies act as one of the main sources of information on violations of human rights and have mobilized a substantial international public to promote the cause of human rights.

The principle of equality of the sexes is asserted in the United Nations Charter. One of the functional commissions of ECOSOC, the Commission on the Status of Women, has been active for more than forty years in trying to bridge the gap between words and deeds in making this principle effective.

The General Assembly proclaimed 1975 as International Women's Year, and a world conference was convened in Mexico City from June 19 to July 2 as a focal point of the year's activities. The theme of the conference was "Equality, Development, and Peace." The Mexico City meeting was the first global intergovernmental conference on women's issues ever held.

The conference produced the usual types of documents—a declaration of principles, a world plan of action, regional action plans, and miscellaneous resolutions. The action plan, subsequently approved by the General Assembly, set minimum targets by 1980 for substantial gains by women in the areas of literacy; vocational training; education; career opportunities; political participation and employment; health education; and parity in civil, political, and social rights.

The Mexico City conference was marked by more than usual dissension primarily because of the insistence by representatives of developing countries that the issues of establishing a new international economic order and of racism receive as much attention as the traditional aspects of women's rights. If, as the conference proclaimed, the role of women is a major factor in achieving development, it is noteworthy that the seventh special session of the General Assembly, which was devoted to development and economic cooperation and to which the Mexico City recommendations were submitted, almost totally ignored the possible contributions of women. During this same year, an analysis of the role of women in United Nations Secretariat positions revealed that the percentage of women employees in professional or higher categories was less than one-third that of men employees in those categories. These few indicators signal the manifold difficulties of achieving the degree of equality of status for women targeted at Mexico City. Another world conference was held in Copenhagen in 1980 to assess progress and to set priorities for the second half of the United Nations Decade for Women (1976–85).

In July 1985 the Conference to Review and Appraise the Achievements of the United Nations Decade for Women met in Nairobi, Kenya. The Conference received abundant publicity and was accompanied by a forum of more than 13,500 representatives of nongovernmental organizations who attended in excess of 1,100 workshops. The Conference itself had 2,000 delegates, mostly women, from 157 governments.

In addition to a review of the progress of the Decade for Women, the Nairobi Conference unanimously adopted a document of Forward-Looking Strategies to Improve the Status of Women over the fifteen-year period until the end of the century. As a means of implementing the Forward-Looking Strategies, the fortieth General Assembly requested that the Commission on the Status of Women be strengthened so that it could monitor progress and recommend further action. The General Assembly also suggested that increased funding be supplied in support of the International Research and Training Institute for the Advancement of Women (INSTRAW). Another world conference on women's issues is planned for 1995.

One of the most divisive global conferences was the first World Conference to Combat Racism and Racial Discrimination. The divisive issue was not racial discrimination in itself but the pressures by the third-world countries to include anti-Israeli declarations in the final document and to propose unacceptable measures against South Africa in order to punish that country for its continuation of apartheid. The conference was held in Geneva, August 14–25, 1978, as a part of the Decade for Action to Combat Racism and Racial Discrimination (1973–83). It was attended by representatives of 123 governments, but 12 withdrew on the last day and the Nordic states dissociated themselves from the final document because of the inclusion of anti-Israeli and pro-Palestinian declarations. Only eighty-eight states approved the document.

In addition to the anti-Israeli provisions, the final document (1) declared that any doctrine of racial superiority is scientifically false, morally condemnable, and socially unjust; (2) asserted that any government policy based on racial superiority is a violation of human rights and jeopardizes international peace and security; (3) stated that those who profit from racism and exploitation or help regimes that practice apartheid are accomplices to crimes against humanity; (4) emphasized the need for elimination of racial discrimination as it affects special groups, including women and migrant workers; (5) urged the Security Council to consider mandatory sanctions against the apartheid regimes of southern Africa; (6) asked UNESCO to organize a multimedia campaign to fight racism and racial discrimination; and (7) recommended that at the end of the Decade for Action to Combat Racism and Racial Discrimination the General Assembly should provide for holding another world conference to review and evaluate the work done and to chart new measures where necessary.

The Second World Conference to Combat Racism and Racial Discrimination met in Geneva in August 1983, at the end of the decade devoted to this subject. Efforts were made to avoid the conflict and acrimony of the 1978 Conference. The Conference reviewed the progress of the past decade, adopted a new Declaration and a Programme of Action, and requested the General Assembly to declare a second decade against racism to end in 1993. The Assembly complied with this request during its 1983 session. The Conference expressed an "unalterable determination to mobilize maximum international pressures in obtaining the objectives of the Decade." In recognition of the persistence of widespread racial discrimination policies, the General Assembly in 1993 proclaimed a Third Decade to Combat Racism and adopted an eight-part Programme of Action for the Decade.

In the late 1980s, two special anniversaries of human rights documents were observed by the UN General Assembly. On the fortieth anniversary of the Universal Declaration of Human Rights in December 1988, the UN launched a World Public Information Campaign for Human Rights using the mass media for information and education. In 1989, on the thirtieth anniversary of the Declaration on the Rights of the Child, the General Assembly approved for ratification by governments a Convention on the Rights of the Child.

A landmark of the human rights movement was the World Conference on Human Rights held in Vienna in June 1993. The global commitment to human rights was indicated by the participation of eleven heads of state or government, one vice president, seventy foreign ministers, and sixteen ministers of justice. Representatives from nearly every country in the world took part as well as observers from 95 international organizations and 840 nongovernmental organizations (NGOs). The conference produced the Vienna Declaration and Programme of Action for Human Rights. Among the principles emphasized in the Declaration were (1) the universality of human rights, (2) the right to development, (3) the protection of indigenous peoples, (4) the need for strengthening women's rights, and (5) a recommendation for the establishment of a High Commissioner for Human Rights and the strengthening of the Centre for Human Rights in Geneva. The Conference also expressed strong concern for continuing acts of genocide, "ethnic cleansing," systematic rape of women in war situations, and the effects of wars in producing large number of refugees and displaced persons. In December 1993 the General Assembly authorized the creation of the position of UN High Commissioner for Human Rights, and in February 1994 José Ayala Lasso of Ecuador was confirmed for a four-year term as High Commissioner.

A paradox confronts humankind in its efforts to promote human rights. On the one hand, the need to protect individual and group rights is apparent from history, and the state is likely to be the perpetrator or silent partner in any infringement of those rights. At the same time, each state is jealous of its sovereign prerogatives, and guarantees of rights have traditionally been a subject almost solely of domestic jurisdiction. Any effective international means for implementation is, therefore, revolutionary in nature and likely to be resisted by conservative nationalist forces.[8] In the United States these forces of resistance were led in the 1950s by Senator Bricker and the American Bar Association and so influenced Secretary of State Dulles that he announced a policy of refusing to submit all human-rights conventions to the Senate for approval. A dramatic change of attitude was initiated in 1977 by the Carter administration by making the promotion of human rights a prominent issue in United States foreign policy. However, President Carter was accused of selectively applying pressures to end foreign government persecution of individuals and groups and of meddling in the internal affairs of other states. Moral declarations of rights have much appeal, but the invasion of accepted areas of domestic jurisdiction in order to provide international sanctions against state abuse is quite another matter. The Reagan administration, whose spokespersons announced early that a concern for terrorism would replace the emphasis on human rights and that the United States could tolerate "moderately repressive regimes," obviously placed international human rights near the bottom of its foreign policy agenda. However, in 1986 the United States finally ratified the Genocide Convention, albeit with several reservations.

The international community and regional organizations are ill-equipped to enforce uniform standards of human rights on individual states. As previously noted, the ILO, the Council of Europe, and a few INGOs have been the most effective agencies in monitoring compliance with human-rights standards. Their methods fall short of compulsion and involve primarily persuasion, publicity, and the pressure of public opinion.

Prior to the entry into force of the International Covenants on Human Rights in 1976, the United Nations procedures for supervising compliance with human-rights standards and treaties were not satisfactory. Responsibilities were dispersed among the General Assembly and its Third Committee, the Economic and Social Council and its Commission on Human Rights, the Commission on the Status of Women, and the Sub-Commission on Prevention of Discrimination and Protection of Minorities. In more recent years, some reform of procedures and attitudes has strengthened the effectiveness of these agencies, particularly the Commission on Human Rights, which was expanded from thirty-two to forty-three and later to fifty-three members.

The International Covenants on Human Rights provide their own means of review of compliance. The Covenant on Economic, Social and Cultural Rights provides standards for "achieving progressively the full realization of the rights recognized in the ... Covenant." Governments report periodically to the Secretary-General. Prior to 1987 the Economic and Social Council

---

[8]Both William Korey, "The Key to Human Rights—Implementation," *International Conciliation*, no. 570 (November 1968), and Vernon Van Dyke, *Human Rights, the United States, and World Community* (New York: Oxford University Press, 1970), stress the problem of implementation as the great obstacle to the achievement of international protection of human rights.

acted as the coordinating agency for the review of compliance, with the aid of the Commission on Human Rights and appropriate specialized agencies such as the ILO. In 1987 an expert Committee on Economic, Social, and Cultural Rights assumed this monitoring and review role.

The Covenant on Civil and Political Rights emphasizes the rights of the individual that are not to be violated by any subscribing state. A reporting system is provided and a new Committee on Human Rights of eighteen experts is created to study the reports, question government representatives, and submit its own reports to the Economic and Social Council, the General Assembly, and the states that are parties to the Covenant. The Committee has held regular sessions since 1977. Another expert committee monitors implementation of the Convention against Torture and Other Cruel, Inhuman, or Degrading Treatment or Punishment, which entered into force in 1987.

Human rights is an area in which controversy over international authority will continue for some time. The present period represents a transition from purely domestic jurisdiction to increasing international concern. The transition will be complicated by differences over internal sovereignty and standards of human rights and by the problems of trying to develop international instruments and models for implementation and enforcement. The emphasis upon human rights in the Charter, the Declaration of Human Rights, and the creation of effective agencies by the Council of Europe are indicators of change toward the universalization and internationalization of rights. But as long as major powers are unenthusiastic in their endorsement of international enforcement, and as long as nations can defy international pressures against their practices such as disappearances, religious persecution, arbitrary detention and executions, torture, and persecution of minorities, the new age of human freedom under effective international guarantees will not have dawned.

16

INTERNATIONAL ADMINISTRATION AND THE SEARCH FOR LEADERSHIP

The establishment of many international organizations creates demands met completely or partly by the formation of secretariats as part of their structure. Among these demands are (1) the efficient administration of programs authorized and supported by the organizations, (2) the provision of leadership and guidance for emerging world community forces, (3) the practice of neutralism among competing national interests, and (4) the provision of an international perspective on international problems and programs.

Secretariats certainly do not provide the only leaders of the world community, but international statespeople are rare among those committed to protect national interests. Although several possibilities for leadership will be examined in this chapter, the unique position of the international civil servant will be emphasized. Other roles performed by a secretary-general and his staff also will be outlined. The development of modern administrative structures through precedent-setting practices provides the justification of combining historical and analytical methods of investigating these matters.

THE DEVELOPMENT OF THE INTERNATIONAL CIVIL SERVICE

Although civil-service traditions at the national level date back many centuries, international secretariats have a history of only approximately 100 years. The first suggestion for a neutral international body of civil servants was incorporated into William Penn's proposal for a general parliament in Europe, published in 1694. Penn suggested a body of clerks modeled after the clerks of the British House of Commons. The first actual use of secretariats attached to permanent international organizations developed in the 1860s and 1870s with the establishment of the International Telegraphic Union, the Universal Postal Union, and the International Bureau of Weights and Measures. However, the secretariat personnel for these organizations did not represent a multinational group of civil servants but were either recruited from the host country or seconded by member governments. The concept of a truly international secretariat with primary responsibility to the organization rather than to national governments was put into practice only with the establishment of the League of Nations.

In planning for the League of Nations, two possible roles were foreseen for the Secretary-General. One of these was the role of international statesperson and political leader, as contrasted with that of efficient administrator limited to carrying out the will of the delegate bodies of the League. The role of dynamic leader and innovator was tied to the possibility of recruiting a widely recognized national personality respected internationally for statesmanship and ability. The most frequently mentioned person for this position was Eleutherios Venizelos of Greece, who refused the post. In these early stages the title of Chancellor was suggested as appropriate for the leadership role. President Wilson briefly considered the possibility of accepting the position but decided against it. Before offering the office to Sir Eric Drummond, the decision was made to drop the title of Chancellor in favor of the more indeterminate title of Secretary-General.

The Covenant of the League of Nations provides little insight into the intended nature and role of the Secretariat. The relevant clauses from Article 6 are tersely stated as follows:

1. ... The Secretariat shall comprise a Secretary-General and such secretaries and staff as may be required.
2. The first Secretary-General shall be the person named in the Annex; thereafter the Secretary-General shall be appointed by the Council with the approval of the majority of the Assembly.
3. The secretaries and staff of the Secretariat shall be appointed by the Secretary-General with the approval of the Council.
4. The Secretary-General shall act in that capacity at all meetings of the Assembly and of the Council.

The first Secretary-General named in the annex to the Covenant was Sir Eric Drummond, and it was his personality and vision of the office that shaped the role of the League's Secretariat. Sir Eric was immersed in the tradition of anonymity and nonpartisanship of the British civil service, and he carried these attitudes into the League Secretariat.

Sir Eric Drummond was known to his most intimate associates as an efficient and capable administrator, a man of unimpeachable integrity, and one who effectively practiced quiet diplomacy. Some of the adjectives most frequently used by these associates to describe his qualities are discreet, prudent, modest, quiet, shy, impartial, tactful, cautious, well-informed, and judicious. Because of these personal qualities, combined with the tradition of the British civil service of impartially serving any political party in power, it is no surprise that Sir Eric visualized his role more as an administrator than as a leader. The assumption of this role smoothed his relationships with representatives of governments in the Assembly and Council. They trusted his judgment and appreciated his support and counsel. He never addressed the Council or Assembly, seldom made public speeches, avoided publicity, and limited his reports to a factual accounting of the work of the League.

The description above might lead to the erroneous assumption that Drummond failed to practice any form of leadership in League affairs. He believed that quiet diplomacy behind the scenes was often more effective than public statements. Dag Hammarskjöld later expressed his admiration of this approach by Drummond and partially followed a similar practice. Drummond spent much time in private, behind-the-scenes consultations with government representatives, and his wise counsel, combined with his tact and discretion, inspired their confidence and trust in him. He traveled extensively to world capitals, but again he shunned publicity. He believed in the principles and purposes of the League and furthered them without assuming the role of outspoken advocate.

Drummond is frequently contrasted with Albert Thomas of France, whose term as director of the International Labor Office of the International Labor Organization approximately coincided with the tenure of Drummond as League Secretary-General. Thomas was dynamic and outspoken and used his office to assert leadership on behalf of measures he personally advocated. Thomas was an activist who took the initiative in suggesting policy. He was forceful, controversial, and eloquent. He suggested measures and programs to the ILO Conference and Governing Body and vigorously defended his initiatives. He promoted support for his programs by establishing direct contact with constituencies in labor unions, in governments, and among employers. Thomas was a fighter for social justice for labor. He also established a precedent and a model for the later relationship of the specialized agencies to the United Nations by insisting on the autonomy of the ILO and its freedom from undue control by the League Assembly.

To compare and contrast Drummond and Thomas may be both unfair and inappropriate. The foreign ministries, in all probability, would not have tolerated an Albert Thomas as Secretary-General of the League. In a functional organization, dealing with the special problems of labor, he was both accepted and effective. Each man seemed uniquely suited to the demands of his situation and each, then, was able to contribute to the advancement of the cause of international organization.

In one most important respect, Sir Eric Drummond was an innovator and pioneer in the development of precedents for secretariats of international organizations. He rejected the concept that personnel of the League Secretariat should be government representatives, that they should be seconded for their positions by their governments, or that they should serve the international agency while being temporarily detached from national civil service. Drummond insisted from the earliest stages that the League Secretariat should be truly international in composition, responsibilities, loyalties, and spirit. He was supported in his principles by the Balfour Report to the League in 1920 and by several subsequent reports on administrative policies. The Balfour Report stated that "members of the Secretariat once appointed are no longer the servants of the country of which they are citizens, but become for the time being the servants only of the League of Nations. Their duties are not national but international."

This development of an international civil service was the first experiment of its type. It necessitated appointment of personnel by an international authority. It enabled the assemblage of a competent body of persons from more than thirty states working as an administrative team. Secretariat members were selected on the basis of qualifications for each position and devotion to the principles of the League rather than on the basis of nationality. Reasonable assurances of security of employment and tenure were given, and a corporate spirit was developed under Drummond's leadership.

An exception to the complete internationalization of the Secretariat was made at the undersecretary-general and assistant secretary-general level. Each of the major powers insisted on having one of its nationals in a key position on an assigned basis, so that a Frenchman would always be replaced by a Frenchman, an Italian by an Italian, and so forth. Germany and Italy, in particular, insisted on home government approval of major appointees and on the duty of their nationals to report important matters to their foreign offices. The degree of national interference at the top level is cogently summarized by Arthur W. Rovine.

> By this time [1926], it was obvious enough that the upper strata of the Secretariat were filled with political appointees responsible in fact not to Secretary-General Drummond, but to their respective foreign offices, with their primary functions being advisory, representative, and liaison with home governments.[1]

[1]Arthur W. Rovine, *The First Fifty Years: The Secretary-General in World Politics, 1920–1970* (Leiden, Netherlands: A. W. Sijthoff, 1970), p. 38.

Drummond gently but determinedly resisted undue encroachment of these practices upon the international independence of the Secretariat. The experience of the League in this regard is closely paralleled by the later situation in the United Nations, both in the matter of the distribution of top administrative posts and in the attacks upon the neutrality of the Secretary-General accompanied by proposals for collective leadership operating under the limitations of a veto power. These United Nations developments will be examined in other sections of this chapter.

The League of Nations Secretariat always operated under conditions of severe limitations of budget and personnel. The number of personnel was a small fraction of the present total for the United Nations Secretariat and was actually less than the administrative staffs of several regional organizations and United Nations specialized agencies today. These circumstances, in addition to the philosophy of exercising primarily an administrative role for the Secretariat, set limits on the impact which the Secretariat could have.

Joseph Avenol, who in 1933 succeeded Sir Eric Drummond, and Sean Lester, who presided over the vestiges of the Secretariat from 1940 to 1946, retained, for the most part, the Drummond philosophy of the role of the Secretariat. Avenol, a French financial expert, was less capable than Drummond of inspiring the confidence of government representatives and the esprit de corps of Secretariat personnel. Because he believed that during most of his term as Secretary-General the League had lost its political impact, he emphasized the technical work of the organization. Sean Lester had the thankless job of holding together a skeleton Secretariat of a practically defunct organization.

THE INTERNATIONAL CIVIL SERVANT IN THE UNITED NATIONS

The Secretariats of the United Nations and of the specialized agencies are the beneficiaries of the principles established by Sir Eric Drummond. The substance of the practices initiated by Drummond was incorporated into the United Nations Charter and into the treaties establishing each of the specialized agencies to entrench these principles firmly into the basic concepts of the new organization rather than to leave them open to later negotiation or doubt.

The international character, loyalty, and independence of the Secretariat are fundamental to the effectiveness of an international civil service. The principle of national representation is carried out in the United Nations through the several delegate bodies. The Secretariat's role can only be performed satisfactorily if its members impartially serve the organization as a whole, are loyal to Charter principles, and take their direction from the Secretary-General, not from their home governments. In Dumbarton Oaks and in San Francisco, no fundamental disagreement was expressed with the principles underlying the international loyalty and independence of the Secretariat.

If a secretariat is international in character, its members must be recruited on a broad geographical basis. Article 101 of the Charter provides that geographical distribution shall be considered but shall be secondary to the more essential requirements of high standards of efficiency, competence, and integrity in recruitment of personnel; no necessary conflict exists between these two sets of principles. Member states of the United Nations have insisted on a distribution of Secretariat posts that allots to each state a reasonable "quota" of those posts with regard to both total number of positions and their grade level. This insistence reflects national pride as well as an attitude that national representation should, in a limited sense, carry over into the Secretariat. The Secretaries-General, buttressed by General Assembly support, have contended that efficiency, competence, and integrity must take precedence over geographical distribution, but that a wide variation of national backgrounds, cultures, and experiences among Secretariat personnel enrich the contributions that the Secretariat can make to the work of the organization. The intrinsic value of diversity of staff establishes the compatibility of geographic distribution with the primary standards of efficiency and integrity.

The issue of international loyalty raises some interesting questions. Must national loyalty be sublimated in favor of international loyalty for Secretariat personnel? Are the two loyalties incompatible? What are the demands of international loyalty on the staff members? How do temporary or permanent appointments to the Secretariat affect the attitudes of appointees toward their roles as international and as national actors? Can a member state demand of its nationals a certain standard of national loyalty as a requirement for employment by an international organization?

International loyalty demands that the staff member accept and adhere to the purposes and principles of the organization and faithfully and impartially further these standards in the performance of his or her duties as an international civil servant. The oath required of United Nations Secretariat personnel includes the promise that the employee will discharge assigned functions and regulate his or her personal conduct "with the interests of the United Nations only in view." The international civil servant must abjure the promotion of national interests in favor of impartially serving the interests of the international community. This is a difficult task in a nationalistic world. The staff member must also faithfully serve the Secretary-General or designated head of the secretariat of an international organization and must take instructions only from authorities internal to the organization.

The international civil servant is not required to forswear national allegiance in order to become an effective international agent. In fact, national loyalty, if not carried to the extreme of ethnocentrism and national prejudice, may serve as an effective prerequisite qualification for the international staff member. In general, the narrow or intolerant nationalist will not be inclined to seek employment with an international organization. The United Nations preparatory commission declared that "Loyalty to the Organization is in no way incompatible with an official's attachment to his own country, whose higher interest he is serving in serving the United Nations."

If international loyalty is to be fostered in a secretariat, at least two-thirds of the personnel must have permanent status. A career service with adequate pay, promotion, and retirement benefits is essential to the building of an esprit de corps and a devotion to the purposes and principles of the organization that result only from continued experience and interaction among personnel of diverse backgrounds. The career civil servant gradually absorbs the spirit of cooperative enterprise that will ideally dominate the secretariat under skilled and intelligent leadership. The temporary employee, seconded by his or her government for a one- or two-year term, generally cannot achieve the same degree of loyalty to the organization to which he or she is briefly assigned, since his or her permanent career is with a national government or in his or her home state. Communist countries have favored short-term international assignments for the majority of their nationals. This attitude is consistent with Communist states' attempts to convert international secretariats from independent to representative agencies. African states, because of internal demands for administrative talent, have been reluctant to release substantial numbers of qualified personnel for long-term careers in international secretariats. Technical experts recruited for field missions in a particular country are often on short-term contracts, but the main burden of the continuous work of international organizations is most effectively borne by career personnel of long experience who have acquired a high degree of impartiality and a sense of international loyalty to the organization and its purposes.

The greatest crisis pertaining to questions of loyalty of United Nations Secretariat personnel involved the dismissal of eighteen United States citizens in 1952–53. Investigations and charges of past or current Communist affiliations of employees in the United States government, particularly in the State Department, spilled over into allegations of Communist leanings among United States nationals in the Secretariat. A federal grand jury, without handing down any indictments, charged that "an overwhelmingly large group" of disloyal Americans had infiltrated the United Nations. Several weeks later, Senator Joseph McCarthy, as chairman of the Internal Security Subcommittee of the Senate Judiciary Committee, directed hearings in New York involving eighteen American United Nations civil servants, half of whom were on permanent contract. The number of Americans called to testify amounted to 1 percent of the total number of United States employees of the Secretariat. On the basis of their United States constitutional rights and the independence, under the Charter, of the Secretariat from national jurisdiction, the Americans, on the advice of legal counsel, refused to testify before the grand jury and the subcommittee.

Secretary-General Trygve Lie was caught in the crosscurrents, on the one hand, of American anti-Communist hysteria and official pressure from the host country and, on the other, of the need to protect the independence and integrity of the Secretariat. In spite of the acknowledged right of United States citizens against self-incrimination guaranteed in the Fifth Amendment of the United States Constitution, Lie seemed to feel that refusal to testify represented an overriding threat to the reputation of the Secretariat. He stated that he did not want to employ any United States citizens under suspicion of dedication to the overthrow of their government by force or violence.

Lie first dismissed the temporary employees—those on fixed-term contracts—who had refused to testify. He then sought the advice of a special three-member international panel of eminent legal experts, on which several persons refused to serve. On the advice of the panel, the staff members on permanent contract were also dismissed. The United Nations Administrative Tribunal, in an appeal from those dismissed, found no grounds for misconduct on the part of the accused staff members and awarded substantial compensation to several of them. Early in his term as Secretary-General, Dag Hammarskjöld received approval for changes in the staff regulations clarifying the obligations of staff members and strengthening the Secretary-General's powers of dismissal of employees whose conduct is interpreted as violating the Charter's standards of integrity, independence, and impartiality. At the same time, Hammarskjöld asserted that he would be the final judge of the validity of evidence presented from national sources and that he would refuse to act on unsubstantiated charges against a staff member.

Under an executive order issued by President Truman on January 9, 1953, the United States Civil Service Commission and the FBI were authorized to carry out loyalty investigations concerning all United States nationals employed by or applying for employment with the United Nations. Trygve Lie succumbed to pressure to allow the investigators to carry on their work on United Nations premises. Dag Hammarskjöld later rescinded this permission since such an invasion by national agents violated the international character of the headquarters. The loyalty investigations delivered a severe blow to the morale of the Secretariat as a whole from which recovery was slow and painful.

Questions of dual loyalties and wide geographical recruitment of staff members are closely related to the international independence of the Secretariat. This interrelatedness is clearly illustrated by the preceding paragraphs. However, the principle of independence merits further consideration.

Articles 100 and 101 of the United Nations Charter are basic to the establishment of the principle of Secretariat international independence. The essential elements in guaranteeing independence are the following: (1) the staff shall not seek or receive instructions from any government or other authority external to the organization; (2) reciprocally, each member state shall respect the exclusively international character of the responsibilities of the staff and not seek to influence them in the discharge of their responsibilities; (3) staff members shall refrain from any action reflecting on their position as international officials responsible only to the organization; (4) the Secretary-General shall have the final power of making staff appointments under regulations established by the General Assembly.

Perhaps the best analysis of the elements relating to the independent position of the Secretariat was made by Dag Hammarskjöld in a lecture at Oxford University on May 30, 1961.[2] In this lecture Hammarskjöld recognized the dependence of the Secretary-General upon the services of governments to obtain suitable applicants for positions and to provide information concerning their competence and integrity, but he asserted the right of the Secretary-General to make final choices on the basis of the information furnished. He further stated that mere suspicion concerning an employee or withholding of evidence from the Secretary-General by a government provided insufficient grounds for dismissal. In summary,

> The interest of the governments in placing certain nationals and in barring the employment of others had to be subordinated, as a matter of principle and law, to the independent determination of the Organization.[3]

Hammarskjöld also pointed out that yielding to pressures from governments to increase substantially the proportion of Secretariat staff on short fixed-term contracts would convert the Secretariat from an "international" to an "intergovernmental" body, would compromise its independence, and would reverse the principles established by the League of Nations and confirmed in Articles 100 and 101 of the Charter. With regard to the integrity of the international civil servant, Hammarskjöld asserted that the staff member must be guided by the common aims and rules of the organization and by recognized legal principles rather than by personal preferences. The staff member must subject himself to self-examination to balance personal judgment against respect for law and truth on behalf of the organization as a whole.

In his Oxford lecture Hammarskjöld also discussed the independence of the Secretary-General in implementing controversial political decisions. This aspect will be discussed in a subsequent section of this chapter dealing more specifically with the office of the Secretary-General.

To safeguard the independent position of Secretariat members, they must be free from national jurisdiction in the performance of their official duties. Article 105 of the Charter, and similar provisions in the basic treaties establishing the specialized agencies of the United Nations family, accord to staff officials "such privileges and immunities as are necessary for the independent exercise of their functions in connexion with the Organization." Instead of conferring traditional diplomatic privileges and immunities, this clause establishes a functional basis for the privileges and immunities of Sec-

---

[2]"The International Civil Servant in Law and in Fact," reproduced in *Servant of Peace: A Selection of the Speeches and Statements of Dag Hammarskjöld*, ed. Wilder Foote (New York: Harper & Row, 1963), pp. 329–49.

[3]Ibid., p. 339.

retariat personnel. Such an indefinite standard requires supplemental treaties to identify the extent and limitations of privileges and immunities that are "necessary" for various levels or categories of personnel. In 1946 the General Assembly approved a General Convention on the Privileges and Immunities of the United Nations, which has been ratified by more than two-thirds of the members. This convention enumerates the privileges and immunities that shall be accorded to categories of personnel specified by the Secretary-General but excludes from coverage those locally recruited persons paid on hourly rates. The Secretary-General and Assistant Secretaries-General and their immediate families are accorded full diplomatic privileges and immunities.

Special agreements have been worked out between the United Nations and certain host countries. One such agreement between the United Nations and the Netherlands covers the personnel associated with the International Court of Justice. Switzerland, as a nonmember of the United Nations but as host to the European headquarters of the United Nations, has acceded to a special arrangement with the United Nations. The United States did not ratify the general convention until 1970, but in 1947 approved, together with the General Assembly, a Headquarters Agreement. The Headquarters Agreement fails to accord exemption from taxation of salaries of United States nationals. Staff assessments have been necessary to reimburse United States nationals employed in the Secretariat in order to maintain equality in salary scales.

THE ROLE OF THE SECRETARIAT

In much of the literature on the United Nations there is a tendency to treat the role of the Secretariat primarily in terms of the Secretary-General. This tendency is a natural outcome of, among other factors, the publicity accorded to the Secretary-General, the direct confrontations and consultations between him and government representatives, the delegation to him by other organs of broad responsibilities, his constitutional position as head of the Secretariat, and the personal qualities of leadership of successive occupants of the office.

Charles Winchmore has pointed out that, in spite of a close linkage between the Secretariat and its chief officer, the treatment of the Secretariat exclusively in terms of the Secretary-General is to confuse the whole with one of its parts.[4] In evidence of this distinction one can cite Article 7 of the Charter, in which the Secretariat and not the Secretary-General is designated as a

[4]Charles Winchmore, "The Secretariat: Retrospect and Prospect," *International Organization*, 19 (Summer 1965), 622–39.

major organ of the United Nations; Article 97, in which the Secretariat is defined as comprised of both the Secretary-General and the staff; and various clauses of Articles 97–101, which deal with both elements of the Secretariat. Drawing this distinction in no way denigrates the importance of the Secretary-General in the theory or practice of the United Nations, and his activities and leadership deserve special treatment in other sections of this chapter.

One problem of meeting the Charter standard of efficiency reaches beyond the recruitment of competent personnel into the establishment of a rational administrative structure for the assignment of tasks, for the maintenance of lines of communication, for the performance of work requirements, and for the provision of working conditions, equipment, and services that expedite the completion of assignments. The attainment of the goal of efficient organization and management is complicated by the size of the Secretariat, the diversity of cultural backgrounds and language abilities, the range of tasks to be performed, budgetary limitations, the demands for conformity to standards of neutrality, and the dispersal of personnel in many centers around the globe. In other words, the administration of the Secretariat is subject to all of the problems of other complex organizations plus special difficulties relating to worldwide recruitment and dispersal of personnel.

The complexity of the organization of the Secretariat may be appreciated by a reexamination of Figure 4–1 (page 63). The organization problem has come under periodic scrutiny by the Secretary-General, the General Assembly, and special committees during the life span of the United Nations. Each Secretary-General has proposed changes in structure to suit his own style and interest in the administrative processes. Trygve Lie, by his own admission, was bored by administrative details, while Dag Hammarskjöld, in contrast, concentrated the supervision of administrative functions in his own office. The preparatory commission worked out detailed prescriptions for administrative organization of the Secretariat, and these were approved by the first session of the General Assembly, thus limiting the freedom of the first Secretary-General to formulate his own structure. The hectic initial recruitment of personnel resulted in geographical imbalances that had to be subsequently corrected. Major reviews of administrative structure and related problems were made in 1954–55, 1960–61, the mid-1970s, 1985–89, and 1992–94. In 1974 the General Assembly created an International Civil Service Commission of fifteen experts to advise the Assembly and the Secretary-General on personnel matters and on the coordination of services within the United Nations family of agencies. Their first set of recommendations in 1977 resulted in a 17-percent reduction in the salary scale for general service personnel in United Nations agencies in Geneva.

Although the United Nations Secretariat is dwarfed by comparison with the 3 million employees of the United States government or the work force of giant corporations, it is large and complex when compared with the 700 employees of the League of Nations. The number now approximates 25,000, About one-third of this number work in New York, and the other two-thirds are dispersed in the Geneva office, in the regional commissions, as United Nations country representatives, and in field operations in more than 140 countries. Supervising, controlling, and coordinating such diverse activities and personnel require the application of considerable expertise in administrative skills.

The recruitment of staff on a wide geographical basis, on the one hand, enriches the international character of the Secretariat, but, on the other, complicates the smooth functioning of administrative processes. Communication is hampered when any two people in the Secretariat make oral or written contact in a language in which both are not equally proficient. The necessity to reproduce documents in the six working and official languages (English, French, Russian, Chinese, Spanish, and Arabic) is a requirement not demanded of national administrations. Administrative methods and standards of efficiency vary from one country and region to another. Variations in cultural values and ways of life affect the working relationships of personnel both positively and negatively. Achieving an acceptable standard of administrative efficiency among persons of lingual and cultural diversity and with varied administrative training and experience is a difficult task.

Only a minority of the total employees of the Secretariat are subject to international recruitment on a geographical "quota" basis. Language specialists must be employed on the criterion of necessary skills. Positions below the professional level are also exempt and are filled mainly through applications from persons in the local job market. Nevertheless, the most responsible posts are filled by recruitment on a worldwide distribution basis.

Budgetary penury has been a problem of international organizations since the days of the League of Nations. The policy organs assign new tasks to the Secretariat but are less than generous with financial support. Tardiness in paying national assessments and refusal on the part of some members to pay for certain peacekeeping expenses have reduced the organization to pauper status despite annual pleas by the Secretary-General to the members to revitalize the United Nations with a much-needed infusion of funds. Secretariat personnel have faced the constant threat in recent years of paydays without paychecks because of the virtual bankruptcy of the organization. Such uncertainties most assuredly affect the morale of the staff. Financial stringencies also limit the means available to most effectively carry out the multiple tasks assigned to an often-overworked staff.

Secretariat personnel must be constantly on guard concerning the national sensibilities and interests of each of the member states of the United Nations. Each staff member must keep in mind that, in reality, he or she has more than 180 bosses to please in addition to his or her superiors in the Secretariat hierarchy. Neutrality demands that each word of a study or report produced within the Secretariat be scrutinized to assure that no offense can be taken by any government delegation. Imagination, creativeness, and literary flair frequently must be stifled in favor of established legal jargon, which has precise and accepted meaning based on past practice and experience. As a result, most United Nations documents and reports make for fairly dull reading.

Certain large tasks occupy the energies of most United Nations Secretariat personnel. One of these is the servicing of the 5,000 or more meetings or conferences held annually by United Nations organs or other agencies convening under its auspices. In addition to supplying physical facilities and preparing documentation, studies, and reports, the Secretariat provides highly competent language specialists and translators for both consecutive and simultaneous translation of speeches and debates and for the written reproduction of documents in the six official languages.

In the substantive areas of United Nations programs, the bulk of the personnel is engaged in economic and social activities and projects. As the United Nations has instigated more and more operating programs, in addition to the previous tasks of gathering data and issuing studies and reports, the number of employees in the economic and social areas has increased and a larger proportion of this number has been widely dispersed throughout the world. As technical assistance and economic aid have been expanded, United Nations personnel have become closely associated with large numbers of experts engaged by the specialized agencies for field projects. Teamwork between these agents and local governmental personnel is also a necessary consequence of the increasing emphasis on economic and social development.

A third major area of activity of Secretariat personnel is the range of internal housekeeping chores necessary in all complex administrative organizations. These activities include financial and accounting services, personnel services, maintenance of physical facilities, supplies, records, library, transportation, security, and other similar services.

Other activities of the United Nations are important or even essential but engage the efforts of smaller numbers of staff members. Some of these areas include political and Security Council affairs, non-self-governing territories and trusteeship affairs, legal matters and public information. The Secretary-General also maintains a staff of personal advisers and assistants whose role will be discussed in the following section.

TASKS AND INFLUENCES
OF THE SECRETARY-GENERAL

Although the staff of the United Nations Secretariat and the Secretary-General are interdependent in their functions, the Secretary-General's position and responsibilities are, in many respects, unique, and he is assigned a central role as an administrator and leader in the organization. The Charter specifies several powers and functions that the Secretary-General is expected to exercise. Article 97 designates him as the "chief administrative officer of the Organization." Article 98 requires that he submit "an annual report to the General Assembly on the work of the Organization," and Article 101 empowers him to appoint the staff "under regulations established by the General Assembly." These functions were all previously exercised in the practice, if not in the mandate, of the Secretary-General of the League of Nations. The expansion of the United Nations Secretary-General's role into the political realm is based primarily on a broad interpretation of the provision of Article 98 that the Secretary-General "shall perform such other functions as are entrusted to him" by the General Assembly, Security Council, the Economic and Social Council, and the Trusteeship Council, and on the succinct statement comprising Article 99 that "the Secretary-General may bring to the attention of the Security Council any matter which in his opinion may threaten the maintenance of international peace and security." Although Article 99 has rarely been specifically invoked to call meetings of the Security Council, its implications, when added to the delegation of authority under Article 98 and the other general powers of the Secretary-General, have served as a basis for political activism by the Secretary-General.

The evolution of the role of the Secretary-General in the area of executive leadership has resulted more from other factors than from deliberate grants of power in the Charter. Any constitutional document becomes a living instrument only through practice and application to a series of actual events and circumstances. The role of the Secretary-General has expanded beyond the intentions of the architects of the Charter in response to demands that could not have been foreseen in 1945. This expansion has come about through broad interpretation of the general and specific terms of the Charter, through delegation of responsibilities to the Secretary-General by the Security Council and General Assembly (usually with either the approval or the acquiescence of the major powers), and through the initiative of successive Secretaries-General in seeking freedom of maneuver and in enhancing possibilities for leadership by all available means within the limits of each political situation. The personality, philosophy, and diplomatic skills of each incumbent of the office have affected the parameters of his action and influence in expanding executive leadership.

One factor affecting the Secretary-General's ability to exercise leadership is his relationship with other top-level administrators and executive personnel in the Secretariat. In San Francisco a proposal to elect a number of deputy directors in the same manner as the Secretary-General was rejected on the grounds that such a procedure would limit the freedom of the Secretary-General and subject him to political restraints. However, the Big Five proceeded to reach agreement on a distribution of top posts among their countries and to put forward the names of particular candidates whom they expected the Secretary-General to appoint. The Soviet Union was allotted the position of Assistant Secretary-General (later Undersecretary) for Political and Security Council Affairs; the United States took the post in Administrative and Financial Services; the United Kingdom was assigned to Economic Affairs; Social Affairs went to France, and Trusteeship to China. Such an arrangement would have gone far toward negating the Secretary-General's independence from political control if each Secretary-General had not taken steps to bypass these chief assistants and to centralize decision making in his executive office. Andrew Cordier of the United States served as executive assistant to both Lie and Hammarskjöld. When Hammarskjöld reorganized the Secretariat, he added two Undersecretaries for Special Political Affairs to serve as special assistants without portfolio. U Thant, in another reorganization, stated that he would consult his eight principal advisers or other officials individually or collectively according to circumstances. Thus, the successive Secretaries-General maintained some flexibility of control in spite of the pressures from major powers to dilute the principle of international independence of the Secretariat.

The Secretary-General is chief administrator or manager of the organization. His strategic position at the intersection of the political and administrative sectors of the organization provides him with opportunities for offering initiative and leadership in both sectors. He maintains contacts with governments and their representatives in the United Nations delegations. He has available an independent, substantial, and usually adequate communications system, including telephone, telegraph, television, radio, press, library, and documentation facilities. He personally performs those administrative tasks in which he is most interested and that most enhance his position of leadership, and he delegates the remainder to others. He appoints Secretariat personnel, within the constraints previously outlined, and is the primary source of plans for restructuring the administrative framework, a process fundamental to improvement of administrative effectiveness and efficiency. In carrying out his administrative functions, the Secretary-General must represent the epitome of discretion and neutrality among member states. At the same time he must uphold the principles and purposes of the organization.

In attempting to unify the staff as an efficient administrative unit, the Secretary-General confronts a paradoxical set of factors. Centrifugal forces (in addition to the representational basis for appointment of heads of major departments and offices and short-term contracts for a minority of employees) include the compartmentalization of the Secretariat into its specific functions and activities. Each employee tends to identify with his or her own unit and to develop a loyalty to his or her administrative chief. In stimulating changes of policy, the Secretary-General is frustrated by attitudes of immobility and resistance to innovation by staff members who cling to established procedures and whose security is protected by staff regulations enforced with the aid of a Staff Association and a Staff Council.

Opposed to these centrifugal forces are the unifying factors available to the Secretary-General. Insofar as the Staff Council has been utilized to develop policy concerning staff welfare, an esprit de corps has been established for the entire Secretariat. The staff members are inclined to rally behind the maximalist philosophy of the Secretary-General because an expansion of executive power is shared by all members of the Secretariat. The career international civil servants also develop, in common with the Secretary-General, a devotion to the broad principles and purposes of the organization, which binds them together in a sense of mission. Finally, the Secretary-General must inspire his staff by his leadership and by seeking their support in their common efforts.

In preparing the budget the Secretary-General is addressing both political and administrative implications of the document. Allocation proposals determine changes in program emphasis and affect the tasks to be performed by Secretariat personnel. The Secretary-General by no means has a free hand in budgetary matters. His proposals are subject to review by the General Assembly through the Advisory Committee on Administrative and Budgetary Questions and the Fifth Committee, where attitudes of conservatism and economy prevail. The near-bankrupt condition of the United Nations since 1962 has had a serious impact on staff morale and on budget planning.

Article 63 of the Charter assigns to the Economic and Social Council the task of coordinating the activities of the specialized agencies and the United Nations in economic and social projects, but, of necessity, the Secretary-General is the chief coordinator. In its first year of operation, the Economic and Social Council authorized the Secretary-General to establish an Administrative Committee on Coordination composed of the administrative heads of the specialized agencies and to serve as its chairman. This committee attempts to prevent duplication of effort and any working at cross-purposes and to allocate tasks among the diverse agencies and subagencies. Other efforts at coordination by the Secretary-General are carried out through the preparation of reports for the Economic and Social Council and through multiagency cooperative activities in such areas as technical assistance and economic development.

The most significant and controversial extensions of the Secretary-General's power have been in the political realm. The history of this development has been marked by periods of euphoria concerning the Secretary-General's accomplishments, followed by bitter attacks upon his person and office by one or another of the member states, including the big powers.

Trygve Lie was, at times, a severe critic of the major powers' failure to live up to Charter principles. In 1950 he interjected his Twenty-Year Program for Peace into the situation of the East-West Cold War in an attempt to restore the United Nations as an effective instrument for peace and collective security. His attempt at negotiation with the major powers to support his proposals received an especially cold reception in Moscow, inspired no efforts at implementation by any major power, and fell victim to the Korean War. In his annual reports to the General Assembly, Lie called upon the great powers to seek agreement on world problems. He also spoke out in press conferences and made public statements against regional security pacts, such as NATO, as inconsistent with Charter intentions concerning regional arrangements and collective self-defense and as inimical to global solutions of global problems.

In the first dispute to come before the Security Council, the Secretary-General was criticized, at various stages, by the Soviet Union and the United States but managed to establish an important principle concerning his political prerogatives. When, in 1946, Iran and the United States insisted, with Lie's reluctant acquiescence, that the dispute over failure of the Soviet Union to withdraw troops from Iranian territory by an agreed deadline be placed on the Security Council agenda, the Soviet representative walked out in protest. When both Iran and the Soviet Union wished to drop the item from the agenda before the troop withdrawal was complete, Lie supported this position in a document based on legal opinion, but the United States mustered sufficient votes to retain the question on the agenda. At the same time, Lie's assertion of authority under Article 99 to intervene in Security Council affairs with oral or written statements at any time during debate was opposed by the United States but subsequently upheld and established as a general rule of procedure. In ensuing months his right to make similar statements to the General Assembly on his own initiative was established along with his right to conduct investigations to determine whether matters should be brought before these bodies. These tools gave the Secretary-General political powers unprecedented in the experience of the League of Nations.

In the early stages of the Palestine dispute, Trygve Lie strongly supported the partition plan approved by the General Assembly and urged the major powers to enforce it through Security Council action, including, if necessary, the furnishing of military forces. As in other situations, Lie felt a duty to speak for the collective interest of the United Nations as a whole. He procured several hundred personnel for observation and truce supervision in Palestine and worked closely with the mediator and other United Nations agents in arranging a truce.

Lie alienated first the United States and later the Soviet Union by his stand on other major United Nations issues. In 1950 he strongly endorsed the seating of Communist Chinese delegates in the United Nations and thus incurred the wrath of the United States. With the outbreak of the Korean War, his support for military measures under the aegis of the United Nations evoked hostility by the Soviet Union to the point of its opposing the extension of his term and of totally boycotting him throughout the remainder of his tenure in office. In the loyalty investigations during the last months of Lie's tenure, he was severely criticized by the delegates of many states for his failure to oppose strongly the overzealous activities of agents of the United States government, which critics saw as a threat to the independence and integrity of the Secretariat.

Dag Hammarskjöld as Secretary-General contributed more to the position of executive leadership of that office than any other incumbent. His contributions came as a result of circumstances to which he responded by building a body of theory and practice that expanded the role of the Secretary-General in unprecedented directions and dimensions. In the end, his actions and ideas brought him and his office under bitter attack from the representatives of the Soviet Union, who perceived his claims as inimical to great-power sovereignty and dominance in world politics.

One of Hammarskjöld's earliest assignments that allowed him some leeway in exercising his diplomatic talents was a request from the General Assembly that the Secretary-General seek the release of fifteen American flyers downed on United Nations missions and imprisoned in China. The Assembly resolution provided no specific guidelines and permitted Hammarskjöld to use "the means most appropriate in his judgment." Since the resolution also condemned the Chinese action, Hammarskjöld wisely decided to use, instead, as his basis of authority for a mission to Peking, his general authority as Secretary-General. Although no dramatic announcement followed his four-day visit, all the flyers were released within the next seven months.

The Suez Canal crisis of 1956 provided much broader mandates and opportunities for the exercise of discretion and initiative by the Secretary-General. The Security Council was deadlocked by British and French vetoes requiring an emergency session of the General Assembly under the Uniting for Peace Resolution. The General Assembly called for a cease-fire and a withdrawal of forces behind the previously established armistice lines, and directed the Secretary-General to submit within forty-eight hours plans for the recruitment and dispatch of a United Nations Emergency Force to the Middle East to secure compliance with these provisions.

All the guidelines, details for raising a peacekeeping force, and the actual direction of the operations were delegated to Hammarskjöld by the General Assembly. Negotiations with the governments that were to furnish personnel as well as with the belligerents for the withdrawal of their forces were necessary. Egypt finally agreed to the deployment of United Nations forces upon parts of its territory after Israel's refusal to accept such an occupying group, and the first UNEF troops reached Egyptian territory eleven days after the adoption of the General Assembly's resolution.

A new principle and concept evolved with the formation of the UNEF. Peacekeeping by a police-type force was substituted for collective-security action dependent upon the might of the major powers. "Preventive diplomacy" and "peacekeeping" entered the lexicon of the United Nations. The Secretary-General directed the forces through his appointee, General Burns of Canada, in contrast to the earlier arrangement in Korea that the United States furnish the direction of the combined forces there.

Hammarskjöld also assumed responsibility for the clearing of the Suez Canal, which had been blocked by ships sunk by the Egyptians. The task was completed within four months (which was ahead of all predictions) by a salvage operation involving personnel or equipment from at least eight countries.

The Hungarian crisis, which occurred almost simultaneously with the Suez dispute, provided no opportunity for the Secretary-General to widen his powers or display his ability to carry out successfully a mission assigned by the political organs of the United Nations. The General Assembly requested Hammarskjöld to take such initiatives as were available to investigate the invasion of Hungary by Soviet troops and to ascertain the facts concerning the intervention. In the face of Soviet intransigence, no entry to Hungarian territory was possible, and United Nations influence was negligible.

As additional crises faced the United Nations, Hammarskjöld added to his philosophy of an enlarged leadership role for the Secretary-General. Not only were specific mandates from the political organs to be flexibly and generously interpreted, but an independent role for the Secretary-General was asserted for situations in which the resolutions lacked specificity or in which authorization was totally lacking. Hammarskjöld proclaimed his right and duty to fill vacuums when no basis of authority existed except the general principles and aims of the Charter and a broad interpretation of the Secretary-General's grants of power in that document.

The Lebanese crisis of 1958 demonstrates Hammarskjöld's interpretation of his independent position. In response to a Security Council directive, he formed an observer group to investigate Lebanese charges of infiltration across its border with Syria by United Arab Republic partisans. After the dispatch of United States Marines to Lebanon at President Chamoun's invitation, all subsequent proposals in the Security Council to provide additional guidance and authority for further action by the Secretary-General failed because of Soviet vetoes. Hammarskjöld declared that under these circumstances he would fill the vacuum by taking such additional measures as he judged appropriate. He increased the observer group sufficiently for effective border surveillance. After he instigated a pledge of mutual nonintervention by the Arab states and after the observers made a further report on minimal infiltration across Lebanese borders, all foreign forces and the observer group were withdrawn from Lebanon.

Independent action by Hammarskjöld without first requesting guidance from the political organs of the United Nations was demonstrated by the situations in the dispute between Cambodia and Thailand in 1958–60 and in the internal conditions in Laos in 1959–61. In the Cambodia-Thailand dispute Hammarskjöld advised against taking the matter to the Security Council in order to avoid any possible hardening of conflicting East-West positions. With informal consent from the major powers, he appointed a personal special representative who brought about a reconciliation between the two countries. When a further dispute flared up in 1960, another special representative of the Secretary-General conducted negotiations with Cambodian and Thai diplomats at United Nations headquarters in New York, which led to the signing of terms of settlement.

In the Laotian situation Hammarskjöld twice made personal visits to Laos to urge a position of neutrality in accordance with the Geneva agreements of 1954. Hammarskjöld resisted requests from the Laotian government for the establishment of a peacekeeping force in Laos, but following his second visit, he appointed a series of personal representatives who were only temporarily successful in delaying the effects of outside intervention.

Hammarskjöld's assumptions of independent authority reached their highest peak and met their greatest challenge in the Congo crisis of 1960–61. In 1960, to meet the Congo emergency, he invoked, for the first time, his authority to call a meeting of the Security Council. In the early stages of the crisis the Security Council provided broad guidelines under which Hammarskjöld raised a peacekeeping force to aid the central government in restoring order and to supervise the withdrawal of Belgian and mercenary forces from the Congo. When the internal political situation became confused and when the secession of Katanga and other provinces was threatened, Hammarskjöld repeatedly returned to the Council for clarification of his instructions. In the face of inadequate guidelines and the necessity for quick decisions in emergencies, he did not hesitate to use his own judgment or to support the decisions of his deputies in the Congo. When the Security Council became deadlocked and when the outside forces were intervening to influence the internal political situation, Hammarskjöld turned to the General Assembly for support and direction.

Because of the confused political situation in the Congo and the clash of external interests, the guidelines furnished by both the Security Council and the General Assembly became increasingly inadequate, and Hammarskjöld was faced with making personal decisions or refusing to act at all. In assessing his responsibilities, Hammarskjöld rejected the course of inaction. He declared instead that his decisions, regardless of offense to any member states, should be based on (1) Charter principles and purposes; (2) widely accepted legal rules and precedents, especially those found in United Nations resolutions; (3) consultations with the personnel of the permanent missions to the United Nations or with advisory committees of the type established for the UNEF and Congo operations; and (4) his own personal judgment based on his integrity and exercise of conscience with self-examination concerning his objectivity and neutrality.[5]

[5]Foote, *Servant of Peace*, pp. 346–48.

When the Soviet Union's representatives decided that Hammarskjöld's policies in the Congo were inimical to Soviet interests, they mounted an attack upon him personally and upon the office of Secretary-General. Asserting that no man is neutral, Khrushchev demanded in the General Assembly that Hammarskjöld resign and that the single office be modified to a "troika," or three-member collective executive body, representing the socialist, Western, and neutralist groups of states. Under this arrangement the interest of each bloc would be safeguarded by vesting each member of the "troika" with veto power. Thus, the arena for political struggle would be broadened to include the Secretariat, and the independent international role of the Secretariat, established forty years earlier by Drummond, would be abandoned.

Hammarskjöld refused to resign and defended the integrity of his office. He declared that "this is a question not of a man but of an institution."[6] He reminded the members of the organization that the Congo was their operation, not his, but if they failed to furnish positive direction, he had no choice but to follow his own conviction.[7] He asserted that the Soviet proposal for a triple executive would destroy the effectiveness of the United Nations. Hammarskjöld appealed to the small nations on the basis that they, not the big powers, needed the protection of the organization, and that he would remain in his post if the large majority wished him to do so.[8] He repeatedly received what amounted to overwhelming votes of confidence in the General Assembly, and the neutralist states rejected the Soviet proposal for giving them representation in the leadership of the Secretariat by substituting a "troika" for a single Secretary-General. However, Hammarskjöld's effectiveness, from September 1960 until his death a year later, was diminished by the active hostility of the Soviet Union.

U Thant, during his ten years as Secretary-General, did not further develop the philosophy of the office or establish startling precedents, but he acted discreetly in a series of crises, consolidated the gains of his predecessors, kept the support of the big powers, and acted as spokesman on the issues of greatest concern to the developing nations. Throughout his tenure of office he was plagued by the financial crises that the members were unable or unwilling to resolve. He played a constructive role in political disputes such as those involving the Congo, Cyprus, West Irian, and the Cuban Missile Crisis. He was criticized in some quarters for the rapid withdrawal of UNEF troops from the Middle East in 1967. He was outspoken but ineffective in trying to bring an end to the Vietnam War. In general, he maintained the principles established by Lie and Hammarskjöld and judiciously exercised the previously established prerogatives.

---

[6]Ibid., p. 316.
[7]Ibid., p. 317.
[8]Ibid., pp. 318–19.

Kurt Waldheim also served for two five-year terms and continued the role of caretaker and administrator. He was caught in the cross-pressures of reconciling the demands of the Third World for new programs and expenditures with those of the affluent states for economy and prudent fiscal management. The big powers, partially through the instrument of the Security Council, also continued to safeguard their own interests in controlling political situations against incursions by either the Secretary-General or the General Assembly. Waldheim participated in numerous crises, including the placing of peace-keeping forces in the Middle East and Lebanon, Soviet occupation of Afghanistan, Vietnam's invasion of Cambodia, mediation of the Cyprus dispute, the future of Namibia, the Iran-Iraq war, and a series of other Middle East crises. In November 1979 he used his authority under Article 99 of the Charter to call a Security Council meeting on the hostage crisis in Iran. This was only the second time a Secretary-General had exercised this authority. Although frequently criticized by interested parties for failure to achieve quick final resolution of disputes, he was more generally respected for his evenhanded, quiet diplomatic efforts. If the charges concerning Waldheim's World War II possible connections to Nazi atrocities, which surfaced at the time of his election as the President of Austria, had been revealed before his selection as Secretary-General, there is no doubt that he could not have won approval for his two terms in office. His conduct in office provided no hint of ideas inimical to administrative neutrality and efficiency.

When Javier Pérez de Cuéllar succeeded Waldheim on January 1, 1982, his acceptability to all major powers and factions in the United Nations was never in question. Although he suggested measures for strengthening the role of the Security Council in dispute settlement and crisis management, and conferred with the Reagan administration to try to prevent the emergency resulting from drastic reductions in United States financial support for the United Nations, he generally conformed in the early years of his tenure to the low profile of the Secretaries-General of the previous twenty-year period. However, the trend, beginning in the late 1980s, to bring major disputes to the Security Council not only revived global interest in the role the United Nations could play in conflict resolution, but also put the Secretary-General in the spotlight of world affairs. Pérez de Cuéllar was called upon to mediate the necessary conditions for and the management of new peacekeeping forces or observers in Namibia, Afghanistan, the Iran-Iraq border, Angola, El Salvador, and Western Sahara. He also presided over the UN executive and administrative functions involved in the Iraq-Kuwait war, in which the Security Council legitimized the repelling of the Iraqi invasion and the application of sanctions against Iraq. He also streamlined the United Nations bureaucracy in response to member pressures and financial stringency. In general, he received support and praise for his judicious and patient diplomatic and management skills.

Boutros Boutros-Ghali began his first term of office in January 1992. As a scholar-statesman from Egypt he satisfied the demand of African and Arab states for a Secretary-General from their region of the world. Boutros-Ghali is an activist but a more discreet one than Trygve Lie. In peacekeeping and its more coercive forms, Boutros-Ghali inherited a dozen ongoing missions from his predecessors, but, under his tenure, has carried out the mandates necessary for fielding a half-dozen new ones including the large and costly operations in Cambodia, Somalia, and Yugoslavia. He has appeared to be an enthusiastic supporter of UN involvement in several internal crises including the use of peace-enforcement measures. In response to a request from a Security Council summit meeting of heads of governments, Boutros-Ghali in June 1992 issued a report entitled "An Agenda for Peace" which outlined his recommendations under the categories of preventive diplomacy, peacemaking, peacekeeping, and post-conflict peace-building. In response to continued pressure from member states to streamline the structure of the Secretariat bureaucracy, Boutros-Ghali, one month after assuming office, announced the merging of twelve major departments or offices, and the elimination of fourteen of the highest-ranking administrative posts. These steps could improve the efficiency and effectiveness of the UN and cut administrative costs, but simultaneously the financial burden of maintaining large-scale peacekeeping and peace-enforcing operations creates a UN financial crisis. In the early years of his tenure, Boutros-Ghali generally received approval for the several aspects of his leadership role.

BASES OF INFLUENCE AND LEADERSHIP

In an international organization such as the United Nations, leadership is shared by the personnel in the Secretariat and the governments of the member states. The unique position of the Secretary-General has been detailed and illustrated in the previous section. As the major spokesperson for an international, objective approach to problems, based on Charter principles and goals, the Secretary-General epitomizes the advocacy of the utilization of the United Nations for the maintenance of peace and for the improvement of the human condition through economic and social cooperation.

Other members of the Secretariat sometimes share in this leadership role. Ralph Bunche, who served as Director of the Division of Trusteeship Affairs of the Secretariat prior to his appointment as Acting United Nations Mediator in Palestine, received the Nobel Peace Prize in 1950 for his mediation efforts in the Middle East. Andrew Cordier, who served as executive assistant to the Secretary-General from 1946 to 1961, and C. V. Narashimhan, who succeeded to the post and served for twelve years, were key figures in decision making in the Secretary-General's office. Paul Hoffman, as director of both the United Nations Special Fund and its enlarged successor, the United Nations Development Program (UNDP), left his mark on the economic and social development efforts of the United Nations. In the same area of concern, Gunnar Myrdal, as executive secretary of the Economic Commission for Europe, and Raul Prebisch, as executive secretary of the Economic Commission for Latin America and first Secretary-General of the United Nations Conference on Trade and Development (UNCTAD), established reputations as vigorous leaders and innovators. Much leadership credit for economic and social activities of the United Nations must also be given to Philippe de Seynes, Undersecretary-General for Economic and Social Affairs in the administrations of Hammarskjöld, Thant, and Waldheim. In this position he directed the largest and most active segment of the Secretariat. Other recognized leaders with distinguished service records include Brian Urquhart, who retired in 1986 as Undersecretary-General for Special Political Affairs after forty years in the Secretariat; Bradford Morse, who served first as Undersecretary-General for General Assembly Affairs and then as administrator of the UNDP; and Kenneth K. S. Dadzie, who was the first United Nations Director-General for Development and International Economic Cooperation and in 1986 became the fourth Secretary-General of UNCTAD.

In many cases the Secretary-General requires the services of a personal representative to go to a crisis area to investigate, mediate, and report on conditions and events. In these instances he often selects a trusted, capable, and judicious member of the Secretariat. Among those who have ably served in this capacity is Pier Spinelli, who during his ten-year tenure as director of the European Office of the United Nations in Geneva was given assignments to the Middle East, Yemen, and Cyprus as special representative of Hammarskjöld and of Thant. Secretary Thant also relied on José Rolz-Bennett to act as his personal representative in West New Guinea in 1962, in Cyprus in 1964, in the dispute between Guinea and the Ivory Coast in 1967, and in Algeria in 1968.

Several able and distinguished leaders have headed the secretariats of the specialized agencies affiliated with the United Nations. Among the many who might be cited for their leadership qualities, Eugene R. Black, who served as president of the International Bank for Reconstruction and Development for fourteen years, and Robert S. McNamara, who served in that capacity from 1968 until 1981, are noteworthy. McNamara engaged in a vigorous campaign to funnel a much larger share of the bank's loans into the International Development Association with the goal of speeding up the development process in the countries that most need financial aid.

If the United Nations is to make progress toward achieving its goals, leadership must come from the member governments as well as from the Secretariat. Heads of delegations, if they have a firm basis of support within their governments, may make major contributions to the success of the organization. Lester Pearson of Canada has distinguished himself as an innovator in United Nations affairs. He served as president of the General Assembly in 1952. He is credited with being the father of the idea for the United Nations Emergency Force. In recognition of his contributions, he received the Nobel

Peace Prize in 1957. Another Canadian head of delegation, Stephen Lewis, took a vigorous leadership role in the 1980s in focusing global attention on the critical economic situation in Africa.

Charles Malik of Lebanon and Eleanor Roosevelt of the United States worked persistently in the Commission on Human Rights to produce the Universal Declaration on Human Rights. Carlos P. Romulo of the Philippines is another head of a national delegation who distinguished himself as a spokesperson for a strengthened United Nations. Adlai Stevenson combined outstanding talent with an enthusiasm for the role of the United Nations, but he was frequently frustrated by a lack of support from Washington for his personal preferences on the United States stance in the organization.

Heads of governments have occasionally utilized the United Nations to carry out proposals for the achievement of universal goals. Two such proposals are noteworthy. In 1949 the General Assembly developed the Expanded Program for Technical Assistance in response to the multilateral aspects of President Truman's Point Four Proposals in his inaugural address of that year. In 1953 President Eisenhower used the General Assembly as a forum for his Atoms for Peace proposal, and this culminated in the formation of the International Atomic Energy Agency.

Secretaries-General sometimes reach into national government services to recruit talent for special assignments. An example is Robert K. A. Gardiner of Ghana, who was appointed as chief of the United Nations Congo Operation in 1962–63 and in the latter year was chosen executive secretary of the Economic Commission for Africa. Major-General Indar Jit Rikhye of India served as chief of staff of the UNEF in 1958–60 and became military adviser to the Secretary-General in 1960. During his eight years in the latter post, he also was assigned to United Nations forces in the Congo, West Irian, Yemen, and Cyprus. Of special note is the service of Gunnar Jarring, who, while serving as Swedish ambassador to the USSR, took on, in 1967, a prolonged and difficult assignment as special representative of the Secretary-General to attempt to mediate the dispute in the Middle East. Maurice Strong of Canada was the prime mover behind the Stockholm Conference on the Environment and served as the first executive director of the United Nations Environment Program (UNEP).

Many other individuals could be cited for meritorious service on behalf of United Nations goals. Restraints imposed within the larger arena of world politics have limited the leadership roles exercised by the individuals who have participated in this work.

THE NEED FOR INTERNATIONAL LEADERSHIP

Since 1970 both the United Nations and its Secretariat have been subject to increased criticism. A series of appraisals of United Nations personnel policies generally agree that the quality of Secretariat personnel has fallen below optimum standards. One critical study concentrates a large share of the blame on member states' advocacy of unqualified candidates for appointment to positions and the Secretariat's lack of resistance to such pressure.[9] Some corrective measures in recruitment policies have been initiated, including competitive examinations for certain junior posts; but important tasks will be assigned to the United Nations only if there is confidence in its competency to perform those tasks. This requirement also applies to other international organizations.

A landmark study was published in 1990 on the need for leadership in the United Nations. The study resulted from grants by the Ford Foundation and the Dag Hammarskjöld Foundation and was entitled *A World in Need of Leadership: Tomorrow's United Nations.* Its authors were Brian Urquhart and Erskine Childers who had been senior administrators in the UN Secretariat for forty and twenty-two years respectively. A key paragraph of the study states:

> In the United Nations leadership comes, or can come, from a number of possible sources. Member states, either singly or in groups, are one such source. Imaginative political leaders are another. Nongovernmental organizations and other expressions of the opinions and aspirations of the people are yet another. The UN system also has its appointed leaders—the Secretary-General and the heads of the various specialized agencies and programmes. The calibre and team-work of these leaders, led by the Secretary-General, are essential to the future effectiveness of the system.[10]

In a chaotic and increasingly interdependent world, more orderly processes for settling disputes and for achieving economic and social cooperation are needed. States that insist on a myopic national view of the international scene can contribute little to the resolution of international problems. International organizations provide one set of existing channels through which such problems can be cooperatively attacked. Since the opportunities for leadership within international agencies are so restricted by the attitudes and policies of governments, it is from within these governments that an impetus toward utilizing the full potential of international organization must originate. One reason international leadership is constrained is that there is no international constituency to lead. There are only national constituencies. Therefore, the need is for national leaders with enough vision to recognize both the threats and the means toward removing those threats that exist in an interdependent world. But creative and farsighted global statespersons of the caliber of Robert Schuman of France, Willy Brandt of Germany, and Gro Harlem Bruntland of Norway are rare. The exercise of leadership in and

[9]Seymour M. Finger and John Mugno, *The Politics of Staffing the United Nations Secretariat* (New York: The Ralph Bunche Institute on the United Nations, The Graduate School and University Center of the City University of New York, 1974).

[10]Brian Urquhart and Erskine Childers, *A World in Need of Leadership: Tomorrow's United Nations* (Uppsala, Sweden: Dag Hammarskjöld Foundation, 1990), p. 8.

through international organizations could help to diminish the sources of tensions and restore confidence in human capabilities for peacefully resolving conflicts and problems.

17

INTERNATIONAL ORGANIZATION IN RETROSPECT AND PROSPECT

It is appropriate at this point in our study of international organization to assess the progress of and the prospects for international organization by examining its problems and accomplishments and by estimating its probable and potential role in world affairs. Several questions establish the outlines of this assessment. How far has international organization progressed since the first international unions or since the League of Nations? Have the principles of international organization been valuable or have they been unrealistic ideals? Has the proliferation, since 1945, of international agencies, both regional and global, caused significant changes in international affairs, or have these agencies operated on only the fringes of the international system without great effect on the principal forces shaping international human relationships? Have international organizations provided services and channels for interaction indispensable to or at least valuable for maintaining an orderly international system? If these services and channels have been indispensable or valuable, have nations and national leaders been willing to and capable of using them wisely? Is international organization of only marginal use, is it the answer to the future, or is it a transitional step in developing a new international order? Of course, not all these questions can be answered definitively, but trying to answer them will be useful in placing the role of international organization into current and future perspective.

SOURCES OF DISCOURAGEMENT

If the major contribution that international organization can make to world affairs is to aid in breaking down barriers that divide the peoples of the world, the progress to date in eliminating those barriers often seems discouraging. Cleavages among nations appear to be nearly as wide and deep as ever in modern history. Deeply ingrained in human consciousness is a sense of loyalty and identity built around the nation-state. This sense of identity compartmentalizes the world into more than 180 sovereign, competing political units. Little evidence exists that substantial numbers of people living in these more than 180 political units feel any strong mutual ties with the whole of humanity or share with them a common sense of values. In spite of lip service accorded to codes of religious, ethical, or moral principles that profess the unity of the human race, the hierarchy of individual and national values assigns priority to the elements of divisiveness, not unity. Humanitarianism is still smothered by particularism. The order of the day is rivalry rather than cooperation. Rivalry among nations is fostered by suspicion, fear, and perceived self-interests. National and individual goals concentrate on immediate economic gain or protection of economic advantage, and any promises of long-range mutual benefits from international cooperation are greeted with impatience and doubt.

In spite of the implications of *perestroika* and *glasnost* in East Europe, the competition of ideologies is far from a dead issue. Divergent networks of political and economic ideas as support for antagonistic political and economic systems have not lost their currency and vitality. Human welfare and freedom are not universally accepted standards as basic concepts for political organization and action. In spite of professions of a willingness to coexist, the basis for cooperation among competing political units remains limited because of fundamental differences in perspectives. Conviction concerning the correctness of the underlying principles and values of one's own system lends impetus to a missionary zeal to bring enlightenment concerning the validity of these "truths" to the entire human race. A sense of historical destiny bolsters up this crusading spirit and hinders the process of accommodation. National barriers are thus reinforced rather than broken down by the influence of ideology.

Perceived economic interests are among the most powerful forces for cleavage among nations. Movement toward economic unity has been limited and tension ridden. Even in the European Community, usually cited as the model for economic unions, the path to cooperation and solidarity has not been smooth. Each country's economic and monetary system elicits the support of individuals to a degree unrivaled at the transnational or international level. Personal economic well-being is identified with the national economic system to the point that foreign economic activities are often perceived as threats to both personal and national economic prosperity in terms of jobs, prices, markets, and profits.

Economic rivalry persists as the dominant attitude over economic cooperation. Among developed states, adversary relationships mark the bargaining process by which compromises can be reached that lead to limited cooperation. In trade and tariff arrangements the interests of internal segments of the working, management, and entrepreneurial population must be protected as a first priority. Individual interest thus becomes linked to and identified with national interest. The state remains as the main instrumentality for safeguarding and promoting individual and group economic welfare.

Economic interests also serve as a basis for the hardening of antagonism between rich, industrial, developed nations and poor, preindustrial, developing nations. The United Nations Conference on Trade and Development emerged as the symbol of the demands of the have-not countries and as the forum for the espousal of their cause. Their frustrations and impatience with economic progress were expressed through resolutions stating recurrent themes—recurrent because so little headway was made toward the achievement of the goals of the development process. Rightly or wrongly, the developing states blamed the affluent nations for much of their plight because the rich states dominated the international economic system and because massive transfers of economic resources were not made from the haves to the have-nots on terms most favorable to the perceived interests of the latter. In 1974–75 the developing countries used special and regular sessions of the General Assembly for the promotion of a "New International Economic Order." This NIEO never emerged, and the developing states became frustrated with the lack of response from the affluent nations. Even the global recognition of the dire economic conditions in most African countries in the 1980s failed to produce promised increased aid from the industrialized North.

Although science and technology continue to shrink global dimensions and problems multiply that demand worldwide solutions, national leaders persist, in their rhetoric and behavior, in emphasizing parochial rather than universal viewpoints and interests. The components of interdependence expand at exponential rates, but traditions and habits linked to the past prevent the application of dynamic and imaginative ideas and techniques appropriate for a new future of which many of the elements have already emerged today. The problems of spaceship earth will not be solved by Neanderthal approaches. A revolution in social and political thinking is required to avoid a series of potential catastrophes whose signs are already evident, but a sense of urgency has not yet permeated the centers of power and decision.

Conflicts and wars flare up in all corners of the globe with alarming frequency. In spite of the ever-increasing destructiveness of weapons and in spite of apprehensions concerning the escalation of the level of conflict from conventional warfare to wars of mass destruction, people wage wars that the

United Nations is unable to prevent or rapidly bring under control. On some occasions, such as in the series of Middle East conflicts, the effects are lessened by action taken through United Nations agencies, while in other cases, such as in Czechoslovakia, Vietnam, Nicaragua, and Bosnia, the United Nations and the principles of the Charter are impotent to resolve the conflict. The desirability of arms limitations and controls is overwhelmed by an arms race in which the nations of the world spend more than $600 billion each year on weapons and means of destruction. Security is sought through a balance of terror and threat, rather than through cooperation for the peaceful settlement of disputes and the elimination of war. World priorities place military preparedness above the values of human life and welfare.

In this highly competitive world climate, international organizations tend to languish rather than flourish. New agencies are created in substantial number but are unable to realize much of their potential. Organizations are based on the principle that the sovereignty of the members will remain intact and undiminished. States retain all their prerogatives of ultimate decision making and cooperate through international organizations when their perceived national interests are enhanced rather than diminished or threatened by such cooperation. International organizations become the convenient tools of foreign policy of the individual states. Most of the energies and resources of each state are reserved for bilateral not multilateral activities. As soon as a regional or global organization is perceived as taking an action or series of actions inimical to the internal interests of one or more members, the spirit of cooperation disappears and the vitality of the organization suffers. The United States' refusal to pay its legally obligated share of the United Nations budget is a prime example of this attitude.

SUMMARY OF ACHIEVEMENTS

In spite of the rather gloomy picture of a sharply divided world painted above, there is a more optimistic view of the contributions of international organization to world peace and human welfare that should be presented. In such a presentation one's expectations should not anticipate a high degree of perfection in the performance of international organizations since humans are fallible and all human institutions are imperfect. In seeking greater harmony and improved standards of justice in an increasingly interdependent yet always competitive international system, the degrees of harmony and justice will always be relative and subject to perfectability. Furthermore, international organizations have never been assigned a major role in an age dominated by national sovereign states. Therefore, in this assessment of achievements, we should look for those elements in the performance of international organizations that have positively, although modestly, moved toward the amelioration of human relations across national boundaries and toward securing a higher standard of justice, especially for that segment of humanity who live under the constant threat of hunger, poverty, illiteracy, and disease or who are denied an effective voice in determining their own political, social, and economic destiny.

One measure of the utility of international organizations is their steadily increasing numbers. Another is the clamor for membership. Almost every eligible state seeks membership in a variety of organizations, and withdrawals are rare. Even for ministates the benefits of participation are judged to outweigh the costs, although these costs are a real economic burden.

In the political area international organizations have a mixed record but some notable successes. Regional organizations such as the OAS and the OAU have served as channels for containing conflicts among their members and restoring peace. When the right combination of conditions and attitudes prevails, the members of the United Nations have used the Security Council and the General Assembly for dispute settlement. The Middle East is a notable example of repeated recourse to the United Nations as an agency for ending hostilities and restoring relative peace. Skeptics were beginning to wonder about the utility of United Nations agencies in any but minor disputes, but a review of major crises since 1979 demonstrates that nations sought the aid of the Security Council and General Assembly in a series of international crises in Afghanistan, Iran, the Golan Heights, Lebanon, the Falkland Islands (Malvinas), the Iran-Iraq War, the downing of the Korean airliner, the downing of the Iranian airliner, Nicaragua, Cambodia, the Chad-Libya dispute, Namibia, Angola, Kuwait, Yugoslavia, and Somalia. Public awareness of the United Nations was renewed as its role in disputes returned to the media headlines. However, as Secretary-General Pérez de Cuéllar pointed out in his annual report to the General Assembly in 1982, there is a tendency to bring critical problems to the Security Council too late for the Council to have any serious influence on their development, and for member states to assume that debate is an adequate substitute for effective action. On the other hand, the United States and the Soviet Union have suggested that the role of the Security Council should be strengthened, and the Soviet Union advocated broad measures for energizing the United Nations as a primary agent in conflict resolution and global security. The United Nations has demonstrated its flexibility and adaptability in controlling conflicts by the selection of appropriate means mentioned in the Charter for the peaceful settlement of all manner of disputes, and by the development of new techniques, including cease-fires, preventive diplomacy, and a variety of forms of United Nations presences, including peacekeeping forces. One of the most significant contributions to peace has involved the insulation of power vacuums from great-power direct involvement or confrontation.

Although international law, because of its nature and sources, develops slowly in a world of sovereign states, the United Nations has fostered modest but significant advances toward building a more satisfactory body of world law. Through interpretations and applications of Charter principles, through the efforts of the International Law Commission, and through decisions and advisory opinions of the International Court of Justice, the right of the international community to concern itself with denials of human rights and justice has been repeatedly affirmed. Special emphasis has been placed on the rights of all peoples to self-government. Treaties exempting areas of potential conflict from national competition contribute much to a vital area of law. Agreements concerning outer space and a number of nuclear-free zones are prime examples. The adoption of a comprehensive law-of-the-seas treaty, including an international authority with jurisdiction beyond national limits, represents a major step toward the expansion of international law.

One of the least tangible, but potentially most significant, contributions of international organizations to a more orderly and cooperative world is the provision of multiple contacts among national representatives so that a greater appreciation of other viewpoints and interests may be developed. Constant exposure to a variety of approaches to world or regional problems will usually enlarge the horizons of the participants. International organizations provide a multitude of forums and negotiating channels for seeking consultation and for the development of common interests. On a personal level these contacts represent a minute, yet important, segment of the present expanding network of transnational forces operating in today's world. Enlargement of human horizons is one basic element in breaking down barriers in a shrinking world. A symbolic recognition of the importance of the United Nations as a forum for international interactions was the historic meeting of the Security Council in January 1992 at the level of heads of state and government. Symbolism is significant, but the true test of government cooperation and UN support is measured by perennial reliance on and financial backing for the organization.

Although the world is armed at a high level of lethality, the United Nations has contributed limited gains in arms control and in assuring restraint against unleashing the holocaust of nuclear war. It is difficult to separate negotiations outside United Nations channels from those under its aegis, but a series of United Nations agencies have worked at arms control continuously over a period of forty years, and many of the agreements not actually hammered out in these agencies have been brought back to them for legitimization. From the setting up of the International Atomic Energy Agency through the test-ban treaty, the outer-space treaty, the nonproliferation treaty, and the seabed treaty, to the efforts begun in the 1980s, the United Nations and many of its members have exerted unremitting pressure for more effective arms control. The INF Treaty (1987) between the United States and the Soviet Union marked a major breakthrough by eliminating, for the first time, an entire category of weapons—intermediate range nuclear missiles. The new political climate in the Soviet Union and East Europe opened the way for further, more drastic reductions in nuclear, chemical, bacteriological, and conventional weapons.

The most notable achievements of international organizations have been registered in the area of assistance for economic and social development. Although East-West and North-South cleavages have sometimes marred the unity of purpose that would most enhance the prospects for development, this area has elicited more harmony and enthusiasm than the political area, in which stalemate is frequent. Proliferation has been noted in the establishment of global and regional agencies that are totally or partially devoted to fostering economic and social development through technical assistance, financial aid, the promotion of trade, or the diversification of the economic base in the developing three-quarters of the globe. Some of the earliest initiatives came from the affluent countries, although in more recent years the clamor for more resources and favorable treatment by the less-developed countries has outstripped the willingness of the industrialized nations to comply with these demands. Nevertheless, the total expenditure of resources and effort of the United Nations, the specialized agencies, and many regional agencies for their economic and social programs represents the bulk of their budgets, programs, and personnel. In comparison with bilateral and private channels, the multinational programs may seem small, and in terms of total needs to effect rapid economic and social change, the sum total of commitments may seem inadequate, but these efforts represent a notable response to the aspirations for a better life for billions of human beings. Problems of coordination and degrees of inefficiency should not obscure both the nobility of purpose and the indispensability of these programs for raising the level of human dignity for the great mass of the world's population.

Fundamental to an understanding of world problems and needs and to the development of rational and appropriate responses to those needs are the processes of data and information gathering and dissemination. Most international and regional organizations engage in these activities, and in many cases intergovernmental organizations are linked with private organizations in an intricate two-way communications network. The information-gathering and publications activities of the United Nations are at the center of this network and provide invaluable services to governments, public and private organizations, scholars, and other individuals.

International organizations help to build gradually the human foundations for a more orderly and just world through the development of a body of personnel devoted to and engaged in programs that serve a broad community of interests. The predominance of the perspective of narrow national interests will never accommodate to the broader outlook appropriate to a world of rapidly increasing interdependence without the emergence of a growing body of individuals whose ideas and attitudes are attuned to a cosmopolitan viewpoint. International organizations provide channels for the development of a corps of international civil servants with a devotion to interests beyond national boundaries. The pronouncements of the United Nations Secretary-General frequently epitomize a world consciousness and commitment. Even national representatives in international organizations are frequently influenced by their constant exposure to the ecumenical climate of the organization. In relation to the imperatives of economic and social development, international organizations are creating a reservoir of talent for aiding developing countries in the solution of their most fundamental problems. Altogether, the human component of the complex set of relationships and factors that affect world adjustment to the reality of interdependence is a vital element, and international organizations provide an important set of channels for enlarging the perspectives and influence of this human component.

Although the study of international organizations generally emphasizes intergovernmental or public activities, these cannot be separated from the role of private actors. With world interdependence increasing at exponential rates, both old and new private actors take on increased importance. New business giants in the form of multinational corporations defy control and analysis in conventional terms. Their impact on future international relations will undoubtedly be significant, but whether, on balance, they will contribute to a better world is still open for debate. Multinational corporations both reflect and contribute to global interdependence. As a subject of continued analysis, they deserve much attention for both their positive and negative inputs into the emerging global system. Other transnational interactions, such as the increased interchange of persons and ideas, probably contribute more positively than negatively to the breakdown of provincial attitudes that compartmentalize the world. Recent acceleration of such transnational forces provides hope for future global security and welfare by helping to build the economic and social foundations for global community without which political cooperation cannot flourish.

Among the most important contributions of international organizations to the security and well-being of humanity is the provision of channels and programs for dealing with short- and long-range crises. If a series of disasters for humankind is to be prevented or contained, it is imperative that means be provided for cooperative action.

The possibilities for disaster range over a broad spectrum of political, social, and economic problems. In the political realm the threat of nuclear destruction still exists. Even in the area of peaceful uses of atomic energy, the IAEA's safety standards for preventing accidents affecting the lives and health of millions of persons living in the vicinity of nuclear power plants do not eliminate all concerns and fears of the possibility of such accidents. For the preindustrial societies of the world, the major long-range crisis is a crisis of development and the elimination of gross inequalities between rich and poor countries. Priorities for speeding the processes of development are expressed through such programs as the four Development Decades, the UNCTAD, UNIDO, the UNDP, the IDA, and the New International Economic Order.

Other transcendent crises of such proportions as to threaten all or substantial segments of humanity include a deteriorating environment, uncontrolled population growth, inadequate food distribution, a broad range of problems relating to the use of the oceans, shortages due to accelerating use and depletion of finite energy and other resources, and illicit traffic in drugs.

A variety of international organizations are concerned with these crises and can and do serve as agencies for cooperative action in avoiding the threats that these crucial problems present to the fragile life-support system of our biosphere. A mental scanning of the range of agencies discussed throughout the previous chapters would remind one of an exhaustive list of regional and global organizations and suborganizations whose major activities include various aspects of present and future crisis management. There is no assurance that the efforts of nations working through this broad range of international agencies will or can prevent catastrophes, but without recourse to international action the endeavors of individual states will surely fail.

Finally, in assessing the positive values of international organizations, their role as agents of integration and aggregation of interests across national boundaries should be noted. Constant interaction among government representatives and international civil servants in the meeting rooms, offices, corridors, and lounges of these diverse organizations gradually build habits and attitudes that facilitate and foster cooperation. As common problems are attacked that obviously will not respond to parochial, national solutions, the advantages of integrated approaches through regional and global agencies become increasingly apparent. International organizations thus serve as instruments for raising the level of consciousness concerning the realities of world interdependence, and they provide the means for an integrated approach to an attack on problems that, through other channels, defy resolution. Unless the objective scientific facts concerning the spaceship-earth concept are matched by a heightened awareness of the political and social implications of those facts, humanity could be faced with conditions that have slipped beyond the point of control. Through a process of integration and aggregation of interests, international organizations provide a most important means of supplying the balance to make humankind the beneficiary rather than the victim of rapid change.

FUTURE NEEDS AND PROSPECTS

The preceding assessment of positive and negative contributions of international organizations to human welfare is not wholly reassuring for future prospects concerning the role of such agencies. International organizations must be viewed within the larger context of the international system. That system is still dominated by national states that arrogate to themselves the claim of sovereignty or ultimate authority in their international relationships and that assign to international organizations a role subservient to their own convenience and interests. Of course, these interstate relationships are responses to the basic parochialism, selfishness, and fears that are engrained in the minds, emotions, and attitudes of the peoples of the world and their leaders.

But, ever since the beginning of the Industrial Revolution, economic, social, and political change in those countries in which this revolution occurred has accelerated with each successive decade; and since the 1950s, those tides of change have revolutionized the demands of the three-quarters of the human race previously untouched by these dynamic forces. At the same time, the further developments of science and technology and the expansion of the industrialization processes have brought about both a shrinking of the globe and a condition of worldwide interdependence. Our growing body of knowledge has furnished the means, if wisely applied, to enhance the well-being of most of the world's people. It also has produced, in its applications, unprecedented problems that threaten the lives and security of all humanity. A catalog of these threats includes nuclear incineration and nuclear, chemical, or biological poisoning; the exhaustion of finite resources; overpopulation; mass starvation; deterioration or destruction of the earth's life-support system; and the denial of justice and dignity to an ever-enlarging mass of humanity who populate the underdeveloped portion of the world. Our knowledge has not only expanded our potential for either disaster or enhanced well-being, but it has also furnished the means for foreseeing, however imperfectly, future trends and problems and for guiding human affairs toward those policies that increase human welfare and avoid disaster.

Throughout this study the increasing role of international organizations in the years since 1945 has been repeatedly noted and documented. The complex system of agencies created by the member states of the United Nations represents as much development over the League of Nations system as the League represented over the sporadic and meager organizational efforts of the nineteenth century. Concomitant with the proliferation of United Nations agencies, regional and nongovernmental organizations have been established in ever-increasing numbers. As global time and distance continue to shrink and as world interdependence becomes more and more apparent, the existing trends toward the creation of international and transnational organizations will continue. The needs of a small, fragile, and interdependent planet cannot be met by the independent activities of more than 180 political units. Cooperation among these units is the minimum essential for promoting the common interests in which each has a share. Collective approaches to problems become increasingly necessary if the world situation is not to deteriorate. International organizations, based as they are on the principle of voluntary cooperation, provide acceptable means of collective consultation and action.

At the present stage of history, the United Nations system of agencies, as well as regional and transnational organizations, provide a bridge between the old and the new world order. On the one hand, they act as a conservative force against radical change by conforming to the status quo and by further institutionalizing the present international framework. On the other hand, they reflect the necessity for orderly, cooperative action in attacking the common problems of humanity. As the range of common problems broadens, organizations spring up in response to the need for united effort toward the possible solution of these mutual problems. Since cooperation is dependent upon the will of the involved parties, and since will is partially shaped by perceived needs, the future utility and increased role of international organizations seem assured. Past trends in the development of international organizations project themselves into the future as forecasts of the formation of more organizations performing a wider range of activities at a constantly accelerating pace.

It may well be that change will occur in the next twenty years at such a rate that revolutionary modifications in the international system will be required to adapt to the new developments. It is also possible that some of the potential sources of global disaster will threaten all or major segments of humanity with extinction. In either case the nation-state system and a system of international organizations based on voluntary cooperation among sovereign states may, of necessity, give way to a radically new international order. The clash between sovereignty and interdependence may require the relinquishment of substantial areas of sovereign prerogatives. Short of such radical threats or changes, both the nation-state and international organizations as instruments of cooperative action will survive and thrive. Both interdependence and the shrinking of global dimensions will require adjustments and will promote the role of international organizations.

A great deal of attention has recently been focused on the many areas of potential threat to human survival in the next quarter- or half-century. Such predictions of doom certainly require our closest scrutiny and our most intelligent and diligent efforts to forestall disaster. This type of prediction reflects pessimism concerning human capability to solve problems, to cooperate in their solution, and to evolve institutions and social frameworks adequate to support the processes of problem solving.

The other side of the coin is the capability of the human race to survive. Humanity has a resilience that has been demonstrated throughout thousands of years of adaptability to change. As thinking creatures, humans have developed an ingenuity of incredible proportions. There is no assurance that humanity will not be overcome by conditions partially of its own making, but ingenuity and adaptability give hope for continued survival.

The short history of international organizations is one demonstration of human ingenuity and adaptability. Their rapid development is a prime example of how humanity responds to changing needs. This development has not yet reached its zenith. If at some future date, other instruments, which are better suited to that time, are required, we should, with some confidence, assume that present forms of organization will then be modified or replaced by more appropriate tools for promoting human welfare. Until that relatively remote period is reached, human reliance on the general type of international organizations familiar today will continue and will increase.

BIBLIOGRAPHY

GENERAL SOURCES

A primary source is the *United Nations Documents*, which include records of meetings, reports, research studies, and communications from governments. The documents of the specialized agencies are also included in the listings in the *United Nations Documents Index*. Regional and other organizations generally publish voluminous records, which are also primary sources of information.

Other basic publications of the United Nations include:

"Annual Report of the Secretary-General on the Work of the United Nations"

Everyman's United Nations (8th ed.), 1968

Everyman's United Nations—Supplement, 1971

Everyone's United Nations, 1986

United Nations Demographic Yearbook

United Nations Statistical Yearbook

United Nations Treaty Series

Yearbook of the United Nations

The documents of the San Francisco conference, which produced the United Nations Charter, appear in *Documents of the United Nations Conference on International Organization,* 22 vols. Volumes 1–16 were published in 1945–46 in London and New York by the United Nations Information Organizations in cooperation with the Library of Congress. Volumes 17–22 were published in 1954–55 in New York by the United Nations.

Privately published sources of fundamental importance include:

Goodrich, Leland M., Edvard Hambro, and Anne P. Simons. *United Nations Charter: Commentary and Documents* (3rd ed.). New York: Columbia University Press, 1969.

Kaleidoscope: Current World Data. Includes an updated chronology of events in the United Nations.

Issues before the General Assembly of the United Nations. Annual volumes. New York: United Nations Association of the United States of America.

"Reports of the Commission to Study the Organization of Peace."

Worldmark Encyclopedia of the Nations, 1, The United Nations (7th ed.). New York: John Wiley & Sons, Inc., 1988.

Yearbook of International Organizations, published biennially. Brussels: Union of International Associations.

Periodicals published by the United Nations Office of Public Information are indispensable in supplying current information. The following series have been published:

United Nations Bulletin (August 1946–June 1954). Weekly through December 1947, then twice monthly.

United Nations Review (July 1954–April 1964). Monthly.

United Nations Chronicle (since May 1964). Monthly through February 1986, then quarterly.

The two most valuable privately published periodicals are *International Organization* and *International Conciliation* (discontinued in 1972).

SELECTED BIBLIOGRAPHY BY CHAPTERS

Chapter 1   Introduction

ARCHER, CLIVE. *International Organizations* (2nd ed.). London: Routledge, 1992.

CLAUDE, INIS L., JR. *The Changing United Nations* New York: Random House, 1967.

DAUGHERTY, JAMES E., and ROBERT L. PFALTZGRAFF JR. *Contending Theories of International Relations: A Comprehensive Survey* (2nd ed.). New York: Harper & Row, 1981.

KAPLAN, MORTON A., ed., *The Revolution in World Politics.* New York: John Wiley, 1962.

LUARD, EVAN. *Conflict and Peace in the Modern International System: A Study of the Principles of International Order.* Albany: State University of New York Press, 1988.

MANGONE, GERARD J. *A Short History of International Organization.* New York: McGraw-Hill, 1954.

MORGAN, PATRICK M. *Theories and Approaches to International Politics: What Are We To Think?* (3rd ed.). New Brunswick, NJ: Transaction Books, 1981.

NICHOLAS, H. G. *The United Nations as a Political Institution* (4th ed.). New York: Oxford University Press, 1971.

Chapter 2   A Great Experiment—The League of Nations

CECIL, LORD ROBERT. *A Great Experiment.* New York: Oxford University Press, 1939.

League of Nations. *The Development of International Cooperation in Economic and Social Affairs.* Geneva: League Secretariat, August 1939.

MILLER, DAVID HUNTER. *The Drafting of the Covenant.* New York: Putnam, 1928, 2 vols.

NORTHLEDGE, F. S. *The League of Nations: Its Life and Times 1920–1946.* New York: Holmes & Meier, 1986.

WALTERS, F. P. *A History of the League of Nations.* New York: Oxford University Press, 1952, 2 vols.

Chapter 3   The Genesis of the United Nations

EAGLETON, CLYDE. "The Charter Adopted at San Francisco." *American Political Science Review,* 39 (October 1945), 934–42.

GOODRICH, LELAND M. "From League of Nations to United Nations." *International Organization,* 1 (February 1947), 3–21.

———, EDVARD HAMBRO, and ANNE P. SIMONS. *United Nations Charter: Commentary and Documents* (3rd. ed.). New York: Columbia University Press, 1969.

LUARD, EVAN. *A History of the United Nations,* Vol. I, *The Years of Western Domination, 1945–1955.* New York: St. Martin's Press, 1982.

"Report to the President on the Results of the San Francisco Conference. . . ." Department of State Publication 2349, Conference Series 71. Washington, D.C.: Government Printing Office, 1945.

RUSSELL, RUTH B., and JEANETTE E. MUTHER. *A History of the United Nations: The Role of the United States, 1940–45.* Washington, D.C.: The Brookings Institution, 1958.

Chapter 4   Basic Principles and Organization of the United Nations

BAILEY, SYDNEY D. *The Procedure of the UN Security Council.* New York: Oxford University Press, 1975.

Basic Facts about the United Nations. New York: United Nations.

Everyman's United Nations (8th ed.). New York: United Nations, 1968.

Everyone's United Nations. New York: United Nations, 1986.

GOODRICH, LELAND M., EDVARD HAMBRO, and ANNE P. SIMONS. *United Nations Charter: Commentary and Documents* (3rd ed.). New York: Columbia University Press, 1969.

Chapter 5   Some Basic Issues of the United Nations

ALKER, HAYWARD R., JR., and BRUCE M. RUSSET. *World Politics in the General Assembly.* New Haven, CN: Yale University Press, 1965.

BAILEY, SYDNEY D. "Veto in the Security Council." *International Conciliation,* no. 566 (January 1968).

JUNN, ROBERT S. "Voting in the United Nations Security Council." *International Interactions,* 9, no. 4 (1983), 315–52.

KAY, DAVID A. "The Impact of the African States on the United Nations." *International Organization,* 23 (Winter 1969), 20–47.

KEOHANE, ROBERT O. "Political Influence in the General Assembly." *International Conciliation,* no. 557 (March 1966).

NEWCOMBE, HANNA, MICHAEL ROSS, and ALAN G. NEWCOMBE. "United Nations Voting Patterns." *International Organization,* 24 (Winter 1970), 100–21.

"The Problem of Membership in the United Nations." Staff Study No. 3, Subcommittee on the United Nations Charter, Committee on Foreign Relations, United States Senate, 83rd Congress, 2nd Session. Washington, D.C.: Government Printing Office, 1954.

"The Problem of the Veto in the United Nations Security Council." Staff Study No. 1, Subcommittee on the United Nations Charter, Committee on Foreign Relations, United States Senate, 83rd Congress, 2nd Session. Washington, D.C.: Government Printing Office, 1954.

"Representation and Voting in the United Nations General Assembly." Staff Study No. 4, Subcommittee on the United Nations Charter, Committee on Foreign Relations, United States Senate, 83rd Congress, 2nd Session. Washington, D.C.: Government Printing Office, 1954.

RUSSELL, RUTH B. *The General Assembly: Patterns/Problems/Prospects.* New York: Carnegie Endowment for International Peace, 1970.

STOESSINGER, JOHN G. *The United Nations and the Superpowers* (4th ed.). New York: Random House, 1977.

———, and ASSOCIATES. *Financing the United Nations System.* Washington, D.C.: The Brookings Institution, 1964.

Chapter 6　Peaceful Settlement of Disputes

CLAUDE, INIS, L., JR., "The OAS, the UN, and the United States." *International Conciliation,* no. 547 (March 1964).

FALK, RICHARD A., and CYRIL E. BLACK, eds. *The Future of the International Legal Order,* Vol. III, *Conflict Management.* Princeton, NJ: Princeton University Press, 1971.

GOODRICH, LELAND M., and ANNE P. SIMONS. *The United Nations and the Maintenance of International Peace and Security.* Washington, D.C.: The Brookings Institution, 1955.

LUARD, EVAN, *A History of the United Nations,* Vol. I, *The Years of Western Domination, 1945–1955.* New York: St. Martin's Press, 1982.

MITCHELL, C. R. *Peacemaking and the Consultant's Role.* New York: Nichols Publishing Co., 1981.

"Pacific Settlement of Disputes in the United Nations." Staff Study No. 5, Subcommittee on the United Nations Charter, Committee on Foreign Relations, United States Senate, 83rd Congress, 2nd Session. Washington, D.C.: Government Printing Office, 1954.

STEVENSON, ADLAI E. *Looking Outward: Years of Crisis at the United Nations.* New York: Harper & Row, 1963.

Chapter 7　Collective Security and Its Alternatives: Theory and Practice

BOYD, ANDREW. *Fifteen Men on a Powder Keg: A History of the United Nations Security Council.* New York: Stein and Day, 1971.

BOYD, JAMES M. *United Nations Peace-Keeping Operations: A Military and Political Appraisal.* New York: Praeger, 1971.

FABIAN, LARRY L. *Soldiers Without Enemies: Preparing the United Nations for Peacekeeping.* Washington, D.C.: The Brookings Institution, 1971.

FINGER, SEYMOUR M. "The Maintenance of Peace." *Proceedings of the Academy of Political Science,* 32, no. 4 (1977), 195–205.

FINKELSTEIN, MARINA S., and LAWRENCE S. FINKELSTEIN, eds. *Collective Security.* San Francisco: Chandler Publishing, 1966.

GOODRICH, LELAND M. *Korea: A Study of the U.S. Policy in the United Nations.* New York: Council on Foreign Relations, 1956.

HARRELSON, MAX. *Fires All Around the Horizon: The UN's Uphill Battle to Preserve the Peace.* New York: Praeger, 1989.

JAMES, ALAN. *The Politics of Peace-Keeping.* Published for The Institute for Strategic Studies. New York: Praeger, 1969.

LEFEVER, ERNEST W. *Crisis in the Congo: A United Nations Force in Action.* Washington, D.C.: The Brookings Institution, 1965.

RIKHYE, INDAR J. *The Theory and Practice of Peacekeeping.* London: C. Hurst and Co., 1984.

STEGENGA, JAMES A. *The United Nations Force in Cyprus.* Columbus: Ohio University Press, 1968.

UNITED NATIONS DEPARTMENT OF PUBLIC INFORMATION. *The Blue Helmets: A Review of United Nations Peace-Keeping* (2nd ed.). New York: United Nations, 1990.

WEISS, THOMAS G., ed. *Collective Security in a Changing World.* Boulder, CO: Lynne Rienner Publishers, 1993.

Chapter 8   The Search for Justice under Law

CORBETT, PERCY E. *The Growth of World Law*. Princeton, NJ: Princeton University Press, 1971.

FALK, RICHARD A., and CYRIL E. BLACK, eds. *The Future of the International Legal Order,* Vol. I, *Trends and Patterns.* Princeton, NJ: Princeton University Press, 1969.

FISCHER, DANA D. "Decisions to Use the International Court of Justice." *International Studies Quarterly,* 26, no. 2 (June 1982), 251–77.

FRANCK, THOMAS M. *Judging the World Court.* New York: Priority Press for Twentieth Century Fund, 1986.

HENKIN, LOUIS. *How Nations Behave: Law and Foreign Policy.* Published for The Council on Foreign Relations. New York: Praeger, 1970.

HIGGINS, ROSALYN. *The Development of International Law through the Political Organs of the United Nations.* New York: Oxford University Press, 1963.

International Court of Justice Yearbook. The Hague: International Court of Justice.

International Organizations and Law. New York: Ford Foundation, 1990.

JENKS, C. WILFRED. *A New World of Law?* London: Longmans, Green, 1969.

JESSUP, PHILIP C. *The Price of International Justice.* New York: Columbia University Press, 1971.

MCWHINNEY, EDWARD. *United Nations Law Making: Cultural and Ideological Relativism and International Law Making for an Era of Transition.* New York: Holmes & Meier, 1984.

Chapter 9   Controlling the Instruments of War

Arms Control: Issues for the Public. Published for The American Assembly. Englewood Cliffs, NJ: Prentice-Hall, 1961.

ART, ROBERT J., and KENNETH N. WALTZ, eds. *The Use of Force: International Politics and Foreign Policy.* Boston: Little, Brown, 1971.

BARGMAN, ABRAHAM, "Nuclear Diplomacy." *Proceedings of the Academy of Political Science,* 32, no. 4 (1977), 159–69.

BLOOMFIELD, BETH. "Strategic Arms Limitation." *Proceedings of the Academy of Political Science,* 32, no. 4 (1977), 184–94.

"Economic and Social Consequences of the Arms Race and of Military Expenditures." Report of the Secretary-General, UN Document A/8469/Rev. 1. New York: United Nations, 1972.

EDWARDS, DAVID V. *Arms Control in International Politics.* New York: Holt, Rinehart and Winston, 1969.

FALK, RICHARD A., and SAUL H. MENDLOVITZ, eds. *The Strategy of World Order,* Vol. IV, *Disarmament and Economic Development.* New York: World Law Fund, 1966.

FREI, DANIEL. *Perceived Images: U.S. and Soviet Assumptions and Perceptions in Disarmament.* Lanham, MD: Rowman & Allanheld, 1986.

SIVARD, RUTH LEGER. *World Military and Social Expenditures 1993.* Washington, D.C.: World Priorities, Inc.

SLOCOMBE, WALTER. "Controlling Strategic Nuclear Weapons." Headline Series, no. 226. New York: Foreign Policy Association, June 1975.

Chapter 10   Varieties of Regionalism

BALL, M., MARGARET. *The OAS in Transition.* Durham, NC: Duke University Press, 1969.

BEER, FRANCIS A., ed. *Alliances: Latent War Communities in the Contemporary World.* New York: Holt, Rinehart and Winston, 1970.

CANTORI, LOUIS J., and STEVEN L. SPIEGEL. *The International Politics of Regions.* Englewood Cliffs, NJ: Prentice-Hall, 1970.

ETZIONI, MINERVA M. *The Majority of One: Towards a Theory of Regional Compatibility.* Beverly Hills, CA: Sage Publications, 1970.

FEDDER, WERNER J. *The European Community in World Affairs: Economic Power and Political Influence.* Port Washington, NY: Alfred Pub. Co., 1976.

GREGG, ROBERT W. "Program Decentralization through the Regional Economic Commissions." In *UN Administration of Economic and Social Programs,* ed. Gerard J. Mangone. New York: Columbia University Press, 1966.

KEOHANE, ROBERT O., and STANLEY HOFFMAN, eds. *The New European Community: Decision-making and Institutional Change.* Boulder, CO: Westview Press, 1991.

KORBONSKI, ANDRZEJ. "The Warsaw Pact." *International Conciliation,* no. 573 (May 1969).

MAGEE, JAMES S. "ECA and the Paradox of African Cooperation." *International Conciliation,* no. 580 (November 1970).

NYE, JOSEPH S., JR. *Peace in Parts: Integration and Conflict in Regional Organization.* Boston: Little, Brown, 1971.

RIVLIN, BENJAMIN. "Regional Arrangements and the UN System for Collective Security and Conflict Resolution: A New Road Ahead?" New York: The Ralph Bunche Institute on the United Nations, Occasional Paper Series, 1992.

SHEMAN, L. RONALD. *The Inter-American Dilemma: The Search for Inter-American Cooperation at the Centennial of the Inter-American System.* New York: Praeger, 1988.

SINGH, MANMOHAN. "Regional Development Banks." *International Conciliation,* no. 576 (January 1970).

TAYLOR, PHILLIP. *Nonstate Actors in International Politics: From Transregional to Substate Organizations.* Boulder, CO: Westview Press, 1984.

TSOUKALIS, LOUKAS, ed. *The European Community: Past, Present & Future.* Oxford: Basil Blackwell, 1983.

WORONOFF, JON. *Organizing African Unity.* Metuchen, NJ: Scarecrow Press, 1970.

Chapter 11 Transnational Relations and International Organization

AGGARWALA, NARINDER, MICHAEL J. FENELLO, and GERALD F. FITZGERALD. "Air Hijacking: An International Perspective." *International Conciliation,* no. 585 (November 1971).

ANGELL, ROBERT C. *Peace on the March: Transnational Participation.* New York: Van Nostrand Reinhold, 1969.

BEHRMAN, JACK, N. *National Interests and the Multinational Enterprise: Tensions among the North Atlantic Countries.* Englewood Cliffs, NJ: Prentice-Hall, 1970.

BERGSTEN, C. FRED, THOMAS HORST, and THEODORE H. MORAN. *American Multinationals and American Interests.* Washington, D.C.: The Brookings Institution, 1978.

KEOHANE, ROBERT O., and JOSEPH S. NYE JR., eds. "Transnational Relations and World Politics." *International Organization,* 25 (Summer 1971).

KINDLEBERGER, CHARLES P., ed. *The International Corporation.* Cambridge, MA: MIT Press, 1970.

MURPHY, JOHN F. *Punishing International Terrorists: The Legal Framework for Policy Initiatives.* Lanham, MD: Rowman & Allanheld, 1985.

ODISHAW, HUGH, "International Cooperation in Space Science." In *Outer Space: Prospects for Man and Society,* ed. Lincoln P. Bloomfield. For the American Assembly. Englewood Cliffs, NJ: Prentice-Hall, 1962, 105–22.

PERLMUTTER, HOWARD V. "The Tortuous Evolution of the Multinational Corporation." *Columbia Journal of World Business,* 4 (January–February 1969), 9–18.

RUBIN, SEYMOUR J. "The Transnational Corporations." *Proceedings of the Academy of Political Science,* 32, no. 4 (1977), 120–27.

SCOTT, ANDREW M. *The Revolution in Statecraft: Informal Penetration.* New York: Random House, 1965.

SERVAN-SCHREIBER, J. J. *The American Challenge,* trans. Ronald Steel. New York: Atheneum, 1968.

TANZER, MICHAEL. *The Political Economy of International Oil and the Underdeveloped Countries.* Boston: Beacon Press, 1969.

"Terrorism: The World at Bay." Transcript of special events production broadcast by WHYY, Philadelphia. Kent, OH: PTV Publications, 1978.

TURNER, LOUIS. *Invisible Empires: Multinational Companies and the Modern World.* London: Hamish Hamilton, 1970.

Chapter 12   Promoting Economic Welfare

ANSARI, JAVED. *The Political Economy of International Economic Organization.* Boulder, CO: Lynne Rienner, 1986.

BROWN, LESTER R. *The Interdependence of Nations.* Headline Series, no. 212. New York: Foreign Policy Association, October 1972.

FERGUSON, C. CLYDE JR. "The Politics of the New International Economic Order." *Proceedings of the Academy of Political Science,* 32, no. 4 (1977), 142–58.

FINLAYSON, JOCK A., and MARK W. ZACHER. *Managing International Markets: Developing Countries and the Commodity Trade Regime.* New York: Columbia University Press, 1988.

The Global 2000 Report to the President: Entering the Twenty-First Century, 3 vols. Washington, D.C.: Government Printing Office, 1980.

GOODE, RICHARD. *Economic Assistance to Developing Nations through the IMF.* Washington, D.C.: The Brookings Institution, 1985.

GREGG, ROBERT W. "UN Economic, Social, and Technical Activities." In *The United Nations, Past, Present, and Future,* ed. James Barros. New York: Free Press, 1972.

HILL, MARTIN. *The United Nations System: Coordinating Its Economic and Social Work.* Cambridge: Cambridge University Press, 1978.

"The International Development Strategy: First Over-all Review and Appraisal of Issues and Policies." Report of the Secretary-General. New York: United Nations, 1973.

"International Development Strategy: for the Third United Nations Development Decade." New York: United Nations, 1981.

MANGONE, GERARD J., ed. *UN Administration of Economic and Social Programs.* New York: Columbia University Press, 1966.

MENON, B. P. *Bridges across the South: Technical Cooperation Among Developing Countries.* New York: Pergamon Press, 1980.

North-South: A Programme for Survival. London: Pan Books, Ltd., 1980.

ROTHSTEIN, ROBERT L. *Global Bargaining: UNCTAD and the Quest for a New International Economic Order.* Princeton, NJ: Princeton University Press, 1979.

SCHACHTER, OSCAR. *Sharing the World's Resources.* New York: Columbia University Press, 1977.

SEN, SUDHIR. *United Nations in Economic Development—Need for a New Strategy.* Dobbs Ferry, NY: Oceana Publications, 1969.

SPERO, JOAN E. *The Politics of International Economic Relations* (4th ed.). New York: St. Martin's Press, 1990.

SYMONDS, RICHARD, ed. *International Targets for Development.* New York: Harper & Row, 1970.

"Towards Accelerated Development: Proposals for the Second United Nations Development Decade." Report of the Committee for Development Planning. New York: United Nations, 1970.

The United Nations in Development. Final Report of the Nordic UN Project. Stockholm: Almqvist & Wiksell International, 1991.

WILLIAMS, DOUGLAS. *The Specialized Agencies and the United Nations.* New York: St. Martin's Press, 1987.

Chapter 13   Managing Global Resources

BROWN, LESTER R. "The Social Impact of the Green Revolution." *International Conciliation,* no. 581 (January 1971).

———, and ASSOCIATES. *State of the World.* Annual volumes. New York: W. W. Norton.

FERARU, ANNE THOMPSON. "Transnational Political Interests and the Global Environment." *International Organization,* 28 (Winter 1974), 31–60.

"The Global Partnership for Environment and Development." New York: United Nations, 1992.

HAAS, PETER M. *International Environmental Issues: An ACUNS Teaching Text.* Hanover, NH: Academic Council on the United Nations System, 1991.

HOLLICK, ANN L., and ROBERT E. OSGOOD. *New Era of Ocean Politics.* Baltimore: Johns Hopkins University Press, 1974.

LOGUE, JOHN J., ed. *The Fate of the Oceans.* Villanova, PA: Villanova University Press, 1972.

"Man's Impact on the Global Environment." Report of the Study of Critical Environmental Problems. Cambridge, MA: MIT Press, 1970.

NANES, ALLAN S. *Beyond Malthus: The Food/People Equation.* Committee Print, Subcommittee on National Security Policy and Scientific Developments, Committee on Foreign Affairs, U.S. House of Representatives, 92nd Congress, 1st Session. Washington, D.C.: Government Printing Office, 1971.

PIRAGES, DENNIS. *Global Technopolitics: The International Politics of Technology and Resources.* Pacific Grove, CA: Brooks Cole, 1989.

SCHACHTER, OSCAR. *Sharing the World's Resources.* New York: Columbia University Press, 1977.

SWING, JOHN TEMPLE. "The Law of the Sea." *Proceedings of the Academy of Political Science,* 32, no. 4 (1977), 128–41.

WEISS, MILDRED. "The Lawless Depths: The Need for an International Oceans Regime." In *The U.S. and the Developing World: Agenda for Action 1974.* Published for the Overseas Development Council. New York: Praeger, 1974.

Chapter 14   Promoting Social Progress

JENKS, C. WILFRED. *Social Justice in the Law of Nations: The ILO Impact after Fifty Years.* New York: Oxford University Press, 1970.

JOHNSTON, G. A. *The International Labour Organization, Its Work for Social and Economic Progress.* London: Europa Publications, 1970.

JOYCE, JAMES AVERY. *World Labour Rights and Their Protection.* London: Croom Helm Ltd., 1980.

JOYNER, CHRISTOPHER C. "The United States' Withdrawal from the ILO: International Politics in the Labor Arena." *International Lawyer,* 12 (Fall 1978), 721–39.

LABOUISSE, HENRY R. "For the World's Children—UNICEF at 25." *UN Chronicle,* 8 (April 1971), 48–60.

MORSE, DAVID A., *The Origin and Evolution of the ILO and Its Role in the World Community.* Ithaca: New York State School of Industrial and Labor Relations, Cornell University, 1969.

PREGEL, BORIS, HAROLD D. LASSWELL, and JOHN McHALE, eds. *World Priorities.* New Brunswick, NJ: Transaction Books, 1977.

QUIMBY, FREEMAN H. *The Politics of Global Health.* Committee Print, Subcommittee on National Security Policy and Scientific Developments, Committee on Foreign Affairs, U.S. House of Representatives, 92nd Congress, 1st Session. Washington, D.C.: Government Printing Office, 1971.

SMITH, ANTHONY, *The Geopolitics of Information: How Western Culture Dominates the World.* New York: Oxford University Press, 1980.

The State of the World's Children. UNICEF annual reports. New York: Oxford University Press.

WADDEL, IAN G. "International Narcotics Control." *American Journal of International Law,* 64 (April 1970), 310–23.

The Work of WHO: Biennial Report of the Director-General. Geneva: World Health Organization.

Chapter 15   Human Rights and the Struggle for Self-Government

ALLEN, PHILIP M. "Self-Determination in the Western Indian Ocean." *International Conciliation,* no. 560 (November 1966).

CHOWDHURI, R. N. *International Mandates and Trusteeship Systems: A Comparative Study.* The Hague: Martinus Nijhoff, 1955.

Conference on Security and Co-operation in Europe. Final Act, Helsinki, 1975, Part 1. (a) VII.

EMERSON, RUPERT. "Colonialism, Political Development and the UN." *International Organization,* 19 (Summer 1965), 484–503.

———. *From Empire to Nation: The Rise to Self-Assertion of Asian and African Peoples.* Cambridge, MA: Harvard University Press, 1960.

FORSYTHE, DAVID P. *Human Rights and World Politics.* Lincoln: University of Nebraska Press, 1983.

———. "The United Nations and Human Rights: 1945–1985." *Political Science Quarterly,* 100 (Summer 1985), 249–70.

HENKIN, LOUIS. "The Internationalization of Human Rights." *Human Rights: A Symposium.* Columbia University, Proceedings of the General Education Seminar, 6, no. 1 (1977), 5–16.

KAY, DAVID A. "The United Nations and Decolonization." In *The United Nations: Past, Present, and Future,* ed. James Barros. New York: The Free Press, 1972.

KOMMERS, DONALD P., and GILBERT D. LOESCHER, eds. *Human Rights and American Foreign Policy.* Notre Dame, IN: University of Notre Dame Press, 1979.

KOREY, WILLIAM. "The Key to Human Rights—Implementation." *International Conciliation,* no. 570 (November 1968).

MCHENRY, DONALD F. *Micronesia: Trust Betrayed.* Washington, D.C.: Carnegie Endowment for International Peace, 1975.

MURRAY, JAMES N., JR. *The United Nations Trusteeship System.* Illinois Studies in the Social Sciences, 40. Urbana: University of Illinois Press, 1957.

VAN DYKE, VERNON. *Human Rights, the United States, and World Community.* New York: Oxford University Press, 1970.

Chapter 16   International Administration and the Search for Leadership

BAILEY, SYDNEY D. *The Secretariat of the United Nations.* New York: Carnegie Endowment for International Peace, 1962.

BERRIDGE, G. R., and A. JENNINGS, eds., *Diplomacy at the UN.* New York: St. Martin's Press, 1985.

CLAUDE, INIS, L JR. "Reflections on the Role of the Secretary-General of the United Nations." New York: The Ralph Bunche Institute on the United Nations, Occasional Paper Series, 1991.

FINGER SEYMOUR M. *Your Man at the UN: People, Politics, and Bureaucracy in Making Foreign Policy.* New York: New York University Press, 1980.

———, and JOHN MUGNO. *The Politics of Staffing the United Nations Secretariat.* New York: The Ralph Bunche Institute on the United Nations. The Graduate School and University Center of the City University of New York, 1974.

FINKELSTEIN, LAWRENCE S. "The Coordinative Function of the United Nations Secretary-General: What, If Anything, Should He Coordinate and How Should He Do It?" New York: The Ralph Bunche Institute on the United Nations, Occasional Paper Series, 1992.

FOOTE, WILDER, ed. *Servant of Peace: A Selection of the Speeches and Statements of Dag Hammarskjöld.* New York: Harper & Row, 1963.

FOSDICK, RAYMOND B. *The League and the United Nations after Fifty Years: The Six Secretaries-General.* Newtown, CN: Raymond B. Fosdick, 1972.

"Leadership at the United Nations: The Roles of the Secretary-General and the Member States." First Panel Report, United Nations Management and Decision-Making Project, New York: United Nations Association of the United States of America, 1986.

"Report of the Group of High-level Intergovernmental Experts to Review the Efficiency of the Administrative and Financial Functioning of the United Nations." UN Document A/41/49, 1986.

ROVINE, ARTHUR W. *The First Fifty Years: The Secretary-General in World Politics, 1920–1970.* Leiden: A. W. Sijthoff, 1970.

SCHWEBEL, STEPHEN M. *The Secretary-General of the United Nations: His Political Powers and Practice.* Cambridge, MA: Harvard University Press, 1952.

"The UN Secretary-General: His Role in World Politics." 14th Report, Commission to Study the Organization of Peace. New York: Commission to Study the Organization of Peace, 1962.

URQUHART, BRIAN, and ERSKINE CHILDERS. *A World in Need of Leadership: Tomorrow's United Nations.* Uppsala, Sweden: Dag Hammarskjöld Foundation, 1990.

WINCHMORE, CHARLES. "The Secretariat: Retrospect and Prospect." *International Organization,* 19 (Summer 1965), 622–39.

ZACHER, MARK W. *Dag Hammarskjöld's United Nations.* New York: Columbia University Press, 1970.

Chapter 17   International Organization in Retrospect and Prospect

BARNABY, FRANK, ed. *Building a More Democratic United Nations.* London: Frank Cass & Co. Ltd., 1991.

BERES, LOUIS R. *People, States, and World Order.* Itasca, IL: F. E. Peacock Publishers, Inc., 1981.

COATE, ROGER. *Unilateralism, Ideology and U.S. Foreign Policy.* Boulder, CO: Lynne Rienner, 1988.

FINKELSTEIN, LAWRENCE S., ed. *Politics in the United Nations System.* Durham, NC: Duke University Press, 1988.

FROMUTH, PETER. *The UN at 40: The Problems and Opportunities.* New York: United Nations Association of the United States of America, 1986.

GOODRICH, LELAND M. *The United Nations in a Changing World.* New York: Columbia University Press, 1974.

GREGG, ROBERT W. *About Face? The United States and the United Nations.* Boulder, CO: Lynne Rienner, 1993.

KAUFMANN, JOHAN and NICO SCHRIJVER. *Changing Global Needs: Expanding Roles for the United Nations System.* Hanover, NH: Academic Council on the United Nations System, 1990.

KAY, DAVID A., ed. *The Changing United Nations: Options for the United States.* Proceedings of the Academy of Political Science, 32, no. 4 (1977).

PUCHALA, DONALD J., and ROGER A. COATE. *The Challenge of Relevance: The United Nations in a Changing World Environment.* Hanover, NH: Academic Council on the United Nations System, 1989.

"Reform and Restructuring of the U.N. System." Department of State Pub. 8940, International Organization and Conference Series 135, June 1978.

TEHRANIAN, KATHERINE and MAJID TEHRANIAN, eds. *Restructuring for World Peace: On the Threshold of the Twenty-First Century.* Cresskill, NJ: Hampton Press, Inc., 1992.

appendix I

COVENANT
OF THE
LEAGUE OF NATIONS*

The High Contracting Parties

In order to promote international co-operation and to achieve international peace and security

by the acceptance of obligations not to resort to war,
by the prescription of open, just and honourable relations between nations,
by the firm establishment of the understandings of international law as the actual rule of conduct among Governments,
and by the maintenance of justice and a scrupulous respect for all treaty obligations in the dealings of organised peoples with one another,
Agree to this Covenant of the League of Nations.

Article 1

1. The original Members of the League of Nations shall be those of the Signatories which are named in the Annex to this Covenant and also such of those other States named in the Annex as shall accede without reservation to

*Texts printed in italics indicate amendments.

this Covenant. Such accession shall be effected by a Declaration deposited with the Secretariat within two months of the coming into force of the Covenant. Notice thereof shall be sent to all other Members of the League.

2. Any fully self-governing State, Dominion or Colony not named in the Annex may become a Member of the League if its admission is agreed to by two-thirds of the Assembly, provided that it shall give effective guarantees of its sincere intention to observe its international obligations, and shall accept such regulations as may be prescribed by the League in regard to its military, naval and air forces and armaments.

3. Any Member of the League may, after two years' notice of its intention so to do, withdraw from the League, provided that all its international obligations and all its obligations under this Covenant shall have been fulfilled at the time of its withdrawal.

Article 2

The action of the League under this Covenant shall be effected through the instrumentality of an Assembly and of a Council, with a permanent Secretariat.

Article 3

1. The Assembly shall consist of Representatives of the Members of the League.

2. The Assembly shall meet at stated intervals and from time to time as occasion may require at the Seat of the League or at such other place as may be decided upon.

3. The Assembly may deal at its meetings with any matter within the sphere of action of the League or affecting the peace of the world.

4. At meetings of the Assembly, each Member of the League shall have one vote, and may have not more than three Representatives.

Article 4

1. The Council shall consist of Representatives of the principal Allied and Associated Powers, together with Representatives of four other Members of the League. These four Members of the League shall be selected by the Assembly from time to time in its discretion. Until the appointment of the Representatives of the four Members of the League first selected by the Assembly, Representatives of Belgium, Brazil, Spain and Greece shall be Members of the Council.

2. With the approval of the majority of the Assembly, the Council may name additional Members of the League whose Representatives shall always be Members of the Council; the Council with like approval may increase the number of Members of the League to be selected by the Assembly for representation on the Council.

2. *bis. The Assembly shall fix by a two-thirds majority the rules dealing with the election of the non-permanent Members of the Council, and particularly such regulations as relate to their term of office and the conditions of re-eligibility.*

3. The Council shall meet from time to time as occasion may require, and at least once a year, at the Seat of the League, or at such other place as may be decided upon.

4. The Council may deal at its meetings with any matter within the sphere of action of the League or affecting the peace of the world.

5. Any Member of the League not represented on the Council shall be invited to send a Representative to sit as a member at any meeting of the Council during the consideration of matters specially affecting the interests of that Member of the League.

6. At meetings of the Council, each Member of the League represented on the Council shall have one vote, and may have not more than one Representative.

Article 5

1. Except where otherwise expressly provided in this Covenant or by the terms of the present Treaty, decisions at any meeting of the Assembly or of the Council shall require the agreement of all the Members of the League represented at the meeting.

2. All matters of procedure at meetings of the Assembly or of the Council, including the appointment of Committees to investigate particular matters, shall be regulated by the Assembly or by the Council and may be decided by a majority of the Members of the League represented at the meeting.

3. The first meeting of the Assembly and the first meeting of the Council shall be summoned by the President of the United States of America.

Article 6

1. The permanent Secretariat shall be established at the Seat of the League. The Secretariat shall comprise a Secretary-General and such secretaries and staff as may be required.

2. The first Secretary-General shall be the person named in the Annex; thereafter the Secretary-General shall be appointed by the Council with the approval of the majority of the Assembly.

3. The secretaries and staff of the Secretariat shall be appointed by the Secretary-General with the approval of the Council.

4. The Secretary-General shall act in that capacity at all meetings of the Assembly and of the Council.

5. *The expenses of the League shall be borne by the Members of the League in the proportion decided by the Assembly.*

Article 7

1. The Seat of the League is established at Geneva.

2. The Council may at any time decide that the Seat of the League shall be established elsewhere.

3. All positions under or in connection with the League, including the Secretariat, shall be open equally to men and women.

4. Representatives of the Members of the League and officials of the League when engaged in the business of the League shall enjoy diplomatic privileges and immunities.

5. The buildings and other property occupied by the League or its officials or by Representatives attending its meetings shall be inviolable.

Article 8

1. The Members of the League recognise that the maintenance of peace requires the reduction of national armaments to the lowest point consistent with national safety and the enforcement by common action of international obligations.

2. The Council, taking account of the geographical situation and circumstances of each State, shall formulate plans for such reduction for the consideration and action of the several Governments.

3. Such plans shall be subject to reconsideration and revision at least every ten years.

4. After these plans have been adopted by the several Governments, the limits of armaments therein fixed shall not be exceeded without the concurrence of the Council.

5. The Members of the League agree that the manufacture by private enterprise of munitions and implements of war is open to grave objections. The Council shall advise how the evil effects attendant upon such manufacture can be prevented, due regard being had to the necessities of those Members of the League which are not able to manufacture the munitions and implements of war necessary for their safety.

6. The Members of the League undertake to interchange full and frank information as to the scale of their armaments, their military, naval and air

programmes and the condition of such of their industries as are adaptable to warlike purposes.

Article 9

A permanent Commission shall be constituted to advise the Council on the execution of the provisions of Articles 1 and 8 and on military, naval and air questions generally.

Article 10

The Members of the League undertake to respect and preserve as against external aggression the territorial integrity and existing political independence of all Members of the League. In case of any such aggression or in case of any threat or danger of such aggression, the Council shall advise upon the means by which this obligation shall be fulfilled.

Article 11

1. Any war or threat of war, whether immediately affecting any of the Members of the League or not, is hereby declared a matter of concern to the whole League, and the League shall take any action that may be deemed wise and effectual to safeguard the peace of nations. In case any such emergency should arise, the Secretary-General shall, on the request of any Member of the League, forthwith summon a meeting of the Council.

2. It is also declared to be the friendly right of each Member of the League to bring to the attention of the Assembly or of the Council any circumstance whatever affecting international relations which threatens to disturb international peace or the good understanding between nations upon which peace depends.

Article 12

1. The Members of the League agree that if there should arise between them any dispute likely to lead to a rupture they will submit the matter either to arbitration *or judicial settlement* or to enquiry by the Council, and they agree in no case to resort to war until three months after the award by the arbitrators *or the judicial decision* or the report by the Council.

2. In any case under this article the award of the arbitrators *or the judicial decision* shall be made within a reasonable time, and the report of the

Council shall be made within six months after the submission of the dispute.

Article 13

1. The Members of the League agree that whenever any dispute shall arise between them which they recognise to be suitable for submission to arbitration *or judicial settlement,* and which cannot be satisfactorily settled by diplomacy, they will submit the whole subject-matter to arbitration *or judicial settlement.*

2. Disputes as to the interpretation of a treaty, as to any question of international law, as to the existence of any fact which, if established, would constitute a breach of any international obligation, or as to the extent and nature of the reparation to be made for any such breach, are declared to be among those which are generally suitable for submission to arbitration *or judicial settlement.*

3. *For the consideration of any such dispute, the court to which the case is referred shall be the Permanent Court of International Justice, established in accordance with Article 14, or any tribunal agreed on by the parties to the dispute or stipulated in any Convention existing between them.*

4. The Members of the League agree that they will carry out in full good faith any award *or decision* that may be rendered, and that they will not resort to war against a Member of the League which complies therewith. In the event of any failure to carry out such an award *or decision,* the Council shall propose what steps should be taken to give effect thereto.

Article 14

The Council shall formulate and submit to the Members of the League for adoption plans for the establishment of a Permanent Court of International Justice. The Court shall be competent to hear and determine any dispute of an international character which the parties thereto submit to it. The Court may also give an advisory opinion upon any dispute or question referred to it by the Council or by the Assembly.

Article 15

1. If there should arise between Members of the League any dispute likely to lead to a rupture, which is not submitted to arbitration *or judicial settlement* in accordance with Article 13, the Members of the League agree that they will submit the matter to the Council. Any party to the dispute may effect

such submission by giving notice of the existence of the dispute to the Secretary-General, who will make all necessary arrangements for a full investigation and consideration thereof.

2. For this purpose, the parties to the dispute will communicate to the Secretary-General, as promptly as possible, statements of their case with all the relevant facts and papers, and the Council may forthwith direct the publication thereof.

3. The Council shall endeavour to effect a settlement of the dispute, and if such efforts are successful, a statement shall be made public giving such facts and explanations regarding the dispute and the terms of settlement thereof as the Council may deem appropriate.

4. If the dispute is not thus settled, the Council either unanimously or by a majority vote shall make and publish a report containing a statement of the facts of the dispute and the recommendations which are deemed just and proper in regard thereto.

5. Any Member of the League represented on the Council may make public a statement of the facts of the dispute and of its conclusions regarding the same.

6. If a report by the Council is unanimously agreed to by the members thereof other than the Representatives of one or more of the parties to the dispute, the Members of the League agree that they will not go to war with any party to the dispute which complies with the recommendations of the report.

7. If the Council fails to reach a report which is unanimously agreed to by the members thereof, other than the Representatives of one or more of the parties to the dispute, the Members of the League reserve to themselves the right to take such action as they shall consider necessary for the maintenance of right and justice.

8. If the dispute between the parties is claimed by one of them, and is found by the Council, to arise out of a matter which by international law is solely within the domestic jurisdiction of that party, the Council shall so report, and shall make no recommendation as to its settlement.

9. The Council may in any case under this article refer the dispute to the Assembly. The dispute shall be so referred at the request of either party to the dispute provided that such request be made within fourteen days after the submission of the dispute to the Council.

10. In any case referred to the Assembly, all the provisions of this article and of Article 12 relating to the action and powers of the Council shall apply to the action and powers of the Assembly, provided that a report made by the Assembly, if concurred in by the Representatives of those Members of the League represented on the Council and of a majority of the other Members of the League, exclusive in each case of the Representatives of the parties to the dispute, shall have the same force as a report by the Council concurred in by all the members thereof other than the Representatives of one or more of the parties to the dispute.

Article 16

1. Should any Member of the League resort to war in disregard of its covenants under Articles 12, 13, or 15, it shall, *ipso facto,* be deemed to have committed an act of war against all other Members of the League, which hereby undertake immediately to subject it to the severance of all trade or financial relations, the prohibition of all intercourse between their nationals and the nationals of the Covenant-breaking State, and the prevention of all financial, commercial or personal intercourse between the nationals of the Covenant-breaking State and the nationals of any other State, whether a Member of the League or not.

2. It shall be the duty of the Council in such case to recommend to the several Governments concerned what effective military, naval or air force the Members of the League shall severally contribute to the armed forces to be used to protect the covenants of the League.

3. The Members of the League agree, further, that they will mutually support one another in the financial and economic measures which are taken under this article, in order to minimise the loss and inconvenience resulting from the above measures, and that they will mutually support one another in resisting any special measures aimed at one of their number by the Covenant-breaking State, and that they will take the necessary steps to afford passage through their territory to the forces of any of the Members of the League which are co-operating to protect the covenants of the League.

4. Any member of the League which has violated any covenant of the League may be declared to be no longer a Member of the League by a vote of the Council concurred in by the Representatives of all the other Members of the League represented thereon.

Article 17

1. In the event of a dispute between a Member of the League and a State which is not a member of the League or between States not members of the League, the State or States not members of the League shall be invited to accept the obligations of membership in the League for the purposes of such dispute, upon such conditions as the Council may deem just. If such invitation is accepted, the provisions of Articles 12 to 16 inclusive shall be applied with such modifications as may be deemed necessary by the Council.

2. Upon such invitation being given, the Council shall immediately institute an enquiry into the circumstances of the dispute and recommend such action as may seem best and most effectual in the circumstances.

3. If a State so invited shall refuse to accept the obligations of membership in the League for the purposes of such dispute, and shall resort to war against a Member of the League, the provisions of Article 16 shall be applicable as against the State taking such action.

4. If both parties to the dispute when so invited refuse to accept the obligations of membership in the League for the purposes of such dispute, the Council may take such measures and make such recommendations as will prevent hostilities and will result in the settlement of the dispute.

Article 18

Every treaty or international engagement entered into hereafter by any Member of the League shall be forthwith registered with the Secretariat and shall, as soon as possible, be published by it. No such treaty or international engagement shall be binding until so registered.

Article 19

The Assembly may from time to time advise the reconsideration by Members of the League of treaties which have become inapplicable and the consideration of international conditions whose continuance might endanger the peace of the world.

Article 20

1. The Members of the League severally agree that this Covenant is accepted as abrogating all obligations or understandings *inter se* which are inconsistent with the terms thereof, and solemnly undertake that they will not hereafter enter into any engagements inconsistent with the terms thereof.

2. In case any Member of the League shall, before becoming a Member of the League, have undertaken any obligations inconsistent with the terms of this Covenant, it shall be the duty of such Member to take immediate steps to procure its release from such obligations.

Article 21

Nothing in this Covenant shall be deemed to affect the validity of international engagements, such as treaties of arbitration or regional understandings like the Monroe Doctrine, for securing the maintenance of peace.

Article 22

1. To those colonies and territories which as a consequence of the late war have ceased to be under the sovereignty of the States which formerly gov-

erned them and which are inhabited by peoples not yet able to stand by themselves under the strenuous conditions of the modern world, there should be applied the principle that the well-being and development of such peoples form a sacred trust of civilisation and that securities for the performance of this trust should be embodied in this Covenant.

2. The best method of giving practical effect to this principle is that the tutelage of such peoples should be entrusted to advanced nations who, by reason of their resources, their experience or their geographical position, can best undertake this responsibility, and who are willing to accept it, and that this tutelage should be exercised by them as Mandatories on behalf of the League.

3. The character of the mandate must differ according to the stage of the development of the people, the geographical situation of the territory, its economic conditions and other similar circumstances.

4. Certain communities formerly belonging to the Turkish Empire have reached a stage of development where their existence as independent nations can be provisionally recognised subject to the rendering of administrative advice and assistance by a Mandatory until such time as they are able to stand alone. The wishes of these communities must be a principal consideration in the selection of the Mandatory.

5. Other peoples, especially those of Central Africa, are at such a stage that the Mandatory must be responsible for the administration of the territory under conditions which will guarantee freedom of conscience and religion, subject only to the maintenance of public order and morals, the prohibition of abuses such as the slave trade, the arms traffic and the liquor traffic, and the prevention of the establishment of fortifications or military and naval bases and of military training of the natives for other than police purposes and the defence of territory, and will also secure equal opportunities for the trade and commerce of other Members of the League.

6. There are territories, such as South West Africa and certain of the South Pacific Islands, which, owing to the sparseness of their population, or their small size, or their remoteness from the centres of civilisation, or their geographical contiguity to the territory of the Mandatory, and other circumstances, can be best administered under the laws of the Mandatory as integral portions of its territory, subject to the safeguards above mentioned in the interests of the indigenous population.

7. In every case of mandate, the Mandatory shall render to the Council an annual report in reference to the territory committed to its charge.

8. The degree of authority, control or administration to be exercised by the Mandatory shall, if not previously agreed upon by the Members of the League, be explicitly defined in each case by the Council.

9. A permanent Commission shall be constituted to receive and examine the annual reports of the Mandatories and to advise the Council on all matters relating to the observance of the mandates.

Article 23

Subject to and in accordance with the provisions of international Conventions existing or hereafter to be agreed upon, the Members of the League:

(*a*) will endeavour to secure and maintain fair and humane conditions of labour for men, women and children, both in their own countries and in all countries to which their commercial and industrial relations extend, and for that purpose will establish and maintain the necessary international organisations;

(*b*) undertake to secure just treatment of the native inhabitants of territories under their control;

(*c*) will entrust the League with the general supervision over the execution of agreements with regard to the traffic in women and children, and the traffic in opium and other dangerous drugs;

(*d*) will entrust the League with the general supervision of the trade in arms and ammunition with the countries in which the control of this traffic is necessary in the common interest;

(*e*) will make provision to secure and maintain freedom of communications and of transit and equitable treatment for the commerce of all Members of the League. In this connection, the special necessities of the regions devastated during the war of 1914–1918 shall be borne in mind;

(*f*) will endeavour to take steps in matters of international concern for the prevention and control of disease.

Article 24

1. There shall be placed under the direction of the League all international bureaux already established by general treaties if the parties to such treaties consent. All such international bureaux and all commissions for the regulation of matters of international interest hereafter constituted shall be placed under the direction of the League.

2. In all matters of international interest which are regulated by general Conventions but which are not placed under the control of international bureaux or commissions, the Secretariat of the League shall, subject to the consent of the Council and if desired by the parties, collect and distribute all relevant information and shall render any other assistance which may be necessary or desirable.

3. The Council may include as part of the expenses of the Secretariat the expenses of any bureau or commission which is placed under the direction of the League.

Article 25

The Members of the League agree to encourage and promote the establishment and co-operation of duly authorised voluntary national Red Cross organisations having as purposes the improvement of health, the prevention of disease and the mitigation of suffering throughout the world.

Article 26

1. Amendments to this Covenant will take effect when ratified by the Members of the League whose Representatives compose the Council and by a majority of the Members of the League whose Representatives compose the Assembly.

2. No such amendments shall bind any Member of the League which signifies its dissent therefrom, but in that case it shall cease to be a Member of the League.

appendix **II**

CHARTER
OF THE
UNITED NATIONS

WE THE PEOPLES OF THE UNITED NATIONS determined

- to save succeeding generations from the scourge of war, which twice in our lifetime has brought untold sorrow to mankind, and
- to reaffirm faith in fundamental human rights, in the dignity and worth of the human person, in the equal rights of men and women and of nations large and small, and
- to establish conditions under which justice and respect for the obligations arising from treaties and other sources of international law can be maintained, and
- to promote social progress and better standards of life in larger freedom, and for these ends
- to practice tolerance and live together in peace with one another as good neighbours, and
- to unite our strength to maintain international peace and security, and
- to ensure, by the acceptance of principles and the institution of methods, that armed force shall not be used, save in the common interest, and
- to employ international machinery for the promotion of the economic and social advancement of all peoples,
    have resolved to combine our efforts
    to accomplish these aims

Accordingly, our respective Governments, through representatives assembled in the city of San Francisco, who have exhibited their full powers found to be in good and due form, have agreed to the present Charter of the United Nations and do hereby establish an international organization to be known as the United Nations.

CHAPTER I
PURPOSES AND PRINCIPLES

Article 1

The Purposes of the United Nations are:

1. To maintain international peace and security, and to that end: to take effective collective measures for the prevention and removal of threats to the peace, and for the suppression of acts of aggression or other breaches of the peace, and to bring about by peaceful means, and in conformity with the principles of justice and international law, adjustment or settlement of international disputes or situations which might lead to a breach of the peace;
2. To develop friendly relations among nations based on respect for the principle of equal rights and self-determination of peoples, and to take other appropriate measures to strengthen universal peace;
3. To achieve international co-operation in solving international problems of an economic, social, cultural, or humanitarian character, and in promoting and encouraging respect for human rights and for fundamental freedoms for all without distinction as to race, sex, language, or religion; and
4. To be a centre for harmonizing the actions of nations in the attainment of these common ends.

Article 2

The Organization and its Members, in pursuit of the Purposes stated in Article 1, shall act in accordance with the following Principles:

1. The Organization is based on the principle of the sovereign equality of all its Members.
2. All Members, in order to ensure to all of them the rights and benefits resulting from membership, shall fulfil in good faith the obligations assumed by them in accordance with the present Charter.

3. All Members shall settle their international disputes by peaceful means in such a manner that international peace and security, and justice, are not endangered.

4. All Members shall refrain in their international relations from the threat or use of force against the territorial integrity or political independence of any state, or in any other manner inconsistent with the Purposes of the United Nations.

5. All Members shall give the United Nations every assistance in any action it takes in accordance with the present Charter, and shall refrain from giving assistance to any state against which the United Nations is taking preventive or enforcement action.

6. The Organization shall ensure that states which are not Members of the United Nations act in accordance with these Principles so far as may be necessary for the maintenance of international peace and security.

7. Nothing contained in the present Charter shall authorize the United Nations to intervene in matters which are essentially within the domestic jurisdiction of any state or shall require the Members to submit such matters to settlement under the present Charter; but this principle shall not prejudice the application of enforcement measures under Chapter VII.

CHAPTER II
MEMBERSHIP

Article 3

The original Members of the United Nations shall be the states which, having participated in the United Nations Conference on International Organization at San Francisco, or having previously signed the Declaration by United Nations of 1 January 1942, sign the present Charter and ratify it in accordance with Article 110.

Article 4

1. Membership in the United Nations is open to all other peace-loving states which accept the obligations contained in the present Charter and, in the judgment of the Organization, are able and willing to carry out these obligations.

2. The admission of any such state to membership in the United Nations will be effected by a decision of the General Assembly upon the recommendation of the Security Council.

Article 5

A Member of the United Nations against which preventive or enforcement action has been taken by the Security Council may be suspended from the exercise of the rights and privileges of membership by the General Assembly upon the recommendation of the Security Council. The exercise of these rights and privileges may be restored by the Security Council.

Article 6

A Member of the United Nations which has persistently violated the Principles contained in the present Charter may be expelled from the Organization by the General Assembly upon the recommendation of the Security Council.

CHAPTER III
ORGANS

Article 7

1. There are established as the principal organs of the United Nations: a General Assembly, a Security Council, an Economic and Social Council, a Trusteeship Council, an International Court of Justice and a Secretariat.

2. Such subsidiary organs as may be found necessary may be established in accordance with the present Charter.

Article 8

The United Nations shall place no restrictions on the eligibility of men and women to participate in any capacity and under conditions of equality in its principal and subsidiary organs.

CHAPTER IV
THE GENERAL ASSEMBLY

Composition

Article 9

1. The General Assembly shall consist of all the Members of the United Nations.

2. Each Member shall have not more than five representatives in the General Assembly.

Functions and Powers

Article 10

The General Assembly may discuss any questions or any matters within the scope of the present Charter or relating to the powers and functions of any organs provided for in the present Charter, and, except as provided in Article 12, may make recommendations to the Members of the United Nations or to the Security Council or to both on any such questions or matters.

Article 11

1. The General Assembly may consider the general principles of co-operation in the maintenance of international peace and security, including the principles governing disarmament and the regulation of armaments, and may make recommendations with regard to such principles to the Members or to the Security Council or to both.

2. The General Assembly may discuss any questions relating to the maintenance of international peace and security brought before it by any Member of the United Nations, or by the Security Council, or by a state which is not a Member of the United Nations in accordance with Article 35, paragraph 2, and, except as provided in Article 12, may make recommendations with regard to any such questions to the state or states concerned or to the Security Council or to both. Any such question on which action is necessary shall be referred to the Security Council by the General Assembly either before or after discussion.

3. The General Assembly may call the attention of the Security Council to situations which are likely to endanger international peace and security.

4. The powers of the General Assembly set forth in this Article shall not limit the general scope of Article 10.

Article 12

1. While the Security Council is exercising in respect of any dispute or situation the functions assigned to it in the present Charter, the General Assembly shall not make any recommendations with regard to that dispute or situation unless the Security Council so requests.

2. The Secretary-General, with the consent of the Security Council, shall notify the General Assembly at each session of any matters relative to the maintenance of international peace and security which are being dealt with by the Security Council and shall similarly notify the General Assembly, or the Members of the United Nations if the General Assembly is not in session, immediately the Security Council ceases to deal with such matters.

Article 13

1. The General Assembly shall initiate studies and make recommendations for the purpose of:

a. promoting international co-operation in the political field and encouraging the progressive development of international law and its codification;
b. promoting international co-operation in the economic, social, cultural, educational, and health fields, and assisting in the realization of human rights and fundamental freedoms for all without distinction as to race, sex, language, or religion.

2. The further responsibilities, functions and powers of the General Assembly with respect to matters mentioned in paragraph 1(b) above are set forth in Chapters IX and X.

Article 14

Subject to the provisions of Article 12, the General Assembly may recommend measures for the peaceful adjustment of any situation, regardless of origin, which it deems likely to impair the general welfare or friendly relations among nations, including situations resulting from a violation of the provisions of the present Charter setting forth the Purposes and Principles of the United Nations.

Article 15

1. The General Assembly shall receive and consider annual and special reports from the Security Council; these reports shall include an account of the measures that the Security Council has decided upon or taken to maintain international peace and security.

2. The General Assembly shall receive and consider reports from the other organs of the United Nations.

Article 16

The General Assembly shall perform such functions with respect to the international trusteeship system as are assigned to it under Chapters XII and XIII, including the approval of the trusteeship agreements for areas not designated as strategic.

Article 17

1. The General Assembly shall consider and approve the budget of the Organization.

2. The expenses of the Organization shall be borne by the Members as apportioned by the General Assembly.

3. The General Assembly shall consider and approve any financial and budgetary arrangements with specialized agencies referred to in Article 57 and shall examine the administrative budgets of such specialized agencies with a view to making recommendations to the agencies concerned.

Voting

Article 18

1. Each member of the General Assembly shall have one vote.

2. Decisions of the General Assembly on important questions shall be made by a two-thirds majority of the members present and voting. These questions shall include: recommendations with respect to the maintenance of international peace and security, the election of the non-permanent members of the Security Council, the election of the members of the Economic and Social Council, the election of members of the Trusteeship Council in accordance with paragraph 1(c) of Article 86, the admission of new Members to the United Nations, the suspension of the rights and privileges of membership, the expulsion of Members, questions relating to the operation of the trusteeship system, and budgetary questions.

3. Decisions on other questions, including the determination of additional categories of questions to be decided by a two-thirds majority, shall be made by a majority of the members present and voting.

Article 19

A Member of the United Nations which is in arrears in the payment of its financial contributions to the Organization shall have no vote in the General Assembly if the amount of its arrears equals or exceeds the amount of the contributions due from it for the preceding two full years. The General Assembly may nevertheless, permit such a member to vote if it is satisfied that the failure to pay is due to conditions beyond the control of the Member.

Procedure

Article 20

The General Assembly shall meet in regular annual sessions and in such special sessions as occasion may require. Special sessions shall be convoked by the Secretary-General at the request of the Security Council or of a majority of the Members of the United Nations.

Article 21

The General Assembly shall adopt its own rules of procedure. It shall elect its President for each session.

Article 22

The General Assembly may establish such subsidiary organs as it deems necessary for the performance of its functions.

CHAPTER V
THE SECURITY COUNCIL

Composition

Article 23

1. The Security Council shall consist of fifteen Members of the United Nations. The Republic of China, France, the Union of Soviet Socialist Republics, the United Kingdom of Great Britain and Northern Ireland, and the United States of America shall be permanent members of the Security Council. The General Assembly shall elect ten other Members of the United Nations to be non-permanent members of the Security Council, due regard being specially paid, in the first instance to the contribution of Members of the United Nations to the maintenance of international peace and security and to the other purposes of the Organization, and also to equitable geographical distribution.

2. The non-permanent members of the Security Council shall be elected for a term of two years. In the first election of the non-permanent members after the increase of the membership of the Security Council from eleven to fifteen, two of the four additional members shall be chosen for a term of one year. A retiring member shall not be eligible for immediate reelection.

3. Each member of the Security Council shall have one representative.

Functions and Powers

Article 24

1. In order to ensure prompt and effective action by the United Nations, its Members confer on the Security Council primary responsibility for the maintenance of international peace and security, and agree that in carrying out its duties under this responsibility the Security Council acts on their behalf.

2. In discharging these duties the Security Council shall act in accordance with the Purposes and Principles of the United Nations. The specific powers granted to the Security Council for the discharge of these duties are laid down in Chapters VI, VII, VIII, and XII.

3. The Security Council shall submit annual and, when necessary, special reports to the General Assembly for its consideration.

Article 25

The Members of the United Nations agree to accept and carry out the decisions of the Security Council in accordance with the present Charter.

Article 26

In order to promote the establishment and maintenance of international peace and security with the least diversion for armaments of the world's human and economic resources, the Security Council shall be responsible for formulating, with the assistance of the Military Staff Committee referred to in Article 47, plans to be submitted to the Members of the United Nations for the establishment of a system for the regulation of armaments.

Voting

Article 27

1. Each member of the Security Council shall have one vote.

2. Decisions of the Security Council on procedural matters shall be made by an affirmative vote of nine members.

3. Decisions of the Security Council on all other matters shall be made by an affirmative vote of nine members including the concurring votes of the permanent members; provided that, in decisions under Chapter VI, and under paragraph 3 of Article 52, a party to a dispute shall abstain from voting.

Procedure

Article 28

1. The Security Council shall be so organized as to be able to function continuously. Each member of the Security Council shall for this purpose be represented at all times at the seat of the Organization.

2. The Security Council shall hold periodic meetings at which each of its members may, if it so desires, be represented by a member of the government or by some other specially designated representative.

3. The Security Council may hold meetings at such places other than the seat of the Organization as in its judgment will best facilitate its work.

Article 29

The Security Council may establish such subsidiary organs as its deems necessary for the performance of its functions.

Article 30

The Security Council shall adopt its own rules of procedure, including the method of selecting its president.

Article 31

Any Member of the United Nations which is not a member of the Security Council may participate, without vote, in the discussion of any question brought before the Security Council whenever the latter considers that the interests of that Member are specially affected.

Article 32

Any Member of the United Nations which is not a member of the Security Council or any state which is not a Member of the United Nations, if it is a party to a dispute under consideration by the Security Council, shall be invited to participate, without vote, in the discussion relating to the dispute. The Security Council shall lay down such conditions as it deems just for the participation of a state which is not a Member of the United Nations.

CHAPTER VI
PACIFIC SETTLEMENT OF DISPUTES

Article 33

1. The parties to any dispute, the continuance of which is likely to endanger the maintenance of international peace and security, shall, first of all, seek a solution by negotiation, enquiry, mediation, conciliation, arbitration, judicial settlement, resort to regional agencies or arrangements, or other peaceful means of their own choice.

2. The Security Council shall, when it deems necessary, call upon the parties to settle their dispute by such means.

Article 34

The Security Council may investigate any dispute, or any situation which might lead to international friction or give rise to a dispute, in order to determine whether the continuance of the dispute or situation is likely to endanger the maintenance of international peace and security.

Article 35

1. Any Member of the United Nations may bring any dispute, or any situation of the nature referred to in Article 34, to the attention of the Security Council or of the General Assembly.

2. A state which is not a Member of the United Nations may bring to the attention of the Security Council or of the General Assembly any dispute to which it is a party if it accepts in advance, for the purposes of the dispute, the obligations of pacific settlement provided in the present Charter.

3. The proceedings of the General Assembly in respect of matters brought to its attention under this Article will be subject to the provisions of Articles 11 and 12.

Article 36

1. The Security Council may, at any stage of a dispute of the nature referred to in Article 33 or of a situation of like nature, recommend appropriate procedures or methods of adjustment.

2. The Security Council should take into consideration any procedures for the settlement of the dispute which have already been adopted by the parties.

3. In making recommendations under this Article the Security Council should also take into consideration that legal disputes should as a general rule be referred by the parties to the International Court of Justice in accordance with the provisions of the Statute of the Court.

Article 37

1. Should the parties to a dispute of the nature referred to in Article 33 fail to settle it by the means indicated in that Article, they shall refer it to the Security Council.

2. If the Security Council deems that the continuance of the dispute is in fact likely to endanger the maintenance of international peace and security, it shall decide whether to take action under Article 36 or to recommend such terms of settlement as it may consider appropriate.

Article 38

Without prejudice to the provisions of Articles 33 to 37, the Security Council may, if all the parties to any dispute so request, make recommendations to the parties with a view to a pacific settlement of the dispute.

CHAPTER VII
ACTION WITH RESPECT TO THREATS
TO THE PEACE, BREACHES OF THE PEACE,
AND ACTS OF AGGRESSION

Article 39

The Security Council shall determine the existence of any threat to the peace, breach of the peace, or act of aggression and shall make recommendations, or decide what measures shall be taken in accordance with Articles 41 and 42, to maintain or restore international peace and security.

Article 40

In order to prevent an aggravation of the situation, the Security Council may, before making the recommendations or deciding upon the measures provided for in Article 39, call upon the parties concerned to comply with such provisional measures as it deems necessary or desirable. Such provisional measures shall be without prejudice to the rights, claims, or position of the parties concerned. The Security Council shall duly take account of failure to comply with such provisional measures.

Article 41

The Security Council may decide what measures not involving the use of armed force are to be employed to give effect to its decisions, and it may call upon the Members of the United Nations to apply such measures. These may include complete or partial interruption of economic relations and of rail, sea, air, postal, telegraphic, radio, and other means of communication, and the severance of diplomatic relations.

Article 42

Should the Security Council consider that measures provided for in Article 41 would be inadequate or have proved to be inadequate, it may take such action by air, sea, or land forces as may be necessary to maintain or restore international peace and security. Such action may include demonstrations, blockade, and other operations by air, sea, or land forces of Members of the United Nations.

Article 43

1. All Members of the United Nations, in order to contribute to the maintenance of international peace and security, undertake to make available to the Security Council, on its call and in accordance with a special agreement or agreements, armed forces, assistance and facilities, including rights of passage, necessary for the purpose of maintaining international peace and security.

2. Such agreement or agreements shall govern the numbers and types of forces, their degree of readiness and general location, and the nature of the facilities and assistance to be provided.

3. The agreement or agreements shall be negotiated as soon as possible on the initiative of the Security Council. They shall be concluded between the

Security Council and Members or between the Security Council and groups of Members and shall be subject to ratification by the signatory states in accordance with their respective constitutional processes.

Article 44

When the Security Council has decided to use force it shall, before calling upon a Member not represented on it to provide armed forces in fulfillment of the obligations assumed under Article 43, invite that Member, if the Member so desires, to participate in the decisions of the Security Council concerning the employment of contingents of that Member's armed forces.

Article 45

In order to enable the United Nations to take urgent military measures, Members shall hold immediately available national air-force contingents for combined international enforcement action. The strength and degree of readiness of these contingents and plans for their combined action shall be determined, within the limits laid down in the special agreement or agreements referred to in Article 43, by the Security Council with the assistance of the Military Staff Committee.

Article 46

Plans for the application of armed force shall be made by the Security Council with the assistance of the Military Staff Committee.

Article 47

1. There shall be established a Military Staff Committee to advise and assist the Security Council on all questions relating to the Security Council's military requirements for the maintenance of international peace and security, the employment and command of forces placed at its disposal, the regulation of armaments, and possible disarmament.

2. The Military Staff Committee shall consist of the Chiefs of Staff of the permanent members of the Security Council or their representatives. Any Member of the United Nations not permanently represented on the Committee shall be invited by the Committee to be associated with it when the efficient discharge of the Committee's responsibilities requires the participation of that Member in its work.

3. The Military Staff Committee shall be responsible under the Security Council for the strategic direction of any armed forces placed at the disposal of the Security Council. Questions relating to the command of such forces shall be worked out subsequently.

4. The Military Staff Committee, with the authorization of the Security Council and after consultation with appropriate regional agencies, may establish regional sub-committees.

Article 48

1. The action required to carry out the decisions of the Security Council for the maintenance of international peace and security shall be taken by all the Members of the United Nations or by some of them, as the Security Council may determine.

2. Such decisions shall be carried out by the Members of the United Nations directly and through their action in the appropriate international agencies of which they are members.

Article 49

The Members of the United Nations shall join in affording mutual assistance in carrying out the measures decided upon by the Security Council.

Article 50

If preventive or enforcement measures against any state are taken by the Security Council, any other state, whether a Member of the United Nations or not, which finds itself confronted with special economic problems arising from the carrying out of those measures shall have the right to consult the Security Council with regard to a solution of those problems.

Article 51

Nothing in the present Charter shall impair the inherent right of individual or collective self-defence if an armed attack occurs against a Member of the United Nations, until the Security Council has taken measures necessary to maintain international peace and security. Measures taken by Members in the exercise of this right of self-defence shall be immediately reported to the

Security Council and shall not in any way affect the authority and responsibility of the Security Council under the present Charter to take at any time such action as it deems necessary in order to maintain or restore international peace and security.

CHAPTER VIII
REGIONAL ARRANGEMENTS

Article 52

1. Nothing in the present Charter precludes the existence of regional arrangements or agencies for dealing with such matters relating to the maintenance of international peace and security as are appropriate for regional action, provided that such arrangements or agencies and their activities are consistent with the Purposes and Principles of the United Nations.

2. The Members of the United Nations entering into such arrangements or constituting such agencies shall make every effort to achieve pacific settlement of local disputes through such regional arrangements or by such regional agencies before referring them to the Security Council.

3. The Security Council shall encourage the development of pacific settlement of local disputes through such regional arrangements or by such regional agencies either on the initiative of the states concerned or by reference from the Security Council.

4. This Article in no way impairs the application of Articles 34 and 35.

Article 53

1. The Security Council shall, where appropriate, utilize such regional arrangements or agencies for enforcement action under its authority. But no enforcement action shall be taken under regional arrangements or by regional agencies without the authorization of the Security Council, with the exception of measures against any enemy state, as defined in paragraph 2 of this Article, provided for pursuant to Article 107 or in regional arrangements directed against renewal of aggressive policy on the part of any such state, until such time as the Organization may, on request of the Governments concerned, be charged with the responsibility for preventing further aggression by such a state.

2. The term enemy state as used in paragraph 1 of this Article applies to any state which during the Second World War has been an enemy of any signatory of the present Charter.

Article 54

The Security Council shall at all times be kept fully informed of activities undertaken or in contemplation under regional arrangements or by regional agencies for the maintenance of international peace and security.

CHAPTER IX
INTERNATIONAL ECONOMIC
AND SOCIAL CO-OPERATION

Article 55

With a view to the creation of conditions of stability and well-being which are necessary for peaceful and friendly relations among nations based on respect for the principle of equal rights and self-determination of peoples, the United Nations shall promote:

a. higher standards of living, full employment, and conditions of economic and social progress and development;
b. solutions of international economic, social, health, and related problems; and international cultural and educational co-operation; and
c. universal respect for, and observance of, human rights and fundamental freedoms for all without distinction as to race, sex, language, or religion.

Article 56

All Members pledge themselves to take joint and separate action in co-operation with the Organization for the achievement of the purposes set forth in Article 55.

Article 57

1. The various specialized agencies, established by intergovernmental agreement and having wide international responsibilities, as defined in their basic instruments, in economic, social, cultural, educational, health, and related fields, shall be brought into relationship with the United Nations in accordance with the provisions of Article 63.

2. Such agencies thus brought into relationship with the United Nations are hereinafter referred to as specialized agencies.

Article 58

The Organization shall make recommendations for the coordination of the policies and activities of the specialized agencies.

Article 59

The Organization shall, where appropriate, initiate negotiations among the states concerned for the creation of any new specialized agencies required for the accomplishment of the purposes set forth in Article 55.

Article 60

Responsibility for the discharge of the functions of the Organization set forth in this Chapter shall be vested in the General Assembly and, under the authority of the General Assembly, in the Economic and Social Council, which shall have for this purpose the powers set forth in Chapter X.

CHAPTER X
THE ECONOMIC AND SOCIAL COUNCIL

Composition

Article 61

1. The Economic and Social Council shall consist of fifty-four Members of the United Nations elected by the General Assembly.

2. Subject to the provisions of paragraph 3, eighteen members of the Economic and Social Council shall be elected each year for a term of three years. A retiring member shall be eligible for immediate re-election.

3. At the first election after the increase in the membership of the Economic and Social Council from twenty-seven to fifty-four members, in addition to the members elected in place of the nine members whose term of office expires at the end of that year, twenty-seven additional members shall be elected. Of these twenty-seven additional members, the term of office of nine members so elected shall expire at the end of one year, and of nine other members at the end of two years, in accordance with arrangements made by the General Assembly.

4. Each member of the Economic and Social Council shall have one representative.

Functions and Powers

Article 62

1. The Economic and Social Council may make or initiate studies and reports with respect to international economic, social, cultural, educational, health, and related matters and may make recommendations with respect to any such matters to the General Assembly, to the Members of the United Nations, and to the specialized agencies concerned.

2. It may make recommendations for the purpose of promoting respect for, and observance of, human rights and fundamental freedoms for all.

3. It may prepare draft conventions for submission to the General Assembly, with respect to matters falling within its competence.

4. It may call, in accordance with the rules prescribed by the United Nations, international conferences on matters falling within its competence.

Article 63

1. The Economic and Social Council may enter into agreements with any of the agencies referred to in Article 57, defining the terms on which the agency concerned shall be brought into relationship with the United Nations. Such agreements shall be subject to approval by the General Assembly.

2. It may co-ordinate the activities of the specialized agencies through consultation with and recommendations to such agencies and through recommendations to the General Assembly and to the Members of the United Nations.

Article 64

1. The Economic and Social Council may take appropriate steps to obtain regular reports from the specialized agencies. It may make arrangements with the Members of the United Nations and with the specialized agencies to obtain reports on the steps taken to give effect to its own recommendations and to recommendations on matters falling within its competence made by the General Assembly.

2. It may communicate its observations on these reports to the General Assembly.

Article 65

The Economic and Social Council may furnish information to the Security Council and shall assist the Security Council upon its request.

Article 66

1. The Economic and Social Council shall perform such functions as fall within its competence in connexion with the carrying out of the recommendations of the General Assembly.

2. It may, with the approval of the General Assembly, perform services at the request of Members of the United Nations and at the request of specialized agencies.

3. It shall perform such other functions as are specified elsewhere in the present Charter or as may be assigned to it by the General Assembly.

Voting

Article 67

1. Each Member of the Economic and Social Council shall have one vote.

2. Decisions of the Economic and Social Council shall be made by a majority of the members present and voting.

Procedure

Article 68

The Economic and Social Council shall set up commissions in economic and social fields and for the promotion of human rights, and such other commissions as may be required for the performance of its functions.

Article 69

The Economic and Social Council shall invite any Member of the United Nations to participate, without vote, in its deliberations on any matter of particular concern to that Member.

Article 70

The Economic and Social Council may make arrangements for representatives of the specialized agencies to participate, without vote, in its deliberations and in those of the commissions established by it, and for its representatives to participate in the deliberations of the specialized agencies.

Article 71

The Economic and Social Council may make suitable arrangements for consultation with non-governmental organizations which are concerned with matters within its competence. Such arrangements may be made with international organizations and, where appropriate, with national organizations after consultation with the Member of the United Nations concerned.

Article 72

1. The Economic and Social Council shall adopt its own rules of procedure, including the method of selecting its President.
2. The Economic and Social Council shall meet as required in accordance with its rules, which shall include provision for the convening of meetings on the request of a majority of its members.

CHAPTER XI
DECLARATION REGARDING
NON-SELF-GOVERNING TERRITORIES

Article 73

Members of the United Nations which have or assume responsibilities for the administration of territories whose peoples have not yet attained a full measure of self-government recognize the principle that the interests of the inhabitants of these territories are paramount, and accept as a sacred trust the obligation to promote to the utmost, within the system of international peace and security established by the present Charter, the well-being of the inhabitants of these territories, and, to this end:

    a.   to ensure, with due respect for the culture of the peoples concerned, their political, economic, social, and educational advancement, their just treatment, and their protection against abuses;

b. to develop self-government, to take due account of the political aspirations of the peoples, and to assist them in the progressive development of their free political institutions, according to the particular circumstances of each territory and its peoples and their varying stages of advancement;

c. to further international peace and security;

d. to promote constructive measures of development, to encourage research, and to co-operate with one another and, when and where appropriate, with specialized international bodies with a view to the practical achievement of the social, economic, and scientific purposes set forth in this Article; and

e. to transmit regularly to the Secretary-General for information purposes, subject to such limitation as security and constitutional considerations may require, statistical and other information of a technical nature relating to economic, social, and educational conditions in the territories for which they are respectively responsible other than those territories to which Chapters XII and XIII apply.

Article 74

Members of the United Nations also agree that their policy in respect of the territories to which this Chapter applies, no less than in respect of their metropolitan areas, must be based on the general principle of good-neighbourliness, due account being taken of the interests and well-being of the rest of the world, in social, economic, and commercial matters.

CHAPTER XII
INTERNATIONAL TRUSTEESHIP SYSTEM

Article 75

The United Nations shall establish under its authority an international trusteeship system for the administration and supervision of such territories as may be placed thereunder by subsequent individual agreements. These territories are hereinafter referred to as trust territories.

Article 76

The basic objectives of the trusteeship system, in accordance with the Purposes of the United Nations laid down in Article 1 of the present Charter, shall be:

a. to further international peace and security;

b. to promote the political, economic, social, and educational advancement of the inhabitants of the trust territories, and their progressive development towards self-government or independence as may be appropriate to the particular circumstances of each territory and its peoples and the freely expressed wishes of the peoples concerned, and as may be provided by the terms of each trusteeship agreement;

c. to encourage respect for human rights and for fundamental freedoms for all without distinction as to race, sex, language, or religion, and to encourage recognition of the interdependence of the peoples of the world; and

d. to ensure equal treatment in social, economic, and commercial matters for all Members of the United Nations and their nationals, and also equal treatment for the latter in the administration of justice, without prejudice to the attainment of the foregoing objectives and subject to the provisions of Article 80.

Article 77

1. The trusteeship system shall apply to such territories in the following categories as may be placed thereunder by means of trusteeship agreements:

a. territories now held under mandate;

b. territories which may be detached from enemy states as a result of the Second World War; and

c. territories voluntarily placed under the system by states responsible for their administration.

2. It will be a matter for subsequent agreement as to which territories in the foregoing categories will be brought under the trusteeship system and upon what terms.

Article 78

The trusteeship system shall not apply to territories which have become Members of the United Nations, relationship among which shall be based on respect for the principle of sovereign equality.

Article 79

The terms of trusteeship for each territory to be placed under the trusteeship system, including any alteration or amendment, shall be agreed upon by the states directly concerned, including the mandatory power in the case of territories held under mandate by a Member of the United Nations, and shall be approved as provided for in Articles 83 and 85.

Article 80

1. Except as may be agreed upon in individual trusteeship agreements, made under Articles 77, 79, and 81, placing each territory under the trusteeship system, and until such agreements have been concluded, nothing in this Chapter shall be construed in or of itself to alter in any manner the rights whatsoever of any states or any peoples or the terms of existing international instruments to which Members of the United Nations may respectively be parties.

2. Paragraph 1 of the Article shall not be interpreted as giving grounds for delay or postponement of the negotiations and conclusion of agreements for placing mandated and other territories under the trusteeship system as provided for in Article 77.

Article 81

The trusteeship agreement shall in each case include the terms under which the trust territory will be administered and designate the authority which will exercise the administration of the trust territory. Such authority, hereinafter called the administering authority, may be one or more states or the Organization itself.

Article 82

There may be designated, in any trusteeship agreement, a strategic area or areas which may include part or all of the trust territory to which the agreement applies, without prejudice to any special agreement or agreements made under Article 43.

Article 83

1. All functions of the United Nations relating to strategic areas, including the approval of the terms of the trusteeship agreements and of their alteration or amendment, shall be exercised by the Security Council.

2. The basic objectives set forth in Article 76 shall be applicable to the people of each strategic area.

3. The Security Council shall, subject to the provisions of the trusteeship agreements and without prejudice to security considerations, avail itself of the assistance of the Trusteeship Council to perform those functions of the United Nations under the trusteeship system relating to political, economic, social, and educational matters in the strategic areas.

Article 84

It shall be the duty of the administering authority to ensure that the trust territory shall play its part in the maintenance of international peace and security. To this end the administering authority may make use of volunteer forces, facilities, and assistance from the trust territory in carrying out the obligations towards the Security Council undertaken in this regard by the administering authority, as well as for local defence and the maintenance of law and order within the trust territory.

Article 85

1. The functions of the United Nations with regard to trusteeship agreements for all areas not designated as strategic, including the approval of the terms of the trusteeship agreements and of their alteration or amendment, shall be exercised by the General Assembly.

2. The Trusteeship Council, operating under the authority of the General Assembly, shall assist the General Assembly in carrying out these functions.

CHAPTER XIII
THE TRUSTEESHIP COUNCIL

Composition

Article 86

1. The Trusteeship Council shall consist of the following Members of the United Nations:

a. those Members administering trust territories;
b. such of those Members mentioned by name in Article 23 as are not administering trust territories; and
c. as many other Members elected for three-year terms by the General Assembly as may be necessary to ensure that the total number of members of the Trusteeship Council is equally divided between those Members of the United Nations which administer trust territories and those which do not.

2. Each member of the Trusteeship Council shall designate one specially qualified person to represent it therein.

Functions and Powers

Article 87

The General Assembly and, under its authority, the Trusteeship Council, in carrying out their functions, may:

a. consider reports submitted by the administering authority;
b. accept petitions and examine them in consultation with the administering authority;
c. provide for periodic visits to the respective trust territories at times agreed upon with the administering authority; and
d. take these and other actions in conformity with the terms of the trusteeship agreements.

Article 88

The Trusteeship Council shall formulate a questionnaire on the political, economic, social, and educational advancement of the inhabitants of each trust territory, and the administering authority for each trust territory within the competence of the General Assembly shall make an annual report to the General Assembly upon the basis of such questionnaire.

Voting

Article 89

1. Each member of the Trusteeship Council shall have one vote.
2. Decisions of the Trusteeship Council shall be made by a majority of the members present and voting.

Procedure

Article 90

1. The Trusteeship Council shall adopt its own rules of procedure, including the method of selecting its President.
2. The Trusteeship Council shall meet as required in accordance with its rules, which shall include provisions for the convening of meetings on the request of a majority of its members.

Article 91

The Trusteeship Council shall, when appropriate, avail itself of the assistance of the Economic and Social Council and of the specialized agencies in regard to matters with which they are respectively concerned.

CHAPTER XIV
THE INTERNATIONAL COURT OF JUSTICE

Article 92

The International Court of Justice shall be the principal judicial organ of the United Nations. It shall function in accordance with the annexed Statute, which is based upon the Statute of the Permanent Court of International Justice and forms an integral part of the present Charter.

Article 93

1. All Members of the United Nations are *ipso facto* parties to the Statute of the International Court of Justice.
2. A state which is not a Member of the United Nations may become a party to the Statute of the International Court of Justice on conditions to be determined in each case by the General Assembly upon the recommendation of the Security Council.

Article 94

1. Each Member of the United Nations undertakes to comply with the decision of the International Court of Justice in any case to which it is a party.
2. If any party to a case fails to perform the obligations incumbent upon it under a judgment rendered by the Court, the other party may have recourse to the Security Council, which may, if it deems necessary, make recommendations or decide upon measures to be taken to give effect to the judgment.

Article 95

Nothing in the present Charter shall prevent Members of the United Nations from entrusting the solution of their differences to other tribunals by virtue of agreements already in existence or which may be concluded in the future.

Article 96

1. The General Assembly or the Security Council may request the International Court of Justice to give an advisory opinion on any legal question.

2. Other organs of the United Nations and specialized agencies, which may at any time be so authorized by the General Assembly, may also request advisory opinions of the Court on legal questions arising within the scope of their activities.

CHAPTER XV
THE SECRETARIAT

Article 97

The Secretariat shall comprise a Secretary-General and such staff as the organization may require. The Secretary-General shall be appointed by the General Assembly upon the recommendation of the Security Council. He shall be the chief administrative officer of the Organization.

Article 98

The Secretary-General shall act in that capacity in all meetings of the General Assembly, of the Security Council, of the Economic and Social Council, and of the Trusteeship Council, and shall perform such other functions as are entrusted to him by these organs. The Secretary-General shall make an annual report to the General Assembly on the work of the Organization.

Article 99

The Secretary-General may bring to the attention of the Security Council any matter which in his opinion may threaten the maintenance of international peace and security.

Article 100

1. In the performance of their duties the Secretary-General and the staff shall not seek or receive instructions from any government or from any other authority external to the Organization. They shall refrain from any action which might reflect on their position as international officials responsible only to the Organization.

2. Each Member of the United Nations undertakes to respect the exclusively international character of the responsibilities of the Secretary-General and the staff and not to seek to influence them in the discharge of their responsibilities.

Article 101

1. The staff shall be appointed by the Secretary-General under regulations established by the General Assembly.

2. Appropriate staffs shall be permanently assigned to the Economic and Social Council, the Trusteeship Council, and, as required, to other organs of the United Nations. These staffs shall form a part of the Secretariat.

3. The paramount consideration in the employment of the staff and in the determination of the conditions of service shall be the necessity of securing the highest standards of efficiency, competence, and integrity. Due regard shall be paid to the importance of recruiting the staff on as wide a geographical basis as possible.

CHAPTER XVI
MISCELLANEOUS PROVISIONS

Article 102

1. Every treaty and every international agreement entered into by any Member of the United Nations after the present Charter comes into force shall as soon as possible be registered with the Secretariat and published by it.

2. No party to any such treaty or international agreement which has not been registered in accordance with the provisions of paragraph 1 of this Article may invoke that treaty or agreement before any organ of the United Nations.

Article 103

In the event of a conflict between the obligations of the Members of the United Nations under the present Charter and their obligations under any other international agreement, their obligations under the present Charter shall prevail.

Article 104

The Organization shall enjoy in the territory of each of its Members such legal capacity as may be necessary for the exercise of its functions and the fulfillment of its purposes.

Article 105

1. The Organization shall enjoy in the territory of each of its Members such privileges and immunities as are necessary for the fulfillment of its purposes.

2. Representatives of the Members of the United Nations and officials of the Organization shall similarly enjoy such privileges and immunities as are necessary for the independent exercise of their functions in connexion with the Organization.

3. The General Assembly may make recommendations with a view to determining the details of the application of paragraphs 1 and 2 of this Article or may propose conventions to the Members of the United Nations for this purpose.

CHAPTER XVII
TRANSITIONAL SECURITY ARRANGEMENTS

Article 106

Pending the coming into force of such special agreements referred to in Article 43 as in the opinion of the Security Council enable it to begin the exercise of its responsibilities under Article 42, the parties to the Four-Nations Declaration, signed at Moscow, 30 October 1943, and France, shall, in accordance with the provisions of paragraph 5 of that Declaration, consult with one another and as occasion requires with other Members of the United Nations with a view to such joint action on behalf of the Organization as may be necessary for the purpose of maintaining international peace and security.

Article 107

Nothing in the present Charter shall invalidate or preclude action, in relation to any state which during the Second World War has been an enemy of any signatory to the present Charter, taken or authorized as a result of that war by the Governments having responsibility for such action.

CHAPTER XVIII
AMENDMENTS

Article 108

Amendments to the present Charter shall come into force for all Members of the United Nations when they have been adopted by a vote of two-thirds of the members of the General Assembly and ratified in accordance with their respective constitutional processes by two-thirds of the Members of the United Nations, including all the permanent members of the Security Council.

Article 109

1. A General Conference of the Members of the United Nations for the purpose of reviewing the present Charter may be held at a date and place to be fixed by a two-thirds vote of the members of the General Assembly and by a vote of any nine members of the Security Council. Each Member of the United Nations shall have one vote in the conference.

2. Any alteration of the present Charter recommended by a two-thirds vote of the conference shall take effect when ratified in accordance with their respective constitutional processes by two-thirds of the Members of the United Nations including all the permanent members of the Security Council.

3. If such a conference has not been held before the tenth annual session of the General Assembly following the coming into force of the present Charter, the proposal to call such a conference shall be placed on the agenda of that session of the General Assembly, and the conference shall be held if so decided by a majority vote of the members of the General Assembly and by a vote of any seven members of the Security Council.

CHAPTER XIX
RATIFICATION AND SIGNATURE

Article 110

1. The present Charter shall be ratified by the signatory states in accordance with their respective constitutional processes.

2. The ratifications shall be deposited with the Government of the United States of America, which shall notify all the signatory states of each deposit as well as the Secretary-General of the Organization when he has been appointed.

3. The present Charter shall come into force upon the deposit of ratifications by the Republic of China, France, the Union of Soviet Socialist Republics, the United Kingdom of Great Britain and Northern Ireland, and the United States of America, and by a majority of the other signatory states. A protocol of the ratification deposited shall thereupon be drawn up by the Government of the United States of America which shall communicate copies thereof to all the signatory states.

4. The states signatory to the present Charter which ratify it after it has come into force will become original Members of the United Nations on the date of the deposit of their respective ratifications.

Article 111

The present Charter of which the Chinese, French, Russian, English, and Spanish texts are equally authentic, shall remain deposited in the archives of the Government of the United States of America. Duly certified copies thereof shall be transmitted by that Government to the Governments of the other signatory states.

IN FAITH WHEREOF the representatives of the Governments of the United Nations have signed the present Charter.

DONE at the city of San Francisco the twenty-sixth day of June, one thousand nine hundred and forty-five.

appendix III

MEMBERS OF THE UNITED NATIONS

MEMBERS OF THE UNITED NATIONS: DATE OF ADMISSION, AREA, POPULATION, AND ASSESSMENT

NAME OF COUNTRY	DATE OF ADMISSION	TOTAL AREA (SQUARE KILOMETERS)	ESTIMATED POPULATION	PERCENTAGE OF UN BUDGET ASSESSMENT
Afghanistan	19 Nov. 1946	652,090	16,433,000	0.01
Albania	14 Dec. 1955	28,748	3,250,000	0.01
Algeria	8 Oct. 1962	2,381,741	25,324,000	0.16
Andorra	8 July 1993	480	53,000	0.01
Angola	1 Dec. 1976	1,246,700	10,020,000	0.01
Antigua and Barbuda	11 Nov. 1981	440	77,000	0.01
Argentina	24 Oct. 1945	2,766,889	32,609,000	0.57
Armenia	2 Mar. 1992	29,290	3,376,000	0.13
Australia	1 Nov. 1945	7,686,848	17,086,000	1.51
Austria	14 Dec. 1955	83,853	7,823,000	0.75
Azerbaijan	2 Mar. 1992	86,528	7,137,000	0.22
Bahamas	18 Sep. 1973	13,878	253,000	0.02
Bahrain	21 Sep. 1971	678	503,000	0.03
Bangladesh	17 Sep. 1974	143,998	104,776,000	0.1
Barbados	9 Dec. 1966	430	258,000	0.01
Belarus	2 Mar. 1992	207,601	10,297,000	0.48
Belgium	27 Dec. 1945	30,519	9,845,000	1.06
Belize	25 Sep. 1981	22,965	194,000	0.01
Benin	20 Sep. 1960	112,622	4,889,000	0.01

(continued)

NAME OF COUNTRY	DATE OF ADMISSION	TOTAL AREA (SQUARE KILOMETERS)	ESTIMATED POPULATION	PERCENTAGE OF UN BUDGET ASSESSMENT
Bhutan	21 Sep. 1971	47,000	1,517,000	0.01
Bolivia	14 Nov. 1945	1,098,581	7,400,000	0.01
Bosnia and Herzegovina	22 May 1992	51,142	4,300,000	0.04
Botswana	17 Oct. 1966	581,730	1,348,000	0.01
Brazil	24 Oct. 1945	8,511,965	153,322,000	1.59
Brunei Darussalam	21 Sep. 1984	5,765	266,000	0.03
Bulgaria	14 Dec. 1955	110,912	8,977,000	0.13
Burkina Faso	20 Sep. 1960	274,200	9,242,000	0.01
Burundi	18 Sep. 1962	27,834	5,620,000	0.01
Cambodia	14 Dec. 1955	181,035	8,246,000	0.01
Cameroon	20 Sep. 1960	475,442	11,834,000	0.01
Canada	9 Nov. 1945	9,976,139	26,992,000	3.11
Cape Verde	16 Sep. 1975	4,033	370,000	0.01
Central African Republic	20 Sep. 1960	622,984	3,039,000	0.01
Chad	20 Sep. 1960	1,284,000	5,679,000	0.01
Chile	24 Oct. 1945	756,945	13,386,000	0.08
China	24 Oct. 1945	9,596,961	1,160,017,000	0.77
Colombia	5 Nov. 1945	1,138,914	32,987,000	0.13
Comoros	12 Nov. 1975	2,235	551,000	0.01
Congo	20 Sep. 1960	342,000	2,271,000	0.01

Costa Rica	2 Nov. 1945	51,100	3,030,000	0.01
Côte d'Ivoire	20 Sep. 1960	322,463	11,998,000	0.02
Croatia	22 May 1992	56,552	4,700,000	0.13
Cuba	24 Oct. 1945	110,861	10,695,000	0.09
Cyprus	20 Sep. 1960	9,251	707,000	0.02
Czech Republic	19 Jan. 1993	78,902	10,300,000	0.42*
Democratic People's Republic of Korea	17 Sep. 1991	120,570	21,773,000	0.05
Denmark	24 Oct. 1945	43,077	5,140,000	0.65
Djibouti	20 Sep. 1977	23,200	409,000	0.01
Dominica	18 Dec. 1978	751	83,000	0.01
Dominican Republic	24 Oct. 1945	48,734	7,170,000	0.02
Ecuador	21 Dec. 1945	283,561	9,623,000	0.03
Egypt	24 Oct. 1945	1,001,449	54,609,000	0.07
El Salvador	24 Oct. 1945	21,041	5,252,000	0.01
Equatorial Guinea	12 Nov. 1968	28,051	356,000	0.01
Eritrea	28 May 1993	93,679	3,318,000	0.01
Estonia	17 Sep. 1991	45,111	1,565,000	0.07
Ethiopia	13 Nov. 1945	1,157,585	56,700,000	0.01
Fiji	13 Oct. 1970	18,274	736,000	0.01
Finland	14 Dec. 1955	338,127	4,986,000	0.57
France	24 Oct. 1945	551,500	56,720,000	6.00
Gabon	20 Sep. 1960	267,667	1,172,000	0.02
Gambia	21 Sep. 1965	11,295	861,000	0.01
Georgia	31 July 1992	69,718	5,400,000	0.21

(continued)

NAME OF COUNTRY	DATE OF ADMISSION	TOTAL AREA (SQUARE KILOMETERS)	ESTIMATED POPULATION	PERCENTAGE OF UN BUDGET ASSESSMENT
Germany	18 Sep. 1973	356,910	79,973,000	8.93
Ghana	8 Mar. 1957	238,537	15,028,000	0.01
Greece	25 Oct. 1945	131,990	10,269,000	0.35
Grenada	17 Sep. 1974	344	85,000	0.01
Guatemala	21 Nov. 1945	108,889	9,197,000	0.02
Guinea	12 Dec. 1958	245,857	5,756,000	0.01
Guinea-Bissau	17 Sep. 1974	36,125	965,000	0.01
Guyana	20 Sep. 1966	214,969	796,000	0.01
Haiti	24 Oct. 1945	27,750	6,625,000	0.01
Honduras	17 Dec. 1945	112,088	5,105,000	0.01
Hungary	14 Dec. 1955	93,032	10,341,000	0.18
Iceland	19 Nov. 1946	103,000	258,000	0.03
India	30 Oct. 1945	3,287,590	843,931,000	0.36
Indonesia	28 Sep. 1950	1,904,569	179,322,000	0.16
Iran (Islamic Republic of)	24 Oct. 1945	1,648,000	58,798,000	0.77
Iraq	21 Dec. 1945	438,317	18,920,000	0.13
Ireland	14 Dec. 1955	70,284	3,523,000	0.18
Israel	11 May 1949	20,770	5,037,000	0.23
Italy	14 Dec. 1955	301,268	57,690,000	4.29
Jamaica	18 Sep. 1962	10,990	2,420,000	0.01
Japan	18 Dec. 1956	377,801	123,921,000	12.45
Jordan	14 Dec. 1955	97,740	4,010,000	0.01

Kazakhstan	2 Mar. 1992	2,718,135	16,793,000	0.35
Kenya	16 Dec. 1963	580,367	25,905,000	0.01
Kuwait	14 May 1963	17,818	2,143,000	0.25
Kyrgyzstan	2 Mar. 1992	198,554	4,422,000	0.06
Lao People's Democratic Republic	14 Dec. 1955	236,800	4,139,000	0.01
Latvia	17 Sep. 1991	64,508	2,686,000	0.13
Lebanon	24 Oct. 1945	10,400	2,701,000	0.01
Lesotho	17 Oct. 1966	30,355	1,774,000	0.01
Liberia	2 Nov. 1945	111,369	2,705,000	0.01
Libyan Arab Jamahiriya	14 Dec. 1955	1,759,540	4,083,000	0.24
Liechtenstein	18 Sep. 1990	161	29,000	0.01
Lithuania	17 Sep. 1991	65,207	3,739,000	0.15
Luxembourg	24 Oct. 1945	2,586	385,000	0.06
Madagascar	20 Sep. 1960	587,041	11,197,000	0.01
Malawi	1 Dec. 1964	118,484	8,556,000	0.01
Malaysia	17 Sep. 1957	329,749	17,756,000	0.12
Maldives	21 Sep. 1965	298	223,000	0.01
Mali	28 Sep. 1960	1,240,192	8,156,000	0.01
Malta	1 Dec. 1964	316	356,000	0.01
Marshall Islands	17 Sep. 1991	181	48,000	0.01
Mauritania	27 Oct. 1961	1,025,520	2,036,000	0.01
Mauritius	24 Apr. 1968	2,040	1,070,000	0.01
Mexico	7 Nov. 1945	1,958,201	87,836,000	0.88

(continued)

NAME OF COUNTRY	DATE OF ADMISSION	TOTAL AREA (SQUARE KILOMETERS)	ESTIMATED POPULATION	PERCENTAGE OF UN BUDGET ASSESSMENT
Micronesia (Federated States of)	17 Sep. 1991	700	99,000	0.01
Monaco	28 May 1993	2	30,000	0.01*
Mongolia	27 Oct. 1961	1,566,500	2,190,000	0.01
Morocco	12 Nov. 1956	446,550	25,061,000	0.03
Mozambique	16 Sep. 1975	801,590	15,656,000	0.01
Myanmar	19 Apr. 1948	676,552	41,675,000	0.01
Namibia	23 Apr. 1990	823,363	1,781,000	0.01
Nepal	14 Dec. 1955	140,797	18,916,000	0.01
Netherlands	10 Dec. 1945	40,844	15,131,000	1.50
New Zealand	24 Oct. 1945	268,676	3,380,000	0.24
Nicaragua	24 Oct. 1945	130,000	3,999,000	0.01
Niger	20 Sep. 1960	1,267,000	7,732,000	0.01
Nigeria	7 Oct. 1960	923,768	108,542,000	0.20
Norway	27 Nov. 1945	323,895	4,262,000	0.55
Oman	7 Oct. 1971	212,457	1,502,000	0.03
Pakistan	30 Sep. 1947	796,095	115,520,000	0.06
Panama	13 Nov. 1945	77,072	2,466,000	0.02
Papua New Guinea	10 Oct. 1975	462,840	3,699,000	0.01
Paraguay	24 Oct. 1945	406,752	4,277,000	0.02
Peru	31 Oct. 1945	1,285,216	21,998,000	0.06
Philippines	24 Oct. 1945	300,000	61,480,000	0.07

Poland	24 Oct. 1945	312,677	38,244,000	0.47
Portugal	14 Dec. 1955	92,389	9,868,000	0.20
Qatar	21 Sep. 1971	11,000	486,000	0.05
Republic of Korea	17 Sep. 1991	98,510	43,500,000	0.69
Republic of Moldova	2 Mar. 1992	33,710	4,373,000	0.15
Romania	14 Dec. 1955	237,500	23,201,000	0.17
Russian Federation	24 Oct. 1945	17,079,792	148,485,000	6.71
Rwanda	18 Sep. 1962	26,338	7,165,000	0.01
St. Kitts and Nevis	23 Sep. 1983	261	44,000	0.01
St. Lucia	18 Sep. 1979	622	151,000	0.01
St. Vincent and the Grenadines	16 Sep. 1980	388	116,000	0.01
Samoa	15 Dec. 1976	2,831	164,000	0.01
San Marino	2 Mar. 1992	62	24,000	0.01
São Tomé and Principe	16 Sep. 1975	964	121,000	0.01
Saudi Arabia	24 Oct. 1945	2,149,690	14,870,000	0.96
Senegal	28 Sep. 1960	196,722	7,327,000	0.01
Seychelles	21 Sep. 1976	280	68,000	0.01
Sierra Leone	27 Sep. 1961	71,740	4,151,000	0.01
Singapore	21 Sep. 1965	618	3,003,000	0.12
Slovak Republic	19 Jan. 1993	48,995	5,300,000	0.13*
Slovenia	22 May 1992	20,256	1,974,000	0.09
Solomon Islands	19 Sep. 1978	28,896	321,000	0.01
Somalia	20 Sep. 1960	637,657	7,497,000	0.01

(continued)

NAME OF COUNTRY	DATE OF ADMISSION	TOTAL AREA (SQUARE KILOMETERS)	ESTIMATED POPULATION	PERCENTAGE OF UN BUDGET ASSESSMENT
South Africa	7 Nov. 1945	1,221,037	35,282,000	0.41
Spain	14 Dec. 1955	504,782	39,025,000	1.98
Sri Lanka	14 Dec. 1955	65,610	16,993,000	0.01
Sudan	12 Nov. 1956	2,505,813	25,204,000	0.01
Suriname	4 Dec. 1975	163,265	422,000	0.01
Swaziland	24 Sep. 1968	17,364	768,000	0.01
Sweden	19 Nov. 1946	440,945	8,642,000	1.11
Syrian Arab Republic	24 Oct. 1945	185,180	12,116,000	0.04
Tajikistan	2 Mar. 1992	139,946	5,357,000	0.05
Thailand	16 Dec. 1946	513,115	57,196,000	0.11
The former Yugoslav Republic of Macedonia	8 Apr. 1993	25,548	2,050,000	0.02*
Togo	20 Sep. 1960	56,785	3,531,000	0.01
Trinidad and Tobago	18 Sep. 1962	5,130	1,253,000	0.05
Tunisia	12 Nov. 1956	163,610	8,180,000	0.03
Turkey	24 Oct. 1945	779,452	57,326,000	0.27
Turkmenistan	2 Mar. 1992	488,127	3,714,000	0.06
Uganda	25 Oct. 1962	235,880	16,583,000	0.01
Ukraine	24 Oct. 1945	603,700	51,944,000	1.87

Country	Date		
United Arab Emirates	9 Dec. 1971	83,600	0.21
United Kingdom	24 Oct. 1945	244,100	5.02
United Republic of Tanzania	14 Dec. 1961	945,087	0.01
United States of America	24 Oct. 1945	9,372,614	25.00
Uruguay	18 Dec. 1945	177,414	0.04
Uzbekistan	2 Mar. 1992	447,409	0.26
Vanuatu	15 Sep. 1981	12,189	0.01
Venezuela	15 Nov. 1945	912,050	0.49
Vietnam	20 Sep. 1977	331,689	0.01
Yemen	30 Sep. 1947	532,010	0.01
Yugoslavia	24 Oct. 1945	101,036	0.14*
Zaire	20 Sep. 1960	2,345,409	0.01
Zambia	1 Dec. 1964	722,614	0.01
Zimbabwe	25 Aug. 1980	390,580	0.01

*Provisional

INDEX